THE IRISH LABOUR

VOICE OF LABOUR

NEW SERIES. VOL. VII. No. 13.   DUBLIN, SATURDAY, MARCH 28, 1925.   ONE PENNY.

".WE AIN'T GONNA WAIT NO MO', NO MO'."

VOTE 1 FOR LABOUR.

THE IRISH
LABOUR PARTY

1922–73

NIAMH PUIRSÉIL

UNIVERSITY COLLEGE DUBLIN PRESS
PREAS CHOLÁISTE OLLSCOILE BHAILE ÁTHA CLIATH
2007

First published 2007
by University College Dublin Press
Newman House
86 St Stephen's Green
Dublin 2
Ireland
www.ucdpress.ie

ISBN 978-1-904558-67-5 pb
978-1-904558-68-2 hb

CIP data available from the British Library

Typeset in Ireland in Adobe Caslon and Bodoni Oldstyle
by Elaine Burberry, Bantry, Co. Cork
Text design by Lyn Davies
Printed in England on acid-free paper by
MPG Books Ltd, Bodmin, Cornwall

Contents

—

Illustrations

—

Cover photograph: Labour Party annual conference, Wexford, February 1972. *Front row, left to right:* Seamus Scally, Brendan Halligan, Roddy Connolly (standing), Brendan Corish, Niall Greene, Donal O'Sullivan; *back row, left to right:* Paddy Devlin (SDLP), Brian Garrett (NILP), Zui Harmour (Israeli Labour Party), Liam Kavanagh, Michael O'Leary, David Thornley and Barry Desmond (reproduced with permission from the *Irish Times*, with thanks to Brendan Halligan and Sheila O'Mahony).

Frontispiece: *Voice of Labour*, front page, 28 March 1925.

Between pp. 176 and 177

Acknowledgements

—

Research for this book took on the character of a treasure hunt from an early stage and I owe an enormous debt of gratitude to all those who helped by searching for documents in their attics and garages and to those who shared with me the results of their own research. I would like to express my thanks in this regard to Barry Desmond, Donal Nevin, Professor John Horgan, Peter Rigney and Dr Tara Keenan Thompson. I would also like to thank D. R. O'Connor Lysaght and the family of Gilbert Lynch for allowing me access to unpublished memoirs.

I would like to thank the staff in the libraries and archives for their all their assistance over the years: Seamus Helferty and all the archivists in University College Dublin Archives Department, the staff of the National Archives of Ireland, Trinity College Dublin's Manuscript room, the National Archives, Kew, and Stephen Bird in the Labour History Archive and Study Centre, Manchester. The staff of the National Library of Ireland have been most helpful, not least for allowing me access to the uncatalogued collections of Brendan Corish and Owen Sheehy Skeffington, and I would like to thank Dr Diarmuid Whelan for his assistance in this regard. My thanks to Dr Jack McGinley in Trinity College library and I am especially grateful to all the library staff there for showing such good humour when confronted with deluges of illegible dockets. Finally, my thanks to my colleagues in the Irish Labour History Society for their help, especially Theresa Moriarty. Without the sterling work of ILHS members over the years to preserve the documents of the labour movement, this book would have been impossible.

Thanks to the Labour Party, especially Mike Allen and Marion Boushell for permitting me to look at the party's records recently deposited in the Irish Labour History Museum and Archive, Beggars Bush and the minutes of the Administrative Council held in the party's head office in Ely Place. Also thanks to Fianna Fáil and Fine Gael for access to their papers held in UCD archives and to Declan Costello for permission to consult his father, John A. Costello's papers which are held there also.

Thanks to everyone who agreed to be interviewed, and to those who spoke informally or off the record.

I would also like to thank everyone who helped me in my quest for photographs and illustrations: the *Irish Times* for the use of the cover photograph and other illustrations, Barry Desmond, the late Aidan McNamara, Betty Dowling, Paul Rouse, Brendan Halligan and Sheila O'Mahony. My thanks to Frank Kelly and the Reverend J. Anthony Gaughan for permission to reproduce illustrations from *Dublin Opinion* and *Thomas Johnson* respectively.

Several people have read all or part of this work in its various forms. My research on the Labour Party began with a doctoral thesis, which is present in chapters five to nine in significantly revised form. Thanks to my doctoral supervisor Professor Ronan Fanning for all his assistance while I was under his tutelage. The timely completion of my thesis was made possible by the Irish Research Council for the Humanities and Social Sciences award of a Government of Ireland doctoral scholarship. I would also like to thank Professor Fergus D'Arcy, Dr Gary Murphy and Francis Devine for their comments on all or parts of the dissertation. I would like to thank Tom Garvin for his remarks on a draft of the manuscript. Geraldine McCarter did a fantastic job of proofing and my thanks to her for all her suggestions and improvements. The usual proviso applies, and responsibility for errors or otherwise remains with the author. My thanks also to the external reader whose observations were most helpful.

My thanks to Professor Eunan O'Halpin, who was external examiner of the original dissertation and later my colleague in the Centre for Contemporary Irish History, for his advice and encouragement. From hand-me-down notes to very practical assistance, he has been a driving force in getting this book started and, more importantly, finished, and I owe him a huge debt of gratitude.

Writing a book such as this is not easy, but the task was made infinitely more agreeable by Dr Anne Dolan's co-habitation of the sixth floor. Dr Dolan was there throughout the long gestation of this manuscript, and somehow managed to put up with constant queries on everything from Catholic doctrine and constitutional law to spelling without ever throwing anything across the desk – and it was not for want of objects! Similarly, Dr Joseph Clarke and Mícheál Ó Fathartaigh provided much encouragement and levity when needed.

For tip-offs, insight and support, my thanks to Dr Emmet O'Connor, Dr Daithi Ó Corráin, Dr Martin Maguire, Dr Susannah Riordan, Dr Tom Feeney, Dr Noreen Giffney, Deirdre Bryan, Dr Brian Hanley, Dr Claire Mitchell and Dr Gillian O'Brien. Thanks also to Professor Jane Ohlmeyer, head of the School of Histories and Humanities, TCD. My comrades and sparring partners in the outside world did so much to keep spirits lifted: thanks to Sineád Burt, Anna Womersley, Antje Jaeger, Brian Cowzer, Joe Doyle, Dave O'Leary and to Brendan O'Toole and Gerry Martin whose lessons on perseverance and indomitable spirit proved invaluable.

My deepest thanks to Barbara Mennell who was so positive about this project from the outset and has shown a level of patience I can only dream of.

Finally, I would like to thank my family for all their love and support over the years. My sister Clíodhna and my parents Séamus and Olwyn must be almost as delighted to see this finished as I am. I could not have done it without them.

NIAMH PUIRSÉIL
Dublin, October 2006

Abbreviations

—

AC	Administrative Council of the Labour Party
ATGWU	Amalgamated Transport and General Workers Union
BLP	British Labour Party
CDMC	Common Market defence Campaign
CIU	Congress of Irish Unions
CPGB	Communist Party of Great Britain
CPI	Communist Party of Ireland
DCC	Dublin Constituencies Council
DD	Dáil Debates
DDA	Dublin Diocesan Archives
DHAC	Dublin Housing Action Committee
DO	Dominions Office
DTUC	Dublin Trades Union Council
DRC	Dublin Regional Council
EEC	European Economic Community
FCO	Foreign and Commonwealth Office (UK)
FPTP	First Past the Post
FF	Fianna Fáil
FI	Fourth International
HMG	His/Her Majesty's Government
ICA	Irish Citizen Army
ICTU	Irish Congress of Trade Unions
IHA	Irish Housewives Association
ILHM&A	Irish Labour History Museum and Archive
ILHS	Irish Labour History Society
ILP&TUC	Irish Labour Party and Trade Union Congress
IMA	Irish Medical Association
INTO	Irish National Teachers' Organisation
IPOOA	Irish Post Office Officials' Association
IRA	Irish Republican Army
ITGWU	Irish Transport and General Workers' Union
ITUC	Irish Trade Union Congress
ITUC&LP	Irish Trade Union Congress and Labour Party
IWL	Irish Workers' League
IWP	Irish Workers Party

IWV	*Irish Workers' Voice*
IWWU	Irish Women Workers' Union
L & H	Literary and Historical Society
LHASCM	Labour History Archive and Study Centre, Manchester
LP	Labour Party
LPC	Lower Prices Campaign
NAI	National Archives of Ireland
NAM	National Archives, Maryland
NE	National Executive (ICTU)
NFA	National Farmers' Association
NHIS	National Health Insurance Society
NIEC	National Industrial Economic Council
NILP	Northern Ireland Labour Party
NLI	National Library of Ireland
NPD	National Progressive Democrats
NUR	National Union of Railwaymen
OEEC	Organisation for European Economic Co-operation
OIRA	Official Irish Republican Army
PIRA	Provisional Irish Republican Army
PLP	Parliamentary Labour Party
POUM	Partido Obrero de Unificacíon Marxista (Workers' party of Marxist Unification)
POWU	Post Office Workers' Union
PUTUO	Provisional United Trade Union Organisation
PR-STV	Proportional Representation by the Single Transferable Vote
RUC	Royal Ulster Constabulary
RWG	Revolutionary Workers' Group
SD	Seanad Debates
SDA	Students for Democratic Action
SDLP	Social Democratic and Labour Party
SLA	Socialist Labour Alliance
TCD	Trinity College Dublin
TCDM	Trinity College Dublin Manuscripts Room
TD	Teachta Dála
TNA	The National Archives, Kew
UCC	University College Cork
UCD	University College Dublin
UCDAD	University College Dublin Archive Department
WUI	Workers Union of Ireland

Glossary

—

Oireachtas	Irish legislature comprising the President, the Dáil and the Seanad.
Dáil	Lower house of the Oireachtas
Seanad	Upper house of the Oireachtas
Ceann Comhairle	Chairman of the Dáil
Leas Cean Comhairle	Deputy Chairman of the Dáil
TD (Teachta Dála)	Member of the Dáil

Administrative Council (AC)   This is the Labour Party's ruling executive. It is made up of nominees elected at the party's annual conference, members of the Parliamentary Labour Party elected by same and *ex-officio* members.

Congress   This refers to the collective organisation of affiliated trade unions. Established in 1894 as the Irish Trade Union Congress, it became the Irish Trade Union Congress and Labour Party (ITUC&LP) in 1914 and subsequently changed its name to the Irish Labour Party and Trade Union Congress (ILP&TUC) in 1918. The division of the political and industrial wings of the movement saw it revert to the name ITUC once more in 1930. In 1943 some Irish-based unions split to form a rival Congress, the Congress of Irish Unions. In 1956, the two groups came together in a provisional umbrella organisation, the Provisional United Trade Union Organisation (PUTUO). The two ultimately reunited in 1958 as the Irish Congress of Trade Unions (ICTU).

Introduction

History has been unkind to the Labour movement in Ireland. Consigned, as it often was, to the margins of Irish life because of the national struggle and its aftermath, and confined to relatively small pockets of industrialisation in an otherwise agricultural society, neither the movement nor its leaders have attracted the attention of conventional historians to the extent that they deserve.[1]

—

There is some truth to this observation by former Labour Party General Secretary Brendan Halligan. 'Conventional historians' have tended to play little heed to the labour movement generally and the Labour Party in particular. While some Labour characters such as Big Jim Larkin and James Connolly are among the most recognisable figures in Irish history – the iconic image of Larkin, arms aloft, mid-oration looms large over Dublin's O'Connell Street and Connolly's face is recognisable from the photographs of the 1916 signatories as well as Harry Kernoff woodcuts – but other central figures are less well known. It is a situation, however, which cannot be attributed to conventional historians alone. All political parties are selective in their memories of the past, but Labour has tended to be more selective than most. Take, for instance, a poster published by the party in 1993 which was co-designed by Ruairí Quinn. The poster, a pictorial history of Labour, was a montage of images dating back to the eighteenth century: Liberty leading the People; a pikeman from 1798; Tom Paine; Michael Davitt; one hundred years of Congress; James Connolly; the 1913 Lockout; Tom Johnson; 1916; the old Liberty Hall; Jim Larkin (1928); President Mary Robinson; a starry plough and the stars of the EU flag; head shots of some women deputies; the 'Spring Tide' Labour deputies entering the Dáil in October 1992; Dick Spring himself; a rose. It was an interesting choice of images, as notable for its omissions as its inclusions. Eighteenth-century republicans, be they French, Irish or English, figure more prominently than most of the men and women who toiled under the banner of Labour – a party that marks its inception as 1912. Labour's earliest years are there, but for the decades between 1928 and 1990 there was nothing. William Norton who led Labour for nearly 30 years was nowhere to be seen, and the only concession to Brendan Corish, leader for 17 years (and Wexford man through and through), was the pikeman. Why was it that two of the men who led the party for almost half a century between them were painted out of the party's history? Perhaps it is not fair to read too much into the poster's content. After all, one person's Stalinism is another's artistic licence and maybe the substitution of proud Liberty's heaving bosom for Norton's jowly visage made aesthetic sense, but a similar selectivity is evident elsewhere nevertheless. A section on the Labour Party's website entitled 'Labour's Proud History', for instance, devotes more attention to the party's failure to contest the 1918 general election than to what it did afterwards. The decades until the 1960s are glossed over in a flash, Labour's participation in two governments between 1948 and 1957 covered with indecent haste.

Far from being proud of its history, Labour seems more than a little ashamed. If Labour is critical of itself, it is in good company. Described by one scholar during the early 1960s as 'probably the most opportunistically conservative Labour party in the known world', it was dominated according to Conor Cruise O'Brien by 'dismal poltroons on the lines of O'Casey's Uncle Payther'. Indeed, over the years, writers and politicians have excelled in their descriptions of Labour's reactionary tendencies. In 1930, for instance, Fianna Fáil's Seán Lemass stated that 'the outstanding characteristic of the Labour Party is that it is the most respectable Party in this State . . . So long as they cannot be accused of being even pale pink in politics they seem to think they have fulfilled their function towards the Irish people.'[2] Some 25 years later, when the second inter-party government featuring Labour and Fine Gael had left office, a former Fine Gael minister was asked by a journalist if there had been any ideological differences between his party and its Labour colleagues. 'Yes', he concluded eventually, 'the four Labour members, Corish, Keyes, Everett and Norton were to the right of Gerry Sweetman', the government's notoriously conservative Minister for Finance.[3] Around the same time, Jack White, then deputy editor of the *Irish Times*, was asked by a foreign colleague to explain the irrelevance of the left–right cleavage in Irish politics to a foreign colleague. 'Draw a line, and put all the parties well to the right', he told his companion. When his tutee asked where he should locate the Labour Party, White responded, 'Put that furthest of all'. Nor were the cynics any more satisfied when Labour swung leftward in the sixties. Few people nowadays can say 'the seventies will be socialist' without smirking. Labour was damned if it didn't and damned if it did.

Ireland is, of course, nothing if not a nation of begrudgers: always the bitter word from the barstool analysts. Beyond the pub talk, however, Labour's opponents to its left and right have always had a vested interest in making the party appear insipid and impotent. Labour is lily of liver, they say, forget them. Fianna Fáil/the Communist Party of Ireland/the Socialist Workers'

Party/Sinn Féin, even Fine Gael, is the *real* Labour party: vote for us! That is very well as propaganda, but as a critique it leaves something to be desired. Repeating something, however often, does not make it true. In Labour's case, however, repetition has turned into folkloric fact the notion that it existed as a right-wing monolith until the end of the 1960s. For instance, the political scientist Michael Gallagher asserted in his 1982 study *The Irish Labour Party in Transition, 1957–82*, that there was no truth in the idea put forward by Labour since the mid-1960s that it was a 'secretly or potentially radical party' before that time,[4] but his evidence for this was based for the most part on public pronouncements by senior party representatives. However, what people articulate on platforms and what they say behind closed doors can be quite different, while the views of the leadership and those of the rank and file are often at odds. So often painted as little more than the political wing of the Society of St Vincent de Paul, it is little wonder that one recent history of twentieth-century Ireland made the claim that Labour was the 'most difficult of the Irish political parties to understand'.[5] This claim is fairly dubious, but the fact that it can be made at all begs the question of how, in a political system so often painted as a deviant case by writers of comparative politics, Labour should be singled out as being particularly anomalous. Was Labour *really* so strange?

The answer is no. Part of Labour's problem is that it is wilfully misunderstood. Commentators tend to judge it according to their own preconceptions of what a Labour Party should be. It receives short shrift from those on the left who castigate it for its lack of radicalism and mundane social democratic tendencies. Commentators from a more centre-left or liberal perspective, on the other hand, have an idea of what a Labour Party ought to be which is often based on woolly notions of the British Labour Party. Neither perspective allows for the climate in which Labour operated which was far from liberal or open to radical ideals. A more quixotic party might have been nobler, but it would not have been more successful. What differentiates Labour from the short-lived but much written about Republican Congress, for instance, is that Labour actually had sizeable public support. The leftist republican, Peadar O'Donnell, for all the books written about him, never deigned to put himself before the people while Frank Ryan, who did, managed fewer than 900 votes when he stood at the 1937 general election. Similarly, within Labour itself, few on the left in this period stood for election, and fewer still were successful. Regarded in the context of its time, and for what it was instead of what it ought to have been Labour is very easy to understand indeed.

It is difficult to comprehend something, however, when we cannot see it fully, and this presents us with a second problem in understanding Labour, namely, that until now it has never been the subject of a full length academic study. Arthur Mitchell's *Labour in Irish Politics*[6] and J. A. Gaughan's *Tom*

Johnson[7] remain very valuable works, but cover the party's earlier years, as do most of the articles and unpublished theses on Labour. When it comes to Labour in the post-war period, there are now quite a number of memoirs and more journalistic studies (most notably John Horgan's *Labour: The Price of Power*,[8] which paints a particularly vivid portrait of the party from the 1970s) as well as Michael Gallagher's book. These studies are valuable, but selective in their scope. This book aims to take in the big picture, dealing as it does with Labour's first fifty years in Dáil Éireann. It also differs in the wealth of new sources which were available. Using a host of private papers, state records from Ireland and abroad, newspapers and interviews, this book traces Labour's progress, or lack thereof, and endeavours to evaluate Labour's performance in the context of the times. Much of the new material opens a new picture of a party that has been hidden for decades, highlighting the relationship between the Labour leadership and the party's members, the existence of a left wing – albeit one which remained silent in the face of a climate of Catholic anti-communism, and the often sharp discourse within the party on every issue that came before it.

This was not an easy book to research, not least because most of what would have constituted Labour's archive went up in smoke at the back of its head office in Earlsfort Terrace when a change in personnel there in 1967 prompted some over enthusiastic spring cleaning. Nevertheless, this lack of a central archive was a problem which eventually begat rewards. Forced to look beyond the official records of the party, I soon came upon a host of papers of party activists which shone a very different light on the party from the one with which I was familiar. Yes, the party leadership was conservative, as was its parliamentary party and, arguably, most members, but there was a tradition of left-wing activism in the party throughout the decades which, while not influential, was nevertheless an important aspect of the party. Moreover, apart from identifying those in the party who were on its left, it was extraordinary to note the regularity with which external groups, be they republicans, communists, Trotskyists or Catholic Actionists, attempted to infiltrate and influence the party. Many are aware of Militant Tendency's campaign of entryism in the 1970s and 1980s, but few are familiar with similar attempts which began some four decades earlier. Similarly, while the red scares waged against Labour in the 1940s are well known, there has been an unwillingness on the part of most Labour historians to admit that the many of the accusations of communist entryism were well founded. While none of these efforts ended in success (it is only in recent years that the party succumbed to entryism in a significant fashion), they are important nonetheless. Of course, Labour has not only been subject to entryism but to schism too, most notably in the case of the Larkin split in 1923 and later the breakaway by members of the Irish Transport and

General Workers' Union to form the National Labour Party 20 years later. Labour often spent as much time fighting itself as its opponents.

Riven by factions throughout its existence, Labour often seemed as though it was its own worst enemy, although there were many rivals for this title. Labour had the unfortunate ability of being able to please none of the people all of the time. During the civil war, for instance, Labour was attacked by republicans for being collaborators with the Free State but regarded by the government as bleeding-heart liberals. In the 1940s it was regarded as reactionary by leftists and as a hotbed of communists by the Catholic Church.

What follows, then, is an examination of the Irish Labour Party's course over its first fifty years in parliamentary politics. It does not try to put Labour into any paradigms or subject it to Marxist critiques. Nor does it look at what Labour ought to have been, merely what it was: how it operated in the context of Irish society and political culture as it developed from the foundation of the state to more contemporary times. It is hoped that what emerges is a party that is easy to understand, if not always easy to like.

ONE

A VERY CONSTITUTIONAL PARTY

'IF IT'S SOCIALISM YOU WANT, JOIN SOME OTHER PARTY'[1]

—

All too often, analyses of the Irish Labour Party begin with the wrong question. A prime example is David Thornley's 1963 paper in which he asked how 'the militantly Marxist movement of Connolly and Larkin [became] the gradualist and scarcely socialist party of today'.[2] The fact is that while Connolly and Larkin were themselves socialists, Labour, as Larkin's son Young Jim noted, was 'not formed as a socialist party'.[3] Delegates to the 1912 Irish Trade Union Congress (ITUC), itself established some 18 years earlier, passed a resolution to establish a political wing and adopted a new constitution at the annual congress two years later.[4] Congress had resisted setting up a party until then, but with a Home Rule Bill on the statute books in Westminster it looked as though self-government would be a reality within a couple of years, and, as Connolly suggested, the labour movement should be ready to enter an Irish parliament 'to represent a definite organised labour opinion' rather than tacking the movement on to a 'political party of their masters'.[5] Established as the Irish Trades Union Congress and Labour Party (ITUC&LP), its primary objective was

> To organise and unite the workers of Ireland in order to improve their status and conditions generally and to take such action in the industrial and political fields with that end in view as may be decided upon at its Annual Meetings.[6]

In other words, although many of its founders were themselves socialists, Labour was established as the political wing of the trade union movement and its core value was labourism (the pursuit of workers' rights, rather than social- ism) – the restructuring of the economy whereby the state, on behalf of the community, has control of the means of production, distribution and exchange.

The labourist ethos was reinforced by the new party's structure with membership limited to trade unions and trades councils. Unlike the Labour Party in Britain, which was an amalgamation of trade unions, the Fabians and the Independent Labour Party, the party excluded co-operatives and socialist societies. There were two reasons for limiting membership to trade unions.

The need for the unions to retain control of the party was paramount and there were fears that the new party would be 'swamped' if it allowed co-operative societies to join and that careerist politicians would take over.[7] However, the second reason for excluding the socialist organisations was the belief that the adoption of an expressly socialist ethos would hinder the fledgling party. This was not a view put about by reactionaries within the party, but by convinced socialists such as James Connolly who had first-hand experience of the public's antipathy to that ideology fostered, in large part, by the Catholic Church. The Church's hostility to socialism had been most clearly enunciated in Leo XIII's 1891 encyclical *Rerum Novarum* (known in English as *On the Condition of Workers*) which concluded that it was not possible to be a socialist and a good Catholic. Connolly had gone to great lengths to proclaim that this was not the case but it was a view that found little support. Elsewhere, and in Britain in particular, socialism was a vague but benign ideology, George Orwell noting that 'to the ordinary working man, the sort you would meet in any pub on Saturday night, Socialism does not mean much more than better wages and shorter hours and nobody bossing you about'.[8] In Ireland, however, the word as much as the ideas behind it had profoundly sinister connotations, and this was before anyone had even tried it, with the Russian revolution still some five years away. Connolly for one had already founded a socialist party. His reason for establishing a new Labour party was that this one might actually garner popular support.[9] If it was to secure the support of ordinary workers, it would have to tailor its programme to their beliefs which is why Labour's first constitution was 'in all respects a mild political outline of trade union demands, without reference to social, political or economic change in society, although the men who drafted it were all far from being moderate'.[10]

Its constitution or programme, however, remained largely irrelevant while the Labour Party remained, for the most part, an organisation only on paper. The ITUC&LP had contested local elections with a modicum of success, and had contested a single by-election in Dublin in 1915 where it polled very respectably,[11] but that was the extent of its electoral activities until 1922. Without elected representatives or an organisation of individual members, Labour was no more than a notional extension of the trade union movement, obscured, in effect, by the shadow of the unions. It thus spent its first decade, in Michael Laffan's words, 'a delicate and neglected creature, vulnerable, and totally lacking in self-confidence'.[12]

'LABOUR MUST WAIT'

During its earliest years the question of whether or not Labour ought to be socialist was eclipsed by the national question. The Easter rising of 1916 had a profound effect on Irish politics in general and a massive impact on the Irish labour movement in particular. The Irish Citizen Army's participation in the rising resulted in the loss of some of the Irish labour movement's most significant figures, not least James Connolly, whose execution lost Irish workers' their greatest thinker. It is impossible to know how Labour might have fared had Connolly lived. It would almost certainly have taken a very different direction under Connolly's leadership than that of his successors, for Connolly was a Marxist–republican revolutionary and his successors were constitutional social democrats. In death, however, Connolly was able to become all things to all people, in W. K. Anderson's words, 'a vessel into which each man could pour his own dream'.[13] His voluminous writings in which he set out his beliefs unambiguously did not stop Connolly from being invoked across the left-wing spectrum. It would be uncharitable to suggest this was merely a case of the many devils citing scripture for their purpose, but when those purporting to be his successors – regardless of where their politics stood – asked themselves the question 'what would Connolly do?' they invariably found that Connolly would chose the same course of action as they themselves were adopting. Labour was thus able to hold up its founder James Connolly as its patron saint, quoting him at any given opportunity, using his image and his name, commemorating him at Connolly Day celebrations every May, while adopting policies and strategies which bore little resemblance to the path Connolly might himself have chosen. Certainly, without him, there were 'no Lenins, Trotsys, Krassins, Radeks, or Litvinoffs' to take up where Connolly left off, as his successor Tom Johnson noted (anonymously) in 1922.[14]

Apart from the loss of vital personnel there was a paradigm shift in popular support away from Home Rule towards separatism, of which the rise of Sinn Féin was such a vital part. The ITUC&LP, or the Irish Labour Party and Trade Union Congress (ILP&TUC), as it became known in 1919, was certainly not inactive during this time – it was involved in the anti-conscription campaign and many trade unionists were actively involved in the war of independence as they had been in the 1916 rising – but it stood aside from the political fray. In 1918, Sinn Féin successfully prevailed upon Labour not to contest the December general election[15] arguing that 'Labour must wait'. As a sop for standing aside, Sinn Féin turned to the leaders of the Labour movement to draft a statement of social and economic policies for the new parliament – known as the 'Democratic Programme' – which consisted of policies which, as Brian Farrell has observed, Sinn Féin had 'neither the means nor the intention of implementing'.[16] Sinn Féin found it easy to promise the world when they were not in a position to repay, and it became clear when elements of the Sinn Féin party subsequently gained power, that Labour's leaders had been more humoured than heeded.

Of course, while Ireland was undergoing its tumult, the rest of Europe was going through its own turmoil after the First World War, while the Russian revolution marked the greatest political upheaval in a century. In light of what was going on at home and abroad, it is unsurprising that Labour's rhetoric and policies should lurch to the left for a time. This was evident in the ITUC&LP's 1918 constitution which was socialist in all but name,[17] its (unused) 1918 manifesto proclaiming 'we adopt the principles of the Russian Revolution', and the content of the Democratic Programme echoing Labour's support for dictatorship of the proletariat over parliamentary democracy at the 1919 meeting of the Socialist International in Berne. Just how hollow these 'occasional dramatic gestures'[18] were, however, is illustrated by Labour's stance in Berne: the party may have stepped back from parliamentary democracy but it was doing nothing to bring about a dictatorship of the proletariat either. Like Sinn Féin and the Democratic Programme, it found it very easy to lend its weight to promises that it could not keep. For as long as the war of independence continued, Sinn Féin retained its political dominance. The ILP&TUC was growing increasingly restive, but faced with another general election in May 1921, Labour demurred reluctantly once again. By the time negotiations had begun to end the war of independence, however Labour's peripheral position and its impotence had become increasingly obvious. Negotiations were beginning between representatives of Dáil Éireann and the British government, as Labour looked on from the sidelines. As one delegate put it at the 1921 Congress, 'I feel humiliated that in all we read about this great peace movement we appear nowhere in the negotiations'.[19] By now, as Arthur Mitchell noted, 'brutal reality was dawning on Labour: although the leaders were sought after and consulted when they could be useful to the leaders of the national movement, they were to be excluded from the exercise of political power until they could claim a portion of it in their own right'.[20] Labour could wait no more.

LABOUR ENTERS THE FRAY

Negotiations between the British and Irish delegations ended in December 1921 with the signing of the Anglo-Irish Treaty in London, thus ending the war of independence and paving the way for the civil war. Sinn Féin, which had functioned as an uneasy monolith until now, was riven by division over the treaty. For Labour, however, the treaty provided one significant development in the short run – a general election would have to be held during 1922 using proportional representation rather than the first past the post system used in Britain and before then also in Ireland. This meant two things: firstly that the election could not be regarded as a plebiscite on the treaty, and secondly, under the new voting system, Labour would have a better chance than ever of picking up seats. By now, the party's officials – Tom Johnson, William O'Brien, Cathal O'Shannon – were convinced that Labour's influence would remain negligible as long as it stood back from the electoral fray, but others remained unconvinced. On 21–22 February 1922, a special meeting of the ILP&TUC was held in Dublin to decide the issue, where the level of opposition to contesting the election became clear. The leadership's push to fight the election was resisted by labour men and women on four very different grounds. Some, such as the Irish Women Workers' Union, felt that industrial issues were more pressing and that Labour should avoid parliamentary diversions. A Larkinite group which was predisposed to object to anything the leadership suggested did just that, while those of a revolutionary syndicalist or commu-nist outlook wished to restrict labour's struggle to the front line of Ireland's factories and services rather than risk compromise in the political sphere. As Walter Carpenter put it, 'Russia did not bring the Workers' Republic into operation by going to Parliament . . . but through direct action by Lenin and Trotsky'. The fourth group were the republicans, who argued, as they had done in the past, that Labour ought to leave Sinn Féin a clear run once again, and it was the Republican Helena Moloney who moved the amendment that the party should not take part in the forthcoming election.[21] Speaking against the republican amendment, one delegate, Richard Anthony, complained that Labour was always being asked to 'wait until the next election', but wondered when this waiting would stop.[22] The delegates responded that the waiting would stop now. The republican amendment was defeated by 115 votes to 82, a slim enough majority in the circumstances.

Internal division over whether Labour ought stand was not the only significant obstacle as it faced into its first general election. The fact that the Labour Party was still effectively a paper organisation with 'practically no electoral machinery in the political field either nationally or locally' provided further hindrance.[23] With polling due to take place in June, Labour had four months to turn itself into an effective political organisation. The ILP&TUC's weekly newspaper, *Voice of Labour* (edited by Cathal O'Shannon), called on members to tackle the business of organising finance, propaganda, canvassing and acquainting themselves with the electoral register as a matter of urgency. Above all, Labourites were warned against attaching themselves to the electoral machines of either Sinn Féin faction in the course of the campaign. It would, O'Shannon explained, prove difficult to disassociate from such alliances afterwards.[24] Of course, Labour could not contest the election without candidates, and so from March local trade union branches and trades councils across the country held selection conferences. In all, 22 candidates were selected, meaning there were Labour candidates in just over half of the potential 28 constituencies. For a party without local roots or organisation, this was not a bad start, but with Labour's leaders confident of popular support, the small number of candidates seemed a little surprising, though it can be explained by two factors. Firstly, the Labour leadership were inclined to be cautious, and fielded candidates only where they were felt to have a good chance of success,[25] lest widescale defeat bring ignominy at such an early stage. Secondly was the problem of finance. Elections were a very expensive business, not least having to find the £150 deposit for each candidate.[26] ILP&TUC financial appeals to its affiliate unions met with a poor response.[27] Unions were happy to support certain candidates at a local level but their benevolence did not go far.

Arrangements for the election continued as the spectre of civil war loomed increasingly large over the country. On 14 April, units of the IRA's Dublin Brigade led by Rory O'Connor and Liam Mellows took over the Four Courts. Subsequently, their anti-treaty colleagues took over several other buildings in the capital and elsewhere, thus beginning a stand-off which was to last until the end of June. Once again, Labour donned the mantle of honest broker. Tom Johnson, Thomas Foran and Cathal O'Shannon met with O'Connor, Mellows and Joe McKelvey in the Four Courts in an effort to persuade them to vacate the building and avoid confrontation, but to no avail. William O'Brien also ventured there, as did his colleague Frank Robbins, with a similar lack of success.[28] With private talks proving fruitless, the Labour leadership changed tack and called a Strike Against Militarism for 24 April in an effort to put the weight of the country, or at least of its workers, against a descent into civil war. Though the strike was observed with enthusiasm by many workers,[29] it had little effect on those whom it was hoped to sway.

With both sides apparently unwilling or unable to compromise, there was general surprise when on 20 May Michael Collins and Eamon de Valera announced that there would be a pact between their respective sides in the forthcoming poll. Under the terms of this agreement, voters would be presented with a united Sinn Féin panel on which pro- and anti-treaty factions would be represented at their current levels. Furthermore, it was intended that the two groups would form a coalition government after the election. Much to the annoyance of many Sinn Féiners, the pact did not preclude non-Sinn Féin candidates from standing and, taking the matter into their own hands, supporters from both factions exerted moral pressure and intimidation on non-Sinn Féin candidates. Independents (unionists for the most part) and

Farmers' candidates bore the brunt of this. Labour came under less pressure to withdraw,[30] but there were notable instances of intimidation. Dan Morrissey in Tipperary refused the request made by Dan Breen and posse to stand down despite, he claimed, Breen's 'gun levelled at [his] temple'.[31] Patrick Hogan in Clare found it more difficult to decline, despite his best intentions. Not long before the deadline for nominations, Hogan had gone to Ennis Courthouse to register his candidature where he was met by a mob of republicans calling for him to withdraw. Eventually he relented and withdrew on the steps of the courthouse, but not before the legal assessor there had turned the hands back on his watch to give Hogan more time to make the 'correct' decision.[32] In the event, only four of Labour's original 22 candidates stood down but as William Davin, taking his seat for Labour after June 1922, later told the Dáil 'many of the members sitting in these benches had revolvers and guns used against them by people who were party to that pact'.[33]

The campaign itself was short but strenuous.[34] Labour may have lacked electoral organisations at the outset, but within two or three weeks it had it managed to establish machines in 16 constituencies. What it lacked in resources or experience it made up for in energy and enthusiasm, prompting comparisons with Sinn Féin's 1918 performance.[35] Obviously the treaty remained the central issue at hand, not least after Michael Collins repudiated the pact two days before the election on 16 June. Although one Farmers' candidate complained that Labour 'had been spared the general intimidation that was being aimed at them'[36] the party was by no means immune from smear campaigns and dirty tricks during the contest, with William O'Brien, Tom Johnson and Cathal O'Shannon bearing the brunt of such attacks.[37] Johnson's English birth saw him described as a 'loyal son of the Empire', while canvassers in Louth–Meath went about accusing O'Shannon of atheism.[38] In the latter case it would appear that the Louth–Meath electorate were either unusually broadminded or were disinclined to believe such slurs for not only did Cathal O'Shannon top the poll there, but he did so with more than two quotas of first preference votes. In all 17 of the 18 Labour candidates were elected. Five topped the polls, six came second and the other four were elected third. The only unsuccessful candidate, J. T. O'Farrell standing in Dublin North West, lost out by only 13 votes on the last count. Labour blamed dirty tricks for his defeat, but displayed a stoicism that would serve the party well in the years to come: O'Farrell was 'the first Labour candidate to be defeated', remarked the party's annual report of the matter, 'but he won't be the last'.[39]

In the end, voters did not pay undue heed to the pact. Two votes in every five went to non-Sinn Féin candidates and those who voted for Sinn Féin plumped overwhelmingly for the pro-treaty faction which won 38.5 per cent of the national vote (losing five outgoing deputies), compared with just over

21 per cent for the anti-treaty side (which saw 22 outgoing deputies defeated). This meant that non-republicans won just over 78 per cent of the popular vote. Labour benefited most from the republican losses.[40] Garnering over 21 per cent of the poll, Labour had actually overtaken anti-treaty Sinn Féin in terms of votes, although not seats. It was a performance which surpassed all expectations. After years of standing on the political sideline Labour, as the *Irish Times* editorial put it, had '"arrived" as an important and highly organised factor in national affairs'.[41] But if Labour was rightly heartened by the result there was a danger of taking the party's breakthrough at face value. Yes, it had come close to having all its candidates elected and would almost certainly have won even more had it contested more seats, but in reality many of the its votes had been cast primarily in protest against the pact, which was seen by many as an arrogant gesture by Sinn Féin, and as a way to punish 'the patriots who have talked for six months and done nothing but driven the nation ever more rapidly along the road to chaos and ruin'.[42] In this way Labour gained sympathy on the rebound, the electorate responding positively to the party's cry of 'a plague on both your houses'.[43]

The formal transfer of power from the provisional government to the second Dáil was to take place two weeks after the election but by then the uneasy truce between supporters and opponents of the treaty had begun the slide into civil war. On 28 June government troops began bombarding the Four Courts where anti-treaty forces had been in situ for more than two months. After three days of shelling the garrison surrendered. Once again, the Labour leadership endeavoured to prevent an escalation of the conflict, meeting with government and republican sides in an effort to broker a deal, but without success.[44] The civil war had begun. Politics now took a back seat to the hostilities, as the provisional government repeatedly postponed the first meeting of the new Dáil (in all, five times), much to Labour's concern. After five weeks of delays Labour gave the government an ultimatum that its deputies would resign their seats if the Dáil did not meet by 26 August. This deadline was missed, although in view of the sudden deaths of two of the provisional government's most senior members – Arthur Griffith of a brain haemorrhage on 12 August and Michael Collins in an ambush in Cork ten days later – and on the assurance of W. T. Cosgrave, the new president of the executive council, that the Dáil would meet 9 September, Labour was loath to carry out its threat.

The abstention of the Republican deputies meant that the Dáil had a total of 92 deputies of which the government party had 58, giving it a 2:1 majority in the House. Labour was the second largest party with 17 seats, followed by the Farmers' Party with seven deputies, and Independents holding the remaining ten. Even if the opposition parties united to hold the government to account on any issue, they would have found themselves powerless. The opposition ran the full ideological gamut on every issue – from large farmer to labourer, from republican to unionist. In effect, the Farmers and Independents supported the government, making Labour its only opposition in the Dáil. As long as the Republican deputies remained outside the confines of parliament, the government's majority was safe as houses. The role of opposition was assumed with tremendous energy from the outset, although the vast majority of the work was undertaken by certain members, namely, Tom Johnson (Leader), Cathal O'Shannon (Deputy Leader), William O'Brien and T. J. O'Connell (whips), as well as William Davin from Laois–Offaly and the Wexford deputy Richard Corish. The work of the Dáil consisted for the most part of constitutional issues arising from the treaty and security issues arising from the civil war. Labour found a great deal to be critical of in the government's treatment of both questions. The new Free State constitution was lambasted for diluting the state's sovereignty and failing to fulfil the socio-economic promises of the Democratic Programme passed by the First Dáil in January 1919. The constitution passed easily without amendment.[45]

Labour proved equally impotent in its efforts to oppose the government's more draconian security measures as the civil war waged on. It opposed establishing military courts which would have 'the power to inflict sentences of death, penal servitude, imprisonment or fine on persons tried before them and convicted of attack upon the national forces, looting, arson and other destruction or damage to property, possession of explosives or firearm, or the breach of any general order or regulation made by the Army council'.[46] As well as arguing against allowing an inexperienced army to have such untrammelled power over the civilian population, Labour reasoned that such legislation would only play into the hands of republicans.[47] The courts were set up regardless. When the government embarked on a policy of executing republican prisoners, beginning with Erskine Childers on 17 November, Labour protested in the strongest terms and the government turned a deaf ear. To make matters worse, while the government ignored Labour's well-intentioned entreaties on behalf of the Republicans, the Republicans, for their part, had decided that the presence of Labour deputies in the Dáil rendered them collaborators. As the IRA Chief of Staff, Liam Lynch put it in a letter to Tom Johnson, 'the continuing participation of your Party in the proceeding of this illegal parliament can only be construed by us as intentional co-operation with enemy forces in the murder of our soldiers'.[48] Lynch informed Johnson that he would be held *personally* responsible if any further executions took place.[49] On this occasion, Cosgrave offered Labour's deputies accommodation in Buswell's Hotel across the road from Leinster House where they would stay, along with a number of other deputies, under armed protection.[50] In the event, the invitation was declined. In fact, the Labour men were able to continue about their work unmolested, although the threats against their persons did not stop, with the Englishman Johnson attracting more than his share of intimidation.[51] Later, William O'Brien noted that the fact that the Republicans had never carried out their threats against Labour attested to the fact that they were not viewed in the same light as the Cumann na nGaedhaeal (as pro-treaty Sinn Féin were now calling themselves) representatives,[52] although O'Brien's magnanimity was by no means shared by his all his colleagues.[53]

LARKIN'S RETURN

On 30 April 1923 Frank Aiken, the chief of staff of the anti-treaty forces, ordered his men to suspend all offensive operations but on another front a civil war of a very different sort was about to begin. Among the passengers carried by the Dun Laoghaire steam train which arrived into Westland Row that same evening was Jim Larkin, who was returning to Dublin after almost a decade's absence. Some 4,000 supporters were there to welcome him, and with Larkin leading the way in a horse and trap, they made their way towards Liberty Hall accompanied by the O'Connell fife and drum band.[54] Having reached Beresford Place, Larkin made his way inside Liberty Hall, and addressing his supporters from an upstairs window, engaged in 'veiled criticism' of the Transport Union's leadership:[55] complaining that 'there had been a lack of faith and a limitation of vision' within the union, of late.[56] But if William O'Brien's ears were burning, they did so at a distance. Relations between the officers and their general secretary were poor, communications even worse (the first Liberty Hall knew of Larkin's return was an advertisement in an evening newspaper), and only Tom Foran had turned out to meet (rather than welcome) his old boss. O'Brien was not inclined to indulge Larkin, and boycotted the event.[57]

The ITGWU leaders had good reasons for their antipathy towards their general secretary. During Larkin's American sojourn (throughout which he was paid his full salary and his family was supported by union funds), O'Brien and his colleagues had laboured to build up the union from the verge of collapse with considerable success. By Larkin's return the union's finances were reasonably strong, and its membership close to 100,000. Disinclined to let Larkin take up where he had left off, the secretariat had held a conference some days prior to his return, at which changes to the union's rules diluting the general secretary's powers and transferring them to a five man group were ratified. Larkin reacted with public denunciations of O'Brien et al. for maladministration and betrayal and attempted to unseat O'Brien at a meeting of the union's executive. By 10 June Larkin had moved from strong words to direct action when he and a group of around 100 followers seized the Transport Union's headquarters in Liberty Hall and Parnell Square.[58] It was a provocative act, and, at a time when the occupation of strategic buildings was a precursor to open war, a highly symbolic one. The occupations did not last long,[59] but his willingness to relinquish these properties in no way signalled a diminution in hostilities. In fact, Larkin widened his broadside to include the Labour Party, an obvious target in light of its close relationship with the Transport Union at this time. Larkin's re-launched *Irish Worker* was filled with diatribes against the 'God Save the King Labour Party' and its 'English anti-Irishman' leader, but the Larkinite attacks were not merely propagandist, as the violent scenes outside the LP&TUC annual congress that August where Larkinites and republicans tried to block delegates from entering the Mansion House attest.[60]

Larkin's return, and the conflict which ensued marked a serious setback for Labour, and in particular for the party in Dublin. His status and influence were far greater in the capital – where he was regarded as a working-class messiah – than elsewhere, and though his appeals to Transport Union members to reject the O'Brienite leadership were ignored by almost all workers beyond the Pale, they received a more favourable response from the Dublin membership. In one fell swoop, Larkin detached so many of the workers who might otherwise have formed the backbone of Labour organisation in Dublin at precisely the time it needed to establish its roots. Nor did the movement's descent into very public in-fighting do the party's image any good, and the timing could not have been worse. A general election had been set for 27 August. There were 153 seats at stake (increased from 128) and, in the absence of any electoral pact, there was now double the number of candidates compared with the last election.[61] It was only weeks since fighting in the civil war had come to an end, and the prisons were filled with over 12,000 Republican prisoners, including Sinn Féin leader Eamon de Valera, who had been arrested during the campaign. Clearly a state of normality was some time away.

Labour went into the election confident of improving on its position. Though the Larkin feud was a distraction, and sundry disturbances on the industrial front were taking up a great deal of energy, the belief prevailed that Labour's strong performance in the Dáil and workers' discontent about the government's failure to address their economic needs, could only result in more seats and accordingly nominated twice the number of candidates as the previous year. Labour's confidence was shared by many commentators who predicted it might pick up 30 to 35 seats.[62] Others were more circumspect. The London *Times* painted Labour as the 'dark horse' of the parties, suggesting that while Labour had been very active throughout the campaign, it had faced significant problems including the withdrawal of Johnson from the campaign under doctor's orders, the constant attacks from the Larkinites and the increased public annoyance at the disruption caused by the various ongoing labour disputes, making its result difficult to call.[63] In the event, *The Times*'s prediction proved prescient. The poll showed increases for parties across the board – Cumann na nGaedheal picked up five seats, anti-treaty Sinn Féin eight, while the Farmers more than doubled their seats to 15 – apart from Labour. Far from doubling its seats, Labour's vote collapsed by half and its deputies fell to only 14. Among the four outgoing TDs to lose their seats were deputy leader Cathal O'Shannon and ITGWU leader and party whip William O'Brien. More than a quarter of Labour's candidates lost their deposits and the party failed to top the poll in a single constituency.[64] Perhaps most ominously, Labour found itself without a single representative in the cities of Dublin or Cork. The extent of Labour's decline was alarming, but why had its vote collapsed in such a spectacular fashion? First of all, it should be remembered that Labour's vote in 1922 had been artificially high, having attracted many anti-Sinn Féin protest votes which would not otherwise have gone to it. A certain amount of slippage was probably inevitable, but this was ignored by a party which early success had made unduly optimistic. The industrial situation was a significant factor militating against Labour success. Some contemporary observers argued that voters, already tired of the conflict of the civil war, had rejected Labour in protest at being further discommoded by the rash of strikes which followed the ceasefire, although another view is that the party had in fact done too little for the striking workers, who had abandoned it as a result.[65] Labour itself placed most emphasis on the impact of the Larkin split, which undoubtedly cost the party votes especially in Dublin.[66] But in another sense Larkin provided Labour with a convenient scapegoat. Some of the blame had to be levelled at the party's candidates. Take, for example, the failure of O'Brien and O'Shannon to be re-elected. Both were very capable men who had worked reasonably hard to represent the party in the Dáil but neither had the personality of a successful politician. O'Brien, a slight, lame figure, shy and uncharismatic (dubbed the 'mangy rat' to Larkin's 'lion' by the staunch Larkinite Seán O'Casey), lacked the personal touch. O'Shannon was more personable but a little lazy and disinclined to play the game of local powerbroker. Even at this early stage in the new state's development, deputies were already being seen by their constituents as power-broking intermediaries rather than legislators. Deputies from all parties recognised from an early stage that establishing themselves as parish pump politicians gave them the best foothold if they wished to hold on to their seats at the next election. But not all were so cunning. Cathal O'Shannon's response to a man who wrote to him seeking assistance with finding a job in the army belied either a surfeit of integrity or a crass lack of cunning. Rebuking his correspondent for his failure to understand either the position of the party or that of individual deputies he explained:

> It is not part of our job to assist individual men to get posts in any army or indeed in any other establishment. The job imposed on us is to secure the all round improvement of the conditions etc. of any and every section of the workers and eventually to raise the general standard and status of the workers as a whole.

Concluding, O'Shannon suggested that if the man wanted such a post he should 'apply to the authorities concerned in the ordinary way'.[67] It should come as no surprise then that O'Shannon, elected on two quotas in 1922, merely won his marching orders this time around.

LABOUR AND THE FOURTH DÁIL

With the Republicans still abstaining and Cumman na nGaedheal still by far the largest party, the election had done little to alter the make up of the chamber and the fourth Dáil continued in much the same vein as its predecessor, with Labour once again in the unenviable position of acting as official opposition to a government which happily ignored it without fear of defeat.[68] It is not surprising, then, that the Labour Party which entered the new Dáil in 1923 was particularly dejected. Tom Johnson, who had been subjected to Larkin's brickbats throughout the campaign and had suffered a breakdown in its latter stages, had taken his party's electoral collapse particularly to heart and signalled that Labour would focus exclusively on economic issues since the electorate had intimated 'fairly and clearly' that it did not want Labour to take any responsibility for criticising the government on constitutional or security issues.[69] In the event, this policy was soon abandoned, as Johnson's sense of responsibility proved too great to let the government act without criticism on such important issues as its failure to release thousands of republican prisoners long after the civil war had ended.[70]

The fourth Dáil proved a particularly difficult time for Johnson as party leader. He had lost two of his most active parliamentarians at the last election, and his colleagues had little inclination to take up the brunt of their work. Admittedly, Tom Johnson's management style may have had something to do with his comrades' silence. Johnson continued to do the lion's share of Dáil duties, which created resentment in some quarters at least, with William Davin complaining at Congress that Johnson said 'all there was to be said' on most issues.[71] Others did not agree, however. T. J. O'Connell recalled that he and his colleagues were perfectly happy to let Johnson dominate the stage, while Gilbert Lynch (first elected in June 1927) wrote fondly of how, when it came to new deputies,

> Johnson mothered us all like a hen mothering her chicks. He watched over us all the time. He knew we were new and not used to looking up for material when debates were on. He generally either told us where we could find the information we were looking for or found it for us. The first deputy to arrive each day at the Dáil was Tom Johnson and the last deputy to leave was Tom Johnson. He was a wonderful man.[72]

It is impossible to say whether the more retiring deputies might have blossomed had they not been in their leader's shadow, but on balance it is unlikely. By the summer of 1925, his heavy workload, continued frustration at Labour's complete lack of progress in the Dáil and the unrelenting personal attacks against him (by Larkin in particular) had become too much for Johnson, who submitted his resignation as leader of the Labour Party in the Dáil and secretary of the ILP&TUC.[73] The Party/Congress executive refused to accept his resignation and told him to take an extended holiday.[74] Refreshed after his time off and heartened by his comrades' support, Johnson returned to the Dáil with a renewed sense of purpose. His priority at this time was to get the Republican deputies to enter the Dáil. Johnson had always believed that Irish politics could never reach a state of normality unless the republicans abandoned absentionism, and under the current circumstances not only would their entry to the Dáil help to reconcile them with the new state, it would also provide a more effective opposition against the government. Johnson's policy was not universally popular among his colleagues, not least because the republicans' support seemed to be on the verge of collapse. Their vote in recent by-elections and local elections had declined significantly, while the number of affiliated cumainn had decreased markedly (there were half as many in July 1925 as there had been a year earlier) and they were beginning to experience significant problems with finance as funding from the United States began to dry up.[75] For many Labour men it seemed more sensible to let the republicans wither on the vine rather than encourage them to join the fray.

Johnson's efforts proved fruitless in the short run, but they might have helped to bolster the efforts of Seán Lemass. Lemass had seen the writing on the wall, and was trying to push Sinn Féin to abandon some of its sacred cows and establish a more bread and butter agenda to regain public support. In December 1925 Johnson renewed his appeals in an effort to defeat the report of the Boundary Commission, but once again de Valera refused. Although

sympathetic, he argued it was impossible for the Sinn Féin TDs to act against
their abstentionist mandate. By March 1926, however, de Valera was ready to
make his move. A special Ard Fheis was held to discuss the Sinn Féin president's proposal that in the event of the Oath of Allegiance being removed it
would be a question of policy rather than principle whether republicans
entered the Dáil. It was defeated by a very narrow majority (223–218) and the
following day, de Valera resigned as president of the party.[76] Moves to establish
a new party followed almost immediately and after a few weeks of frantic
preparation the inaugural meeting of Fianna Fáil–The Republican Party took
place in Dublin's La Scala theatre on 16 May 1926. De Valera's address to the
gathering must have served as something of a shot across the boughs for
Labour's leaders. Having dealt with the questions of the oath and partition
rather summarily at the beginning, de Valera devoted the best part of his speech
to social and economic issues. Labour saw its key issues of unemployment,
housing and poverty adopted by de Valera, who while he was at it decided to
adopt Labour's founder, James Connolly, as Fianna Fáil's own.[77] Beware of
false prophets, was the *Voice of Labour*'s response to events, as it warned that
Fianna Fáil had no more to offer than Sinn Féin. Yes, it conceded, there were
many in the new party's ranks who were some of Labour's 'sincerest sympathisers', but while its heart may have been in the right place, it lacked 'real
understanding of working class problems, needs and aims'.[78]

One serious advantage enjoyed by the new party was that it understood
how to organise. While Labour had one man trying to build up a local branch
network single handed, a crack team of Fianna Fáil volunteers led by Seán
Lemass and Gerry Boland were travelling the length and breadth of the
country to establish a cumann in every parish. One observer noted at the
time that on many weekends as many as twenty motor cars, with four or
five speakers in each, could be seen departing from Fianna Fáil's O'Connell
Street headquarters to spread the party's gospel throughout the state.[79]
(Several decades later Labour's great leap forward in this direction saw
the Administrative Council purchase a bicycle for its national organiser.[80])
Fianna Fáil's emphasis on building up a grass-roots membership was somewhat unusual among Irish parties. Labour was for the idea in theory and,
although wary of allowing careerists or troublemakers into its ranks, had it the
personnel and the wherewithal to organise systematically undoubtedly it
would have done so. Cumann na nGaedheal, on the other hand, was apparently trying to wind down what little organisation it had,[81] while Sinn Féin
was finding it hard to retain its organisation let alone build on it. Ultimately
this meant that the new party was able to cut a swathe through the country,
building up support and establishing machines to be put into operation at the
next election.

Although Labour's organisation paled in comparison with Fianna Fáil's, it was becoming more and more optimistic around this time, and with good reason. There had been success in the local elections of 1925, followed in February 1926 by the party's first by-election success when William Norton, the 26-year-old general secretary of the Post Office Workers' Union, took the seat in Dublin County. Significantly, the party had become much more relaxed of late since Larkin's attacks had peaked the previous summer, and now felt it was possible to go on the offensive against the government rather than defend itself from the Larkinites. With an election on the horizon, Labour's new-found confidence was much needed. The fourth Dáil was dissolved on 20 May 1927, leaving less than three weeks until polling day on 9 June, although in effect campaigning had begun in mid-April. At the outset, it seemed as though it might prove an interesting contest. Three new parties were standing: Fianna Fáil (which nominated 87 candidates compared with Sinn Féin's 15), Clann Éireann, a tiny splinter group of Cumann na nGaedheal origin which nominated eight candidates, and the National League, established by Captain Willie Redmond in September 1926. Described as 'a party of malcontents representing nothing fundamental in Irish political divisions',[82] the National League lacked a significant programme but provided a welcome home for those who wished to vote against the government party but for whom Labour was too left wing or working class. It fielded 30 candidates, of whom 12 were former Nationalist MPs.[83] Labour fielded the third largest number of candidates, after the government party and Fianna Fáil, at 44, three fewer than in 1923. Its failure to nominate sufficient candidates to be able to form a government was criticised in the press, but as Tom Johnson countered, the party simply could not afford to hand over to the government three or four thousand pounds in forfeited deposits.[84] Labour went before the country with a programme little different to those of earlier contests. It pointed to its role in the Dáil as the 'defenders of liberties of the people [and] opponents of every tendency towards autocracy',[85] and outlined its usual demands for the right to work, the development of industry and agriculture, and improved education provision, housing and social insurance for all. On this occasion, however, Labour found itself competing against a Fianna Fáil party whose programme had been culled 'without acknowledgement' from Labour.[86] In fact, Johnson alleged at the time, of the 15 items in the new party's programme, 12 had been filleted wholesale from Labour.[87]

The campaign itself attracted little interest,[88] but its results proved fascinating. Cumann na nGaedheal's vote fell by almost a third and with only 47 seats in the new Dáil, it found itself without a majority of *sitting* deputies. Fianna Fáil, on the other hand, held practically all of the old Sinn Féin vote and found itself with 44 seats. (Sinn Féin held five, having nominated 15 candidates). Labour was returned as the third largest party, its 22 seats representing a 50 per cent increase on its 1923 figure, a result which matched what the party's leaders had expected, if less than some had hoped for.[89] It did so, however, on an increase of only two per cent of the national vote. Its gains in Tipperary, Leix–Offaly, Wexford and Limerick came from fielding second candidates in areas where it was strong.[90] One place where there was a significant swing towards Labour was Dublin which, in the midst of the Larkin split, had seen the most spectacular collapse at the last election. This time it more than doubled its vote to over ten per cent which meant that its representation in the capital had increased from none to two, an improvement on a sorry state of affairs, but considering the number of working-class votes for the picking, it was little cause for celebration.

Cumann na nGaedheal was four seats short of a working majority provided that the abstentionist deputies remained just that. Fianna Fáil did attempt to enter the Dáil, armed with counsels' opinion that deputies could take their seats without taking the oath, but when their effort was rebuffed by the clerk of the Dáil, they withdrew,[91] leaving the way clear for W. T. Cosgrave to be re-elected as president by 68 votes to Labour's 22 against. The National League deputies – who had ostensibly fought the election as an opposition party – abstained on this occasion, which seemed to bode more of the same, with the government able to operate oblivious to outside influences. This, however, did not last long. On the morning of 10 July, Kevin O'Higgins, minister for justice and external affairs and Cosgrave's deputy in the cabinet, was fatally wounded after he was set upon by a group of three gunmen. The assassination of the second most senior member of the government was shocking, particularly after a period of relative calm. The following day, Thomas Johnson and T. J. O'Connell met with Cosgrave to offer Labour's sympathy and pledge support for the government. Should Cosgrave feel it necessary to form a national government to safeguard national security, Labour would be a willing participant. Cosgrave declined, however.[92] Instead the government responded by introducing three pieces of legislation intended to break the republicans' backs: a new public safety bill, a bill to remove the initiative from the constitution thus preventing the republicans from scrapping the oath in such a fashion; and finally, and most significantly, a bill which would compel prospective Dáil candidates to pledge that they would take their seats upon election. If the public safety bill was an attack on the IRA, the latter two pieces of legislation were designed to force Fianna Fáil to decide between going to hell or Kildare Street, and to do so on Cosgrave's terms. Labour, sensing danger in the hastily put together legislation, tried to delay the reading of the bills, but to no end.[93] The debates on the legislation were fraught, at one point the Labour deputies walked out of the chamber in protest after one government minister accused the party of trying to make political capital out of O'Higgins's death, Johnson's customary decorum was absent for once as he called the president a liar across the floor of the House.[94] Labour's opposition, along with that of the Farmers' Party and the National League, was not enough to stop the public safety bill or the pre-electoral pledge, which had passed all stages by 4 August.

In the meantime, talks had begun between Labour and Fianna Fáil to discuss the current impasse. Labour's efforts to get Fianna Fáil to enter the Dáil had effectively been ongoing, with Labour deputies 'who had any influence with any Fianna Fáil deputy using [their] influence', only to see de Valera and 'and a few of the more extreme members' unwilling to swallow the oath.[95] Towards the end of July, the newly elected Galway deputy Gilbert Lynch, a trade union official with strong republican links, was approached by Charlie Ridgeway, an ITGWU branch secretary, who had been imprisoned during the civil war.[96] Ridgeway was concerned that the situation arising from O'Higgins's shooting and the legislation which followed could lead to a resumption of civil war. In the belief that this would be avoided if Fianna Fáil entered the Dáil, he contacted a number of republicans, including Seán MacEntee and Peadar O'Donnell, before asking Gilbert Lynch for his help.[97] Lynch agreed to assist, subject to Johnson's approval which was readily given, and several meetings between Lynch (accompanied by Wicklow deputy James Everett) and MacEntee ensued.[98] Lynch recalled that he and Everett were making good progress, until they met with the Fianna Fáil leader. De Valera had agreed to the Labour proposals that his party would enter the Dáil, support a Labour-led coalition and raise no controversial issues during the lifetime of the fifth Dáil in exchange for Labour's efforts to remove the oath, but the negotiations very nearly fell apart when Lynch suggested that they should put this agreement in writing. De Valera 'hit the ceiling' at the inference that he could not be taken at his word, and although he subsequently obliged, he remained furious at what he felt had been Lynch's slight.[99]

Other negotiations were taking place at the same time. Late on the evening of 1 August, Gerald Boland had called to Tom Johnson's house for the first in a series of meetings with the Labour leader in an effort to establish what his party's attitude to the oath would be were it to form a government. Johnson's first response – that he would seek to remove it with the agreement of the British government, and would resign if this was not possible – was rejected by Fianna Fáil as not going far enough. More meetings ensued – de Valera saying he would enter the Dáil, then almost immediately changing his mind 'irrevocably' – but eventually agreement was reached. In a memorandum outlining Labour's position on a number of queries raised by Fianna Fáil, Johnson now promised that a Labour administration would seek to get rid of the oath through agreement with the British government, but if this approach were to fail the question would be left to a referendum for the people to decide.[100] This was enough for the Fianna Fáil leadership, who agreed to lend its support to a Labour-led government when it entered the Dáil. Once Fianna Fáil had declared themselves on side the matter was put to Labour's national executive, where it was approved with Louie Bennett's the sole dissenting voice.[101] Finally, on 11 August, the Fianna Fáil deputies signed the Dáil register and took their seats. Subsequently, Tom Johnson gave formal notice that he was calling a motion of no confidence in the government for the Dáil's next sitting on 16 August.

By now Labour and Fianna Fáil held 66 seats between them and needed at least nine more seats to achieve an overall majority.[102] The National League was prepared to make up the shortfall, although at a price. Distrustful of Fianna Fáil's influence and wary that Labour might implement some overly radical legislation, the League demanded a proportional number of seats in the new government; Labour was prepared to offer two ministries, which turned out to be enough for Redmond at least. Not all his colleagues were satisfied with this state of affairs, however: one, Vincent Rice, resigned from the party to support the government and a number of other deputies were looking a little uncertain. This meant that when the Dáil met to debate the confidence motion on 16 August, no one could predict what the outcome of the vote would be with the two sides so closely matched.[103] The debate was a subdued five hours. Johnson, in particular, was exhausted and gave an unconvincing performance, although this had little bearing on the result of the vote, since none of the independent deputies was prepared to vote against the government. With the two sides evenly split, the matter was settled by the Ceann Comhairle's casting vote in favour of the government. The absence of Sligo independent Alderman John Jinks is often credited with having scuppered the vote for the coalition, but some of the blame rested closer to home. Had Labour not given its deputy leader, T. J. O'Connell, leave to attend a conference in Canada at the time of the vote, Jinks's absence would have had no consequence. Moreover, at least one of the independents on whom Labour had been counting, was not prepared to see an Englishman become president of Ireland.[104]

It is difficult to see this defeat as anything but a lucky escape for Labour. Had it succeeded in the vote, its administration would certainly have proved short lived and ineffectual. It was too ideologically diverse – the only thing shared by the three constituent parties was their dislike of Cumann na nGaedheal, after that they disagreed on everything. Indeed, socially and economically Labour and the National League were polar opposites; Johnson had to promise not to 'press contentious legislation upon the coalition'[105] but with the League representing profoundly bourgeois interests it is doubtful if any reforming legislation put forward by Labour would be seen as anything other than contentious. So what would the government have done in office once the oath had been dealt with? Very little, it can be surmised, which meant that in the end defeat spared Labour the embarrassment of trying to make this unstable lame-duck administration work, which was no small blessing but provided little consolation at the time. After five years of being criticised as overly cautious and too inclined to do the right thing, Labour was now vilified as irresponsible. But did Labour have any alternative? In reality it did not. Its credibility had been questioned at the opening of the fifth Dáil when it objected to Cosgrave's election as president, yet did not offer itself as an alternative. It is difficult to see how it could have justified refusing to take power when presented with the chance.

The government held on this time, but its position was far from secure, and it was only a matter of weeks before Cosgrave announced he was dissolving the Dáil and calling an election for 15 September 1927. This time, Cumann na nGaedheal and Fianna Fáil nominated the same number of candidates in the previous election, but the smaller parties and independents were caught on the hop, having expended their relatively meagre resources earlier in June. The AC agreed that all of Labour's outgoing deputies should stand again[106] along with a handful of others, leaving it with 28 candidates compared with 44 in June. On this occasion, the Transport Union informed all of its candidates that it would be unable to fund them because it was too soon after the last election, leaving many candidates with practically no funds for the campaign.[107] Nor was Labour's impecuniousness its only problem, for Larkin was back on the scene. He had taken no interest in the June 1927 election, but had become prominent afterwards with his public denunciations of the legislation introduced in the wake of the O'Higgins's shooting. Now faced with another general election, Larkin entered the fray once more. Under the banner of the Irish Workers' League, Larkin stood in Dublin North himself, his eldest son Jim junior (popularly known as Young Jim) stood in County Dublin while John Lawlor, the general president of the WUI stood in Dublin South.[108] Where there was no Workers' League, voters were urged to cast their vote for Fianna Fáil. Nor were the attacks on Labour directed only from the left. Since the no confidence motion, Labour had found itself under a barrage of criticism from Cumann na nGaedheal for its part in trying to bring down the government. Cosgrave accused it of socialism,[109] with several members of the clergy making similar pronouncements.[110] In a tense and emotional contest, Labour was subjected to a particularly personalised vindictive campaign. In scenes reminiscent of the 1923 general election, Labour speakers found themselves harassed by Larkinites at every given opportunity, with Tom

Johnson singled out for particular abuse. When one meeting in Rathfarnham degenerated to the point of physical violence, poetic justice declared that it was Larkin who emerged injured from a scuffle involving the Johnsons *en famille*.[111] There was also a smear campaign which accused the ILP&TUC's assistant general secretary R. J. P. Mortished (another Englishman, although of Irish parentage) of being a Black and Tan. Members of the Communist Party of Great Britain who had travelled to Dublin to assist with Larkin's campaign were astonished by the behaviour of Larkin and his supporters, and consulted with non-Larkinite communists on the matter. Larkin, furious at the CPGB's meddling, complained to Moscow, and asked that the British contingent be instructed to break its links with the Workers' Party. Moscow issued an edict accordingly but advised Larkin to be more critical of Fianna Fáil and less hostile towards Labour in the future.[112]

The campaign could not have been any worse for Labour. Under-resourced, demoralised, attacked in the press and by its opponents on the left and right, Labour tried in vain to position itself as a responsible party which had merely sought to prevent a reactionary government from going too far. And, it argued quite rightly, coalitions were the natural form of government under proportional representation, so why should Labour be maligned for attempting to form one.[113] Once the results came in, however, it became clear that the electorate was unconvinced. The poll showed an unmistakable swing towards the two larger parties. Cumann na nGaedheal's vote rose by over ten per cent, increasing its number of seats from 47 to 62, while Fianna Fáil's vote increased by nine per cent, bringing its seats from 44 to 57. All the minor parties fared badly – the Farmers' Party saw its number of seats almost halved to six, while the National League was returned with only two deputies. Twelve independents were returned, compared with 16 in the previous election. Of the three Workers' League candidates, Big Jim Larkin alone was successful, although he was prevented from taking up his seat as an undischarged bankrupt. (This had arisen following his failure to pay damages awarded against him in a libel case taken by Tom Johnson two years earlier after Larkin had accused Johnson of 'encouraging the Government to shoot unemployed demonstrators'.[114]) Labour's vote fell two and a half percentage points to 9.1 per cent, its lowest level yet, its number of seats falling from 22 to 13. Tom Johnson was among the fallen. He had held on to his seat in June with some difficulty and his vulnerability was recognised by the decision that he alone should stand in the County Dublin constituency in September, but this was not enough to save him. Labour's vote in that constituency crashed by two thirds. Some of the blame can be laid at the feet of the Larkinites; Young Jim Larkin garnered an impressive 2,126 votes but even if these votes had gone to Johnson his first preference vote would still have been half that of three months earlier. Nor was there any chance of him being elected on transfers – he did not get any. It is difficult to see Johnson's performance as anything other than the electorate punishing him for the events of the summer.

Having endured its most bruising campaign yet, Labour returned to the Dáil half the size it had left it, its leader among the losses and its baker's dozen of a parliamentary party understandably demoralised. Nevertheless, if comfort, however slight, could be drawn from the situation it was that perhaps a new Labour leader might prove more popular with the electorate. The fact was that while Johnson was a conscientious parliamentarian and an individual of the highest integrity, his brand of rather austere, over earnest Englishness was never likely to gain support for Labour and, privately, after he had lost his seat, he admitted that another leader might have better success at building the party's organisation around the country.[115] What Labour needed now was someone with energy, focus and charisma who could guide it in the Dáil while fostering its support among the voters. Unfortunately, there was not a very large pool from which to choose, but in the end, it was T. J. O'Connell, deputy leader of the PLP since 1923, who was nominated for the job. O'Connell was a reasonably diligent parliamentarian and had been a regular contributor to Dáil debates, but his performances were far from exceptional and it seemed he was unlikely to set the Dáil ablaze with his attacks on the government. Moreover, as general secretary of the Irish National Teachers' Organisation (INTO) he found himself with a heavy union workload to distract from his party business. At best, it looked as though O'Connell might be able to keep the party's level of support stable but with Fianna Fáil making significant inroads into the working-class vote this was not an option. Labour needed to adopt a more aggressive stance if it had any hope of survival.

Though 15 seats short of a working majority, Cosgrave was elected president of the executive council by a majority of six votes with the help of the Farmers' Party and independents. Fianna Fáil's presence in the chamber and the relatively unstable nature of the government's majority meant that the mood of the seventh Dáil became particularly tense and fractious. Although economic and social issues dominated the parliamentary agenda, the civil war cast a long shadow and it took very little provocation for debates to descend into name calling. As if making up for lost time, Fianna Fáil took up the role of official opposition with gusto, although it took a little while before it found its feet, and for the first eight months of the new Dáil Labour continued to table most of the opposition amendments and motions while Fianna Fáil

were more active in the debates.[116] This diminution in Labour's role was not
helped by the pronounced lack of discipline within the parliamentary party
which often saw Labour deputies dealing with issues on the basis of personal
preferences rather than the party line. Such was the tendency towards individualism that Tom Johnson remarked privately that 'strictly speaking there
was not a Labour Party in the Saorstát because, of the party's thirteen TDs
and five senators, no two of them would agree even on fundamentals'.[117] (In
fact, by the end of the fifth Dáil, two of the 13 Labour deputies elected in
September had left to sit as independents and two had been expelled for
breaches of discipline.[118]) With the issue taken up by delegates at successive
Congresses, T. J. O'Connell was prompted to complain that the critics were
ignoring the majority of occasions when the PLP voted together to harp on
about the few occasions they had not, arguing that Labour discipline was as
good as, if not better than that of the two larger parties.[119] This was not
entirely accurate, for although Cumann na nGaedheal and Fianna Fáil suffered
occasional absenteeism, when their deputies *did* vote (and they usually did)
they did so along party lines. However, the government's knife-edge majority
made such issues of paramount importance. Fianna Fáil and Labour were to
be found on the same side in divisions more often than not, but each party
nonetheless accused the other of propping up the government.[120] Setting out
grounds for attack on this matter, Seán Lemass wrote to Frank Gallagher,
then editor of Fianna Fáil's newspaper *The Nation*:

> I think you should make reference to the fact that on practically every occasion on
> which the government was in difficulties since we went into the Dáil and a tight
> division was imminent members of the Labour Party left the House so as not to
> defeat the Government. On the occasion of many divisions I have seen members
> of the Labour Party sitting in the public Gallery while the voting was going on
> and returning to the House after the announcement of the result was made. They
> have saved the Government repeatedly in this way.[121]

Labour countered by citing instances where Fianna Fáil deputies had
apparently done the same.[122] In reality, following on from the confidence
motion debacle of August 1927, neither party was in a hurry to bring down the
government just yet. The issue unexpectedly came to a head, however, after a
successful reading of an opposition private member's bill to amend old age
pension legislation prompted Cosgrave to resign as president.[123] De Valera
announced he would stand against Cosgrave in the presidential vote, and,
rather than pick sides between the two, the PLP decided to nominate
O'Connell. Initially, Seán Lemass suggested that were de Valera to prove
unsuccessful, Fianna Fáil would support O'Connell, but when the Labour

whip William Davin launched an angry attack on de Valera, accusing Fianna Fáil of creating 'uncertainty, unrest and uneasiness in the minds of the public', his remarks provoked a volte-face from Lemass. Far from supporting a Labour administration, he found the very notion of a Labour administration 'ludicrous'.[124] By the time the Dáil met on 2 April for the presidential vote, the debate had come to focus on the differences between the two opposition parties. Speaking against de Valera's nomination, O'Connell cited Fianna Fáil's refusal to accept the legitimacy of the Dáil as Labour's primary reason for its opposition, and accused it of putting constitutional issues over the economic welfare of the Irish people. He acknowledged that the two parties shared many policies, but O'Connell said he was not prepared to admit the suggestion 'that there are no essential differences between their programme and ours'.[125] His speech was effectively an attempt to place his party equidistant between the two larger parties, promising to vote against de Valera as they had voted against Cosgrave but it was less than convincing, not least because O'Connell seemed to spend more time talking about de Valera and the treaty than where he and his party stood in April 1930. In so doing, O'Connell merely highlighted Labour's tendency towards rigid constitutionalism – the London *Times* had once called it a 'very constitutional party'[126] – which looked staid in comparison with Fianna Fáil's 'slightly constitutional' character, a term coined by Seán Lemass in response to earlier clashes with Labour during a debate on civil war prisoners.[127] Naturally Lemass was forthright in castigating Labour's attitude. 'I have said already', he remarked,

> that the outstanding characteristic of the Labour Party is that it is the most respectable Party in this State. The members of that Party desire to be respectable above everything else. So long as they cannot be accused of being even pale pink in politics they seem to think they have fulfilled their function towards the Irish people. That is why, with the exception of the National League Party, they are the smallest Party in the House.[128]

Once de Valera had been comfortably defeated (93 votes to 54), it was O'Connell's turn to be nominated. This time Lemass kept his comments brief, but he said everything he needed to say. The notion that a party which held 13 of the 153 seats in the Dáil would aspire to government was ridiculous. Fianna Fáil would not support O'Connell's nomination, nor would it waste time by debating the issue.[129] In the event, not one deputy outside Labour deigned to lend their support to O'Connell whose nomination as President was roundly defeated by 13 lowly votes to 78. Eventually, Cosgrave was re-elected with a comfortable majority.

Labour's performance that day earned it plaudits from the London *Times*, which felt it had earned the honours of the debate with its 'respect for constitutionalism and a common sense which promise well for its political future'.[130] For an Irish working-class party to earn praise from such quarters should have sounded alarm bells. It certainly underlined Lemass's remarks about its pale pink respectability. Labour had set itself up as a bastion of conformity and Fianna Fáil was only too happy to adopt the mantle of radicalism in its wake. Time would tell which would prove more popular with Irish voters.

THE FOUNDATION OF 'THE IRISH LABOUR PARTY'

Labour's drubbing at the September 1927 election prompted renewed focus on the party's organisation. The fact was, as William Norton maintained, that 'not one of the 13 deputies held his seat with trade union votes'.[131] (Norton was by this time a former deputy, unable to repeat his by-election victory in the following general election.) Indeed, the unreliability of the union vote was highlighted by Tom Johnson's defeat in a constituency with sufficient trade union votes to return at least two candidates.[132] As Johnson himself put it:

> Trade unionism cannot hope to cover more than one sixth of the electorate at the utmost and a Labour Party based on trade unions would require to have not only the unanimous support of the members of unions but great additional support from outside before it could obtain a majority . . . there is also a common idea not yet worn down that the Labour Party is a labourer's party – with no objective or purpose but work and wages, pensions and insurance benefits. This conception may be dissipated in time but the trade union control helps to perpetuate it . . . there is a growing feeling on my part that the trade union appeal is too often narrow, anti-social and unduly selfish.[133]

If trade unionists were resistant to Labour's charms, the solution, as far as Norton and others were concerned, was to abandon the party's narrow union appeal and look elsewhere for votes. This was the thinking behind William Norton's resolution, passed by the 1929 congress, to establish a committee to consider the merits of separating the political and industrial sides of the movement into two autonomous organisations. A special conference to be held not later than February 1930 would then decide on the committee's report.[134]

The Committee on Re-organisation decided at its first meeting that the two arms of the movement should go their separate ways (as its report argued, 'a trade union is essentially an organisation of wage earners . . . a democratic political party must make a wider appeal'), and its subsequent meetings were spent hammering out the logistics of the split such as the division of personnel, assets and liabilities. There was an implicit acceptance that the split would have little significant effect on Congress and that the reason behind the move was first and foremost to revive the party. The committee thus paid quite a lot of attention to the structure and image of the new party. The constitutions of other social democratic or labour parties were examined, including the Social Democrats in Germany and the South African Labour Party,[135] but the committee's final report was bereft of any of the advances (such as quotas for women on the party executive) to be found elsewhere. But if the committee seemed predisposed to conservatism, it did consider one quite radical – albeit superficial – proposal to broaden the party's appeal. Such was the desire for the party to move away from its image as the 'Labourers' Party' that the committee considered changing its name to something less sectional, with the Social Democratic Party, the Progressive Party, the Constructive Party, the Democratic Social Progressive Party, the People's Party, the Party of Social Justice and the Democratic Liberty Party (or League) among the alternatives.[136] In the end, however, the committee plumped for the familiar and decided upon the National Labour Party. The use of the term 'national' in the party's title was significant, for it was in line with the nationist, community-centred rhetoric in the new party's constitution and literature; sectional language was entirely abandoned and there was to be no talk of workers or capital. The deeply moral, civic republican tone of the document could best be described as Christian socialist, although there was no mention of socialism, and any references to Christianity were excised from the final draft.[137]

The plan for separation met with wide approval when the special conference met in Dublin on 28 February 1930, although the response to the new party's constitution was less favourable, with Cathal O'Shannon urging Labour to 'pitch its banner a little nearer to the skies', and William McMullen criticising its 'pale pink, bourgeois objects that anybody could subscribe to'.[138] Of course, it was precisely the idea that anybody could subscribe to Labour's objects that was behind the new constitution, and Norton in particular was keen to stress that retaining the status quo was simply not feasible, noting that 'if the experience of 1927 is not to be repeated, we must create a Labour Party which will make a really serious bid for the reins of government'.[139] This meant, as least as far as Norton saw it, tackling Fianna Fáil on its populist terms. It was a dangerous strategy, however, for in trying to broaden its appeal the party risked diluting its message to the point where it was effectively pointless. It also provided ammunition to the republican leftists, such as Peadar O'Donnell and Frank Ryan, and the proliferation of communist front groups that were mushrooming in Dublin and beyond around this time, and which preferred to attack the easy target of Labour than the more appropriate enemy of Cumann na nGaedheal. While these fringe groups were politically insignificant and enjoyed virtually no popular support they were an unwelcome irritation to the new party. Indeed, when the newly constituted Labour Party held its inaugural meeting in the Mansion House in April 1930, Peadar O'Donnell played evil fairy at the event, leading a ragtag of Fianna Fáilers and communists in scenes of organised hooliganism outside and in the hall of the meeting.[140] What was intended as a bold declaration of Labour's intent turned into a fiasco, with the spectacle of Labour leaders vying to be heard over pro-Soviet slogans and cries of 'Up Dev!' marking an inauspicious start.

In its desire to broaden the class basis of the new party, Labour planned to approach not only professionals such as 'lawyers and professors', but also 'manufacturers' to join its ranks. It also proposed issuing personal invitations to James Coburn, the National League deputy and other potential converts from the Fianna Fáil and Cumann na nGaedheal benches but, if in fact any of these deputies were actually approached, none of them joined.[141] Claims made a year after Labour's launch that its members included 'hundreds of small farmers, shop keepers, professional men and other classes of citizens who [had] had no previous association with our party previous to the adoption of the new constitution'[142] are unsubstantiated and unlikely, but there was something of a need to exaggerate Labour's gains as a response to continued complaints about the party's diluted objectives. *The Irishman*, edited (and mostly written) by Cathal O'Shannon, was one of the loudest voices on this subject. It complained the new party was 'too apologetic', that it needed to 'go back to socialism' and to be 'more audacious',[143] with one correspondent arguing:

> Our programme has been adulterated, our visions obscured, our viewpoint modified – in every way we are but the remnant of a party that was. Even the word 'socialism' if not entirely eliminated from our vocabulary is now used with greater circumspection.

Labour had abandoned its 'resolute class character' and with it its vigour, because 'we chose to be "regular guys" in the orthodox political sense; because we preferred to wash our little necks and faces, don nice clean collars, and pride ourselves that we had as much claim to the support and sympathy of the upper and middle class as any lanky de Valera . . . or frail Cosgrave'.[144] The prevailing view among Labour's leaders, however, remained that the middle group would yield the greatest gains, and unless there was tangible evidence to the contrary, this was the course which would be adhered to.

Since no individual membership figures were kept at this time it is impossible to gauge how successful Labour was in attracting new members. The situation at branch level is much clearer, however, and the fact is that only a year into the new party's existence the number of affiliated Labour branches in existence was lamentable. A full-time organiser was appointed in September 1930 with a view to organising the Labour Party generally and carrying out propaganda work on its behalf, but without great effect. Within a year Labour still only had 124 fully paid up affiliated branches, which is particularly poor considering they were concentrated almost entirely in areas with sitting Labour deputies. In Dublin, for instance, where there was no sitting deputy, Labour had only a single branch.[145] Contrast this with Fianna Fáil's performance during the same period, its cumainn increasing from 550 to 759 in the twelve months which followed October 1930.[146] Nor was the next year any better. 'The work of establishing branches did not run too easily', it complained. 'It was found difficult to arouse sufficient interest in the party in the constituencies to get meetings arranged. Some of the deputies were not entirely faultless.'[147] With the combination of lazy deputies, an ineffectual organiser, an insipid programme or the lure of other parties, the fact was that Labour's separation from Congress had yielded no significant benefit in terms of attracting active supporters to the party. Not only did it prove difficult to establish a broader based membership, but keeping the old support bases was also problematic. Only 13 unions affiliated to the new body after the split, with another two, with a combined membership of 1,419, joining during the following year.[148] On the other hand, the unions which had dominated the party prior to the split, particularly the ITGWU, continued to dominate afterwards which meant that in effect the structure of the party was even more narrow than previously, with the larger unions exerting even greater influence.

THE RED SCARE AND THE 1932 GENERAL ELECTION

With Cosgrave's government sustained by such a slim majority, there was constant speculation that a general election was imminent.[149] The government's response to the dire state of the economy was greater retrenchment, which did nothing to ameliorate the economic situation but was very effective in fostering popular discontent. Cumann na Gaedheal's chances of re-election on its economic record were slim and, in need of another issue on which to court support, it looked towards law and order, which had been a large part of its appeal in every election since 1922, but which had declined as an issue as the country returned to a state of all but normality. However, if Cumann na nGaedheal was to gain votes from law and order politics, it had to highlight the threat from lawlessness and disorder. The relative rise of the republican left at this time provided the government with its target.

The late 1920s saw an increase in the activities and visibility of various communist groups and republican leftists, such as those present at Labour's inaugural. This radical milieu was minuscule. A special branch memorandum from April 1930 showed the Friends of Soviet Russia as having a membership of 'about 12', the Irish Labour Defence League had 190, the Women Prisoners Defence League around 20, the Irish National Unemployed Movement just over 300 while there were around 50 women in Cumann na mBan in the Dublin area. Considering that most of these groups enjoyed a single transferable membership, the sorry state of the Irish radical left becomes painfully apparent.[150] However, it was the links being developed between the communist groups and armed republicans (which, according to the Department of Justice files, numbered around 1,300 officers and 3,500 rank and file from April 1931)[151] that were of most concern to the authorities, and when the IRA Army Council gave its approval for establishing a new socialist group, Saor Éire, which made its first public appearance in September that year, the government's fear of conspiracy was kindled,[152] a fear which was heightened all the more by an increase in IRA violence, including a number of fatal shootings during the summer.

As soon as the Dáil resumed in October after its summer recess, the government went about pushing through its Constitution (17th Amendment) Bill. Among the far reaching security measures provided for in this legislation was the setting up of a five-man military tribunal, from which no appeal could be taken, whose powers included the death penalty. It also gave gardaí the power to arrest on suspicion without a warrant and gave the government the power to proscribe organisations.[153] Believing the 'menace of armed conspiracy' to be exaggerated and the new legislation to be over the top and unnecessary, Labour opposed the bill. Before its first reading, T. J. O'Connell tried to work towards a compromise, by bringing together the leaders of different parties in an effort to find consensus on the issue. Fianna Fáil was supportive but Cosgrave had no interest in diluting the legislation and rejected the idea outright.[154] In fact, far from reaching a cross-party consensus on the bill, O'Connell was having difficulties keeping his own house in order. On the morning the Dáil reassembled, the PLP met to establish its position on the legislation. All present opposed the legislation, but two deputies, Daniel Morrissey from Tipperary and Richard Anthony from Cork, declared they would support the government in any powers which it asked for, regardless of the party's position. Later that day the two men proved as good as their word. Cosgrave introduced the bill by cataloguing recent IRA activity as reason for passing the legislation, while pointing to the Saor Éire leadership's 'training in the authentic Soviet gospel' at first hand in Russia as further cause for concern, arguing that the sugar coating of Muscovite teachings on Irish extremism had the potential for success.[155] O'Connell argued against the proposed legislation in typically constitutional, liberal terms. It made a farce of parliamentary institutions, he claimed, and suggested it would be simpler if the government stopped messing around and just established a dictatorship. O'Connell was followed by Morrissey who warned of the dangers of anti-national and anti-Christian forces at work in the country,[156] but Richard Anthony's contribution which followed was more barbed. Exasperated with his party's legalism he argued, 'to me the lives of that humble labourer and that superintendent of the Civic Guard who were murdered, brutally murdered, were of more consequence and were more sacred than every Article of your Constitution'.[157]

The legislation having passed comfortably, Labour found itself embarrassed by Morrissey and Anthony's support for it. Lapses of discipline were by no means unusual, and usually went without sanction (indeed, when the two were called before the Administrative Council to explain themselves, Morrissey complained that in the past when his colleagues had voted against party direction they had not been called on to account for their behaviour),[158] but they had never occurred on such an important vote. Moreover, there was a distinct lack of contrition with both men insisting that they would act the same way if the issue arose again. Unable to agree on a compromise strategy for reprimanding the men, the Administrative Council decided by 12 votes to three to expel the two. Among those most insistent on this course of action were T. J. O'Connell, who felt his position as leader would be 'impossible unless strong action were taken', and the chairman, William Norton, who was 'very insistent upon discipline if the party [was] to be a party'. Similar sentiments were expressed in the *Watchword*, which lauded the expulsions for making it clear 'once and for all that it is a party and a movement and not just a conglomeration of individual TDs and senators'.[159] Tom Johnson, on the other hand, was more circumspect. His position on the issue is particularly interesting for the way in which it belied his suspicion of his own party. Johnson had been reluctant to impose such strict discipline on deputies for acting in accordance with their conscience, seeing the possibility of a conflict between himself and the party over religious issues and, privately, he expressed his dislike of strict majoritarianism in view of the 'shortcomings of the Party's equipment in intellect and experience (not to say character)'. In the end, while he felt the action taken by the AC was the only option open to it, and that most Labour supporters approved, he anticipated that the pro-treaty Labourites would 'silently turn away' from the party.[160] The episode ultimately saw Labour act in a dignified and reasonable manner, but it was an unenviable situation to be involved in, coming as it did only weeks before a general election. Not that the poll had yet been announced, but the timing of the 17th amendment legislation left few people in any doubt that an election would take place in the immediate future.[161] The Dáil was eventually dissolved in January 1932 and 16 February set as polling day.

With the two larger parties going into the contest very evenly matched, it was set to be the most closely fought election since the foundation of the state, and the campaign was as a result particularly tense. The tone was set at the launch of Cumann na nGaedheal's manifesto, when W.T. Cosgrave warned voters about the need to protect the country from the 'conspiracy solemnly condemned by the hierarchy'. Voters were led to believe that they had before them a choice between democracy under Cumann na nGaedheal or anarchy under Fianna Fáil. Speakers for the government party were instructed to paint Fianna Fáil as 'a communistic, pro-IRA, state socialist party intent upon Bolshevising the structures of the Irish state', while its election posters portrayed de Valera as a puppet for sinister gunmen.[162] Fianna Fáil's campaign, in contrast, was a positive one. While the removal of the oath of allegiance and the non-payment of subsidies were the first two planks of Fianna Fáil's manifesto, it concentrated for the most part on economic policies, with its poster campaign featuring the slogans, 'speed the plough' and 'speed the wheels'. Fianna Fáil's campaign was conducted with remarkable confidence and the party managed to give every impression that it was a government in waiting. The campaign in effect became a two-horse race and Labour found itself left behind. In its first election since separating from Congress, Labour failed utterly to capture the public imagination. Labour's behaviour at the 1932 election belied any notions that it wished to increase its support. The party ran only 33 candidates (a paltry increase of five on September 1927) who for the most part ran particularly lacklustre campaigns; in most cases, it would be more accurate to say that they stood in the election rather than fought in it. Lacking organisation, finance and, most importantly, interest and with the two larger parties fighting it out with each other, Labour remained on the sidelines, so irrelevant that neither of the larger parties bothered attacking it. While Cumann na nGaedheal painted Fianna Fáil the brightest vermilion, Labour remained untouched, for the most part because it posed no electoral threat but also because it had become so insipid of late, that accusing it of radicalism would merely serve to highlight the ludicrous nature of the charges.[163] Labour's prospects were further damaged by its failure to keep pace with the sharp propaganda being produced by its rivals. Its programme in comparison was turgid and unoriginal.[164] Nor was it merely in quality, but in volume and reach that Labour lagged behind, for while Cumann na nGaedheal had the support of the *Independent*, and Fianna Fáil now had its own paper, the *Irish Press*, Labour had only its small circulation weekly *The Irishman* at its disposal. Labour implicitly acknowledged its status as a minor party throughout the campaign and appealed for support on the basis that it would 'endeavour to compel whatever party came into power to use the powers given by the treaty for the purpose of reorganising the economic life of the people',[165] or in other words that it would try to stop Fianna Fáil going off at the constitutional deep end when it got in. Labour's experience during the campaign left it in little doubt that Fianna Fáil would get in.[166] Through its economic policy and its security legislation, Cumann na nGaedheal had successfully alienated itself from Labour, and the party did not bother with pretence at neutrality; Labour called on its voters to transfer their lower preferences to Fianna Fáil, and the larger party reciprocated.[167]

The election was Fianna Fáil's great leap forward. Its national vote rose by almost ten percentage points to 44.5 per cent – the first time any party had won over 40 per cent of the vote[168] – garnering it an extra 15 seats and bringing it up to 72. Fianna Fáil was now comfortably the largest party in the Dáil, although it was five seats short of an overall majority. Cumann na nGaedheal's vote fell by over three percentage points, and its number of seats dropped by five to 57. Labour's performance was atrocious. Of Labour's 33 candidates, just under half lost their deposits. Seven were successful. To look at this perform-ance in a more positive light, it is worth remembering that Labour had already lost one third of its parliamentary party in the course of the fifth Dáil through death, resignation and expulsion, so although it had won 13 seats in September 1927, it actually went into the 1932 contest with only eight. But there was little succour to be gained in looking at that particular bright side, especially when, to add to Labour's woes, T. J. O'Connell was numbered among the party's losses, confirming that the party had moved from the realms of misfortune to carelessness.

THE WORST OF TIMES, BEST OF TIMES?

There were, however, shafts of light in the darkness. Paradoxically, at just the moment Labour hit rock bottom, it found itself holding power for the first time in its history. Fianna Fáil was looking for a majority, and Labour alone was willing to provide it with one, and so ended the pretence of neutrality or equidistance between Labour and the two larger parties. Moreover, while Labour had lost one leader, it had gained a new one. The party had managed one gain in the election, with the party chairman William Norton returning to the Dáil after an absence of five years. At the age of only 32, he was young, energetic, confident, pugnacious (vide his attitude as party chairman towards

Anthony and Morrissey) and above all, determined to succeed.[169] Although he was the most junior member of the parliamentary party in terms of Dáil experience, and was the youngest deputy by far, Norton's clear ability and the crucial role he had played in bringing about the separation between the party and congress made him the obvious man for the job. That none of his six comrades were willing to take it on was irrelevant. It was clear from the outset that Labour under Norton was about to take a very different shape. Exactly what that shape would be, however, was less obvious.

TWO

COULD LABOUR BECOME SOCIALIST?

LABOUR IN THE HUNGRY THIRTIES

—

THE MAGNIFICENT SEVEN: LABOUR IN THE SIXTH DÁIL

William Norton, Labour's third leader in four years, could count his Dáil colleagues on the fingers of two hands. A second hand was only just necessary. Labour had reached its lowest ebb in a decade of parliamentary politics but its role supporting the new Fianna Fáil government gave it influence that went far beyond its seven deputies, while in its new leader it possessed a character capable of supplying much needed drive and momentum. Norton, according to one profile, was 'a fighting man, so self-confident that he is apt to succeed in the most unexpected places simply because he cannot anticipate defeat'.[1] On past performance it could be said that the ability of a Labour Party leader to anticipate defeat should be part of the job description, but in this case it saved Labour from dwindling from its tiny form to nothing at all. Labour had to keep its organisation together, but it would also have to carve out a new niche for itself. Having spent the last ten years as a progressive opposition party, it was now an adjunct to a progressive government. Could Labour maintain an independent identity, and, more importantly, take credit for the government's successes while avoiding flack for contentious issues?

There were heady scenes on the afternoon of 9 March as deputies assembled for the first meeting of the seventh Dáil. Fianna Fáil supporters had thronged the streets approaching Leinster House, greeting their party men with loud cheers, treating passing Cumann na nGaedheal deputies with stony silence or jeers as the mood took them.[2] Inside, the atmosphere was more subdued, although there was obvious tension in the air. There were fears within Fianna Fáil that the outgoing government would refuse to hand over power. Only days earlier the *Irish Press* had reported that two government ministers were plotting some kind of putsch, and the recent formation of the Army Comrades Association, a shadowy group of Cumann na nGaedheal supporters, was seen as a sinister portent.[3] There was sufficient concern for many of the Fianna Fáil deputies to carry revolvers with them on the day.[4] With Fianna Fáil anxious to take over, there was no appetite for grandstanding when it came to the nomination for president of the executive council. Brevity characterised the speeches, apart from William Norton's lengthy, bombastic contribution. Explaining that Labour was prepared to support a Fianna Fáil government on the basis of its declared social and economic policy, Norton then enunciated his party's shopping list, which ran from reducing unemployment, to issues of housing, widows' and orphans' pensions, transport, flour milling, profiteering and economic and industrial development generally.[5] Moreover, in contrast to his predecessors, he couched his speech in staunchly republican terms, with, for instance, references to the 'struggle to drive out the foreign invader', which would have been unthinkable coming from either Johnson or O'Connell.

'TIN-WHISTLE PLAYERS IN THE FIANNA FÁIL BAND'?[6]

If Norton's references to aiming towards 'that life of frugal comfort which Pope Leo XIII laid down as the God given right of every man and woman'[7] seemed designed to appeal to de Valera, the courting was going both ways. De Valera consistently appealed to Labour's sensibilities (as well as those of its voters), emphasising the links between his party and Labour's founder. In April 1932, for instance, he famously told the Dáil:

> I never regarded freedom as an end in itself, but if I were asked what statement of Irish policy was most in accord with my view as to what human beings should struggle for, I would stand side by side with James Connolly. The thing that was most heartbreaking in this Dáil since I came into it was to find the two Parties who should have stood side by side trying to secure the freedom in order that they might have power to order their own policy, divided. I am speaking of the Fianna Fáil Party and the Labour Party. These two Parties had, naturally, the same programme, and when I differed with the Labour Party after the Treaty it was because I thought that that Party was making a mistake and that they did not see what James Connolly saw, and what he told me he saw, that to secure national freedom was the first step in order to get the workers of Ireland the living that they were entitled to in their own country.[8]

Besides such public displays of affection, close contacts also built up between the two parties, with meetings between representatives of the two on a fairly regular basis, with Tom Johnson, now a full-time senator,[9] especially close. This closeness, not surprisingly, proved less than popular with a sizeable section within the party. As Luke Duffy, Labour's general secretary, wrote to Ronald Mortished that summer, 'I do not know whether the party is very happy about this intimate contact with the government people, but Johnson is firmly wedded to it.'[10] Just how intimate Johnson envisaged this contact becoming is apparent from remarks to his friend Ronald Mortished, when he suggested 'we shall have to coalesce some day either with an independent party or as an integral part of FF (Unless, not an impossibility, FF and Labour re-form as a new party! This by the way is being mooted in hitherto unsuspected quarters on our side).'[11] Johnson's perception of the esteem in which he and his party were held by the government party betrayed more than a little naïveté, but it is easy to understand how he would be flattered by dialogue after years of being roundly ignored by Cosgrave's regime.

OATH AND ANNUITIES

The incoming government wasted no time before moving on some of the more repugnant aspects of the Anglo-Irish settlement. On 12 March the cabinet decided to introduce legislation to remove the oath of allegiance from the Free State constitution, with the bill receiving its first reading the following month.[12] Predictably, the British government was not best pleased.[13] These were difficult and uncertain times in British politics. After two uneasy years in office, the minority Labour government led by Ramsay MacDonald had resigned in August 1931, to be replaced by a broad-based coalition known as the 'National Government', of which MacDonald remained prime minister. Opposition within Labour to its participation in the government led to MacDonald's expulsion (along with Lord Snowdon and J. H. Thomas), following which the prime minister and his renegade comrades established the National Labour Party. MacDonald found himself at the head of a cabinet dominated by Conservatives, as well as Liberals, National Liberals and members of his own (new) party, National Labour, among whom J. H. Thomas was secretary of state for dominion affairs. Solid trade union and Labour credentials notwithstanding, Thomas had developed a soundly establishment outlook which included a firm commitment to Empire.[14] As Dominions Secretary during the Boundary Commission fiasco in 1924, he had shown a distinct lack of sympathy with the Irish case. It was unlikely that he would prove any more amenable this time around. Indeed, the signs were that he would prove even more stringent than before, having predicted prior to the election that a 'difficult situation' would arise between Britain and Ireland in the event of de Valera's success.[15]

Of course, whether the minority Fianna Fáil government could dismantle the Treaty with any degree of success depended on Labour's support, support which William Norton had made it clear would be forthcoming only as long as the government concentrated on economic issues. Certainly, Cumann na nGaedheal believed (and further conveyed this belief to the British government) that Labour was divided on the question, and all it would take was for the London government to stand firm against de Valera for Labour to withdraw its support.[16] It did not take long, however, before it became obvious that this was merely wishful thinking on Cumann na nGaedhael's part. Though Norton had blustered that the oath's removal would not 'provide work for one unemployed man or woman',[17] the fact was that to resist its removal would have been incongruous with his vocal republicanism during this time. Norton's description of the oath as a 'relic of feudalism' managed to put it in class terms as well as nationalist ones, while he emphasised Labour's consistency on the issue on the grounds that the party had argued against putting the oath in the constitution in the first place. Naturally, this did not stop accusations from the Cumann na nGaedheal benches that Labour was making a volte-face on the issue, and had sold out to Fianna Fáil, or as one deputy put it, 'when the dog barks the tail wags'.[18] But in Labour eyes, it was a simple trade off: as Tom Johnson put it 'we ought to back up the Government in respect to its political programme on the understanding that they will proceed resolutely and rapidly with its programme of social reconstruction'.[19] Though Norton's enthusiasm for abolishing the oath was not shared among all his parliamentary colleagues, talk of a split was misplaced, and Labour was quick to disabuse any British notions that they were about to leave the government high and dry on the issue.[20]

It did so, significantly, through her sister party in London. Links between the Irish Labour Party and the Labour Party in Britain had never been particularly strong, and by the early 1930s they were all but non-existent.[21] However, with trouble brewing between the Irish and British governments, it was an opportune time to become reacquainted. In this regard contact was initiated by Dublin, and was directed towards the Labour opposition only (rather than to National Labour). Tom Johnson wrote to British Labour Party organiser, Jim Middleton, in early April in an effort to shine some light on affairs. Outlining the Fianna Fáil government's stance on the oath and the annuities, and the extent of support within the Irish Labour Party on the two questions, he left the Labour opposition with the unambiguous message that Irish Labour would continue to back the government.[22] From this point on the two parties kept closely in touch on the question of the oath and the annuities.[23] Following the 1931 split and subsequent election, the British Labour Party had been reduced to a rump of only 46 MPs against a National Government of 554 MPs, but though it was numerically insignificant it was disproportionately vocal and its MPs provided the only opposition to the government's policy on Ireland. British Labour was keen to arrest the deteriorating relations between the two governments and so two days after the Free State government withheld its annuities payment due on 1 July, Norton travelled to London for talks with Labour leaders George Lansbury, Clement Attlee and Stafford Cripps to discuss the possibility of finding a settlement. He met without success.[24] The next day Norton sat in the House of Commons gallery during the debate on the Special Duties Bill, as Labour battled against it alone and in vain. Attlee and Cripps, in particular, were vociferous in their opposition, the latter deploring the spirit of 'reprisal and revenge' in recent government statements, but to no avail. The Bill passed easily and the new tariffs came into law on 11 July.[25]

This did not end Labour's involvement, however. Almost two weeks later, on 13 July, Norton made a dramatic impromptu second visit to London, with a view to bringing about a compromise. The British government had been adamant that an Imperial tribunal was the only acceptable forum for examining the annuities, while de Valera, mindful of the Boundary Commission fiasco, was fixed on an international tribunal to be held in the Hague. Norton's plan was that both countries should set up a commission consisting of two representatives from each country and a chairman nominated by the four representatives, and its report would form the basis for negotiations between the two governments.[26] Norton put his proposals to Lansbury, Cripps, Attlee and Arthur Greenwood in the course of a long meeting on 13 July which continued late into the evening.[27] The next day, Norton accompanied by the four Labour leaders met the Prime Minister Ramsay MacDonald, the Lord Chancellor Lord Sankey and the attorney general for a lengthy discussion. It cannot have been a comfortable gathering. MacDonald, whose relations with his erstwhile Labour colleagues were far from convivial, attended the meeting more because he felt he could not refuse rather than with a view to coming to a solution, and was suspicious that he was being pressured into making concessions to the Irish by the Labour men.[28] In the end, the only thing to come out of the meeting was an invitation extended to de Valera by MacDonald through Norton to attend talks in London the following day.[29] De Valera accepted the invitation, but a three-hour meeting between him and MacDonald in 10 Downing Street only raised the hackles of both premiers, as it became clear early on that there were no grounds for negotiation.[30] Norton had persuaded both premiers to agree to talks and each went into the meeting believing the other had sought the interview. De Valera left Downing Street furious, while in private an angry MacDonald fumed that Norton had completely misrepresented the British attitude to the president.[31] The London *Times* was keen to stress that 'the initiative definitely came from the Free State' and that, without question, any misunderstandings arising between MacDonald and de Valera were to be laid on the shoulders of Norton.[32]

Norton's role as a go-between ended here, as did contact between the Irish and British Labour Parties, which was not to be resumed until well into the next decade.

Labour's faith in the government was repaid at an early stage as the summer saw a raft of progressive legislation passing though the Dáil. This included a much needed Housing Act which led to an average of 12,000 houses per annum being built with public subsidy between 1932 and 1942, compared with 2,000 a year between 1923 and 1931,[33] as well as an Old Age Pensions Act and a Control of Prices Act. The administration's first budget, delivered on 11 May, and which included a range of progressive tax measures as well as increases in welfare allowances, was described by William Davin as the kind of budget that might be expected 'from a minister with a truly Christian outlook'.[34] In June, Seán Lemass introduced his Control of Manufacturers Act which protected Irish-owned industry behind a series of high tariff barriers. Labour support for Fianna Fáil's economic policy was qualified by a concern about the effect of tariffs on the Irish economy, fearing that the creation of monopolies under these conditions would lead to the exploitation of Irish workers and consumers. This exception aside, on economic matters the two parties spoke with the same voice. Similarly, Labour was so pleased with the government's performance on social questions that the former had little to do but commend the government for its actions. It did not take long before Fianna Fáil's legislative bonanza began to affect Labour on the ground, as by the summer months of 1932 (in the words of Labour's annual report), 'slackness set in. It was found difficult to arrange for organising meetings. The reason appears to be that the workers expected Fianna Fáil to fulfil all their wishes'.[35] Alarmed by this turn of events, Labour's ardour cooled by the autumn, its attitude towards Fianna Fáil becoming more standoffish, while the weekly *Watchword* began emphasising the fundamental difference between Norton and de Valera, namely that while the latter supported private enterprise the Labour leader believed 'the present system' could not work.[36] If the word 'socialist' never made an appearance, a great deal of Norton's rhetoric and talk of the impending collapse of capitalism in the pages of *Watchword* endeavoured to portray the party as socialist in all but name.[37]

Of course, by the autumn there was more cause for complaint as the adverse effects of the economic war became increasingly apparent. Labour released a statement on 12 September calling for 'more courageous [economic] leadership',[38] and articulated its grievances on profiteering and more generally at a meeting of representatives of the two parties four days later.[39] The government humoured Labour by establishing weekly meetings between the two parties from October, but these were designed as one-way briefings rather than consultations. The 'policy for the crisis', featuring a 14-point list of suggestions including special emergency legislation to break up ranches, the national-isation of railways and a call for all proposals for reduction of public servants' pay to be postponed indefinitely, which was jointly drawn up by the PLP and the AC,[40] was roundly ignored by the government. Labour was particularly angered by the government's point blank refusal to consider proposals for railway nationalisation,[41] a point which came up at the annual conference in October (the first since the election) although most speeches were supportive of the government.[42] There were occasional words of warning, however, with Senator J. T. O'Farrell accusing speakers of seeming 'to show that Fianna Fáil had done all that a Labour Government would do'.[43] In an effort to get around this problem, Norton tried to turn his weekly meetings with de Valera to his advantage. As Lemass later recalled:

> If I, for example, told this conference that I was going to introduce the Unemployment Assistance Act, within a few days there would be a speech from Norton demanding that the Government should produce an Unemployment Assistance Act . . . he was trying to exaggerate the influence of his party on gov-ernment policy and to take the credit in advance for everything the Government did that would be popular from his party's point of view.[44]

Not surprisingly, the meetings did not continue for long.[45]

1933 GENERAL ELECTION

By the end of November 1932, rumours that Labour was considering bringing down the government began to appear in the press. Norton issued blank denials,[46] but within weeks Labour was pushed to breaking point when December saw the government announce it was going to reduce public service pay bonuses. Labour could not agree to such a cut, not least because the members of Norton's own Post Office Workers Union would be among the worst affected, and so Norton communicated to de Valera that Labour would vote against the government on the issue. By this stage, however, Fianna Fáil was finding its reliance on Labour increasingly tiresome. De Valera felt the time was right to seek a new mandate and, with any luck, an overall majority, and so before Labour had a chance to vote against the wages cut, he pulled the rug from under them by dissolving the Dáil and calling a snap election for 24 January 1933.[47] Though hopeful he would not require its co-operation after the election, de Valera was careful to keep Labour on-side just in case. He told Norton that his decision had nothing to do with public service pay, but rather that he needed a strong majority in order to deal with the British, who would not enter negotiations while the government could be defeated, while in a statement to the press he expressed the hope that future relations would be as happy as they had been in the past.[48]

Though it lasted only three weeks, the 1933 general election campaign was 'arguably the most bitter, turbulent and colourful in the history of independent Ireland'.[49] The parties' platforms were effectively the same as they had been a year earlier, except for the added dimension of the economic war. The only change in Fianna Fáil's manifesto was its promise to reduce the amount of annuities by half, while Cumann na nGaedheal ran a wholly negative campaign which effectively promised nothing except that Cosgrave would end the economic war in three days.[50] Labour, with remarkable hubris, claimed the outgoing government's reforms as its own, maintaining that 'where the government accepted Labour's programme of social and economic reconstruction, they have admirably succeeded. Their failures are to be found where they departed from the lines laid down in that programme'. Its manifesto was completed by a few pieces of radical rhetoric and anti-British sloganeering, not least the reference to 'the most foreign thing in Ireland – the capitalist system'.[51] It looked like crass political opportunism, and there was little in it to hold the existing Labour voter, let alone make any converts. The election was one of two blocs, Fianna Fáil and Labour on one side, Cumann na nGaedheal and the Centre Party – a new conglomeration of anti-Fianna Fáil independents and Farmers – on the other. In effect this meant the two larger parties canvassed for government with the smaller two aiming to hold the balance of power in the next Dáil.[52] Political enmity regularly spilled into violence at the hustings as IRA men, declaring there should be 'no free speech for traitors', and Fianna Fáil supporters disrupted Cumann na nGaedheal public meetings, prompting retaliation from members of the Army Comrades Association.

The election caught Labour on the hop. Short notice of the poll combined with a lack of funds meant Labour nominated only 19 candidates in 17 constituencies, the smallest number since 1922.[53] (Even the newly formed Centre Party was able to put up 26 candidates, of which six were outgoing TDs.)[54] Labour simply did not have the resources to fight a strong campaign, and compared with the larger parties which were spending heavily on posters and newspaper advertisements, it was hard pressed to afford a handful of advertisements in the *Irish Press*. Had Labour enjoyed better resources it would have been starting off on the back foot nonetheless since the election was very much a two-horse race, and Labour's case that voters should return it in sufficient numbers to keep an eye on a Fianna Fáil government seemed slightly desperate. Political forecasters had found the election hard to call, but one thing that the opposition press, at least, agreed on was that Labour faced annihilation.[55] On this point, however, the naysayers were proved wrong. Although the party's national vote did fall by two points to a new low of 5.7 per cent, transfers from sympathetic Fianna Fáil voters meant that Labour in fact picked up one extra seat, bringing it to a total of eight deputies.[56] On a record turnout of 80 per cent, Fianna Fáil increased its share of the vote by five per cent, and an increase of eight seats which mirrored Cumann na nGaedheal's losses. The new Centre Party performed quite respectably, winning over nine per cent of the national vote, giving it 11 seats. What this added up to was Fianna Fáil returning with simple majority of one vote. The incoming government would be more secure than the last Dáil, but only just.

LABOUR IN THE EIGHTH DÁIL

Before the first meeting of the new Dáil, de Valera had stated that there would be no need for any formal alliance between his party and Labour, explaining that the two parties were virtually at one on all the major points and that they were 'natural allies'.[57] While opposition press predicted a stormy relationship between a Fianna Fáil government and its would-be Labour allies over the unresolved questions of public service pay and, more significantly, rail nationalisation,[58] with its already meagre resources depleted at the last election, its first preference vote down by one third and reliant on Fianna Fáil transfers for its survival, it was unlikely that Labour would try to force any significant government defeats, let alone try to take the government down in the near future. This did not stop rumours that there might be a possible coalition between the two parties, but on 3 February the Administrative Council and the PLP met before issuing a statement on Labour's position in the new Dáil which would be to 'give full support to measures which are in accordance with the national and economic policy as laid down in its programme' but there would be no coalition.[59] The new Dáil met on 8 February to elect a new president. Norton's contribution was unusually brief. First, he expressed his belief that Fianna Fáil in co-operation with Labour would 'initiate a bold economic and social policy, and, in the realms of national endeavour, a no less bold policy so far as the national rights of this country are concerned', after which he devoted his speech to attacking Cumann na nGaedheal for predicting Labour's demise.[60] It certainly was not designed to keep the prospective government on its toes. In fact, it must have been music to its ears. When it came to the vote, de Valera was comfortably elected president by 82 votes to 54.

GROWTH OF EXTREMES

The heightened political atmosphere that had characterised the January election did not end when the ballots had been counted. If anything, it became worse and the following year, at least, would be characterised by an atmosphere of tension that permeated the body politic and was to have a direct impact on Labour and its relationship with the government. One notable feature of Irish life at this time was the wave of anti-communist hysteria which reached its zenith in the capital in March 1933. The growth of communism in Ireland which had begun at the beginning of the decade had reached its high point by the end of 1932. As a movement it was still small – the Revolutionary Workers' Groups (RWG), for instance, had a membership of some 339 nationwide[61] – but its growth in numbers, its move into previously unorganised parts of the country and its apparently burgeoning confidence (visible in its announcement in November that it was going to reform itself as a fully fledged communist party the following year[62]) were cause for alarm in certain quarters. The communist menace became practically the sole subject of pastoral and sermon, as the Catholic Church demanded action by the state and the vigilance of its flock to rid Ireland of this pernicious anti-Christian doctrine. This was not, of course, a position unique to the Catholic Church in Ireland and the Church's antipathy towards communism and socialism had been reinforced by Pius XI's 1931 encyclical *Quadragesimo Anno*, which updated and reaffirmed the teachings in *Rerum Novarum*. Occasionally, more than vigilance was called for, with instances of sermons being delivered in Dublin city instructing the congregation to engage in preemptive action and attack the communists before they could burn down the churches.[63] The clergy's message was promoted heavily in popular Catholic publications such as the *Irish Rosary* and the *Standard* and met with a receptive audience; with the renewal in devotion surrounding the Eucharistic Congress, combined with the sense of crisis and instability at home and on the continent, a host of Catholic Action groups such as the Catholic Young Men's Association and the newly formed St Patrick's Anti-Communist League were only too happy to assist.[64] In rural Ireland, the RWGs fell apart in the face of clerical condemnation. In Leitrim a hall owned by a local RWG organiser and former IRA man Jim Gralton was burned down, and in February 1933 the minister for justice made an order for Gralton's deportation on the basis that he was an undesirable character and a naturalised citizen of the United States. Gralton went into hiding until late summer before finally being deported to the United States in August, but in the meantime he became a cause célèbre for the Irish left, with the Gralton Defence Committee holding public meetings and demonstrations in Leitrim (where veteran republican

Peadar O'Donnell was physically attacked on the instigation of the local parish priest) and in the capital.[65] There were extraordinary scenes in March in areas of Dublin's north city when anti-communist vigilantes took to the streets. A meeting of the communist front organisation, the Irish Unemployed Workers, was violently broken up in O'Connell Street on the evening of 26 March. The next evening members of the congregation at evening mass in the Pro-Cathedral were sufficiently riled by an anti-communist sermon that they set off towards Connolly House, the headquarters of the RWG, some minutes away. For the next three days and nights they laid siege to the building to the accompaniment of 'Faith of our Fathers' and only moved on having finally laid waste to the house by setting fire to a bedding factory next door whereupon they moved on to their next targets: the Workers College in Eccles Street and the WUI headquarters Unity Hall.[66] Reports had 33 people injured in street fighting. It was a secular miracle that no one was killed.

The communists believed the state had acted in collusion with the vigilantes, pointing to the irregular deportation of Gralton, the failure to protect Connolly House and the lack of arrests in the aftermath of the attack (with the exception of one of the building's defenders), as evidence of a lack of concern for legality or due process, but they found themselves without allies. Labour, ordinarily a champion of due process, now stood utterly aloof. At Labour's annual conference later in October, the PLP's failure to raise the Gralton deportation in the Dáil prompted one Dublin branch to table a motion of censure against it and the AC, but Norton's response was scathing. Describing the motion as a burlesque, Norton stated flatly that the issue was none of the party's business.[67] Once Norton had vented his spleen, a motion to move to next business was passed and no more was said on the matter.[68] Nor was Norton alone in his lack of sympathy. One of his Dáil colleagues, Limerick deputy T. J. Murphy, went so far as to call upon the government to deport 'the two or three foreign communists who are in the country'. [69] Effectively, where Labour's voice was heard on such issues it tended to be on the side of the red baiters. In light of the fractious relations between the communists and the Labour Party – originating in the former's attacks on the latter – it is easy to understand why Labour was disinclined to act as the communists' advocate, even when fundamental issues of civil and political liberties were involved.

The crusade of anti-communism was a bandwagon readily mounted by the leaders of the Army Comrades Association which began as a representative group for Army pensioners and quickly developed into something more sinister. By April 1933 the group had a new leader, former Garda Commissioner Eoin O'Duffy, and a new uniform including a blueshirt. The type of uniform was cause for alarm – it was only three months since Hitler had taken power in Berlin flanked by his Brownshirts, while Mussolini's Blackshirts had long been in existence in Italy – and the adoption of a fascist style salute shortly afterwards did nothing to assuage the fears of observers. Contemporaries and historians have debated whether the Blueshirts were actually fascist, but certainly as far as the Irish labour movement was concerned the appearance of an organisation with all the trappings of fascism, with a constitution declaring its 'commitment to effectively prevent strikes and lock-outs and harmoniously compose industrial differences', led by a man who declared that party politics were redundant in Ireland, represented serious cause for concern.[70] (In the same month that the Blueshirt uniform made its first appearance, Hitler banned trade unions in Germany, and they had long since been sidelined in Mussolini's corporate Italy.) By late August the government had already had enough. A Blueshirt parade to the cenotaph on Leinster Lawn was proscribed on the morning it was due to take place. Just over a week later on 21 August the National Guard itself was banned and the military tribunal, which had been suspended by the Fianna Fáil government on coming into office, was reintroduced.

The Blueshirt ban had an immediate political impact. Negotiations about a merger had been taking place between Cumann na nGaedheal and the Centre Party with some progress, but when O'Duffy was approached with a view to joining this new party, he declined. Once the Blueshirts had been proscribed, O'Duffy was faced with two options: to operate outside the law and face the consequences, or to seek legitimacy and allies by accepting the overtures of the Centre Party and Cumann na nGaedheal.[71] He chose the latter, and on 8 September 1933 a new party named the United Ireland Party or Fine Gael was unveiled to the Irish public. This put de Valera in an extremely vulnerable position. The government had been engaged in a delicate balancing act since the 1933 election, relying on Labour support to pass progressive legislation and on Centre Party votes to put through cutbacks. It had managed this with great success although there had been a few very close shaves.[72] The Centre Party's merger with Cumann na nGaedheal cut this lifeline and placed Labour once again in the position of holding the balance of power. This was a particularly uncomfortable scenario for the government at this time. Labour had been very critical about specific points of government policy during the new Dáil and the trade union movement's disenchantment with Fianna Fáil had been plain to see at the 1933 Congress.[73] De Valera wanted security for his government; obtaining Labour's support was the only way he was going to achieve this without an election. Having the government over a barrel, Labour felt it was in a position to strike a hard bargain.

There were some preliminary talks between de Valera and Norton before representatives of the two parties met the following week on 12 September for a two-hour discussion in the president's room in Government Buildings. De Valera, Lemass and Jim Ryan for the government were treated to a tour de force of Norton bluster in which he outlined their failure to implement election pledges on social legislation. It was obviously quite some show; leaving the meeting, the Labour men refused to comment to the waiting press outside, with the exception of a jocular William O'Brien who asked journalists assembled outside to venture how many seats they felt Labour should be entitled to at cabinet.[74] Others were more circumspect and favoured retaining Labour's independence at all costs.[75] As they saw it, the alliance with Fianna Fáil had brought little in the way of electoral benefits at the last election – what was there to say that anything would change in the future? Over the course of a four-hour meeting, Labour's leaders discussed their position, with Cork deputy T. J. Murphy and Wicklow deputy James Everett representing the strongest line of resistance,[76] but ultimately Norton had his way and predictions of a split in the party over an alliance with the government came to nothing.[77] It was almost a week before Norton broke Labour's silence on the issue at a party meeting in Kildare, announcing that Labour would indeed give its support to de Valera in exchange for guarantees on social legislation and regular consultation over the government's programme.[78]

THE SPECIAL POWERS BILL

If there was general unease within the parliamentary party about this agreement, one issue was causing particular anxiety, namely the government's re-enactment of the Special Safety Bill. Fianna Fáil had opposed the legislation when it had first been introduced by the Cosgrave government in 1931, but it had few scruples about using it against the increasingly visible Blueshirt movement. Labour had also opposed the act, and had expelled deputies Anthony and Morrissey when they broke the whip and voted for it. Propping up the government meant Labour would have to support the act, a prospect no one relished and which, it seemed, most of the PLP were not prepared to do. With most Labour deputies suggesting they would vote against the government on the matter,[79] Norton decided to play things safe; when Fine Gael tabled a motion of censure against the government for its use of the legislation, Norton allowed a free vote, thus avoiding the embarrassment of having to expel any of his deputies for showing the temerity to remain consistent.

When the Dáil met to debate the censure motion on 28 September there were extraordinary scenes as 14 opposition deputies sat through the debate resplendent in their Blueshirt uniforms. Splenetic Fine Gael speakers railed against the government, and against Labour too, which was reminded time and again of its perfidy on the question. Deputies Anthony (Independent Labour, still) and Morrissey (now Fine Gael) were particularly exercised on this point,[80] and understandably so. Norton, the only Labour deputy to speak on the motion, delivered a 'heavily jocose' speech which relied more on personal attacks on a number of deputies than on trying to deliver any plausible explanation for his party's change of heart. In a misjudged reference to the Centre Party's merger with Cumann na nGaedheal, Norton cited a limerick in which 'a young lady from Niger/Who smiled as she sat on a tiger/they came back from the ride with the lady inside/and the smile on the face of the tiger'.[81] It was, remarked Dan Morrissey, a rather double-edged story, to great laughter on the opposition benches as Norton was asked if in fact he was the lady in question. In an extremely unedifying performance, Norton had managed to make himself a laughing stock as well failing to put forward a good reason for Labour's U-turn, but he enjoyed a victory of sorts when in the event there were no defections. Six Labour deputies voted with the government against the censure motion while the other two, William Davin and T. J. Murphy, were absent. Nevertheless, while most of the parliamentary party backed the government in the end, there was obvious discontent at the turn of events. The matter was discussed at length when Labour's annual conference met in Dublin the following month, although a motion objecting to the use of the Special Powers Act tabled by the Dublin Central Branch was defeated by 31 votes to 50.[82]

Labour had gone into its arrangement with Fianna Fáil in bullish form but the limits of its influence were apparent from an early stage, Labour's annual report emphasising 'the Government were not always responsive to the representations of the Party [and] in some cases there was obvious lack of sympathy'.[83] Nevertheless, if the government did not always come up with the legislative goods, Labour's continued support could be justified by the ongoing activities of the Blueshirt movement which was becoming increasingly belligerent. Its leaders took to making speeches which denounced democracy and drew explicit parallels between their movement and continental fascism and Nazism; as the Cumann na nGaedheal deputy John A. Costello told the Dáil during the debate on the government's Wearing of Uniform bill in February, 'The Blackshirts were victorious in Italy, and the Hitler shirts were victorious in Germany, as assuredly . . . the Blueshirts will be victorious in the Irish Free State'.[84] Such provocative language engendered little in the way of response from Labour, however. In October 1933, the AC and the National Executive of the ITUC published a joint statement on the 'Fascist Danger', promising to organise public meetings throughout the country to 'crystallise the hostility of the Trade Union and Labour Movement to the realities of Fascism', but their promise to hold these meetings some six months hence belied any sense of urgency on the part of the organisers.[85] Labour's failure to mobilise against fascism at a street level contrasted with the CPI which began its anti-fascist campaign under the Labour League Against Fascism front in early 1934.[86] Violent anti-communism made open communist meetings difficult, and so anti-fascism gave the CPI the opportunity to meet, and try to recruit publicly. When the Labour–ITUC demonstrations finally took place around the country on Connolly Day (6 May) 1934, the largest of 10,000 held in College Green was the occasion of a noisy counter-demonstration led by Jim Larkin (quiet of late) who denounced Labour as a fascist organisation.[87] Similarly, the CPI secretariat proclaimed that in encouraging workers to let the forces of the state take on the Blueshirts instead of taking to the streets themselves, the leaders of the Labour Party and the ITUC were 'the worst enemies of the workers' struggle against the fascists'.[88] This view had nothing to do with circum-stances in Ireland, and everything to do with the Comintern's policy of class against class which put social democratic reformism on a par with fascism.

At the same time, the IRA was undergoing schism. In an effort to bring the increasing closeness between republicans and the far left to its logical conclusion, Peadar O'Donnell and George Gilmore had put a motion before the IRA's March 1934 convention to adopt a left-wing agenda. When their motion was defeated by a single vote, O'Donnell and his supporters quit and began to organise a Republican Congress which they hoped would unite left wingers and republicans in one organisation. Though optimistic of achieving a reasonably broad-based membership, the Republican Congress never developed beyond an umbrella group for left-wing IRA people and members of the CPI and CPI fronts, such as the Labour League Against Fascism and the League Against Imperialism. Unsurprisingly, in view of the CPI's attitude towards the labour movement earlier on in the year, the trade union movement on the whole remained aloof. A motion sought to unite the labour movement with the Republican Congress at the ITUC's annual conference in 1934, but was defeated. It had been tabled by Roddy Connolly, son of James, who had been active in the Irish communist movement and the Citizen Army and was now one of the few non-CPI leaders of the Labour League Against Fascism/ Labour Defence League.[89] As far as Cathal O'Shannon was concerned, the new movement was a 'varnish for socialism and communism', and anyone wishing to fight fascism could do so from within the Labour Party.[90] Nor did efforts by Republican Congress to bring the Labour Party on board, either by personal approach or at conference, meet with any success. Once again it was Roddy Connolly who was the champion of Republican Congress, this time at the Labour Party annual conference in October 1934. His two motions of note – one calling on the AC to take 'every possible step in conjunction with all forces' opposing the Blueshirts, the other calling for 'a

truce among all who stand for an Irish Workers' Republic and a united front
against the common enemy' in view of the dangers from 'capitalism, fascism,
international war and imperialism'[91] – both met with short shrift, and noting
his association 'with another movement', William Davin advised Connolly
that the time had come for him to make up his mind where exactly his loyalties lay.[92] Others were similarly unimpressed. Tom Johnson, referring to the
second motion, argued that the real meaning of the resolution was to unite
with the Communist Party and that 'the whole propaganda for a united front
was merely an attempt here as in England, France and other countries to nobble
the Labour Party under the name of and by the officials of the Communist
Party'.[93] Labour's willingness to engage any kind of popular front, however,
began and ended with Fianna Fáil. Not only were Connolly's motions shot
down but another resolution which 'strongly [opposed] any attempt to introduce anti-Christian communistic doctrines into the movement' passed, albeit
after a long debate. Many speakers were unhappy that the motion had been
moved at all. Frank Robbins argued that 'Labour should not be baited with
this insidious propaganda', with Cathal O'Shannon complaining that the
Irish Labour Party did not require a certificate of good character. The fact
was, many delegates wished that the motion had not been put before the
conference, but felt that since the issue was before them, they could not vote
against it.[94]

THE WORKERS' REPUBLIC

It would be a mistake to read these motions as evidence of Labour's reactionary tendencies. In fact, the truth was quite the opposite. While declaring
their outright opposition to co-operation with communism – a movement
which had done nothing but attack the Labour movement and its leaders –
the party actually began to shift leftwards. Conference passed a resolution
which declared that 'personal liberty, political freedom and social justice are
unattainable under any from of Capitalistic Imperialism' and that the party's
aim was to 'continue Connolly's efforts for the establishment in Ireland of a
Workers' Republic founded on equal justice and equal opportunities for all'.[95]
As a result of this, the decision was made to revise the party's constitution and
draft a new programme which would be put to a party conference for
adoption in the future. More than one speaker showed candour about the
reason for the change: Fianna Fáil had stolen Labour's programme and it was
necessary for Labour to draft a new one 'in order to be in advance of any other
political party'.[96] There were, of course, other factors at work. The continued
breakdown of capitalism at an international level was cited as cause for a

rethink,[97] and the existence of the Blueshirt movement had undoubtedly had an impact on Labour's sense of identity. But more than anything it was the desire, or perhaps more accurately the *need*, to put clear red water between itself and Fianna Fáil which saw Labour commit itself to the Workers' Republic at this time. The move originated from the leadership of the party and was supported by the ITGWU, and was not, as some have suggested, the result of leftist Republican Congress influences within the party. As Roddy Connolly's experience that year illustrated, any push to the left would inevitably come to nothing without leadership support.

Labour seemed to be emerging from a lengthy sleep around this time. Though the movement was extant, the prospect of any serious Blueshirt threat to the state seemed to have passed, and with it did the honeymoon between Labour and Fianna Fáil. Labour became increasingly critical of the government's failure to move on areas of social legislation, including the Widows and Orphans Bill which had been agreed in the deal between the two parties in September 1933.[98] Work began on a new constitution and programme for the party along the lines of the Workers' Republic motion at the 1934 conference, and, following a long period of stagnation, it looked as though organisation was improving, with a 'large number' of new branches formed around the country.[99] Admittedly, a small number of new recruits were the result not of any organising drive by Labour but rather from developments in the ongoing saga of Republican Congress and its military ancillary the Irish Citizen Army (ICA). In June 1935 the ICA army convention instructed its members and supporters to join the Irish Labour Party or the Northern Ireland Labour Party.[100] The only prominent new arrival into Labour as a result of this move was Michael Price, who had made a significant transformation from a rather right-wing IRA man only a couple of years earlier before joining the Republican Congress. The ICA leader, Roddy Connolly, was already a Labour member. How many joined as a result of this initiative is difficult to say, although the ICA numbered around 200 members by this point.[101] Their first instruction was to get their branches active, with meetings to be held every fortnight, and to complain to Labour's general secretary, Luke Duffy, if the local Labour people did not oblige. The primary aim in this strategy, however, was to get its members to push for a declaration of a Workers' Republic in the party's new constitution. In the event that this did not happen, the ICA men would split and form a new organisation called the Republican Brotherhood Party which would unite republican and labour elements,[102] the irony of splitting for unity seemingly lost at the time.

Luckily, the prospect of a Republican Brotherhood Party evaporated when Labour's annual conference adopted its new Workers' Republic constitution and programme in February 1936. The programme put before delegates included the nationalisation of basic industries and calls for economic planning, the breaking up of ranches and promotion of co-operative farming, better social services and a review of banking in the state. There was little that Labour had not said before, nor much difference in the way it said it. The most significant change was the appearance of the two little words in its constitution: 'Workers' Republic'. Outlining this section to the conference, Norton spoke of how the party was already being condemned in the press for this objective, and that they would be 'bitterly assailed by the Imperialist elements in the country', but Labour made no apologies for supporting this aim.[103] Norton's attempt to talk up the Workers' Republic section of the constitution failed to convince at least one sceptic, the ITGWU's Gilbert Lynch, who pointed out the inconsistency of the constitution's claim that it followed the ideals of James Connolly, a revolutionary socialist, with the reformist objectives which followed. The new constitution was not merely cant but a dilution of the previous constitution's aims and objectives, Lynch argued and while he had always thought that 'Labour and Nation' was a very 'wishy-washy' document, which some people suggested was only 'pale pink', the new programme had 'even washed out the pink, leaving it a pale white'.[104] Tom Johnson said clearly the whole point of the passage was to give the impression that Labour was taking a line further leftwards than it had previously, pointing out that 'if they were standing by the workers' republican faith of James Connolly they would have a very different kind of document before them. Debate on the documents carried on throughout the last two days of conference with surprisingly little acrimony. There was precious little enthusiasm for the documents but very little hostility towards its provisions either. On right, left and centre, the attitude was one of 'it will do'. As Nora Connolly O'Brien wrote to Leon Trotsky afterwards: 'The LP recently adopted a new programme and constitution, the first step towards achieving the leading role in the revolutionary movement in Ireland. The new programme is not yet a correct revolutionary one, but it is such an enormous advance on the previous one, that we are not indulging in any carping or cavilling criticism. Through it they can supply an alternative to FF'. Trotsky sent her a copy of *In Defence of Terrorism* by way of thanks. [105]

The Workers' Republic caused little fuss beyond the conference either. The national newspapers made little comment about it and even the *Irish Rosary* found it difficult to take it particularly seriously, although it did warn the party's leaders that 'both the letter and the spirit of Labour utterances which echo Marxian socialism and Sovietism fill us with some alarm for the future of that party'.[106] This reflected a decline in some of the more hysterical anti-communism of late which had come about since the government's aggressive stance against the IRA and the Republican Congress had disintegrated at its inaugural meeting in Rathmines on 29 September 1934.[107] Lenten pastorals published on the eve of Labour's conference reflected the change in mood, for while many warned of the dangers of communism, far more attention was devoted to the dreadful evils of dancing.[108] No doubt emboldened by this lack of censure, Labour's rhetoric, and that of Norton in particular, continued on its leftward path. 'We declare ourselves as being unsatisfied with any measure of freedom other than the living Irish Republic for which Connolly died to achieve', Norton told a large Connolly Day rally in Dublin, adding that 'industrial development would not make the people any happier if it were under capitalist control'. Claiming the nationalist high ground from the government he promised that 'the Irish Labour Party would not stand for the bartering of nationhood in exchange for bullocks'.[109] Connolly Day speeches elsewhere took a similarly critical tone,[110] and by late summer local elections in Dublin and Cork and a by-election in Wexford saw Labour devote a great deal of energy at the hustings and in the Dáil to denigrating the government, attacking Fianna Fáil on its economic and employment policy, its use of the military tribunal and accusing it of putting up slum landlords as candidates.[111] Beginning in August, Labour began holding monthly public meetings on the corner of Abbey Street where crowds of over 200 listened to speeches dealing with slum housing and unemployment.[112] Labour showed signs of confidence and energy. It also showed signs of delusion, with Luke Duffy telling the ITUC's annual congress in Tralee that 'if Labour secured a victory in the Wexford by-election the time would not be far distant when the party would have a majority in the Dáil'.[113] As it was, far from winning in Wexford (where the party was relatively strong), Labour came third out of four candidates, with almost three thousand fewer first preferences than at the previous general election.[114] Nor did the local elections bring much joy with Labour picking up one of seven vacancies in Cork and a single extra seat on Dublin Corporation; the gap between expectation and reality was very wide indeed.[115]

REACTION AND RETREAT

Labour's leftward shift had been remarkably smooth so far but all that changed with the outbreak of the Spanish Civil War in the summer of 1936. The war in Spain received massive coverage in the national press, particularly the *Irish Independent*, and in Catholic periodicals in which it was portrayed as a battle between atheistic communists and God-fearing protectors of Christian values, with stories of desecrated churches and nuns being raped causing widespread revulsion. Unsurprisingly the stories from Spain reignited the popular anti-communism which had been relatively dormant in the previous year or so.[116] For the most part, this consisted of clerical warnings to exercise caution against the perils of communism, while not long after the outbreak of the conflict, the Irish Christian Front was established by Patrick Belton TD in support of Spanish Nationalists and to 'unmask communism in Ireland'.[117] Labour was not the target of any red-scaring during the summer but it was conscious of the threat nonetheless and was very sensitive about anything which could be construed as an association with, or accusation of, communism. For instance, when the CPI announced that it was not putting up any candidates for the local election in Dublin and called on its supporters to vote for Labour or Republican candidates, Labour released a statement declaring that it had no connection with the CPI or any of its members.[118]

Labour's initial response to the war in Spain was undoubtedly muted.[119] When Fine Gael tabled a motion in the Dáil to recognise the Franco government, Labour deputies remained silent, although they voted against it, while the party's weekly paper *Labour News* ignored the issue entirely, apart from one book review of Peadar O'Donnell's *Salud!* Some within the party supported Franco, and did so on religious grounds,[120] while those who supported republican forces kept it to themselves. This silence was not confined to Labour, with Jim Larkin's Workers' Union of Ireland, regarded by many as a 'red' union, barring its officials from speaking on pro-republican platforms.[121] In fact, open support for the republican forces in Spain was restricted to communist and leftist-republican circles, the same circles from which came the relatively small numbers of volunteers who ventured to Spain. Irish Labour's failure to support the republican government has been contrasted unfavourably with social democratic and socialist parties in Europe, but it is worth bearing in mind that, in the British case at least, Labour's response to the war in Spain was tempered by an unwillingness to alienate its Irish Catholic supporters.[122] Some Catholic groups did break away from the British party in protest,[123] but the fact that it was able to go as far as it did on the issue was because of the relatively small number of Catholics in its organisation, not to mention the lack of an alternative party so that many dissenters stayed within Labour and fought the Spanish nationalist case from within.[124]

It is significant that Labour avoided the glare of the country's anti-communists in the political tumult of the early 1930s. For instance, in James Hogan's 1935 treatise *Could Ireland Become Communist?* the party warranted barely a mention. This had been achieved, however, only through the diligent pursuit of blandness. Now its support for a 'Workers' Republic', deliberately vague as it was, made the party a target for the first time. Labour's problems began in earnest at its annual conference in February 1937. Though much of the conference was spent looking at workaday issues, unsurprisingly the debates dealing with ideology and foreign affairs attracted most outside attention.

Among the motions attracting interest was one tabled by Michael Price of the Dublin North West Branch condemning the Limerick TD Michael Keyes for speaking on a platform of the Irish Christian Front.[125] The motion was debated in private session, but this precaution became unnecessary as what could have turned into quite an altercation turned out to be a damp squib, when Keyes admitted that he had indeed addressed a meeting of the Christian Front in Limerick in November, but claimed he had been unaware of its anti-labour attitude at the time. Price accepted his assurances, requested that the Administrative Council make a statement about the politics of the Christian Front, and the matter rested there. It was an astonishingly low-key debate, prompting thanks to delegates from Chairman William O'Brien for their tact on the issue.

Tactful as the Irish Labour Party delegates were, they had not counted on the indiscretion of their fraternal delegate, Cllr A. H. McEvoy, from the Northern Ireland Labour Party (NILP). Referring to attacks on northern Labour for its support for republicans in Spain by 'that rather infamous rag, the *Independent*', he said it was

> tragic that Irish workers who had experience of the Black and Tans and had seen the horrors that Franco and his Moors were perpetrating on the defenceless people of Spain, did not realise that Franco was doing in Spain what British Imperialism had done in Ireland.[126]

Digging a hole deeper still, he mentioned the *Independent*'s references to the relationship between the NILP and the CPI, and argued that his party was democratic and constitutional but 'if, perchance, they and the Communist Party did occasionally find that there was something they had in common, there was no reason why they should not unite on that particular point'. He may have been wet behind the ears (thanking him for his remarks William O'Brien described him as 'a very recent . . . recruit to the Labour movement'), but this did not stop the *Independent* taking advantage of his naïveté; the next day its conference report appeared under the headline: 'PROUD TO SUPPORT REDS'.[127]

The *Independent*'s disingenuous headline was an unhelpful start to the last day of conference which was to consider a motion declaring Labour's opposition to fascism (submitted by the Rathmines branch), and an amendment (submitted by the Tipperary branch) looking to extend the party's opposition to 'Godless communism'. The motion was introduced by Séamus O'Brien (formerly of the Republican Congress)[128] and seconded by the ITGWU's Frank Robbins who stressed the irreligious character of continental fascism. The Tipperary delegate moved the amendment by arguing that it was 'unfair to condemn one undemocratic system and by their silence give tacit approval to another system which was, if anything, more undemocratic than Fascism'.[129] William Norton, bemoaning the fact that it should be necessary at this stage for the conference to debate a resolution condemning Fascism and Communism when it should be obvious to all that the party condemned both alike, complained that it 'had become fashionable during the past twelve months to address admonitions to Irish workers warning them of the dangers of Godless Communism', which was an insult to the intelligence and religious convictions of the Irish working class. Referring to the disruptions at the inaugural meeting of the Labour Party in 1930, Norton complained that 'those who profess to warn us of the dangers of Communism ought to know that as far as the Communist Party is concerned it has selected the Labour Party as the target for its bitterest criticism and vilest abuse'. He drew parallels with the dictatorships in Nazi Germany and Soviet Russia, both of which were maintained only through intimidation and terror, and contrasted these with social democratic administrations in Sweden and New Zealand where Labour governments ruled with positive effect. Thus far all were in agreement but the mood changed when a delegate from the newly established Trinity College branch rose to speak against the amendment, veering almost immediately into the territory that, until that point, all speakers had been careful to avoid, namely, Spain. Criticising the PLP for their failure to speak against Franco in the Dáil, he spoke against 'that filthy rag', the *Independent* for misquoting the NILP delegate's remarks about Spain and its labelling of the democratically elected legitimate government of the country as 'Red'. Hackles were raised when the Trinity delegate expressed his view that anyone at conference who was not prepared to support the republican government was there under false pretences, but further discussion on Spain was prevented by adroit chairing by William O'Brien. In the end, it was decided to publish Norton's speech in lieu of passing any more resolutions on the subject and the motion was withdrawn.

What comes across most forcefully throughout is the delegates' exasperation that they were wasting so much time on ideological debates, particularly when a general election was on the near horizon. One delegate complained that they were paying 'far too much attention to all those "isms"', while another from the ITGWU asked why 'alone among all parties, was the Labour Party asked every day in the week and every week in the year, to denounce something which everybody knew it hated?' Far from silencing Labour's critics, however, the conference merely stirred up more unwelcome interest. In the Dáil there were rowdy scenes when Richard Anthony accused the Labour conference of refusing to condemn communism, ending in a walk out by Norton.[130] In the press the *Limerick Leader* was now joined by the *Standard,* the *Irish Rosary* and the *Irish Catholic* in expressing concern over the 'down-ward sloping ground' on which some Labour people were slipping.[131] A press campaign at home was bad enough, but when the Vatican's newspaper *Osservatore Romano* reprinted the *Irish Catholic*'s contention that the 204,000 Irish workers affiliated to the ITUC were 'tacit supporters of communism' William Norton felt he could not let is pass. Norton wrote a letter to the Papal Secretary of State, Cardinal Pacelli, protesting about *Osservatore Romano*'s repetition of the *Irish Catholic*'s false accusations, and drew attention to the motion adopted at the 1934 conference which 'strongly opposed any attempt to introduce anti-Christian doctrines into the movement'.[132] Norton's complaint garnered a retraction from the Vatican paper but did nothing to stop press critics at home.[133] It also garnered protest from an appalled Thomas Johnson, for whom the letter represented an unreasonable blurring of the boundary between politics and personal morality.[134] Johnson was disgusted that anyone wanting to know the political views of organised Irish workers should not consult Congress or the Labour Party but, as Norton put it in his letter, instead approach a 'recognised Catholic authority qualified to interpret authoritatively such tendencies'. Johnson protested that a person expressing belief in an economic creed could be accused of being guilty of a moral offence which should be pronounced on by the Catholic hierarchy or any other recognised Catholic authority. 'If the Party adopts the position that this question is one concerning faith and morals and in consequence is a matter for the Hierarchy to pronounce authoritatively upon', Johnson warned, 'I for one will have to reconsider my position as a member'.

Nor was Johnson the only one reconsidering his position. By late 1936, the Irish National Teachers' Organisation executive had grown sufficiently con-cerned about the character of Labour's constitution that it sought the Catholic hierarchy's advice on the matter.[135] The reason for their anxiety was two-fold. The vast majority of national schoolteachers were directly employed by the Catholic Church which made avoiding unnecessary conflict with the Church very desirable. However, it would be wrong to suggest that the unions' objec-tions were raised only in pursuit of a quiet life. Most of the executive were practising Catholics and its treasurer, M. P. Linehan, was an active Catholic Actionist.[136] The INTO was one of Labour's largest affiliated unions and a significant contributor to party funds – in fact in the early 1930s its financial backing to the party had been greater than that of the largest affiliate, the ITGWU. The teachers' concerns would have to be taken very seriously.

ANOTHER CONSTITUTION

The limelight soon shifted towards an altogether different constitution. De Valera had been working on a new national constitution since 1936, with the draft of Bunreacht na hÉireann finally published on 1 May the following year.[137] Labour criticised the timing of its introduction (believing economic problems were more urgent)[138] and several of its more illiberal provisions (in particular, its provision for special courts along the lines of the Military Tribunal, as well as the those dealing with the freedom of the press),[139] and concluded that its contents were merely the product of Fianna Fáil's conservatism. It was, as Norton put it, 'an innocuous document compared with the Democratic Programme of the first Dáil'.[140] This contrast between the promise of radical social republicanism and the underachievement of the government was a theme played out at length by Labour over the next few months, for with the promise of a referendum on the draft constitution came the prospect of a simultaneous general election and, for the first time, Labour identified Fianna Fáil as its primary target in the campaign. Fianna Fáil had failed in its economic policy and its social policy. Unemployment was rising and thousands were emigrating. Wages were low and the cost of living high. Fianna Fáil promised plenty to the working classes at election time, but when in office had failed to deliver.

Not content to attack Fianna Fáil on economic grounds, Labour donned its green cloak and endeavoured to outdo it on nationalist grounds as well. In December 1936 the two parties had differed over the Irish response to the abdication crisis in Britain. Following Edward VIII's abdication, de Valera had received notice from London that for the abdication to be effective, and for the King's brother to succeed him, it would be necessary for Dáil Éireann to pass legislation to that effect. Seeing this as his chance to remove the King and the governor general from the Saorstát constitution (and hence his own), de Valera was eager to oblige, but when he informed William Norton of his plan at a meeting on 10 December, the Labour leader urged him to hasten slowly. Norton felt that they had Britain over a barrel on this issue, and that rather than rush into anything they ought to 'obtain from the British the maximum advantages on such matters as the economic war, partition and national independence before introducing legislation in the country to extricate the British from a difficult situation'.[141] De Valera was not, however, inclined to change tack. After lengthy discussions the following evening, a meeting of the PLP and AC decided that despite the party's reservations, Labour's deputies would vote in favour of the Constitutional Amendment No. 27 Bill although they would do so under protest.[142] Between then and the vote, however, there was a change of plan. When the matter was put before the Dáil later that evening, Norton complained that the house was being 'asked to appoint a British King of Saorstát Éireann under a guillotine motion in the Parliament of Saorstát Éireann',[143] but though he and his party voted against the bill (as Fine Gael did for quite different reasons) the Constitutional Amendment No. 27 Bill passed comfortably.

Labour took great pleasure subsequently in contrasting its refusal to recognise the King with the stance taken by Fianna Fáil.[144] On the occasion of George VI's coronation, Labour took to the streets in Dublin where its anti-imperialist meeting in College Green attracted a crowd of 2,000. Under a banner proclaiming 'Labour Repudiates Coronation' Helena Moloney told listeners that the spirit of flunkeyism was still abroad in high places in Ireland but the Labour Party and the Irish Citizen Army had sworn to upset the social order.[145] Fianna Fáil were painted as the new establishment; it found 'soft jobs for its followers', paying off Domhnall Ó Buachalla, the now redundant governor general, with a lump sum of £2,000 and a pension for life, while one of his late employees had been dismissed without compensation.[146]

The constitution successfully expunged of the British monarch, it was now ready to go before the public. To kill two birds with one stone, de Valera decided to wed an election to the referendum on the constitution, and so on 14 June he dissolved the Dáil and called another election, announcing that polling day would take place on 1 July. Niggardly unemployment benefits in comparison with Ó Buachalla's bounty and the government's disgraceful treat-ment of Old IRA men – which had never troubled Labour in the past, but it was more than happy to adopt this cause while it was busy riffling through Fianna Fáil's wardrobe[147] – became the themes of Labour's election campaign. Despite its attacks on the government party, one thing remained clear. Labour sought to hold the balance of power so that it could keep an eye on Fianna Fáil. There could be no return for the Cosgrave government.[148]

Labour News instructed its readers to prepare for battle, predicting a dirty fight: 'our enemies have been marshalling their forces and getting ready their poison gas', it warned, 'so let Labour be ready to give as good as it gets'.[149] Efforts were made to get the party machine working. In April the AC appointed a former Lord Mayor of Limerick to oversee its organisational drive,[150] and by July there were almost 60 new branches affiliated, as well as two new unions (the Irish Union of Distributive Workers and Clerks and the Irish Women Workers' Union, with combined membership of 15,000).[151] Another fillip from the trade union movement came with the Dublin INTO's pledge of support for the party at the end of May, where, citing conditions in schools and threats of pay cuts for teachers, it urged its members to vote and canvass for Labour, and join the party if they had not done so already.[152] The party's appeal for subscriptions met with a positive response, and turnout at street meetings and the popularity of the newly launched Labour Youth Movement in Dublin also seemed to indicate a new support for the party.[153] By the middle of June *Labour News* was enjoying a circulation of 65,000. 'Nearly everywhere', it wrote, 'the signs are most encouraging'. It seemed as though Labour's green flag waving was proving a success:

> National elements that did not throw themselves wholeheartedly in to the fight on our side in previous elections are working for our candidates . . . They realise now that the one definitely and uncompromisingly Republican Party in the Dáil and in the election is the Labour Party. We serve neither King nor Empire but Labour and Ireland.[154]

Compared with the antagonism of the previous election in 1933, this contest was quiet. Though keenly contested by the parties the electorate was reported to be generally apathetic.[155] The number of seats in the new Dáil had been reduced by 15 with the larger seat constituencies broken up mostly into three seaters. The revision increased uncertainty about the result of the poll, although all things being equal it should have led to increases for Fianna Fáil,[156] and overall observers – and indeed the outgoing government itself – were confident of a comfortable return for the government. A quiet polling day reflected the quiet campaign,[157] but the results of the contest came as a surprise to many. De Valera had apparently got his maths wrong. Far from sweeping up the bonuses due from the constituency revision, Fianna Fáil and Fine Gael both saw their votes fall by around five per cent, losing nine seats apiece on their pre-dissolution figures.[158] Labour, on the other hand, saw its vote almost double to over ten per cent, garnering an extra five seats (including two in Dublin) to give it a total of 13, a result which took many, not least Fianna Fáil, by surprise.[159] Moreover, although the draft constitution was approved in the accompanying referendum, its 57 per cent level of support was somewhat less than resounding. Joe Lee has concluded that most Labour supporters probably did support the constitution in the end, but it is likely that one in three did not, as the combined Fianna Fáil and Labour vote was 50,000 greater than the 'yes' vote for the constitution.[160]

One writer has suggested that Labour's 'flirtation with socialism' in the form of the Workers' Republic constitution may have paid off electorally in this election;[161] in fact its gains came *in spite of* this dalliance. The Workers' Republic rarely featured in Labour's campaign; it was its protest about economic and social problems at a time when country was punch drunk from five years of the economic war that actually won Labour votes. As one delegate at the subsequent Labour conference recalled:

Candidates for election were afraid of the Workers' Republic talk. How many of them had included the Workers' Republic in their election addresses last Summer? He could ascertain only one case. . . . The fact was that if they wanted to frighten the life out of a man seeking election last summer they would tell him they were going to talk of the Workers' Republic from his platform. He would say, 'for Heaven's sake, give it a miss, don't mention it'.[162]

Independents on the whole lost out, but there was one significant addition to their ranks in the shape of Jim Larkin who was elected in Dublin North East without reaching the quota, depriving Fine Gael's Richard Mulcahy of a seat in the process. Larkin was still an undischarged bankrupt, but on this occasion there was no attempt to debar him,[163] indicating something of a détente between himself and Labour, which had not been so magnanimous in 1927. That he had managed to get through this election without rhetorical or physical attacks on Labour no doubt had something to do with Labour's silence on the issue.

So it was that with de Valera returned yet again without a majority, Labour was kingmaker once more. Of course, Labour's choice of king was never in doubt: it had made it plain throughout the campaign that it wanted a return of a Fianna Fáil government, just one that it could keep an eye on and soon after the result had become clear Luke Duffy told reporters that a Fianna Fáil government could rely on the assistance of the Labour Party so long as it made every effort to improve social legislation. Labour would retain compete independence in the new Dáil and would only support government legislation with which it was in agreement.[164] De Valera was making no promises, however, and declared that Fianna Fáil would assume the responsibility of government on the clear understanding that it would 'pursue its own policy and none other'.[165] Unsurprisingly, with Labour and Fianna Fáil both taking a hard line, an early election was predicted, perhaps as soon as in a couple of months but certainly no later than a year.[166]

The ninth Dáil conducted little business of consequence. The government's attentions lay elsewhere as de Valera now sought an end to the economic war. There were a number of reasons for his choosing this time to resolve the matter. Some were opportunistic; for one thing, J. H. Thomas had been replaced as dominion secretary by the altogether more amenable Malcolm MacDonald, while the war clouds looming on the continent made Britain eager to tie up its loose ends in Ireland. Moreover, the knowledge that Fianna Fáil had fared so badly at the general election largely owing to the economic war's impact could only have encouraged de Valera in starting moves to reach a settlement.[167] Labour's criticism of the government continued in much the same vein as it had during the election. Norton was publicly indignant at talk of early elections,[168] but by October was already beginning Labour's selection process.[169] There were signs of the pre-election momentum continuing as new branches were established, and various initiatives were started, such as a Labour lecture campaign and a drive to get 1,000 new members in Dublin by May 1938.[170] In all 105 new branches were formed during 1937, many of which covered new ground.[171]

It was noticeable around this time that prurient interest in Labour policies and scaremongering about its communist tendencies began to wane. The quiet shelving of some of Labour's more alarming rhetoric during that contest may have had something to do with this, and beyond the party the communist spectre had diminished, with Franco in the ascendant in Spain and the failure of republican candidates at the general election. By 1938 the Lenten pastorals had returned to denouncing the dangers of dance halls, with the menace of communism receiving little notice at all.[172] Labour leaders remained on their guard nevertheless, and one area in particular was causing regular headaches. *Labour News* had been published weekly by the party since November 1936. It was a reasonable publication as far as Labour newspapers went. It was lively, well laid out, and concentrated on politics and agitprop rather than rehashes of Connolly's life story or lengthy transcripts of Dáil debates as most of its predecessors had done. That *Labour News* was the first labour publication to be edited by a full-time professional journalist (Christopher O'Sullivan) rather than a trade union or party official contributed in no small part to its success, but it also led to a number of problems, for the editor's eye for a good story or headline, and his lack of sensitivity about what might get the party in trouble, saw the paper sail dangerously close to the edge on a regular basis.[173] Although the Spanish civil war remained an unbreakable taboo, O'Sullivan was less circumspect in his treatment of the Catholic Church. The tone of editorials was often belligerent, particularly in relation to the misrepresentation of Labour policy by the Church, as too was its reportage. It had a propensity to throw fuel on the fire of controversy, as evidenced during its controversy with the *Limerick Leader* over the Workers' Republic, and with no concept of how far it could reasonably go, as demonstrated by its use of a poster proclaiming 'CHURCH HAS NO SOLUTION FOR LABOUR' to advertise one particular issue.[174] A week later, *Labour News* ran an article relating how Catholic clergy in Youghal had issued an edict that no women would be admitted to church if they were bare-legged. *Labour News* argued that they were only likely to be bare-legged if they could not afford stockings and so the issue was not one of modesty but low pay. O'Sullivan was warned to pay more heed to the party's particular sensitivities after a number of such incidents, but he paid scant notice to these entreaties.[175]

The final straw came in March 1938 with two very different pieces. The first was a report of a lecture on the control of finance by a Dominican priest which ran contrary to Labour's economic policy; the second was a short piece of verse entitled 'Poem by a Negro boy to God', which featured the line, 'you must have a great laugh up there in your big sky, Lord!'[176] The directors of *Labour News* met on 1 April to consider the two pieces. As Norton put it, 'the views of the two clergy men quoted in the article . . . were bad from our standpoint but the poem . . . was a million times worse' and was 'a piece of blasphemy'. By now the directors were determined to take a strong line, and the editor's services were dispensed with immediately. Publication of *Labour News* was consequently suspended until a replacement could be found.[177] The last issue appeared on 2 April and the paper was never revived. This move could not have been easy – only three months earlier the party, a number of unions and several individuals had put up extra capital to keep the paper afloat when mounting debts saw it face collapse,[178] and to wind it up so soon after must have been galling in the extreme – but ultimately, however important its propaganda role, Norton argued that the party would actually lose more seats if it was kept going.[179] Norton was conscious that both the suspension of the paper, and the reasons for so doing would be controversial but he was prepared to broach no arguments. As he put it to one colleague, 'certain individuals – who are non-Catholic – will probably disagree with our attitude but we cannot help that and must meet any criticism they make'.[180] Not that any effort was made either to explain or placate the paper's subscribers, prompting angry complaints (to no effect) at the party's conference the following year.[181]

YOUTHFUL ENTHUSIASM AND ITS PROBLEMS

Labour's 1938 conference took place days after *Labour News* was closed down. No doubt sensing an impending election, the party was on its best behaviour. There was inevitably a motion calling on the AC to 'press upon the government the need for radical measures directed towards . . . a Workers' Republic'. The debate was wound up without a vote owing to to lack of time, although not before perennial grouse J. T. O'Farrell had pointed out the distinct reluctance of any of the party's candidates to mention the Workers' Republic at the last election. To his question 'what was then the use of having an ideal of which nearly every candidate for election was ashamed?' no answer was provided. Controversy on this issue had been avoided, but arose later during debate on a motion on Abyssinia tabled by the Trinity College branch. The motion itself was uncontroversial, but in introducing it, the Trinity delegate, a young graduate student named Conor Cruise O'Brien, had ignored his Aunt

Mary's warning beforehand not to 'say anything silly or extreme as it wouldn't do [him] any good',[182] and adverted to the 'clique of Fascist generals . . . [who were] wantonly waging a civil war' against the people of Spain. This drew a troubled response from County Dublin TD Gerrard McGowan, who claimed that such talk would bring the party into contempt throughout the whole country. (It certainly brought him into contempt with his Aunt Mary who felt he had made a 'communist, anti-God speech', and wrote him a 'nasty note' accusing him of 'trying to gain notoriety'.[183]) Norton appealed to McGowan for discretion, reminding him that the press was present, but McGowan continued, accusing O'Brien of proposing the motion 'in a manner that was *calculated* to harm the party more than anything else', adding that he would be 'lacking in his duty as a citizen and a Catholic if he did not enter a protest', but 'with respect to everybody's religious beliefs, they were Catholics first and politicians afterwards'.[184] A full-scale commotion was only avoided when the Chairman put the resolution to an immediate vote, thus ending the debate. For Labour, as Fearghal McGarry has described it, when it came to Spain, it was still a case of 'don't mention the war',[185] and whether delegates agreed with Cruise O'Brien's sentiments or not there must have been collective eye-rolling in the hall as he galloped headlong into rhetorical Indian territory. That Labour's omertà on Spain had been broken by a young recruit for the second year in a row illustrated the problems created by inviting youths to become active in the movement. During 1937 there had been an attempt to establish a Labour Youth Movement, with the aim of providing young recruits for the party.[186] It was set up eventually, after long delays in formulating a constitution and structures which would keep it under the watchful eye of head office and prevent it from being used as a conduit for communist infiltrators. Even so, as *Labour News* noted, young members were not without their problems:

> It may be argued that its enthusiasm and want of experience will carry youth with its idealism far ahead of the main body of the party, that its thinking is far in advance of the general line of thought that it is liable to make serious mistakes and to use language and express ideas that will draw damaging fire from opponents of the party . . .[187]

In the event, the Labour Youth Movement was wound up almost before it started, as the party proved unable to prevent it becoming dominated by communist voices. The problem as Labour saw it was not merely with young people, but with intellectuals generally. The late 1930s was the time when poverty and anti-fascism led many intellectuals in the direction of communism and fellow travelling. This happened a lot less in Ireland than elsewhere, but a strong middle-class leftist milieu did flourish in enclaves such as Trinity College. That these types were not exactly welcomed with open arms, is well illustrated in a complaint by Michael Price (who was far from reactionary) to Cathal O'Shannon. Price lamented that:

> the pseudo intellectuals of the Left Book Club and of Trinity College – who are no damned good when you want a flag sold, a poster put up, etc. – are just about *thirty* people in a population of 3,000,000. The thirty will have had all their excitement and be finished with us in about a year: the 3,000,000 are always there to be appealed to.[188]

Negotiations between the British and Irish governments began in January 1938 with an agreement signed on 25 April. It was a triumph for de Valera. The British government did not give any leeway on the issue of partition, but it was never likely that it would. What de Valera did secure, however, was the writing off of £100 million in annuities and other payments in return for a £10 million lump sum, the return of the three treaty ports in Berehaven, Cobh and Lough Swilly, and a number of significant trade provisions, including an end to all restrictions on Irish agricultural products,[189] marking 'the culmi-nation of a remarkably successful guerrilla diplomatic campaign to revise the Treaty out of existence'.[190] During negotiations de Valera had sought to convince the British side that Ireland's political stability rested on him, and played up Fianna Fáil's reverses at the previous election. Essentially, he had put it up to the British side to give him a deal he could win the country with, and London had acceded to his request. On 25 May, exactly a month after the Anglo-Irish agreement was signed, the government was defeated by a single vote on compulsory arbitration for civil servants. The government should heed the Dáil instruction, said Norton, and abandon this measure.[191] De Valera read the Dáil's instruction rather differently, however, and two days later called a general election for 17 June, to general surprise all round.[192] Fianna Fáil contested the election on its record, not least its recent success in London. Fine Gael was bankrupt in terms of policies, and merely carped about how the government could have ended the economic war many years earlier. They were said to be 'quietly optimistic' going into the contest,[193] a fact belied by its fielding only 76 candidates, 20 fewer than in the last election, and barely enough for an overall majority even if all were returned.[194] Labour, in contrast, actually increased its candidates by almost a third to 30, contesting 25 constituencies in all and hoping to maintain or even increase its represen-tation.[195] This increase in candidates seemed to show Labour on the ascendant, although some of the nominations were idiosyncratic to say the least.[196] It effectively ran the same campaign as the previous year. Once more, it tried to outflank Fianna Fáil nationally and economically. It wheeled out the issue of Old IRA pensions and the 1936 recognition of George VI once again, to which was added de Valera's £10 million tribute to the British government and his promise to restore the treaty ports as proof of his lack of republican credentials.[197] Its campaign on social and economic issues was largely identical to that of the previous election, criticising the government for not dealing with unemployment, cherry picking Fianna Fáil's successful reforms as their own, and promising more of the same when they held the balance of power once more.

Essentially, then, Labour wanted a Fianna Fáil government, but with Labour pulling the strings and, naturally enough, Fianna Fáil wanted to govern alone. This was the real crux of the election. Labour portrayed de Valera's rational and reasonable desire for a single party government as a tendency towards megalomania; there was 'no doubt that de Valera is aiming for dictatorship', he was 'posing as a super-democrat but had the make up of a dictator', his democracy was a veneer and 'beneath it truculence and intolerance of dictatorship'.[198] Unsurprisingly, when de Valera announced that he would take steps to abolish proportional representation if he did not win an overall majority,[199] both Labour and Fine Gael (which had wanted to abolish it themselves not long before) were apoplectic. 'Every dictator in Europe holds his country in subjection only because at one period the people succumbed to his plea for a "strong government"', warned Labour's manifesto.[200] There was no little irony (as Seán Lemass and others were happy to point out) in Labour holding itself up as the champions of democracy, when it believed that a party which won less than a tenth of Dáil seats should be able to have a veto on all issues and dictate matters of general policy.[201] Certainly the electorate thought so. Fianna Fáil's vote increased in all but two constituencies and they won 52 per cent of the national vote, the first time any party had won a majority of the popular vote in the history of the state.[202] Fine Gael and Labour's votes remained stable but made a net loss of three and five seats respectively. Labour lost both of its precious newly won Dublin seats, and 11 deposits.[203] A significant development was the extent to which Labour had been abandoned by Fianna Fáil voters. Fianna Fáil to Labour transfers were now at 27.5 per cent, down from 42 per cent at the last election which itself was down 91.7 per cent on 1933.[204] Having defined themselves for the last six years as allies of Fianna Fáil, Labour was now once more on its own and on the political sidelines.

THREE

LABOUR'S RISE AND FALL
1938–44

—

Labour under Norton was like a teenager, its character changing with the company it kept. Over the next few years, Labour started hanging with some very different crowds, and the party veered rightward and leftward with dizzying results. It enjoyed some of its greatest advances and suffered probably its worst ever setback, but the events which are examined in the course of this chapter were to influence the party for decades.

RETREAT FROM THE WORKERS' REPUBLIC

At its April 1939 conference, the party's first since the general election, Labour buried the Workers' Republic. It happened with very little ado and marked the culmination of the INTO's careful attempts which had been continuing behind the scenes for nearly two years to remove the offending clause. Profound concerns among the INTO's executive about the character of the party constitution led the teachers' union to refer the it to the Catholic hierarchy for its opinion. The hierarchy sought the advice of a committee of experts, comprising Bishop Kinane of Waterford, the bishop-elect of Galway Michael Browne, and two senior clerics, Patrick O'Neill and Cornelius Lucey, which presented its report to the hierarchy at the end of the year.[1] The committee's findings – that the constitution contained several aspects that were contrary to Catholic teaching – were endorsed by the hierarchy and put to the INTO executive, which then communicated this advice to the AC early in 1938.[2] The union tabled an amendment for Labour's 1938 conference seeking the 'deletion of the objectionable features' from the constitution, but was persuaded to withdraw it by the AC, which informed the INTO that its amendments would not be carried at conference.[3] The teachers and the hierarchy bided their time. In the year that followed, the hierarchy lobbied the AC to support the necessary changes while the INTO lobbied Labour's affiliated unions and branches.[4]

When Labour's annual conference met in April 1939, the party's constitution came under review. William Norton, on behalf of the AC, moved that 'in

view of certain misunderstanding of Labour Party policy, Conference autho-
rises the AC to make such amendments in the constitution of the party as will
obviate the misunderstanding'.[5] The problem, as Norton explained, revolved
around two issues: firstly, the term 'Workers' Republic' had proved open to
misinterpretation, and secondly, there were objections to the constitution's
principles and objects on the grounds that they made insufficient provision
for private property. Norton rebutted the objections, arguing that while
Labour's use of the phrase 'Workers' Republic' was portrayed as trying to ape
the rhetoric of Mexico and Russia, the term had been used by Connolly in
Ireland first of all, and then emphasised that Labour's support for the
nationalisation of certain industries did not extend towards generally taking
over the business of shopkeepers and small trades. Acknowledging that 'there
would be considerable feeling on the matter' he put it to delegates that 'if they
wanted to avoid the misrepresentations – and deliberate misrepresentations –
which opponents would employ against them' all references to the 'Workers'
Republic' would have to go. In all other ways, he said, the programme would
remain unaltered.

Perhaps predictably, opposition came from the more republican ranks and
some Protestant delegates. Séamus O'Brien (Inchicore branch), a former
Republican Congress man and the husband of James Connolly's daughter
Nora, opposed the motion, arguing that once they had started on the slippery
slope of reaction, they could not say where they would stop. Michael Price
called for resistance against this undemocratic procedure, arguing that the
Irish hierarchy had been against nearly every popular movement. 'What about
the Penal days?' enquired an INTO delegate, 'What about Parnell?'countered
Price. Sam Kyle (a Northern Protestant) explained that he had voted against
the constitution before, but on this occasion would vote against the changes
on principle since he felt the powers which the AC was seeking were too open
ended and, furthermore, only conference had the power to change the
constitution or the party's aims and objectives. He took issue with the notion
that outside bodies such as the hierarchy had the right to say that Labour
must act in accordance with their ideas.

The debate seems to have been astonishingly temperate:[6] the chairman
congratulated delegates on their 'splendid restraint', which reflected credit on
everybody present and which augured well for the future of the movement,
sentiments echoed by an obviously relieved Norton. In his last word to
delegates on the subject he appealed to their sense of pragmatism, arguing
that 'while it might be popular to defeat a motion of this kind, in the long run
it would be a more courageous course to adopt it'.[7] Norton explained that 'his
aim had been to prevent the Party foundering on a rock which might mean its
political end. If they wanted to make artificial martyrs of themselves, it would

be easy.' In effect, Labour could accept retreat or face immediate and terrible war with the Church on the issue. Of course, Labour could, if it chose, stand on principle and refuse to make the changes demanded of them, but since the Workers' Republic had been adopted as an opportunistic measure to differentiate the party from Fianna Fáil, and, more importantly, had proved of little use in gaining Labour seats, the only principle involved was survival and by that measure the clause had to go. This view was reflected in the voting, with the AC's motion passed by a margin of more than three to one.[8]

The controversy over the Workers' Republic constitution, and Labour's apparently craven kowtowing to the hierarchy's demands have become one of the most infamous episodes in the party's history. Any claims to a radical mantle certainly slipped as a result. 'You have killed the idealists in your party. There is no future in it for them', Seamus O'Brien told the conference after the vote.[9] It is impossible to gauge how many members may have left,[10] or even how many potential recruits may have been put off because of it, but what is quite evident is its influence on the rhetoric of the party for decades to come. The lasting impact was in the way it provided Norton with a salutary lesson in how attempts to *appear* radical could create more trouble than they were worth. Labour never attempted to use such rhetoric again while Norton was leader. Henceforth the Labour Party, which *was* predominantly conservative, went out of its way to make sure that it was *seen* to be conservative. Anything which could be misconstrued by the enemies of the party was avoided at all costs, unless, that is, it was quite clear that there were votes in it.

One study described the scrapping of the Workers' Republic constitution as Labour's 'formal separation from the ideology of socialism',[11] but this overstates its significance. For one thing, there were questions as to whether the Workers' Republic constitution was socialist in the first place. For another, Labour's refusal to mention the document in the course of two successive general elections indicated that it had been informally separated from its notional socialism. Nevertheless, what was truly remarkable about this episode was not conference's compliance in ditching the Workers' Republic, but its decision effectively to write the AC a blank cheque on what would go in its place, authorising the AC to 'make such amendments in the constitution of the party as will obviate the misunderstanding'. Labour's socialism may have been half hearted at best, but once it was gone it became evident that the party which ceased to believe in socialism would believe in anything, with policy documents beginningh to adopt an altogether different character, as we shall see later on below.

WAR IN EUROPE

The irrelevance of debates on a notional Workers' Republic was highlighted by events outside Ireland. Europe was sliding inexorably into war. The Munich agreement signed by Britain, France and Germany in September 1938 was in tatters by the March 1939 as German troops marched into Czechoslovakia. All out war between Germany and the two allies was inevitable, the only question seemed to be when would it start. In February de Valera had announced that the central tenet of government policy would be to keep Ireland out of the war.[12] It was a policy which enjoyed broad political consensus, and Labour was no exception with Norton telling the April 1939 conference that the party's policy was one of 'peace and neutrality'.[13] Many within Labour took the view of a 'plague on all your houses' towards the would-be belligerents, regarding the forthcoming war as a battle between competing varieties of imperialism, as Labour had looked on the conflict of 1914–18.[14] This was the point of view put forward by *Torch*, a weekly news-paper published by the Dublin Constituencies Council of the Labour Party, when its first edition announced: 'Labour backs neither Chamberlain nor Hitler'.[15] Indeed, some weeks later its editor, Cathal O'Shannon, wrote of the protracted Anglo–French–Russian negotiations: 'We may not agree with [the Soviets'] principles or their practice. But we can understand, even admire, their suspicions of the British and French imperialists and capitalists.'[16]

Labour's support for the government on neutrality was steadfast, but its stance on related security issues was not. Events in Europe had had an imme-diate political impact closer to home. Resurrecting the old adage about Britain's difficulty and Ireland's opportunity, the IRA (now under the leadership of Sean Russell) began preparations for a new campaign and in December 1938 the IRA Army Council issued a formal declaration of war against Britain. The following month a series of bomb attacks in Britain started a campaign which continued sporadically throughout the year and beyond. The response to the renewed IRA activity by the Stormont government was immediate; on 22 December 1939 a number of known republicans were arrested in a sweep under the Special Powers Act and interned indefinitely in Crumlin Road prison.[17] Meanwhile in Dublin in November, the Department of Justice had begun drafting legislation to deal with the Special Criminal Court, unlawful organisations and treason,[18] resulting in the Treason Bill and the Offences Against the State Bills being introduced to the Dáil in February and March 1939 respectively.

With the exception of the use of the military tribunal against the Blueshirts in 1934, Labour had consistently opposed the type of provisions included in these two bills, and this time was no different. Norton took greatest exception to the fact that the legislation was pre-emptive, arguing that it came 'at a time when the country, so far as its internal administration is concerned, was never more peaceful',[19] and he contrasted Britain's failure to introduce similar legislation even though it was actually under attack.[20] Though the government could easily pass the legislation without Labour's support, de Valera appealed for it nonetheless and urged the party not to play politics with the issue. A less emollient Frank Aiken suggested that some of Labour's speeches might be read as favouring the continuance of 'a certain armed organisation'.[21] This accusation was particularly repugnant, and for the Labour men who had held their seats since 1922 it was particularly galling to hear it from the former Irregular Chief of Staff. As William Davin put it, he and his colleagues had entered 'this House in spite of threats of assassination, dictated probably and directed to us by some of the people who are now making these allegations against us'.[22] The character of the debates illustrates the degree to which the relationship between Labour and Fianna Fáil had soured: Fianna Fáil patently fed up with what it saw as Labour's opportunism, and Labour alarmed by Fianna Fáil's willingness to don the mantle of Cumann na nGaedheal's old policies (while detecting more than a little opportunism on de Valera's part for good measure). Ultimately both bills were passed with the support of all sections in the Dáil apart from Labour. Labour's opposition to the measures remained constant over the following years with one significant exception. Following the German invasion of Poland, the Dáil met on 2 September to debate the Emergency Powers Bill. Drafted during the Munich crisis the year before, the Emergency Powers Bill was based on a blueprint circulated by the British government to its dominions, with anti-subversive provisions taken from Cosgrave's 1931 Constitutional Amendment Act.[23] It went far further than the Offences Against the State Act or the Treason Act which Labour had voted against earlier that year, but what had changed was the context. Labour deputies objected strongly to the bill's abrogation of civil liberties, press censorship, and the rights of parliament,[24] but now that war was a reality they did not vote against the bill. The labour movement, a *Torch* contributor wrote subsequently, would have the privilege of seeing that the emergency powers with which the government had been equipped were not abused.[25]

While there was narrow consensus on neutrality, there would be no political truce in the Dáil between the government and opposition parties. There was never any question in de Valera's mind of a national government and the opposition parties felt no compunction to pull in their horns on any issue. Outside the Dáil, *Torch* maintained a militant stand, declaring that 'specious talk' about '"national unity"' ought to be ignored, and proclaiming with banner headlines: FIGHTING CONTINUES ON THE HOME FRONT and WAGES WAR: NO NEUTRALITY in the early stages of the Emergency.[26]

This fighting talk did not last very long, however, as the Emergency censorship was deepened and widened from covering issues directly related to maintaining Ireland's neutrality to 'keeping the temperature down' more generally. Under the Emergency Powers (No. 5) Order 1939 made on 13 September, 'authorised persons' could prohibit publication of any specified matter permanently or for a specified period, and could ban publications which did not adhere to directions issued on these matters. Furthermore, they could not give any indications that such orders had been issued in the first place.[27] In July the following year the Emergency Powers (No. 36) Order 1940 augmented the operation of wartime censorship by giving authorised persons the power to direct the seizure of matter which 'would be prejudicial to the public safety or the preservation of the State or the maintenance of public order'. On 17 February 1942 existing orders relating to censorship were revoked and replaced by the Emergency Powers (No. 151) Order 1942 which sought to close any loopholes in existing provisions, including the extension of censorship to printed matter of all kinds, including pamphlets.[28] Within the Dáil Labour protested against the censorship (as did Fine Gael deputies) from the outset, although the extent to which the censorship would be used for political means had not yet become apparent.[29]

Another feature of Emergency legislation which was taken up by Labour was the internment of known republicans. Beginning in early September, Special Branch had begun to arrest suspected troublemakers to put them out of circulation. Their intelligence was not always au courant, and while most *were* active IRA men, others such as Con Lehane (the veteran republican and associate of Seán MacBride who was estranged from the Russell leadership of the IRA) were unlikely to pose a threat at this time.[30] Lehane, a solicitor, who had, according to *Torch*, been 'arrested while visiting a prisoner in a professional capacity', went on hunger strike on 12 October to effect his release. The case was raised by Norton in the Dáil who engaged in some political point scoring when he asked the Minster for Justice if he was to take it that 'hunger strikes . . . of this nature which were right in 1922 and 1923 are wrong in 1939?'[31] The case, which had been largely ignored in the press was also taken up in *Torch*,[32] as was that of the 1916 veteran Paddy McGrath and others who were also on hunger strike at the time. *Torch* was able to get away with publishing on such issues where other newspapers with greater circulation figures could not.[33] Labour lobbied the government on the occasion of subsequent hunger strikes, with Senator Seán Campbell, who was on the visiting committee of Mountjoy acting as go-between for the prisoners and their families with the government's permission.[34] Undoubtedly, some of the Labour men genuinely believed that individuals' civil liberties were being usurped by the state, but it is difficult to deny that Norton, in particular, was not engaging in what Joe Lee has described as 'insidious opportunism'.[35] Whereas other Labour deputies were quite able to make cogent arguments against the use of internment, Norton's constant refrain that the country was at peace, ignoring entirely the appetite and capability for subversion by republicans, seems disingenuous at best. Certainly the government (predictably) felt Norton was engaged in irresponsible populism, accusing him in one instance of thinking 'that he is on a bit of a popular wave'.

RELATIONS BETWEEN THE GOVERNMENT AND TRADE UNION MOVEMENT

If there was one single issue on which relations between Labour and the government were charged it was that of trade union regulation and the emergency regulation of wages. The matter of how trade unions in Ireland should be organised had dominated discussions in Congress throughout the 1930s.[36] The multiplicity of unions in single sectors regularly led to inter-union disputes. As Emmet O'Connor has put it, 'sometimes unions fought over their respective merits, sometimes over the advantages of craft or industrial unionism, sometimes over the principles behind Irish or British based unions; always they fought about members'.[37] O'Connor further notes, 'The most strike prone sectors, transport and construction, were also the most faction ridden areas of trade unionism. Sixteen unions operated in transport, twelve of them British based, making it a cockpit of the general friction in the movement between the ITGWU, the WUI and the amalgamateds'.[38] The situation as it stood was intolerable for the government, with the long-time Minister for Industry and Commerce Seán Lemass increasingly frustrated at having to deal with a trade union 'hydra' instead of a single coherent organisation.[39] By 1936 he had instructed Congress that if it did not get its house in order and do something about inter-union friction the government would have to intervene.[40]

In April 1936, Congress responded with the age-old delaying tactic of establishing a commission to look into the movement's reorganisation.[41] The speed with which the proposals were submitted to the commission was indicative of their authors' desire for change. The ITGWU general secretary, William O'Brien, was most anxious to consolidate the movement in Ireland. For one thing, he held firm to his own organisation's syndicalist aim of OBU (One Big Union) and saw the profusion of unions as the antithesis of this goal and detrimental to the interests of the Transport Union. Many of the smaller unions were British based and, from the point of view of O'Brien's and the Transport Union's traditional nationalism, the number of foreign unions operating in Ireland could not be tolerated. Before the year was out, O'Brien had set out a plan for swingeing rationalisation which would see all members grouped in around ten industrial unions (at that time there were 49 unions affiliated to Congress alone).[42] In contrast, it was another *year* before Sam Kyle of the British based ATGWU put forward an alternative, which amounted to retaining the status quo, albeit with some of the smaller unions being amalgamated. Eventually, a special meeting of Congress met on 9 February 1939 to choose one of three proposals: O'Brien's fundamental reorganisation (Memorandum No. 1), Kyle's status quo with some rationalisation (Memorandum No. 2) and a third proposal submitted by William Norton, which was effectively the same as Kyle's document (which Norton felt precluded from supporting for reasons of diplomacy).[43] Unsurprisingly in view of what was at stake, the conference was an extremely fractious gathering. After much procedural wrangling, Memorandum No. 2 was put before conference as the key motion. Supported in a card ballot by 21 unions with an aggregate membership of 85,211, with 18 unions representing 70,836 members voting against, Kyle's motion was declared carried without O'Brien's proposals being put to a vote, prompting a furious O'Brien to lead a walkout.[44] Incensed that he had been outmanoeuvred on such a crucial issue and determined to tackle British-based amalgamateds' influence within the Irish trade union movement, O'Brien established a faction within Congress – the Council of Irish Unions – to pursue national policy interests. It was a fissure which would ultimately sunder the labour movement for the next two decades, and would have the most profound influence on the Labour Party itself.

The plan to tinker with the unions' organisation approved by Congress fell far short of the fundamental reform which Lemass sought and meant that Congress had reneged on its unspoken agreement to reform itself or be reformed from above. Legislation was, then, inevitable, but the shape this legislation was to take was further influenced by the Emergency. For one thing, a cabinet reshuffle in September 1939 had moved Seán Lemass from Industry and Commerce to the Department of Supplies, replacing him with the altogether more abrasive Seán MacEntee. Secondly, the government had promised that it would 'set its face against the efforts of any class to obtain compensation for the rise in prices at the expense of the community',[45] a warning resolutely ignored as the early months of the Emergency saw a rash of strikes in disparate industrial sectors from shopworkers to railwaymen.[46] Of these the most notable was that of 2,000 Dublin Corporation workers who went out in February 1940 for an increase of eight shillings a week.[47] Dublin Corporation had been inclined to meet some of the demand submitted by the Irish Municipal Employees Trade Union earlier in January, but had been encouraged to adopt a more intransigent stance by the government. The strike, which ultimately involved eleven unions, and affected essential services including water works, street cleaning, sewerage and the fire brigade, lasted 20 days before it was called off following the intervention of the Auxiliary Bishop of Dublin, Dr Wall. As far as Seán MacEntee was concerned, this type of action could not be tolerated. 'Quite clearly', he wrote to his secretary in Industry and Commerce, R. C. Ferguson, 'if the State and our economic system here are to survive, the most effective measures that can be devised to defeat this accelerating tendency on the part of workers to irresponsible action must be taken by the State'. MacEntee, always the bull in a china shop, set his officials about drafting legislation which would radically curtail the right to strike and introduce compulsory arbitration while providing for massive penalties against not only unions but their individual members who breached the legislation. It was roundly rejected by cabinet as being too contentious when it was presented in May, and a subsequent revision put before cabinet in June suffered a similar fate.[48] Twice foiled, the Department of Industry and Commerce now changed tack, opening behind the scenes talks with William O'Brien and Tom Foran of the Transport Union in an effort to come up with something feasible. By autumn, under O'Brien's covert guidance, the emphasis of the department's legislation had shifted from industrial disputes to union regulation and when the new bill was published some months later in April 1941 it bore all the hallmarks of O'Brien's original proposals, which Congress had rejected two years earlier. It had three main aims: 'to clarify the legal position of trade unions, to whittle away the smaller unions, and to eliminate trade union multiplicity'.[49] Among the means by which these aims would be achieved were the obligation for all unions to obtain a licence before it could negotiate wages or conditions of employment which would involve lodging a deposit of between £2,000 and £10,000 with the High Court, and a proposal to establish a tribunal which could award one or more unions sole negotiating rights for a category of workers where that union represented the majority of workers.[50] The legislation inevitably provoked a storm of reaction within the unions that would find themselves worst effected, in particular the smaller unions for whom it would be impossible to raise the price of a negotiating deposit. The WUI was one of the single largest unions under threat and, with Jim Larkin as general secretary, it was certainly the most vocal. On 6 May 1941 on Larkin's proposal, the Dublin Trades Council (DTUC) established a Council of Action composed of the DTUC's executive committee with co-options including Young Jim Larkin and John Swift of the Bakers' Union[51] to campaign against the proposed legislation.[52]

'NOT SINCE 1913 WAS SUCH A SPIRIT OF COMRADESHIP AMONGST THE WORKERS OF THIS COUNTRY'[53]

The bill would probably have resulted in quite limited agitation by affected unions had it not been for an astonishingly mistimed move by the government. The day after the Council of Action was established, MacEntee announced Emergency Order No. 83, or the Wages Standstill Order, as it was more popularly known, which froze wages indefinitely. The Council of Action used the pay freeze to move its campaign beyond sectional trade union interests into a general protest against wartime conditions. It lobbied TDs, held well attended public meetings in working-class areas, distributed hand-bills and produced a newspaper, *Workers' Action*, with an average circulation of 6,000,[54] which was co-edited by John Swift, Owen Sheehy Skeffington (then a member of the Pearse Street branch of the party and of the Administrative Council) and Paddy Staunton (a journalist on the *Irish Press*), all socialist members of Labour.[55]

A mass meeting in College Green on 22 June 1941 marked the apex of the Council of Action's campaign. With an estimated 20,000 people representing some 53 trade unions, it was one of the biggest demonstrations remembered in Dublin and '[the] biggest demonstration of working class resolve since 1923'.[56] The speakers included a number of trade union leaders as well as William Norton, Roddy Connolly and James Hickey representing the Labour Party, but the greatest impact on proceedings was made by Big Jim Larkin, who concluded proceedings with customary flourish. Larkin had not actually been due to speak but the crowd demanded he do so, and by the time he rose to address the meeting, the shouts and cheers which met him were so great that he could barely be heard. Denouncing the 'rotten fascist government' he pulled from his pocket a copy of the Trade Union Bill and striking a match on the seat of his pants set it alight.[57] (Considering the supposedly impromptu nature of his contribution, it is worth noting that Larkin had come well prepared, having soaked his copy in paraffin and attached sandpaper to the seat of his trousers.[58]) The occasion was certainly a heady one; Big Jim Larkin was to remark of it, 'I never felt so lifted up as I was that day in Dublin',[59] and he was not the only one to be moved by the proceedings. James Hickey, usually quite a moderate type, declared that they would take down capitalism.[60] From his seat on the platform at College Green, William Norton was most taken by the sheer size and the vehemence of the crowd. Norton, who had hitherto been somewhat half-hearted about opposition to the bill took the issue up with gusto. Labour, he announced, would refuse to table any amend-ments to the Trade Union Bill so that its total opposition to it could not be compromised.[61] This ran directly contrary to the wishes of the Congress executive, which wrote to the AC to complain about the party's change of policy on the matter without consultation.[62]

When the bill began its committee stage in the Dáil on 24 June, each and every aspect from its title down was opposed by the Labour deputies who forced a division on every section.[63] The party's new-found militancy is well illustrated by contrasting the speeches of Richard Corish (himself an ITGWU man): on 5 June he told the Dáil that he was 'not one of those who would advocate that there should be disregard of the law'. On 24 June, two days after the College Green rally, he declared that he for one would 'advocate that the law will not be observed when this bill is passed, and I will take the consequences'.[64] This fighting talk fell foul of the censors, who then prohibited publication of 'matters relating, directly or indirectly' to Norton and Corish's remarks in the Dáil.[65]

William O'Brien was incensed by the party's behaviour regarding the bill – no doubt the appearance of several Labour deputies (including the party leader) on the same platform as his old adversary Jim Larkin did not help – and was not backward about making his displeasure known. When a Labour deputation arrived at O'Brien's headquarters for a meeting, he refused to meet it on a spurious technicality, but sent them away with the assurance that the officers of Congress

> were anxious to maintain friendly relations with the Labour Party and . . . that objective would be best served by each organisation recognising that the other had special functions to fulfil . . . The Labour Party should have regard to the point of view of the National Executive *if harmonious relations were to be preserved between the two organisations*'.[66]

If O'Brien's communications with the Labour Party were characterised by a tone of barely concealed hostility, his relations with most of his comrades within Congress were in a state of open warfare and the ITUC's annual conference in July 1941 (which O'Brien, as ITUC President, chaired) turned into something of a bloodbath.

A minor cabinet reshuffle saw Seán Lemass return to his old stomping ground in Industry and Commerce the following month. This change in personnel and the government's alarm at the furore generated by the bill were enough to see that it was never implemented in its original form.[67] Though never enacted, it nonetheless had a profound impact. For one thing it mobilised the trade union movement in a way that had not been seen for decades and revived a leadership (outside the ITGWU) which had become increasingly somnolent and cynical. In the Dáil it saw the PLP gain a member as the independent deputy Dr Joseph Hannigan joined, impressed by Labour's recent performance.[68] It brought Big Jim Larkin back into active political life,[69] and his son Young Jim with him, and in so doing did much to rehabilitate him with his former Labour colleagues with whom he had enjoyed fractious relations for so long. Lastly, it completed the process of alienation between the Transport Union and Bill O'Brien and the rest of the labour movement, including the Labour Party, which had begun during the previous decade. Relations between the ITGWU and Labour once soured would prove extremely difficult to repair.

WHITHER LABOUR? THE FIGHT FOR POLICY

Since its foundation Labour had been a coalition of disparate political opinions, in which the middle ground tended to hold sway. As Ronald Mortished put it in the mid-1920s, the party ought to be 'wide open to all genuine Labour adherents – left wing, right wing, centre – provided that they all realise that no bird could fly if its left and right wings flew off at tangents to the centre'.[70] In effect, the party was more of a pendulum: sometimes it swung leftward, and sometimes to the right, but it always returned to a dull equilibrium before long. Norton, who was really the guardian of the centre, was always happy to swing in whatever direction would bear fruit. This had been evident with his support for the Workers' Republic, and his decision to drop it, and more recently with his decision to take a more militant stand against MacEntee's Trade Union Bill. Whether this was pragmatism or expediency was in the eye of the beholder, but as he is reported to have told one AC meeting, 'We should be slowest in doing anything that might make difficulties for us later on and prevent us from being in a position to manoeuvre. The political party which can't manoeuvre is dead.'[71]

Nor was Labour short of people or factions trying to manoeuvre it. Labour had already become home to Republican Congress/Irish Citizen Army members in the 1930s, who had endeavoured to move the party leftward and in a more republican direction. Catholic Actionists within and without the party had then moved successfully to counter this by having the Workers' Republic clauses removed from Labour's constitution. There was also a very small number of communists. At least one, John Breen, joined at the behest of the CPI in October 1936;[72] others, such as the International Brigade veteran Peter O'Connor, did so of their own volition, regarding Labour membership as a case of working 'with the tools at our disposal', as Lenin had advised.[73] Over the course of the Emergency, Labour became home to many new recruits who had a tremendous effect on the character and fortunes of the party. Many ordinary members were attracted into Labour by its stand against the privations of the Emergency. A smaller number, who were ultimately more influential, joined the party's ranks to further the agendas of outside bodies, but became pawns in the ensuing battle between Labour and the ITGWU.

In September 1939, a young Trotskyist named Patrick Trench returned to Dublin after a decade abroad. The elder son of the former Provost of Trinity College, Trench was a some-time painter who had worked as a journalist alongside the Trotskyist POUM during the Spanish civil war until poor health compelled him to leave for London.[74] From the early 1930s, Leon Trotsky had encouraged his followers to pursue a strategy of entryism and so it was natural that on his arrival Trench would join the Irish Labour Party. He also tried to groom young republicans and communists for the cause, although his early converts only amounted to two at this time. Still, having adopted two recruits, Trench began holding meetings which were soon attended by Labour Party members. Within weeks they were joined by four members of the Fourth International (FI) who had fled wartime Britain fearing arrest.[75] Each of the British Trotskyists joined Labour, having first made contact with Nora Connolly O'Brien. The British comrades did not stay long (the last one had returned home by 1941) and their efforts at building up a Trotskyist movement bore little fruit. Their most notable endeavour was a short-lived campaign under the auspices of the Dublin Unemployed Workers Movement to prevent Dublin men from joining the Clonsast work scheme, for which Steve Daly and Tom Dunne were arrested and interned.[76] The two men's stay in the Curragh was short lived, however. As Bowyer Bell put it, 'a sufficient number of those who mattered were outraged – the IRA and the Communists were one thing, honest Irish agitators another – and the two were released in less than a week'.[77] Apart from the handful of Trotskyists in Dublin there was a small group in Belfast based around Bob and Elsie Armstrong, who had moved there from London at the end of 1939.[78] The Belfast group remained in close contact with their Dublin comrades, and were responsible for bringing the young Matt Merrigan into the Trotskyist movement in the Autumn of 1942.[79]

One way in which the Dublin Trotskyists made their presence felt was in the pages of the Dublin Constituencies' Council weekly paper, *Torch*. Though its first editor, Cathal O'Shannon, was not sympathetic himself, the need to fill a weekly paper made him receptive to regular contributors and when O'Shannon was replaced as editor by Joe McGlinchey in mid-1940 the number of pieces increased still more.[80] The paper's columns became crammed with their ideological musings, particularly those of Patrick Trench who wrote under his own name (most *Torch* pieces were pseudonymous or without any byline) on almost a weekly basis. Within the Labour organisation itself, the handful of Trotskyist comrades were scattered in a small number of Dublin branches of the party (including Tommy Reilly in Dublin North West), but it did not take long before the Pearse Street branch, which Trench joined in January 1940[81] and becoming secretary soon after, was the centre of socialist agitation within the party. For such a small faction they made an awful lot of noise, giving the Labour leaders a nagging pain in the head from the time they first made their presence felt at their debut party conference in April 1940.

CATHOLIC ACTION?

Labour's 1939 conference had abandoned the Workers' Republic constitution and had given the AC carte blanche to revise the party's constitution and programme to remove anything which might leave the party open to clerical attack. Labour needed a new programme, while the trade union movement felt that it needed to put forward an economic blueprint for the course of the Emergency, so to this end the executives of Labour and Congress decided to formulate a joint statement of policy regarding 'the unemployment problem as affected especially by the war situation'.[82] The secretaries of the respective organisations, Luke Duffy and Eamonn Lynch, were ostensibly in charge of formulating a draft, which was ultimately put before a joint conference of the two bodies on 10 January 1940, but the document bore the imprint of Duffy's pen. Duffy had recently finished a stint as a member of the Banking Commission, which sat from late 1934 and had finally presented its report to the government in 1938. Three minority reports were presented alongside the main report, the first of which, calling for a break with sterling and the use of credit to fund national development,[83] had been written by the UCC Professor of Philosophy, Alfred O'Rahilly, and was signed by the two labour representatives on the Commission, Luke Duffy and William O'Brien.[84] O'Rahilly was a committed Catholic Actionist (his ostentatious piety garnered him the nickname 'Alf the Sacred River Ran'[85]) who saw himself as something of a polymath. He was forever expounding his learned thoughts in pamphlets and newspapers, and economics happened to be one of his favourite hobby-horses. Already on very friendly terms with the Labour Party in Cork (although as a vigilant anti-communist, O'Rahilly was keen that the party did not adopt any suspect political ideas[86]), he similarly developed a good relationship with his labour colleagues on the Commission, and with Duffy in particular.

Duffy was once described by American intelligence as 'a well-meaning man who is incapable of independent action and is used to the methods of his real masters: the O'Brien–Norton group. He is an efficient Secretary for the Party as it exists and seems to be on the Right'.[87] This assessment is perhaps a little harsh, but it does seem as though Duffy became overly influenced by the economic ideas propounded by O'Rahilly at this time; indeed, the latter's biographer has described one lecture delivered by Duffy on 'Currency, credit and poverty' in October 1939 as 'a classic example of applied O'Rahilly monetary theory'.[88] The same could be said of the policy statement which Duffy presented to delegates from Labour and Congress in January 1940. Duffy's policy effectively abandoned any semblance of socialism, with any notions of large-scale nationalisation being replaced by a system of social credit, a cranky school of economics. No substantial changes were made to the document following the consultative conference although Duffy did tinker with it a little in an effort to make it more palatable to socialists and 'doctrinaire republicans' and, as he put it, 'meet criticism of those outside who might be inclined to say we were opening the gates of the citadel to a fascist regime!'[89] The end result was 'Planning for the Crisis', an 18-page pamphlet published by Labour and the ITUC in February 1940.

It was with this in mind that Patrick Trench spent the entirety of the 1940 Labour Party conference trying to keep the citadel's gates bolted. He had already circulated a letter predicting that the AC's 'treachery' in trying to cut all socialist principles from the party's programme would 'lead to apathy in the workers' movement and pave the way for fascism'. 'We must not fall away from the party', he continued,

> but become on the contrary more active than before, recruiting new members on the basis of those socialist principles which were accepted when we joined. Thus with more active branches fighting for day to day for the workers' demands and rights, we can defeat any proposal to abandon socialism. By serious work we can build a party whose impetus will smash capitalism and obliterate reaction in our own ranks. The N.A.C. [National Administrative Council] proposals won't wash. The party members will fight for a Workers' Republic.[90]

Over the next three days of conference, Patrick Trench, assisted by the delegates of the Dublin North West branch (including Joe McGlinchey and Michael Price who was regarded by the Trotskyists as a Trotskyist fellow traveller) took on the AC on almost every motion. The Pearse Street amendment to scrap 'Planning for the Crisis' was defeated by 49 votes to 33, and the document adopted by 51 votes to 29.[91] This was the closest the left came to success during proceedings. Time and again, Trench and his small band of allies tabled motions and resolutions to no avail. Most failed to reach a vote, let alone be passed, but Trench et al. managed to dominate proceedings to the growing frustration of the other delegates. One delegate from Tullow summed up the attitudes of many:

> a good deal of talk went on in Dublin, but when supporters of Labour wanted anything done, they had to fall back on the Nortons, the Corishes and the Davins, who were elected in the country. [Labour's] greatest evil was that they spent so much time talking about useless things . . . [I am] surprised at the attitude of supporters of Labour in Dublin. If it were not for the country, who would they have to fight their battles?'[92]

This view was echoed later by the chairman, after a Dublin delegate was absent when his motion on housing was due to be moved: 'If a new constitution was being drafted, they would all be here!' he mused.[93] If the correspondent from *Torch* complained afterwards that the spirit of the conference was not 'of the fraternal striving for greater things',[94] it is remarkable that the atmosphere was not worse, with most delegates showing considerable restraint in the face of Trench's attempt to hijack proceedings. The conference represented only the beginning of Labour's problems with the far left, although there was a period of calm before that storm. The left failed to make any significant advances in influence or numbers until the summer of the following year when two very different campaigns took place which had a profound impact on the party. The first was that of the Council of Action, the second was Operation Barbarossa.

COMMUNISTS

The Council of Action's campaign had a number of consequences, of which two were particularly significant: the chasm between the ITGWU and the rest of the ITUC and Labour, and Big Jim Larkin's rehabilitation. After two decades attacking the Labour Party, Larkin signalled his willingness to work with it; the question was, was the Labour Party willing to work with Larkin? Larkin and his son, Young Jim, both applied for Labour membership in the aftermath of the Council of Action campaign during the summer,[95] and were eventually admitted in December 1941.[96] Both had been active in the communist movement for many years; Larkin senior had effectively been estranged from it since the mid 1930s, while Larkin junior had ceased attending Communist Party meetings in 1938,[97] although he remained on good terms with his erstwhile comrades. In fact, by the time the two

Larkins actually joined the Labour ranks, many of these comrades had actually preceded them into the party.

On 22 June 1941, Operation Barbarossa saw Germany overrun the Soviet Union's western border, breaking the German–Soviet non-aggression pact in a spectacular fashion. The impact of this on the international communist movement was, understandably, immense. Having spent the last two years decrying the European war as one of competing imperialisms, each national communist party was now forced to make a volte-face and call on its supporters to join in the fight against fascism. Justifying this U-turn was a difficult enough task, but it posed particularly keen difficulties for the Communist Party in Ireland. Public opinion was overwhelmingly in favour of neutrality, and there was generally a strong vein of anti-British feeling. For the CPI (which was never exactly popular at the best of times) to adopt a pro-British line would have been to court a level of opprobrium that even the veterans of the red scares of the 1930s had not experienced. Moreover, to do so would have led to a breach with the IRA, at this time allied with the Germans, which the leadership of the CPI was at pains to avoid.[98] The solution put forward by the CPI's National Committee was to liquidate the Dublin branch (one of only two branches of the CPI at this time, the other in Belfast), upon which members would join the Labour Party. The CPGB endorsed this scheme. It recognised the Irish comrades' problems with the new policy, but could not countenance the CPI taking an independent stance on a fundamental issue. However, if there was 'no party, [there was] no problem'.[99] Still, not all of the Dublin comrades were as sanguine when this plan of campaign was put before a meeting of the Dublin branch on 10 July. After strong opposition from a number comrades, a second meeting was held a number of days later, at which Barney Larkin (the youngest of Big Jim's four sons), led efforts to put a stop to the move.[100] (His misgivings were shared by his brother Jim, who had been consulted about the move and who had counselled against it.[101]) In the end, however, the London leadership had its way.[102] The Dublin branch was dissolved, the cadre instructed which branches they were to join and told to present their membership cards for inspection at the next meeting.[103]

With this, the small ranks of the CPI's Dublin branch began to trickle into the Labour Party. Their entry generated little or no attention at a time when Labour was becoming home to relatively large numbers of new members generally and, as Emmet O'Connor has remarked, 'the rapid growth and radicalisation of Labour after 1940 facilitated entryism'.[104] The government party provided many of the new recruits. One Labour man from Trim noted how 'the most active and enthusiastic members of the Fianna Fáil organisation at the last election had now joined the Labour Party and were among its officers in the provinces'[105] and among the more prominent Fianna Fáil people who joined Labour around this time were Con Desmond from Cork (whose son Barry would be a future Labour minister) and Senator Jim Tunney in Dublin.[106] Though Labour was happy to have these Fianna Fáil defectors (for kudos, if nothing else), many were regarded with suspicion; indeed, the only evidence of Labour's fears about entryism revolved around the new-comers from the Republican Party. During the local election in 1942, one new arrival was summoned before the Election Committee to pledge that he was not a member of Fianna Fáil, and had not been for some time.[107] Labour speakers were, moreover, instructed by the DCC to have a 'proper attitude' on platforms and solicit support for Labour candidates only,[108] presumably in order to stop Big Jim Larkin from engaging in his usual habit of calling for transfers for some of his Fianna Fáil chums.[109]

It is worth noting that as well as becoming the favoured destination for those who had left other parties, Labour was consolidating its support by fostering links with other parties and groups. In the west, for instance, there was a certain amount of co-operation with Clann na Talmhan, the western-based small farmers' party founded before the war.[110] Labour also had links with the republican movement, which had been strengthened by Labour's defence of republican internees and hunger strikers. A new party, Coras na Poblachta, was founded in March 1940 by a number of republicans,[111] among them Con Lehane who remained very close to Labour.[112] However, like many of its predecessors Coras na Poblachta never really took off[113] and in the absence of a viable party, many republicans turned to Labour. Labour's erstwhile foe Peadar O'Donnell, as well as Noel Hartnett (a member of Fianna Fáil) and former IRA Chief of Staff Seán MacBride, were mooted as candidates for the local elections by Labour's head office[114] (although none of them stood), while intelligence sources reported that IRA volunteers had been instructed to vote for Labour although 'there [was] no reason to suppose that the Labour Party have solicited this support'.[115] True enough, it was probably going too far to say Labour had 'solicited' IRA support, but in private the party's secretary Luke Duffy was candid about his party's courting of the republican vote. In March 1943, Duffy attended a conference of Old IRA men (and was appointed a treasurer of the organisation) in an effort to throw the Labour Party net as wide as possible in order to defeat de Valera at the election. He judged that his presence at the conference with a number of the more extreme members of the old IRA would add strength to the Labour Party and demonstrate that de Valera had not the monopoly of talk about the Irish Republic.'[116] Duffy's colleagues in the Labour leadership were distinctly unhappy about his behaviour, however, and following a complaint to the AC, the AC passed a motion requesting that Duffy relinquish his position in the organisation by eight votes to two.[117] It is difficult to assess the impact that this strategy may have had on ordinary voters in view of the censorship's media blackout on the hunger strikes, particularly, but contemporary opinion suggests that it was very successful. Speaking in July 1943 after a general election in which Labour had made significant gains, the new Labour deputy Roddy Connolly expressed the view that 'it should be obvious . . . that the 80,000 extra votes which the Labour Party obtained at the election were, perhaps, due very largely to the fact quite a number of Republicans . . . had come over towards the Labour Party'.[118] Labour's assiduous adoption of the prisoners issue garnered it at least one new seat at the 1943 election, where Dan Spring won a seat for Labour in the republican heartland of Kerry North. It may have been opportunistic, but in terms of winning votes it worked.

At least 35 new branches were formed between April 1941 and 1942 (an increase of a third on the previous year), and anecdotal reports noted an influx of young people into the party.[119] It is worth pointing out, however, that while Labour membership did grow because of discontent with the government, it might have grown more had the party been better organised to take advantage of this resentment. As one Donegal trade unionist wrote to Head Office:

> The young men and indeed the old are fed up with FF and FG. I would not say they are coming over to the LP, because through lack of foresight and direction and organisation, that chance has not so far been provided for them. The laxity of the Labour Party has created the impression in many minds that the whole concern is to keep a few of the leading lights in the Dáil and the remainder in executive positions; concentrate on a few convenient centres and let the rest of the country go be [damned]. Whether or not this is the case, it amounts to about the same thing once it becomes the opinion of too many people, and the sooner the party wakes up and gets new life and blood into the ranks the better. Otherwise it must die.[120]

As the Emergency wore on, then, Labour found its membership and general support growing, while in Dublin, it had become something of a broad church with old-Labourites operating side by side with Larkinites, Communists and Trotskyists. Under Young Jim Larkin's leadership, the Council of Action had broadened its remit to include unemployment, housing and prices,[121] and had become the centre of party's activities in the capital. Young Jim had extended the campaign, partly as a vehicle for his father,[122] but its role as an instrument to mobilise disgruntled workers into a militant rank and file movement was very important.[123] If the different ideological factions managed to work with each other in remarkable harmony, there were inevitable differences in strategy. For instance, as far as Labour's communist element was concerned, the most important task was to build up the party's rank and file. Once they had built up the numbers sufficiently, they would lead a breach between the rank and file and leadership and establish a new party, but they had no wish to take on the party's leaders before it was necessary. Others were less patient. For instance, Owen Sheehy Skeffington, who was not aligned with any particular socialist faction but happily worked in a united front with them,[124] was becoming an increasingly vocal critic of the party's conservative, union dominated leadership. When an article headlined WHAT IS WRONG WITH THE LABOUR PARTY?, attacking the unions' control over the party and the timidity of the leadership, appeared under his byline in *Workers' Action* in May 1942,[125] Sheehy Skeffington found himself censured by a vote of the AC (of which he was a member) by 13 votes to two.[126] Skeffington's own branch in Pearse Street was appalled by what it saw as the censorship of free debate, but its attempt to get the DCC to take up the issue came to naught when, on the advice of the newly formed Central Branch and the Dublin North West branch, it was decided that 'it would not be helpful for the Council to get involved in the controversy at this time'.[127]

By the summer of 1942, the municipal elections, due in August, had become the focus of all Labour attention. It was the first significant election since the beginning of the war and Labour was determined to put up a good fight. Despite suggestions that several high profile republicans would stand for Labour,[128] in the end the party's ticket was solidly trade unionist, with Mícheál Ó Maoláin, an associate of Big Jim Larkin since before the time of the 1913 Lockout, director of elections, while Michael Price advised on publicity and organisation although ill health had prevented him from taking a more active role.[129] Characterised by enormous energy and drive, the campaign for the municipal election in Dublin was highly effective. Having printed and distributed over 100,000 pieces of election literature, and with open air meetings taking place in wards throughout the city, the Labour campaign did great work in conveying their message and their enthusiasm to Dublin voters. Speakers were instructed to be constructive, and emphasise Labour's positive policies and the practical benefits they would bring about, rather than spend too much time attacking opponents – who included not only Fianna Fáil, but also Fine Gael, independents, Coras na Poblachta, and the new nationalist, quasi-fascist party Ailtirí na hAiséirghe. Labour was the party of the working class, speakers were to emphasise, while all others represented and were financed by the employer class. Those active at the time recalled the unanimity of purpose among the 'Connollyites, Trotskyites, Stalinists, and all kinds of social democrats' who co-operated 'in a comradely way, and consciously so'.[130]

'THE LION AND THE MANGY RAT'[131]

There was, however, one glaring absentee from this popular front. Since the breach between the Transport Union and the Labour Party had begun over the Trade Union Bill, the former had begun to withdraw its practical support for the latter incrementally, for instance withdrawing the use of its premises for meetings of the Dublin Constituencies Council.[132] On this occasion, the ITGWU which had 'lavished money and energy on such conflicts' over the years did not nominate any of its members for election and played no part whatever in the campaign.[133] Even if bad blood had not arisen already between the union and the party, Big Jim Larkin's presence on the Labour ticket made it inconceivable that the Transport Union would campaign for the party. For the Transport Union, it was not merely a question of Larkin's candidacy but his very membership of Labour which was at issue. On 18 June William McMullen, a long-time Transport Union official, tabled a motion at the AC stating:

> That in view of the campaign of disruption carried on in the Labour movement since 1923 by Jim Larkin the Administrative Council is of the opinion that he should not be permitted to be a member of the Labour Party and hereby cancels his membership of the Dublin Central branch and directs that he shall not be admitted to any branch of the party.[134]

In response, the AC deputed three party officers, Michael Keyes, Roddy Connolly and Luke Duffy to Liberty Hall to ask the union to reconsider their position on Larkin's membership, but they found the union's officers unyielding.[135] The Transport Union officials from the AC pressed for an early decision, and 'made clear to the deputation *that the ITGWU would not remain in affiliation with the party if Mr Larkin's membership was not cancelled*.[136] When the AC was informed of this, party organiser Peadar Cowan suggested that 'the matter be referred back to the ITGWU with a request that they specify the acts charged against Larkin *since he was a member of the party*', but in the end the AC decided upon appointing a sub-committee which would prepare a case for legal counsel.[137] The brief was given to A. C. Overend, KC whose opinion was put to the party officers some two months later, at a meeting in September.[138]

The Transport Union's attempt to remove Larkin stalled in the short run, and in the absence of an alternative plan of campaign, Larkin was free to contest the election, while the union stood back. The union's absence failed to hinder the onward march of Labour on this occasion. Labour's vote soared across the country. The party had a majority in Kildare and topped the poll in unlikely areas such as Castleblaney, Macroom and Castleconnnell, and after the poll there were reports of independent councillors joining the Labour group.[139] It was in Dublin, however, that its success was most marked. Having gone in to the election with only two seats, Labour was returned with twelve councillors and a majority on the Corporation. This sent alarm bells ringing in Liberty Hall as Transport Union leaders noted Labour's success, due entirely to the work of the combined Dublin left. As Desmond Ryan wrote of the result, 'If Fianna Fáil was astounded it was also certainly true that the Labour Party leadership and the ITGWU were even more so. The victory went, it is to be feared, to the heads of the Labour Party leaders and deep down into the livers of the ITGWU leaders.'[140] Larkin's membership remained a live issue at meetings of the AC after the local elections until, eventually, counsel's opinion was put before the AC on 18 September.[141] Its conclusion was that expulsion on the basis of the ITGWU's motion would leave the party open to legal action, and would have to be abandoned.[142] This merely meant that the O'Brienites would have to find another way of ridding themselves of their old foe, but there was little time to spare, since so long as Councillor Larkin remained a member, he was eligible to stand for the party at the next general election. The indignity of seeing Larkin on the Corporation on a Labour ticket was nothing compared with seeing him in the Dáil.

As rumours abounded that a general election was imminent, the AC instructed its constituency councils to hold its selection conferences on set dates between 28 November and 8 December. Apart from decreeing the dates on which the conferences would be held, the AC also bypassed all of the local organisations in arranging the events, and, in a bizarre move, authorised representation by corporate members with less than three months affiliation,[143] a move which was unambiguously contrary to Labour's constitution. On the evening of 30 November, the selection conference for Dublin met in the Catholic Commercial Club on O'Connell Street, with DCC secretary, Fred Cowan, and Peadar Cowan representing the AC on the door checking delegates' credentials. When Fred Cowan began to challenge those entering with brand new membership cards (in accordance with the party constitution), he was told by his colleague that this was in order, and when he went inside and approached William Norton, who was there to chair proceedings, about the 'phoney cards', Norton merely responded that he was not there 'to hold a post mortem but to select Dáil candidates'. Fred Cowan replied that such things would cause a post mortem on the Labour Party.[144] Ultimately there were 192 votes in the room: 103 of these were controlled by two unions, of which the majority were ITGWU. The result of this was that with nine councillors before the meeting, five were deemed unsuitable to stand for the Dáil, with Big Jim Larkin – naturally – one of the rejects. Instead, Michael Price was nominated in absentia as the candidate for Dublin North East.

Price was undoubtedly popular with his Labour comrades and would have appealed to the republican constituency, but his health had been in decline for some time, and he had played no part in the local election campaign for this very reason.[145] On being told of his nomination, Price wrote to the Labour's chairman to express his gratitude for the 'great honour' but declined because of ill health, and suggested that the runner-up in this constituency be chosen in his stead.[146] The runner-up was Larkin.

Immediate although unco-ordinated efforts were begun to undo the decision of the conference. Owen Sheehy Skeffington, put a motion before the AC (of which he was a member) to overturn the results of the 'rigged "conference"',[147] and planned to resign if the AC did not substantially agree to this. His comrades in the Pearse Street branch counselled him to stay put, however, as he was more useful to the left-wing ginger group within Labour if he retained his vantage point in the AC. Patrick Trench expressed the view that the left-wing group would be 'kicked out of the party sooner or later but it would be made clear that it would be on a socialist issue', and advised that Skeffington's resignation should be 'boosted and used against the leaders'. Skeffington himself was unsure if anyone outside the Dublin party would notice. Labour's communist contingent, however, was quite against any such move. Harry Craig, a member of the faction in Pearse Street, argued that 'the time was not yet ripe for a split'.[148] It was a view echoed by George Pollock, a long-time communist activist who had made his way into the Labour Party,[149] and who was working as an organiser at this time. Pollock's letter (written on Labour Party notepaper) outlines the Communist Party strategy on Labour and is worth quoting at length:

> I've been thinking over the position arising out of the selection conference and I don't think the position is such that we should do anything to split or leave the party *yet* (emphasis added). I've a feeling that that is just what they would like us to do, and would play into their hands. I understand you were considering resigning from the AC. I think you should hang on at all costs, at least for the present. After all we can't expect to win every ground in our efforts to get control, and I think we should rather concentrate in getting the branch movement in Dublin built up to at least treble its present strength in preparation for the annual conference. . . We could make a bid to get a majority on the AC of what we consider to be the right people. I don't think that we have a basis for a new party at present anyhow, a break will only be justified when we feel that there is no hope of pushing the gang from the control of the party.[150]

The AC met on 11 December to discuss, among other issues, Skeffington's motion to amend the list. Although this was defeated by nine votes to two, with three abstentions, Skeffington did not resign.[151] The AC did accede to a request for an audience by a deputation from the DCC, and having heard its arguments the AC decided to consider the matter once again at its next meeting. Within days, however, matters had escalated beyond control.

An account of the controversy from a distinctly Liberty Hall perspective appeared in the *Irish Times* on 16 December, and similar reports appeared in the *Irish Press* days later.[152] Owen Sheehy Skeffington, anxious that the leaks from the AC be stopped, tried to contact Norton and others without success. He took matters into his own hands and made a statement to the *Irish Press* in which he set the record straight, as he saw it. His remarks appeared, attributed, in the *Irish Press* on 19 December.[153] This action, though, left him open to accusations of a serious breach in discipline as only weeks earlier a complaint that he had been leaking AC business to the Pearse Street branch had resulted in the AC passing a motion binding members to secrecy on its business.[154] Skeffington was by no means the only member leaking information to the press, but he *was* the only one to do so on the record. The AC reacted immediately, summoning Skeffington:

> [to] explain the publication of subversive propaganda designed to disrupt the Labour Party and to inform him that in the absence of a satisfactory explanation of his conduct a motion will be moved at the next meeting of the AC for the purpose of having him expelled from the party.[155]

In a letter to the party secretary, Luke Duffy, Skeffington denied he was engaged in any campaign of disruption and insisted that none of the information he had divulged to the press had been confidential. He accused the Transport Union of having been engaged in 'disruptive tactics' ever since the campaign against the Trade Union Bill in 1941. He continued:

> I think it will be a lamentable thing if any split occurs in the party now, and I believe that the AC realises this and will amend the Dublin list at its next meeting. Any attempt to disrupt the unity of the party, or to suggest that the AC has already been told which way it will vote, will be vehemently opposed by me, not merely in private but right out in the open. Of that the Officers Committee may rest assured and I believe that my attitude will have the approval of the entire branch movement in Dublin and throughout the country and of the vast majority of the unions.[156]

Peadar Cowan moved a motion for Skeffington's expulsion when the AC met on 12 January. It was seconded by Norton. Several members called for the motion to be withdrawn but Cowan was prepared to do so only if Skeffington made a public apology, which he subsequently diluted to an *official* one. Being firmly of the opinion that he had done no wrong, and no doubt sure there was more to be gained from martyrdom than compromise, Skeffington refused the lifeline and the motion went to a vote. The Council proved evenly split on the question, but when the chairman used his casting vote Skeffington's fate was sealed, and by eight votes to seven he found himself expelled with immediate effect, although he had the right to a written appeal at the next annual conference.[157] Skeffington bristled at the injustice of his treatment and began, in characteristic fashion, to bombard the newspapers with correspondence on the subject, and he set about putting together his case for appeal at conference that April. It was read in private session (he was not allowed appear himself), and was dismissed by 131 votes to 79.[158] So ended Skeffington's time in Labour. His wife recalled later that he had 'reluctantly agreed' to let his name go forward for readmission some seven years later, 'but was thankful that it was turned down'.[159]

Was this much ado about nothing? The controversy was not one of Labour's more edifying episodes, and it is difficult to disagree with Skeffington's contention that he was expelled on trumped up charges because he was a troublemaker. This was patently true. However, his transformation into one of the plaster saints of Irish liberalism, and the castigation of Labour for his expulsion, are more tendentious.[160] It is true that Skeffington did not sit easily within the Labour Party. He was no politician, a man more used to debating chambers and intellectual discourse in the parlour than the pragmatic wheeler-dealer nature of politics in general, and the more backroom nature of trade union and labour politics in particular.[161] But was his problem merely one of being too parlour pink to get on with the union apparatchiks? Not really. Skeffington was a socialist who was prepared to work in a united front to oust the then current leadership of the Labour Party and transform it into a strongly left-wing party. He may not have been aligned with any single leftist tendency (although the perception of Special Branch and at least one of his colleagues was that he was essentially Trotskyist)[162] but he was aware of, and worked with, an informal conspiracy within Labour to deploy an entryist strategy to take the party over, which meant that the allegations that he had engaged in a campaign of disruption were in fact true.

Events soon went from bad to worse. The AC decided that the Dublin party had grown out of control and needed to be reorganised from branch level upwards. Branches were to be reorganised on a ward-by-ward basis and membership would be strictly enforced on the basis of residency.[163] Furthermore, the Dublin Constituencies Council was to be wound up and a new executive for Dublin established. There was some resistance to this on the part of established DCC members, but the Larkinite/communist element seized on this as an opportunity to consolidate their own position in the movement. In the run up to the new Dublin Executive's first meeting in February 1943, there were rumours that Young Jim Larkin would be moved for the chair, and that named (former CPI) members would be moved for the other offices. Some of the older Labour members such as Michael Price and Fred Cowan, erstwhile secretary of the DCC, were unhappy at what looked to them very like a communist putsch of the Dublin organisation and so, when the time came for nominations, Fred Cowan stood before the meeting and made his case against Young Jim. The DCC, he explained, had always operated as an independent organisation which had refused association with doctrinaire sects, but this independence now seemed under threat. Cowan couched his words, but his meaning was quite clear to all present:

> If Comrade Larkin were made chairman the prejudice would be created that the DCC had come under the Larkinite tutelage and while I recognised the Comrade's ability I was certain that he was not a free agent. And if the particular 'union' he belonged to decided to break from the Labour Party, we had no guarantee what he would do. And what effect would there be down the country if the leaders of the Dublin movement went with a split?[164]

John Breen, a Labour member since 1936 (at the CPI's behest, if intelligence reports are to be believed[165]) protested that Cowan's remarks were unfair and unhelpful, before Young Jim gave a measured, although not altogether reassuring, response. Larkin explained that he had been 'helpful in preventing a split' in the past and had done everything to keep the unity of Labour, which '*for the moment* fits the bill', an astonishing admission, in Cowan's eyes. When Larkin asserted his desire for 'a unified party' instead of the present situation with different groups, Cowan had heard enough: 'he actually said this! – and it was his group "Larkin-CP" that had rigged the meeting'. In the end, the Larkinites had a clean sweep of the officerships, leaving Cowan in a state of despair. 'Instead of an executive carrying on in the tradition of the old DCC – pioneer work, giving the working class an alternative to personalities and great man thesis . . . we are going to enter a stage of opportunism and expediency, the worshipping of idols, and abasement of individual self-respect and the febrile growth of branches.' 'Had you submerged your ego', he complained to Owen Sheehy Skeffington, 'you would have been in the party and a delegate to the Executive, which would have told a different tale'[166]

In the meantime the AC was still embroiled with the Larkin issue. In April 1943 the AC agreed to the adoption of a party pledge,[167] and appointed a sub-committee consisting of James Hickey, William Davin and William Norton to try and bring the matter to some sort of agreement.[168] Scenes at

Labour's annual conference which took place that month showed no cause for optimism, however. A proposal to send the annual report back so that Larkin senior could be added to the Labour ticket was defeated in the union block vote by 94 to 85, leading one Dublin delegate to point to the perversity of selecting the candidate who polled lowest in the area at the local elections, and refusing to select the candidate who topped the poll.[169] There was also a contretemps between Larkin and O'Brien, which would have been more at home in a playground. Larkin proclaimed himself to have been a founder of the party, prompting shouts of 'that's a lie'.

> *Larkin*:   In Clonmel in 1912, I drafted the resolution, proposed by James Connolly.
> *O'Brien*: I deny that. I drafted it and James Connolly moved it.
> *Larkin*:   You never drafted anything in your life except something disturbing.
> *O'Brien*: I drafted you.

The Chairman, James Hickey, appealed for order amidst shouting through-out the hall. Larkin, like a boy appealing to the master before he got a lash of the cane, contended he had said nothing of personal abuse.[170] Larkin, by his own standards, was on his best behaviour, but his mere presence was still enough to cause a near riot in the hall. Getting O'Brien to put aside his animosity towards his old foe would be nothing short of miraculous.

Still, Larkin seemed amenable to doing whatever it took to bring about détente. Following a meeting with the AC's three-man sub-committee, he submitted a written statement, in which he asserted:

> My attitude to the party since I renewed my active membership should be clear from my activities since I again took up membership, based as it has been on my acceptance of the constitution and policy of the party, loyalty to its decisions and a willingness to serve the party in any position or in any form of work. . .For myself, I assure you most sincerely that I am willing to work loyally with any member of the party regardless of previous personal differences and antagonisms and to put aside all division and conflicts. In all my activities in the party in whatever sphere of work I may find myself I will act as a loyal member of the party within the constituency and in conformity with the leadership of the party and will be no party to the engendering of personal differences or conflicts in the movement. You may be assured that this declaration will be scrupulously observed by *me* and I shall at all times accept the judgement of the AC as to whether or not I have been faithful to that declaration.[171]

Once in receipt of this letter the sub-committee approached William O'Brien and Thomas Kennedy of the ITGWU. Notwithstanding his pledge of good behaviour, the Transport Union officers pointed out that Larkin had failed to express remorse for his part in earlier conflict with the union.[172] O'Brien and Kennedy made it clear they would not accept Larkin's assurances and stated, furthermore, that if he was adopted as an official candidate, the ITGWU would withdraw all their members from Labour's panels of candidates.[173] Once again, the matter was discussed and deferred by the AC, with the sub-committee instructed to approach both Larkin and the Transport Union on the matter. After a second meeting with the AC's sub-committee, Larkin wrote another letter to Norton. Expressing his awareness of the lengths to which Norton and his colleagues had gone to 'resolve the present difficulties', he continued:

> I have fully considered the points you put to me in our last conversation and I will respond to your viewpoint by stating that if in the heat of past conflicts statements were made by me, I regret having made such statements if those statements today appear as obstacles in the way of a united effort by all members of the Party at the present moment.
>
> In conclusion may I say that I on my part have set aside all personal feelings and antagonisms in order that I may work loyally with any and every member of the Party but if such a gesture is rejected, then I at least, am willing to have the Party and its members pass verdict on whether or not I have placed the Party and its welfare before any personal feelings and personal position.[174]

Norton, Davin and Hickey felt that, taken together, the letters had removed all reasonable grounds of objection to Larkin's candidature, and so when the AC next met on Tuesday 25 May, Roddy Connolly (seconded by William Davin) proposed a motion 'that Jim Larkin senior be endorsed as a candidate for North East Dublin and that the AC give assurances to the ITGWU that they will take the necessary steps to enforce discipline'. The motion was defeated by seven votes to eight.[175] Every vote against Larkin's candidature came from the ITGWU members, every vote for Larkin from members of other unions.[176]

Naturally the matter did not rest there, and as soon as the AC had reached its decision the Dublin Executive set about overturning it. The following morning, telegrams were dispatched to members of the Dublin executive summoning them to a meeting in the Bakers' Hall that evening. Under the chairmanship of Young Jim, the meeting passed a resolution selecting Big Jim as a candidate for North East, and subsequently called upon the other candidates to endorse the decision of the meeting. This they did, with Thomas Farren (a candidate in South Dublin from the ITGWU) the sole dissenter, protesting that the meeting had no authority for such action.[177] A meeting to launch the campaign in Dublin had already been organised for the next night at the Mansion House, and it was at this event that Big Jim's candidacy was announced. Norton (almost certainly briefed beforehand) sat on the platform as this was done, in tacit acceptance of the 'Dublin mutiny'.[178] Thomas Farren withdrew his candidature in protest at Larkin's selection through 'methods of intimidation in defiance of the constitution' while Michael Colgan of the Irish Bookbinders (who had been selected for Dublin North East alongside Michael Price) apparently did likewise,[179] but there were no official attempts by the union to put a stop to this, and in the short run the party simply got on with the business of trying to run an election campaign.

1943 GENERAL ELECTION

On 26 May 1943 de Valera ended the phoney war, and began the campaign proper when he announced that the general election would take place on 26 June. A year earlier Labour had relished the prospect of a general election, predicting it would be the occasion of a phenomenal breakthrough for the party. Even before its sweep in the local elections, head office was privately expecting to return with forty deputies at the next poll[180] and by December 1942, Michael Price was predicting that the forthcoming general election could end up being 'the most momentous general election since 1922'.[181] If recent controversies saw Labour's estimates shift downward (it was predicting between 20 and 30 seats before the poll),[182] the party remained confident nonetheless, and put up a record 70 candidates. In fact, there was a record number of candidates all round, a total of 354 by the close of nominations on 8 June. Fianna Fáil was appealing to the electorate on the basis of security and continuity – its slogan this time was 'don't change horses when crossing the stream' – and was once again identifying itself as the only party capable of providing strong government. Another echo of its 1938 campaign was its strategy of singling Labour out for attack. The *Irish Press* made great play of Labour's faction fighting, while government speakers argued that Labour's policies were inherently pie in the sky.[183]

Nothing, however, could compare with the campaign being run against Labour by Seán MacEntee. After throwing a few feints at Larkin and Norton on the Trade Union Bill at the beginning of the campaign,[184] he embarked on a campaign of heavy duty scurrility. Although he had a long-standing reputation as a political bruiser, MacEntee truly surpassed himself on this occasion, combining information from Special Branch reports with his own penchant for mischief. He began in early June with an outlandish speech in Ballinasloe, in which he informed his audience of 'many sinister happenings' at work in Ireland and the presence of alien forces – allies of communism – who were working to overthrow democratic rule in the state. A struggle over who would control the Irish Labour Party was going on in Dublin, and MacEntee was able to report that Moscow had, in fact, won. This should be of particular concern to the people of Galway because Labour and Clann na Talmhan had entered into an 'unholy alliance' which had been negotiated by 'Hitler' Donnellan and 'Stalin' Duffy.[185] He developed this theme the following day, when, speaking at Harold's Cross bridge, he claimed that although the Comintern had been dissolved in Russia, 'Muscovites' were active in Dublin who had captured William Norton and were keeping him captive. This time, he related how a meeting of 'Field Marshal Davinoff' and 'Herr Von Donnellan' had resulted in an agreement between Labour and the farmers' party, although the result of the conference was no more known than the result of the Hitler–Stalin pact.[186] MacEntee did not continue in this vein for long, however, as his apparently bizarre attacks on the Labour Party were decried by a number of senior colleagues in Fianna Fáil. Following conversations with Oscar Traynor and Dr Jim Ryan, among others, Seán Lemass wrote to MacEntee on 10 June relating a view that 'we should modify our attacks on Labour', as Labour was gaining from them and not the reverse. 'I am passing this on to you', Lemass continued,

> I may say I think there is a great deal in this. The canvassers in my area all report that we will get the majority of the Labour vote unless we irritate them by unduly severe attacks on the Labour Party. Sean T. [O'Kelly] reports the same. I [hear?] you have agreed to speak in Crumlin. I do not think this is wise. It will have the wrong result in my opinion. Crumlin is a Labour stronghold, insofar as they have such. Also your meetings at Naas and Newbridge . . . should not be devoted to attacking Norton. This will help him and not otherwise. I know you have your own views and methods but you have a different type of constituency to others and on this account I think you may perhaps overlook the reactions of your campaign elsewhere. Dr Ryan intended to phone you today to express similar opinions but had to rush away and requested me to write you this note. I hope it won't cramp your style.[187]

MacEntee assured Lemass that he would endeavour to bear what he said in mind, 'but remember this', he added, 'elections are not won by billing and cooing at your opponents'.[188] For the most part, however, MacEntee did heed colleagues' counsel, and although he continued his attacks on Labour for the rest of the campaign, he did so on the basis of its policies rather than any more outré factors, although he could not resist the occasional swipe at Young Jim Larkin's Moscow-based education, and such like.[189]

Pre-election predictions put Fianna Fáil at a loss of perhaps ten seats, with Labour winning up to 30, and gains for Clann na Talmhan as well.[190] These proved correct in the directions of the swings for each party, if not the extent. The bigger parties were the bigger losers. Fianna Fáil's vote dropped by ten per cent nationally, as did Fine Gael's, resulting in losses of ten and 13 seats respectively. For the most part, the anti-government vote went to Labour in the east and Clann na Talmhan in the west. Labour's vote went up by five per cent nationally, almost doubling its seats from nine to 17, while Clann na Talmhan, contesting its first general election, won nine per cent of the national vote and 11 seats.[191] Among the new deputies who would be joining the Labour benches in the new Dáil were the Jims Larkin, senior and junior, in Dublin, and Roddy Connolly in Louth, while other gains were made in traditional republican heartlands in Munster, where Labour's attitude towards Fianna Fáil's security measures had made it the natural home for those protesting against the government's hard-line measures.[192] Each and every one of Labour gains was made at the expense of Fianna Fáil. It was obviously an improvement for Labour, but fell far, far short of the advances envisaged before the poll.[193] Fianna Fáil's losses prompted MacEntee to draft a letter of resignation from the government to de Valera. 'It will surprise none, I am sure, that a party which has suffered a reverse at the hands of the electorate should look for a scapegoat', he wrote. 'I venture to say, however, that it will surprise many to learn that the person chosen as the vicarious delinquent is myself'.[194] Prone to melodrama (he was in the habit of writing, and even sometimes sending, resignation letters to his Chief), MacEntee remained a member of the Fianna Fáil front bench until the mid-1960s.[195]

LABOUR IN THE NEW DÁIL

Despite these setbacks, Fianna Fáil was still by far the largest party (albeit one without a majority) and when the new Dáil met on 1 July de Valera was easily elected taoiseach after Labour and Clann na Talmhan abstained from the vote. The only thing that stopped Labour voting against him was the prospect of a Fine Gael government, which was still a bridge too far.[196] Labour did, however, oppose de Valera's new cabinet when it came before the house, owing to MacEntee's presence.[197] Young Jim Larkin made his maiden speech on the resumption of the debate the following day. A lesser man, having borne the brunt of MacEntee's attempted witch hunt, might have taken the opportunity to settle some old scores, but Larkin's contribution was intelligent, measured and insightful,[198] qualities characteristic of the junior Larkin, who was in so many ways the polar opposite of his showman father. Not that

Young Jim avoided MacEntee's smear campaign, but his main focus was not on personalities or playing politics, but on the very real need for the government to begin addressing the question of post-war economic reconstruction, a constant theme for Larkin in the years to come. Nevertheless, despite Young Jim's willingness to brush off the accusations hurled at him in public, he does seem to have become more cautious after his election. Intelligence reports recorded that the communists had decided that 'Larkin should not openly identify himself with the CP in Dublin',[199] but even in private correspondence he was guarded. Responding to a congratulatory note from Andrée Sheehy Skeffington (wife of Owen), he expressed the hope that she was 'not building up too exaggerated hopes of overlooking my own personal shortcomings, and particularly the fact that *I am a pledge-bound party member – with all its implications*'.[200] He did raise his head above the parapet in spectacular fashion soon after he entered the Dáil, however, when he addressed the House on the desirability of opening up trade with the Soviet Union.[201] It was applauded by some as a highly courageous move, but a number of his colleagues were less impressed and let it be known if he ever wanted to come out with anything similar again, he could do so as an Independent.[202]

Larkin's caution was by no means unjustified. In fact, he had replaced his father as public enemy number one in Liberty Hall after his stunt at the Mansion House at the beginning of the campaign. Public enemy number two was John de Courcy Ireland, who was Young Jim's right hand man on the Dublin Executive. When the AC met on 16 September it had before it motions tabled by Thomas Kennedy of the ITGWU which called for the expulsion of the pair for disloyalty to Labour by promoting and assisting the candidature of Larkin senior after he had been rejected by the AC. It was decided in the end that John de Courcy Ireland would be informed of the motion relating to him and asked to respond, while the question of Young Jim's membership would be put before the PLP before it was dealt with further. Three days later a meeting of the PLP voted to expel Larkin junior,[203] on the basis of Transport Union votes,[204] which put the matter back in the hands of the AC. On 3 December a compromise suggestion that Larkin be reprimanded rather than expelled, was rejected by Thomas Kennedy who moved once again (seconded by P. J. O'Brien of the ITGWU) that Larkin junior, be expelled from membership. In all, six members of the AC, each one a member of the Transport Union, supported Larkin's expulsion; eight of their colleagues (including Young Jim himself) voted against. Frank Robbins then moved that a special delegate conference be called to 'consider all the implications of the matter', but the chairman refused to accept the motion and thus brought the issue to a conclusion.[205]

This was not a conclusion acceptable to Liberty Hall, however, and on 7 January 1944, the ITGWU officers finally carried out their threat, and wrote to Labour giving notice of their disaffiliation. When the AC's next meeting took place almost a week later on 13 January, it was boycotted by its ITGWU members. James Hickey, party chairman and member of the Transport Union, resigned his position.[206] The following day five (of the eight) ITGWU deputies and two senators seceded from the parliamentary Labour Party, upon which the Transport Union finally broke its silence and sent a circular to its branches explaining that it had disaffiliated because of Larkin's ancient enmity towards the union, and that his acceptance into the party had been facilitated by communists. Since the union's members had neither been consulted nor informed of their leaders' intentions prior to the breakaway, this came as something of a surprise. Nor was the discomfort confined to the rank and file with many of the union's officials very unhappy with the situation.[207] Noting that there was increasing alarm caused by his vendetta against Larkin, O'Brien made an abrupt change of tack. Larkin's presence in the party was demoted to a secondary reason for disaffiliation, with the failure of the Labour leaders to tackle the communist conspiracy now cited as the primary reason for breaking away. This was recognised by all involved for what it was – an attempt by O'Brien to knit an excuse less shabby than Larkin's mere presence in the party. As AC member Louie Bennett noted at the time, 'the Larkin issue [had] dominated every other subject' ever since she had been elected to the council in April 1943; any efforts to get rid of Larkin were personal and, she concluded, 'the communist bogey [had] nothing to do with it'.[208] Nevertheless, specious and opportunistic as the Transport Union's use of the 'communist bogey' may have been, it did not mean that their accusations were untrue. Certainly, after paying a visit to Ireland at the end of 1943, CPGB secretary Harry Pollitt left under the impression that 'comrades in the South seem to be doing a good job of work in the Labour Party'.[209] The CPI leaders seemed optimistic about the effectiveness of their action. In July 1943 a CPI meeting was told that 'since they had decided to work through the branches of the Labour Party more contacts had been made and they had gone a greater distance towards building up the Communist Party as a force than ever before',[210] while Seán Murray expressed the hope that their activities within Labour might bring about 'a restatement of that party's principles, including the formal and public recognition of the principles of the Soviet Social System'.[211]

Labour's leadership was in an invidious position: it knew that the Transport Union's accusations of communism were a smokescreen, but it felt compelled to address them nonetheless, and so on 13 January a joint meeting of the PLP and AC voted unanimously to establish a committee of enquiry, consisting of William Norton, Michael Keyes, William Davin, Martin O'Sullivan and Senator Michael Colgan to look into the allegations that there were communists in the Dublin branches and that they were using the Labour Party as a cover for communist activities. The committee of enquiry met at least weekly over three months, beginning on 19 January, 'for the purpose of collecting information and interviewing persons likely to be in a position to assist' and signed off on its report for the AC on 20 April.[212] As the committee began its enquiries, weekly exposés began to appear in the *Standard* based on similar (if not identical) sources to those made available to Seán MacEntee at the general election the previous year. The vast majority of the *Standard*'s articles were written by Alfred O'Rahilly, who, as we have seen, was close to a number of senior Labour men and regarded himself a staunch friend of the labour and trade union movement. As a long time Catholic Actionist and anti-communist, O'Rahilly genuinely believed his muckraking was in the best interests of the party and of the movement,[213] arguing that it was important to do 'the necessary cleaning up' then rather than 'when a crowd of communised emigrants return [from Britain after the war and] avoid damaging the Labour cause as much as possible'.[214] O'Rahilly was identified early on as a most useful ally of the ITGWU in its battle for hearts and minds, and before long he had become a willing stooge of Liberty Hall. This meant the *Standard*'s features on Labour were a potent cocktail of Special Branch intelligence and Transport Union black propaganda.

Labour's committee of inquiry had been charged with establishing the veracity of claims that communists had infiltrated Labour, but had no real means at their disposal to investigate this with any degree of rigour. It was an unenviable task. The modus operandi decided upon was to interview a number of people about the claims and base their report on their answers. In all, 17 people were called before the committee (by no means an exhaustive trawl), of whom 13 appeared. Only two of those 13 'were in a position to produce statements or material [most likely police reports[215]] in support of their allegations' which the committee felt were reliable. Others, the committee reported, 'considered it sufficient to make us aware of the rumours and suspicions associated in certain quarters with the names of some prominent, some obscure, persons in Dublin who may, or may not, be members of the Labour Party; others expressed their own suspicions or beliefs'.[216] At least one merely adverted to the material being published in the *Standard*, arguing that 'the mass of evidence adduced in the articles . . . is so well documented that no further evidence from me or from anybody else appears to be necessary', an attitude shared by a number of others who went before the committee.[217] The material in the *Standard*, however, was disregarded on the basis that it had been 'collected through the activities of *agents provocateurs* planted at the head of the so-called communist organisation [and] material of such a character, collected in such a manner [and ultimately used in such a political fashion] must be viewed with the gravest suspicion'.[218] 'In a matter of such grave importance', the committee continued, 'it seems to us that natural justice imposes on all responsible people an obligation to suspend judgement until there is available to them an abundance of evidence derived from untainted sources, on which to base a balanced judgement.' The committee conceded that there were 'a few members [in the Dublin Labour Party] who, at one time or other were members of the Communist Party', but so too were there significant numbers who had previously been members of Fianna Fáil, Fine Gael or the IRA. Labour was prepared to accept their bona fides because:

> when a person formally and publicly breaks off association with a political party of which he has been a member and, in an equally public manner associates himself with another party, it would be the height of folly, on the part of the latter, to refuse him admission to its ranks. So long as political freedom remains to us, men and women must be free to join the Labour Party once they are willing to pledge their loyalty to it without reference to their former political associations.

Effectively, in the absence of evidence to the contrary, former members of the CPI would be seen as just that.

After three months of meetings, the committee of inquiry decided there was sufficient evidence to make a case against four members of the party in Dublin. The committee had been made aware that John Nolan, Charles Kennedy, John de Courcy Ireland and R. N. Tweedy had attended the CPI's conference in Belfast the previous October, and it was further suggested that all four were communists. Nolan, Kennedy and Ireland were interviewed on the matter (Tweedy refused to appear), and admitted to having been in Belfast at the time, but denied they were members of the CPI. (Nolan admitted that he had been a member in the past, but said his relations with them had ceased three years previously.) The committee concluded that the four men had undoubtedly been 'present at certain functions organised by the CPI, that they had contact with the promoters and organisers of the conference and thereby held themselves out as persons sympathetic to Communism'. Concluding that their action was incompatible with Labour Party membership, the committee recommended that their membership of the party be cancelled. This view was soundly endorsed by Labour's annual conference in April 1944, when it voted to expel the four men by 203 votes to ten.[219] Outside Dublin, the Liam Mellows branch in Cork city which had been formed by two recently released communist republican internees, Michael O'Riordan and Jim Savage, was dissolved and O'Riordan expelled,[220] while in Drogheda, Roddy Connolly endeavoured without success to expel another suspected communist, although the man in question subsequently resigned.[221]

Left-wing commentators then and since have tended to paint Labour's inquiry into the matter, and the subsequent expulsions, as yet another example of the leadership's craven behaviour in the face of attack, but is this really fair? Did Labour have an alternative? Did the committee behave in a way which would justify such a description? It is nonsense to argue that Labour could have brazened out the accusations coming from its former colleagues and in the *Standard*; they had no alternative but to look into the matter. Nor did the committee of inquiry engage in anything approaching a witch hunt; where members denied they were communists, and where there was no reasonable evidence to contradict this, they were taken at their word. Far from carrying on an 'inquisition', Labour did the least they could possibly get away with. Certainly Martin O'Sullivan's addendum to the report was not the work of a man who felt the issue had been resolved. Recognising the difficulties in procuring direct evidence of communist activities, he concluded that the movement in Dublin, which could not be trusted, would have to be supervised by a special committee. Ultimately, though, when moving beyond the talk of witch hunts and timidity, the arguments of those who criticised the inquiry and the resultant expulsions really boiled down to the belief that it was wrong to expel the communists, who ought to have been allowed to operate with impunity within Labour's ranks. To criticise Luke Duffy's comment that 'Communists have no right in the Labour Party; anyone pursuing communist tactics will speedily leave'[222] is only another way of arguing that entryists should have carte blanche to do as they please.

Something had to be done, but not too much, lest credence be lent to some of the more outrageous accusations. The Belfast four were scapegoats, whose expulsion made a wider purge unnecessary. Nevertheless, it was obvious that things could not continue as before. The question of the branch organisation in Dublin had to be addressed, the more visible forms of radicalism had to be suppressed, and Labour's political and religious orthodoxy reinforced. A week after the committee of inquiry signed its report, the last edition of *Torch* was published, wound up on the orders of the AC.[223] Since described as 'without question one of the most popular and stimulating labour papers ever produced in Dublin',[224] *Torch* was, in fact, a rather turgid publication. Hamstrung by the wartime censorship, dependent on party and union funding, and overly reliant on a handful of Young Coveys for most of its copy, the paper was an unsatisfying combination of lightweight agitprop and overly theoretical articles. Even among activists on the ground, there was a belief that while a real working-class paper was needed to educate and organise the working class for the struggles ahead, *Torch* was not it;[225] indeed the Labour Party Dublin Executive instructed its secretary, John de Courcy Ireland, to protest to the party's Administrative Council for:

The inadequacy and incompetence of its reports on municipal affairs . . . its incomplete handling of the news sent in from various sections of the Dublin Labour movement, and its lack of policy and drive concerning most of the vital matters facing the party today as well as bad editing, dull get-up, lack of news generally, and superfluity of academic and long winded articles.[226]

According to the newspaper, '*Torch* replied to John Ireland informing him that most of the long academic articles were his own – and he sent a most disarming apology'![227] Too cautious for radicals, too radical for conservatives, *Torch* ended up pleasing no one, as was so often the case with the Labour Party itself. What is surprising is not so much that *Torch* was wound up, but that the it was allowed to continue for so long. Nor was it the only casualty. *Signpost*, published monthly by the Dublin Executive from April 1943, was also wound down around this time,[228] as was the Waterford divisional council's monthly, *The Spark/An Splanc*.[229] The left may not have been purged, but it had been silenced very effectively indeed.

1944 GENERAL ELECTION

De Valera had been operating without a majority in the Dáil since the 1943 election and was naturally eager to remedy this situation. In February 1944, he gained considerable kudos from his performance during the 'American note' episode, when he resisted demands from the American ambassador, David Gray, to expel Axis diplomats from the country, a demand that would have fundamentally compromised Irish neutrality had it been obliged. Keen to capitalise on this boost and on the opposition's disarray (Labour was in crisis, Fine Gael was more than usually demoralised since W. T. Cosgrave had stepped down as leader in January[230]), de Valera took the first chance he could to call an election. When the second reading of the government's Transport Bill was defeated by one vote on 9 May the fate of the eleventh Dáil was sealed, and election was called for three weeks hence. The opposition was understandably angry about the election, not least William Norton who now faced a campaign before the dust had even settled on the split.[231] Though relations were obviously poor between the two parties, the hope remained that the rift could be mended before it was too late, but the election, and National Labour's decision to contest it, scuppered that, 'polarising attitudes to the point of no return'.[232] There was, moreover, the issue of logistics; snap elections were difficult enough at the best of times, but now that the Transport Union had disaffiliated from Labour, the party had lost its biggest benefactor.

Overall, the campaign was subdued. The electorate was distinctly uninterested and the opposition parties were in such a shambles that Fianna Fáil was the only party to fight the election as though they meant to win it.[233] In fact, it was the only party *capable* of winning it, since none of the others fielded sufficient candidates to win a majority.[234] This meant, of course, that the key election issue was a familiar one: vote Fianna Fáil for strong government, or for the others and see what you get, or at least that was how the government party put it. Fine Gael's campaign bore the hallmarks of its malaise, while Labour, though keen to push its economic policies and attack the government, found itself unwilling to do so in any way that might leave it open to attack on the 'red' front. De Valera's penchant for 'dictatorship' was attacked,[235] as Norton stressed that the country was in greater need of good government than strong government.[236] The breach between Labour and Fianna Fáil was summed up by Labour's new weekly, *The Irish People*:

> For many of us, Mr de Valera represented ten or fifteen years ago, the upright, courageous leader who knew all the answers; who stood firmly on the rock of Irish nationality; who in office would subordinate the claims of the rich to the needs of the nation. That phase has passed. Today, he represents the most incompetent group of political adventurers in Ireland.[237]

Even when criticising the government, Labour seemed to do it more in sorrow than in anger. The party was obviously on the defensive and, recognising the problems it was facing, fought a 'very restricted and concentrated campaign, based on protecting existing seats as much as possible'.[238] MacEntee was back to his old tricks, joined now by the *Standard* and National Labour, the latter choosing to run a generalised red scare rather than engage in the kind of personalised attacks that had become the mainstay of the *Standard*. Politically, MacEntee was alone in using the red scare; his colleagues did not adopt his tactics,[239] nor did candidates from the other parties, if for no other reason than that they had nothing to gain by attacking Labour.[240] For the most part, Labour candidates ignored their collective jibes and accusations,[241] but there were also exceptions to this restraint. Richard Corish, Labour's longest serving deputy, ran quite an aggressive campaign in Wexford,[242] where he faced two National Labour candidates 'spending money like water' on their campaign. Corish was a Transport Union man of over thirty years standing, but his decision to stay loyal to Labour left him with practically no resources for the campaign.[243]

The result, when it came, was as expected. Fianna Fáil swept the boards, winning a majority of votes in all but two constituencies.[244] It picked up nine seats and with them a Dáil majority. With the exception of Clann na Talmhan, every other party saw its vote fall,[245] but Labour came out the worst. In Cork, National Labour lost one of its five outgoing deputies, while Labour saw its national vote halve, and five of its outgoing deputies defeated – Roddy Connolly in Louth, Patrick Hogan in Clare, Richard Stapleton in Tipperary, Jim Tunney in County Dublin, and Big Jim Larkin in Dublin North East[246] – leaving it with eight seats. Its gains from the last election had been lost almost to a man, but this merely meant that it had one seat less than 1938, the same number of seats as 1933, and one more than in 1932. To put it another way, between schism, red scare, and the continuing fall off in transfers from other parties, Labour faced the very real prospect of being wiped out at this contest; instead, it merely fell back to its core level of seats. Nevertheless, the 1944 election marked a very definite end to Labour's advance.

FOUR

PICKING UP THE PIECES
1944–8

—

LABOUR DURING THE TWELFTH DÁIL

The twelfth Dáil met for the first time on 9 June 1944. Three days earlier Allied troops had landed on the beaches of Normandy, finally opening up a second front in Europe after more than a year of steady Soviet advances in the east. This momentous offensive marked the beginning of the end of the conflict in Europe, but at home it signalled that the new government would be entrusted with guiding Ireland safely into the new political, social, economic and military context that would arise after the war. De Valera had been elected taoiseach with a solid majority, and it was clear that his new government would be able to hold on to the reins of office for the next five years, if it so wished. However, if it was clear that the Fianna Fáil government would be in power for another five years, it was less clear what it was going to do during this time; the government's agenda was vague, to say the least, having been elected on a platform quite lacking in concrete policies. That is not to say that it was without ideas; Seán Lemass had been pushing his plans for economic development at the cabinet table for some time now, but was facing stiff resistance from Seán MacEntee, and a lack of enthusiasm from most of the others. Still, if the government gave the impression of lacking direction, the opposition were little better, with Fine Gael and Labour preoccupied with keeping themselves from falling apart.

PARTY

The split had left Labour (what was left of it) badly shaken. Over the previous few years, the leadership had given the party membership a greater degree of autonomy than it had enjoyed previously. Despite left-wing complaints about Labour's reactionary leadership, leftist factions had been allowed to operate unchecked within the party during the Emergency, while the content of *Torch* was much more radical and openly socialist than anything which had appeared in *Labour News* for instance (although the ban on criticism of matters religious continued). This ended after the split, and the party's replacement newspaper for *Torch*, the *Irish People* which appeared three weeks after *Torch*'s last issue, illustrates the sudden shift in the party. Unlike *Torch*, which was published by the Dublin Constituencies Council (although it received substantial funding from head office), the *Irish People* was an official party paper, and was expected to read accordingly. Its first editor was Mrs B. Berthon Waters, an economist whose main claim to fame was that she was one of those responsible for the Third Minority Report to the Banking Commission.[1] Undoubtedly an intelligent, educated woman, it seems likely, nevertheless, that her political and religious credentials (she was a practising Catholic and follower of social credit economic theory) had a great deal to do with her appointment. If she was chosen as a safe pair of hands, she did not disappoint. The tone of the *Irish People* could not have been more different from its predecessor. The turgid theoretical treaties so beloved of the Young Covey element were thankfully absent from the new paper, but in their stead appeared selected papal pronouncements that were reprinted practically on a weekly basis. Its first leading article was typical of this style, stating that Ireland's greatest threat came not from communism but 'the gross abuses of the individualistic Capitalist system, which abuses are most stringently condemned in the Papal Encyclicals'.[2] 'Socialism' never raised its gory head. As far as many members were concerned, the *Irish People* was wholly unsatisfactory, and the complaints were immediate.[3] A discussion in the Inchicore branch found most members expressing 'dissatisfaction with its lack of vigour and militancy, while it was inclined to be much too academic'.[4]

Berthon Waters edited the *Irish People* for 18 months, relinquishing the post because of ill health at the beginning of 1946. Her replacements signalled that the leadership might have become more relaxed about the position. George Pollock, who took over the editorship in a temporary capacity, was a former CPI man – regarded in intelligence circles as 'a well known and active communist',[5] and he was soon followed by Sheila Greene, who was appointed editor as a permanent position. Greene was a highly intelligent, lively young woman. Married to the Trinity College Professor of Irish, David Greene, she was a social science graduate, and former Alexandra College girl, characterised in her Department of Justice profile as 'a friend of Schrodinger and lapsed Quaker', and in another profile as an 'active communist sympathiser'.[6] More significantly, she was part of Dublin's tiny 'Bloomsbury intelligentsia'[7] which was beginning to take shape at this time. Although this group was small it was vocal beyond its size, consisting as it did of a handful of journalists, literati and senior trade union officials who were socialists of a slightly bohemian bent. Included among them was Peggy Rushton (who later succeeded Sheila Greene as editor of the *Irish People*), Christy Ferguson of the WUI, Brian Inglis of the *Irish Times* and later Donal Nevin who became Research Officer of the ITUC in 1949.

Sheila Greene's arrival at the *Irish People* had little effect on the paper's politics however, and while the *Irish People*'s editor and contributors were to be found on Labour's left, their room to manoeuvre was dictated by finance and by self preservation. With a circulation barely into four figures and practically no advertising, the paper was utterly dependent on the leadership's goodwill for survival.[8] The contributors also faced the problem of what could actually be put in the newspaper once it had avoided taboo subjects, which were numerous. Brian Inglis who wrote for the *Irish People* around this time recalled that 'to keep on the [leadership's] right side, it was not just a question of avoiding the kind of explicit socialism Connolly had promised . . . We also had to avoid writing about any subject in which criticism, even if justified, could be construed as criticism of the Church.'[9] Among the issues which this veto put beyond the pale were health and education, and as a result the two issues which received the most attention in the paper were housing and prices – important issues, certainly, but not necessarily the recipe for rousing mass enthusiasm in the party. A belief in the pre-eminence of intellectuals among the writers also meant that the paper was insufficiently trade union conscious, and thus not completely representative of the labour movement as a whole.[10] Where there was mention of the trade union movement it was often in the form of criticising the schismatic tendencies of the ITGWU;[11] indeed the amount of space devoted in the *Irish People* to attacking the National Labour Party rather than the government serves as a sad reminder of the energy wasted by the movement during the years of the split. The split and the continued red scare meant that the *Irish People*'s editor could not make it a genuinely representative organ of the party reporting the often sharp discourse among activists. As the editor Sheila Greene explained to the author of a letter critical of the party's leader,

> I didn't publish it for reasons which I'm sure you will appreciate. However much the Administrative Council or the party officers annoy us we *can't* criticise them publicly. God knows I suffer the most intense irritation every day, but I wouldn't dream of letting off steam in the paper. You see *Irish People* is read by all sorts of outsiders – enemies as well as friends and we can't afford to give them extra ammunition.[12]

When Seán O'Casey submitted an article which contained criticism of the Roman Catholic Archbishop of Westminster, Greene had to write to him and explain that she could not print it as it stood, as 'without putting a tooth in it, it would be harmful to the Labour Party . . . I think if you lived here you would understand what I mean'.[13] Greene asked O'Casey to resubmit the article without reference to Cardinal Griffin, but O'Casey was unsympathetic to her plight. 'Goethe's last words were, "More light. More light,"' he wrote, 'Mine will probably be "more courage. More courage".' His conclusion was damning, 'I am not out to force the Labour Party of Ireland. Their ways rest with their own conscience. Please let me have the article back. No wonder Bill O'Brien has had his way.'[14]

If the subjects which Labour could tackle were limited, so too was its vocabulary. The use of the word socialism was completely avoided in public. As Paddy Bergin, who joined Labour in this period, recalled of public speaking at the time, '[I had] the knowledge that the minute you use communist jargon that you're gone. "That's it, he's giving us a line", if you're in Dublin, and down the country the minute they hear anything Red, that's it. So I preached unadulterated socialism – without ever using a word of jargon.'[15] This was not a case, then, of a heavy handed leadership telling people what they could or could not say; it was *self* censorship which came from an acute appreciation of what the party could hope to get away with.

This was not merely the case for ordinary rank and file left-wingers, but also for the communist contingent which remained in the party. (The Trotskyist element had, by now, dissipated through a combination of ill health and schism.[16]) Ever since the April 1944 expulsions, the Labour communists had kept a low profile, intent on not rocking the boat within the party, while communist activity outside Labour still centred on New Books on Pearse Street, and on publishing, with its newspaper *Irish Workers' Weekly* being replaced by *Review* in April 1945. *Review*, edited at different times by Seán Nolan and John de Courcy Ireland (both of whom had been expelled from Labour in April 1944, although the latter was readmitted on appeal), took a critical line against Labour – it was too timid and uninspiring – but was careful not to go too far. Its caution infuriated the always forthright Owen Sheehy Skeffington, who wrote to Ireland in 1947 after Ireland had censored an article by him, on the 'Keep Left' ginger group in the British Labour Party. 'I . . . refuse to have my name used over articles which have been toned down to suit what I believe most strenuously to be wrong policy', he wrote.

> You have operated, between you, your policy of loyalty to Norton and Duffy and Murphy for over four years now. Is it really mere 'egotism' on my part that makes me dubious of your results? To me it seems clear that to pretend to the public that Nortonism can build a real Labour movement is to stultify that very movement and the very thing you accuse me of making good effort.[17] . . .
>
> I am not sure that if I were harder hit materially I would not be out on the streets denouncing the Nortonites for telling the workers that Irish Labour had

nothing better to offer them than Nortonism. I think in justice you might recall that even in the heat of the moment when I made a public statement after my expulsion, I reaffirmed my conviction that the only hope for the Irish workers lay (in spite of all its defects) in the Labour Party. But if I had been told then that the militant wing would use all its strength in the coming years to keep the reactionaries in control even after O'Brien's departure, I would have felt a sense of despair.[18]

Many on the communist and non-communist left had pinned their hopes on Young Jim Larkin to take over the leadership of the party.[19] By 1944 he had survived at least one attempt to have him expelled from the party and had managed to hold on to his seat in the general election in the face of heavy Labour losses. From the outset, he distinguished himself as one of the few intelligent voices in Leinster House, the Dáil chamber filling at the prospect of a Larkin speech, not because he was a great orator, or a showman like his father – he was not – but because of the depth of thought and intelligence that he brought to bear on the subject in hand.[20] Lemass, in particular, had him marked out as an intellectual force to be reckoned with and held him in very high esteem indeed.[21] Evidently his popularity was also growing within his party as in 1945 the annual conference elected him vice-chairman of the party, a development described in *Review* as marking 'the end of the old reactionary domination of the Party's AC'.[22] This is an exaggeration, but it is true, nevertheless, that Larkin would never have been able to get to that position were the ITGWU still the dominant faction within the Labour Party. *Review* continued that Larkin's election 'ought also . . . mark the end of "red baiting" inside the party, and the beginning of a new era of vigour and enlightenment in the party's leadership. Whether it will or not depends largely on the new vice-chairman himself.' The truth is that, while the left might have wished that Larkin would use this position as a springboard to the party leadership, Larkin himself had other ideas. He showed no sign of initiating a putsch against Norton, and resigned from the AC only a year after being elected vice-chairman. He cited lack of time as his primary reason – Larkin's priority was helping run the Workers' Union of Ireland, and he was finding it difficult to balance his political workload (constituency, party and parliament) with his union activities. 'I am not a good cook', he explained to his friend John de Courcy Ireland, 'and to change the proverb even a good cook can spoil too many broths if he tried cooking them all at the same time, and a lot of people lately seem to find a bad taste in some of my broths'.[23] But there was more to it than that. Though Larkin remained friendly with his erstwhile communist comrades, he had stepped back from any political association with them by this stage, and had adopted an evolutionary approach to socialism. If Larkin was a socialist first and foremost, he was a pragmatist too, and it seems that the success of British Labour in the 1945 general election had a profound effect on him, with British workers in the socialist vanguard implementing socialist policy.[24] Larkin was fast coming to the conclusion that politics was the art of the possible, a philosophy which was clear from his words a couple of years later to one young man who had left Labour to join the communist Irish Workers' League: 'you can pass all the resolutions you like', Young Jim counselled, 'but resolutions are what they will remain'.[25] His refusal to countenance leadership was repeated time and again. Diffidence and an acute awareness of just how divisive a figure he could be saw him reject such a role outright, as is clear from his firm words to John de Courcy Ireland:

> Finally – please get it out of your head about 'big men'. I am not one, I don't like them, and if I felt that any one person merely was in the party because I was in it and in the AC then I'd certainly leave the AC and possibly cease all activity in the party. I've had my belly full of big men. I have never said it but the one thing I can't stomach even in the USSR is this cult of Joe Stalin. Perhaps I am getting too serious and developing a swelled head to ever suggest such comparisons but I do want you to realise that I am not of the stuff of which leaders are made, and even if I was foolish enough to let you and the other short sighted persons convince me, and try to live up to it, I'd fail at a critical moment and the cost to be paid might be very heavy. I have ability, I can do certain jobs, I am not exactly a fool, but I have a very good idea of my own ability and I only wish I could get some other people to take the same view, not for my sake but for their own peace of mind and the good of the movement.[26]

Larkin was forever the left's lost leader. His refusal to challenge the centre-right leadership, and the absence of a alternative figure meant that the left remained subdued and demoralised. There was always hope that he would change his mind,[27] but he never did. Norton remained secure, then, not because of his own popularity or cunning, but because no one challenged him. Larkin's reticence came from a combination of complex factors, but that of his parliamentary colleagues was mere apathy, for as Norton admitted in a moment of candour, the only reason he managed to lead the party for so long was because the other Labour deputies were 'too engrossed in their constituencies and county councils to challenge him'.[28] Larkin, meanwhile, remained active within Labour, his stature growing among his party colleagues and political opponents alike. There is little doubt that Larkin's political ties to the communist movement had ended by the mid to late 1940s, even if the belief in some quarters was that it was impossible for a communist to give up his ould sins. Unable to point to any evidence of communist activities a Department of Justice dossier resorted to supposition. Jim Larkin (junior), it said, 'remains in the background but *there is little doubt* that he would resume his identity as "comrade" Larkin if it were politic to do so'.[29] Or as National Labour Party leader Jim Everett was reported to have put it, 'If Larkin politically ever shows the whites of his eyes, we'll blow the top of his head off'.[30]

POLICIES AND POLITICS

It is probably unsurprising that Ireland's political scene immediately after the war lacked the sense of drama evident elsewhere in Europe. Ireland had been spared the upheaval associated with war, from conscription and civilian bombing to forced labour or occupation. In contrast to so much of the continent – and beyond – Ireland emerged from the conflict unscathed. This was obviously 'a good thing', but in social terms there was a downside to neutrality. Elsewhere the war had served as a catalyst for change. Sir William Beveridge in Britain argued in his 1942 report on *Social Insurance and Allied Services* that 'now, when the war is abolishing landmarks of every kind is the opportunity for using experience in a clear field. A revolutionary moment in the world's history is a time for revolutions, not for patching.'[31] In Ireland, the inclination of many Irish politicians was to reach for their darning needles.

Arguments on the subject of economic policy were often as pronounced within parties as between them. This was particularly the case in Fianna Fáil, where Seán Lemass's lobbying within the cabinet for the adoption of a policy of full employment, and Seán MacEntee's wholehearted resistance to it, were taking place behind closed doors.[32] Labour's policy developed little in this period. Although a committee on financial policy had been established towards the end of 1943, it does not seem to have produced any working papers or documents. If it did not so far as to adopt any new policies, it was, perhaps, a positive sign that it was engaging in serious thinking and open to new ideas. After Arnold Marsh, headmaster of Drogheda grammar school and a sometime contributor to *Torch*, published a book entitled *Full Employment in Ireland* in December 1945, he was approached by the party to assist in policy formulation in a number of areas, including farming, social services and housing.[33] As was so often the case in politics generally, and in the labour movement in particular, the committees were slow to produce, and it was late 1947 before any of their recommendations came before the party.

The year 1944 saw the publication of two notable reports. The first was the report of the Commission on Vocational Organisation published in August, a year after it had been presented to the government. The thinking behind the commission's appointment in 1939 had been to silence the proponents of vocationalism while the report was being researched, rather than any idea that the government would heed its findings. Of the 25-person commission, four were labour representatives; two of these, Louie Bennett (IWWU) and Senator Seán Campbell signed the final report. Of the other two, Luke Duffy became embroiled in a spat over the report,[34] while Jim Larkin senior signed nothing and kept his counsel on the issue.[35] The government was far from enamoured with the report's findings, much to Labour's relief, as there were elements to the report which Duffy, for one, thought close to fascism. This was one political football with which Labour would not be playing. Some weeks later, however, another report was published with which Labour had much greater sympathy. On 11 October Dr John Dignan, Bishop of Clonfert, and chairman of the National Health Insurance Society (NHIS) presented a paper entitled *Social Security: Outlines of a Scheme of National Health Insurance* to a meeting of the society's committee of management, a summary of which was published in the national newspapers a week later.[36] In it, Dr Dignan engaged in a trenchant critique of the social services as they existed in Ireland, writing that 'the system is tainted at its root and it reeks now, as it did when introduced, of destitution, pauperism and degradation', a situation which could be rectified only by a fundamental reform of their provision. He argued that the chaotically organised social services should be unified under a single scheme which would be run on an insurance basis, and would be administered, not by a government department, but by an enlarged version of the NHIS. This, Dignan argued, would represent the genuine implementation of vocational principles into Irish life,[37] since by basing the scheme on insurance principles and administering it through the enlarged NHIS, it would not lead to any excessive increase in state power, and would thus be in accordance with Catholic social teaching. Though Dignan's paper contained much that was popular it garnered a frosty reception from Seán MacEntee, then minister for local government and public health, who ignored it publicly until forced to address the issue in response to a parliamentary question tabled by William Norton. MacEntee reported that, upon examination, his departmental officials had found that the 'paper in general did not take due cognisance of the several very complex fundamental difficulties which the author's proposals involved, that many of these proposals were impracticable, and that accordingly no further action on the basis of the paper would be warranted'.[38] Such a response from the notoriously prickly MacEntee is not surprising: the government had already decided to ignore the Report of the Commission on Vocational Organisation which it had actually appointed. Why should it pay any more attention to a report which was unsolicited? It had arrived on the minister's desk on the same day it was published in the national press,[39] a move which showed the bishop and his colleagues to be either astonishingly arrogant or injudicious in the extreme. There was more to the minister's response than

pique (although William Norton suggested that his obvious annoyance whenever there was mention of the report was 'because he got only a compliment
slip with it'[40]), but the manner in which it was published did lead MacEntee
and his officials to read the report as 'part of a campaign to undermine public
confidence in, and challenge the authority of, the Department of Local
Government and Health', as Susannah Riordan has observed.[41] For one thing,
MacEntee opposed extending welfare provisions anyway, as he believed they
encouraged a derogation of personal responsibility, and opposed the compulsory nature of the contributions.[42] But if MacEntee did not want to see the
introduction of a nanny state, he had no wish to see a nanny committee
established either. It was a point taken up by *Irish Times* columnist Myles na
gCopaleen (Brian Ó Nualláin to his colleagues in the Department of Local
Government and Local Health, where he worked as an official), who remarked
that the Dignan report and the Report on Vocational Organisation advocated:

> what one might call a neo-fascism. Both assail the fitness of the Government to
> carry out several of its most material duties, and demand that these should be
> transferred to certain 'voluntary' and 'vocational' bodies not directly answerable to
> your Oireachtas.[43]

Labour had always pressed for large-scale increases in benefits and provisions; indeed, increased social welfare was one of the cornerstones of Labour
policy, but it was an issue that was not always exploited to the degree it might.
For instance, after the Beveridge report had been published in Britain in 1942,
Hugo Flinn, parliamentary secretary to the minister for finance, had warned
the taoiseach that 'every wildest claim' made by Labour would seem feasible,
as it could argue that 'if this can be done by England after a horribly costly war,
what could not be done by a country that has remained at peace'.[44] But Labour
never did this. Although constantly eulogising the government and economy
of New Zealand or Sweden, the Irish Labour Party never felt comfortable
extolling the virtues of anything advocated by its sister party closer to home.
There may have been 'strong echoes of Beveridgean ideas' in Labour policies
and propaganda,[45] but there was no likelihood of the party hitching itself to
British reforms explicitly, no matter how popular they might have been. Dignan
was thus a godsend for Labour. Here was a home-grown scheme (albeit vague
and uncosted) with the imprimatur of a bishop to improve and increase welfare provision.[46] For Labour, it was ideal, and it was only natural that the party
should become a vocal proponent of the scheme, not least when it provided a
'political blackthorn' with which to beat the government.[47] The fact that the
scheme was based upon the very same principle as the Report on Vocational
Organisation which Labour had deemed fascistic was conveniently ignored.

POLITICAL COMPETITION

If the result at the 1944 election seemed to confirm Fianna Fáil's position as the dominant party in Irish politics, there was mounting evidence that its pre-eminence was far from secure. It was a victory won on a very low turnout, while it had managed to win back only half of the votes which it had lost the previous year.[48] Undoubtedly the government party had profited from the sorry state of the opposition parties, so that ultimately it was only as strong as the opposition was weak. For the opposition, then, any strategy for power could be summed up in two notions: first, the hope that the next five years would see the government's popularity continue to wane, second: try to last that long and then pick up the pieces. It was looking as though the second strategy would be a tough proposition for Fine Gael, then going through the 'most dismal' period in its history.[49] Suffering the longest political losing streak in the history of the state (it had lost seats at almost every election since September 1927[50]), by the end of 1945 it had to stand aside in a series of by-elections because it could not find any half decent candidates.[51] Clann na Talmhan's position was more difficult to gauge, for though its vote at the last election had increased, it had lost seats. Perhaps more significantly, it saw itself as a sectional party and had no interest in moving beyond its support base as it stood,[52] and hence seemed unlikely to grow any larger than it had to date. Nevertheless, its performances in two head-to-head by-elections with Fianna Fáil in December 1945 were particularly impressive, winning a seat from the government party in Mayo South, and coming a very close second in Kerry South.[53] Labour's fortune was also difficult to predict. It was impossible to tell how much of the mud flung by the *Standard* et al. had actually stuck in the public's mind, but for the most part it seemed Labour had done quite a good job of getting back to normal since the split, even if there was no sign of a reconciliation in the short run. If anything, the split had reached its logical conclusion when the ITGWU (and others) split from the ITUC to form a rival Congress of Irish Unions (CIU) in January 1945. If there was one positive sign for the prospects of an end to the split, it was National Labour's singular failure to turn itself into anything approximating a real political party, rather than a rump of Transport Union deputies. Moreover, rumours circulated in Dublin of financial and sexual misconduct within the CIU which was dam-aging its reputation, at least in government circles. In contrast, Fianna Fáil acknowledged that although Labour 'had its imperfections' it was at least 'a clean group'.[54] Still, any residual coolness or antipathy between the two sides had little effect on voters going to the polls in Dublin and Wexford in December 1945. The latter contest, which came about following the death of Richard Corish, saw Labour keep the seat, with Corish's son Brendan succeeding his father into the Dáil. Meanwhile the party came a decent second in Dublin.

The political field after the 1944 election was wide open, and was all to play for. This was a view held at the time by Seán Lemass who related his thoughts on the matter to London-based Jack Carney in October 1946.[55] Lemass painted a fascinating picture of political change over the next few years. There was 'general agreement that if Labour unites there will be a LABOUR GOVERNMENT IN IRELAND at the next election' (emphasis in the original), he told Carney. For one thing, government leaders were of the opinion that 14 years was 'too long for a political party to be in power,' but added to this was, in Lemass's mind, the fact that a *united* Labour Party would benefit from the formation of a new Catholic Party. Carney recorded:

> This party will be composed of the followers of Rev. Dr Dignan, who drew up a social insurance scheme he stole from Labour, and Rev. Dr Browne, who had his report on Vocational Organisation scrapped by Lemass. The latter was the framework of a Fascist State. This party will take votes from FF and FG which will help Labour. Some of the clergy, notably the Bishop of Wexford, oppose any idea of a Catholic Party and prefer Labour.[56]

Lemass, Carney felt, would welcome a Labour government, observing, 'he does not want a fascist state and he would like to see Labour take power'. Not that Lemass was disinterested in this scenario, for as he saw it, Labour would last five years 'then *we* [Fianna Fáil] would come back'! As it turned out, Lemass could not have been more wrong. The Catholic Party, crypto-fascist or otherwise, never materialised, and his prediction of how a reunited Labour would have fared remains consigned to the realms of conjecture. The one sense in which he was utterly correct, however, was in anticipating a radical shake up in the Irish body politic in the very near future.

Some months before Lemass spoke with Carney, a new political party had arrived on the scene, the latest in a line of republican groups that appeared every few years with very little consequence.[57] Clann na Poblachta, as the new party was called, was mostly made up of IRA men, many of whom had been interned during the Emergency, while its leader, Seán MacBride, was a former Chief of Staff. There was also a reasonably strong contingent of former Fianna Fáilers, many of whom had left the party after the government's treatment of republicans during the Emergency. There were few high profile defections from Fianna Fáil to the new party, but one such example was that of Noel Hartnett, formerly close adviser to de Valera.[58] Labour converts were very few, the most well known being Captain Peadar Cowan, whose loss to the party was something of a blessed release.[59] The primary reason for Clann na Poblachta's appearance had much to do with Fianna Fáil's steady descent into respectability, and especially its security policy during the Emergency, which alienated many of the party's traditional republican voters (many of whom, as we have seen above, appear to have turned to Labour in protest), we might ask why a new party was necessary or, to put it more precisely, why not Labour? The split, or more accurately the leadership's consequent determination that the party should give no cause for alarm, did nothing to attract people to Labour, its increasingly insipid appearance prompting Louie Bennett to remark with grim understatement, 'the Labour Party isn't a very inspiring organisation these times'.[60] This was a view held by those on the left, with London-based communist C. Desmond Greaves writing that 'the new party comes from Labour's failure [as well as Fianna Fáil's]',[61] while Labour member Harry Ryan argued in *Review* that 'if Labour had not become disunited and had continued to grow and develop as it was showing signs of doing in 1943–44, Clann na Poblachta would not have come into existence'.[62] But was it because Labour's *policy* was too timid that people were turning to the Clann? In a word, no. If imitation was the sincerest form of flattery, Labour had reason to be pleased since Clann seemed to have adopted much of its social and economic policy. In truth, however, Clann's policy was less progressive than Labour's. Where Labour advocated elements of Catholic social teaching in an opportunistic fashion such as the Dignan plan, Clann's support (or more accurately that of Seán MacBride) seemed more genuine. While Labour, controversially within the party, had a policy which encompassed elements of social credit and the second minority report on banking (see p. 84 above), Seán MacBride was a fervent proponent of social credit and based his party's policies on the even more cranky third minority report, which proposed that the Irish economy be completely restructured in accordance with papal encyclicals. In the case of the Clann, radicalism was in the eye of the beholder. It was merely re-hashing an ultra-Catholicised version of Labour policy, but, significantly, with a vigour quite lacking in the older party.

There was also the question of class. In terms of organisation and of support, Labour had always been a profoundly working-class party with a strong trade-union character. Although the purpose behind the labour movement's 1930 division into a separate congress and party had been to extend the latter's appeal to non-trade unionists, little had been done beyond this to create a more catch-all party. As one Labour activist had admitted during the Emergency:

> The attitude of the Labour Party to the black-coated worker needs examination. Hitherto the Party has directed nearly all its propaganda to the industrial worker and the small farmer. If it is to become the party of the workers it will need to

show a keener appreciation of the needs of the white-collar worker. Many of these workers, quite unjustly, it is true, have come to think that the Labour Party is not interested in their problems and that the machinery of the Labour and trade union movement is not for them.[63]

Not that the lack of white-collar workers was entirely due to Labour's failure to appeal to this group ('of course, such things as snobbery and "professional honour" are responsible too', conceded the same critic), but the truth was that the experience of middle-class people in Labour tended to be an unhappy one. Culturally, they found the trade unionist character unappealing, and politically they tended to be isolated far to the left of their more labourist comrades. Frustrated at the party's bureaucratic culture and its failure to embrace socialism or anything like it, Labour's middle-class strays rarely rested long in the party's ranks, drifting out disillusioned and annoyed. Owen Sheehy Skeffington lasted longer than most, unusually being expelled before he could leave. Labour's perceived class bias was later cited by Noël Browne as one reason for joining Clann, to which he was an early recruit, for although he looked upon Labour as his 'natural party', he was, he said, put off by its timidity and its perceived antipathy towards professionals.[64] There was also a generational aspect in Clann's initial success. It was a new party (albeit one with many familiar faces), and it marketed itself as such. This newness appealed to younger people, who saw the established parties as having been sewn up by the 1916 generation. However, if these elements accounted for much of Clann na Poblachta's early attraction, they did not explain why it was founded. Whatever else about its politics, Clann na Poblachta was established as a new *republican* party. If Labour had become increasingly green during the 1930s and in the course of the Emergency, republicanism remained far from its raison d'être. Prior to the foundation of the Clann, MacBride had come close joining Labour, but had been talked out of it by Louie O'Brien and others because 'a new republican party was called for'.[65] As far as the republicans were concerned, Labour could never fit the bill.

Ultimately, Labour's problem was not so much that people were *leaving* it, but that a cohort of bright young things was ignoring it to join the new party. As Labour activist Brian Inglis put it (writing in his guise of Quidnunc from the *Irish Times*), it was

those who have been deterred from coming in, that really matter; the number of Clann members I know, who have admitted that they would like to have joined Labour, but who were put off by the moribund state in which they found the party, is astonishing.[66]

Far from Labour making a late sprint for the radical high ground, it became, if anything, even more cautious around this time, as talks between the two Labour parties opened in the spring of 1947. These talks were made possible by the exit from the main stage of two of the key protagonists in the split; William O'Brien had retired as General Secretary of the ITGWU in 1946, while his long time adversary Big Jim Larkin died suddenly at the end of January 1947. Even in death, passions ran deep. As the taoiseach and his cabinet colleagues were leaving St Mary's church in Haddington Road after the funeral mass, a woman in black rushed forward and shouted: 'There's your godless man you attacked during his life. You never thought he would have this funeral. God forgive you all'. It was an incident which, Larkin's old comrade Jack Carney felt, set the tone for the funeral on the whole.[67] If the woman's anger was misplaced (and it was, for Larkin enjoyed better relations with Fianna Fáil than with most[68]), it was because those who had fought hardest against Larkin were absent from this occasion. The writer James Plunkett, a one time official of the Workers' Union, recalled how he, as one of the thousands of mourners who came out that day, made his way through the snow filled streets of Dublin, 'all the shops were closed, the flags along the route were at half mast, [and] traffic was at a standstill'.[69] There was one notable exception to this show of respect, however. As the cortège made its way across town from Haddington Road to Glasnevin, it stopped outside Liberty Hall for some moments. Perhaps unsurprisingly, the building displayed no sign of mourning. After everything that had happened between Larkin and his old union, it is easy to understand why, but the fact remained that despite his often reckless and irresponsible behaviour Larkin had always remained a hero to the Dublin working class, who thronged the icy streets of the capital to say their goodbyes. Such were the numbers who turned out that 'the tail end of the procession had not reached Parnell's statue in O'Connell Street as the procession entered Glasnevin', Carney recalled. This dramatic display of Dubliners' devotion to Larkin goes a long way to explaining why William Norton was prepared to accept Larkin back into the fold in 1941 in the face of opposition from his largest affiliated union.

Still, Larkin's death opened the prospect of détente between the two factions. On the day Big Jim was buried, Young Jim published a letter calling for unity in the movement, but when the ITUC made the first move to establish a dialogue subsequently, it met with a sharp rebuff from the CIU.[70] On the political side though, the National Labour Party seemed more agreeable. On 22 April 1947 a Labour Unity Committee was established by a group of Labour men in Wicklow in an effort to reach an agreement between the two sides. (County Wicklow was effectively partitioned by the split. It was the constituency of National Labour leader James Everett, whose heartland lay in the south county, while a number of senior Labour men, including Roddy Connolly and Jim Larkin, lived in Bray.[71]) Discussions continued for some months until eventually a document, 'Document no. 6', was drawn up and put before the two parties in July. This saw Labour reiterate its strong and unanswerable opposition to communism, and that in accordance with this a united Labour Party would 'not admit or retain in its membership any person who is a communist or who participates in communist activity'. Continuing in something of a sectarian vein, it then stated that,

> Having regard to our religious and political policy, and as evidence of good faith, [the united party] agrees to take such steps as will effectively prevent the party branches from being used by the communists or any disruptionist organisa-tion. [The meeting] considers that this understanding provides the basis for the National Labour Party to amalgamate their organisations and to reform a united Labour Party.[72]

National Labour agreed to the resolution 'provided that satisfactory machinery is set up to implement the agreement *and that the plan is remitted to the unity committee in consultation with each side to make further suggestions.*[73] This decidedly vague proviso referred to the British control of unions, which had been an important factor in causing the split in the first place. However, the ambiguity of the wording led to a profound misunderstanding between the Unity Committee, which was under the impression that Document no. 6 had been accepted, and National Labour which believed it had accepted it on condition that the issue of British ownership was resolved. On 30 August Labour wrote to the Unity Committee to say that the 'proposed draft was acceptable', but it was another month before they heard from National Labour to say 'no deal'. The Unity Committee wrote back pointing out that if political unity were established, industrial unity would inevitably follow, and National Labour's demands would be met, but this cut no ice with the renegades. On 10 October, National Labour's executive issued its last com-munication to the Unity Committee on the matter. After full consideration, it declared it was insistent that 'industrial unity was an essential preliminary to political unity . . . the two matters are linked together and cannot be treated as separate and unrelated problems'.[74] And that, effectively, was that. Labour felt it had given practically every concession which was asked for – to the extent that sections within the party were critical of having given away too much; National Labour, on the other hand, had offered nothing. Even on the issue of British-based unions, Norton promised that the party would 'do its utmost' to bring about a transfer of power from England, but added, perfectly reasonably, that 'it would be a most undemocratic step to force unions to give up the benefits they had under powerful English unions'. By the end of October 1947, Roddy Connolly, the committee's secretary, effectively conceded defeat. James McCrea, a National Labour man who chaired the talks was sufficiently disenchanted with the behaviour of his party and its leader that he rejoined the ranks of official Labour and stood as a candidate for that party at the next general election.[75] Perhaps the failure of the unity talks was a blessing in the long run as the shelving of Document no. 6 meant that the witch hunt feared by the left never came to pass.[76] Still, Labour's willingness to countenance such a thing seemed to show it on the defensive, as in the face of the MacEntee, *Standard*, and the National Labour triumvirate, the Labour leadership continued to protest its innocence and the party's left kept quiet.

Labour nevertheless had reasons to be positive. The depression which had settled over the party in the aftermath of the split had lifted somewhat, with John de Courcy Ireland remarking that the 'despondency' felt by many members that the party could never pose a threat to Fianna Fáil as an alternative government had now passed.[77] For a start, the government's popularity was waning steadily. Though it had put in place a number of far reaching pieces of legislation in health, social welfare and post-war planning, none of these had been enacted. In fact, far from enjoying the benefits of progress, Irish people were facing increasing austerity. Rationing of bread and fuel was reintroduced, the latter causing considerable hardship during a particularly bad winter. The wages standstill order was lifted in 1946, resulting in an immediate outbreak of strikes from laundry workers to national schoolteachers. The cost of living was going up and up, and a supplementary budget removing some food subsidies, while increasing taxes on beer, cigarettes and cinema tickets, was introduced in October. The budget's economic impact was negligible, but its political effect was massive.[78] To add to its economic woes, the government was also beset by, as David McCullagh put it, 'a series of "scandals" which, it was claimed, demonstrated a certain ethical laxity on the part of Fianna Fáil ministers. In fact, it was more a sign of carelessness (and arrogance) after so many years in office, and of the opposition's eagerness to use anything to discredit the government.'[79] A scandal of a more serious kind was the treatment of IRA man Seán MacCaughey, who spent four and a half years in Portlaoise prison until his death on hunger and thirst strike in May 1946. MacCaughey was in prison for his part in the sadistic torture of former IRA chief of staff, Stephen Hayes, but when details emerged of his treatment in prison – he spent the duration without access to fresh air or sunlight, a year of which was spent in solitary confinement – there was a wave of public revulsion, all the stronger for the fact that news of this sort had been suppressed by the wartime censorship. The information came to light in the report of the inquest on his death, at which Seán MacBride, appearing as senior counsel for

MacCaughey's family, forced the prison's medical officer to concede that he would not have treated a dog in such a fashion.[80] (His junior counsel in the case was Noel Hartnett, and both were briefed by Con Lehane. All three were founder members of Clann na Poblachta.) MacBride's performance at the inquest was a tour de force and the launch of his new party only weeks later was no coincidence. By the close of the year it was difficult to imagine anyone voting to re-elect this government for a sixth consecutive term, and it is easy to see how opposition parties of all hues were becoming increasingly confident that Fianna Fáil would be rejected by the electorate at the earliest opportunity.[81]

Still, seeing Fianna Fáil put out was only half the battle; now the question became one of what would go in in its stead? It was clear that none of the opposition parties was capable of forming a government on its own and that a coalition of sorts was going to have to be fashioned if an alternative government was going to be possible, but what would it be? Fine Gael had spent much of the Emergency calling for a national government, and perhaps it is unsurprising then that it was the first party to fly the coalition kite. In September 1946 the Fine Gael vice-president, T. F. O'Higgins, called upon his own party, Clann na Talmhan and independents to amalgamate or present a common panel of candidates, arguing that their policies had always been much of a muchness.[82] Though there seemed little appetite for any kind of merger, the idea of a rapprochement between the opposition parties was said to have gained adherents in the months after O'Higgins first mooted the idea.[83] O'Higgins did not include Labour in his suggestion, identifying it as 'a special case because of its relations with the trade unions', and indeed, as one senior Labour deputy put it, while he welcomed a combination of the non-Labour opposition parties Labour was more concerned with uniting its own forces, which would not 'be easy of accomplishment'.[84] This was somewhat disingenuous, as around this time Labour's eye roved towards Clann na Poblachta, with informal, unofficial talks about some sort of agreement opening between the two parties. Roddy Connolly alluded to the talks at a Connolly Day commemoration in mid-May when he spoke of the need for a united opposition to the left of the government,[85] although the discussions between Labour and the Clann did not become public until the end of the month.[86] Though there was some favourable comment on the far left,[87] debate within Labour did not begin in earnest until October, when Clann na Poblachta, on its first electoral outing, won two of three seats in a cluster of by-elections. Roddy Connolly started the ball rolling with an article in the *Irish People* in which he called for a Labour–Clann na Poblachta–Clann na Talmhan alliance, on the basis that Labour lacked sufficient popular support to go it alone against Fianna Fáil.[88] (The question of coalescing with Fine Gael was rejected without serious consideration: 'we have least in common with Fine Gael – a party of the dead past'.) There was a very mixed response to Connolly's article, although those against any Clann–Labour alliance made up the majority of respondents in the *Irish People*. Though some were roused by a long-standing antipathy towards coalition, many were just profoundly suspicious of the new party, which was seen as unreliable and fundamentally bourgeois. One Labour man questioned whether his party would be able to agree on a minimum programme 'with a party whose members seem so incompatible one to another, whose policy is so similar to that of Fianna Fáil and whose course in the last year has been as rickety as a butterfly', while Louie Bennett was of a similar point of view, suggesting that such an arrangement would amount to selling 'our birthright for a mess of pottage'.[89] This point of view was given short shrift by some of the party's younger members, for whom getting rid of the Fianna Fáil government was of primary importance. The young Dublin Trotskyist Matt Merrigan (recently returned to Labour after a sojourn in the Revolutionary Socialist Party[90]) poured scorn on the notion that coalition would interfere with Labour's 'glorious' or 'fundamental heritage' on the basis that these phrases attributed 'qualities and virtues of a profoundly class nature to the Labour Party – when in fact they don't exist'.[91] A less brusque analysis was offered by Joe Deasy, then the youngest member of Dublin Corporation:

> I sympathise with the reluctance of many of our party members to accept this policy, but I would urge upon them the consideration that an 'over-purist' complex might easily unduly influence us in solving a problem of this nature. It must be remembered that a continued term in office for the present Government will do irreparable damage to the nation, not only economically but more especially culturally and spiritually.[92]

In the end though, while relations between Labour and the Clann remained cordial, they never came to any official agreement about cooperation. The efforts to bring about a unity of the right (if we can call it that), either as a loose arrangement or a new party,[93] were perhaps even less successful, with James Dillon announcing in December that talks had come to naught.[94]

Noting Clann na Poblachta's successes at the October by-elections, de Valera decided to put the party to the test before it had a chance to consolidate its position, and called a general election for 4 February 1948. The campaign was in stark contrast to the one that had preceded it; the patent lack of interest which had characterised the 1944 election was now replaced by an excitement not seen in years. A record number of candidates (405 up from 248 in 1944) stood for 147 seats.[95] There was real sense that change was in the air, but nobody knew how it was going to manifest itself. The general feeling at the time was that Fianna Fáil would lose seats and Clann na Poblachta would do well (its own confidence apparent from the fact that although it was the newest party it fielded the largest number of candidates (93) after Fianna Fáil) but beyond that no one could say. Reporting that de Valera was fighting for his political life, the London *Times* correspondent quoted an old political hand as saying that more money would be won and lost in bets on this general election than on any since the Free State had been established.[96] Rather than talk up its plans for post-war economic development and its legislation for social services, it ran on its record, foremost of which was its successful defence of neutrality.[97] Naturally, de Valera and Fianna Fáil spent a great deal of the campaign decrying the dangers of coalition, as they had done in every contest since 1937, making the government's ticket seem particularly negative, an impression bolstered by MacEntee getting up to his old tricks again, with Clann na Poblachta now joining Labour in his red scare.[98]

Although there were press reports that a common agreement between Labour and Clann na Poblachta was 'considered almost certain' were the two parties to return to the Dáil with enough deputies,[99] both fought the election independently. Labour promised to reduce prices and improve housing and social services. Clann na Poblachta's platform was little different, although it utilised modern campaigning techniques to sell itself, excelling at style over substance. Having said that, the two did differ in their economic policies, with Clann's leader Séan MacBride concentrating on issues such as the repatriation of sterling assets, much to the bemusement of the vast majority of the electorate, and, more than likely, his own party colleagues.[100] Ultimately, though, the central tenet of each and every opposition party (with the exception of National Labour) could be summed up in a single phrase: put Fianna Fáil out. The government was the enemy, and none of the opposition parties saw fit to attack each other. None, that is, apart from the two Labour factions which took time out every once and a while to disparage each other, or to stress their respective Christian, anti-communist credentials.[101]

In the end, the result was closer than might have been imagined. Fianna Fáil's vote dropped by seven per cent to its 1943 level and the party lost eight seats while the opposition parties (with the exception of Clann na Talmhan whose vote halved with the loss of two seats) all made gains. Fine Gael returned with one extra seat (an unspectacular result but the first time it had improved its position in two decades) and the independents did likewise. The result everyone had been waiting for turned out to be something of an anticlimax. The excitement surrounding Clann na Poblachta had begun to dissipate towards the end of the campaign, as what the public had once seen as enigmatic began to look more like a dog's breakfast, MacBride recalling in his memoirs of how he 'could feel, day by day, the tide slipping back, to such an extent that at the end of the campaign I thought that I'd be lucky if I got five seats'.[102] In fact, his prediction was not that far off, with the Clann winning only ten of the 40 or so seats predicted some weeks earlier.[103] Labour and National Labour both held their first preference votes, but increased transfers between the opposition parties saw them win an extra six and one seats, giving them a total of 13 and five seats respectively. All of this meant that, as had been expected, no party had enough seats to form a government. Despite its losses, Fianna Fáil remained by far the largest party, returning with 68 seats, which left it six short of a majority. National Labour had voted for de Valera as taoiseach the last time around, and there was a belief (not least within the outgoing government) that it would do so again, in which case all Fianna Fáil needed was the support of a couple of independents and it was in. When one unsuccessful Labour candidate wrote to head office in a flap about possible coalition partners a week after polling, he was told by Luke Duffy, 'we need not worry about the next government. Dev will be elected'.[104]

Having raised their hopes before the poll, however, the opposition parties were not going to give up that easily. The death of a Fine Gael candidate in Carlow–Kilkenny meant that the election there was delayed until 10 February, and it was during that campaign that the opposition parties began to discuss the possibility of a broad-based coalition. Fine Gael took the initiative, announcing on 8 February that it would endeavour to form a government and inviting the other party into discussions on the matter.[105] Meanwhile, Seán MacEoin, a Fine Gael deputy for Longford–Westmeath and unsuccessful candidate for the presidency in 1945, who had travelled to Carlow–Kilkenny for the campaign, met there with senior activists from Labour (including Jim Larkin), National Labour (including James Pattison), Clann na Poblachta and Clann na Talmhan and gauged that there was wide support for such a plan. Later, he recalled that 'in a discussion to assess the political situation it was agreed that Fine Gael and its leader had a responsibility to form a government as it was clear that the majority of the people had rejected Fianna Fáil and their government'.[106] Formal negotiations commenced on 13 February when representatives from Fine Gael, Labour, Clann na Poblachta and Clann na Talmhan met to deliberate Fine Gael's proposal. Beyond platitudinous talk about reducing emigration, unemployment, and so on there was little real discussion of policy. There was really only one potential stumbling block, on which Clann na Poblachta and, to a lesser extent, Labour had made their feelings quite clear, namely, that while they were quite prepared to sit in a government with Fine Gael, they drew the line at serving under Richard Mulcahy, a man who had earned the sobriquet 'Dirty Dick' for his role in the execution of republican prisoners during the civil war more than two decades earlier.[107] William Norton put the issue more delicately, however, when he explained to the meeting that Labour would not be prepared to serve in a government in which the leader of another party was taoiseach. Mulcahy was agreeable to standing down and so the question now became who else would take the helm. A number of Fine Gael names were suggested,[108] but only one seriously, that of John A. Costello, a senior counsel who had served as Cumman na nGaedheal attorney general, 1926–32. Crucially, Costello was untainted by any civil war involvement, and although his dalliance with the Blueshirt movement in the 1930s made him unpopular with some on the far left, this opinion was very much in the minority. He was held in very high esteem within Labour, having acted as senior counsel to the trade union movement for many years,[109] and had a 'close association' with the Limerick deputy T. J. Murphy and, through Jim senior, 'an old association' with the Larkin family.[110] Approached by Costello just before the vote for taoiseach, Young Jim was heard stating decisively, 'don't you know that we would do anything for you'.[111] The only real resistance to having Costello as taoiseach came from Costello himself. Having reached the peak of his profession, he was extremely reluctant to forego the remuneration of a top barrister for the lowly salary of a taoiseach, but was eventually worn down by his colleagues. His eventual capitulation, albeit on a provisional basis,[112] meant that the embryonic inter-party group, now consisting of Fine Gael, Labour, Clann na Poblachta, Clann na Talmhan and independent deputies (who had been brought on board by James Dillon[113]) had a leader, but as yet, no majority. On 14 February, the day after the would-be sweethearts had met, a two-hour joint meeting of the Parliamentary Labour Party and the Administrative Council at the party's head office rubber-stamped Labour's decision to go into the proto-coalition, reasoning that the people had put Fianna Fáil out and this was the only alternative.[114] That morning the *Irish People*'s front page proclaimed 'LABOUR WILL AGREE TO ACT IN COALITION GOVERNMENT AND PUT PEOPLE'S DECISION INTO EFFECT'.[115]

The five National Labour deputies now found themselves holding the balance of power, and faced the most important decision of their political lives. National Labour, as we have seen, was in effect little more than the political wing of the ITGWU/CIU. It had been formed and it operated to serve the interests of the union, and act in accordance with its orders.[116] Prior to the election, the CIU had written to Fine Gael, Clann na Poblachta and Fianna Fáil seeking a pre-election statement of policy on whether each party supported the CIU's fundamental aim of expelling British-based unions from Ireland. Only Fianna Fáil came out in favour of an 'Irish self-contained trade union movement'.[117] It was only logical, then, that the Transport Union/CIU would want its deputies to vote for a Fianna Fáil government. However, unbeknown to the union officials (or to Fianna Fáil), National Labour had been in talks with Fine Gael about supporting the new coalition. James Pattison had already been approached informally by Seán MacEoin, but MacEoin's next move was significant. He and Senator Patrick Baxter drove to Cork city where they met with 'a prominent Cork citizen of great quality' (it is difficult to imagine that this could be other than Alfred O'Rahilly) to whom they explained the position. This sagacious Corkonian pronounced the coalition 'a great experiment in democracy', and gave the project his 'active blessing', whereupon he rang James Hickey, who held Cork City for National Labour, and invited him to meet with his visitors. Hickey duly joined the three men around midnight, and having listened to what they had to say expressed approval with a single proviso – that Patrick McGilligan be minister for finance in the new government. Thereafter, the three other National Labour deputies, James Everett (the party's nominal leader), Dan Spring and John O'Leary were each contacted and gave their approval, on the basis that their decision would remain secret for the time being.[118] Subsequently they expressed a desire that their members would be Irish delegates to the International Labour Conference in Geneva,[119] which until then had been the preserve of the Workers Union of Ireland, but Costello declined to make such a promise, arguing he was unable to give any assurances though 'if an inter-party government was formed National Labour would get "a square deal"'.[120]

Whether National Labour's silence on their decision was because it relished the element of surprise, or feared the wrath of their union superiors, is hard to say, but even when Fianna Fáil's Gerry Boland went to visit James Everett a short time before the taoiseach's vote, he found the Wicklow man unwilling to give a straight answer, an equivocation which he took to mean 'no deal',[121] although his colleagues remained confident that National Labour would come good.[122] Similarly, it is difficult to tell whether it was arrogance or cowardice which saw the five National Labour deputies turn up an hour late for a meeting with the CIU on 17 February, at which they were to be instructed to vote for de Valera the next day. On their belated arrival, they rejected this instruction and informed their executive of their decision to vote for Costello, which they justified on the basis that they were answerable only to their constituents and not to their union.[123] In so doing, they were, in fact, making it quite clear that they were answerable to no one. Having betrayed their party in 1944, they now betrayed their union, and happily, for the chance of a seat at cabinet. When they decided to act on their own initiative to support the coalition rather than de Valera it sealed the fate of the government and their own. The inter-party group was in, and National Labour's days were numbered, for in pulling the rug from under Fianna Fáil it had lost its long-time ally as well as its raison d'être. That was for the future, however. For now, though, office beckoned. At nine o'clock on the eve of the new Dáil's first

meeting, Richard Mulcahy released a statement on behalf of all the constituents of the would-be government, setting out ten policy goals which the
government would pursue.[124] When the new Dáil met on 18 February Costello
was comfortably elected by 75 votes to 68. Fianna Fáil was out of office for the
first time in 16 years, and in its stead the state's first coalition government.

FIVE

IN OFFICE OR POWER?

—

LABOUR IN GOVERNMENT

If John A. Costello was a reluctant taoiseach it would be a hard man who would blame him, for managing this 'great experiment in democracy' would take patience and skill hitherto unseen in an Irish government. All political parties are coalitions, in politics and in personalities, and the role of the taoiseach is to balance factions and interests within a government to allow the cabinet to operate effectively. To do so in a single party government was difficult enough; to do so in a government made up of five different parties (including the two Labour parties who were not on the best of terms) as well as a raggle-taggle of independents, was another story entirely. Not only that, but while Costello was held in high esteem by his colleagues and enjoyed a great moral authority, he lacked some of the more fundamental powers usually enjoyed by a head of government, not least the ability to nominate his own ministers. The method of appointing the new cabinet was quite different from that used in previous single party governments. Each party was allocated a number of ministries proportionate to its Dáil presence and could appoint individuals from its ranks in a manner of its choosing. For most parties this meant the post was filled on the leader's nomination, except in Labour's case, where it was allocated on a vote of the parliamentary party. Labour had been given two ministries, Social Welfare and Local Government, which were filled by William Norton (who was also appointed Tánaiste) and T. J. Murphy respectively. Rumours abounded, then and since, that Jim Larkin was going to be made a minister (the *Irish Times* went so far as tipping him for Education) but that he was vetoed by Fine Gael.[1] It is difficult to establish if there was any truth in this.[2] Noël Browne was of the view that the *Irish Times* piece was 'black propaganda',[3] and as David McCullagh has pointed out, the timing of the article, appearing as it did 'on the morning of a crucial meeting of the National Labour Party . . . was hardly coincidental',[4] but Donal Nevin recalled that Larkin *had* been offered the job and the executive council of his union had agreed to allow him leave of absence, before he was told that it was not to be. Larkin, however, never spoke about it, Nevin recalled, as he was understandably sore about the episode.[5] Young Jim was, however, appointed leader of the Parliamentary Labour Party in place of Norton (who would be preoccupied with his ministerial duties) having proved himself an accomplished parliamentarian during his relatively short time in the Dáil. Labour was also allocated one of the three parliamentary secretaryships, which saw the youthful Brendan Corish, just entering his third year as a deputy, ensconced in Local Government. National Labour was allocated Post and Telegraphs, a position taken by party leader James Everett.

The cabinet was made up as follows: Fine Gael had six ministries; Costello was taoiseach with Richard Mulcahy in education, Patrick McGilligan in finance, Dan Morrissey in industry and commerce, Seán MacEoin in justice and Dr T. F. O'Higgins in defence; Labour had its two, Norton as tánaiste and minister for social welfare and the Cork deputy T. J. Murphy in local government; Clann na Poblachta had two, with Seán MacBride in external affairs and Dr Noël Browne in health, while Clann na Talmhan, National Labour and the Independents held one ministry each with Joseph Blowick in Lands, James Everett in post and telegraphs and James Dillon in agriculture. Support for Labour's participation in the government was by no means universal. As the *Irish People* acknowledged, there were many who accepted the 'situation with serious reservations',[6] but these people kept their criticisms to themselves and overall the response of party and trade union branches was very positive.[7] In contrast, quite a few branches of Clann na Poblachta resigned en masse rather than support a government which included Fine Gael.[8] There was a real sense of excitement at the prospect of Labour having power, when, after three years of watching the Attlee government's advances in Britain, Irish Labourites could enjoy the prospect of similar progress here. Obviously Labour held only two of 13 seats at cabinet, but it was confident nonetheless that it could punch well above its weight. National Labour and Clann na Poblachta, whose social and economic policies were very similar to Labour's, had three ministries between them, and of the Fine Gael contingent it was said that two were 'at least as left . . . as most Labour men'.[9] (This was particularly true of Patrick McGilligan, the minister of finance, who was said to be seen by his Labour colleagues as 'nearer to them than his own party'.[10]) 'While Fine Gael is therefore numerically the strongest party in the government,' summed up Arnold Marsh, 'Labour may be the most effective.'[11] Labour, he reasoned, was the only party to have formulated policy documents for, among other things, housing and social welfare, and as most of the other parties had not done so, they would be likely to follow Labour's leadership 'at least part of the way'. Furthermore, the ten points of policy set out the night before the government was elected were cause for optimism. The ten-point plan was as follows:

1   Increased agricultural and industrial production.
2   Immediate all-out drive to provide houses for the working and middle classes at reasonable rates. Luxury building to be rigidly controlled.
3   Reduction in the cost of living.
4   Taxation of all unreasonable profit-making.
5   Introduction of a comprehensive social security plan to provide insurance against old age, illness, blindness, widowhood, unemployment, etc.
6   Removal of recent taxes on cigarettes, tobacco, beer and cinema seats,.
7   Immediate steps to provide facilities for the treatment of sufferers from tuberculosis.
8   Establishment of a Council of Education.
9   Immediate steps to launch a National Drainage Plan.
10 Modification of means test as present applied to old age, widows and orphans, and blind pensions.[12]

Though lacking any mention of nationalisation and being distinctly vague about the economy, the plan nevertheless contained a great deal with which Labour could be content – arguably Fine Gael had made significant concessions to its partners on many of these points. It was not that there was nothing with which Labour could argue although, as Costello pointed out when the Dáil met, this was because the government's programme was based on points on which all were agreed, 'any points on which we have not agreed have been left in abeyance.'[13]

Nevertheless, if Labour was optimistic, it was not naïve. It recognised the importance of retaining its independence and being a 'vigilant' partner in the government; it was 'Labour's right – and duty – to criticise the government', as the *Irish People* put it.[14] Archie Heron, Labour's organiser, made a similar point in a document submitted to the AC two months after the government was formed. It was vital, he argued that Labour's 'independent position as a working class party' be clearly established and maintained, and that Labour demonstrate this independence in government by pressing 'its programme within the limits set by the existence of a coalition government, but if necessary to break with such a government should continued participation necessitate sacrifice of basic policy'. The first thing Labour ought do was restate its party policy in an official statement to 'clearly identify . . . and distinguish it from other parties in the coalition'. Then it should publicly identify itself with certain key areas (housing, transport, agriculture and social security) and show that

These are policies it intends to fight for, and by seeking to enlist popular support, secure their adoption by cabinet. Contrariwise there would be official and informed criticism, from a party view point, of government decisions on administrative

decisions or acts not fully in keeping with party policy, the purpose of which being
to continually emphasise the separate, independent position of the Labour Party.[15]

Labour had to offer a 'counterpoise to Fine Gael's continual emphasis on
economy, to their hostile attitude to state enterprise and special favouring of
private enterprise; to their declaration that reduced taxation is the only effective way to reduce the cost of living', and it certainly could not 'supinely swallow
a Fine Gael budget'. Heron then warned that Fine Gael and Seán MacBride
were getting 'continuous publicity' and that to balance this 'the ministerial
positions of Deputies Norton, Murphy and Corish must be fully exploited'.
Labour's problem in attracting attention from the press had been exacerbated
by the decision to wind up the *Irish People* in March 1948, Norton apparently
deciding that it had 'served its purpose'.[16] Valuable as a party newspaper might
have been in opposition, it was vital in government and Heron advised that
the establishment of a new paper should be 'tackled at once'. However, financial pressures and logistical problems meant that it would be well over a year
before a specifically Labour journal, *The Citizen*, would see the light of day and
so Labour continued to have to rely on coverage from the mainstream press.[17]

Scant notice was paid to Heron's advice. In fact, in a government which
had effectively abandoned collective responsibility,[18] Labour remained perhaps
the most disciplined party. Ministerial statements, inside and outside the Dáil,
often 'revealed differences of view on policy matters' with some ministers
inclined not only to speak as individuals on policy issues, but to make a virtue
of this.[19] The worst offenders in this regard were some of the Fine Gael ministers and Seán MacBride and Noël Browne of Clann na Poblachta. Labour's
discipline was due largely to the role which William Norton ascribed himself
in the cabinet. More than two decades as a trade union leader and 16 years
leader of his party meant that Norton was an accomplished wheeler-dealer,
'streetwise'[20] and described by a contemporary as 'perhaps the most skilful
"fixer" and experienced manager of all Irish politicians'.[21] Norton took his role
as Tánaiste very seriously indeed, and was inclined to use his skills as a 'fixer'
for the good of the government rather than the good of the party. As the
historian of the first inter-party government, David McCullagh, put it,
'[Norton] played a key role in keeping the government together, a role
appreciated by Costello who later said, "any time I ever had any trouble, any
problems to solve, and there were many, I always sent for my friend Bill
Norton for his sage and wise advice and counsel, and it was never lacking."'[22]
Noël Browne recalled that 'throughout the lifetime of that Cabinet Norton
played an invaluable role for his conservative Fine Gael colleagues. Whenever
I chose to contest some issue which merited a radical solution, the taoiseach
would turn aside my criticism with the unanswerable, "But the Labour leader,

Mr Norton, agrees; what is your difficulty, Dr Browne?'"[23] In his effectiveness as government troubleshooter and his refusal to play the party card in public, as Heron and others had advocated, Norton might have displayed an admirable lack of opportunism but this created problems within his own party, as we shall see later.

Ironically, one of the new government's first accomplishments was not included in its ten-point plan, namely the External Relations Act, which was announced by the taoiseach on a visit to Canada in April 1948.[24] It was a move with which Costello's colleagues were in full support; Clann na Poblachta had campaigned for its repeal during the 1948 election and Labour, although less vocal on the subject, concurred.[25] National Labour, which painted itself as more nationalist than its former comrades, could not have objected had it been inclined so to do (and it was not), while Clann na Talmhan was assuaged after assurances that the move would not have an adverse effect on cattle exports.[26] However, the repeal of the External Relations Act combined with the renewed anti-partition campaign had other implications for Labour.

For years the NILP endeavoured to operate as a non-sectarian party within which all Labour men and women could co-operate regardless of their constitutional beliefs. That this represented a particularly difficult balancing act seems, however, to have been wasted on its southern counterparts who broke off relations with the NILP on two occasions during the late 1930s because its members would not commit the party to an anti-partitionist policy. At the same time, there was pressure within the NILP, particularly from the Belfast MP Harry Midgley, for the party to adopt a unionist policy, and its refusal to do so ultimately saw Midgley leave the party in 1942 to establish his own Commonwealth Labour Party.[27] Once the war had ended, and with Midgley out of the way, relations between the NILP and the Irish Labour Party resumed – in late 1945, representatives of the two parties met to discuss future liaison,[28] and a joint committee of both parties was established which held its first full meeting in May 1946[29] – but little came out of these links, and the détente proved very short lived. A shift in the NILP executive's balance of power towards the unionist side was consolidated by events in the South, namely the repeal of the External Relations Act and the revival of an anti-partition campaign. Unionist opinion in the NILP felt it was in the party's best interests to abandon its status as an independent party and apply to become a regional affiliate of British Labour, a prospect which was clearly abhorrent to the anti-partitionists within the NILP, not to mention its sister party in the

South. By November 1948 all hell broke loose. The NILP executive disaffiliated
its West Belfast and South Down branches and expelled their members after
they had begun to organise opposition to a merger with the British Labour
Party,[30] while in Dublin the AC was alarmed to learn through a leak to the
Belfast News Letter that the NILP executive had invited the British Labour
Party's organiser and general secretary to Belfast for a meeting on 19 December
to discuss the logistics of the merger. If the proposed merger was consum-
mated, Luke Duffy advised in a letter to the NILP's secretary, the Irish
Labour Party would have no choice but to organise in the north to 'fight for
the overthrow of Partition and . . . [promote] the interest of the working class
in the Six Counties pending the reintegration of that area in a United
Ireland.'[31] On 10 December, representatives of the NILP travelled to Dublin
for a meeting at the Irish Labour Party's invitation but it was clear there was
no common ground. Over the next week, a number of nationalists resigned
from the NILP, including the party's chairman and secretary, and many those
who left looked to the Irish Labour Party for support.[32] Luke Duffy sought a
meeting with the British Labour Party's National Executive to resolve the
matter but to no avail, the NE apparently of the 'unanimous opinion . . . that
the time was not opportune'.[33] In February 1949, on the advice of the AC, a
small number of those who had disaffiliated from the NILP and members of
the Socialist Republican Party met to set up a 'Provisional Committee for the
establishment of an Irish Labour Party in the Six Counties.'[34] As a result the
NILP broke off all ties with the Irish Labour Party. Thereafter the Irish
Labour Party began to describe itself as Ireland's only '32 county party'. Of
course, it was nothing of the sort – with branches in Derry and Newry as well
as a couple of wards in Belfast, it was a '29 county party' at best – but the fact
remained that for all its rivals' anti-partitionist claims, the Irish Labour Party
was the only constitutional party organised north of the border at that time.

Predictably, none of this did anything to foster goodwill between the Irish
and British Labour parties, which although far from intimate at this time had
at least improved their relations after over a decade of silence.[35] Naturally, the
fact that British Labour was in government after 1945 gave Norton et al. good
reason to resume friendly relations, as was evident during the cold spell of
spring 1947 when Norton and Young Jim travelled to London to lobby the
Labour government for more coal.[36] Later that year, British Labour sent a
fraternal delegate to Labour's conference in Wexford[37] for the first time in 15
years, although any closeness between the two ought not be exaggerated, and
it is perhaps more significant that when British Labour convened a conference of European socialist parties which supported the Marshall plan, Ireland
was one of three countries excluded (the others being Portugal and Turkey)
because they were 'not considered to have any Socialist party suitably

qualified'.[38] Constitutional issues were even more complex. Labour was the most sympathetic towards Ireland of the British political parties for reasons of heritage, anti-imperialism or the demographics of its constituency, but the Irish question was certainly not a priority. For instance, when Labour's Friends of Ireland group was established in 1945 by the Manchester MP Hugh Delargy, it had only 30 members and although this had reportedly grown to 120 by May 1948 it has been suggested that 'the bulk of its membership must have been purely nominal'.[39] Moreover, in the policy-making echelons of the party where it mattered, there was little sympathy for anti-partitionism. On one occasion, the British Labour Party's general secretary warned the party's MPs against pledging support for legislation that they could not keep, he highlighted as an example any move for a united Ireland, which attracted a predictably irate response from his opposite number in Dublin.[40] In fact, not only did British Labour decline to promote a united Ireland, but, in response to the repeal of the External Association Act, introduced the Ireland Act in May 1949 which effectively copper fastened partition.[41] Irish Labour responded by sending a small anti-partition delegation to the British Labour Party's's conference in Blackpool the following month. Former internee Seán Dunne, *Irish People* editor Peggy Rushton, Kay McDowell of the IWWU and Jack Macgougan from Belfast were accompanied by Conor Cruise O'Brien who was there as the Department of External Affairs liaison. The group established a headquarters in one of the hotels and, Macgougan recalled, 'had leaflets galore and held a very big press conference',[42] but beyond the Friends of Ireland, the group failed to make any positive impact among delegates. On the last day of conference, Seán Dunne made a final effort to have his voice heard. From his seat on the balcony he stood up and roared 'Up the republic!' while attempting to unfurl a tricolour. As he was bundled out of the conference hall, two of his colleagues endeavoured to dispose of their remaining leaflets by scattering them from the gallery over the delegates seated below.[43] Contact between the two parties ceased thereafter and the Friends of Ireland group fell asunder. It took another two decades for relations between the Irish Labour Party and her sister parties to be resumed.

BILLY THE QUID

In February 1949 the *Irish Press* published a piece which claimed that the Tánaiste spent 'most of his time with party matters', leaving his Department 'to run itself.' Norton took great umbrage at this and, in an astonishing lapse of judgement, sued the paper for libel, against the strongest legal advice.[44] The case went to trial in the High Court some months later, whereupon Seán

Lemass, on whose notes the piece had been based, appeared to defend the libel. Back-tracking somewhat, Lemass argued that 'the general view was that his function was not so much to administer the Department of Social Welfare but to look after the government and hold it together in so far as there was a danger of dissension arising in it'. Norton won his case, but it was a Pyrrhic victory. He was awarded a princely £1 in damages, prompting Seán MacEntee to bestow on him the nickname 'Billy the Quid'. Libel cases of this kind are notoriously double edged, and most lawyers worth their salt would counsel their client not to pursue one, as Norton's solicitor had done. Why, then, would a man so experienced in public life be so sensitive to criticism that he would chose to pursue such a perilous action? Perhaps it was because, even if the *Press*'s accusation was not true, it was plausible. After all, when the article was published, Norton had been minister for social welfare for a whole year, and there was still no sign of any legislation, although there had been some improvements in widows' and orphans' pensions.[45] In fact, his white paper for the reform of the social insurance system did not appear until October 1949, close to two years after he had become minister. For an issue which had always been so crucial to Labour, his lack of progress was something of an embarrassment, although to suggest that the delay was caused by Norton playing hatchet man for the taoiseach underestimates the obstacles faced by Norton in preparing this legislation and the delicacy with which he had to act. Setting up a scheme to replace the labyrinthine system of social security provision was always going to be a painstaking task and, in the case of Norton's ambitious plans, a lengthy one. Norton's greatest problem in this regard, however, was the degree of opposition he faced, both inside the cabinet and without.

Aware that his proposal would be resisted by the Church because it would increase state control of social services, Norton met with Church leaders in a effort to gain their support. Thus, when Norton's proposals were finally published, they 'evoked a barrage of criticism from exponents of Catholic social teaching' from prominent members of the clergy as well as from publications such as *The Standard* and *Christus Rex*, but the hierarchy was silent for the most part, although Dr Dignan was 'mildly critical'.[46] By ensuring the Church's non-intervention on the plan, Norton had removed a significant obstacle to its progress but his biggest problem remained closer to home. Although the fifth point in the ten-point plan on which the government was formed promised the 'introduction of a comprehensive social security plan to provide insurance against old age, illness, blindness, widowhood, unemployment, etc.', it was obvious that the parties were divided on this question. It is difficult to imagine Labour agreeing to a programme for government in which swingeing reform of the social services was not included. Fine Gael, on the other hand, was happy to see the system reformed, but was profoundly antipathetical either to its extension or to its coming under state control. When Norton submitted a memorandum to cabinet in June 1948 expressing his intention to dissolve the National Health Insurance Society (NHIS) and have its functions taken over by the Department of Social Welfare, this was strongly resisted by the Minister for Finance, Patrick McGilligan, who was of the view that the society had performed its functions well, and that 'the NHIS might with more profit absorb the Department of Social Welfare'. McGilligan's objections on this matter were scotched, however, and the government agreed to the dissolution of the NHIS on 12 July 1948, meaning that in Norton's first 'set-piece battle' with his Fine Gael opponents, as David McCullagh put it, 'the Labour leader won'.[47] If Norton felt that the ease with which he had achieved this success would characterise his future dealings, he was quite mistaken.

The final draft of Norton's Social Welfare Bill went before the cabinet in April 1949. Predictably, it came up against immediate opposition, beginning with the Department of Finance and followed by the Departments of Industry and Commerce and Agriculture. This was reflected at cabinet level for the most part, with Patrick McGilligan and James Dillon the most vociferous opponents of the scheme, subsequently joined by Seán MacBride who complained about the lack of provisions for farmers and agricultural workers.[48] Nor was this opposition confined to the private sphere, with Norton's claims of cabinet unanimity on the issue laid bare by McGilligan's remarks in the Seanad on how the welfare state constituted 'a good step towards a servile system'.[49] McGilligan's fight against the bill centred on religious issues. At a meeting of the cabinet committee which had been established to examine the draft of the white paper, he proposed securing the views of Rev Dr Peter McKevitt, Chair of Catholic Sociology and Catholic Action in Maynooth on the matter.[50] In a confidential memorandum, which he subsequently sent to the taoiseach, McGilligan laid out his opposition to Norton's plan in terms of Catholic social teaching. It was, he said, 'a centralised bureaucratic type of scheme following the well known lines of doctrinaire socialistic teaching', continuing that it was well known that 'one of the most important of the principles of Catholic sociology is the principle of allowing subordinate bodies in a community to do work which they can do well and not bring the State to the exclusion of these bodies'. Furthermore 'it might be objected that a comprehensive scheme such as the one proposed, implies the *virtual abandonment of any intention to progress towards vocational organisation*'.[51] McGilligan's entreaties to Costello failed to convince, however, and Norton's scheme was finally approved, for the most part, by the cabinet on 21 October 1949,[52] and the White Paper, *Social Security*, was published four days later. Six months had elapsed since Norton had first put his proposals before cabinet and, as Noël Browne saw it, much of this time could be accounted for by the delaying tactics of the Fine Gael ministers.[53] While Browne's view was perhaps jaundiced, his conclusion was shared by David McCullagh, and it is difficult to imagine that there was not a conscious decision to try and hold up the legislation for as long as possible. The fact was that Labour was utterly committed to the scheme, and had Fine Gael (which was utterly opposed to it) objected to it outright it could have brought down the government. Norton stressed the government's pledge to introduce a comprehensive scheme of social security in its ten-point plan each time he distributed a memorandum on it to his cabinet colleagues,[54] as if to remind them of this. Norton was finally authorised to draft the long and short titles of the bill on 30 June, introducing the bill on 7 July, but the text of the bill was not approved by cabinet until December 1950,[55] and did not receive its second reading until April 1951. Thus after three years in government the primary plank of Labour's policy had still not been passed. It was an extremely uncomfortable time for Labour supporters, having to watch Norton's failure to prevent Fine Gael slowing the progress of the much heralded scheme down to a crawl.

Norton's colleague T. J. Murphy, and following Murphy's death in April 1949, the Limerick deputy Michael Keyes, proved much more successful. Their work in increasing the levels of house building during the government's time in office did a huge amount to improve the quality of life for many of the country's most disadvantaged and marked the fulfilment of one of Labour's key pledges. Neither Murphy nor Keyes was particularly publicity hungry, however, and though their achievements were admirable, Labour did not reap the benefits as it might have done, in comparison with Norton their achievements were greater than their publicity. Little was heard of their backbench colleagues either, although their silence owed little to diffidence. Labour backbenchers were conspicuous by their absence in the Dáil (leading James Dillon to christen the PLP 'the Quiet Mice'[56]) at votes and debates, to the point where the whips, Brendan Corish and Tom Kyne, had threatened to resign on the basis of the 'difficulties they were encountering in the matter of enforcing general discipline'.[57] Of course, the lack of a Labour-friendly newspaper since the *Irish People* had been wound up in early 1948 made publicity for the party even harder to come by, and if a paper had been important while Labour was in opposition, it was vital now it was in government. As part of a broad-based coalition Labour needed to put its own side across, take credit for its achievements and disclaim blame for the government's failures. Moves to establish a new paper began in the autumn of 1948. The view expressed by Labour members in Inchicore that the new paper ought to be a more ambitious publication than its predecessors, that it be 'less "political" in tone and should be "newsy" in the style of *Reynolds News* [the popular British left-wing paper] without losing its Labour standpoint',[58] was shared by those charged with bringing out the new paper. Its directors expressed their objective as being to 'bring out a newspaper making the widest possible appeal to readers. In this way only can a circulation and an advertising revenue big enough to ensure success be secured. The purely propagandist sheet is fore-doomed to failure.'[59] Besides, if the paper were really to be an effective instrument of propaganda it had to appeal beyond the converted.

First envisaged as the *Irish Freeman*, then the *Nation*,[60] the *Citizen* eventually appeared on 18 November 1949. An eight-page broadsheet, it was much larger than any previous Labour paper, and although it had an obvious Labour leaning, it lacked branch reports or Connolly tracts or the usual agit prop (the party's new status as gamekeeper rather than poacher precluding the latter). Instead, the *Citizen* tried to position itself as a populist newspaper with a great deal of sports coverage, radio schedules and reviews, a cartoon strip and a women's page complete with knitting patterns and make-up tips; in fact, entertainment took up more column inches than politics and the Labour content was drastically scaled back after the first edition. This was not a problem in itself – after all a spoonful of sugar could help the politics go down – but it was the nature of the political reportage which was more questionable. For instance, the appearance on the front page of the fifth edition of a tribute to John A. Costello in terms so gushing they were embarrassing must have caused alarm bells to ring for most Labour readers,[61] although subsequent profiles of Seán MacBride and James Dillon were less obsequious.[62] Whatever the populist aspirations of the paper, it looked as though any Labour journalist practised in the black arts of propaganda had been kept well away from the paper's copy. Before the editor could get further through the non-Labour members of the cabinet, it was announced that the publication of the *Citizen* would have to be temporarily suspended owing to the illness of the editor.[63] In reality, the paper had run up heavy losses over its seven issues, and there was no prospect of this turning around. Any chance of survival it might have had ended with the launch of the *Sunday Press* in the same month that *Citizen* hit the newsstands. It had similar format but enjoyed far greater resources, better writers and more exciting content. 'Scrupulously anodyne'[64] *Citizen* with its puff pieces on Fine Gael politicians could not hope to compete. *Citizen*'s launch was laudably ambitious, but when it folded it left Labour with a mountain of debt and, more importantly, no paper at a time when there was a growing sense among Labour members that Fine Gael was gaining the upper hand in the administration.

If, initially, Labour's participation in government had looked as though it might revive the party's fortunes,[65] this honeymoon was short. By autumn 1948, when the party held its first conference while in government, dissatisfaction was being expressed about the party's perceived lack of independence and loss of identity[66] (elsewhere one pensioner lamented that in times past 'we would not tolerate McGilligan [or] Costello . . . or any other snobs trying to force us back on our knees'[67]), and this merely grew as time went on, particularly in light of the delays in introducing the social welfare bill, but also in view of the government's failure to tackle rising prices or unemployment.[68] If frustration was growing in the Labour ranks generally, it was particularly strong in Dublin. The Dublin membership had been kept under close surveillance ever since the split, and, once in government, the leadership had kept it on an even tighter rein. The situation is perhaps best described by Brian Inglis, who recalled of the time:

> So far from stimulating a new enthusiasm, Labour's decision to join the inter-party government generated only apathy. All that William Norton and the other party leaders were concerned about was that the branches should not pass any resolutions that might identify the Irish Labour Party with the Labour Government in England; such resolutions might get into the papers, and make people thing we were a gang of dangerous socialists. 'Look at it this way,' the party leaders in effect told the branches; 'the first time since the war we have the party united again. You wouldn't want to scare away those fellows, would you? ('those fellows' being the National Labour deputies, the right wing that had provoked the split in the first place). And don't forget, Norton's drafting a new social security Bill. It can't go far, because Fine Gael won't vote for it if the Bishops don't like it, and if they won't vote for it we can't get it through; if you go rocking the boat and get people scared that we're all a lot of fellow travellers, we'll get nowhere. People have got to realise we're an Irish party, not taking our orders from Moscow. [69]

How, it would be reasonable to ask, might the leap be made from not identifying with the British Labour government to looking like a puppet of the soviets. There was a deliberate blurring of the boundaries between the two by Irish conservatives and, during the escalation of the Cold War, socialism was identified as a stalking horse for communism. As the Archbishop of Dublin John Charles McQuaid explained in 1948:

> Atheistic Communism has not yet attempted violence in this land. It has not openly pronounced its brutal sentence on all the principles of our Catholic Faith and culture. Its agents have been content to disguise their aims under the mask of Socialism, which seems to look only for fair conditions of a decent livelihood.

Socialism was thus portrayed as being, to all intents, the same as communism, except a more insidious variety – as one Catholic newspaper later remarked, 'the Welfare State is diluted Socialism and socialism is disguised communism'.[70] For the purposes of Irish Catholicism, Clem Attlee was placed on an ideological par with Joe Stalin.

Even if Labour's record in office should have proved its reformist credentials (for many of its supporters, it had not even gone that far), and the party was on its best behaviour, still it remained the subject of suspicion. The continued presence of many of the purported entryists in Labour's ranks did not help matters. Though the left collectively kept its head down for the most part, there was an awareness both within and without the party that while its influence appeared to be minimal (albeit 'out of all proportion to their numbers in the Labour Party'[71]), it had not gone away. For instance, one ordinary Labour member found himself being sent communist literature after he had appeared before the AC on a disciplinary matter. 'How did this brood of vipers know of the difference between the AC and myself?' he asked. 'Evidently some of the AC passed on the word and tried to enlist me then as '*a good labour man*'. I know of at least three on the AC whom I could suspect.'[72] In contrast, the type of 'communist' antics that took place after drink had been taken could be viewed much less seriously: a tribute dinner held for Lord Mayor John Breen ended in a mêlée when a group including E. J. Tucker and the future TD Maureen O'Carroll insisted on singing the Red Flag and the Internationale after the National Anthem in the face of vigorous protest from some of their Labour comrades. Tucker's behaviour may have been ridiculous, but it was taken very seriously by at least one Labourite present, who complained that 'much harm has been done by Mr Tucker and his type within recent years . . . for it is a well known fact that there is that hidden attachment to communist ideas, which, of course, are never openly expressed.'[73]

If all the Labour based communists were guilty of was some drunken play-acting their presence in the party still attracted unwelcome attention. Anti-communism had long been a part of Irish political and religious life, as we have seen, but now with Cold War hysteria starting to manifest itself, red scares came to the fore once again. It is worth remembering that in this Ireland was merely following the lead of the Catholic Church internationally, which, under the papacy of Pius XII, had identified communism as the greatest threat facing the Church or modern society. Catholics' relationship to communism was codified in July 1949 when the Holy See published the answers to four questions regarding faith and communism, which declared unambiguously that Catholics could *not* join or support any communist party, read communist literature, or be admitted to the sacraments if they professed communism. In the event of any of these strictures being breached, excommunication would be automatic.[74] As had been the case in the communist scares of the early 1930s, the Catholic Church was to the fore in encouraging vigilance in the face of the red menace, with the laity, for the most part, only too happy to oblige. The evils of communism became the regular stuff of sermons and Lenten pastorals once again, and when, in April 1948, it seemed as though the Communist Party was on the cusp of victory in the Italian general election, Archbishop McQuaid made a public appeal for funds to aid the Christian Democrats in their campaign, garnering very large sums indeed.[75] The anti-communist sentiment showed its most public form in the enormous street demonstrations that took place in Dublin to protest against the imprisonment by communist regimes of Cardinal Stepinac of Zagreb in 1946 and of Cardinal Mindzenty of Hungary in 1949.[76] Such was the force behind these demonstrations, that to refrain from taking part was a very dangerous thing indeed, and when an estimated 150,000 people marched through the streets of Dublin against Mindzenty's incarceration they were led by their Lord Mayor, John Breen, himself a former member of the CPI.[77] There was a popular compulsion to take part in such demonstrations and it is unlikely that Breen would have participated in such a demonstration had he not felt he had to.[78] Moreover, Young Jim Larkin also marched ahead of his union, with one contemporary recalling, 'he daren't do otherwise. It would smash the union if they were seen not to be wholly part of this. It would split the union. They would have lost all their members.'[79] In fact, Labour's participation in the proceedings that day could only be described as ostentatious, and they would have been happy to hear that their presence had been noted. 'The political parties, in particular, the Labour Party, aligned themselves firmly on the side of loyalty to the Faith and to our Holy Father' noted Archbishop John Charles McQuaid. 'And what I had never seen before: the Papal flag flew, alone, on the headquarters of the Irish Transport and General Workers Union, where the Citizen Army had flown its Plough and Five Stars in former times'.[80] McQuaid related this to a superior by way of showing off; in fact he was far from convinced by Labour's performance. McQuaid was profoundly suspicious of Labour, and held Norton in particularly low regard.[81] Norton, in McQuaid's eyes was soft on the communist question and a man without principle, his only tenet being 'votes from anywhere and how to get them'.[82] Ultimately, however, McQuaid's strategy against communism had two parts, firstly to educate and advise the laity against the pernicious doctrine of atheistic communism, and secondly to keep an eye on what any of the 'tentacles of communism' (to use the Knights of Columbanus's description[83]) were up to, with a Vigilance Committee established under McQuaid's auspices to monitor the activities of a number of named groups. Apart from the broadly defined 'left wingers' (mainly Labour Party members), this also included groups such as the People's College, an adult education centre set up by the ITUC in 1948, and the Irish Housewives Association (IHA). It might seem absurd that the IHA, a group which devoted much of its time to campaigning against high food prices, should be singled out as a tentacle of the communist octopus,[84] but this can be largely explained by the fact its joint secretaries were Hilda Tweedy and Andrée Sheehy Skeffington, women identified in their own right with left-wing politics, but whose marriages to R. N. Tweedy and Owen Sheehy Skeffington respectively undoubtedly led to them being viewed with suspicion. Also included in this surveillance was the Irish Workers' League, the new Communist Party launched in November 1948, led by Seán Nolan and Michael O'Riordan, and consisting for the most part of old CPI people, ex-Curragh communists, and Trinity College leftists.[85] Nevertheless, if this kind of intelligence gathering was somewhat sinister, the information collected by these lay spies went no further than Archbishop's House, and Labour remained safe from the red brush for the time being.

In fact, it seems as though some zealots felt the Church was not doing nearly enough on the issue. In June 1949 an article appeared in the British newspaper *Cavalcade* purporting to be 'an informative and factual article proving there is . . . COMMUNISM – BUT DISGUISED – IN EIRE!'[86] Actually, the piece was far from factual. A piece of red-scaring schlock worthy of the *Standard* at its worst, the article was a combination of information derived from a short piece in the *Sunday Independent* some weeks earlier[87] and alarmist calumnies with no basis in fact. Apparently, wrote *Cavalcade*'s special correspondent, as a consequence of there being no official communist party in Ireland (untrue – the Irish Worker's League had been in existence for seven months by this time), 'most Irish people are convinced that communism does not exist in Ireland under any form and this sense of false security has enabled the communists to infiltrate into many branches of Irish life'. 'During the last year, the Irish communists [had] greatly intensified their activities along three main lines of advance, towards three separate but complementary objectives', namely, the creation of isolationist and anti-NATO sentiment through anti-British propaganda; the 'infiltration of cultural organisations, the Press etc. in order to undermine the fabric of Irish society and to suppress criticism of their manoeuvres'; and finally the conversion of the working classes, especially the unemployed, to communist doctrines, 'carefully disguised as "social justice" or at worst "socialism"'. In order to achieve their first objective they had utilised their 'strongly entrenched positions in the Republican and Labour parties where powerful communist minorities exercise a considerable influence over policy by the implied or open threat of withdrawing their support, and that of many followers should the party leaders not accede to their demands.' Apparently, the Minister for External Affairs, Seán MacBride was at the heart of this, implementing a communist foreign policy from his vantage point in Iveagh House (although he must have been engaged in an elaborate double bluff, since his enthusiastic support for Ireland's use of Marshall Plan funds was distinctly at odds with the Party line). The writer really went to town, however, when he came to the question of the infiltration of cultural organisations. This, apparently, was the task of the '"intellectual" wing' of the communists, who, with the help of their fellow travellers, had recently founded the Association of Civil Liberty [*sic*] in co-operation with the British National Council of Civil Liberty.

> The aim of the association is, as in Great Britain and other countries, to promote free speech for communists – although this is carefully obscured by campaigns in favour of objects as legal adoption, free legal aid and prison reform.

A glance at the Society's sponsors would go a long way to ascertaining just how ludicrous a claim this was. The usual suspects, such as they were, were entirely absent (apart from Owen Sheehy Skeffington), and in their stead were figures such as the taoiseach, John A. Costello, Robert Collis, MD, Senator James Douglas, Seán O' Faoláin, Sir John Keane, Professor T. W. Moody, Gerard Sweetman TD and Michael Yeats, a member of the Fianna Fáil National Executive.[88] Far from being a selection of notorious reds, there was a distinctly blue hue surrounding this bunch, with one or two notable exceptions. Further calumny was heaped on to this, when the author then went on to libel Owen Sheehy Skeffington and the 'Housewives League', a misnomer used, no doubt, because 'Leagues' have a more Stalinist connotation than 'Associations'. Finally, the article concluded that the country was reasonably safe because Fine Gael had cleverly held the key ministries of Defence and Justice when the government had been formed, even if action on the communist question 'may be somewhat delayed for political reasons', although, damningly, the Catholic Church,

> which could exercise a very considerable influence on communist infiltration, [had] so far held its hand. It has no wish to incur the inevitable accusations of 'interfering in politics' and, in any event, it genuinely feels the time has not yet come for it to take decisive action.

The end result of this was that the months 'go by and communism continues to make considerable headway on all three fronts, while Irish people remain fatally convinced that "communism just could not happen in Ireland"'.

It was a shocking piece of work, sending the British National Council for Civil Liberties running to their lawyers, followed soon after by Owen Sheehy Skeffington and the Irish Housewives Association. (They had been unaware of the piece when it came out initially, because *Cavalcade* was banned in Ireland. It carried advertisements for the British football pools, and was hence prohibited under the Gaming Acts.) After some stiff solicitors' letters, *Cavalcade* published a full retraction and apology on the matter in its 5 November edition.[89] One effect of this was that it made the Irish Council for Civil Liberties extremely wary of dealing with any issues which related to communism. Only three years later, Joe Deasy, then an active member of the communist Irish Workers' League, approached the Council after he and others had been subjected to a venomous red scare when a co-operative grocery shop was opened in the Ballyfermot and Inchicore area. The Council refused to take on his case, because it was associated with communism.[90] The episode would also seem to have had quite an impact on its young author, Garret FitzGerald,[91] who abandoned the more sensational variety of journalism in favour of infinitely drier prose. It would be several years before he began to style himself as that rarest of things, the great Irish liberal.

A PARTY ONCE AGAIN

The young FitzGerald and Archbishop McQuaid were evidently more exercised with communists in the Labour Party than was National Labour. Having worked alongside each other without difficulty for two years, the two groups finally announced the end of the split on the evening of 6 June 1950. The re-unification of the party would be based on a four-point plan, the content of which would leave no one in any doubt as to the nature of the disagreement between the two parties. The main terms of the agreement were that both parties would work together as a united party in accordance with Christian principles and national ideals, and that the united party would accept the principle of Irish-based and Irish-controlled unions to cater for Irish workers.[92] The agreement was really the reverse of what had been formulated at the unity conference three years later, there being no references to rooting out communist elements from the party but a commitment that it would deal with the issue of British-based unions, on which the talks had fallen down the last time. Within a week, the reunited party established a sub-committee consisting of Norton, Everett, Corish, Hickey and Kyne to approach both congresses once again, but nothing came of it, the initiative appearing to 'fade completely'.[93] Fianna Fáil's first move following Labour's reunification was to request the Clerk of the Dáil to requisition National Labour's old office.[94]

Meanwhile, the erstwhile National Labour leader James Everett's first move was to become embroiled in one of the most infamous political scandals of the period, the 'Battle of Baltinglass'. This involved the minister's inter-ference in the awarding of a sub-post office licence in Baltinglass, a village in south County Wicklow which was in the heart of his constituency. Towards the end of 1950, the sub-postmistress of Baltinglass, Katie Cooke attempted to transfer the licence to her niece Helen Cooke. The licence had been held by the Cooke family since the 1880s and Helen Cooke had worked alongside her aunt for some 14 years, so it had been assumed that the transfer would be straightforward. At the end of November, however, Miss Cooke was informed of a recent amendment to the rules governing such licences which meant that succession rights to the licences were now restricted to immediate blood relatives. Helen Cooke, as Katie Cooke's niece was not covered, and so a 27-year-old local man named Michael Farrell was awarded the licence instead. Everett had made the decision in favour of Farrell against departmental advice and aroused a storm of controversy which went well beyond the confines of the small village in Wicklow, for the injury he had caused the younger Miss Cooke by taking away her livelihood had been compounded by his decision to transfer it to a young man whose suitability for the job seemed to be that his father had been a Labour councillor and was part of Everett's machine. The issue bitterly divided the tiny community. A local protest committee was established which waged a national campaign in support of Miss Cooke as well as instigating a boycott against the new sub-post office. In the meantime, the local Labour Party organised counter-demonstrations in support of Farrell which took on an unpleasant air of sectarianism. Miss Cooke was a Protestant, as were many of those who had rallied to her defence. Farrell painted himself as a poor Irish labourer being harassed by rack-renting landlords and the descendants of Yeomen and Tans.[95] This theme was reflected on the placards in evidence as a Labour Party demonstration, numbering around 100, made its way through Baltinglass on 5 January. The proclaimed 'DOWN WITH IMPERIALISM', 'ORDINARY PEOPLE ON THE MARCH', 'DID JAMES CONNOLLY DIE FOR CAPITALISTS WITH LOUD-SPEAKERS AGAINST LABOUR', and 'REMEMBER CONNOLLY AND SUPPORT EVERETT AND NORTON'. In case anyone had missed the point, the national organiser Paddy Bergin went further when he told the meeting which ended the demonstration that 'this was a fight really between the ordinary people and the hard core of Toryism and West Britonism which still remained in this country through the great charity of Irish revolutionaries who had freed this country'.[96]

Few, if any, were inclined to view the matter as anything other than a simple case of jobbery, and the sectarian overtones and the notion of treating a woman in such a shoddy fashion only made the matter worse. In Wicklow, the former Fine Gael deputy The O'Mahony resigned from his party,[97] Noel Hartnett resigned from Clann na Poblachta, and one branch of that party dissolved itself in protest at the government's corruption.[98] Meanwhile in the Dáil, the independent deputy Patrick Cogan withdrew his support for the government until the issue was resolved, while Fianna Fáil attacked the government for its misuse of power. With Everett refusing to budge, the government unwilling to move against him and opinion within the other government parties becoming increasingly antagonistic, the issue could well have spiralled out of control had it not been for Farrell's resignation as sub-postmaster at the end of December. By then the damage had been done. So much of the election campaign in 1948 had focused on Fianna Fáil's lack of fitness for government, but now Labour had proved that it was as capable of corruption and jobbery as any party, given half the chance.

'THEY SHOULDN'T BE ALLOWED DO THIS': THE MOTHER AND CHILD SCHEME

By 1951 the inter-party government had been in office three years. During this time, Labour had increased pensions benefits and overseen a much-needed housing drive, as well as seeing a number of significant pieces of legislation introduced with which it could be very pleased, including the establishment of the Industrial Development Authority in 1949 and the nationalisation of the railways into Coras Iompar Éireann. (The fact that these developments were overseen by a Fine Gael minister – Dan Morrissey – may have curtailed their potential as propaganda.) All in all, though, it was not much to show after three years. Still, as disgruntled Labour supporters were reminded repeatedly, it would all be worthwhile as soon as Norton's social welfare reforms were put in place. The saga of this legislation finally appeared to be nearing its end in April 1951 when Norton's bill was due its second reading. The timing could not have been worse. If the Social Welfare Bill had suffered a difficult conception, it was nothing compared to the tortuous gestation of what was popularly known as the Mother and Child scheme, a piece of legislation that would divide the country and effectively bring down the government.

No Irish government, as Joe Lee has observed, 'took much interest in health until the Second World War',[99] and it was not until the Emergency that the government began to take stock of the appalling levels of illness, particularly among the poorer sections of Irish society. Squalor and malnutrition were responsible for a dramatic rise in the numbers of children with rickets, and serious outbreaks of gastro-enteritis, the latter responsible for the deaths of 506 children in Dublin in 1941,[100] while the high levels of TB were also the source of grave concern. In 1946 two new departments were established, Health (which until now had been under the remit of the Department of Local Government and Health) and Social Welfare (an entirely new department) in an effort to bring their administration to a level more in line with other developed states. This reform was vital, but as in the case of William Norton's efforts in social welfare, often resisted by those who felt that the sphere of the state should not be increased. Centralised provision and compulsory treatment were at issue in Dr Conn Ward's Public Health Bill 1945. It was a wide-ranging piece of legislation designed to tackle every aspect of public health but it was most concerned with mother and child welfare and infectious diseases.[101] The provisions for mothers and children were sweeping: a free-for-all scheme, without means test, would be available to mothers and to children under 16 years, and administered by dispensary doctors and nurses, while compulsory school inspections would also be instituted.[102] When the bill reached committee stage in March and April 1946, a record 642 amendments were put down, of which almost 500 came from Fine Gael, compared with 25 from Labour. Fine Gael's opposition was based on the grounds that it violated Catholic social teaching because of its centralising tendency and its degree of compulsion, with Richard Mulcahy, John A. Costello and Patrick McGilligan among the most vocal opponents. In opposing the bill, McGilligan told the Dáil he was upholding the 'Christian tradition that there are individual rights which no State can take away'.[103]

In the end, though, the legislation had to be withdrawn and redrafted after the reorganisation of the relevant departments. By this stage Dr Jim Ryan had been appointed minister for health. When the new health bill was put before the Dáil, Fine Gael's response had become 'quite cordial', as John Whyte put it, with the baton of opposition having been taken up by James Dillon, who opposed the compulsory aspects of the legislation and argued the 'proposal infringed the natural rights of the parents'.[104] Dillon was joined in his opposition by the Irish Medical Association (IMA) which complained about patients' lack of choice of doctor and the loss of earnings doctors would face as a result of the scheme. Another significant body throwing its weight against the legislation was the Catholic hierarchy, which privately wrote to the government in October 1947 to warn that the mother and child provisions in the bill were 'without qualification . . . entirely and directly contrary to Catholic teaching on the rights of the family, the rights of the Church in education, the rights of the medical profession and of voluntary institutions'.[105] Soon after, James Dillon made a constitutional challenge to the Act on the grounds of its elements of compulsion, his legal team including Patrick McGilligan and John A. Costello.[106] This meant the legislation was stalled until the general election which followed a couple of months later,when the issue became the problem for the inter-party minister for health, Noël Browne.

The full extent of the inter-party government's pledges on health was contained in the seventh point of its ten-point programme, which promised 'immediate steps to provide facilities for the treatment of sufferers from tuberculosis'. Beyond this there was nothing. Still, it was an important issue, and one on which the inter-party government's Minster for Health was well equipped to deal. Noël Browne found himself nominated minister for health by his party leader Seán MacBride on his first day in Dáil Éireann. A political neophyte, having joined Clann na Poblachta only shortly before he stood in the 1948 election, Browne was a potent mixture of youthful idealism (he was only 32 years old when elected) and inexperience. His family had been ravaged by tuberculosis and he himself had been struck down by the disease several times.[107] As a doctor he had specialised in the treatment of TB, working in Newcastle sanatorium, County Kildare, and had developed a high public profile for his work in the area; indeed, it was because of his work and his reputation that Clann na Poblachta approached him to stand at the 1948 election. As a minister his energetic tackling of the tuberculosis problem attracted public acclaim, even if most of his successes were more the culmination of other factors than of Browne's personal endeavours. Browne came to tackle the problem at an auspicious time – Fianna Fáil had already passed legislation to deal with the issue, and it was largely up to Browne to put the last government's provisions into operation, not to mention the breakthrough in the treatment of TB using streptomycin at this time. The propitious timing of Browne's tenure as minister did not, however, hinder his development as a folk hero then or since. Browne may have been unversed in the ways of politics, but he was canny enough to publicise each and every advance made by his department for all it was worth. It was not by accident that Browne came to be seen as something of a latter-day St Patrick, who banished consumption from Ireland.

Browne's other priority once in office was to proceed with the implementation of the Health Act 1947. He reintroduced the scheme to cabinet in June 1948, but with two significant changes to the original proposals: the clauses providing for compulsory inspection and treatment were dropped in an effort to deal with the concerns of the bishops and Dillon; and there would be nominal charges for treatment in order to placate the medical profession. His amendments were sufficient to see the revised bill approved by the cabinet, apart from the proposed charges which were scrapped in the face of Labour opposition,[108] with Norton, according to Browne, roaring at him down the cabinet table, 'Yer not going to let the doctors walk on ye, Noël?' in the 'proletarian voice which he affected on such occasions'.[109] Browne had passed the first hurdle, but he now faced the doctors empty handed, and was yet to see if his removal of some of the Act's compulsory aspects were enough to satisfy the Church. It was almost a year and a half later, on 4 November 1949, that the cabinet approved the text of the revised Health Bill.[110] In this time Browne had singularly failed to assuage any of the difficulties which had been voiced by either the IMA or the Hierarchy, the minister refusing to meet with the former and choosing not to seek the support of the latter. However, while the doctors were quite open about their opposition to the legislation, the bishops kept their concerns to themselves.

Eventually, on 10 June 1950, the draft of the Mother and Child scheme was sent to the IMA and to the rest of the cabinet,[111] although it was not until October that the doctors sought an audience with the minister. When Browne met the doctors on 24 October they expressed their profound opposition to the lack of any means test in the scheme, objecting to a situation where those who were in a position to pay would be provided with a free service. Browne, however, was unyielding. Subsequently, on 23 November, when the IMA asked its members if they would agree 'to work a mother and child scheme which includes free treatment for those who could pay for themselves', 78 per cent of respondents (and only 54 per cent of members took part in this referendum[112]) replied in the negative.[113] The overwhelming opposition of IMA members alarmed Browne's cabinet colleagues, who were acutely aware that with Browne digging his heels in over the means test and the doctors doing likewise, a compromise looked unlikely. This state of affairs was naturally deemed unsatisfactory by the taoiseach and the tanáiste, who concluded between themselves that there might be a chance of agreement if Browne were sidelined. From December Costello, Norton and the Minister for Defence, Dr T. F. O'Higgins (a member of the IMA), took it upon themselves to engage in confidential talks with the doctors.[114] Browne was himself engaged in occasional negotiations with the IMA during January and February before announcing on 5 March, without any warning, that the IMA was engaging in delaying tactics, and so he was going to continue with the scheme regardless.[115]

The IMA had for a long time been the only real body of opposition to the scheme, but by October 1950, in what John Horgan described as 'what now looks suspiciously like a pincer movement', the Catholic bishops entered the fray. On 10 October, the Bishops wrote to the taoiseach expressing their opposition to the Mother and Child scheme, as well as to other aspects of Browne's bill. The following day, Browne travelled to Archbishop's house in Drumcondra to meet with McQuaid, Michael Browne of Galway and James Staunton, Bishop of Ferns,[116] where he was read the letter sent by the bishops to the taoiseach, in which they outlined their objections to the scheme. Their problems were not insubstantial. For one thing, the Church was one of the main service providers in the area of medicine, being responsible for the running of most hospitals in the state and as such the scheme was thus regarded by the Church as an unwelcome intrusion by the state into the Church's sphere of influence. The issue of health education was also regarded with suspicion, with the possibility that it could lead to the dissemination of information about birth control to women. But the issue which seems to have exercised the greatest concern for the bishops was the political implications of the scheme's enactment. In 1948 John Charles McQuaid had warned that 'Atheistic communism' would attack the Church in Ireland, disguising its 'aims under the mask of Socialism';[117] now as McQuaid saw it, this scheme presented exactly the kind of showdown that the left had sought. After McQuaid had read the bishops' letter to Browne, the minister sought to put their minds at ease by explaining that he had dealt with the compulsory aspects with which they had taken issue. From the bishops' point of view, however, Browne was merely arguing the toss. This meant that Browne left the meeting thinking he had pacified the hierarchy, when he had left them seething, a fact of which John A. Costello was made quite aware when he paid a visit to McQuaid the next day.[118] From this point on, the bishops were kept fully briefed by Costello on the progress of negotiations on the legislation and its progress generally.

Costello had effectively told the bishops that the scheme being promoted by Browne was not government policy, and would not be enacted in the form that it stood and so it was with some concern that the bishops (not to mention the doctors) noted Browne's announcement on 6 March 1951, that the Mother and Child scheme was to go ahead as was. Naturally taken aback by this turn of events, McQuaid wrote to Noël Browne reiterating the hierarchy's objections to the scheme, as he had laid out to the minister at their meeting some five months earlier, and concluded by stating that he was copying this letter to the taoiseach. Browne decided there was nothing to the letter, and despite Norton urging him to act on it, failed to reply. Costello, on the other hand, responded at once.[119] On the same day Browne found himself in receipt of McQuaid's letter, Seán MacBride organised a 'peace conference' between himself, Browne and Norton. Norton (at the behest of the taoiseach and MacBride) was the principal figure in the effort to reach a compromise, but his final suggestion that the scheme would apply only to households with an income of less than £1,000 was rejected by Browne.[120] In the face of opposition he remained obdurately attached to the free for all scheme. Norton, on the other hand, was convinced that a watered-down scheme was better than none. He had, lest we forget, been responsible for getting Browne to remove the proposed fees in the original proposals in 1948, but he was a pragmatist first and foremost, and was appalled that the scheme might falter for the sake of Browne's dogmatic attachment to free for all provision. In his eyes, working-class people would be deprived of health care for the sake of 'fur coated ladies in Foxrock', and Browne was making 'a fetish out of a phrase'.[121]

A fortnight after McQuaid had written to Browne, Norton finally persuaded him to contact the Archbishop,[122] and a meeting between the two men took place on Holy Thursday, 22 March, at which an apparently contrite

Browne was carpeted by McQuaid. Browne spent much of the following week scouting the country for members of the hierarchy to visit, but his belated charm offensive was too little, too late.[123] In fact, with Browne involved, there was never going to be a happy conclusion to this affair. Browne's attachment to free for all provision was doctrinaire, as was the bishop's opposition. The scheme, as promoted by Browne, was in the eyes of McQuaid not merely the not-so-thin end of the socialist wedge, but more accurately a Trojan horse for communism. As McQuaid put it:

> If we reject this particular scheme we shall have paused the country from advancing a long way towards *socialistic* welfare. In particular, we shall have checked the efforts of Leftist Labour elements, which are approaching the point of publicly ordering the Church to stand out of social life and confine herself to what they think is the Church's proper sphere.[124]

The Hierarchy held a meeting on 4 April during which it considered Browne's response to the bishops' letter which he had articulated to McQuaid at their meeting of 22 March. The following evening, McQuaid called on the taoiseach to convey the bishops' opinion that the particular scheme for a Mother and Child health service proposed by the minister for health was opposed to Catholic social teaching. During their conversation, Costello informed McQuaid that Labour was beginning to become 'worked up to a defence of the scheme' to the point where he had had to 'deal very firmly with misconceptions of several Labour people, including Mr Seán Dunne TD' during the course of an inter-party meeting. McQuaid was also informed that there had been similar scenes at a meeting of the PLP, but that the Chairman, William Davin, had managed to counter a vote in favour of the scheme.[125] According to Costello, Noël Browne had used Noel Hartnett and Owen Sheehy Skeffington ('both Trinity College men') to work up the Labour people, while Louie Bennett ('Protestant') had been working on the Irish Women Workers. Norton, however, 'was going to put things right with Labour' and would be the one to explain the bishops' letter to the party.[126] The following day, Costello read the bishops' letter to a meeting of the government, and, having concluded, looked down the cabinet table towards Browne and stated 'This must mean the end of the mother and child scheme'. There was solemn nodding by all assembled. Browne, perhaps having seen too many courtroom dramas, insisted on making each minister state one by one whether he concurred with the taoiseach's conclusion. All answered in the affirmative, Browne recalled, with the exception of Michael Keyes, who nodded his agreement with the taoiseach, but opined as he did so, 'they shouldn't be allowed to do this'.[127] The cabinet had made its decision and the following day a letter was despatched by the government expressing the order that the existing scheme 'should not be further pursued,' and that an alternative scheme should be drawn up which was not in contravention of Catholic Social Teaching.[128] The government having made its pronouncement on the issue, Norton set about extinguishing any rebellion in his own party, and put things right he did. Speaking to Owen Sheehy Skeffington some days before Browne was compelled to resign, Roddy Connolly remarked that it would be unthinkable for the party to turn against the minister, adding 'If Browne goes, I go,' but when Skeffington asked Connolly, some days later, what had happened, he was informed that 'there had been a "bit of a barney" with Norton . . . and there would have been "difficulties" in supporting Browne'.[129] And, as far as the Parliamentary Labour Party was concerned, that was the end of the matter.

With Labour effectively silenced, Congress now became involved. As rumours began to circulate that as Browne was threatening resignation the scheme as a whole might be pulled, the National Executive sent a deputation to the minister on 8 April to try and hammer out a compromise scheme based on insurance.[130] There was a further meeting between Jim Larkin and Congress General Secretary Ruadhraí Roberts with Norton on the issue two days later.[133] Browne seemed amenable to the suggestions from Congress, but his fellow ministers could take no more and on 10 April Seán MacBride requested his resignation. Browne obliged but he did not go quietly. Though he lacked most of the attributes of the natural politician, Browne was, nevertheless an adept self-publicist. By way of an apologia, he decided upon publishing the correspondence on the issue which had taken place between the government and the bishops; indeed when the letters appeared in the *Irish Times* there was uproar.[132] The controversy filled the press, with most of the sentiments expressed profoundly inimical to the government, and sometimes to the hierarchy. Huge public meetings were held, such as one held by the Irish Housewives Association in the Mansion House in early May, which kept the issue in the public eye. McQuaid was concerned at this, but not unduly, believing the campaign for the scheme to be 'inspired' by communists rather than the outcry of appalled members of the faithful.[131] It is impossible accurately to gauge public opinion on this question more than half a century later, but on balance its does seem that in this case most people felt that the bishops were wrong and had over stepped the mark. As Tom Garvin has observed, 'the incident generated a considerable *sotto voce* resentment in middle class and working class circles. A common remark of the period was "this time the bishops have gone too far."'[134]

The whole business certainly left Labour looking very shabby indeed. Many Labour members felt badly let down by the party's failure to support

Browne and his no-means-test scheme, and the issue became an open bone of contention between the Dublin left in particular, and the leadership for years to come. In addition, the behaviour of Norton during the episode created tension between the party leadership and the ITUC.[135] It made health the cornerstone of the left's agenda and, in so doing, it highlighted the ideological distance between most Labour Party members and Fine Gael. In opposition and later in the second inter-party government the two parties continued to be on opposing sides over health legislation. David McCullagh has noted that the crisis demonstrated the limitations on minority parties in a coalition: all parties except Fine Gael were in favour of the Mother and Child Scheme, but opposition by the doctors and the hierarchy, allowed that party to frustrate the plans for its introduction.[136] Finally, and perhaps most importantly, it added further to the public perception that Labour was a conservative party. The leadership's success in establishing a united front (with the exception of the Dublin Constituency Council) over the crisis meant that most people took it for granted that Labour supported doctors and bishops over the mothers and children of the workers it purported to represent. That Norton had been the most active in trying to keep the scheme afloat counted for little. In the end, not least because of Browne's adroit propaganda, it looked as though he had sold out to Fine Gael, the doctors and the priests. It was the foremost example of how Norton's 'fixing' could damage his own party, for as one commentator remarked soon after, 'the direction [the government] were going in was not always Labour's direction and the Labour Party paid the price of Norton's success'.[137]

THE BEGINNING OF THE END

Browne, and others, withdrew their support for the government, leaving its majority perilously slim. The administration continued for another month, but in the face of an incipient revolt by some of the independent farming deputies over the price of milk, Costello eventually called it a day. The government's last budget was introduced on 2 May, and the following day the taoiseach announced that the Dáil would be dissolved at the weekend and that polling would take place on 30 May.[138] Now, facing the electorate after three years in office, what had Labour to show for itself? Perhaps Labour's most important achievement during this time had been purely political, since the two Labour factions' participation in the government facilitated an end to the split. There had been outstanding progress in house building under T. J. Murphy and subsequently Michael Keyes, but Labour's other two ministers had been less successful. James Everett was an assiduous local politician, but had done little of note as a minister, apart from turn the name of Baltinglass into a by-word for political jobbery. Norton had proved an adept tánaiste but a less successful minister, his Social Welfare Bill impeded by cabinet colleagues for two whole years before it fell at the last hurdle. Finally, though there were some incremental benefits such as the half-day holiday for agricultural workers and increased wages for road workers,[139] there were no comparable improvements for urban, industrial workers (the very people who had most to gain from the Social Security Bill). Ultimately, there was 'no decisive measure' which could be pointed to as a success for the party.[140] This was the conclusion of the short-lived Labour monthly *Impact* (whose editorial board and contributors were all prominent members of the Labour left), which argued that Labour had done its very best to agitate for its legislation. 'True, not a great deal was achieved', it stated baldly, but 'the results merely indicate the actual power given to the party and no more could have been expected.' Its advice for the general election was simple – go as an independent party and blame Fine Gael for every unfulfilled promise. 'It would be a great mistake indeed for Labour to enter the campaign under the "inter-party umbrella". . . we must show that we have clean hands'.[141]

Norton had other ideas, however. In the administration's early days, he had promised that Labour would contest the next general election as a free agent,[142] but when the time came he put his signature on the inter-party manifesto, much to the shock and disappointment of many Labour members.[143] Labour's notes for speakers during the campaign extolled the virtues of inter-party government, declaring single-party government to be 'purely a British concept'.[144] This was the salient issue in the campaign: you could vote for single party government (Fianna Fáil) or for the rest. Jim Larkin in Dublin was alone in emphasising that 'the Labour Party entered the last stage of the election campaign as it had begun it – an independent party', adding that it was 'not committed to any other party, or parties or any combination of parties',[145] a statement completely at odds with the view of his party leader.

It was a lacklustre campaign, and though crowds turned out for public meetings, there was none of the usual heckling.[146] The number of candidates contesting the election fell to 295, which was high compared with most previous contests, but was over 100 fewer than in 1948. Clann na Poblachta's collapse accounts for much of the difference, putting up almost 70 fewer candidates this time around. Labour's campaign was summed up by one observer as simply 'miserable'.[147] Norton, as usual, confined his campaign to his own constituency, and overall it was said of the party that 'lack of funds and inspirational leadership, or indeed common tactical competency were notable throughout the country'.[148] It had not gone into the campaign all guns blazing by any means, and fielded only 37 candidates, which were twenty

fewer than Labour and National Labour combined at the previous poll.[149] Its
first preference vote held up for the most part, but by the time the counts were
complete four of the outgoing deputies had lost their seats. Two of these were
rural-based deputies: James Pattison's defeat in Kilkenny was unexpected, as
he was considered 'reasonably safe', but that of Roddy Connolly in Louth was
much more predictable.[150] Neither was there good news in Dublin. Former
Lord Mayor Martin O'Sullivan surprised party observers by losing his seat in
Dublin North Central,[151] while Labour's newest deputy, Dr J. P. Brennan,
who had defected from Clann na Poblachta during the government's final
days, also failed to hold Dun Laoghaire–Rathdown. In fact, the only Labour
candidate returned in Dublin city was Jim Larkin in South Central, leading
one commentator to remark that 'the name of Larkin alone' stood between
the Labour Party and 'electoral extinction' in Dublin.[152] Furthermore,
Labour's losses in the capital were put in stark relief by the success of the three
Brownite independents, consisting of Browne himself, Peadar Cowan, and
Michael ffrench O'Carroll.

Inter-party transfers meant that although Fianna Fáil's vote increased by
almost five per cent this resulted in only a single extra seat, bringing it to 69
deputies. There were mixed blessings for Labour's erstwhile partners. Clann
na Poblachta collapsed to two deputies, Clann na Talmhan's first preference
halved, and only Fine Gael came out of the election stronger than it had gone
in, returning with 40 seats, compared with 31 the last time around. This merely
bolstered the view that only the largest party could benefit from coalition, or
as the *Sunday Press* later remarked mischievously, each minor party that had
joined the inter-party government had 'vanished, leaving Fine Gael fattened
by a blood transfusion fatal to the donor'.[153]

Still, 74 was the magic number, and the figures did not add up to a
majority on either side. The new Dáil would meet on 13 June, which gave the
parties a little under two weeks to find the deputies to make a majority, one
way or another. On 3 June Seán MacBride suggested the formation of an
(almost) national government consisting of Fianna Fáil, Fine Gael, Labour
and Clann na Talmhan, which was never a likely scenario but, significantly,
he signalled that his party (all two deputies) would not participate in another
administration.[154] Nevertheless, it looked to many as though the inter-party
grouping, in some shape or form, would most likely form the next government.[155] Labour put its hat officially in the ring on 7 June, when its 16 deputies
held a joint meeting with the AC. It was agreed that Labour would
participate in a new inter-party administration, provided that there was an
agreed programme which would prioritise Labour's policies, and that Labour
would have at least as many ministries as it had held in the outgoing government.[156] Fianna Fáil was not, however, going to let the coalition steal a march

on it, and set about wooing some of the independent deputies. Of the 14 independents in the new Dáil, five had confirmed their support for the coalition, and three others seemed likely, leaving six unaligned.[157] The six comprised four Brownites (Browne, Cowan, ffrench O'Carroll and former Clann na Poblachta deputy Jack McQuillan) and two others. In the case of the four Brownites, at least, it seemed that a government featuring Fine Gael was unlikely to gain their support. Fianna Fáil approached Noël Browne to assure him that if it was elected to office the health services would be reformed.[158] In the meantime, Michael ffrench O'Carroll, who had already decided to support Fianna Fáil, was being courted by the coalition. He was taken to a rendezvous at Costello's residence in Leeson Park where Norton tried to convince him of the virtues of a compromise health scheme based on social insurance (no doubt one very similar to that advocated by the ITUC during the crisis). Ffrench O'Carroll remained unimpressed, however,[159] and left the meeting determined to support Fianna Fáil.

The first business before the fourteenth Dáil when it met on 13 June was the election of a new Ceann Comhairle. Frank Fahey, the Fianna Fáil deputy who had held the post for almost two decades, had indicated his unwillingness to serve again. Paddy Hogan, a Labour deputy from Clare, who had been Leas Ceann Comhairle for many years, was unanimously elected in his stead, which effectively handed Fianna Fáil two precious votes.[160] When it came to the taoiseach's vote, Richard Mulcahy spoke first, nominating Costello, who was then seconded by Norton in an unusually brief and succinct speech.[161] Lemass followed, nominating de Valera. The ensuing speeches were acrimonious, and often personally abusive, with accusations of jobbery flying across the floor of the house. The most absurd exchange, however, was that prompted by the Wicklow deputy Patrick Cogan's claim that he was supporting de Valera as taoiseach because the holder of that post 'must not be hampered by any group who may have affiliations with those who seek to weaken the defences of this nation [and] the Minister for Posts and Telegraphs on a number of occasions . . . proved beyond all shadow of a doubt that the Labour Party is closely associated with international Communism'.[162] Naturally, this provoked uproar on the inter-party benches, but Seán Keane, Labour's deputy in Cork North East, could not let such a slur pass without comment. Keane began to recount how 'as one of the rookies of the Irish Labour Party, on the 6th or 7th January, 1937, I was in charge of 250 men to go out to fight with General Franco in Spain . . .'.[163] Before he could continue any further with his story (which, according to contemporary reports, ended in ignominy after the ship on which Keane and his colleagues were to sail failed to arrive in Cork harbour[164]), he was stopped dead in his tracks by his party colleague, the new Ceann Comhairle, who advised Keane to stick to the matter in hand of electing a taoiseach. [165] After several lengthy speeches, the question was finally put, and John A. Costello was rejected as taoiseach by 74 votes against to 72 votes for. De Valera's nomination was then put to the vote, receiving 74 votes in favour and 69 against. With that, Fianna Fáil found itself back in office after its three-year hiatus, and Labour returned to the backbenches.

SIX

RETURN TO THE SIDELINES
1951–4

—

Labour's return to the backbenches was not an easy transition. Norton and his colleagues were incensed by the government's defeat at the hands of the independents (in much the same way as Fianna Fáil had felt towards National Labour three years earlier). Labour's annual report referred to the 'usurping of office by the Fianna Fáil party with the aid of certain disgruntled "independents"', while the electorate was criticised for its 'thoughtless' casting of votes.[1] Not everyone within Labour was so belligerent. The view on the left was that the party had brought defeat on itself. An editorial in *Impact* called for a special conference to be summoned 'so that future Labour Party policy be determined and the tactics to be used for the advancement of the working people devised without delay. Unless this is done, and done at once, then clearly Labour's leaders must admit that they have failed lamentably in the job they were appointed to do.'[2] But where the left felt Labour's problems lay in its programme, the leadership was only prepared to take responsibility for Labour's losses insofar as it acknowledged that the party was poorly organised, a fact which had become evident in the course of the campaign,[3] and so the AC established a special reorganising committee to investigate the state of party organisation around the country.[4] This question of whether logistics or policy was to blame for losing power was not unique to the Irish Labour Party. Writing a few years later, Jim Larkin's London-based colleague, Jim Prendergast, outlined the leftist thesis, arguing that it was 'the lack of a "distinctive" radical philosophy, a set of ideals', that provided 'the key to the dilemma of Irish (and British) Labour'. Looking at the situation in Britain, he complained about the British Labour Party's retreat from socialism and criticised the belief on the part of the Labour right that lack of organisation had caused the party's failure. The 'slick boys' were, he said,

holding inquests galore into the 'organisation' of the Party. There it is, they exclaim, the Tories had a better organisation machine than we had. All that is needed is a little drop of oil here, a few full time agents there, a few pounds more from the trade unions, and we'll sweep the boards. Of course, all this ignores the point that the 'machines' were much the same in 1945 – but the electorate voted for a set of men who held aloft the 'vision splendid' of socialism and plenty'.[5]

Although the Irish electorate had never voted for the 'vision splendid of socialism and plenty', the point could equally have been made about the situation here. Part of the reason organisation in some areas was poor – in Dublin in particular – was because people were not attracted to Labour in the first place or had become disillusioned and had left. Dublin members attributed the poor state of organisation there to, among other things, alienation from the leadership and the party's association with Fine Gael during the inter-party government.[6]

Parliamentary co-operation between the former government partners effectively ceased after the election. Revived by its spell in office and the electoral successes which followed, Fine Gael returned to the Dáil an energetic opposition party. Labour, on the other hand, seemed crushed. It went into something of a state of shock, and by Christmas was being described as 'more than usually asleep'.[7] Much of this apathy had its roots in a feeling of hopelessness. Tom Johnson mulled over the situation in November 1951, after Labour's defeat in the British general election. Although optimistic that most of the Attlee government's advances would be retained by Churchill, he was less sanguine about the situation closer to home. 'I wish I were as happy about Labour policies and practice here', he complained, 'but I can't see light'.[8] Johnson was anxious to play a part in Labour's regeneration, as he told John de Courcy Ireland, but the question was how. He wrote that he was

> hankering after some clue or other regarding the future of the Labour Movement in Ireland and to know whether or not I, personally, can do anything . . . to turn things in the right direction? At present I feel as in a fog. I can't see a way clear . . . but the problem I can't solve for myself is how to give practical application to the [socialist] theories in *this country*, in *present circumstances*, with the *human material available*.[9]

Johnson's fatalism about the 'human material available' was shared by Peggy Rushton. Rushton was trying to establish a 'Brains Trust' similar to the one organised by the British Labour Party, but lamented that 'the difficulty of course is to discover brains in the Labour Party'.[10]

In April 1952, Labour held its first conference since 1950, its first since the inter-party government's defeat. For the Labour left it provided an opportunity to hold the leadership to account for its behaviour in office, and on the Mother and Child scheme in particular. (On the latter issue, Sheila Greene, former editor of the *Irish People* and her partner Christy Ferguson, Larkin's right-hand man in the WUI,[11] had been using their pseudonymous 'Aknefton' column in the *Irish Times* to stir trouble for Norton.[12]) On its second day, conference had before it a resolution from the Clontarf branch which reaffirmed Labour's independence, and declared that 'it shall not enter into coalition or alliance with any other party without first obtaining the consent of a special national conference convened for this purpose'.[13] Those supporting the motion complained that only Fine Gael had benefited from the experience, while Labour's vote had declined across the board, that Labour had been 'swamped' and had 'lost its identity in coalition' and had sown 'the seeds of its own destruction'. One Derry delegate argued that the majority of working-class votes which were held by Fianna Fáil would be out of bounds to Labour while it was in an alliance with Fine Gael. Crucially, the resolution received the support of Jim Larkin, who had been one of the most important forces for bringing Labour into the government in the first place. Though he stopped short of condemning Labour's association with Fine Gael, he did suggest that the party's behaviour had been naïve. Larkin was pragmatic, arguing that the days of single-party government were over, which meant Labour had to decide whether it would remain in perpetual opposition or 'utilise such political representation as was given to them to secure concrete positive gains'. Labour, he said, 'could have got a great deal more out of the inter-party government' but had 'failed to take advantage of their own strength and power'. In one telling phrase he observed: 'we were under certain obligations which were translated at certain times into *undue loyalty* to the inter-party government'.[14] In contrast, Fine Gael had 'utilised every opportunity that came, not only in the open light of day but in the dark of night' – next time Labour would know better. The party's participation in the government had been a calculated risk, he said, and that could come out of government weaker than when it went in was no surprise. Thus Larkin supported the right of the party as a whole to decide on the question of coalition but without coming out against such a move again in the future. Norton was outraged by this attempt to diminish the AC's right to rule and defended Labour's right to coalesce, declaring he had 'never been prouder to be associated with the Labour Party than for the last two years.' Delegates remained unconvinced by his argument that 'if you elect an Administrative Council you should trust them',[15] however, and the motion was carried by 47 votes to 31. It was a remarkable result, establishing a 'curious precedent', as the *Leader* put it, with the party leaders having been 'deprived of the power to act as plenipotentiaries in negotiations with allied parties' in what amounted to a virtual vote of no confidence.[16] It was, said the *Irish Times*, a 'tribute to the impermeability of the Labour leaders that they did not resign at once', but that they had disregarded the moves because they had originated in the Party's 'intellectual' fringe.[17]

Further hostility followed when some delegates (the most vocal being Dubliners and IWWU[18]) took issue with the Annual Report's account of the Mother and Child scheme crisis which placed the full blame for the debacle on Browne's shoulders. A furious William Davin rounded on the critics, and accused one delegate of being part of a 'Dr Browne ginger-group' within the party. His opponent denied the accusation, explaining he had 'no interest in Dr Browne except that he made a stand on an issue on which I felt the Labour leaders should have made a stand'. Conference had provided Labour's leaders with the opportunity to assuage the party's discontented elements, to find common cause and re-group after its general election losses, but no effort was made to this end. Instead, conference ended in rancour and merely highlighted divisions, in particular those between the Dublin element within the party and the PLP, with no attempt at conciliation by either side, or any sign of a *via media*. The *Irish Times* conclusion was damning: 'apart from the more obvious dissensions, there were innumerable indications that the Party has no coherent attitude to present day problems, let alone in policy'.[19] Describing the speeches from the platform as 'lamentable' and the proceedings as 'chaotic', the editorial concluded that events could 'only confirm the opinion that Labour, as a parliamentary group, has lost touch with Labour as a social force'. The occasion in Louie Bennett's eyes was 'a wash-out, important matters were shelved and we were cornered by the opportunistic politicians' cliques'. Nevertheless, there was one success for the rank and file, as Bennett gleefully noted, 'We did at least get a spoke in the wheel of another inter-party government.'[20]

'The confusion and lethargy among the ordinary rank and file could not have been dispelled by the discourses of the week-end', remarked the *Irish Times*,[21] but the problem as the leadership saw it was that the rank and file were not nearly lethargic enough. Following the conference, the AC established a sub-committee ostensibly to enquire into organisation in Dublin and advise on how it might be improved, although the actual reason was more ominous. There were two issues at play. First of all, the party leadership had not taken kindly to criticism during the last conference and were disinclined to suffer another annual gathering of inimical motions. Secondly, now that the party was to be compelled to hold a special conference to approve going into coalition, entry into government was now dependent on the AC/PLP securing a majority of members. Since Labour's performance in the inter-party government had engendered strong anti-coalitionist tendencies in the Dublin branches, there was only one thing for it: there ought to be fewer branches in Dublin. The sub-committee was appointed in June 1952, and consisted of three rural deputies, Brendan Corish, William Davin and James Hickey, with the organiser Paddy Bergin as secretary. It reported a general acknowledgment that most branches in Dublin had an active membership of ten or fewer, the same branches being responsible for 'most contentious proposals' at conferences. 'It was admitted and generally agreed', according to the sub-committee's report, that 'minimum membership for affiliation *should* be 20' (this despite there being no stipulated lower limit to the size of a branch in the party's constitution), and so the committee recommended that a minimum membership of 20 for a branch to qualify for affiliation be established, with branches with fewer than 20 members to be merged with others in the same constituency.[22] Unquestionably, the organisation in Dublin was in dire need of repair, but what is patently clear is that the capital's reorganisation was not undertaken to make its branches more efficient but to diminish its presence at conference, not only in terms of 'contentious proposals' but also of the coalition issue when it next arose. The new scheme was to come into being in 1953, with the national organiser authorised to ensure the adoption of the report's recommendations.

MAC THE KNIFE

On 2 April 1952, the Minister for Finance, Seán MacEntee, introduced Fianna Fáil's first budget since returning to power nearly a year earlier. With what soon became known as the 'famine budget', MacEntee tried to tackle a worsening balance of payments deficit by abolishing and reducing food subsidies, as well as increasing duties on tobacco, alcohol and petrol. Labour, naturally, had a field day. It went on the attack in the Dáil and a public meeting held two days after the budget saw thousands gather outside the GPO in Dublin in protest. It was the largest meeting of its kind for some time, but its success was marred by the violent clashes which broke out afterwards. Around 70 people were injured and several arrests were made.[23] At least one publication blamed the violence on the work of Marxists and fellow travellers,[24] while in the Dáil, government deputies made great play of the role played by Labour on the day in inciting the riot with inflammatory speeches,[25] prompting angry demands by Labour deputies that these accusations be withdrawn. Typically, Labour's attempt to go on the attack ended in its going on the defensive.

MacEntee's budget had a catastrophic effect on Fianna Fáil's popularity, which the opposition parties were eager to exploit, but doing so effectively proved difficult. The first by-elections of the fourteenth Dáil were taking place in June 1952 in Limerick, Waterford and Mayo. Ignoring Mayo, where it had no organisation and negligible popular support,[26] Labour contested the Limerick and Waterford to show itself as 'a separate and distinct party', Tom Kyne explained.[27] In fact, far from wanting to demonstrate its independence,

Labour, along with the leaders of the other opposition parties, had wanted to put forward an anti-budget candidate but were prevented from doing so by opposition from local activists from the various parties,[28] proving the breach between the grassroots and leadership on inter-party co-operation was by no means unique to Labour. Nevertheless, the high chance that an agreed candidate would be a member of Fine Gael settled the matter.[29] During this time, there was no hard and fast rule about by-elections, whether they should be contested or the extent of an inter-party line. For instance, when Labour absented itself from a by-election in Dublin North West in November 1952 after a disagreement between the local party and head office over the selection of the candidate, head office urged its supporters to cast their votes against the government, but stressed that it had made no agreements with any of the other parties.

Labour's leaders were anxious to put the question of co-operation on a firmer footing and at the party's annual conference in April 1953, they managed something of a coup in this regard when delegates approved a PLP and AC motion recommending that the party would 'co-operate with another political party or parties in the formation of a government committed to an agreed programme of economic and social measures in broad conformity with Labour Party policy'. This meant that the leadership had at least regained the authority to negotiate a coalition programme without the permission of a special conference, although any decisions made in relation to joining an inter-party government would have to be subsequently approved. The motion did not, however, restore to the party's leaders the status they had enjoyed in 1948 when no consultation with the rank and file was necessary before going into a coalition. Nevertheless it was a significant victory over the left which had sought to tie the leadership's hands on this matter. However, as the *Irish Times* observed, while conference had faced up to the question of Labour joining a new coalition, it had failed to do anything to prepare itself to be an effective government partner. It was 'trying to combine two diverse elements, town and country, into a political unit':

> [but its] preoccupation with the views of the country constituencies, who make up the bulk of the parliamentary party, has led to a decline of Labour's power in Dublin, where normally its influence might expect to be more powerful. There were few signs at this year's conference that the problem will be tackled seriously. Until the Labour Party finds a way to recapture the support of the urban worker, even to the limited extent of 1943, Labour deputies will have to reconcile themselves indefinitely to playing second fiddle to Fine Gael, whether in Government or in opposition.[30]

Indeed, as one letter writer to the *Irish Times* put it:

> The so-called split in the British Labour Party fades into insignificance when
> compared with the divergent views possessed by the two wings of the Irish Labour
> Party, which has never held more than twenty two seats in the Dáil, because it has
> so consistently run with the hare and hunted with the hounds that it could receive
> no general support.[31]

SINGLE-ISSUE CAMPAIGNS

Labour's campaign against the 1952 budget was the first of a number of similar
efforts. Labour associated itself with the Dublin Unemployed Action Group
which began organising street protests in Dublin city centre in the summer of
1953.[32] It was also actively involved in the Lower Prices Council. The reduction
of prices and the restoration of the abolished food subsidies came to dominate
Labour's agenda to the exclusion of any other issue, not least because they
were popular among the public, raised no opposition from the clergy and were
backed by left and right within the party. The benefits of using the prices issue
were outlined by Peggy Rushton, who was a member of the AC at this time:

> the best thing that can be done at the moment is to get everyone . . . and parti-
> cularly Trade Unionists and Housewives, aware of the sharp connection between
> the rising cost of living, and war preparations . . . I am trying to get myself on the
> Lower Prices Council and Donal Nevin and I have been talking of getting public
> meetings going under the LPC auspices . . . it is quite hopeless to start them under
> the auspices of the Labour Party, as one is tied at every turn.[33]

The summer of 1953 also saw two by-elections, one in East Cork following
the death of the Labour deputy (and erstwhile General Franco-phile) Seán
Keane, and one in Wicklow following the death of a Fianna Fáil deputy there.
Labour contested both seats, with Seán Keane junior attempting to take up
his father's mantle in East Cork, and put in a vigorous campaign. It took
almost the same number of first preferences as in the last general election in
Cork, but was hugely outpolled by both Fianna Fáil and Fine Gael, and lost
the seat to Fine Gael, which also won in Wicklow. Both Fine Gael successes
were attributed to 'clever campaigning' which had resulted in its receiving
high levels of second preferences from Labour voters.[34] Still, the loss of a
Labour seat seemed indicative of how the party had lost its way in recent
years. An *Irish Times* editorial was scathing, remarking, 'Labour has no policy;
it seems to teeter between this expedient and that. One day its leaders pretend

to be socialists, the next to be dyed-in-the-wool Roman Catholics, prating Papal Encyclicals which they plainly do not understand.'[35]

This portrayal of Labour as schizoid and disingenuous is unfair and inaccurate; it was true that the party was sending out mixed messages, but they were not coming from the same people. To say that anyone in the party ever 'pretended to be a socialist' is also quite false. Those socialists in the party endeavoured to promote their progressive agenda without ever mentioning the word 'socialism' although that was often what they meant, ever conscious that the use of the word would create more trouble than it was worth.[36] While red smears against Labour had by and large abated since the party reunified in 1950, there were enough zealous anti-communists around to make sure that the party remained on its guard. Only a year earlier the Irish Housewives' Association had had to close its books to new members after it had begun to be infiltrated by Catholic Actionists, while a grocery shop run by a co-operative society, some of whose members had joined the Irish Workers' League, had been closed down following a church-controlled boycott.[37] Furthermore, the *Standard* began to get up to its old tricks again, after two former members of the Dublin Unemployed Movement went to the paper with tales of Workers' League involvement, leading to headlines along the lines of 'REDS EXPLOIT DUBLIN'S UNEMPLOYED'.[38] A great deal of suspicion remained, and it was noted at the time of the Cork by-election that even among Labour *members* there were victims of a 'bomb under the bed mentality'.[39] It was less that the anti-communist hysteria had abated than that it was no longer directed at Labour and those on the left were acutely conscious that it would take very little for it to become the subject of a red scare once more. On the other hand, it was true that the prating of encyclicals was a favoured pursuit of quite a number on the right, and that the extent to which they were understood properly was, overall, slight.

In October, Noël Browne, Michael ffrench O'Carroll and Patrick Cogan gave up their independent status and joined Fianna Fáil. Eighteen months earlier, there had been speculation that Browne might join Labour[40] but this was never a realistic prospect in light of the antipathy felt towards him by senior members of the PLP, and not least William Norton.[41] After his application (which was not made public) had been rejected,[42] Browne made an abortive attempt at establishing a new left-wing party[43] before finally throwing his lot in with Fianna Fáil. For those outside Labour, Browne's joining Fianna Fáil was taken as further evidence of the party's lack of leftist credentials.[44] The Labour Party in Dublin issued a statement accusing him (although not by name) of having 'sadly disappointed' the 'many honest and sincere men and women' who had 'relied on the good intentions and integrity of particular individuals'. The statement's purpose was to dissuade Browne's supporters from following him into Fianna Fáil and urged 'all progressive elements and especially trades unionists to examine their position in the light of recent events and recognise that the way forward for our people lies in a strong Labour Party pursuing an independent policy'. This was an implicit admission that Labour's current image might not make it a particularly attractive party to join but that could change given an influx of new blood:

> The Labour Party is a party with a democratic constitution and structure. Its policy is not laid down by any person, however exalted or by a caucus of individuals but by the membership through the medium of the annual delegate conference. Any shortcomings or deficiencies in party policy, therefore, are open to correction and change by the membership.[45]

The Dublin branches' insistence on Labour's independence was very much in evidence, and Fine Gael was condemned as having the same 'bankruptcy of policy' as Fianna Fáil. Later, it was stated that

> Notwithstanding the misrepresentation of interested politicians, the Labour Party is, of course, a completely independent party. It has no links or ties with any other party or group of parties. It pursues its own policy and programme independently and without reference to any other party.

It was obvious that in spite of the leadership's endeavours to convince the membership of the advantages of co-operation, the Dublin branches remained unenthusiastic about such a prospect.[46]

1954 GENERAL ELECTION

March 1954 saw Fine Gael win two by-elections in Louth and Cork city. The results did nothing to damage the government's majority, but de Valera decided to call an election nonetheless. Labour had begun its electoral preparations the previous June and was well set when the dissolution was announced. Within days of the campaign opening Labour issued a statement reiterating the 1953 conference decision that the party would participate in an inter-party government which was committed to a programme 'in broad conformity' with Labour policy.[47] Speeches by prominent deputies such as Norton and Brendan Corish also made it plain that the party's preference was for another coalition.[48] The situation in Dublin, however, was quite different. There, speakers stressed that Labour was an independent party free from any commitments of 'collaboration'.[49] When, on the eve of his 86th birthday, veteran Labour leader Tom Johnson addressed a meeting of the Dun Laoghaire branch, it was to remind those present that Labour needed to be supported as an independent party,[50] and there was a similar message when the party's Dublin Regional Council published the first edition of its monthly newspaper, *Labour*, in April 1954. But the most vocal adherent of independence was Jim Larkin who continually stressed that his party sought support for Labour *qua* Labour and not as part of any would-be coalition. As he told one meeting in his own constituency, the party would 'not sacrifice its policy for ministerial prestige or administrative control of a few government departments. It has stood alone before, and it can and will stand alone again if that is the price of its political constituency.'[51] Moreover, unlike his parliamentary colleagues who seemed to see the post-election conference as a mere formality, Larkin stressed that it was party members themselves, through the special conference that would 'decide Labour' position in relation to the formation of the next government'. Labour 'was not a "one-man band"', he told another meeting, 'and party policy was not decided by any single individual whether it be Mr Norton, Mr Corish, Mr Larkin or Mr Kyne'.[52] An aspect of the campaign in Dublin was the regular correspondence featured in the *Evening Mail* on the merits (or lack thereof) of Labour entering into government with Fine Gael. Correspondents noted a breach between the Labour leadership and the party rank and file, the fall in support in various by-elections and the problematic nature of an alliance with Fine Gael, and many suggested that support for Fianna Fáil would be more in keeping with Labour's programme. Most were published under pseudonyms and there were accusations – undoubtedly true – that many originated from Fianna Fáil sources, but some *were* genuine nonetheless and they highlight the concern among certain sections within the party that the party was hanging its wagon on the wrong horse. For example, 'Aknefton' in the *Irish Times* wrote of the pro-Fianna Fáil sentiments of 'quite a number' of Labourites in city areas, especially Dublin, while the *Leader* noted strong Fianna Fáil sympathies on the part of 'some Labour deputies'.[53]

So, with most of Labour (with the exception of Larkin and his Dublin colleagues) wedded to the idea of another coalition, the election had effectively become a choice of a return of Fianna Fáil or a coalition featuring Fine Gael and Labour at the least. But were there any policies involved? Not really. All the parties said they wanted to get into office, but none came up with a good reason why they should. One month into the campaign Labour finally issued a manifesto, but it was more of a wish list than a programme for government. There was talk of improving housing, increasing social welfare benefits, creating state control of credit facilities and increasing investment in the national economy, but the issue on which it placed the most emphasis was very basic: it was going to reduce food prices and reintroduce the subsidies which had been removed in the 1952 budget. It was, as the *Irish Times* put it, 'a very nice programme' but perhaps a little over ambitious.[54] For one thing, it promised all sorts of state expenditure without hinting at where it might find the funds, while many aspects of the programme were contrary to Fine Gael policy, not least the proposal to reintroduce food subsidies. That mattered little, as Labour campaigned on its platform of what amounted to little more than 'vote for us, or get MacEntee back'.

In the end Labour never managed to capitalise on its months of preparation, and by polling day the *Leader* wrote that only the lack of press coverage had meant the 'abysmal inadequacy of its campaign' went largely unnoticed.[55] Some of the difficulties during the campaign were Labour perennials. Finance was a problem to the point where the traditional end of the campaign rally had to be scrapped because they could not afford to stage it.[56] Publicity was also a problem. In William Norton the party suffered from a leader who conducted every election campaign within the boundaries of his own constituency, but other senior members were no better, leading the *Irish Times* to note that 'only the Labour Party leaders neglect the opportunity of haranguing the far flung corners of their prospective country'.[57] Even the usually conscientious Jim Larkin had withdrawn from the campaign trail, having been put out of action by a bout of laryngitis. But when Norton complained about the 'deplorable' level of coverage afforded to Labour by the press, and reminded candidates to ensure that the press was issued with scripts of all speeches, he provoked an irate response from Jim Larkin. Larkin was scathing of the parochialism of senior members of the parliamentary party and placed the blame for Labour's lack of publicity with them rather than the party's more lowly candidates. 'It is to be expected', he wrote,

> that the national press would naturally give greater publicity to former Cabinet Ministers and Parliamentary Secretaries than to ordinary deputies, or particularly to those who have not hitherto been successful in securing election to Dáil Éireann. In this regard the volume of publicity secured by those occupying this privileged position is hardly commendable and is readily understandable, in view of the content of many of the speeches. Quite clearly, if the national press is to be expected to give publicity, they will only do so where national issues are dealt with and not where there is merely repetition of the everyday crossroad propaganda points.[58]

The lacklustre campaign was further damaged by local skirmishes. In Drogheda, for instance, a faction opposed to Roddy Connolly's candidature created tensions, and there was a residual problem between Labour and Fine Gael from the April by-election. On the advice of the Louth constituency council, the AC dissolved the Jim Larkin branch, following which a 'New Labour Party' was established in the town. A statement from the new party accused the 'Norton Labour Party' of abounding 'with social climbers and Ministerial post hunters' which was 'now nothing more than an appendage to the Fine Gael party, and can no longer represent the workers'.[59] Scraps such as this did not receive much coverage (except, predictably, in the *Irish Press*) but they were damaging nonetheless, as they bolstered the image of Labour as factious and its leadership as heavy handed. Moreover, while the broadsides against the leadership came from the fringes of the party, the fact remained that some of their accusations, particularly those of careerism in Labour's higher echelons, had a ring of truth about them.

Described as the state's 'quietest election',[60] the voters displayed little interest in the campaign, which began to bear some of the hallmarks of modern electioneering, with, for instance, the first party political broadcasts being put out on Radio Éireann.[61] The decision to agree to the radio broadcasts was just as well, since the crowds turning up for the open air meetings were reported to have been 'smaller and quieter than ever before', much to the dismay of the correspondent from the London *Times*, who complained that 'less zest has been shown in heralding the arrival of speakers with processions and horsemen and bands of pipers. Gone are the days of heckling and free fights'.[62] But the days of fisticuffs between IRA men and Blueshirts at Irish elections were long over. Tricolour waving was now effectively a thing of the past, and the issues of most importance to the Irish voters were literally matters of bread and butter.

Predictions that Fianna Fáil was insecure in the cities but reasonably safe in the country proved correct. The government's vote fell seven per cent in Dublin and an average of two per cent in the rest of the country, leading to a loss of five seats, including the three independents (Browne, ffrench O'Carroll and Cogan) who had joined the party in June 1953. Fine Gael was by far the most obvious winner, its vote having increased by almost seven per cent across the country and it won an extra ten seats. It was a remarkable comeback for a party which had lost seats at successive elections for two decades, having increased its presence in the Dáil by almost two thirds over the previous two elections. As for Labour, its vote remained stable but it managed to pick up three extra seats bringing it up to 19 deputies, its best result since 1922 although equal to the number of seats held by Labour and National Labour combined in 1948. One positive development was that two of the seats were in Dublin where the party had suffered its worst losses last time around. One of the gains was made in Dublin North Central by Maureen O'Carroll, who was known locally for her campaigns against high prices with the IHA and the Lower Prices Council. (She gained national attention the following year after

she took Bachelor's to court for selling inferior-sized marrowfat peas.)
Labour's other gain in the capital was in the neighbouring constituency of
Dublin North East where Jim Larkin's younger brother Denis, also an official
in the Workers' Union of Ireland, was elected for the first time. The third
new deputy to join the Labour benches was James Tully in Meath, an official
of the Federated Rural Workers' Union. If it had gained little in votes, and
only a handful of seats, it was still moving in the right direction. Certainly,
Jim Larkin, not usually one to engage in misplaced optimism, was heartened
by the gains, writing afterwards:

> To some extent Dublin has retrieved its good name from the viewpoint of the
> working class movement and it is to be hoped that we will be able to build solidly
> on our success in the future. The overall picture for the Party is encouraging,
> especially as we have now secured the second highest number of seats in the Dáil
> in the history of the Party. With this strength it is to be hoped that we can look
> forward to a new stage in the building up and development of the political labour
> movement and let us also hope for a parallel strengthening and unification on the
> industrial field.[63]

The *Leader* took a more sceptical view 'Labour unexpectedly gained four seats
rather easily in the election for a additional 8,000 votes and [is] naturally
anxious to make the best of a success which is unlikely to be repeated'.[64]

Making the best of its success on this occasion meant only one thing.
With Fianna Fáil ten seats short of a majority and de Valera adamant that
Fianna Fáil would not enter a coalition, with no party offering external
support and with insufficient independents to make up the numbers, Fine
Gael approached Labour about forming a government.[65] After the two parties
had held several separate meetings,[66] there followed a series of daily meetings
between the leadership of the two parties, as well as with Labour alone.
Eventually, on 28 May, John A. Costello, Richard Mulcahy and Patrick
McGilligan met William Norton and Jim Larkin to discuss an agreed programme and the composition of the new government. Norton and Larkin
demanded an undertaking that Labour receive four ministries and one parliamentary secretary and insisted that Norton would get Industry and Commerce,
so that unlike the first inter-party government, Labour would hold at least
one key economic portfolio. There then began protracted negotiations on
what the principle objects of the new government would be. What emerged
eventually was quite different from the ten-point plan drawn up at the
beginning of the first inter-party government, which amounted to little more
than a vague wish list that might have been drawn up on the back on an
envelope. This time around the programme was more specific, although tiny

in comparison with modern programmes for government.[67] Labour, it seems, had learned from experience that if the devil was in the detail, it was best to summon these demons and deal with them at the outset. Moreover, the Labour leadership was no longer working as a free agent, and Norton would have to sell the programme to his own party. The first paper, which bore distinct Fine Gael hallmarks, promised a reduction in the cost of living, reduced taxes, improved social welfare services, an increase in house building, better organised health services, an expansion of agricultural production (largely through technological improvements) and of industrial production (through a State Capital Development Programme), which would have the effect of increasing employment and reducing emigration. Finally, it would establish a ministry specially concerned to deal with the cultural and economic problems of the western seaboard.[68]

Labour came back with some significant amendments. It opposed a suggestion for the government to look into how it might reduce prices, since this was obvious (reinstate the subsidies removed in 1952, a move to which Fine Gael was firmly opposed). Labour proved unable to secure explicit commitment to bring back the subsidies, although it did inveigle a promise that 'as an earnest of [the government's] intentions in this respect it is proposed to reduce the price of butter in the near future [and] a detailed announcement of the government's proposals will be made in the course of the next fortnight'.[69] It also inserted a promise to maintain protection for Irish industry while keeping 'the whole tariff policy under continuous review so as to ensure that it effectively contributes to the expansion of Irish industry', a policy which had been entirely absent from the earlier document. In addition, it made specific demands in the sphere of social welfare, called for the building of more houses through private and public effort (rather than merely through increased credit facilities as the previous document had outlined) and demanded the setting up of an agricultural version of the Labour Court for agricultural workers. Finally, two new points were added, the first calling for an examination of the 'whole field of education in the light of the experience gained since the establishment of native Irish Government', while the second called for the restoration of democratic rights 'in respect of local government by amending the County Management Acts'. In the end, Fine Gael agreed to all Labour's demands, and with that a 12-point plan for government was drawn up, although its contents would not be made public until it had been put before Labour's special conference on 30 May.

Three hundred and fifty delegates assembled in Dublin on that Sunday afternoon in late May to decide on Labour's next move.[70] This was a huge attendance, and around twice that of Labour's annual conferences. Obviously the question at issue was more important than the usual dull composites dealt

1 *Left to right:* J. H. Thomas, Thomas Farren and Thomas Johnson visiting Mountjoy prison, 1920, to investigate the conditions of hunger strikers. (*Irish Independent*)

2 First administrative council of the Labour Party, June 1931. *Front row, left to right:* William O'Brien, Thomas Johnson, Mary Davidson, William Norton , Michael Keyes. *Back row, left to right:* Luke Duffy, Thomas Nagle, T. J. Murphy, TD, Archie Heron, T. J. O'Connell TD, Senator J. T. O'Farrell, William Davin TD, Robert Tynan. (From J. A. Gaughan, *Thomas Johnson* (Dublin, 1980))

3 William Norton and Eamon de Valera on their arrival at Euston Station in London en route to meeting Prime Minister Ramsay MacDonald for talks about the annuities, 1932. On de Valera's left is Thomas Inskip, British attorney general.
(UCD Archives)

4 Big Jim Larkin in later years.

5 The Committee on Vocational Organisation, 1944. Luke Duffy, Labour's general secretary is second from right in the back row with Alfred O'Rahilly (with 'horns' to his right). The committee in full: *Front row, left to right*: Mr B. P. Boland, Rev. E. J. Coyne, SJ, Miss E. Franks, The Most Rev. Dr Browne (chairman), Miss Louie Bennett (Labour), Rev. Dr J. A. B. Irwin, Mr R. Wilson. *Middle row, left to right*: Mr C. P. McCarthy, Mr P. Gallagher, Rev. J. W. Hayes, Miss W. MacGeechin, Mr F. A. Lowe, Professor Michael Tierney, Mr A. A. Odlum. *Back row, left to right*: Senator Seán P. Campbell (Labour), Dr B. Kennedy, Professor Alfred O'Rahilly, Séamus S. Breathnach, Mr Luke J. Duffy (Labour), Mr P. A. O'Toole (secretary). James Larkin senior (not pictured) was also a member of the committee, although he never signed any of its reports. (UCD Archives)

6 Labour Party annual conference, held in Wexford, 1946. On the platform left to right: William Norton TD, Roddy Connolly TD, T. J. Murphy TD (chairman), Jim Larkin junior TD, Luke J. Duffy (general secretary).

No. 195.   SATURDAY, FEBRUARY 14, 1948   PRICE 2d.

A Coalition Government

Labour Will Agree To Act In Coalition Government and Put People's Decision Into Effect

SPECULATION runs riot in Dublin this week as the various political observers try to gauge the possibility of a new Taoiseach leading the thirteenth Dail Eireann. The electorate have made it quite clear that they do not want Mr. de Valera's "strong" Government, but they are likely to get it all the same, if Fianna Fail can succeed in attracting to its side sufficient Independent Deputies to vote with them, and their National Labour satellites, for the election of Eamon de Valera.

Whether they will succeed or not is not yet clear. In view of Mr. de Valera's declared intention to appeal to the country again if he did not receive his required majority, the Independent Deputies may think twice before giving their support to a Government which would almost certainly mean another General Election within twelve months. Even the handful of National Labour Deputies can hardly face that prospect with equanimity, though it is probable that they intend, in spite of their denial of it, to stand as Fianna Fail candidates next time.

Meanwhile the opposition parties are

No Support For Any Policy Directed Against The Working Class

JAMES LARKIN, T.D.

THERE would not be any support from the Irish Labour Party for the policy of any party directed against the working class, said Mr. James Larkin, T.D., speaking at Kilkenny.

" We will not compromise with those who seek to make the Irish workers carriers of the burden of the emergency."

As far as the people of Ireland were concerned, he said, they had voted definitely against Fianna Fail and the policy they had been conducting for the past seven years.

Question of Hugh Lane Pictures Raised in House of Commons

MR.   SKEFFINGTON-LODGE   (Labour) asked a question in the British House of Commons last week, which reopened a small but irritating wound on the scarred body of Anglo-Irish relations; would the Prime Minister explore at an early date the possibility of handing over to the Government of Eire the pictures at present housed in the Tate Gallery, and bequeathed by the late Sir Hugh Lane to the Dublin Municipal Gallery?

7 *Irish People*, 1948.

8 First inter-party government. *Standing, left to right*: Dan Morrisey, James Everett, Patrick McGilligan, Joseph Blowick, Gen. Seán MacEoin, James Dillon. *Seated, left to right*: Dr Noël Browne, Seán MacBride William Norton, John A. Costello, Gen. Richard Mulcahy, Dr T. F. O'Higgins, T. J. Murphy.

(Getty Images)

9 WUI official and Dublin Labour Party activist, Christy Ferguson, addresses a WUI seminar in the 1950s.

10 Norton steers Labour through stormy waters after Jim Larkin's speech criticising the government's lack of concern. The caption reads: 'Do I feel somebody back there trying to rock the boat?' *Dublin Opinion*, November 1956.

11–15 Candidates and deputies in Dublin in the 1950s: 11 and 12 Sean Dunne and Maureen O'Carroll (from *Labour*, June 1954); 13 Liam Hamilton (from election leaflet, 1954); 14 Matthew Merrigan (from election leaflet, 1954); 15 Michael Mullen (from election leaflet, 1954).

16 Proto-partnership with Jim Larkin: WUI seminarI in Greystones, Co. Wicklow, 1958. *Front row, left to right:* Donal Nevin (research officer, ICTU), Maj.-Gen. Michael Joe Costello (general manager, Irish Sugar Company), Bishop James Kavanagh (aux. Bishop of Dublin), Jim Larkin, junior (general secretary, WUI), Prof. Louden Ryan (Professor of Economics, TCD), T. K. Whitaker (secretary, Department of Finance).

17 First ITUC Executive, 1958. *Seated, left to right*: Jim Larkin, junior, R. Roberts, Norman Kennedy, John Conroy, Leo Crawford, Walter Carpenter, Harold Binks, (unknown); *Standing, left to right*: Jack McGougan, Eddie Dignam, William Irwin, Michael Mervyn, John McAteer, Frank O'Connor, Laurence Hudson, Gerald Doyle, Nicholas Boran, Terence Farrell.

18 Denis Larkin at the hustings in Dublin North East, 1963 by-election.

19 Noël Browne and Baron, with Garda Kelly at the anti-Cuban demonstration outside the American Embassy on Merrion Square, October 1962. (Courtesy *Irish Times*)

20 The national government after receiving their seals of office from President de Valera. *Front row, left to right:* James Tully, Paddy Donegan (Fine Gael), Liam Cosgrave (Fine Gael), President Éamon deValera, Brendan Corish, Richie Ryan (Fine Gael), Mark Cooney (Fine Gael); *Back row, left to right:* Tom Fitzpatrick (Fine Gael), Michael O'Leary, Tom O'Donnell (Fine Gael), Dr Garret FitzGerald (Fine Gael), Dr Conor Cruise O'Brien, Richard Burke (Fine Gael), Peter Barry (Fine Gael), Justin Keating, Patrick Cooney (Fine Gael), Declan Costello (Fine Gael).

21 Brendan Corish addresses the crowd at the Labour Party's final rally outside the GPO, Dublin during the 1969 general election campaign, while Michael O'Leary (to his left) prevents his notes from blowing away. (Courtesy *Irish Times* with thanks to Brendan Halligan)

22 Brendan Corish (left) and Liam Cosgrave

with at ordinary conferences, but this did not explain the overwhelming turn-out, so much as the resurrection of ghost branches throughout the country, with, as Donal Nevin remembers, 'bus loads' of people being brought up from the country to swing the vote.[71] The leadership was not taking any chances. Delegates from the Dun Laoghaire branch (a long-time bastion of anti-coalitionism) were informed 'at the conference door' that their branch had been suspended as of midnight on Saturday and they were refused admission.[72] (A subsequent attempt to reorganise the branch involved the suspension of committee members and an apparent endeavour to 'paper' the membership.[73]) The treatment meted out to the Dun Laoghaire branch was almost certainly unnecessary – the anti-coalitionists were vastly outnumbered and it is unlikely that they would have caused significant disruption – but it certainly left no one under any illusions about the party leadership's attitude towards dissenters, and it caused a great deal of resentment among members, in Dublin at least.

Over the course of four hours, those lucky enough to have made it inside were presented with the 12-point programme agreed with Fine Gael and told of the party's allocated ministries. Then, according to the Annual Report, a motion authorising Labour's participation in government on the basis of the plan presented to conference was passed 'unanimously and with acclamation'. What the report did not mention is that it was only passed unanimously because the entire Dublin contingent had abstained. They had turned up with the intention of voting against the proposal, but when they saw the degree to which they had been outnumbered, concluded that since opposition was futile, and would only widen the cleavage between the Dublin party and the rest of the country, they would do well to hold their counsel.[74] The only sign of any possible disquiet on the coalition question was the absence of Jim Larkin and his brother Denis from the conference. The Larkin brothers' absence was attributed to a clash in timing, as the special conference had been scheduled for the same day as the WUI's Annual General Meeting, but the fact that two meetings were taking place around the corner from each other in Dublin meant that, as the *Irish Press* noted, if they had really wanted to attend they could easily have done so. It reported that on the issue of coalition, it was felt that Young Jim dared not oppose, but 'did not want to seem to take responsibility for Labour support of a Government dominated by Fine Gael'.[75] It might seem odd that Young Jim declined to support the new government publicly after he (along with Norton) had negotiated its entry, but on this issue Larkin was nothing if not a pragmatist. Though opposed to a new coali-tion, he was determined that if Labour was to enter government again it would be on the best terms possible, and Larkin was nothing if not a superb nego-tiator. For him it was a question less of whether Labour went into government, but how it performed once in there, and certainly on the basis of the 12-point programme which he had helped draw up, it seemed as though Labour could perform very well indeed. As the front page of the *Irish Press* announced the day after the special conference had approved of the coalition motion, 'FINE GAEL PROMISE EVERYTHING'. Time would tell.

SEVEN

NEVER HAD IT SO BAD

—

Labour now entered government for the second time in six years. It returned to office confident that it had extracted very favourable terms from Fine Gael and would not be outmanoeuvred this time around. On 2 June, John A. Costello was elected to head a government – consisting of Fine Gael, Labour and Clann na Talmhan, supported externally by Clann na Poblachta – by 79 votes to 66. Labour's four ministries were allocated by an election of the parliamentary party, as they had been in 1948.[1] The three ministers who had served in the first inter-party government returned with new portfolios – Norton in Industry and Commerce, James Everett in Justice and Michael Keyes in Posts and Telegraphs – while, Brendan Corish (a parliamentary secretary the last time around) was promoted to a full ministry and was put in charge of Social Welfare. Finally, William Davin was made a parliamentary secretary. The only noteworthy aspect of Labour's nominations was Jim Larkin's absence. Suggesting it was 'unlikely that if Larkin wished to take part in the Government, [that] his party would refuse to nominate him', the *Leader* concluded that Larkin must have chosen to remain aloof from the government because at some time in the future 'he might find it convenient to be a leading man of the Labour Party who had not actively collaborated with Fine Gael',[2] a view corroborated by Mina Carney who noted that Young Jim had 'refused to take office in the new Costello government. He prefers to remain on the outside adopting a critical role for the danger is that the Labour Party may get too close to Fine Gael.'[3]

Among the Fine Gael ministers, John A. Costello and James Dillon (who had rejoined Fine Gael in 1952) returned as taoiseach and minister for agriculture respectively, and were joined by T. F. O'Higgins in Health and Pa O' Donnell in Local Government. Patrick McGilligan had been offered Finance,[4] but refused, citing ongoing health problems. According to one later account, Costello had sought to put Norton in Finance instead, but this was vetoed within Fine Gael. After James Dillon turned down the job, Costello turned to Gerard Sweetman. Sweetman was a man of great intelligence and enormous energy, and had proved himself 'a very forceful personality' in his party.[5] Sweetman was eminently capable, but an economic liberal of the old school, prompting his description as 'one of the keenest minds of the nineteenth century'.[6] Little was made of it at the time, but his appointment effectively meant that control of the Finance portfolio had shifted to a doctrinaire conservative, and when McGilligan learned of his successor he privately regretted not taking the job.[7] Lastly the Clann na Talmhan leader Joe Blowick returned to Lands.

Labour had been warned against painting itself as the tail wagging the compliant dog before it went into government, especially on the question of health.[8] Labour had supported Jim Ryan's 1953 Health Bill, while Fine Gael had opposed it, and though Labour liked to suggest that it had managed to secure Fine Gael's support for the Bill's implementation (set for 1 August), in fact, the reference to health in the 12-point plan had been so vague as to be meaningless.[9] Sure enough, only a fortnight after the government had been sworn in, the issue raised its head. On arriving in his new department, the Fine Gael Minister for Health, T. F. O'Higgins, who was himself a medical doctor and had been involved in some of the negotiations during the Mother and Child scheme crisis, concluded that the Act's implementation would have to be delayed because the health service was not ready. O'Higgins was, however, acutely aware that his decision could cause 'serious political difficulties' within the Labour Party and went about circumventing a crisis. After holding meetings with individual Labour deputies, O'Higgins addressed the PLP as a whole. He promised that the legislation would be implemented unamended within a few months, and received a vote of confidence, on Jim Larkin's proposition, for his trouble.[10] O'Higgins had targeted Larkin's support, knowing that once the man who 'in many ways was the socialist conscience of the Labour Party' had given his support, there would be little opposition from the PLP. He then sought advice from the National Health Council in order to 'insulate the Labour Party from political attack in the Dáil', and only when he had received the advice he wanted, tabled the legislation to delay implementation.[11] When the second stage of the Health Bill was debated in the Dáil on 7 July, it was Jim Larkin who spoke for Labour, supporting the delay but making it clear that neither he nor his party could agree to an indefinite postponement in the legislation and called for a definite date for implementation to be arrived at soon.[12] Again, Larkin's backing was important, in that it would inoculate the government against criticism on the matter either from the trade union movement, who would be watching carefully, or from the Dublin left, for whom the health question had a special resonance after 1951. As the Dublin Labour party's paper noted:

The Minister for Health is on trial in this matter. But what is more important from our point of view, the Labour Party too is on trial. Questions of health schemes and health legislation have become focal points of political controversies over recent years. In the eyes of the public, Labour has been caught on the wrong foot as it were. Labour supporters can be assured that this will not happen again.[13]

In fact the *Leader* had suggested that the country as a whole was 'indifferent' to the Health Act and implied that it was only 'the "intellectual" wing of the party (such as it is)' that had any interest in it.[14] Labour's position attracted only minimal reproach and a showdown between Labour and Fine Gael was averted by the minister's careful diplomacy.

A week after the Health Bill had been put on ice, the Dáil adjourned for three months. All was quiet during the recess, the only development of any significance being the 5*d* reduction in the price of a pound of butter in August, with hints that, despite the minister for finance's opposition, more subsidies were to come.[15] Still, Labour head office warned its members not to expect too much too soon,[16] a call that appears to have been taken to heart if the party's annual conference that autumn was anything to go by. This time around, conference came and went without any of the rancour of recent years. By the time the Dáil resumed in October, the *Leader* remarked that the political scene 'could not have been calmer over the last three months',[17] a sentiment echoed by the *Fine Gael Bulletin* which boasted that after the atmosphere of sustained hysteria created by Fianna Fáil, 'calm prevails in every aspect of our national life'.[18] The emphasis on 'settled conditions' and 'peace and calm' were, perhaps, an early indication that this might not turn out to be a very dynamic administration. By December, after six months in office, the government had achieved nothing apart from making butter cheaper.[19] One tenth of the government's lifespan had passed, and the time for action had come. It was a message which Larkin was to articulate from this point on in his column in the Dublin monthly *Labour*, and before long in the chamber of the Dáil.[20] Having enjoyed a fairly lengthy honeymoon after the election, the government began to come in for increasing criticism from the trade unions, although more so for its failure to tackle the cost of living, than for its general lack of a positive macroeconomic policy. It was very difficult to ascertain though what the government was actually doing. When Norton addressed his party's annual conference in May 1955, the only achievement he could point to by his administration was that people in Ireland could buy butter more cheaply than anywhere else in the world.[21] Norton enjoyed another sedate conference, although the *Leader* (the only publication to deal with the conference at any length) felt that the lacklustre conference was symptomatic of a lacklustre party, Labour having lost its way entirely. The *Leader*'s profile of the party was damning. 'The appearance every now and again of a lively little propaganda sheet called *Labour* is a welcome reminder that an Irish Labour Party is still with us', it remarked.

> A stranger visiting this country might well have his doubts on the point. He would find in office a government recognisable to any student of politics as conservative; he might discover that certain Ministers bore the label 'Labour' after their names, but he would be unlikely to pick them out from their colleagues on the strength of their public utterances.[22]

One would be hard pressed, the profile continued, to discern from the reports of Labour's conference

> any shadow of a relationship with the parties that represent the Labour interest in Britain and elsewhere. The fact is that the Irish Labour Party has fallen with a thump between the two stools of political idealism and political tactics. To Mr Norton and some of his colleagues, it seems, the gaining of an ever increasing number of Ministerial posts is a worthy objective of Labour policy . . . But there are a good many members of the party who wonder whether the watering-down of their policy necessitated by this desire for compromise has not produced, in fact, a totally different beverage. [23]

Noting the preponderance of wishful motions on social services and prices the *Leader* commented, 'one cannot help wondering if Mr Norton and his friends have ever tried to think out a policy at all, or whether they merely try to string together a number of sentiments which will look nice on paper'.

If the government and the Labour Party did not have a policy, it was not for want of suggestions. Calls for improvements and changes to Irish macro-economic policy were coming from all sorts of bodies, at home and abroad. For instance, in January 1955, the Ministerial Council of the OEEC met to discuss extending trade liberalisation between member states, an issue of no little alarm to the government which was still firmly wedded to protection. Ireland's 'severe misgivings', were shared by Belgium,[24] but these two were no match for the larger countries and the attempt by the Irish delegation to postpone the decision[25] came to nought. Closer to home there were the recommendations of the Report of the Commission on Emigration and Other Population Problems, which had been presented to the government in July 1954 but which was not published until October 1955.[26] The Commission had been established by William Norton in 1948, in his capacity as minister for social welfare in the first inter-party government. Although its report had taken so long to produce that some wags had begun to wonder if the Commission had itself emigrated,[27] the Commission heard a vast amount of evidence from different sectors of Irish society, in what has been described as 'an exhaustive (if not the most complete) examination of the economy and social structure of Irish rural society in the first half of the twentieth century'.[28] The majority report was inclined first and foremost to put forward measures to prevent the flight from the land, suggesting the decentralisation of government departments and the setting up of a body to oversee the use of agricultural land as two ways of tackling this, as well as calling for an Investment Advisory Council to be established to offer guidance on state investment,[29] (itself a neglected aspect of the government's 12-point plan) as well as the setting up of an export corporation.[30]

The most vocal critic of the government's economic policy at this time, however, was the trade union movement. The movement has often been criticised by commentators for having taken a myopic view of the Irish economy, and being more interested in pay rounds for its members than in the state of the economy at large, and at an individual level this was generally true. Statements coming from the ITGWU during 1955, for instance, consisted of criticisms of the government's failure to address high prices and low wages, in an attempt to prepare the way for the fifth round of pay increases since the wages standstill was lifted.[31] This is only half the picture, however, and ignores the longstanding commitment of both the ITUC and the CIU to economic planning (which included a strong emphasis on investment and research in agriculture), for which it lobbied long and hard, if without great effect. In July 1953, for instance, a joint deputation from the ITUC and the Labour Party had met with Seán Lemass (then minister for industry and commerce) and de Valera to discuss problems of unemployment and emigration. Then, Lemass and Congress were singing from the same hymn sheet in their economic policy objectives,[32] although this meant Lemass was out of tune with his cabinet colleagues. Once the inter-party government had returned to office, and Norton began his tenure in Industry and Commerce, however, it seemed as though Congress's access to government actually decreased. Perhaps Norton felt that formal liaison was not necessary and that, as a trade union leader of long standing, all he had to do was look into his own heart to see the movement's needs, but he might have tried to give the impression that he was open to consultation nevertheless. Instead, Congress found their efforts to confer with Labour rebutted, and when Congress economic policy was put to the minister (in writing), the response was indignant and defensive.[33] Failing to humour the unions was not a clever tactic, especially since the two Congresses were well on their way to mending the breach that had left the trade union movement hamstrung in the previous decade. The CIU had begun to soften its position on reunification in 1953, and by June 1955 a sub-committee had been appointed by the CIU and the ITUC which commenced talks later that autumn. The potential impact of a united trade union organisation was one that seemed to have been overlooked by Labour, which now appeared ill-placed to benefit from such a development. However, if the PLP as a whole showed no inclination to abandon the politics of drift, Jim Larkin was becoming increasingly restless. In an article published in the August 1955 edition of *Labour*, entitled 'Has Labour a policy?' Larkin argued that the party needed to work out a blueprint for economic development and criticised the party at every level for its lack of vision, noting that 'quite frequently, leaders of the party are sharply criticised for speaking in general terms . . . [but] maybe the party gets the standard of leadership it deserves.' Nor was this critique confined to the pages of his party's newspaper, with the weekly *Times Pictorial* running a four-part series of articles in October, under the rubric of 'Labour's Dilemma', which kicked off with a piece of provocative analysis from Larkin himself. Larkin argued that Labour 'of which so much was expected, [had] so far failed to measure up to the needs of Irish political development', and while its members could 'no doubt find many reasonable and even satisfactory explanations outside the party' for its failure, 'honesty and the best interests of the Labour Party compel the admission that the cause of such failure be sought inside rather than outside the party'.[34] Larkin argued that Labour had to get away from the tinkering reformism of butter subsidies and espouse genuinely progressive politics, establishing itself as 'a radical party seeking radical and basic changes in the present social and economic system'. Though it would continue the political struggle for reforms, it had to 'strive at all times to hold aloft the Vision Splendid of a new social order based on social justice', which was as close as he felt he could come to calling for the adoption of a socialist policy.[35] Similar sentiments were expressed by the ITUC research officer and Dublin activist Donal Nevin, and the *Irish Times* journalist Michael McInerney in subsequent weeks, Nevin stressing the need for Labour to become something more than 'an umbrella under which individuals who eschew the two main parties can shelter in their pursuit of a political career for themselves'.[36] If Larkin, Nevin and McInerney had been helpfully critical, however, the final article, which appeared under Brendan Corish's by-line, showed a leadership unwilling to concede that the party was in any difficulty whatever. It was only natural that a government minister would try to portray the situation in a good light, but Corish failed to address the concerns of the many Labour members and supporters who felt the party had lost sight of its raison d'être, and his assertion that it was 'beyond question that the Labour Party [was] functioning as a virile entity' convinced no one.[37]

Numerous words could be used to describe Labour at this time, but 'virile' was not one of them. Corish was less confident in private, but the bumptious tone evident in his article and in the pronouncements of his colleagues, led many Labourites to see their leaders as arrogant and remote. The Labour veteran Mícheál Ó Maoláin was incensed at being patronised by an aloof leadership. 'I rather think Brendan Corish is a young man who imagines that everybody looks up to him but they *don't* even look *down* on him', he told Jim Larkin. 'I think the great fault of the Labour Party (like all the other parties) is that they don't give 'the *great unwashed*... credit for having any *brains* at all.'[38] Ó Maoláin's prognosis was pessimistic, concluding that Irish politicians of all parties had failed the people and 'the present political parties...are things of the past,' and warned of the increasing allure of militant republicanism. Larkin's old friend Jim Prendergast was more optimistic. Unlike Ó Maoláin, he thought all was not lost, and that change was possible. Reminding Young Jim of the allegiance his father had commanded in the movement, Prendergast encouraged Larkin to persist in his attempt to bring the party back to its socialist roots.[39] Acknowledging Larkin's 'deep sense of responsibility' and fear of making a false step – 'since you are the cynosure of so many hostile eyes' – he reminded Larkin of his 'many, many friends who wish you well, and who will give you loyalty in the days ahead'. Larkin's realism stopped him from taking his friend's kind words too much to heart, however. Try as he might to get Labour to reassess its position, he was acutely aware of the left's lack of strength within the party and his hopelessness is clear in his response to Ó Maoláin:

> Yes! The present position of Labour is not a happy one, nor is it likely to commend itself to many who have a background in the movement like yourself. But what to do? Those whom you castigate in your letter [Corish, Norton and Kyne] secure and maintain the widest popular support as representatives of Labour – others barely managing to hang on by the skin of our teeth.[40]

What made the current situation all the more pressing was that while Labour gave the impression of drifting aimlessly, seemingly impervious to the concerns of the unions or its own members, a challenge was opening up on another front. Larkin's calls for a proper plan to tackle Ireland's economic malaise may have been studiously ignored by his own party but on the other side of the house, Fianna Fáil's Seán Lemass was thinking along similar lines. Just as Larkin had called on his party to engage in ideological soul searching, so too had Lemass, making speeches at conference, writing articles in party publications and establishing Comh-Chomhairle Átha Cliath (Dublin consultative council) made up of Fianna Fáil members and supporters as an informal think tank to this end.[41] It was to a meeting of Comh-Chomhairle Átha Cliath, held in Clery's Ballroom on 11 October 1955, that Lemass publicly laid out his proposals for economic planning which he argued would lead to the creation of 100,000 jobs within five years. Lemass's plan was influenced by European post-war planning, and particularly by the Italian government's Vanoni plan, which had been designed to tackle similar problems (high unemployment and emigration, unequal regional development) to those of the Irish economy.[42] The Clery's Ballroom speech attracted a great deal of attention, not all of it positive, but any criticism was theoretical. Lemass made his private battle with his less progressive colleagues public but had yet to convince his party colleagues of the value of his proposals; and even if he did convince his party, they were not in government, so they could not implement them even if they wanted to. It was highly significant, nevertheless, that Lemass had effectively put economic planning at the centre of political debate. Had Labour been paying attention, it would have seen this as a shot across the bows for two reasons: firstly that a senior member of Fianna Fáil was urging the adoption of progressive economic measures when Labour appeared to be napping on the job, and secondly, that Lemass was making a move within his own party against the more conservative, economically orthodox views of Seán MacEntee which had held sway for the past decade and had done so much to diminish Fianna Fáil's popularity among the electorate. Although this potential Fianna Fáil revival was at an incipient stage, the fact that any change in thinking was afoot merely highlighted the lack of any equivalent movement in the government. To add insult to injury, University College Dublin's's L&H debating society (a body scarcely known for its radicalism) could be found tackling the motion 'that the Labour Party is too conservative to justify its own existence',[43] demanding remarkable resourcefulness from those speaking against the proposal.

The year of 1955 had not been a good one for the government, but worse was to follow. A balance of payments deficit had arisen during 1955, due mostly to external trade factors, but attributed by the government to increased consumer spending following the fifth round of pay increases awarded during the year. Sweetman believed that swift deflationary action should be taken to rectify the situation, while his colleagues were inclined to sit tight and let the imbalance work itself out.[44] The tánaiste and the minister for finance were at loggerheads over the issue throughout 1955, but eventually, in early 1956 (while Norton was out of the country on a trade trip to the United States), Sweetman had his way, and introduced a number of measures to curb consumer spending including an increase in the bank rate, and various credit restrictions. In fact, those who had counselled sitting out the crisis were correct. The situation was beginning to rectify itself by this time,[45] and Sweetman's measures merely ravaged the economy, sending the already high levels of unemployment, and hence emigration, rocketing. This was exactly the scenario painted by the

Provisional United Trade Union Organisation (PUTUO), the umbrella group of the ITUC and CIU which had been established in January, when it looked at the measures, which it said were formulated on 'a superficial examination of the balance of payments position'.[46] Far from deflating the economy, it argued, the government ought concentrate on investment and expansion. It was a sentiment echoed by Jim Larkin at the time who complained:

> Nearly two years have passed since the present Government took office and we have yet to see any major policy on basic economic or social problems translated into an act of the Oireachtas . . . Administration is important but the voters at the last election were asked to put out the Fianna Fáil government because its *policy* was wrong and in order to permit the inter-party government to apply its correct policy.[47]

This lack of any apparent policy was also articulated by Aknefton. Criticising Labour for never having 'given the lead that its natural supporters hoped for' the column argued:

> It is all practice based upon no theory, and without an intellectual basis political discussion is likely to resolve around whether WX, whose uncle owns a pub, would be a more suitable candidate than YZ the champion footballer. Nobody sits down and says, 'Look, we're in an economic mess; how do we get out of it?'[48]

But by mid-March, the 'economic mess' showed no signs of abating, leading Gerard Sweetman to introduce a series of import levies,[49] with Larkin, once again, at the forefront of the attack. Unsurprisingly, by the time Labour's annual conference was held a few weeks later, the cracks in the party were very much in evidence with calls for radical economic action dominating proceedings.[50] The most overt sign of rank and file unrest came in a motion tabled by the North Wicklow Divisional Council which called on the PLP 'to withdraw from the inter-party government as this government has failed to implement the 12-point programme, the basis on which they agreed to co-operate in forming a government'.[51] There were other signs of discontent, but the most open display of hostility broke out during a discussion on the health services when an uncontentious motion relating to the minimum qualifying rate for the health services,[52] turned into a fracas between the floor and the platform after one delegate referred to T. F. O'Higgins, as the 'Fine Gael Hitler for Health' and others complained of absenteeism by the PLP in important debates.[53] Nevertheless, while the conference was often ill tempered and delegates critical of the Party's achievements (or, rather, lack thereof) the leadership survived it relatively unscathed.

On 30 April, the day after the conference closed, the voters of Dublin North East and Laois–Offaly went to the polls following the deaths of two government supporters, the independent Alfie Byrne and Labour's William Davin. In Laois–Offaly, Labour insisted on putting forward a single candidate, Davin's son Michael, rather than the government parties fielding one each. Similarly in Dublin there was a straight fight between Byrne's son and the Fianna Fáil candidate, Charles Haughey, an accountant and son-in-law of Seán Lemass. Following lacklustre campaigns,[54] both contests saw inter-party majorities slashed. Patrick Byrne managed to hold on to his father's seat in Dublin but Michael Davin was less fortunate. A number of factors had contributed to his defeat in Laois–Offaly, but none more than Labour's decision to go it alone.[55] Despite calls from their own party, Fine Gael voters stayed at home rather than vote Labour. This mirrored events in Dublin, where the Labour leadership proved unable to marshal their apparatchiks to work in the government's interest – having agreed to head office's request that they not put forward a candidate against Byrne, the local Labour people then refused to campaign on Byrne's behalf.[56] The by-elections showed that inter-party loyalty had broken down on the ground as well as providing tangible evidence that the government had lost the confidence of the public. The *Irish Times* counselled the government to take the election's message very seriously: 'The sooner it begins to govern, instead of merely sitting in office, the better its prospects will be'.[57]

One week later Gerard Sweetman announced his second Budget proper.[58] The balance of payments deficit remained foremost in his mind as he introduced various indirect taxes, mostly on luxury goods, in an effort to curtail consumption. Balancing these tax increases with a number of increases in benefits (although not old age pensions), Sweetman's budget did not lead to Labour losing much face, but neither did it provide anything for those who wanted the government to adopt a positive policy to halt the economic crisis. Aknefton's summing up of the budget was a damning indictment of the lack of vision on the part of the Irish body politic in the mid-1950s:

> The inter-party government came into power on the threat of price increases to the working man's pint. Fianna Fáil may have inflated his pint, but the inter-Party Government has blown up his tobacco. Pipes or pints – this appears to be the issue in Irish politics today. You can drink a little more under Fine Gael or smoke a little more under Fianna Fáil. If you are an old age pensioner and want to eat on 24s. a week, you will do neither and the budget will mean little to you.[59]

Although there were sharp differences of opinion at cabinet, the *apparent* degree of consensus between the coalition partners puzzled observers. As one writer in the *Irish Times* put it, 'even on subjects where normally there should be deep disagreement there is harmony'.[60] The author, a 'student of politics', wrote of the 'growing similarity of policy' between the two main government parties, which had serious ramifications for Labour. 'It would appear', he wrote, 'that the Labour Party is in the midst of its deepest crisis – without even realising it or with only very few being aware of it'. Not only was it losing its identity within the coalition, but by becoming so close to Fine Gael it was losing its raison d'être. Labour, dominated by a parliamentary party which was becoming increasingly detached from its grassroots, appeared to be amalgamating with its larger coalition partner. The ending of the split in Congress with the establishment of the PUTUO added an extra dimension, however, as it meant that 'there must be the ultimate possibility of the development of a Labour Party of the classical kind based on the unions and with fundamental aims of securing important social and economic gains'. Whether this union-based Labour Party would develop around, or separate from the existing Labour Party was not clear, but it was likely that there were more than a few within the trade union movement who would have been quite willing to write off the present party and start all over again. There was certainly little desire to establish any closer ties in the present circumstances.[61]

Just how bad the present circumstances were was only becoming apparent. The preliminary figures from the 1956 census were released in June. Recording the lowest population on record, they showed that net emigration in the previous five years had reached 200,000 – a figure significantly higher than had been expected.[62] It gave the government something of a jolt. Having mused on the various recommendations of the Report of the Commission on Emigration for *two years*, it finally *established a cabinet committee* on the subject.[63] This dilatory approach was due less to callousness than ineptitude; those responsible for tackling the issue were simply at a loss as to what they should do. Many years later, a party colleague asked Brendan Corish what it had been like being minister for social welfare in this administration. 'I used to lie awake at night, worrying about the unemployed', Corish replied. The response was ungenerous, but understandable, 'Brendan, the difference between you and me is that I would sleep at night – and I'd do something about them during the day.'[64] For the trade union movement, the implications of the report were clear and calls from the ITUC and the PUTUO followed, asking the government to transfer its energy away from tackling the balance of payments towards investment to create full employment, a case the PUTUO put to the government at a meeting on 21 June.[65] The government showed no sign of heeding the unions. The Clann na Poblachta leader Seán MacBride joined the calls for action with a motion in the Dáil on 9 July requesting the formulation of a co-ordinated economic programme.[66] Nothing came of this.

By the end of the month with no evident improvement in the balance of payments deficit, and with the unfolding crisis in Suez adding to a sense of economic unease, Sweetman introduced another round of import levies. In the Dáil the Labour benches were silent and remained so as the Dáil went into recess until late October. (This silence may have been due to the chronic absenteeism of the Labour deputies, which had led Norton to introduce a scheme of fines for offenders, with £1 the going rate for absence from the Dáil without the whips' permission, while missing PLP meetings 'without a reasonable excuse' was rated at 10s.[67]) Reaction would come from elsewhere, for as Sweetman announced his new measures the ITUC's congress was debating a motion calling on the government to adopt full employment as its economic policy and that it should 'implement practical programmes that will bring this about and to reject policies inimical to its achievement'.[68] Jim Larkin proposed the motion, his anger palpable. He quoted from that day's newspaper where, he said, Costello had complained that nobody had 'given him and his government a blueprint of how to deal with these basic economic problems'. Larkin argued that in order to draw up a blueprint it was necessary to establish an objective, and to engage in practical measures such as gathering information before planning could commence. This had not happened: 'I do not think it unfair to say . . . that the most outstanding feature of their contribution to economic problems is their refusal to plan, their refusal to set priorities and, generally, their refusal to even correlate the basic information.' Instead, he said,

> We live in a kind of 'Alice in Wonderland' atmosphere; we have a continued high level of unemployment. So instead of providing more jobs we decide that people will be restricted in what they can buy . . . If there are less goods bought there is less need to make goods; if less goods are made, less goods are required, so that to solve unemployment we make unemployment. Everything that we want is distorted in this peculiar economic looking glass, and the very things that we set out to do, to reduce unemployment, to reduce emigration to give greater opportunities to our people at home, all of these things are twisted and become their opposite because we will not plan, because we insist on everybody going their own way and then we complain we have no blueprint, as Mr Costello had done this morning.[69]

If the general trade union uproar seemed to be cutting little ice with the government, perhaps the message of the Cork borough by-election was one which it could understand more readily. Caused by the death of a Fianna Fáil deputy, it was contested by the three largest parties and two independents. Fianna Fáil held the seat coasting in on the first count with a surplus of almost 2,000 votes, although the turnout of 56 per cent belied any enthusiasm on the electorate's part. By the middle of August, with two more by-elections looming in Carlow–Kilkenny (on the death of a Fianna Fáil deputy) and Dublin South West (an outgoing Fine Gael seat), a general election within six months was looking likely[70] especially when Clann na Poblachta, on whose support the government depended, was becoming increasingly vocal on the need for action on the economy.[71] Only now, with the government's hold on power looking ever more tenuous, did there seem any inclination to act. According to his memoir, it was the Minister for Health T. F. O'Higgins who set the ball rolling, by submitting a memorandum to cabinet urging 'a fresh declaration of government aims and a new policy for development',[72] a task subsequently taken up by the taoiseach. Beginning in August,[73] Costello – or perhaps more accurately his kitchen cabinet of Patrick Lynch and Alexis FitzGerald[74] – began drafting a plan for the 'positive steps' to be taken 'without delay to bring about a radical cure'.[75] It would be crass to suggest that Costello was uncon-cerned about the dire state of the economy, but it is quite clear that the plan was being formulated at this time for party political purposes, and was an exercise as much in propaganda as anything else. 'A clear and bold policy must . . . be announced in broad outline within the next few weeks . . . Such a policy would give hope, show that the Government is alert and alive to the necessity not merely of restriction but of expansion which they appreciate is the real and only permanent remedy for present difficulties.'[76] Lest there be any doubt at the reasoning behind the decision to produce the policy document, and its timing, the taoiseach's draft laid it out in plain terms: 'The [policy] decisions so far as is reasonably possible should comprise new ideas, show originality, create public interest, *and be different from Fianna Fáil policy.*'[77]

Costello, Lynch and FitzGerald were working on their document with-out the aid (and seemingly without the knowledge) of cabinet. From the outside it seemed as though the government was still failing to take the crisis seriously. Jim Larkin was finding the situation increasingly difficult to tolerate, and when he came to address the annual meeting of the Dublin Regional Council on 26 September, he made his most trenchant attack yet. He castigated the public lack of concern shown by political Labour, and contrasted it with the increased agitation of the trade union move-ment. Warning of the undesirability of 'any divergences of policy and action' developing between the two wings of the Labour movement, he argued that the government's economic policy was completely contrary to Labour's tradi-tional stance and that it was vital that Labour 'declare for progress as against retrogression and decline . . . before it was too late'.[78] His speech was front-page news, and the responses he received afterwards give a sense of the despair long felt by ordinary supporters of the party. Messages of support flooded in from branches across the country. Writing from Galway, one member told him of how

The members of this branch are with you one hundred per cent and your speech has given us new hope that our leaders may stir themselves and return to, and act, according to the principles of Labour. It is our opinion that the leaders are losing touch with the plain people and are living in a fool's paradise and it is to be hoped that your splendid speech will have the desired effect. It is a matter of gratification that we have still men with reason in the party, keep it up please, you will not lack support.[79]

Another Labour member wrote that when she had tried to urge action at party conferences and while she had been on the AC she had felt 'like a voice crying in the wilderness'. Reminding him of the heritage he had to live up to she told Larkin 'you have behind you the backing and trust of the workers'.[80] Larkin's candour and obvious concern contrasted sharply with the *apparent* indifference shown by his party colleagues. For some, Larkin had become an almost Messianic figure, the only politician capable of leading either the country or the party out of the economic and psychological mire it was now in. A worker from Tipperary congratulated Larkin for his 'outspoken criticism' of the government, writing that

at present this country is being run solely for the cattle-ranchers and the farmers. The welfare of the workers or his family do not apparently cause any concern to those in power. The honest worker in the country needs the outspoken criticism and the honesty of purpose which you are capable of giving them, I ask you to look for the leadership of our party before it loses its identity by close association with conservatism namely Fine Gael . . . If you consider standing out as an independent Irish Workers Party you can rely on us for full support. I ask God to guide you. For the Irish workers' sake break with those who have neglected the workers' needs.[81]

Evidently, Larkin's remarks to the DRC had struck a chord among party members but what of his colleagues in the parliamentary party? Larkin had long been railing against the government's inactivity and its deflationary policies to no avail. Now, finally, his party sat up and took notice and a special meeting of the AC and the PLP met the day after Larkin's speech in order to 'review and decide on party policy' before the Dáil reconvened.[82]

Things seemed to progress shortly afterwards. On 4 October (some five weeks before the two upcoming by-elections) the taoiseach submitted the draft of the speech on general policy which he proposed presenting to a meeting of inter-party deputies the following day. The speech was approved, and so on 5 October the inter-party deputies met in the Engineers' Hall on Dawson Street to hear Costello outline the government's priorities for investment and development for the future, of which the proposal to establish immediately a capital investment committee of experts to advise on public investment – a basic demand of planning advocates for some time – was the most important point.[83] It represented a significant step in the right direction – not least in its implicit rebuff to Sweetman's devotion to deflation – and received the unanimous approval of the inter-party meeting. Hyperbolic deputies reported that the taoiseach had 'won over the most courageous and sceptical opponents and restored the unity of the inter-party members to a degree never reached before'.[84] The vote of confidence in the inter-party leadership, supported by MacBride, was a welcome boost for the government and the support of Jim Larkin was very welcome. Nevertheless, it is difficult to disagree with the *Irish Times* when it remarked, 'the pity is that we have had to wait . . . until a moment of "crisis"'.[85] The fact was that a great deal of the taoiseach's speech was made up of government policy – featured from the outset in the government's 12-point policy programme – but which it had failed to pursue.

The PUTUO welcomed Costello's statement for being on the right lines,[86] but for many trade unionists it was too little too late. A resolution saying so was put before a meeting of the DTUC but did not go far enough for many delegates and shouts calling for the Labour Party to withdraw from the government met with loud applause.[87] Moreover, if the taoiseach's speech had been designed to win the government votes in the upcoming by-elections in Carlow–Kilkenny and Dublin South-West, which were to be held in mid-November, it failed to have the desired effect. There was a massive swing towards Fianna Fáil, which picked up almost 60 per cent of the first preferences in both constituencies. In the case of the Dublin contest, where Seán Lemass's son Noel was standing in a straight fight against the Fine Gael candidate, the 'government candidate' received an 'almost complete lack of support' from Labour and Clann na Poblachta in the constituency.[88] Furthermore, the turnout in Dublin was horrendously low at just 38 per cent, prompting Peadar Cowan to warn that democracy was 'in danger, and the Labour and Clann na Poblachta parties must share a lot of the blame'.[89]

T. K. Whitaker has recalled the impact a cartoon on the cover of *Dublin Opinion* had on him at this time. In it, a young woman consulted a fortune teller, instructing her to 'get to work, they're telling me I don't have a future'.[90] This sense of hopelessness and national malaise was amplified by the fact that Ireland was falling by the wayside at a time of relative prosperity elsewhere, be it Canada, Australia or the USA, a time when voters in Britain were being told they had 'never had it so good'.[91] After three decades of independence, Ireland had never had it so bad, and colonial mismanagement could no longer be blamed. We had done it to ourselves. Is it fair or correct to blame the electorate for the quality of their government? Did the country, to paraphrase Jim Larkin,[92] get the leadership it deserved? Perhaps, but the people had never really had a choice in the matter. Neither of the two largest parties had a properly worked out economic policy. Within Fianna Fáil, Seán Lemass was fighting a rearguard battle against Seán MacEntee to have his party adopt a more state-led policy on economic investment. Within Fine Gael there was the battle between the economic orthodoxy of Sweetman and the more progressive approach of figures such as Patrick McGilligan and John A. Costello, influenced by advisers such as Patrick Lynch and Alexis FitzGerald. Ultimately both parties adopted the practice of fire-fighting the last crisis, with the more Victorian-minded thinkers getting their way in the end. In Labour's case, if it did have a constructive policy, it hid it very well. It was the politics of 'pipes or pints' and it had many people, as census figures showed, voting with their feet.

It is unlikely that politicians at any time before, and rarely since, have ever been held in such low esteem, so what political choices were there for those who stayed? The short answer, as far as parties were concerned, was not much, with many of the disillusioned looking outside party politics to find a solution to the country's depression. For middle-class bright young things, there was Tuairim, a liberal discussion group which had been established by, among others Donal Barrington, which set itself the not insignificant task of solving 'the social, economic, political and cultural problems of modern Ireland'.[93] Its members shunned party politics, which they saw as unresponsive to ideas and resistant to their precocious talents. Many of those who became involved with Tuairim might otherwise have been expected to join Fine Gael or Fianna Fáil, but what of those whose natural home might have been Labour? Unlike the two larger parties, which were having problems attracting new blood but which had fewer problems holding on to their existing members (even if, as the lifeless by-elections of recent times seemed to indicate that their activists were not particularly active at this stage), Labour was haemorrhaging members. Labour had been losing members since the beginning of the decade, and by 1953 Peggy Rushton remarked that it was 'very difficult to pull back people who have left the party. Heaven knows that I don't blame those who got out. I only stayed in myself by the skin of my teeth',[94] but this was nothing compared with the situation Labour found itself in by the time it was nearing the end of its second stint in office.

By the autumn of 1956 plans were afoot by a number of Labour people and Brownites to form a new party. In late October, around a dozen people met in Dublin to discuss the idea, at Matt Merrigan's instigation.[95] Among those present were Noël Browne (who was at this time a member of the Fianna Fáil National Executive), Jack McQuillan, who was still sitting as an Independent deputy for Roscommon, and May Keating, a radical who had come close to starting a party with Browne in 1952.[96] There were at least two current members of the Labour Party there, Merrigan himself and Maureen Lee (then assistant editor of *Labour*), and another two who had been expelled in the purge on the Dun Laoghaire branch in 1954.[97] Browne and McQuillan made it clear from the outset that while they were agreed on the need for a new political party, the time 'was not opportune', and they suggested that the group concentrate on starting an outspoken left-wing newspaper in the meantime. Their disagreement about just how left wing the paper ought to be is a vivid illustration of the ideological constraints which were still very much in operation at this time. McQuillan opposed taking an *openly* socialist line because, he said, 'Such a policy would not get the support of the people [and] his Parish Priest would be on his trail if he became publicly identified with socialism. Despite this, however, he had been able to advance socialism in his own district without using the name.'

It is significant that McQuillan – perhaps because of his rural constituency – was disinclined to use the word, while Browne tended to be quite profligate with it. Neither did McQuillan ever change his mind about its status as a taboo, for as he told John Horgan, the people who supported Browne voted for him *in spite* of his socialism, not because of it.[98] A month after this initial meeting, a circular was sent around would-be subscribers seeking support for *The Plough*, a monthly socialist newspaper that would be independent of any political party.[99] Its first edition was published in 1957, with a print run of 3,000.[100] *The Plough* was run as a co-operative out of an office on Parliament Street, a fact which one seasoned veteran of the left-wing paper business blamed for its poor quality – '*Plough*, of course, has a Committee, God help it! or any paper that has one'[101] – but despite its 'obvious marks of amateurism',[102] it managed to keep going on a regular basis until 1965, a remarkable feat for a paper without party funding.

It might be expected that at a time of economic crisis that parties on the extremes of politics might benefit. The Irish Workers' League was counting on this being the case. The IWL had seen its already tiny membership diminish still further through the decade – between June 1952 and October 1954 its membership had fallen from 102 to 59 in Dublin (with seven members in other parts of the country[103]) – and Khrushchev's attack on Stalin's record in early 1956 did little to improve the public's view of communism. The summer of 1956 had seen the IWL confident that it might capitalise growing unemployment levels to mobilise support and had gone as far as publishing a pamphlet in September entitled *Emigration CAN be ended*.[104] Their optimism was short lived. On 4 November Russian tanks rolled into Hungary to put down a national uprising which had begun a week earlier to international protests. In Ireland, the mistaken belief that Cardinal Mindszenty was involved in the revolt gave the cause of popular anti-communism a new boost. Petitions and motions in support of the Hungarians were passed in organisations throughout the country, including branches of the Labour Party and many trade unions. There were popular protests in Cork and Belfast, while in Dublin a crowd of some 3,000 marched on New Books in Pearse Street, which was ransacked by a section of the crowd.[105] In the face of this attack, the IWL went underground. The bookshop remained closed for some time and publication of the *Irish Workers' Voice* (which was already being printed in Derbyshire because no Irish printer would touch it[106]) was suspended. (Meanwhile the Irish government agreed to allow around 500 Hungarian refugees into the country,[107] housing them in an old army camp in County Limerick. The refugees, for their part, were nonplussed by their surroundings and within a month were petitioning the government to allow them to leave for another country.[108]) Although the IWL had thought it politic to disappear from public view for the time being, it took the opportunity to direct its energy elsewhere. It had already decided that the unemployment issue had the potential to yield political results, and in January 1957 the Dublin Unemployed Protest Committee was established in the south inner city, the latest in a long line of communist front groups on the issue.[109] Of the committee's 12 members, five of the most senior were members of the IWL, but cognisant that their presence would damage the campaign, they chose as their figurehead a former IRA internee Jack Murphy, an earnest, if distinctly uncharismatic unemployed carpenter. The group took to the streets demanding the implementation of the PUTUO's *Planning Full Employment* document, published in November. The movement soon attracted the support of many within the trade union movement, but in contrast to its precursor in 1953–4, not of Labour. Then, it had served as a stick with which to beat the Fianna Fáil government of the day,[110] now it was an indictment of the inter-party government's failure.

Finally, what about the republican movement? Although fears had been expressed by some observers that the failure of politics would lead to an upsurge in the popularity of militant republicanism, there was for the most part an air of complacency about this. Wartime internment had left the IRA effectively crippled, but by the mid-1950s it had begun to mobilise once more. British security forces were naturally anxious about this development, but Irish administrations showed little inclination to act on the matter, Costello's especially, since it was entirely reliant on Clann na Poblachta votes to remain in office.[111] Nor was it a case of increased military activity alone, but also political success, with an abstentionist Sinn Féin candidate winning a seat in Westminster in 1955. Nevertheless, there was little evidence of significant public support for the IRA's actions until the beginning of 1957. The IRA announced the beginning of Operation Harvest, a campaign of attacks on border fortifications on 11 November and 9 December, with further raids in Derry, Antrim, Down, Armagh and Fermanagh on 12 December. On the evening of 1 January 1957, a flying column launched an attack on Brookeborough RUC station resulting in the deaths of two IRA men, Seán South and Feargal O'Hanlon, and an extraordinary outpouring of sympathy followed throughout the south, fostering a sense of republicanism which had lain dormant until now. As Bowyer Bell put it, 'the Brookeborough raid became a legend overnight, Seán South and Feargal O'Hanlon martyrs within a week'.[112] The funeral of South, in particular, which saw crowds line the streets of Dublin, provided tangible evidence of a shift in support towards militant republicanism, something confirmed by security figures in March, which showed IRA membership at its highest level since 1945.[113] It seems unlikely that the deaths of these two IRA men would have provoked quite the same expression of grief had there not been a feeling that the country as a whole was standing quite close to the precipice. 'It is easier to find a teetotaller than an optimist in the 26 counties', was the somewhat flippant observation of the London *Times*' correspondent.[114]

Gardaí were instructed to round up known republicans under the Offences Against the State Act, and within days senior IRA personnel were being arrested in Garda raids.[115] This sent alarm bells ringing within Clann na Poblachta, and when the Clann National Executive met on 26 January, Con Lehane and Fionan Breathnach led the charge calling for the party to withdraw its support for the government.[116] MacBride opposed this, arguing that a Fianna Fáil government would, if anything, be worse, but the republicans were in the majority on the executive and MacBride was outvoted. Left with no option but to table a motion of no confidence in the government, MacBride argued that he be allowed do it on his own terms, insisting that if Clann was going to bring down the government, it should not do so on the Northern question alone.[117] With that, the fate of the second inter-party government was sealed. Two days later, MacBride tabled a motion of no confidence in the government on the basis of its failure to 'formulate and implement any long-term economic development to ensure full employment, and its failure to make any effort towards the reunification of Ireland'.[118] It was a bolt out of the blue for the government. Personal relations between MacBride and the government remained excellent, and even if MacBride was often critical, his conviction that the alternative – a Fianna Fáil government with Seán MacEntee – would be far worse, meant that the government felt it could safely count on him and his two fellow deputies. It was with some surprise then that the government learned of his volte face. A Fianna Fáil no confidence motion followed immediately. The Dáil was set to remain in recess until February, but, deciding not to delay the inevitable and wait and return to certain defeat, Costello called it a day.

1957 GENERAL ELECTION

It was, said Costello, 'an unwanted election', and the fifth time in 12 years that the country had gone to the polls. Taking place in a mood of abject gloom, the government parties, at least, were unable to muster any enthusiasm for the campaign. Indeed, none of the parties went so far as to issue manifestos for the contest, although much of Fianna Fáil's publicity centred on Lemass's 100,000 jobs speech in Clery's Ballroom some 18 months earlier, with Fine Gael concentrating on Costello's speech the previous October.[119] In reality, though, what the electorate were being faced with was a choice of parties rather than policies. Labour was distinctly ambiguous about whether or not it was standing on an inter-party ticket – Brendan Corish was alone of the more prominent members of the party in taking a distinctly independent line[120] – but Fianna Fáil campaigned against the outgoing government as a unit none-theless,[121] while in the press Labour found itself painted as a lame duck party, with parallels drawn with Ramsay McDonald's impotent regimes rather than those of Attlee.[122]

One early setback was the failure of three of Labour's most popular deputies to stand for re-election. The North County Dublin deputy Seán Dunne had become embroiled in financial difficulties and was unable to go forward, while ill health had forced the well respected Minister for Local Government, Limerick man Michael Keyes to stand down. The decision of Young Jim Larkin not to go forward again in Dublin South Central was more significant. The WUI had recently suffered the loss of two key members of staff: Jimmy Kelly (better known by his pen name James Plunkett) had left, and soon after-wards in February 1957, Christy Ferguson, Larkin's right hand man in the union, died. Larkin, who had always regarded his union activities as more important than party politics, felt he was needed more by the WUI.[123] Whatever the residual syndicalism on Larkin's part, his decision to leave active politics would have been more difficult had he felt that he exerted any genuine influence.[124] As one profile of Larkin had noted in 1954, 'he undoubtedly has the ideas, but where is the policy that they have determined?' – a point which remained equally valid three years later,[125] for while Larkin had the support of many within the party, there were at this point no structures for translating this into policy. As it was, his decision robbed the Dáil of one of the best brains in Irish public life and was a blow to those who had always hoped he would shake off his reticence to lead the party to salvation. This never happened and Larkin remained 'the prince in exile'. As one activist later remembered 'we were waiting for Bonnie Prince Charlie to come back. He never did.'[126]

If the national mood of depression had permeated the election, Fianna Fáil's campaign, masterminded by Lemass, sought to inject a note of optimism,

'Let's go ahead again' and 'Beat the crisis – let's get cracking!' its slogans for the campaign. It looked to all intents as though Lemass was alone in actually wanting to get in to power this time, with the outgoing government parties reluctantly going through the motions.[127] The latest 'dullest election on record'[128] was, however, notable for a number of developments. For one, there was the Dublin Unemployed Protest Committee decision to field Jack Murphy as a candidate in Dublin South Central. Murphy's chances of success were bolstered by the fact that this had been Young Jim Larkin's constituency since 1943. He had been replaced by Roddy Connolly, another scion of a great Labour leader. Connolly had no relationship with the constituency, and his name alone was not enough. Nor were his prospects improved by the decision of many Labour men and women to forsake their party to campaign for Murphy. As *Plough* editor Mary McConnell lamented in *Protest* (the Dublin Unemployed Association's short-lived newspaper) 'there are a great many people in the country who feel as I do and have been trying for many years to find a way to work for the beginning of the establishment of Connolly's Ireland. Some of us hoped to do it inside the Labour Party, by trying to change or influence the leadership, but I now believe that that is a hopeless case.'[129]

There was another significant development in the neighbouring constituency of Dublin South East, where the election marked the end of Noël Browne's sojourn in Fianna Fáil. When Browne's constituency colleagues met to select their two candidates for the election Browne found himself jilted. He appealed to Fianna Fáil's national executive to be added to the ticket, but this failed after Seán MacEntee threatened that if Browne's request was acceded to that he (MacEntee) would resign.[130] Once again, a number of Labour activists defected to Noël Browne's campaign, for which they were subsequently expelled.[131] Finally, following on from the public show of support after the border campaign, Sinn Féin put up 19 candidates, seven of whom were behind bars throughout the campaign.[132]

Despite adverse criticism in the press and some defections from its ranks, Labour appeared relatively confident.[133] This was misplaced. In spite of concentrated canvasses in Dublin, its result there was appalling. Roddy Connolly polled fewer than 2,000 votes and failed to retain Jim Larkin's seat in Dublin South Central, which went instead to Jack Murphy. The seat formerly held by Seán Dunne in North County Dublin was also lost,[134] as was Maureen O'Carroll's in North Central, her vote halved. Only Denis Larkin held on in Dublin, managing only half a quota of first preferences. Elsewhere, Labour lost John O'Leary in Wexford, James Pattison in Carlow–Kilkenny and James Tully in Meath while Michael Keyes's son, Christopher, failed to hold on to his father's seat in Limerick.[135] The party's only gain was Patrick Tierney in Tipperary North. Labour returned to the Dáil with 12 deputies, having gone into the election with 18.[136] The crisis which preceded the election meant that any party aligned with the government would fare badly. Compared with 1954, Fine Gael won ten fewer seats, and Labour seven, while both Clann na Talmhan and Clann na Poblachta lost two each. Although Fine Gael may have lost the greatest number of seats (one fifth of its 1954 figure), the smaller parties were disproportionately affected: Labour lost over one third, Clann na Talmhan two fifths and Clann na Poblachta two thirds. Fianna Fáil's vote went up by five per cent, but weakened inter-party transfers meant it picked up a disproportionate 13 seats. Returning with 78 seats – its best ever result – Fianna Fáil had won an overall majority for the first time since 1944. But this was not a victory for Fianna Fáil, whose manifesto contained nothing new and whose personalities were the same as ever, but rather a resounding defeat for the inter-party government.

The experience of the second inter-party government had borne out the fears of those who had opposed Labour's participation. With the exception of subsidies and a few small pension increases, Labour left no footprint on government policy. Moreover, Labour had appeared to condone Sweetman's austerity measures which led to massive increases in unemployment, particularly in the building trade. On this issue especially, Norton's loyalty to the government, as opposed to promoting his own party's policy, is evident. Norton was no less a government man in the second coalition than he was in the first, except that his talents as a 'fixer' were not as necessary. Nevertheless, the *Leader*'s comment in 1952 that 'the direction [the inter-party government] were going in was not always Labour's direction and the Labour Party paid the price of Norton's success' was could be equally said of his second period in government.[137] Neither had Labour ministers taken to publicising their achievements: they would have been hard pressed to find any achievements to publicise. Any informed criticism of government policy which came from the Labour benches was studiously ignored by the leadership and Labour backbenchers remained, for the most part, silent. In a government which lacked 'freshness'[138] the Labour contingent looked as stale as the rest.

The failure to embark on a positive economic policy was the government's gravest mistake. Although Norton's attempt to attract foreign capital was a start, what was needed – as Larkin and the trade unions kept reminding the government – was a proper plan for economic development. Rather than take action, the government, including Labour, seemed content to sit in office, apparently doing nothing, justifying its existence on the basis that coalition butter was cheaper. It was an administration characterised by inertia and austerity. Joe Lee has observed that Fine Gael managed to increase its vote and return to office in 1954 'by the simple device of doing nothing in opposition',[139] and the same could be said of Labour. Perhaps it is not surprising then that having discovered a strategy for success the parties would choose to pursue it once in power. By 1957, Labour was certainly not socialist, but it was no longer labourist either, having abandoned any working relationship with the trade union movement. Jim Larkin's warnings that Labour had to stand for something, to develop a positive policy, had been ignored and after three years in government Labour left office with high unemployment, high emigration and high prices – vindication for those who had warned that if a party did not stand for something, it was liable to fall for anything.[140] Ultimately, having lost all semblance of a recognisable labour identity, it was difficult to see how Labour could justify its existence for much longer at all.

EIGHT

LABOUR'S WAY

—

The year 1957 marked the return of de Valera and Fianna Fáil to office with a comfortable majority. Few if any expected this to result in immediate or dramatic changes, and they were right, for the beginning of 'the long sixties', seemed to be just more of the same. Nevertheless, the tide had already turned, as the critic Brian Fallon has well described:

> The Fifties were in every way a watershed, in which an entire epoch ended and the modern one emerged. This is not, perhaps, fully understood yet, because the Sixties – in retrospect, a less gifted, less substantial age – have claimed much of the credit for Ireland's supposed quantum leap in to modernity . . . But things do not change overnight like that, and what happened in the Sixties was largely the culmination of a process which had begun well before that. As in Britain and other countries, the Sixties – so outwardly colourful and challenging, yet in many ways meretricious and opportunistic – have taken credit for more than they achieved in reality. Most of the battles had already been fought, stubbornly, bloodily and over a long period, and the walls and bastions of conservatism had been steadily mined from underneath, so that in the end they collapsed with a suddenness which surprised most people, but which in retrospect was quite inevitable.[1]

The seeds for the changes that would become apparent had been sown during the disastrous administrations of the 1950s.

POLITICS IN THE SIXTEENTH DÁIL

Fianna Fáil returned to government with Lemass determined that MacEntee would not be responsible for Finance. De Valera agreed and appointed Dr Jim Ryan, who was politically close to Lemass, to the department instead. Ryan's first budget was distinctly retrenchist, but changes were afoot nonetheless. The government had given its approval for the secretary of the Department of Finance, T. K. Whitaker, and a team of economists to draw up a plan for national development. Published as *Economic Development* in May 1958, it formed the blueprint for the First Programme for Economic

Expansion. The First Programme and its successors guided the government's macro-economic policies over the next decade, and, for the most part, took economics out of Irish politics for the rest of the 1960s.

The former government partners returned to opposition in a state of some disarray. Fine Gael had lost ten seats and its front bench was even more bitterly divided after the collapse of the government than it had been before. Gerard Sweetman had fallen out with most, if not all, of his Fine Gael colleagues in cabinet,[2] and had a particularly frosty relationship with John A. Costello. Sweetman's opinion of Norton was as low as it could be and he was vehemently opposed to another coalition with Labour as long as he was Labour leader.[3] The antipathy ran both ways. Sweetman was universally hated within Labour and Brendan Corish, for one, swore he would never again serve in a government in which he was present. Nevertheless, if Sweetman was blamed for so much that had gone wrong in the last administration, Labour stopped short at making him a scapegoat. Slowly, it began to come to terms with its own inadequacies – both in tactics and policies – and began to come to the conclusion that there were limits to what could be achieved from the association of Labour with an inherently conservative party.

Unsurprisingly, Norton bore the brunt of the membership's resentment. Antipathy towards him had spread beyond its traditional Dublin base across the country, but efforts to coax Jim Larkin into initiating a heave against him came to nought;[4] Larkin was firm in his refusal to go forward, and no one else was willing to go in his stead. When Labour's first post-election conference met in June 1957, the rank and file anger was palpable. There were 'noisy scenes' as delegates rejected the annual report (for the first time), prompting the resignation of the Standing Orders Committee. Chairman James Tully, a veteran of many such occasions, accused the conference of 'making more trouble than any he had ever experienced'.[5] Notwithstanding such remarks, however, the leadership was clearly in a reflective mood as he painted a picture of Labour at the crossroads, asserting that this conference 'would prove to be the most important one ever held by the party'.[6] Exaggerated as this claim undoubtedly was, the gathering was momentous nonetheless. In the course of the private session which followed, delegates resolved by an overwhelming majority for the party to make 'a comprehensive statement of policy on the basis that the Labour Party will not take part in an inter-party government'.[7] The branches also demanded that a special consultative conference be held to examine the future direction of the party. Some months later, an 'organising committee' was set up by the AC 'to prepare a document setting out the party's approach to the situation at present facing the country and the Party's role in future years',[8] with a number of individual sub-committees charged with feeding policy ideas to it. Welcome as this exercise was, its execution pointed to the dearth of expertise within Labour. Jim Larkin found himself the first port of call for convenors of every committee, including those on agriculture and on fisheries;[9] remarking wearily as he declined the invitation to sit on the agricultural committee, 'I am somewhat at a loss to know why I should be thought suitable . . . frankly I know nothing about agriculture and never pretended to do so.'[10] Those entrusted with the job of policy renewal obviously relished the opportunity to get the party working again, but some, at least, must have wondered if it was not already too late. As one member of the agricultural committee wrote:

> Candidly I am of the opinion that the Labour Party is finished, in our time anyway. Perhaps on the ashes of their dead selves a virile party might arise which would have some kick in it. I don't know. They have the ball at their feet now, all they have to do is kick it, and even that I doubt if they are able to do.[11]

This was more than cynicism. The depths to which Labour's popularity had sunk should not be underestimated, as a by-election in Dublin North Central illustrated. In a five man contest Labour managed to come bottom of the poll with a miserable 761 votes; Sinn Féin's Seán Garland, who came second lowest, won more than twice that. Not only did the contest illustrate the lack of support for the party, but also the degree to which its organisation, in that constituency at least, had fallen apart.

'LABOUR'S WAY'

At the 1957 conference, delegates demanded a special consultative conference, and it was to this end that around 200 delegates from across the country met in Dublin on 8 February the following year. They were treated to something of a mea culpa by Norton. Where, at the last conference in June, he had seemed unrepentant about Labour's record in government, this time he looked to the future. He frankly admitted that 'so far as the broad economic and social programme of the Labour Party is concerned, it would be true to say that it had been a correct one insofar as it related to the *immediate* needs of the people, but that as *long term* policy it had been inadequate'. 'So far as the basic problems of the Irish economy are concerned', he continued, 'our programme has been inadequate. We have tended to treat the symptoms rather than the disease, to deal with results rather than tackling causes.' Economic success would only come through planning, through 'a combination of public enterprise, co-operative endeavour and private initiative' with gains in employment through 'large scale capital investment'. The latter would require 'radical changes' in the financial field and 'only a strong Labour Party can overcome the opposition that will inevitably arise from vested interests'.[12]

Most delegates had heard this before. What made the speech significant is that they had never heard it from Norton. The text had been written by Donal Nevin, who as research officer in the ITUC and a senior activist in Dublin, was a staunch ally of Jim Larkin. Only now, ironically after he had withdrawn from parliamentary politics, could Larkin finally say that his thinking, or his agenda, had been taken up by the party. The speech marked a real watershed, its trenchant criticism of the government's record was utterly necessary if Labour was to retain (or claw back) any credibility, with the party's failures laid squarely at the feet of Labour's lack of courage or imagination. It was also important because it saw a shift towards a more overtly social democratic approach in policy and language, with its emphasis on planning and warnings of 'vested interests'. Norton was far from waving a red flag, but the rhetoric did constitute a slight, although nonetheless important, shift to the left. Norton's new found humility saw him abandon his overbearing leadership style in favour of telling the membership what it wanted to hear, and acknowledging their long felt disillusionment with the party, the importance of which was noted by former National Organiser Paddy Bergin, writing in the *Plough*:

> For some years now there has been dissatisfaction of a vague kind among the members, a feeling that the party was not expressing the aspirations of the working class movement generally. This dissatisfaction had nothing to do with electoral success or failure but rather came from the branches that the policy of the party was not radical enough.[13]

Elsewhere in the same paper, however, the prognosis was more circumspect. Announcing that 'Labour may turn "left" again', *Plough*'s correspondent observed that 'for the first time in years Labour Party members and supporters are allowing themselves a cautious hope that Labour, if not yet on its proper road, is at least in sight of it'. A notable aspect of the conference was the fact that despite the lead given by Norton and other senior party members, it was the delegates who had dominated proceedings providing 'keen discussion with much useful criticism',[14] but *Plough*'s correspondent was more sceptical of the leadership's turn around, counselling that the next few months would 'show whether control in the Labour Party is, as its members maintain "exercised from the bottom up and not from the top down"'.[15]

It would, though, take more than a few speeches for Labour to move in the right direction. Larkin effectively drew up an informal three-point plan to revive the party, which was key to Labour's progress until the 1965 election, which saw all three elements realised. The three points can be summed up as identity, quality and unity. Labour had to establish a strong identity as a progressive party with a strong trade union consciousness, something that could not be done within a coalition. The calibre of the parliamentary party had to improve if Labour was to show that it was a national party with a policy, rather than merely an umbrella for independent-minded deputies. It therefore had to 'develop a national minded outlook rather than it is at present, individual politicians representing local political bodies'.[16] Within the PLP, only one or two deputies stood out as having either the ability or the desire to be other than local representatives. Moreover, because of the nature of the organisation of the party in the country where machine-based politics was the norm, there was no question of injecting new blood there, which in effect meant that Dublin would be the base from which new Labour talent would be fostered. Candidates would be taken from within the trade union movement, as this was seen as a testament to their sympathy for the cause rather than a quest for power, and to their having sufficient discipline to work within the party structure. This was all very well, but without an organisation to get them elected or increased popular support they would remain candidates rather than deputies.[17] Finally, the fragmentation of the left had to end. There was, as we have already seen, widespread disillusionment with established politics by the late 1950s, from which Labour was badly affected. For the more ideologically inclined, moreover, Labour's image had become so conservative that no one with left-wing inclinations could possibly think of joining. Labour's one saving grace was that, as things stood, there was no alternative to it: Clann na Poblachta's organisation was defunct, its parliamentary party consisting of a single deputy and any of its radical credentials had been lost at the time of the Mother and Child crisis; Noël Browne and his coterie were still floating around, but Browne, although he consistently displayed great capacity to inspire, still showed no ability to lead or work within the more disciplined confines of a party. Sinn Féin was still unorganised, without a policy and abstentionist; the Irish Workers' League faced insurmountable popular opposition and the unemployed movement's success was never going to be other than a flash in the pan. None of these groups had much chance of success on their own, and as was so often the case, at least as much time and energy went into sectarianism and faction fighting as into challenging the parties notionally of the right. Larkin wanted to see an end to this, but not through any kind of alliance or merger between the groups, but by making Labour, rather than its smaller rivals, the obvious destination for those on the left. Only when progressive forces had united *within* the party, would Labour have any chance of success.

Just how difficult this task would be should not be underestimated. The depth of antipathy between the various groups was well illustrated at a by-election in Dublin South Central in June 1958, caused by the resignation of the Unemployed deputy Jack Murphy, only a year after his election. The contest marked the entry into the fray of the National Progressive Democrats (NPD), Noël Browne's new party with his long-standing political partner, Jack McQuillan. The NPDs had been unveiled the previous month to general uninterest (the platitudinous programme and the false starts which had preceded it producing a sense of anti-climax) but they still represented an obstacle to a united left, as they demonstrated in their maiden electoral outing.

The by-election was contested by five parties – Fianna Fáil, Fine Gael, Labour, Clann na Poblachta and the NPD (contrary to speculation beforehand, neither Sinn Féin nor the Unemployed Protest Committee put up candidates) – it was the three smaller parties who received most of the attention. Frank Cluskey, a trade union official and protégé of Jim Larkin was contesting the seat for Labour, while one-time confidantes now bitter adversaries, Seán MacBride (who had lost his seat in South West the previous year) and Noel Hartnett stood for Clann na Poblachta and the NPDs respectively. MacBride had done his best to cosy up to Labour, making a speech at his party's Ard Fheis which called for a 'republican–labour' combination,[18] but Labour did not bite, much to his chagrin. He complained privately that he had made the same point 'on several occasions and never received any response from the Labour Party'. Still, he mused, 'One can only do one's best and hope that possibly some form of cohesion may result ultimately. I have studiously avoided any criticism of the Labour Party and will continue to do so in the bye-election. I hope that they will do likewise.'[19]

There was no appetite on Labour's part for such a move, however: as Donal Nevin, Labour's director of elections in this contest, explained, a single candidate was desirable, but it would have to be a Labour candidate.[20] The voters of South Central were treated to one of the most unpleasant campaigns in then recent memory, mostly attributable to the youthful exuberance of some of the NPD workers, including future Labour deputy David Thornley, who devoted most of their efforts to attacking Labour on everything it had done since the Mother and Child scheme, while Labour rounded on Noël Browne for voting to abolish food subsidies in 1952. The whole thing had much of the character of student union hustings, with the candidates and their teams engaging in name-calling and occasionally fisticuffs to the apathy of voters, which was reflected by a turnout of 35 per cent. Fianna Fáil's candidate eventually got in on the fourth count, having taken just over 30 per cent of first preferences. Labour, Clann na Poblachta and the NPDs, on the other hand, had almost a quota between them (although the NPDs had fared abysmally, and Hartnett had lost his deposit, much to Labour's delight). It showed quite clearly the potential of a unified left, and the danger of allowing fragmentation to continue.

FIGHTING FOR SURVIVAL: THE PR REFERENDUM, 1958

Ever since the general election, Labour had been to trying to work out how to prevent its own collapse but towards the end of 1958 it was faced with something which had the capacity to wipe the party out more quickly than anyone had anticipated. De Valera had decided to stand down as taoiseach and run for the presidency. While his colleagues welcomed the change in leadership, they were concerned that Fianna Fáil would be less popular with voters without him. In late October, following months of speculation, the government announced that it was going to introduce a bill to hold a referendum to abolish proportional representation.[21] The referendum dominated the political agenda from the time it was called on 2 November to polling day on 17 June 1959. The government made some attempt to attract Fine Gael and Labour support: the former was somewhat favourable, but the latter vehemently against. Labour as the smallest of the main parties felt it had the most to lose with Norton predicting they would be 'wiped out' by the straight vote. The former Cumann na nGaedheal minister Ernest Blythe had taken an active interest in the issue, having been a long time opponent of PR. Blythe canvassed Norton's support for the straight vote, assuring him that Labour would only lose seats in three-way contests, and also that having co-operated with Fine Gael twice in the past it could do so again. Recounting his efforts to Seán MacEntee, Blythe reported that the Labour leader had 'scouted the idea and seemed to me to indicate that while the party leaders and even local candidates might make such an arrangement, their supporters amongst the voters would not or might not act up to it'.[22] There was no deal, and in the end the campaign was fought by opposing sides, Fianna Fáil against Fine Gael, Labour, the print media (except for the *Press*, naturally) and the trade union movement, with some ancillary assistance from Enid Lakeman of the London-based Proportional Representation Society.

De Valera was elected President by a slim margin of six per cent, and the referendum defeated by less than two per cent of the vote. One of the notable aspects of the campaign was the co-operation between the Irish Congress of Trade Unions (ICTU), which had been formally inaugurated in February, and the Labour Party, Congress's foray into such a political campaign led to speculation about its motives. Was it because organised labour wanted to create 'a new firm link with a revivified Labour Party'? asked the *Irish Times*,[23] to which the answer had to be, not really. Neither Congress nor the individual unions had any wish to see Labour annihilated; neither were they eager to establish 'firm links' and it was not for want of trying on Labour's part. The political side of the movement was under no illusion as to how far relations between it and the unions had deteriorated during its period in government, leading to almost desperate courting from Labour. For instance, when Labour Chairman James Tully addressed a special PUTUO conference in 1958, he told delegates that 'the Labour Party was the political wing of the trade union movement *and if necessary the trade union movement should take over its leadership*'.[24]

But what was the likelihood? Though relations between the unions and the party had improved a little, they were still not close, and Labour never managed to make the case for joining.[25] It was clear what Labour would derive from union affiliation, but it was more difficult to see what was in it for the unions. The fact was that despite their speeches and sub-committees, and having stated their willingness to change, Labour had actually done nothing and was in as poor a state as it had ever been after the election. This was clearly laid out in an article published to coincide with Labour's 1959 conference by the ITGWU journal *Liberty*. The piece contrasted the vigour of the newly united trade union centre with the Labour Party, arguing that while 'the power and strength of the trade union movement has grown to a point never before reached . . . it becomes clear also that at the same time the political arm of the movement is withering and dying'.[26] Now that the trade union movement had been revitalised through unity it was the turn of the political wing which would have to be

> Born anew with new leadership and new policy backed by the trade unions and linked tightly with the trade unions. The new congress is both the opportunity and the instrument. The arguments for a political wing are over-whelming but there must be absolute conviction that this political wing will work.

When Labour's conference met in October, it was only natural that the party's relations with the unions would be one of the dominant issues. The defeat of the PR referendum had come as a welcome boost, prompting a rare outbreak of self-congratulation and delegates passed a motion calling on the unions to 'take a more active part in the political life of the state'.[27] Nevertheless, *Liberty*'s description of delegates as being in 'vigorous and courageous mood', ready to face 'up to many difficult problems, political, social and internal',[28] was a euphemistic way of saying that the members were in critical form, and seemed itching for a scrap. From the outset, there were complaints about the way by-elections had been run, the quality of the annual report (described by one member of the AC as 'a disgrace') as well as the PLP being 'castigated' for its atrocious performance in the Dáil.[29] It was not until the private session on the second day, however, that the gloves came off. The session had begun with some 'lively' discussion on trade union affiliation during which the article on the subject from *Liberty* (which had also been reprinted in the Dublin Regional Council's paper *Labour*) was often cited, but it was in the debate that followed that the simmering tension really boiled over. The issue at stake was William Norton's decision to accept a paid directorship of the Irish subsidiary of the General Electric Company,[30] a position which Jim Larkin argued was incompatible with his role as Labour leader. Norton was incensed, and rounded on Larkin. In a profoundly misjudged response, Norton held his membership card aloft and sneered that at least it was the only such card he had ever owned.[31] This crass allusion to Larkin's old Communist Party membership was deeply hurtful to Larkin and prompted an angry reaction from the floor which, in turn, prompted Norton to threaten his resignation then and there.[32] In the end, the vote was shelved,[33] and Norton remained in situ, but the damage was done. Attacking Larkin in such a fashion was foolhardy, and was further evidence of Norton's detachment from the mood of his party and his lack of sensitivity in dealing with Congress, since Larkin was *the* strongest link between the two organisations. Norton had finally crossed the Rubicon and his days were numbered, a fact which bolstered the growing sense of optimism within the party which grew with the membership's sense of empowerment, prompting the Labour veteran Desmond Ryan to remark, 'the Labour movement is quite alive these days'.[34]

But if the movement seemed alive, the parliamentary party was not, and as 1960 dawned, there seemed to be no end to the complaints about its performance. *Liberty* was back on the attack, protesting that all the work of the party was being placed on the backs of only a couple of deputies, that Labour, as it stood, was still not up to the job, and that the party's representatives risked finding themselves 'out on a limb that has to be pruned to let the fresh boughs come through'. 'By all means let us look to 1960 with hope', it concluded, 'if those now in command are too tired or frail, the solution is simple – move over and give way. If not, they may be pushed.'[35] Rumours that Norton was on his way out had abounded since conference the previous October, but it was not until the new year that he made his move. On 10 February 1960, Norton submitted his resignation to a meeting of the PLP, which asked him to reconsider.[36] He was reported as 'still undecided' a week later, but eventually, on 24 February, it was announced that he had decided to quit.[37] There was speculation at the time, and since, over whether Norton had jumped or was pushed, but the answer really lies in a combination of the two. Norton was not getting any younger and by 1960 he had been Labour leader for 28 years – for almost half his entire life. He had enjoyed his periods in government, but now that he was back in opposition, at the helm of a lackadaisical parliamentary party and a mutinous membership, he could not be blamed for thinking of easier ways to spend his time. All the same, the fact that the unions had made quite clear that they felt a change of leadership was necessary did nothing to bolster Norton's authority, a fact alluded to in the *Irish Times*, which had very reliable sources both within Labour itself and the trade union movement.[38] While some have suggested that Norton was 'deposed',[39] it seems most likely that he knew his position was increasingly untenable, and lacked the will or the energy to fight on.

So ended an era spanning four decades. It was quite a feat; lest we forget, Norton had been taken on as a stop-gap leader in 1932, when he became Labour's third leader in almost as many years. He was a consummate political opportunist, for which he was often roundly criticised, but if Norton's ability to go towards the main chance made him and his party seem somewhat mercenary, it probably saved Labour as often as it damaged it. He re-orientated Labour to a more republican stance and established an alliance with Fianna Fáil in 1932, he backed the Workers' Republic and Labour's move left a few years later, and when it looked like that would cause more harm than good, he moved rightward again. He tried, without success, to prevent the breaches in the trade union movement and in the party, and when given the opportunity to enter government with Fine Gael he took it, not once but twice. What Labour might have been like without him, we can only imagine.

THE NEW REGIMES

Norton's departure was the last in a series of key personnel changes at this time. De Valera was now president, and his long time lieutenant Seán Lemass was now leader of Fianna Fáil and taoiseach. Soon after, Richard Mulcahy announced he was retiring as leader of the Fine Gael party. There was general agreement that the dual leadership of the Fine Gael party and its parliamentary party which had operated since 1948 ought to be replaced a single full-time leader. John A. Costello, who 'would almost certainly have been the automatic successor to Mulcahy',[40] indicated his willingness to serve as leader but was once again reluctant to forego his practice at the bar for politics. His colleagues were insistent, however. Most of the erstwhile Fine Gael ministers had run back to the Four Courts as soon as they returned their seals of office, which left the party with only two or three full-time front benchers. It seemed fair enough for the good of the party, that its leader, at least, should take the job on a full-time basis. Costello was firm, though, that if there were no fees there would be no foal, so that was that. Presented with a choice of Liam Cosgrave and James Dillon, the parliamentary party chose the latter. Though Dillon commanded great respect from his party colleagues, he was faced with rumblings from some of the younger elements within the party from the outset, his most prominent critic being Declan Costello, a deputy since 1954 and son of Dillon's predecessor.

In Labour's case, the choice of a successor to Norton was necessarily limited by the size of the party in the Dáil. There were only a dozen deputies, including the Ceann Comhairle, Paddy Hogan, and Norton himself. Of the remaining ten, few shone and fewer still exhibited any interest in being other than constituency representatives. One person (perhaps even the *only* person) with a reputation as a solid party man was Brendan Corish, whose experience in government was also an asset, prompting the *Irish Times* to dub him the 'obvious choice' for the post.[41] Only two other names were mentioned, Cork deputies Dan Desmond and Seán Casey, but neither was ever regarded a likely contender. Once the level of support for Corish had become apparent, both withdrew,[42] leaving Corish to be elected unanimously at a meeting of the PLP on 2 March. Even against more solid candidates, Corish would have always been a strong contender. In terms of lineage, experience, youth, looks and personality, Corish made an attractive package. Ever since he had inherited his father's seat in 1945 he had displayed a willingness to work which was often absent in his colleagues, be it as parliamentary secretary from 1948–51, minister from 1954–7 or party whip from 1958. In marked contrast to most of his colleagues in the PLP, he had worked hard to gain publicity and support for the party rather than for himself, and he had been one of the most active in trying to win back union support after 1957.[43] He was very much a 'Labour man', lacking the maverick tendencies that were so often evident among his party colleagues. Quite apart from his record, however, was the fact that Corish was very likeable, articulate and handsome, characteristics which were becoming increasingly important as the nature of Irish media, and hence electioneering, transformed. Finally, there was the question of age. Corish was only 41 when he became leader, making him the baby face of a far from youthful Dáil. Whereas both Fianna Fáil and Fine Gael had replaced their old leaders with new ones from the same generation (Lemass and Dillon were contemporaries of de Valera and Mulcahy and Costello, Lemass aged 59 when he took over, Dillon 57), Corish represented an altogether younger generation.

But if it looked as though Corish's leadership had the potential to win votes, in which direction would he lead? How would the character of the party change now that he was in charge? For a start, it looked as though Labour might become a lot less fractious; Corish was considerably less domineering than his predecessor and the fact that he had the support of both Norton *and* Larkin[44] seemed to bode well for the future. Apart from unifying the party, it looked as though he would be in a good position to unify the movement, not least on the basis that he was a member of the ITGWU.[45] There had been a complete reversal in *Liberty*'s reportage, which now trilled that Corish's appointment marked 'a new era' in the party's history. 'Youth and vigour has come to the top at a time when Irish labour is ripe for the enthusiasm and fire of animated leadership' it gushed, in a tone unrecognisable from that of only a few months earlier. It was impossible, however, to tell where his intentions actually lay, since in common with most of his colleagues it was difficult to tell what his politics actually were. It has been said that if he was anything when he took over, he was right wing. One early profile described him as being 'well to the right of the Party and was formerly a strong "Inter-Party" man',[46] which echoes Patrick Lindsay's remark that his politics were 'to the right of Gerry Sweetman'. [47] Michael Gallagher's description of him as an 'unknown quantity' at the time is more accurate, although his evidence to back up the view that his record 'was not encouraging from the viewpoint of those who hoped to see the party move to the left' was based solely on his confessional pronouncements rather than on economic issues. Unquestionably, Corish had a reputation for being a staunch moral conservative. Beyond being a practising Catholic, he was a Knight of Columbanus,[48] and had come out strongly on the side of the Church during the Mother and Child scheme, declaring himself a 'Bishops' man' on the issue. In this respect, he was very much his father's son; whereas Richard Corish had told the 1936 Labour conference 'I am neither socialist, syndicalist or communist. I am a Catholic, thank God, and am prepared to take my teaching from the Church', two decades later Corish the younger told the Dáil: 'I am an Irishman second; I am a Catholic first . . . If the Hierarchy give me any direction with regard to Catholic social teaching or Catholic moral teaching, I accept without qualification in all respects the teaching of the Hierarchy and the Church to which I belong.'[49] Sometimes this manifested itself in a kind of unthinking conservatism. For instance, when *Plough* complained on one occasion that the 'lengths to which [Labour] will go in seeking to identify themselves with reactionary policies is almost terrifying', Corish was singled out for attack because of his support for 'bigger and better censorship' of everything from children's matinees to British television.[50] More alarming was his behaviour during the Fethard-on-Sea boycott in 1958. This was the infamous case where the husband and wife of a mixed marriage in Wexford fell out over where their children would go to school. The mother, who was a member of the Church of Ireland, moved to the North taking the children with her following which the Catholics of Fethard-on-Sea began a boycott of Protestant-owned businesses in the town. It was an extremely bitter episode, made all the worse because it involved the break up of a family, and its resolution required a combination of diplomacy and moral leadership, which de Valera (then taoiseach) showed in spades. Corish, on the other hand, was happy to stoke the bigotry that was fuelling the boycott, and called on de Valera to ensure that 'certain people will not conspire . . . to kidnap Catholic children',[51] a stance which led Noël Browne, in typically jaundiced fashion, to refer to him subsequently as the 'Bastard of Fethard'.[52] Still, if Corish was no secret revolutionary, hiding his radicalism under a cloak of Catholic orthodoxy, it is unfair to judge his politics solely on the basis of his religious beliefs, which were little different from those of most deputies of any party. Ultimately, his social and economic views were not fully worked out; he was, in John Horgan's words, 'a political late developer',[53] but even if he was not a 'socialist' of any variety when he became party leader in 1960, the fact is that his experience as a minister during the difficult times of the second inter-party government had made a huge impact on him and shifted him significantly to the left, albeit outside any socialistic or ideological framework.

The greatest change in Labour after Corish took over was a tremendous boost in morale. There were no sudden policy shifts or organisational developments – indeed, none had been expected – but the degree of continuity from Norton's time was quite notable. Norton had stood down as leader, but he had not retired. He held on to the office in Leinster House which he had used as leader; Corish, now its rightful inhabitant was given the use of another desk in the room, much to the new leader's embarrassment.[54] Nevertheless, if Corish lacked the confidence, or perhaps the vision, to make any significant changes in the party his position made a profound change in Labour's image, from a sort of right-wing, totalitarian style to giving the impression of a more open and inviting entity. This was apparent during the local election campaign during the summer of 1960. Labour's advertisements began to take on an extraordinarily contrite tone in its attempts to gain votes and new members. 'Remember', counselled one advertisement in a special edition of *Labour*:

> That even if you are critical of the Labour Party, so are its own members. We know that the Labour Party has many weaknesses, but we also know why. The reason is that there are not nearly enough ordinary people in it – you, for example – to criticise usefully and constructively from the inside; and far too many grumbling on the touchline.[55]

Those wanting to assist Labour's campaign were advised to talk to their family and workmates about the party's policy, but not to be afraid 'to admit that our party is not perfect'. Whether because of or despite Labour's new-found humility, it performed reasonably well in the poll, holding most of its seats and making some gains in areas where the party had previously been unsuccessful. With its first preference support going up by just over one per cent to a little over ten per cent nationwide, it was obvious that though the party had failed to make any earth shattering advances, at least Labour had put a halt to its decline.[56]

Similarly, when Labour met for its first annual conference under Corish in October 1960, there was every sign that Labour was beginning to enjoy a recovery. Its attendance of around 300 delegates made it the largest for quite some time, while the general air of optimism was remarked on. One first-time attendee reported of the high quality of the debates (especially in comparison with those at Ard Fheiseanna), and of the large number of young people in attendance, even if they remained silent through proceedings.[57] The main issue before conference on this occasion was the question of left-wing unity. Some fortnight earlier the AC had published a statement calling for the creation of a unity of progressive forces in Irish politics to provide a strong alternative to the two main parties.[58] Like so much of Labour's recent discourse, it had combined humility with a confidence in Labour's future role. Though Labour asserted its primacy in age and status, and noted the tendency of other parties to cherrypick its policies, it conceded that there was a great deal of political cynicism among young people, which it blamed, in part, on the 'failure to build a strong political party of progress'.

> Labour has not succeeded so far in appealing sufficiently to the mass of people who have looked to the emergence of a strong progressive party which may have been responsible for the appearance of other smaller groupings hoping to fill the gap. Some of these groupings survive, anxious to play a part in winning social and political progress . . . but, by their divisions, contributing towards the consolidation of support for the conservative parties. Whatever may have been the apparent justification for such separate groups in the past it must be clear that the future demands the unity of progressive forces.

There was no real disagreement between any of these groups on policy, and cleavages were based on personal differences alone, even if these differences ran deep. Labour's desire, then, according to the statement, was that the groups in question be brought together 'on a basis at least of common understanding and co-operation' with Labour declaring its 'willingness to discuss future political action with such groups with the ultimate object of creating a unity of the progressive forces in the country'.

Of course, this notion of a 'third force' was not a new one. Seán MacBride, as we have already seen, had been lobbying publicly for an understanding with Labour at least since 1958 at least, and had returned to the issue at the 1960 Clann na Poblachta Ard Fheis when he suggested that a 'Republican-Labour' party be established, which would be based on 'a realistic economic and national policy'.[59] If he had had any chance of a positive response it would have been soundly diminished by his warning that Labour should be wary of union domination, and the dangers of becoming a 'purely sectional' party. He had returned to the subject at a meeting of the 1913 Club, a left-wing discussion group, the following month, when he complained that his plans for a grand alliance were being thwarted because though the parties in question could be heard crying 'come into my tent . . . none will take the practical step to compromise and step into the other's tent'. [60] This was all very well, but none was so unwilling to venture under another's canvas as MacBride. Through 1959 Donal Nevin had been in informal talks with MacBride and Con Lehane on exactly this subject, but these had broken down because of the Clann negotiators' insistence that the two parties be treated as equal entities, with MacBride to be made leader, or, at the *very least*, deputy leader, of the new party which they wanted to call the Republican Labour Party.[61] That MacBride managed to tally the notion that Labour (with its 12 deputies, five senators, a nationwide organisation and trade union affiliates) could enter into a straight merger with Clann na Poblachta (which consisted of some former-IRA men and a parliamentary party of one), that it rename itself accordingly and that MacBride, who held no elected post of any kind at this time, should become its leader, shows him to be delusional, to say the least, with his egomania belying any suggestion that he was actually interested in a deal. Nevertheless, left-wing fragmentation had the ability to hinder Labour's advance, and MacBride's pretensions notwithstanding, the problem had to be addressed.

This, then, was the background to the unity statement, which was put before Labour's 1960 conference for its approval. It was the first significant proposal to come from Corish, and it was important for his leadership that it should gain approval, but when the statement came up for debate, it met with a mixture of bewilderment and hostility in a particularly fraught session. William Norton was the most vociferous opponent, not least because he was apoplectic at the implication that his party might have any truck with Noël Browne. Norton was particularly angry about the way in which the statement had been published before conference and its coverage in the press, which had confused Labour members and supporters. Labour, he argued, ought to concentrate its efforts on the trade union movement, rather than messing around with a united front.[62] Jim Larkin was less damning than Norton, but his conclusions were very similar. He complained that the statement was full of old clichés about the 'bankruptcy of constructive ideas of the two conservative parties' which ended up in all Labour's policy statements, and had worn thin because Labour had failed to put down in black and white what its own 'constructive ideas' were. The only concrete policy was that of working with other progressive groups, which had been portrayed as a coalition of sorts, leading people to believe that 'having failed in an inter-party coalition with a right wing party [Labour] is now going to have a shot at an inter-party coalition on a smaller scale of the left'. Moreover, there was disquiet among some trade unionists, noted Larkin, at the idea of 'issuing wholesale invitations to other groups and parties made up of predominantly non-trade unionists'.

Ultimately, if people were 'really progressive and believe in a party founded by workers for workers . . . then their place is with us in the Labour Party helping to hammer out and put into practice the progressive ideas they claim to believe in.'[63] First and foremost, Labour had to clarify its own principles and objectives, because the small parties 'only existed because of the failure of the Labour Party within itself'.[64]

In the end, however, the motion passed by 79 votes to 61, with many delegates abstaining, but the slim majority meant that the AC would have to study the issue at greater length before anything could be done.[65] If Corish's aim had been to gain popularity with the non-Labour left, he seems to have been successful, for as *Plough*'s correspondent noted

> Personally, I have always held the Labour Party leader in high regard, but until the first day of the conference I never thought of him as a man of the left. His opening address to the meeting however, convinced me that if Ireland has a left wing leader it is he . . . Corish . . . gave a picture of a man of vision, a leader of quality, a man of high principle, a politician who would lead Labour away from the doldrums in which it has been left following nearly thirty years of Nortonism.[66]

If the resolution lent Corish a certain kudos among the leftists, it amounted to little else. The issue was effectively shelved for another six months after conference until finally, in March 1961, three meetings took place between the two parties.[67] These discussions amounted to very little, however, and by the end of the month a worried MacBride had written to Corish expressing his concern about the lack of progress.[68] A further meeting took place on 18 April,[69] and then nothing. The fact remained there was more in it for the Clann than for Labour. By showing himself and his party to be open to dialogue, Corish had achieved all that he needed.

A much more pressing issue at this time was Labour's relations with the trade union movement. The unions, as Larkin had told conference, were worried about Labour cosying up to non-union parties, but surely the question for the unions was whether they were prepared to enter into a closer relationship with Labour. Earlier in the year, when Norton had stepped down, Michael McInerney of the *Irish Times*, had noted the optimism among Labour supporters 'that the lack of dominant leadership would lead to new fields where the trade unions might be persuaded to play a more decisive role in a revived Congress Labour Party and Council of Labour representing the Congress of Trade Unions and the Labour Party',[70] but by the end of the year Labour still had nothing to show for this speculation. All the talk of closer union between the two arms of the movement had overlooked what Emmet O'Connor described as the 'pervasive wariness [which] discouraged a resumption of the old ITUC ties with the Labour Party.'[71] The ICTU's first delegate conference in 1959 had passed two resolutions, one calling on Congress to 'give clear and prompt advice on all major political questions to its affiliated membership' as well as establishing a 'special committee within Congress for the purpose of examining all projected legislation, particularly in relation to [stabilising] prices and full employment', the other calling for 'effective means [to] be devised to secure the application of the movement's policies' and for the National Executive to look into how this might be done.[72] But when the Congress executive examined the issue, it failed to see the benefits. The problem was that 'so long as the Labour Party is not the Government they cannot do more than publicise our viewpoint in the Dáil . . . [and] so long as the newspapers with the widest circulation are linked with parties other than Labour, the intervention of Labour deputies in this manner is limited in its effect.' Moreover, regardless of whether Labour was in government or not, its deputies would 'represent the trade union viewpoint with varying accuracy depending on their closeness to the movement', with those who were not close more inclined to take direction from their own constituency organisations, and even though Labour had offered Congress direct representation on its AC, Congress felt that the AC did not exercise sufficient control over the PLP for this to be of use.[73] Ultimately, Congress not prepared to go further than a Joint Committee which would see the two bodies liaise on 'matters of mutual importance', and in particular legislation with a bearing on the industrial sector,[74] although its meetings seem to have been sporadic to say the least.[75] If there was little inclination to return to the relationship of old, at least a relationship had been established, which was a vast improvement on the situation of only a couple of years earlier. Indeed, détente had gone so far that by the time Lemass called an election in 1961, Congress was prepared to call on its members to vote Labour. Indeed, when John Conroy expressed such a sentiment at the ITUC congress in 1961, his remarks met with widespread approval, and was apparently one of the few occasions during the conference when the speaker was interrupted by applause.[76]

IRELAND AND EUROPE: THE FIRST APPLICATION

On 31 June 1961 the government published its White Paper on the EEC. Within a fortnight, Lemass had travelled to London to conduct talks with the British government about the issue, and returned home to announce that 'the position now is that if Britain decides to apply for membership, we will apply too'.[77] As far as the two larger parties in the Dáil were concerned, entry into the Common Market was effectively a bi-partisan issue, with the elites of

Fianna Fáil and Fine Gael strongly in favour of membership. Within Labour the issue was less clear. In common with most politicians and the general public, few in the Labour Party really understood the ramifications of membership, although several trade union leaders expressed serious fears about entry, including Ireland's lack of bargaining power within the EEC (Jim Larkin), that the markets for Irish agricultural goods did not exist within Europe which was already self sufficient in this area (Donal Nevin), or the problems that would face industry with the dismantling of tariffs (Ruaidhrí Roberts). There were also vocal opponents of membership among delegates in Congress, although these came for the most part from the Northern Communist faction who complained it was a venture in neo-imperialism in which 'monopolistic capitalism' would reign supreme. A debate on the issue at the July 1961 congress degenerated into a free for all when there were clashes between the communist delegates and those who praised the Common Market as a 'bulwark against communism'.[78]

Labour had no official policy on this very important question, but its outlook on the subject in the Dáil was broadly supportive of the government, a development which came about because of the influence of the former leader William Norton. Norton had been a keen participant in the Council of Europe, which he supported as a 'bulwark of communism',[79] and his views on the Common Market followed in the same vein. While his colleagues in the trade union movement and even in the PLP were expressing grave disquiet about the impact of entry on Irish industry and agriculture, Norton was very positive. He told the Dáil that such was the importance of the issue that it was the task of the government and the other parties to 'try and evolve a common policy so that the question of our membership . . . if it takes place, will not continue to be a source of discord, discussion and acrimony in the years to come'.[80] Arguing that Ireland's close proximity to Britain meant that Ireland would have to join if Britain did, he concluded that entry to the Common Market would necessitate an upskilling of every class of worker and more effective management of industry.[81] In the absence of anyone in the PLP willing or able to argue to the contrary, this effectively became Labour's policy.

1961 ELECTION

By 1961 it was clear that a general election was imminent. Labour's confidence may have increased under Corish, but the picture painted by one contemporary observer showed that in practical terms little had changed for the better: Labour's 'central organization . . . is pitifully weak, particularly on the financial side. In obtaining candidates it has to depend largely upon people who as individuals are willing to stand under the Labour banner and obtain their own financial support, specially from local trade union organisations.'[82] There were some improvements, for instance the parliamentary party benefited from the employment of a part-time parliamentary officer in Catherine McGuinness, a young Trinity graduate, who had recently joined the party after hearing Donal Nevin give a speech on Labour's bright future under Corish.[83] (It is worth noting that McGuinness was then unique among her Labour colleagues in Leinster House in having a third-level education. Arnold Marsh recalled that on one occasion a number of years earlier,[84] when he had a suggestion to make on educational policy, he had been directed to speak to Corish because he was the only member of the PLP who had been to secondary school. By the early 1960s, the barrier to graduate entry into trade union officialdom had been broken by two UCC graduates, Michael O'Leary and Barry Desmond, who were appointed educational officer and industrial officer in ICTU respectively. It was not until 1965 that Labour candidates with university degrees were elected to the Dáil in the form of O'Leary himself and John O'Connell, a medical doctor. By the time the election was called, Labour was reasonably well prepared. Though still chronically under funded, it had candidates in hand and a 12-page manifesto, *The Economic and Social Programme of the Labour Party*, which emphasised the problems of unemployment and emigration and stressed that full employment was the keynote of its policy. Comprehensive as Labour's manifesto may have been, the key plank of its platform – its support for economic planning – was to all intents the same as that of the government, and Fine Gael, and what is more the Labour leaders knew it. Privately, they admitted that there would be 'no startling difference' between how Labour would rule the country and how the others would do so, and were frank in acknowledging that 'the only basis which Labour had for offering itself as a party was its close ties with the trade union movement and the fact that it tried to speak for the basic interest of the trade union movement.'[85] It was just as well, then, that its claim to speak for the unions was given some credibility when the ICTU came out in vocal support of Labour at the beginning of the campaign.[86] In press advertisements placed throughout the duration of the campaign, Congress called on trade unionists to vote Labour, noting that the party's policy included all important elements of the ICTU's economic policy. Ireland's best-known trade unionists[87] were prominent in the campaign, to the extent that they took up most of the platform at Labour's final rally outside the GPO in Dublin, where the only deputies in attendance were Brendan Corish and Denis Larkin.

The election was described (yet again) as the 'dullest on record'. There was a variety of reasons for this: the sixteenth Dáil had been a workmanlike Dáil and had ended in an unremarkable fashion. Nor were there any significant differences between the parties: Fianna Fáil stood on its record and promised more growth and Labour stood for full employment; only Fine Gael ventured into the realms of novelty by supporting the abolition of compulsory Irish, which marked the sole new departure in its manifesto. Perhaps the one question which might have captured the public imagination was that of entry into the Common Market, which, according to Lemass, had been the reason calling the election when he did, but even that failed to surface as an issue during the campaign. In Labour's 4,000-word manifesto, the Common Market did not feature once. Corish did mention the subject in an election broadcast on Radio Éireann, in which he told listeners:

> The emergence of the Common Market in Europe and the problems that must arise from it will undoubtedly involve drastic changes in our economy whatever the outcome of current developments, whatever may be our relationship to the Common Market. In this situation can any of you doubt the need for strong Labour representation in the Dáil?[88]

Voters could be forgiven for wondering what the point was in having a strong Labour representation, when it did not have a strong policy on Ireland's role in Europe, but the fact that the Common Market never established itself as an issue meant that Labour was saved the embarrassment of squaring that particular circle. Voters were not making a choice on policies, but on governments, but Corish's constant emphasis was on Labour as an independent party which would not enter government with Fianna Fáil or Fine Gael under any circumstances, meant that even that option was put beyond the electorate's reach.

The sole remarkable aspect of the campaign was that Fianna Fáil, Fine Gael and Labour were each facing the electorate for the first time with their new leaders. Lemass and Dillon differed from their predecessors by engaging in speaking tours which were substantially smaller than usual.[89] Corish, on the other hand, travelled to party meetings across the country, the first time a Labour leader had done so in 30-odd years. Fianna Fáil's fears over how they would perform in a general election without de Valera at the helm seemed borne out by the result, with the party's vote falling across the board, resulting in a loss of seven seats. Both larger opposition parties did reasonably well. Fine Gael's vote went up by six per cent nationally, and it picked up an extra seven seats on its 1957 result. Labour had gone into the election with 12 seats, and expected to come back with 20, Corish envisaging gains to come at the expense of both Fine Gael and Fianna Fáil.[90] In the end, the party returned with 16 seats (half the gains it had hoped for), which consisted of three of the seats it had lost at the previous election and one gain in Tipperary South.[91]

This was an improvement, but not nearly enough, not least because the situation in Dublin remained dire. After the election, it was left with a single deputy in the capital, Denis Larkin's loss in North East offset by ITGWU man Michael Mullen's win in South West. The workers of Dublin had ignored Congress's call: either they did not vote (the average turnout in Dublin was around 12 per cent below the rest of the country), or if they did, they did not vote Labour. Sinn Féin failed to repeat its 1957 performance and won no seats, while the number of independents also fell, the political fragmentation of recent years beginning to be replaced by competition between the big three.

For Labour, though, it was an election of mixed consequences. It had not lived up to expectations, and though it had regained the rural seats lost in 1957 it had failed to make the breakthrough required in Dublin. The parliamentary party desperately needed new blood, but the relatively poor show meant that for now the PLP would remain, in the words of the newly elected Dublin deputy, Michael Mullen, 'a party of individualists and drunken feckers'.[92] Still, there were some reasons to be cheerful. The campaign had had a positive effect on Labour's identity. Corish had performed well, the unions had been generous in their support and Labour had been steadfast in its declaration of independence. The 1961 election was proof that Labour had turned the corner after 1957, even if the end evaluation was one of 'could do better'. The question before the party was, how?

A 'very noticeable awakening of interest' had been detected in the country after the election,[93] but in Dublin the presence of a single deputy was indicative of the poor state of affairs. As the Dublin Regional Council's secretary conceded, the 'bad showing of Labour in the last general election brought home to the minds of all of us the very real necessity for re-thinking, re-organisation and above all "doing something" in Dublin'.[94] That the first occasion that Corish addressed any meeting of the Dublin Labour Party took place in the spring of 1962, some *two years* after becoming leader, gives some indication of the lack of attention paid to the organisation there.[95] Nevertheless, although the leadership displayed no interest in the capital's development, some of the activists on the ground took a different view. From 1962 the membership in Dublin increased,[96] many of whom were young and idealistic. The problem for many people wishing to join political parties is knowing how to go about it. Applications for membership would often be directed to a party's head office, rather than the local branch of the person concerned, and in Labour's case, such applications would usually end up on the desk of the Acting Secretary, Mary (Molly) Davidson. Davidson was a formidable woman who had been working for the party in one capacity or another since 1922, but when Luke Duffy was appointed to the IDA by the first inter-party government in 1950, she took over the role of party secretary in an acting capacity until she was appointed officially in 1962.[97] Davidson was also a senator, having been nominated by her party in lieu of a salary. Around long enough to be distrustful of youngsters and idealists, she adopted a policy of containment, shunting new recruits in the direction of the Seán Connolly branch which held regular meetings in Eustace Street.[98] This was by no means a new development, the placing of intellectual types in ghetto branches had been going on for years. Recalling his efforts to join Labour in the late 1940s, Brian Inglis told of how he and his comrade had to be specially accommodated by Christy Ferguson, who could 'not have us joining any of the ordinary branches because an influx of intellectuals would scare away the ordinary members, of which there were few enough at the best of times'.[99] Among those active there were the party's parliamentary secretary Catherine McGuinness and her husband, the journalist and broadcaster Proinsias MacAonghusa, Jack Dowling, a journalist, and his wife Betty, both of whom had been active in the British Labour Party while they lived there in the late 1950s, Liam de Paor of the *Irish Times*, Liam Hamilton (later Chief Justice), John O'Connell, a young medical doctor, as well as Donal Nevin and a great many others. Before long the branch had become the energetic hub of the organisation in the capital.

Significantly, while the branch did not want for brains, its members were also prepared to engage in the nuts and bolts stuff of political campaigning which so often put off would-be intellectuals. Its first test came with a by-election in Dublin North East in May 1963, which arose following the death of Fine Gael's Jack Belton. Denis Larkin had lost his seat there in 1961, managing a first preference vote of only six per cent. An embarrassing loss for the party, Labour now set about winning it back, or at least paving the way to getting it back at the next general election. Larkin was standing again, but this time the younger members in the city mobilised to help him, with a contingent from the Seán Connolly branch acting as an electoral flying column.[100] Labour's campaign was impressive for its energy and confidence. The party put itself forward as the country's bright new hope, urging voters to 'take a fresh look at politics', and playing up the image of Corish as their youthful leader. 'Labour is not "the same"', it said, 'Labour is the party with the answer to this disillusionment, the party ready to take a fresh step forward, the party with modern policies for a modern Ireland',[101] in stark contrast to the contrite tone of its literature of a couple of years earlier, when it told voters about how it was unafraid 'to admit that our party is not perfect'.[102] The campaign ended with Fine Gael holding its seat, but Larkin came in with 18.5 per cent of first preferences, three times his vote at the previous election. The work of the 'energetic young people' in the campaign was noted inside and outside the party, with Catherine McGuinness being singled out for praise.[103]

By the spring of 1963, then, there was reason for optimism. Labour was more active in the Dáil, its membership was increasing, the Dublin North East by-election result showed increased support and the appearance of a generally well received policy document on education[104] (written by Catherine McGuinness and Barry Desmond) all seemed to show the party was undergoing something of a revival. Nevertheless, there were already warnings about the party slipping into complacency. Writing in *Hibernia*, for instance, Michael McInerney welcomed the party's advances, but argued that Labour was not enjoying the benefits of a positive swing in its direction, but rather that distrust of Fianna Fáil and Fine Gael and an inability to see the differences between the two were leading 'many young people' to join Labour 'in the belief that they are doing something radical when they do so'.[105] (The Dublin North East by-election is worth mentioning here in this context. Labour undoubtedly ran an excellent campaign, but the swing towards Larkin may have owed as much to the government's introduction of a turnover tax (a form of value added tax), as to the quality of Labour's canvass.) The problem, as McInerney saw it, was that these young recruits became disappointed by Labour's lack of overall aims, leading them to wonder how, in fact, the party was different. It was necessary for Labour's friends to be 'more constructively critical than ever before', he argued, 'because unless this opportunity is grasped another 50 years of isolation will lie before it'.

McInerney was being somewhat naïve, for few of those joining Labour at this time did so because of the character of the party as it was, but rather for what it might become. Jim Kemmy, a young socialist in Limerick at this time, having returned from a period working in Britain, was typical of this thinking. Unable to find a party in his home town which was to his liking, Kemmy joined Labour in 1963 and 'decided to do what [he] could to turn it into a socialist party . . . the time had come to change things', he recalled, and he planned to 'jazz things up a bit in Limerick in the Labour Party and attract young people and be more vigorous and liven things up a bit'.[106] Elsewhere, one critic of Labour's slowness to change consoled himself that 'when Labour grows . . . it will grow naturally to the left'.[107] Jim Larkin had been arguing this thesis for years, and in fact, was still doing so. As Larkin wrote to the author of two newspaper articles which had bemoaned Labour's lack of a socialist philosophy:

> Perhaps I could reiterate the question you addressed to us, namely, 'when are you going to do something about it'? Because, after all, the solution of the problems of the Labour Party . . . lies in the hands of those who believe that there should be [a] strong . . . Labour Party. Those of us who are actively engaged in the movement do what we can, although it may appear to critics to be entirely inadequate but at least

we are seeking to do something, whereas our biggest difficulty has been the fact that so many people are critically helpful or helpfully critical but their efforts remain individual and not directly associated with the organisations they wish to help.[108]

In fact, though, Labour's strategy of getting the critically helpful or helpfully critical was beginning to pay dividends. The new image of the party under Corish undoubtedly had a lot to do with the increase in membership, but the lack of alternatives was also important. At this stage Clann na Poblachta was essentially defunct (although it did not sign its own death warrant until 1965), the Irish Workers' Party (as the Irish Workers' League had renamed itself in 1962) had failed to make any significant advances, and the republican movement had been unable to sustain the popularity it enjoyed in early 1957.[109] The IRA had ceased its border campaign only shortly after it had begun, although it was not until 1962 that it officially called off Operation Harvest, regarded within the movement as something of a disaster. In the period which followed, the republican leadership began a process of reassessment. Cathal Goulding had replaced Ruairí Ó Brádaigh as IRA chief of staff in 1962, and inherited an organisation which was in a very weak state – its funding had dried up, and it was short of ammunition and personnel, with insufficient recruits to fill the natural wastage of those who had been imprisoned, killed or just drifted away.[110] Under the leadership of Goulding, who was himself influenced by the Trinity graduate Roy Johnston[111] and his mentor, London-based communist C. Desmond Greaves (general secretary of the Connolly Association and editor of the *Irish Democrat*), the republican movement began moving sharply towards the left. This had no significant impact on party politics in the short term, but the degree of informal contact between the republican movement and the labour movement and rank and file members of the Labour Party ought to be noted nonetheless. There had, of course, long been a strong tradition of republicanism among Labour deputies from certain areas, most notably the Munster contingent where people like Dan Spring and Seán Treacy were arguably more green than they were red, while in Dublin Michael Mullen and Seán Dunne were both former internees. Quite apart from these individuals, however, there would have been a significant amount of contact between republicans, left wingers and trade unionists through organisations such as Scéim na gCeardcumann, a trade-union based Irish language and cultural group established around 1963,[112] and the Wolfe Tone Society, a republican group founded by Roy Johnston and others in July 1964.[113] Johnston recalls that the Wolfe Tone Society was 'making an attempt to build a group fit to involve people who subsequently became leading Labour Party intellectuals'. Any dalliances of Labour men or women with the republican movement remained subaltern, however, and when Proinsias MacAonghusa (who was active in the Wolfe Tone society at this time[114]) called upon 'progressives' from Sinn Féin to join the Labour Party in 1965, it represented an unusual public concession on Labour's part to the fact that the republican movement remained in existence.[115] Any attempts by the republicans to attract Labourites into their ranks ultimately bore little fruit. For instance, when Johnston tried to enlist the up-and-coming Michael O'Leary he met without success, although O'Leary's then flatmate, Anthony Coughlan, was recruited by way of consolation.[116]

Finally, then, there was the National Progressive Democrats. Consisting of only Browne and McQuillan in the Dáil, it had no constituency organisation and no desire to establish one.[117] It was now well over a decade since Noël Browne had apparently taken on church and state during the Mother and Child crisis, and although he had achieved little or nothing of substance in the interim, he remained an attractive figure for young would-be radicals. This was mostly owing to his 1951 reputation, although his image as the great crusader of the left and victim of state reaction had been reinforced and updated through a judicious photo opportunity in October 1962. Browne had been among a group of his followers, members of Irish CND (along with a number of visiting colleagues from Britain) and Trinity students who had marched to the American Embassy in Merrion Square to protest about US policy during the Cuban missile crisis. This protest would have passed without notice except for the fact that by the time the protesters, numbering around a hundred, had reached the Embassy they were met with a contingent of gardaí, who were assisted on this occasion by two canine colleagues, Duke and Baron.[118] When a number of marchers sat down in the middle of the road on Merrion Square, the gardaí moved in to disperse them, during the course of which the two Alsatians, although kept on short leashes by their handlers, inflicted minor injuries on a couple of protestors. The next day, the *Irish Times* published a photograph of Noël Browne, recoiling from Baron, a look of abject terror on his face. The use of dogs in such a context was unusual in Ireland (garda reports afterwards contended they were present by accident rather than design), and would have been associated in the public consciousness with those used against the civil rights movement in the United States. For dogs to be used against an apparently peaceful protest was horrifying to most people, a reaction which was bolstered by the impact of the picture of Browne. As John Horgan noted:

> the photograph itself almost instantly achieved iconic status; there can be few people who came to political literacy in the 1960s who have not seen it, and been affected by it. For many people it became emblematic of Browne in his role as lone and courageous voice protesting against the Establishment.[119]

Browne recalled in his memoirs the 'sudden realisation that a large and angry animal with sharp teeth was furiously tearing at your clothes, your body, your head, face and arms', and a 'sense of hurt revulsion that men could pervert these dogs to savage a fellow man instead of serve him, to deliberately pervert a generous instinct into a fearsome hurting one'.[120] His melodramatic account ought to be balanced with the pictorial evidence, however, which belied Browne's account of having his clothes, less still his 'body, face and arms' furiously torn with sharp teeth. Indeed, several of the gardaí present at the protest reported that Browne had arranged with the photographer in question to stand behind Garda Kelly, Baron's handler, and once the snapper was in situ had begun waving his hands at the dog in an effort to provoke him. Certainly, one of the resulting photographs showed Browne, not looking towards his attacker, as might be expected, but directly towards the photographer's lens. Horgan's identification of the photograph as emblematic of Browne is spot on, but so too was the manner of his getting it. Browne picked a fight with an easy target and milked the publicity for all it was worth. Nothing concrete was achieved by his actions, but his reactionary persecution and crown of martyrdom were burnished for a new generation.

Although Browne had boosted his notoriety, both he and McQuillan were conscious that their lonely furrow was not getting them much in the way of results. Early in 1962, the pair sought membership of the Labour Party, but Labour was in no hurry to roll out the red carpet for the two, and their application was shelved by Corish.[121] This should not be surprising since the two men (and Browne in particular) were described as 'crackpots' and 'screwballs' by Labour leaders, and certainly for any of those who had served in government with him, Browne was persona non grata. It was a full 18 months before they tried again; McQuillan, influenced by Browne's poor state of health at the time, suggested to Browne that they 'should join the Labour Party and take it over'.[122] This time, they were successful, and on 27 November 1963 Brendan Corish and James Tully announced that there had been a 'unanimous' decision of the PLP and AC to admit the two. In fact, Corish had been dead against Browne's admission and had voted against it at a meeting of the PLP, as had Norton, Pattison, and Dan Desmond, but when the issue came before the AC, none of Browne's opponents voted against him. (There was no such opposition to McQuillan, however; the vote for him was actually unanimous.)[123] While senior party members had opposed their admission, what was more important was that Browne and McQuillan had sought to join Labour and that Labour had (eventually) welcomed them in. The impact of this on public perception was considerable, not least because the presence of two self-professed socialists on the Labour benches had shifted Labour significantly leftward overnight. As one-time party organiser Paddy Bergin put it:

Both of the new members are avowed socialists. Their acceptance has brought the Party back to what it was while Connolly and Larkin lived as members of it. It has shown that there is a place in this sometimes over mundane Party for the idealist who believes in the economic theory of socialism; the economic theory of James Connolly.[124]

This turn of events left Seán MacEntee unable to restrain himself, and he endeavoured to begin a red scare by denouncing the development as 'a political takeover of the most sinister kind'. This strategy lacked the impact it would have had 20 years earlier, however, and in a sign of the times, at least one national newspaper refused to publish his speech following legal advice.[125] The arrival of Browne and McQuillan on the Labour benches coincided with the return of the maverick left winger Seán Dunne, who had been elected as an independent in 1961. The impact of the three strongly leftist deputies was bolstered by the loss of an important right-wing counter balance, when William Norton died on 4 December 1963. Norton had always been the brains of the centre-right in the party, and was still influential among Labour's rural elements. There was no one on the right with the intellect, prestige or, most importantly, desire to take his place, something which would affect the party's character profoundly as the decade wore on.[126] Norton's death also had a huge impact on Corish, who had been literally in his predecessor's shadow since becoming leader in 1960 – Norton, it should be remembered, had never moved out of the party leader's office in Leinster House. Now Corish felt he had the freedom actually to lead the party for the first time since taking over, almost three years earlier.

So much for the changes in the membership profile and image of the party, but what of its politics? In this regard, for the most part Labour made little advance. It was becoming increasingly active in the Dáil and by the latter half of 1963 had begun to take the initiative against the government, but it often gave the impression of its opposition being more a case of belligerence than anything more constructive. The case of the turnover tax, announced in the 1963 budget, is a prime example of this. The introduction of this new tax was hugely unpopular at the time, and the government had just managed only to push the legislation on it through, passing it by a single vote in June. Opposition to the tax, as we have seen, played a part in the huge increase in Labour's vote at the Dublin North East by-election that spring. The bill had been passed in June and the tax was not due to come into force until 1 November. Some four months after the bill had been passed, Labour tabled a motion of no confidence in the government on the basis that 'in view of the widespread public opposition to the turnover tax, the Dáil is of opinion that the government have lost the confidence of the people, and, therefore, considers that they should resign forthwith'. It was an extraordinarily specious basis on which to table such a motion – if governments resigned each time their fiscal policies lacked public support, there would be no such a thing as a stable democracy – but as if the timing of the motion and the vacuity of its reasoning were not bad enough, what was worse was Labour's utterly improper attempt to enlist the Ceann Comhairle, Patrick Hogan, the party's Clare deputy, to vote against the government in the event of a tie.[127] It was an unprecedented move, and one which was, in Maurice Manning's words, 'indicative more than anything else of the fact Labour had been sidelined in the debate up to now and was trying desperately to take the initiative'. It was also an unrealistic strategy, Manning rightly points out, 'since in the event of a government defeat Labour was not going to participate in the formation of a new government anyway'.[128] In the end, however, the no confidence debate ended with the government remaining in situ, to no one's great surprise. Labour's penchant for pointless protest was further illustrated by the public meeting outside the GPO, organised by the Dublin Regional Council and attended by various Labour deputies and senior trade unionists, for the evening of 2 November, the day *after* the tax came into effect.[129] It was described, quite reasonably by the Ireland correspondent in *Tribune*, as 'impressive, but too late'. [130] Certainly, as *Tribune*'s correspondent saw it, Labour was going to have to reposition itself, for how could Labour 'stand forth as the genuine party of change if the people think its social philosophy involves no more than a call for an agreed biennial 12 per cent all-around wages increase'.[131]

Labour had adopted more aggressive tactics, but had still to make any real developments in its policies, with the document on education written by Barry Desmond and Catherine McGuinness representing Labour's only new policy since 1958. Complaints continued that the party's revival was proceeding too slowly, but usually from sources far to the left of the party.[132] If the new recruits were restless, however (the *Irish Democrat* noting the 'young people within the Labour Party who would like to see it return to the philosophy of Connolly, and have ideas on how this could be done'[133]), they seemed happy to bide their time for now. The government's slim majority meant that a general election was expected in the near future, and for the time being any notion of a return to Connolly's philosophy was secondary to the more pressing need to consolidate Labour's organisation before the next election. This was very much in evidence at Labour's annual conference held in July 1964, described by one commentator as having been polite and businesslike to the point where it 'narrowly missed being dull'. It seemed, according to the same writer as though the party was 'marking time, to be waiting for something . . . It is felt that Labour is on the very threshold of a great advance'.[134] There was, nevertheless, one concession to the young and restless, in an interview by

Brendan Corish in June, in which he described Labour's policy as socialist, the first time he had done so without the prefix 'Christian', constituting a small but fundamental change in rhetoric.[135] The Irish Workers' Party paper, *Irish Socialist*, regarded this as cause for comment, remarking that 'the fact that the Irish Labour Party is once again openly proclaiming that it is a socialist party reflects the new atmosphere',[136] but what did this 'new atmosphere' actually consist of? Was it anything more than the use of a new buzzword and, if so, what had made 'socialism' any more acceptable than it had been a couple of years previously? The 'new atmosphere' does not seem to have been much different from the old in the sense that, significant as it was that Corish should gauge the public response to his use of the word, it would be another year before he ever used it again. Still, the very fact that he had tried it out in the first place indicated that the stigma of 'socialism' was diminishing, the result of a combination of factors at home and abroad. Ireland had seen an increase in the state provision of health and social welfare benefits combined with a commitment to economic planning over the previous decade, and the more dire warnings about the dangers of the servile state had failed to come to pass. Indeed, proponents of greater state intervention were to the fore in all of the three main parties. Lemass had spoken in 1963 of his belief that 'national policy should take a shift to the left',[137] while within Fine Gael, Declan Costello and the Young Tiger faction were intent on pushing forward an agenda of social democracy before the next general election. With the taoiseach and the main opposition party encroaching more and more on Labour's would-be policy and language, Labour was faced with the need to assert its identity in more radical terms; if Lemass was 'left', and Costello was 'just', Labour might have to be 'socialist'.

Another important influence at this time was the general thaw in the cold war under Khrushchev (obvious exceptions aside), and not least in terms of the attitude of the Catholic Church under the more conciliatory papacy of John XXIII. Not only did Pope John move away from Pius XII's aggressively anti-communist outlook in international relations (the latter having issued 123 anti-communist proclamations during his 19 years as pontiff[138]), but equally significantly, he managed to reconcile Catholic social teaching with the interventionist aspects of the contemporary state in his 1961 encyclical *Mater et Magistra*, and further enunciated his teaching on social justice in his 1963 encyclical *Pacem in Terris*. For some on the left, this profound shift in Church thinking allowed them to reconcile themselves with the Church, the socialist historian Miriam Daly being one such example.[139] It allowed others to reconcile their politics to their faith. It is difficult to exaggerate the ubiquity of *Mater et Magistra* in so many Irish publications in the months, and even years, after it was published. There were summer schools devoted to it for both religious and laity, and articles in the many Catholic periodicals. That much might have been expected, but it also received heavy coverage in everything from trade union publications to the *Irish Socialist*.[140] In fact, the *Irish Socialist* regularly referred to *Mater et Magistra* to back up Irish Workers Party policy on the economy, showing the devil quite able to cite scripture for his own purpose. Even more bizarre was the *Irish Socialist*'s denounciation of the government because 'its whole line . . . runs contrary to the doctrines of *Pacem in terres*'.[141] There was, it must be said, a certain amount of resistance within the Irish Church to a greater emphasis on social justice and a softer style of Catholicism, but, the new teaching did trickle down nonetheless, not least among younger, more educated Catholics who were involved in organisations such as the Catholic sociology group Christus Rex, the Dublin Institute for Catholic Sociology, or even, as the decade wore on, students of politics in UCD who were being taught by the Rev Fergal O'Connor, lecturer in political philosophy in the Department of Ethics and Politics.[142] On balance it might be said that the influence of Pope John was profound, but very uneven, and if delegates at Christus Rex conferences could quote chapter and verse of *Mater et Magistra*, the same might not be said for the average reader of the *Messenger*.[143]

Finally, in terms of the rhetoric of socialism, an important influence at this time was the language being used across the water by Harold Wilson, who had been leader of the British Labour Party since January 1963. Wilson was identified with the left, but soon took it upon himself to offer up a more fluffy form of socialism to British voters. Edmund Dell has written of how Wilson had used his first conference speech as leader in October 1963 to fill 'socialism with a content intended to be less terrifying to the great mass of Labour and uncommitted voters', which he developed further in a later speech in which he argued: 'Socialism, as I understand it, means applying a sense of purpose to our national life: economic purpose, social purpose and moral purpose.'[144] This kind of inspirational rhetoric was very much of the age. John F. Kennedy had begun the vogue for it with his inauguration speech in 1961, in which his call upon US citizens to 'ask not what your country can do for you – ask what you can do for your country', became the rallying cry for a new sense of optimism and civic mindedness that would come to define the decade.[145] Wilson deftly combined this type of wide-eyed communitarianism with the leftist language of his own party, and in so doing came up with a new form of socialism for the sixties, where it stood for a general sense of niceness, rather than anything more specific. As Dell put it, 'the vagueness which now encompassed the word "socialism" was a gift to all those who wished to exhilarate their followers without being tied down to specifics. Socialism, whatever it means, obviously described an ideal society and, as such, was an appropriate objective of political activity.'[146] Wilson used this to great effect during the

1964 general election campaign, which he won, bringing to an end 13 years of Conservative government. Wilson's 1964 victory was seen by many on the Irish left as an auspicious event which boded well for a Labour resurgence in Ireland, and parallels have since been drawn between the momentum created on that occasion and that which followed Mary Robinson's success in the 1990 presidential eletion.[147] The Irish Labour Party sent a telegram expressing its best wishes to its sister party in Britain (earning the censure of the republican movement in the process).[148] The rhetoric of British political discourse never had much of an influence on Irish politics before this time and the Irish Labour Party had deliberately avoided doing anything to identify them in the public mind with British Labour (see p. 144 above). Suspicion of state intervention was waning, however, and with increasing familiarity with British politics facilitated by changes in the media, it was clear that 'socialism' was becoming less of a taboo, if not quite the kind of language one should use in polite company. The role of television is particularly important in this regard. Telefís Éireann had begun broadcasting on New Year's Eve 1961, but those with television sets on the east coast had been able to receive British stations since the 1950s, and British television was extremely popular among those able to receive it. Moreover, a new pattern of short-term emigration to Britain had developed during the 1960s, not least among the young, and especially among university students who often spent their summer holidays working in British factories before returning to their studies in the autumn. The socialisation of these 'tripper emigrants' is one which certainly had an impact on Irish attitudes and politics, and on the younger generation in particular.[149] (This was remarked upon by the British Ambassador Andrew Gilchrist in 1968, when he had his car repaired in the West of Ireland by a young man who had 'spent five years in Birmingham and had transferred back to Ireland the Labour leanings he had acquired in England'.[150]) Wilson had ultimately diluted 'socialism' into a brew more likely to appeal to the average British palate, and it would seem as though Corish and some of his advisers around this time thought they might offer a drop to the Irish people to see how it went down. Weak as it had become, socialism remained an acquired taste, and one that was going to take a little while before it would be put to Irish lips once again.

1965 GENERAL ELECTION

Lemass had managed to hold on to his slim majority in the Dáil until now, but he was naturally eager to consolidate his position. By 1965, he was ready to make his move. Fine Gael was in turmoil with the young turks of the Just Society practically in open warfare with their party leader, while Labour was still resolute that it would not enter into another coalition. Lemass was confident that once the electorate were faced with shambolic Fine Gael party, which even if it did perform well would not be able to form a government, they would plump for a secure Fianna Fáil administration. The death of Labour's Cork deputy Dan Desmond in December 1964 provided Lemass with just the opportunity he needed. Lemass declared that if the Fianna Fáil candidate did not win the contest he would have to go to the country. Desmond's widow, Eileen had been selected for Labour and, as John Horgan has noted, 'In three of the previous five by-elections the deceased TD's widow had been returned and in a fourth the deceased TD's son. When Lemass declared that Eileen Desmond's election would precipitate a dissolution of the Dáil, it was the shortest odds political bet he had taken in years.'[151] Eileen Desmond was indeed successful, but never took her seat. As soon as the result came in, Lemass dissolved the Dáil and announced that a general election would take place on 7 April.

Labour's manifesto, *The Labour Party: The Next Five Years*, was launched by Corish on 23 March. As Corish candidly admitted, it was not really a new document but rather the party's 1961 policy with a number of additional points;[152] or, as the manifesto put it, 'the basic principles of Labour's policy do not change from one election to another'. *The Next Five Years* emphasised state industry and planning and called for a comprehensive social security system which would include a national health service similar to that in Britain. 'All citizens', it stated, 'have an obligation to help in shaping the society in which we live and in deciding how the community should be organised and the wealth shared.' All in all, it was a standard social democratic manifesto, lacking in any left-wing jargon. It was a perfectly decent, if not particularly stellar document. Unfortunately, its lack of originality led to its being completely eclipsed by Fine Gael's *Just Society* paper, published one week earlier. Declan Costello had managed to steal a march on Labour. With its emphasis on planning and welfare, *Just Society* had so much in common with Labour's manifesto that some said it made it difficult for Labour to 'maintain its position as the most radical party'.[153] Still, Fine Gael's problem was that while Declan Costello had robbed Labour of its clothes, James Dillon and his colleagues were refusing to put them on. The Fine Gael leadership may have grudgingly agreed to go along with *Just Society*, but their lack of conviction was patently clear, and despite anything the manifesto may have said about the economy, Dillon was unambiguous in his assertion that Fine Gael was a private enterprise party.[154] Yes, countered Corish some days later, and Labour is a public enterprise party.[155] Nevertheless, it was not until Lemass engaged in some cynical provocation, maintaining that if there was a hung Dáil then Fianna Fáil would not enter into government with Labour, that Corish gave an unequivocal promise during a speech in Tullamore that his party would not enter coalition with any party in any circumstances.[156] *Just Society* or no, Labour was not for wooing. Thus the election became one where Fine Gael and Labour stood on remarkably similar platforms but were precluded from forming a government together afterwards, leaving Fianna Fáil to run on its record – 'Let Lemass Lead on!' – and its promise that it was the only party capable of forming a government.

The 1965 election was a tactical triumph for Lemass. He had caught Fine Gael at a time when that party was going through a particularly fractious period, and saw it returned with as many seats as it had won in 1961, a total of 47. Lemass's own party, on the other hand, saw its vote increase by four per cent nationwide, and picked up an extra two seats – not a huge increase, but enough for Fianna Fáil to return to office with a majority for the first time under Lemass. Labour enjoyed the biggest gains. It went into the election with 18, and returned with 22 – its highest number of deputies since 1922. It performed well across the board, but its greatest breakthrough came in Dublin. Whereas Labour's vote had gone up by almost four per cent nationally, in Dublin it had leaped from 8.4 to 18.5 per cent, its highest ever percentage vote in the capital. There were three new faces in the city: Michael O'Leary in Dublin North Central; Frank Cluskey in Dublin South Central and Dr John O'Connell (who had only joined the party some eighteen months earlier) in Dublin South West, an area which had always enjoyed an active branch membership but which had proved barren ground for Labour in elections until now. Finally, after a tight election and an epic re-count Denis Larkin managed to take back his old seat in Dublin North East, beating Fianna Fáil's Eugene Timmons by a mere six votes. There was, however, one significant loss. Noël Browne failed to hold on to Dublin South East. Many years later, he attributed this to his ill-fated march on the American Embassy during the Cuban missile crisis; in fact it owed more to successful vote management by Fianna Fáil and Browne's neglect of constituency business.[157] Outside Dublin, Patrick Norton managed to regain his father's seat in Kildare, while Harry Byrne won back the late William Davin's seat in Laois Offaly. There had been some speculation before the contest as to whether Jack McQuillan, who had held his Roscommon seat since 1948, could carry the 'unfamiliar Labour flag into Connaught' for the first time with any success, on the basis that Labour had failed in Roscommon with good men in the past, and that 'western people want little to do with socialism in any form', a sentiment which McQuillan himself had long shared.[158] It seems that this view proved correct. McQuillan's association with Labour, combined with a misjudged libel case the previous year when he had sued a newspaper successfully for reporting a local councillor's claim that he was a communist, but was awarded only a halfpenny damages,[159] dented his popularity. McQuillan joined Noël Browne in defeat, the two representing Labour's only losses in the election.

Having increased its seats by one third, Labour was better represented in the Dáil than it had been in four decades. It received its highest share of the vote since 1943, and had its best performance in Dublin since 1954. Labour had every reason to be heartened by its performance, which was seen by many as vindicating its go-it-alone strategy. On the other hand, as UCD political scientist John Whyte put it, Labour had gone into the contest in 'an exceptionally good position for picking up more seats' and needed only a very small increase in votes to win in constituencies where it had missed out marginally in 1961.[160] As Whyte saw it, Labour had 'reached a plateau', and while it gained seats which it ought to have won long ago it did not break new ground. 'Short of some new and quite unforeseeable break-through', Whyte predicted, 'it does not seem likely to do better at coming elections than it is at the moment'. Nevertheless, the 1965 election result was a major boost to Labour's confidence and had an important impact on the party's direction, as it injected some new blood into the parliamentary party and redressed its urban–rural balance. The Labour leadership was conscious that there could be no room for complacency, with Corish quick to identify the need for the party to build on its success,[161] but for now it seemed that Labour's star was definitely in the ascendant.

NINE

'THE SEVENTIES WILL BE SOCIALIST'

—

The 1965 election marked a sea change in Irish political life. The generational shift, which had been imminent since the turn of the decade, had finally come to pass. The election had resulted in 'one of the largest number of newly elected TDs and Senators ever'.[1] Labour, as we have already seen, had succeeded in having a number of bright young things elected. Fine Gael found itself with a new leader when James Dillon stepped down following the election. His successor was Liam Cosgrave, son of former Taoiseach W. T. Cosgrave, and a deputy since 1943. Cosgrave having only just turned 45, had two decades on his predecessor, although his relative youth had little bearing on his outlook. Cosgrave spent much of the next few years battling against another Fine Gael scion, Declan Costello and his Young Tiger comrades who remained a vociferous presence within Fine Gael throughout the rest of the decade. Finally, Lemass's cabinet became home to a host of new, younger faces such as Donogh O'Malley and George Colley and with them Fianna Fáil began to take on a younger, more dynamic appearance. Along with the change in personalities came a change in reportage. Television was becoming increasingly important, with programmes such as 7 Days and the Late Late Show setting agendas and becoming the fora for political debate, while the style of political journalism in the print media was becoming increasingly sharp and robust. All in all, politics had become more boisterous than it had been for years, whether in the Dáil or on the streets. The political temperature rose across the board although, perhaps unsurprisingly, Labour found itself more affected than most.

LABOUR IN THE NEW DÁIL

In an effort to start the new session on a more businesslike footing, all but a handful of Labour deputies were appointed spokesmen on a number of special subjects.[2] If indeed the assembled cast would made an 'oddly assorted cabinet', as one political correspondent put it, it was true nevertheless that the Labour Party seemed to be 'taking itself far more seriously as a party than heretofore'.[3] Another somewhat misguided effort to mobilise Labour deputes involved a rota being drawn up so that at least one Labour TD would be present at every debate at any given time.[4] As John O'Connell later recalled: 'Time and again I would be told – 'Go in there and say something on "X"'. And I would know practically nothing about X, but it was regarded as important to keep the flag flying, to be seen as saying something and to be part of the wheels going round.'[5]

Labour's naïve attempt to make its presence felt was savaged by John Healy of the *Irish Times* who observed that 'Labour seem to be under the impression that by putting in men to talk this is opposition. It is still a fact of parliamentary life that a man on his feet mouthing clichés is not enough.'[6] It soon became quite clear that despite the new arrivals and the party's more sizeable presence, the prospect of Labour becoming a more unified, proficient party seemed no closer. With the exception of Michael O'Leary and Frank Cluskey, both energetic men with lively minds, the new deputies were not much of an improvement on their more longstanding colleagues, and the absence of the irrepressible Browne and McQuillan in the Dáil chamber was deeply felt.[7] By the end of the year, John Healy had seen enough to remark that 'As long as there is a Labour Party in Dáil Éireann on the lines of the present Labour Party, it is a gross libel to say that the day of support for the Independent deputy has gone; it hasn't, and will not until the day that the Labour Party disappears.' [8]

LABOUR TURNS LEFT

Labour's first conference after the election took place in Dublin in October 1965. The party was obviously pleased with its recent developments – not only the election result but also the recent decision by the WUI to affiliate – but the mood was far from complacent with much of the agenda devoted to practical examination of how the party could improve its performance next time around.[9] One notable aspect of the conference was the continuing decline of the members' age profile. Labour was increasingly becoming a party of the under forties, and many of the delegates were reported to be in their early twenties,[10] who were, according to one account, 'imbued in the spirit of youth which questioned everything'.[11] On this occasion, Corish was prepared to do no more than to hint at a future change in direction. The time had come, he told delegates, 'when the Labour Party must make its policy crystal clear. We must say that Fianna Fáil and Fine Gael cannot do the job because they are against all really social legislation for the people and against any socialistic principles which would give the people more power.'[12]

This was far from the 'rejuvenation of ideas' being demanded by some members, and it was clear that the younger element within the party remained impatient.[13] It was beginning to look as though the momentum which had built up behind Labour was in danger of dissipating and even columnists in *Business and Finance*, far from the most sympathetic of publications, were writing of the 'poor radical souls in the party who are not at all happy' with the right-wing party in which they found themselves.[14]

The first few months of 1966 were dominated by the fiftieth anniversary celebrations of the 1916 Rising. The anniversary was marked in many ways from official merchandise to school pageants and to a military parade through O'Connell Street. The event was very much of its time, however, and amidst the enthusiastic commemorations there were critical voices vying to be heard. Some, not yet dubbed revisionists, complained that the Jubilee was an 'orgy of nationalism' (students from UCD's L&H, for instance, passed a motion condemning their university's decision to confer honorary degrees on the relatives of the proclamation signatories).[15] Others highlighted the disparity of the ideals of some of the revolutionaries and the reality of modern Ireland. The Irish language movement decried the existence of a monoglot Anglophone nation, while the left pointed to the continuing inequalities of Irish society. As many on the left questioned whether independence had amounted to anything beyond the painting green of post boxes, attention began to shift towards the writings of James Connolly. Connolly enjoyed a significant revival during the Jubilee, not only on the left but also in the mainstream media. There were numerous lectures and articles examining his life and teachings, and reprinted collections of his writings proved very popular with young radicals. What was interesting about the treatment of Connolly at this time was that writers were placing greater emphasis on his socialism than on his nationalism, the latter having overshadowed the former for decades. As Donal Nevin put it: 'On the fiftieth anniversary of the Easter Rising, which Connolly did so much to bring about, one must echo the words of Desmond Ryan: "There is no need for any maudlin apologies for the most vital and consistent thing about him: his Socialism."'[16] Socially progressive religious, such as the Dominican Fathers Fergal O'Connor and Austin Flannery, began appearing as commentators on the *Late Late Show* and on other programmes to debate whether the socialist Connolly could accurately be called a Marxist. This was testament to a more sophisticated attitude,[17] and yet, while talk of socialism dominated profiles of Connolly, Labour spokesmen had not yet made the transition to the point where they felt comfortable using the language of Connolly, rather than merely invoking his name. 'Social justice' remained the preferred term, the word 'socialism' entirely absent from the party's vocabulary, a seemingly unbreakable taboo. When one member of the PLP was asked whether he considered himself a socialist by a visiting journalist from the *New Statesman*, the deputy replied, 'Of course I do – in this restaurant'.[18]

Within a couple of months, however, Labour was prepared to move its socialism beyond the citadels of fine dining. Several committees were established to formulate new policies which would appeal to an 'increasingly alert electorate', based on Labour's (new found) 'tradition of democratic socialism'.[19] Similarly, Michael O'Leary had pointed out before Labour's October 1966 conference that the party could not expect to survive on clichés and general statements. 'The electorate demands of us much more than mere knocking of political opponents however Tory their policies', he maintained, 'Without a programme that is clear in expression and intent the trade union voters will not leave Fianna Fáil'.[20] As O'Leary saw it, Fianna Fáil and Fine Gael had 'gone to the left' and had taken on Labour's policies en masse: 'everything we ever looked for, they now seek. On planning, health, education, they speak with the tongues of socialists.' Labour had to differentiate itself from the other parties if it was not to become redundant.

Labour's leftward shift was to be unveiled at conference. The political correspondents had been well briefed that Corish would make an explicit declaration of socialism during his leader's speech. Although this would prove popular with many of the newer members, its reception by most of the longer established Labourites on the right of the party, and the majority of the parliamentary party, was less assured. Imagining what the Cork deputy Michael Pat Murphy's response might be, John Healy noted wryly:

[He] has never found it expedient to burden the House or his constituents with the articles of faith from the catechism according to Connolly. His leader, Mr Corish, may preach with a Calvinistic zeal the Connolly gospel and the importance of the party's taking a stand as a real socialist party and Mr Murphy will nod his head and say: 'Whatever you say Brendan, I'm easy', being fully conscious that a Connolly tract is no substitute for a subsidy for Sherwin butter.[21]

The 1966 conference was Labour's largest to date with 590 delegates representing branches alone expected to attend.[22] The attendance rivalled the figures of a Fianna Fáil Ard Fheis and was greater than that of Fine Gael.[23] The size of the gathering was also indicative of the rapidity of Labour's growth, with over twice the number of ordinary delegates as there had been only two years earlier.[24] Nor did the new recruits add merely to the size of the meeting, but also to its volume, with the majority of the more critical motions coming from the younger branches, representing a more dominant force on proceedings, in contrast to previous years, when their presence had been more muted. Moreover, their views were being reflected in the speeches from the platform, and none more so than that of Brendan Corish at the close of proceedings, in which he stressed both his own and his party's adherence to what he called a 'coherent socialist philosophy'.[25] In fact, there was nothing coherent about it. There were, he explained, 'various degrees of socialism' but neglected to mention what degree Labour was expressing.[26] It was as one report put it a 'firm declaration of socialism – not yet clearly defined'.[27] The ambiguous use of the word seemed to matter little to the assembled delegates, however, who were overjoyed that this previously unbreakable taboo now lay shattered on the floor of Liberty Hall. They were overjoyed to have been present at the most radical (and equally meaningless) speech made by a leader of the Labour Party made since the days of the Workers' Republic, with Corish's performance followed by 'a prima donna's oration', as one of those present recalled.[28] There were no voices of dissent in the midst of the rapture. On the other hand, however, neither was there anything to imply that those on the right of the party had been swept away on the wave of enthusiasm that appeared to have enveloped the rest of the delegates. Rather, John Healy's prediction of the right wing's response has proved prescient: they had no interest in rocking the boat for the time being, merely nodding their heads as if to say, 'whatever you say Brendan, we're easy'.

The conference was a triumph. With an atmosphere characterised by 'anticipation, preparation and idealism', Labour showed every sign of being a confident party on the move. As far as coverage of the event was concerned, it was generally favourable although massively unequal – where Corish's profession of socialism went almost unnoticed in the *Irish Independent*, his speech was front page news in the next day's *Irish Times*, and was dissected in columns and editorials subsequently. The *Irish Times'* treatment of the conference was little less than breathless, with Michael McInerney and Donal Foley positively rejoicing at the events.[29] Significant as the leader's speech undoubtedly was, even more important was the way in which the drive leftward seemed to come from the ordinary members, who time and time again prefaced their contributions with the phrase 'speaking as a socialist'.[30] There was a feeling among some of those present, that Corish's speech at the end of the conference had summed up, rather than led, the tone of proceedings. Corish had '"got the message" of this new explosion from below', said one observer, and few if any of those coming away from the conference would have done so without the 'impression that in this case it was the floor inspiring, and even leading, the leaders'.[31]

Of course, the leaders could only be led willingly. If Corish had not been open to change, it would not have happened,[32] something which becomes very clear when the leadership of the Labour Party is compared with that of either Fine Gael or Fianna Fáil, who had their fair share of radicals at the time. (It ought to be borne in mind that there was a massive increase in political activism across the board at this time, for all ages and for all the main parties. Despite the left-wing radicalism among students, and despite the huge gains enjoyed by Labour in the universities at this time, it is worth noting that in UCD, at least, Fianna Fáil's Kevin Barry Cumman was at least 50 per cent bigger than either of the Labour or Fine Gael societies.[33]) Liam Cosgrave continued his forthright opposition to the Young Tigers of the Just Society and convincingly staved off an attempt to have Fine Gael's name changed to the Social Democratic Party at its Ard Fheis in 1968 by 653 votes to 81.[34] Perhaps unsurprisingly, there was less of this kind of thing in Fianna Fáil, although that party had its share of students using up precious Ard Fheis time to opine the evils of American intervention in Vietnam, call for the opening of diplomatic relations with the USSR, or discuss the merits of industrial democracy.[35] The two larger parties were sufficiently well established to resist, with a leadership determined to stand firm against any shifts or lurches leftward or otherwise, while Labour was weak enough to be overtaken by its new recruits who soon came close to swamping the party. As Michael Gallagher pointed out,

> Few European social democratic parties were pulled much to the left by the wave of student protests. Most of them were too much a part of the political establishment to have any appeal to the radicals, and moreover they had too large a membership, and were too well organised, to be easily taken over.[36]

Labour's malleability came from the combination of the party's previously small membership and a compliant leader, for Corish had undergone something of a conversion himself. The influence of two of the 1965 cohort is relevant here. Michael O'Leary and Frank Cluskey had both become very close to Corish since being elected to the Dáil the previous year and were instrumental in bringing Corish to a more left-wing position, helped immeasurably by the shift in Church teaching under Pope John, whom Corish later described as 'one of the greatest contributors of all to change in Irish attitudes'.[37] Significantly, both O'Leary and Cluskey had become active in Labour politics in the late 1950s. They were older than many of the student types who were joining by the late 1960s, but they were, nevertheless, part of a new generation of members who had not been active during the era of virulent anti-socialism of the 1940s or 1950s, and lacked the inherent caution of those who had had to operate in that time. Their willingness – or even eagerness – to use explicitly socialist rhetoric contrasted starkly with the old left. Donal Nevin, who had been the only member of Corish's kitchen cabinet from that generation, had become increasingly busy with his work in Congress and had become less active in the party as a result. Corish thus found himself surrounded by bright young things who urged him to take a radical stance, and he was happy to oblige. Furthermore, after he had become Labour leader, Corish had indicated that he would be willing to let the membership exert greater control over the party. Having stated in 1960 that he regarded the Annual Conference as the supreme body of the Labour Party,[38] he subsequently went further when he told a meeting of the 1913 Club the following year that 'if the members of the Labour Party wished to restore the object of a workers' republic to the constitution of the Labour Party, they could do so at the Annual Conference. He would abide by their decision and would not do a "Gaitskell"'.[39] This, in effect, was exactly what he had done.

The ease with which Corish could do this, however, was facilitated by the right's acquiescence. Firstly, since the death of William Norton three years earlier, no one of commensurate intellect or personality had emerged to lead the right wing and, as a result, it remained disorganised and incoherent for the rest of the decade. Moreover, as the numbers of ordinary members rose, the right's dominance of conference through the traditional use of paper branches was diminished. It was easier to let the firebrands and progressives make whatever resolutions they liked, on the assumption that once the resolutions had been passed they would be ignored by the PLP. The seeming indifference of the rural members of the PLP belied a strategy of forsaking the national stage (thus avoiding guilt by association) and concentrating on local matters, such as Michael Pat Murphy's 'subsidy for Sherwin's butter' mentioned by John Healy. Of course, Labour's rural deputies had always been accomplished parish pump politicians, who could, as Noël Browne so colourfully (and condescendingly) put it, 'with practised ease, build a nest in your ear while minding mice at a crossroads',[40] and about whom the complaint was so often made that they were not party people but mere independents sheltering under a convenient Labour umbrella. It was therefore eminently sensible that, following the changes in their party's supposed outlook, that they would simply concentrate on their 'parish' work to an even greater extent while endeavouring to ensure that none of the party's new-fangled ideas trickled into their areas. The behaviour of Limerick East deputy, Stevie Coughlan, was a classic example of this. In 1966, a recruitment drive by the local left-wing activist Jim Kemmy had successfully netted around 100 new members to the Limerick city branch. Coughlan, quite rightly, saw this as a threat to his position and began a rearguard action to stem any publicity for the branch, including one occasion when he sabotaged a press conference being held there by Kemmy and his colleagues. When the leadership tried to initiate an investigation into what had transpired, it was blocked by Coughlan.[41] Labour's right-wing TDs were keeping their heads down in the knowledge that their seats had to be protected, not at conference, but on the ground in their constituencies.

MCQUILLAN AND MACAONGHUSA

At the same time, one of the PLP's most active members was facing expulsion. Labour was coming under increasing pressure from the trade union movement to expel Jack McQuillan, now a senator, from the party after he had taken up the post of general secretary in the Irish Post Office Officials' Association (IPOOA) in February 1966. The IPOOA was a breakaway union which had recently split from the Post Office Workers' Union, and McQuillan's appointment was problematic for two reasons: firstly, because the POWU was one of Labour's oldest affiliates; and secondly, because the issue of breakaway unions – always a vexed one within the trade union movement – had become increasingly acute since the early part of the decade. Congress made it clear that it was seriously concerned about any attempts to disrupt the movement by the creation of splinter movements, and stressed that there was no question of its accepting the affiliation of splinter organisations.[42] The IPOOA was the second splinter union to come out of the post office in as many years,[43] and both the POWU and Congress, were anxious that Labour was not seen to condone one of its parliamentarians approving of, let alone working for, a splinter union. The IPOOA, for its part, tried to remedy the situation by applying for affiliation to Congress, but, predictably, this approach was brusquely refused. For the POWU and Congress, the solution was clear: McQuillan had to leave the union or leave the party. There was near unanimity within the PLP on the issue, with maverick naïf John O'Connell, one of only two TDs without a trade union background, alone in supporting the senator.[44] An attempt to expel McQuillan from the party in March failed,[45] but the issue did not end there, and by October the ICTU began to renew pressure on Labour to deal with the situation. Congress refrained from suggesting that Labour take a specific course of action, on the basis that it was 'essentially a problem for the party', but their representatives made it quite clear 'that their affiliated unions felt very strongly about the subject'.[46] A composite motion highly critical of McQuillan's actions was passed by the Labour conference,[47] but no action came out of this in the short term, prompting a complaint from Jim Larkin that, despite conference's resolution, McQuillan was continuing to try to induce the members of his union (which was affiliated to the party) to join the IPOOA, and the demand that 'firm and decisive action' be taken by the AC to put a stop to McQuillan's behaviour.[48] Labour was now faced with losing a hardworking and popular member (not to mention a potential deputy) or risking a serious breach with the unions. So it was that, in time honoured fashion, Labour did nothing for the time being and the controversy was allowed drag on for nearly another 18 months.

Later that autumn, there was further friction with the appearance of the weekly *Labour Newsletter*, a two-page photostat published by the self-styled 'Labour Association', which described itself as 'a social and political discussion group of Labour Party members', and which claimed a circulation of around 450.[49] Written anonymously, the newsletter was a combination of griping, insult, innuendo and gossipmongering. Its first edition accused Labour's chairman, James Tully, of throwing his weight around the PLP, and similar remarks appeared the following week. Within no time the PLP unanimously demanded an investigation into the document and for the author's expulsion.[50] A subsequent meeting of the AC found the newsletter's contents to be 'of a very peculiar nature; in fact, so peculiar that it would be reasonable to suspect that the author may be unbalanced',[51] a statement indicating a certain oversensitivity. It did not take long before Proinsias MacAonghusa came under suspicion, but while he was prepared to accept responsibility for some of the content, and for putting up some of its funding, he denied responsibility for the remarks about the Chairman. An investigative committee was established 'with a view to *proving* who was responsible for the offensive paragraphs, the culprit to be expelled from the party',[52] but unchastened, the *Labour Newsletter* continued to publish, now filled with denunciations of the 'witch-hunt' against it being carried out by the 'party's do-nothing-but-hold-on-to-our-cushy-seats wing'.[53] On 12 January 1967 the AC received the sub-committee's report which detailed how MacAonghusa had refused to meet it, had declined their invitations in colourful language, and had finally threatened legal action against them.[54] The AC responded by voting for MacAonghusa's immediate expulsion by ten votes to three, and then relayed the decision to MacAonghusa and to the press in the same post.[55]

Inadequate communication skills on the AC's part turned what should have been a relatively straightforward disciplinary matter into a public debacle. The expulsion attracted an unwarranted amount of critical press attention. MacAonghusa, broadcaster and journalist by trade, was no shrinking violet and he immediately went on the offensive. He portrayed his ejection as an ideological attack by the right-wing/trade-union rearguard (he had been critical of both) against the forces of progression. Moreover, the AC's failure to relate clearly and fully the circumstances behind the expulsion (a statement from the party on the subject did not appear until *three weeks* after the event) meant that MacAonghusa's conspiratorial thesis was generally propounded.[56] Labour was portrayed as a right-wing party in thrall to the unions, in which 'intellectuals' had no place; indeed an article in the *New Statesman* went so far as to cast MacAonghusa as Ireland's Aneurin Bevan with his 'lively personality, combative oratory and Celtic background', with his wife, Catherine McGuinness, cast as his bold Jennie Lee,[57] a description so complimentary, one would almost think he wrote it himself. The whole business seemed to hark back to the bad old days of internal squabbling and arbitrary expulsions, but the disaster was compounded further by the resignation of McGuinness from her post as parliamentary secretary, which she had held since 1961. McGuinness had been Corish's primary speechwriter and confidante throughout his period as leader and her loss came as a profound blow.[58] Not only had Corish lost one of his most trusted colleagues, but he suffered the further ignominy of being portrayed as a weak leader who was being dominated by stronger personalities[59] (not least because he was said to have been one of the three who had opposed the expulsion), and his behaviour during the affair was described as 'unsure and vacillating'.[60] John Healy painted a picture of him in the *Irish Times* as hiding away in Wexford, 'silent amid a raucous claque of dissident voices . . . *sans* scriptwriter, *sans* Proinsias, *sans* a real Labour Party, he is, I hope, taking a crash course in political leadership'. To help him in this end, Healy guided Corish in the direction of Machiavelli's *Prince*.[61]

Rumours abounded that Corish was considering his resignation,[62] but he stood firm. Corish lost the services of Dr John O'Connell who was so upset by the expulsion and the 'shabby' treatment of MacAonghusa (and by extension McGuinness) that he went AWOL from the parliamentary party for some nine months,[63] although the publicity which ensued was infinitely more damaging than the deputy's absence per se. Indeed, personality clashes which would have taken place behind closed doors were now becoming increasing public, as a fracas on the *Late Late Show* between MacAonghusa, Michael O'Leary and Noël Browne illustrated.[64] All in all, the affair itself had been much ado about nothing: a personality clash that ended with a hamfisted attempt to impose discipline, and to view it in left–right terms would be utterly inaccurate, not least because MacAonghusa was never the doyen of the left he purported to be.[65] Moreover, when the POWU had made formal complaints over an article of MacAonghusa's, in which he had written favourably about breakaway unions, the complaints were rejected by the AC on the basis that to censure MacAonghusa would mean interfering in the freedom of party officers to act in a personal capacity.[66] Nevertheless, the number of branches opposing the expulsion illustrated how susceptible many of the newer members were to the idea that the right was prepared to use dirty tricks to maintain its power base. As one observer put it, 'The more radical elements in the party feel that an inordinate amount of power is wielded by the conservative forces . . . And the recent performance has done little to allay the radical disquiet.'[67] It was to this end that the Limerick deputy, Stevie Coughlan, proposed that the party should issue a statement that Labour 'welcomed intellectuals, contrary to any other view expressed',[68] but his colleagues thought better, and passed on the idea.[69]

The radicals did not have to wait long to have their disquiet allayed, however. On the day the story of MacAonghusa's expulsion broke, Labour announced that it was establishing a position of political director to 'initiate activities aimed at furthering the objectives of the party and to develop an administrative and information service for the party'.[70] Jim Larkin headed a three-man interviewing panel, which interviewed 26 candidates before unanimously recommending Brendan Halligan, a 31-year-old Dubliner, then working as an economist with the Irish Sugar Company, for the position. Halligan impressed the interview panel as being articulate and having 'good ideas' for the party. He was seen as being old enough to bring maturity to the post and young enough to have energy and enthusiasm for the job. Furthermore, the panel felt it was unlikely that if he was successful in his post, that he would try to use it as a springboard for a parliamentary seat.[71] Halligan had joined Labour only a year earlier, having been brought into the party by his friend Niall Greene, a member in Rathmines since around 1963. With calls for the creation of such a position ongoing during the previous few years, the appointment heralded the beginning of a more professional approach at long last – as one observer remarked, 'behind the streamlined Fianna Fáil machine, Labour is an elderly Model T Ford'[72] – but more important were its implications for the balance of power within the party after the MacAonghusa affair. Halligan immediately identified himself as a moderniser on Labour's left wing, and was portrayed as such in the media. As the *Labour Newsletter* observed at the time, his 'interview with the *Irish Times* showed him to have belief in progressive and socialist ideas, or at least to be able to use socialist terminology at will'.[73] The appointment of a young progressive such as Halligan helped assuage the left's paranoia, not least because it looked like a deliberate slight against the party secretary, Mary Davidson, who was widely identified as a reactionary presence in head office.[74] Although it had been envisaged that the political director would work alongside the secretary, it is difficult to imagine that Davidson would have been prepared to tolerate such significant incursions on her territory. Within six months of Halligan's appointment Davidson had called it a day, and announced she would retire at the end of the year.[75] It marked the end of an era, and a fundamental generational shift in head office. Halligan was less than half Davidson's age, and thought in terms of the here and now, and the future, compared with Davidson who was old-fashioned and wedded to the traditions of the party. As Halligan explained in one interview: 'Within the next ten years the complexion of the Irish electorate will change drastically. There will be 300,000 new voters, of a new breed. The environment is already changing, liberalising, the young are restless and dissatisfied with the static political situation.'[76]

Whether such remarks were regarded as those of a far-seeing strategist or an arrogant young man depended a great deal on the age of the audience, but it was looking increasingly as though Labour would soon become no party for old men.

ONWARD AND LEFTWARD

By the summer of 1967 Labour seemed to have recovered its momentum, and the decision by the ITGWU to affiliate, more than 20 years after it had left the party in such unhappy circumstances, represented a very positive sign and a major psychological boost. The union's journal *Liberty* described the move in terms of the need to build a society based on social justice, in language which owed much to the social encyclicals, an editorial expressing the hope that 'during the next decade Ireland will not alone be a religious country but also a practising Christian country for the workers employed in workshops, factories and fields'.[77] Nevertheless, Labour's new vocabulary was evident occasionally. When ITGWU General Secretary, John Conroy – a man not known as a firebrand – was asked what he expected from the Labour Party, he replied: 'socialism'. How genuine this response was is open to question, but it was significant all the same, for, as the young Eamonn McCann was to write at the time, 'it appears that even John Conroy would now rather be called a red by a rat than a rat by a red'.[78] In the meantime, the municipal elections which took place in June 1967 also seemed to show the party on the advance, fielding far more candidates than before, around one third of whom were aged under 30 years. It was, however, a tale of two elections. In Dublin, Labour's first preference vote increased by ten per cent and it won 13 seats, beating Fine Gael into third place,[79] but there was no such breakthrough outside the capital. In fact, Labour suffered a net loss of four seats. The consensus, certainly among the Dublin-based activists, was that this was primarily the result of poor organisation which would have to be tackled urgently if Labour was to make gains at the next general election.[80] The right-wing Labour leadership traditionally tended to blame organisation for setbacks while the left stood on the sidelines shouting that it was all down to policies. Perhaps it was inevitable that once the left found themselves in a similar position, they would do likewise. However, as *Hibernia*'s commentator noted, the party's claim that the poll showed 'the sleeping giant of Labour has awakened', ignored the fact that the party's message 'did not percolate outside of Dublin city'.[81]

One other notable aspect of the local elections was Sinn Féin's re-entry into the political fray. The republican movement's emphasis on leftist political action since 1962 had continued throughout the decade.[82] That year the Sinn

Féin president Tomás MacGiolla also promised that the party intended 'to throw the full weight of the organisation into the local government elections in the twenty six counties . . . and a major effort [would] be made to gain a greater foothold in local councils',[83] which meant that not only did Sinn Féin contest the 1967 local elections, but that it did so on a socialist platform. When this electoral foray proved unsuccessful, the Sinn Féin organisation concluded it would have to raise its profile by other means. Within no time it had established a Central Citizens' Advice Bureau in the city,[84] and the formation of the Dublin Housing Action Committee (DHAC) followed soon after. The DHAC was largely the brainchild of Sinn Féin, although it had a strong Irish Workers' Party element. The DHAC ran a militant campaign of street demonstrations as well as squatting and occupying buildings,[85] and enjoyed a great deal of support from students and young radicals, for whom marching and squatting were popular pastimes as well as means of political communication. Though the DHAC was subject to adverse publicity from quite early on, with the *Evening Herald* running pieces identifying the political groups and personnel behind the campaign,[86] this did little to detract from its appeal.[87] But if its founders' intention had been for it to act as a conduit into the republican movement, it failed and Cathal Goulding complained that it was Labour and not Sinn Féin which was reaping the benefits of the campaign, in perhaps the only example of Labour benefiting parasitically from another group, rather than vice versa. In fact, the republican movement, for all its left wing posturing was completely failing to capitalise on the leftist zeitgeist, and appeared to be haemorrhaging support, with one internal document claiming that the republican movement's membership in Dublin was 'not much greater than that of the IWP' and that sales of its newspaper, the *United Irishman* (which had fallen to 14,000 from 100,000 ten years earlier) were comparable to those of the *Irish Socialist*.[88] Nevertheless, it did help bring the republican movement in from the cold, with Sinn Féin activists (along with IWP General Secretary Michael O'Riordan) being invited on to Telefís Éireann to discuss with Dominican priests the problems of housing in Dublin.[89]

When Labour's annual conference met in October 1967, its business was dominated by moves to consolidate the leftward shift. There were calls to re-write the constitution to 'express clearly the Socialist objectives of the party', to move beyond sloganeering and develop policy along socialist lines, as well as improving the organisation so that it would be prepared for the next election. The Vietnam war was the subject of twice as many motions as agriculture, an indication of how much Labour had become a party of urban youth. Further proof of this could be seen in conference's attitude towards Ireland's proposed entry to the EEC, which was the subject of more motions on the agenda than any other topic. As the report of the American Embassy's observer at the proceedings put it:

> Half the Labour Party's representation in the Dáil comes from urban semi-industrial constituencies in Dublin or Cork; the other half is scattered throughout the rest of Ireland . . . Given the fact that Ireland's entry into the EEC will chiefly benefit the agricultural sector of its economy and that the industrial sector is having some difficulty even in adjusting to the gradual reduction in tariffs on UK goods resulting from Ireland's Free Trade Agreement with the British, it is scarcely surprising that the Labour Party should have the mixed feelings about the EEC that it again displayed at this conference. What is perhaps surprising is that the party, by voicing its doubt collectively, has implicitly recognised that it has little appeal or interest in Ireland's agricultural community.[90]

This neglect of the rural constituency was more than a little myopic at a time when tens of thousands of farmers were marching through the streets of the capital under the banner of the National Farmers' Association, led by the redoubtable Rickard Deasy. The highlight of the conference, for which it became infamous, was the leader's speech, in which Corish informed the assembled throng that the 'seventies will be socialist'. To describe this as a 'speech' would be a misnomer: it was really a sermon. Identifying Irish society as suffering from the prevalence of disquiet, apathy, cynicism and indifference, Corish told delegates that it was up to Labour to remedy the nation's ills. Labour had to stand aside from the other two parties and offer a socialist alternative; there could be no turning back, he affirmed, 'from the position we have progressively taken up in the sixties'.[91] Corish had refused to define what he meant when he had pronounced Labour's socialism at the previous year's conference and this time was no different: it was not the purpose of the address to analyse the philosophy of socialism in depth or to outline detailed policies, but rather to 'assert that no solution exists outside socialism'. Socialism not being 'a set of settled doctrines to be applied dogmatically to every situation, but *essentially an attitude* capable of being developed in many ways. Having committed Labour to the politics of niceness, Corish then promised that the party would follow up by holding a special conference six to nine months hence which would put together a programme of nice policies to match, and with these policies Labour would go on to 'Build the New Republic'.

It was a tour de force. Corish was utterly convincing in his confident assertion of a vague socialist ethos, putting a stellar performance behind a feel-good speech. Noting how in order for any party leader (but especially one in opposition) at conference to 'establish himself as the unchallenged leader, the enthusiasm of the party workers must be roused up and they must be given a sense that the party can achieve power', the observer from the American Embassy remarked that Corish had proved very successful in achieving all of these objectives in the course of his 70-minute keynote speech.[92] It was even more important than usual for Corish to put in a good performance, and to show himself as an inspiring and commanding figure after his authority had been dented a little by the MacAonghusa furore, but few would have disagreed with Barry Desmond's summation of the weekend as a 'personal triumph' for Corish. Doctrinal arguments were absent because, once again, the party's right-wing members had kept their heads down. The *Irish Socialist*, alone in mentioning this, described the 'non-participation of the great majority of the Labour TDs in the debate on the common market, coalition and other questions' as a most disturbing feature of the proceedings.[93]

If delegates left conference on a high, however, it did not take long before they were brought back to earth. Labour faced two by-elections in Cork and Limerick West on 9 November, the former caused by the death of the popular Labour deputy Seán Casey, while the latter had been held by Fianna Fáil. Coming so soon after the party's landmark conference, head office felt a good campaign and a decent result were more than usually desirable. 'Public interest will be intense to see if Labour can maintain the breakthrough of the last few years', members were warned.[94] If this was true, it was unfortunate, because Labour's campaigns were a shambles. An appeal for funds raised practically nothing, electoral flying columns were nowhere to be seen,[95] and the 'glorious euphoria' so evident at conference was conspicuous by its absence. Labour's candidate in Cork did well by increasing the number of first preferences from the previous election but he came in third (behind Fianna Fáil and Fine Gael) nonetheless. The Labour man came in third in Limerick West too, but it was a poor third, which saw him lose his deposit,[96] while Gerard Collins took the seat for Fianna Fáil. There were more woes to follow. In December the Kildare deputy Patrick Norton was summoned before the AC to account for his inactivity during the recent by-elections, but rather than explaining himself to the AC, he announced that he was resigning from the party because it had been taken over by a 'small but vocal group of ambitious fellow travellers'.[97] His decision to quit was no great loss. Patrick Norton had been parachuted into the constituency after his father's death against local wishes. Not only was he an outsider stepping on the toes of a well-liked local would-be-candidate, but rumour had it that he was not even a party member before his nomination.[98] Even after his nomination, Norton junior made no effort to curry favour with the local party in Kildare, which proved only too happy to let him go when the time came. Nor was Patrick Norton lamented by his erstwhile colleagues in the PLP who were becoming increasingly embarrassed and exasperated by his vocal support for private enterprise and the security of its profits (he had refused to vote with Labour in support of a Fianna Fáil proposal to allow personal bank accounts to be examined to see if income tax was being avoided), not to mention his behaviour during the Waterford by-election in December 1966, when he called on Labour voters to give their second preferences to the Fine Gael candidate.[99] The *Irish Socialist* was a little crass, but truthful nonetheless, as it summed up 'the fact is that this successful business man-cum-slum-landlord should never have been in the Labour Party' in the first place,[100] although to be fair, Patrick Norton was neither the first nor last person to end up in the wrong party because of familial loyalties. Significantly, however, while it is true that his remarks about fellow travellers probably reflected 'the conservative viewpoint of some members, particularly in rural areas',[101] the fact that no one else followed him out of the party or even partially agreed with his sentiments in public negated the impact of his claims. It was the first and only breach in the silence of Labour's right wing prior to the next general election.

By now, Labour was being attacked from all sides. While Patrick Norton was accusing Labour of having been taken over by communists, Jack McQuillan was complaining that Labour's socialism was not even skin deep. The contro-versy over his relationship with the IPOOA had finally come to a head. He was suspended from the PLP on 23 April 1968 for breaking a party whip after he tabled a question in the Senate relating to his union, despite having been warned that to do so would result in his expulsion.[102] Like Patrick Norton, McQuillan jumped ship rather than be disciplined. He told a meeting of his local organisation that he was resigning from the party and retiring from public life. In a statement, McQuillan complained about the inaction of the rest of his former colleagues in the PLP, and the cynicism of their recent conversion to socialism. 'A discussion on co-operative farming sent them running for Holy Water', he said, while 'mention of the West of Ireland sent them scurrying for lunch'. He continued:

> To my dismay, it became clear that Socialism was only a gimmick as far as Mr Corish and his colleagues were concerned. The proof of the matter lies in the fact that Fine Gael are more than willing to join forces with them. A few old bones in the guise of minor Cabinet posts will satisfy the Labour doggies . . . The Party stood exposed as a puppet of trade union bosses who pulled the strings in the background. Today it is dependent for its survival on the financial backing of a couple of trade unions.[103]

However valid McQuillan's criticism of the PLP's commitment to socialism or its vigour, his assertion that the party was in the pocket of the trade union movement was far from true. The unions were broadly dissatisfied with

Labour at this point and the party seemed unwilling or unable to address the situation. The unions had been objecting to McQuillan's involvement with the IPOOA for over two years before any measures were taken against him, and even then he was disciplined only when he expressly ignored an instruction which had been given to him on this subject. Quite apart from McQuillan and the splinter union, however, there was a sense among senior trade unionists that Labour was not taking its concerns or interests particularly seriously. The WUI had turned down a request for financial assistance for the November 1967 by-elections citing the absence of Labour deputies during the committee stage of the Redundancy Bill, and the union's executive was profoundly unhappy about the expression of anti-union sentiments at the party's conference the previous October. Writing to Corish, Jim Larkin complained of a mood which 'at best could be termed a blend of cynicism and contempt for trade unions and at worst one of antagonism', an 'unhealthy atmosphere' which, he said, the AC had made no effort to dispel. The WUI executive stressed that Labour had often enjoyed its financial support, even before it was an affiliate, and that there was 'growing apprehension at the trend of opinion and decision revealing themselves at many levels of the party'.[104] Worried about the fissures opening between the two wings of the movement, Congress endeavoured to establish a joint council between the two groups,[105] but found Labour slow to respond to its advances. There was further conflict during the following summer (1968), after the AC instructed the PLP to vote against a government initiative to increase TDs' salaries, and a number of Labour deputies threatened to resign rather than do so.[106] The PLP's support for the pay rise infuriated not only the non-parliamentarians on the AC, but also many ordinary branch members and prompted Congress to make an informal complaint to Corish.[107] The issue gave rise to trenchant criticism at the WUI's 1968 conference in May, which also saw the union's general secretary Jim Larkin rounding on the poverty of the PLP's approach to economic issues. Larkin, who was an active and highly respected union representative on the National Industrial Economic Council, complained that Labour appeared incapable of telling the difference between the NIEC and Fianna Fáil, and had engaged in sterile criticism of the council in order to score cheap political points.[108] Labour was in an unenviable position. Those outside the mainstream trade union movement regarded Labour as the union's lap dog, while the unions felt the party was inadequate and unresponsive to its needs. Accused of being taken over by communists by those on the right, it was accused of mere opportunism by the left. It had managed to achieve the worst of all worlds with remarkable success.

These issues were unwelcome distractions from the many more immediate matters facing the party. Two by-elections would be held in mid-March, one in Clare (a Fine Gael seat), the other in Wicklow following the death of James Everett, who had been Labour's (and National Labour's) representative in that constituency since 1922 and was Father of the House when he died. A degree of conflict occurred in Wicklow about Labour's nomination, with Everett's nephew Liam Kavanagh supported by the local party, and Noël Browne (who was resident in Bray at this time) looking to regain a seat after losing Dublin South East in 1965, supported by head office. There would be no parachuting here, and Kavanagh won the nomination by two votes.[109] While he did not hold the seat, he performed well.[110] The Clare contest saw Labour's vote rise by 60 per cent on the party's 1965 figure there. A by-election in East Limerick a few months later, caused by the death of the charismatic Minister for Education Donogh O'Malley, saw Labour's gains continue. Visiting Labour workers had noticed a groundswell of support during the campaign,[111] but even they were surprised by the extent of the swing to Labour. Labour's candidate, Mick Lipper, doubled the party's first preference vote from its 1965 level, taking over 26 per cent of the vote and coming in second on the first count. Lipper missed out to the late minister's nephew Des O'Malley on the third count by only a handful of votes.[112]

Though the results of the by-elections were very positive, Labour faced a threat which, if successful, could wipe out the party almost entirely. After much rumour and speculation, the government formally announced on 31 January 1968 that it was going to try to replace proportional representation with a first past the post system for the second time in less than ten years. Attention shifted from Labour's new-found socialism towards its go-it-alone strategy. Would it be able to retain its much vaunted independence in the face of a straight vote? For all its talk of realigning Irish politics on a left–right basis, Labour still had most to lose under the 'straight vote' system. Its very existence depended on the retention of PR, and the party was acutely aware that a new referendum campaign would see Labour fighting for its life, but this implicit admission that the party could not survive in a plurality voting system underlined the emptiness of much of its recent bravado. Throughout the early months of 1968, a steady stream of press releases on the inequity of the straight vote flowed from Labour's head office. After a late start, Fine Gael also joined in the opposition to the government's proposals, the delay being due to the fact that the party's leader, Liam Cosgrave, was well known to be partial to the straight vote and was battling with his front bench which opposed the move almost to a man.[113] The question then followed, would there be a united front between the two opposition parties against the amendment? In the end, the answer was no. Informal talks took place during this time between representatives of Labour and Fine Gael, but they were not coalition negotiations and Garret FitzGerald's later claims that Labour was trying to effect a merger with the larger party are patent nonsense.[114] As far as senior party activists were concerned, Labour was on the verge of an electoral advance of the greatest magnitude, and they were going to give up now to merge with Fine Gael. The only part of Fine Gael Labour was interested in merging was FitzGerald himself – and Declan Costello. Both men were approached by Brendan Halligan at the time in an effort to induce them into Labour, but they declined.[115] Costello, for his part, was sympathetic to Labour's policies but believed that it was futile to operate from such a meagre base as that party enjoyed, and not least when it was avowedly anti-coalitionist.[116]

The date for the referendum had been set for 16 October, with the campaign bitterly fought out over the last six weeks before the poll. There were predictions that it would be a close campaign,[117] although most people's money was on a no vote. One factor which was widely felt to have swung support behind a no vote was the special edition of *7 Days* in which Basil Chubb and David Thornley predicted that, based on the levels of support at the last local elections, if a general election was held under the straight vote, Fianna Fáil would win 93 out of 144 seats, Fine Gael would lose ten seats and Labour would be practically wiped out,[118] an analysis which lent credibility to Labour's slogan that 'the straight vote is crooked'. As it was, the amendment was defeated by a three to two margin, with only four out of 38 constituencies voting in favour,[119] in a pattern which effectively replicated the result of the 1959 poll on the same issue.

By this time, the issue of a 'credibility gap' was coming to the fore. Until now the party had been coasting on platitudes, but it was now faced with the task of coming up with the policies to go along with its slogans. There was also the problem of the increasingly obvious chasm between what was still a predominantly rural right wing parliamentary party and the increasingly urban left-wing membership. Labour's 1967 conference had resolved that the issue of policy formulation be dealt with as a matter of urgency and as a result, several policy committees were established to compile discussion documents for the consideration of the members. In keeping with the more inclusive outlook of the leadership, these documents were to be put before delegates at a special conference for their review and input, before the finalised documents would be put before the party's annual conference (the only body with the power to decide party policy) for its approval. This style of policy formulation could not have been more different from the more authoritarian style which had been favoured by Labour in the past (particularly under Norton), or by either of the two larger parties at that time. The policy conference, which was held in Liberty Hall in July 1968, saw 400 delegates sitting on ten workshops, each charged with concentrating on one particular policy area. After a two-hour discussion, their reports were written up for delivery at a plenary session that afternoon, where they were recommended for approval at the next annual conference.[120] Though it sounds like a recipe for disaster, the project worked out in a reasonably straightforward fashion: eight of the documents were approved as they were, while two were amended to make them more radical[121] (and, in at least one commentator's opinion, more incoherent), with the document on Industrial Democracy, described as 'more repetitive and more inconsistent than most', being put down to the process of policy formulation by committee.[122] The conference proved a profoundly disagreeable experience for the right, who 'flinched at demands for nationalising the banks and taking the control of education away from the church',[123] but who kept their counsel nonetheless.

By this point, the PLP were not opposing the changes, but they were certainly not playing ball either, and a sense of concern was growing that the party in the country and the party in the Oireachtas were two entirely different animals. Noël Browne helpfully pointed this out at a press conference on the morning of the policy conference, and accused the leadership of engaging in 'an attempt to create a fictitious socialist posture in order to capture the left-wing activists in the party who are the constituency workers . . . without at the same time moving away in fact from the traditional extremely right-wing conservatism of the "Irish Labour Party"'.[124] Moves were already afoot to rectify the situation, however. In fact, it was the main focus of the constitutional review committee, whose interim report on Labour's organisational structure (written almost entirely by Niall Greene and Roddy Connolly, and apparently without the knowledge or input of most of the AC) was presented to the July conference. The problem as set out in the report was quite clear: how was Labour going to reconcile 'the short term objectives pursued by the parliamentary group with the long term and, let's face it, more ideological objectives of the rest of the party'.[125] The report proposed closer links between the PLP and the party's executive (the AC as it stood would be dissolved), and that the party leader would henceforth be elected at a special conference held after general elections which would also decide parliamentary strategy for the incoming Dáil. Quite apart from its far-reaching recommendations, the report resulted in a great deal of friction because of the secretive way in which it had been drawn up, and because it had not been circulated to the AC prior to being put before the ordinary members. Nor was the opposition merely from the PLP or the right wing, with the document engendering angry counter-documents from figures as doctrinally diverse as Barry Desmond and Matt Merrigan.[126]

Giving the membership more power over the parliamentary party was one way of breaching the 'credibility gap'. Another was to field candidates more in tune with the members and in constituencies where they might be elected. There had been some success in this regard at the 1965 election in Dublin, but it would take a massive swing to Labour at the next election to even up the left–right balance in the PLP. How were they going to manage this? The answer would be twofold. Firstly, they would increase the number of candidates across the board; secondly they would seek out high profile figures to join Labour and stand in the forthcoming general election. Labour's first major recruit, unveiled in Liberty Hall on 12 December 1968 amid great commotion, was Dr Conor Cruise O'Brien. Cruise O'Brien had recently returned to Dublin after four years in New York University. He was internationally famous as a writer and as a diplomat following his time working in the Congo on behalf of the United Nations. Although O'Brien had been a member of the Labour Party as a student in Trinity College,[127] he had had to resign when he joined the Department of External Affairs upon finishing his studies, and since then his only public remarks about the party had been negative; his reference to Labour's domination by 'dismal poltroons on the lines of O'Casey's Uncle Payther', in an essay about 1916 published during the Jubilee had become infamous to the point where he thought it might preclude him from renewing his membership.[128] (O'Brien's antipathy to Labour was informed to an extent by the treatment of his cousin, Owen Sheehy Skeffington, at the hands of the 'poltroons' some 20 years earlier.) He found the party most forgiving, however, and he was welcomed back with open arms. It was quite a coup to have O'Brien as a member, but that he should do so having written of the party in such harsh terms less than two years earlier was testament to the distance travelled by Labour in recent times. Within months, O'Brien was joined by a number of other well-known figures. Two were broadcaster/academics: Dr David Thornley, a political scientist based in Trinity College and a regular face on RTÉ's current affairs programme *7 Days*, and Justin Keating, a lecturer in veterinary medicine in UCD and presenter of RTÉ's agricultural programme *Landmark*. Both had been involved in left-wing politics in the past, Thornley, for a time with Noël Browne and the NPDs and Justin Keating with the Irish Workers' League, although he had been a member of the Labour Party for a short period in the late 1940s.[129] In another belated gesture to rural interests, Labour also managed to bring former NFA president Rickard Deasy on board, although they were less successful in attracting Michael Joe Costello, Brendan Halligan's old boss from the Irish Sugar Company.[130] Others who declined Labour's advances at this time were Owen Sheehy Skeffington[131] and more bizarrely, Padraig O'Halpin, a Dublin based engineer and long-time activist in Fianna Fáil, whom Labour had asked to stand in Donegal.[132]

It was one thing bringing in faces from the television, but quite another to have so many newcomers dripping not only with degrees but with doctorates. Labour was in danger of looking too clever by half, which was a sure-fire way of alienating most Irish voters beyond Dublin 4. (As Basil Chubb noted,[133] anti-intellectualism is an important factor in Irish political culture, and it was something which the consummate man of the people Jack Lynch was adept at playing up to. Asked by a student interviewer what characters from history he most admired, he replied 'the French Revolutionaries particularly', but when asked which type of revolutionaries, he replied, 'Napoleons rather than philosophers, whom I don't understand'.[134]) It was going to take more than a couple of high profile candidates to eclipse the parochial character of the existing parliamentary party. Following O'Brien's entry to the party, *Hibernia's* political commentator observed that while his arrival in its ranks was all well and good, Labour was 'still the party of Tully, Tierney, Spring, Murphy, Pattison, McAuliffe, Larkin and the other deep rooted conservatives. The younger element, with red banners flying may make more noise but the solid conservative elements is the heart of the party.'[135]

It is important to place what was going on in mainstream politics in the context of events generally, both at home and abroad. Arguably, it marked the zenith of the decade, as Fergal Tobin has so well described:

> [1968] was the convulsive year in which were focused all the radical passions of the sixties. From Prague to Paris to Chicago the streets were filled with a new generation weary of the cynical conventions of established politics. In Czechoslovakia the stranglehold of the Soviet empire was broken for a few brave months; in France the Fifth Republic came within an act of collapse; in Chicago at the Democratic Party convention Mayor Richard Daley's city policy ran amok among student protestors. Martin Luther King and Robert Kennedy were assassinated and Richard Nixon was elected.[136]

Closer to home, the street politics continued. Marches in Dublin were commonplace, whether about university fees, Vietnam or housing provision as the Dublin Housing Action Committee's campaign of marches and squatting continued. There was nothing so revolutionary here as *les événements* in Paris or even Berkeley but there were shades of it in the foundation of groups like Students for Democratic Action, founded that summer in UCD, which protested against archaic bureaucracy, irrelevant curricula and poor conditions in the university. Moreover, having spent their early time in college in the confines of the university's Earlsfort Terrace campus, students were (quite rightly) alarmed at the prospect of moving to a greenfield site halfway between the city and the Dublin mountains, not to mention the government's proposals of a merger with Trinity College.[137] It began with some 50 members, eventually increasing to around 200 out of a student body of about 6,000. By this time, the number of leftist sects operating primarily among the student populace in Dublin, but also in pockets around the country, had mushroomed. Where common or garden communists had once looked exotic, there were now Trotskyists and Maoists, each with their own splinter groups. While Maoists operated on their own, the Trotskyists acted within Labour, although without much success. (At the AGM of Labour's UCD Branch that year, the young Ruairí Quinn and his colleagues inflicted a 'crushing defeat . . . on a small but vociferous Trotskyite faction in the annual elections for the executive committee', according to a contemporary account.[138]) The Maoists and one of their splinter groups, the Internationalists, were especially marginal, and were peopled for the most part by expatriate British students[139] in Trinity, who endeavoured to bring down imperialism by disrupting College garden parties – the means by which they first burst into the public consciousness, not least through red scare headlines in the *Evening Herald*[140] – and organising Anti-Imperialist Céilís rather than attending the bourgeois Trinity Ball.[141] The role played by these British students was both noted and resented. After a public meeting in Trinity which he was addressing was disturbed by such a group, the Minister for Education, Brian Lenihan, issued a statement warning that 'the people of this country' could not be expected to 'go on subsidizing the minority amongst them who continue to offend the ordinary code of human behaviour. Students who come from abroad and seek to create disruption in this country should remember that the Irish people will not continue to tolerate either them or their actions.'[142] Left-wing Christian groups such as the Student Christian Movement (eventually established by John Feeney in UCD, after much resistance from College authorities[143]) also made an appearance, as well as an Irish branch of Slant, and a short-lived newspaper, *Grille*, which was largely made up of a heady brew of Marxism and ecumenism, which proved unpopular in some quarters.[144] Following the publication of *Humanae Vitae* and the Russian army's invasion of Czechoslovakia in the same week, the Christian Left staged a 'pray-in' in St Andrew's Church, Westland Row, Dublin, but they had to abort their gathering after being physically set upon by around 20 parishioners who thought they were up to no good.[145] Not long afterwards, when members of the Chicago police visited Dublin soon after their 'now famous neo-fascist brutality' at the Democratic convention some weeks earlier, the Christian socialists showed their displeasure by holding a one day fast.[146]

It is not surprising that the student movement was regarded with more bemusement than fear. Its tendency towards ludicrous stunts and no doubt a sense that many were quite divorced from reality meant that they were never taken particularly seriously. The Irish students would certainly never be as influential or as boisterous as their continental cousins, or the peaceniks in the US campuses, not least because they were numerically insignificant, even though the numbers of Irish young people attending university had increased by around 40 per cent over the course of the decade.[147] But even though their behaviour was often absurd and their numbers relatively small, they were still taken seriously enough to attract the 'very keen interest' of the Special Branch, with the Union of Students in Ireland as well as Connolly Youth, the Dublin Young Socialists, the Republican Clubs at UCD and TCD, the Irish Student Movement, and the Internationalists, not to mention the Labour Party itself[148] subject to surveillance.[149] This included Branchmen infiltrating lectures 'disguised' as students,[150] in addition to the Special Branch's conspicuous surveillance of the republican movement and the DHAC.[151] Labour was faced with a delicate balancing act. How could it benefit from the energy and the excitement surrounding these groups, without alienating the majority who found it distasteful at best. Street demonstrations were taking place with such regularity that the government introduced a Criminal Justice Bill to curtail the incidence of these assemblies, and keep them away from Leinster House. The bill naturally became a cause célèbre among young radicals (it was described as the type of legislation 'which would give the Cabinet the power of a Hitler'[152]), or as Andrew Gilchrist the British Ambassador put it, 'the Criminal Justice Bill, which is an attempt to protect the public from the inconvenience of open-air assemblies and demonstrations by giving greater control to the police, is the hated target of all who think their road to success lies through the streets'.[153]

If the pray-ins and ceidhlís were characterised by naïvety, things soon took a more serious turn. Protests by the Northern Ireland Civil Rights Association and subsequently the People's Democracy (an organisation of students from Queen's University, Belfast for the most part with strong Trotskyist leanings at leadership level) began to come under violent attack from the Northern security forces and loyalists. By January 1969 the situation in the North was on a knife-edge. In the South, people watched closely to see events unfold. Many Labour activists took a particular interest, having established quite strong fraternal ties with their Labour colleagues in the North through the All Ireland Council of Labour, established the previous March. The degree to which the political atmosphere had become heightened could be seen in Dublin on 21 January 1969. The fiftieth anniversary of the First Dáil lacked the pageantry of the Jubilee celebrations for 1916, and was altogether a more solemn and elitist commemoration, marked only by a special sitting of the Oireachtas in Leinster House which proceeded in a 'dignified but dull' fashion.[154] Outside, however, was another story, as around a thousand students marched through the city centre protesting against the 'total failure of the state to implement the Democratic Programme'.[155] Meanwhile an assortment of left wingers and republicans engaged in noisy protests over the imprisonment for contempt of court of Dennis Dennehy, chairman of the DHAC. Dennehy was on hunger strike, and his action had prompted a 'well publicised appeal' by Frank Cluskey, then lord mayor of Dublin, for his release. Subsequent to Cluskey's appeal Gilchrist wrote:

> The Lord Mayor is a member of the Labour Party and it is the Labour Party which, after toying with temptation for quite some time, has now made a determined attempt to cash in on the success of the left-wing activists. I do not know just why Mr Brendan Corish, the leader of the Labour Party, has lent himself to this manoeuvre. He is a moderate man of no great intellectual pretensions and I find him one of the most agreeable people in Irish politics . . . The general comment in Dublin is that Mr Corish has tried to move too fast in bad company and has in effect gone for a ride on a tiger.[156]

Days later, Labour held what would almost certainly be its last annual conference prior to the next general election. Taking place in Liberty Hall on 24–27 January, it was a massively important gathering, not only because the party needed to put its best face forward before the poll, but because this conference was charged with approving the policy documents on which Labour's next manifesto would be based. The various policy documents had been trickling out of head office throughout January, garnering a massive amount of press attention both individually and collectively. The *Irish Times* had described the documents as 'an enlightened contrast' with previous 'makeshift, half baked' manifestoes. Elsewhere, the reception was less positive, with the document on worker democracy particularly vilified; the *Cork Examiner* branded it communistic, the Federated Union of Employers said it was a 'watered down version of Russian ideas', and the *Irish Independent* said it was 'drastic'.[157] The conference organisers were concerned about how the 'solid conservative elements' in the party would react, although they feared an overt lack of enthusiasm rather than an actual revolt.[158] It was vital that the conference not only approve the documents but be seen to do so unanimously. The tone of proceedings was upbeat from the start, however. There had been several notable successes of late – the defeat of the PR referendum in October, Conor Cruise O'Brien joining some weeks later, and the very positive performances in the recent by-elections – which meant the enthusiasm which had characterised Labour gatherings of recent times was still very much in evidence. As conference opened in a packed Liberty Hall that Friday evening to the strains of 'Watchword of Labour' played by the ITGWU brass band, the atmosphere seemed 'more reminiscent of a revivalist meeting than a political conference'.[159]

Corish began proceedings with passionate speech in which he reiterated Labour's key articles of faith. First and foremost was its point blank refusal to enter into a coalition after the next election, an issue to which Corish dedicated a third of his address. Muttering about the advisability of Labour continuing its anti-coalition stance had been getting louder in recent times, although not in polite company. By now, as John Horgan records, 'not only had some of the original anti-coalitionists, such as James Tully, become increasingly disenchanted by the long and fruitless years in opposition, but some of the newer faces in the PLP were not as strenuously opposed to the idea of coalition'.[160] Fine Gael TD Paddy Harte recalls Dr John O'Connell and himself doing private head counts in their respective parties at this time, only to discover that 'anti-coalition was not the true position of a large majority of deputies' in *either* party.[161] Michael O'Leary, who had proposed an anti-coalition motion, was worried enough about losing the vote that he asked Corish to put his personal weight behind it.[162] This Corish did, in an unequivocal championing of the go-it-alone policy, put in starkly personal terms. Delegates were free to vote in favour of coalition if they wished, Corish explained, and he would accept that decision, but were that to happen he would relinquish his leadership 'and support socialism from the backbenches'. Labour, he said, did not exist to 'give the kiss of life to Fine Gael'. If the coalitionists had had any chance of turning the tide on this question, it vanished at that moment amidst a heartfelt standing ovation in the hall, although Corish's intervention, as Horgan has remarked, was to 'haunt him for years afterwards'.

Having tied the twin aims of socialism and independence to the mast, the 840 assembled delegates started about the business in hand. No Labour conference had ever had to deal with a programme as significant in size or scope as on this occasion, a fact reflected in the heavy schedule before delegates that weekend. Discussion on the policy documents began on Friday evening and continued until 9.30 p.m. the next day. The right-wing counter-attack never happened, despite there being much with which it could find fault, and after a gruelling day and a half of debate, all 12 policy documents – agriculture, workers' democracy, health, social welfare, education, foreign policy, local government, banking and financial policy, housing, taxation, maritime policy and industrial development – were passed. The closest conference came to an outright confrontation was during the discussions on the health and education documents. The education document proposed that the existing system of management for primary and secondary education be abolished and replaced by multi-denominational, co-educational schools under community management, while the health document similarly called for all voluntary hospitals to come under community control, both effectively seeking to wrest control of the two main sectors in which the Catholic Church wielded its greatest influence. The education debate was tense, with some delegates opposing community management of schools, as well as the document's proposal to abolish corporal punishment. At one point it looked as though Senator Timothy McAuliffe might stage a demonstration, but the situation was diffused when Eileen Desmond articulated her support for the document, arguing that as a devout Catholic mother she did not feel there was anything in the policy that the church could object to. In the end, the anticipated hostilities never materialised, and the debate turned out to be a damp squib.[163]

The marked reluctance of the right to engage in the debates continued over the weekend, and left-wing voices continued to dominate proceedings. This was apparent during private session on Sunday when many ordinary members vented their displeasure about the recent behaviour of the parliamentary party. Their refusal to vote against TDs' salary increases the year before was criticised in several motions: one called for the expulsion from the party of each deputy who had voted against the AC's instruction, another called for all issues of 'national importance' (including deputies salaries) to be decided by a referendum of delegates at the annual conference, while two others reiterated that decisions made at conference were binding on *all* members of the party, including the PLP. (There were two addenda proposed to this last motion: one called for the establishment of a sub-committee which would monitor whether members of the PLP were abiding by conference decisions; the other called for one member of the PLP to be charged with presenting conferences with a month by month account of the activities of each deputy over the previous year.)[164] The lack of trust was palpable.[165] The PLP was criticised during the discussion of the Constitutional Review Committee's paper on expanding the role of the party membership, which stressed the need to improve (or even introduce) the PLP's accountability to the members. The authors of the report were open about the mutual distrust between the two sides, conceding that they were

> Reconciled to the fact that some people will be highly selective in choosing examples from the document to illustrate how 'anti-parliament' we have been in putting forward certain ideas; equally others will select portions in an attempt to uncover some vast complex 'parliamentary' plot to gain control of the party.[166]

Among its proposals was the idea of replacing selection conferences with special meetings of *active* members and a consolidation of branch structure at constituency level which would ultimately lead to the elimination of paper branches, both of which would represent a significant attack on the power bases of the vast majority of the PLP as it stood. To do so would be a very dangerous manoeuvre, for as Michael McInerney warned, 'it is often forgotten that it was not the Sinn Féin party which split in 1922 . . . it was the Republican Party deputies in the Dáil who split while the Sinn Féin Party itself remained formally intact'.[167] Any such move would be some time off, however, as the proposals to tackle the local fiefdoms remained just that. The document was discussed for half an hour in private session, but there was no vote.[168] Once again, the right remained silent.

Apart from the nuts-and-bolts issues of policy and organisation before conference, there was also the need for some rabble rousing, of which there were some fine examples. In his update on recent political activity in Ireland, which focused for the most part on Labour's conference, British Ambassador Andrew Gilchrist included extracts from the weekend's 'three most popular speeches' which he graded in ascending order of applause.[169] In third place was Noël Browne's speech opposing the Criminal Justice Bill, in which he appealed to trade union leaders to consider using a political strike to stop the legislation, and proposed that Labour deputies and leaders should end up in the streets to fight it if necessary. 'Neither housing or unemployment nor any of the other issues of protest would matter any longer, if the right to protest itself were removed', Browne claimed, concluding, 'We must fight this to the death' to great acclamation. Browne was beaten in the oratory stakes by newcomer Conor Cruise O'Brien, now Labour's spokesman on foreign policy, who suggested that Ireland close its embassy in Portugal and open one in Cuba instead, as well as calling for diplomatic relations with the Eastern bloc. In the end, though, the best received speech of the conference was not actually made by a member, but by Gerry Fitt, as fraternal delegate from the Republican Labour Party. Returning to Noël Browne's theme, Fitt told delegates that 'Any Labour leader who is intimidated by the sight of a baton, whether it be wielded by an RUC man or by a member of the Garda, is unworthy of the name of Labour', and called upon Labour to go all out against the Criminal Justice Bill. 'Law and order as in the eyes of Governor Wallace of Alabama means to keep down the blacks and law and order in both the North and the South of this country means exactly the same thing.' 'The responsible leaders of the party did not themselves attempt to match such intemperate language', Gilchrist noted, 'but it is clear that they hope to harness the enthusiasts and the activist to their chariot . . . whether . . . Mr Corish will in fact switch the Labour Party from the Dáil to the streets, as the extremists wish, is one question. Whether it will provide the party with a big access of votes at a general election is another.' Naturally, delegates returning home after this euphoric gathering were disinclined to think in these terms and were convinced that a major breakthrough was only months away. It almost seemed as though many of the delegates had experienced a rapture, leaving some of those who were present 'wondering what had hit the Labour Party over the weekend'.[170] Even commentators displayed an unusual lack of cynicism towards the delegates' zeal. Pondering whether Labour was displaying 'emotionalism or sincere but aimless militancy', the Irish Workers' Party observer concluded that it was actually a 'genuine feeling for socialism'.[171] But perhaps the shocked British onlooker summed up the thoughts of many when he exclaimed, 'Good God! They really mean it!'[172]

'I WON'T VOTE FOR LABOUR BECAUSE O'BRIEN AND THORNLEY ARE COMMUNISTS AND SHOULD BE SHOT': THE 1969 GENERAL ELECTION

With conference over, and the policy documents approved, attention turned at once to the preparations for the imminent election. Brendan Halligan was planning a highly centralised campaign and had at his disposal greater resources than Labour had ever enjoyed in such a contest. Head office was well staffed, and there was outside help from an advertising agency, which built its campaign around two slogans first used at the 1968 conference: 'Let's build the new republic' and, more infamously, 'the Seventies will be socialist'. The campaign was also aided by information garnered from a specially com-missioned Gallup poll on political attitudes (the first professional poll of its scale in Irish politics).[173] Conducted in April 1969, with a sample of 2,000 voters nationwide, the poll put Labour's support at 29 per cent in Dublin, an increase of ten percentage points on the 1965 result. Outside Dublin, the figures for those intending to vote Labour was less marked at 18 per cent, an increase of just over three percentage points on 1965. The results confirmed the view of Labour's campaign managers that the party was on course for a major breakthrough, albeit one which would be concentrated in the capital.[174] Two or more candidates were selected in all but seven constituencies, where the sitting deputies had successfully resisted head office's two-candidate strategy. Otherwise, 19 constituencies had two candidates, ten had three, and six, all in greater Dublin, had four, making a total of 99 in all.[175] This was the largest ever number of candidates fielded by Labour – more than double the 1965 figure, and nearly half as big again as the figure for 1943, the previous record – and the first time the party had ever put up sufficient candidates to form a single party government. From this number, Labour expected to win 30 seats, at the very least.[176]

It was important that Labour convey that it was serious about wanting and expecting power, but the two-candidate strategy was a disaster for the party. It created horrendous intra-party rivalries in the Labour camp, making a stressful election even more fraught and fostering resentments between can-didates and head office. As the general secretary's post mortem noted, 'team work is called for under PR at constituency level. It was remarkable only by its absence in a great many Labour campaigns'. Dun Laoghaire–Rathdown was singled out as the worst case of infighting in Dublin, where all but three constituencies were censured.[177] Dublin North Central, which ran three candidates, was one of the exceptions. In fact, its Clontarf branch had the honour of being the only branch which complained to head office that it was not being allowed to field as many candidates as it wished.[178] Elsewhere, however, it was each man to his own, prompting head office to complain afterwards that too many individuals had put 'their own personal interest very much before that of the party'.[179]

The growth in Labour's membership enabled it to conduct wide-scale canvasses, but it also made it more important than usual that they would sing from the same hymn sheet. To this end, head office printed 10,000 copies (although only half of these were ever collected)[180] of its *Canvassers' Notes*, a 25-point catechism of answers to questions which effectively boiled down to one issue: was Labour communist?[181] For Labour, this was to be *the* question of the election, and it was played for all it was worth by the outgoing Fianna Fáil government in what was a particularly grubby contest. It is no exaggeration to say that the 1969 election was 'all about the Labour Party'.[182] Fianna Fáil ran an especially aggressive campaign against Labour, orchestrated by its director of elections, Charles Haughey. The strategy was simple: to exploit the suspicion that most people outside Dublin had of what was going on with the 'hooligans' in the big smoke, and the strange people in the Labour Party with their funny new ideas. Anyone trying to run a red scare against the likes of Dan Spring would have their work cut out for them, and so an only slightly more subtle approach had to be taken. As one newspaper advertisement warned: 'There are two Labour Parties – the traditional one . . . and a new group of extreme left-wing socialists preaching class warfare and who want total state control and all that goes with it',[183] or as Brian Lenihan put it to one woman in Roscommon, 'your local candidates are decent fellas but what could they do with those dangerous men at the top'.[184]

For their part, the 'decent fellas' did their damnedest to avoid guilt by association. Railway stations in Cork and Tralee became homes to uncollected posters bearing the Labour legend, while some candidates were said to have resorted to dumping head office literature in local lakes.[186] Many of the rural deputies forswore not only Labour's new slogans, but the very name of the party itself. Dan Spring's literature was typical: 'He helps you. Now you help him'.[187] But the Fianna Fáil campaign was hysterical. Its language was grotesque, playing to the lowest common denominator: sectarianism, anti-intellectualism and inverted snobbery. One Fianna Fáil candidate running against David Thornley in Dublin South West promised to 'chase him back to Trinity where he belonged'.[187] The Minister for Justice, Mícheál Ó Moráin was somewhat more explicit when he referred to the 'political queers from Trinity College and Telefís Éireann' who had taken over the party.[188] In fact, Ó Moráin had adopted not only the language of MacEntee, but also his tactics, having instructed Peter Berry, the secretary of the Department of Justice, to trawl Special Branch files for information which could be used against Labour activists.[189] Berry, who had compiled dossiers on communist activities in the Department of Justice during the 1940s, tried to dissuade his minister, in the belief that MacEntee's use of the red smear in 1943–4 had meant that decades later 'an elder statesman who deserved respect, was being sneered at as "Old Mischief MacEntee"', but Ó Moráin would not be put off. (Indeed, MacEntee, who had retired from political life with the Dáil's dissolution, could not resist the opportunity to engage in a valedictory go at Labour, telling voters that the party stood for Lenin, Stalin and the 'red flames of burning homesteads in Meath'.[190]) The MacEntee red scares had been solo runs, however, conducted to his colleagues' chagrin. This was different. If Labour had been angered by Mischief MacEntee in the past, it would be furious about what it correctly identified as 'not the product of local over-zealous Fianna Fáil enthusiasts acting on their own initiative but . . . rather . . . a deliberate and calculated directive issued at national level'.[191] As Michael Gallagher points out 'almost every Fianna Fáil attack included the allegation that Labour wanted to impose "Cuban socialism" on Ireland', bringing to mind Conor Cruise O'Brien's now infamous proposal that Ireland should open an embassy in Havana. For his part, Cruise O'Brien spent much of the campaign attacking Charles Haughey (both were standing in Dublin North East), who had recently derived a very large sum of money through land speculation. The whys and wherefores of this deal, and others, remained the stuff of political speculation over two decades, but Cruise O'Brien's strategy was not entirely popular at the time. Even the *Irish Times,* the most supportive towards Labour of any of the national newspapers, accused him of engaging in the 'politics of envy',[192] and, as Gallagher has noted, criticising land speculation was guaranteed to alienate many rural votes (although whether these would have gone to Labour anyway is another question). Moreover, the fact that one of O'Brien's running mates (Justin Keating) had recently 'made a nice little bargain'[193] on land in south county Dublin made the issue something of a double-edged sword. At least one of his supporters was of the opinion towards the end of the campaign that 'Conor may just about pull it off if he stops harping on Haughey's property which is getting him down a cul-de-sac'.[194]

Fianna Fáil was endeavouring with some success to paint Labour as a crowd of dangerous revolutionaries, but it had a further trump up its sleeve. If the red scare was the negative side of the campaign, the positive side was the sight of a doe-eyed Jack Lynch being ferried by helicopter across the country.

It was a thoroughly presidential campaign, without policies on the government side. Although Fianna Fáil promised 'Progress with stability', its best known slogan was actually 'Let's back Jack'. In fact, the party made a virtue out of its failure to put its policies before the people: Fianna Fáil had not issued a manifesto, Charles Haughey explained, because 'Manifestoes have a Marxist ring about them'.[195] In an election run on slogans, however, it was another of Fianna Fáil's which summed up the election best, when it put it to people that 'There is no alternative'.[196] And there wasn't. A banner which simply stated 'Fine Gael will win' was described by one journalist as a 'sick joke from the outset',[197] for it did not have a hope. For one thing, the party remained ravaged by internecine warfare between the Young Tigers and the more conservative elements. Liam Cosgrave had deliberately moved his party's Ard Fheis to immediately before the election to prevent more clashes taking place.[198] It was Cosgrave's first general election as leader, and although Gerard Sweetman tried to run a muscular campaign on his behalf, it seemed as though Cosgrave's heart was really not in it. But the divisions within Fine Gael were only half the problem, for, since Labour had ruled out coalition once again at its January conference, relations between it and Fine Gael perhaps reached their lowest ebb. Cosgrave was particularly angry. Labour's programme was 'for 1984', he said, their policies 'too doctrinaire and unrealistic'.[199] Fine Gael had precious little chance of getting in on their own, and none of getting in with Labour. Whatever the merits of backing Jack, there simply *was* no alternative.

Facing brickbats from both of the larger parties, and a red scare even greater than it had anticipated, Labour began to emphasise the correlation between its policy and current Catholic social teaching, beginning with a speech by Brendan Halligan on the influence of John XXIII to a Catholic social studies group in Limerick. John Healy began joking about how Labour was 'running among the faithful with a brace of popes', had christened its general secretary 'Pope Halligan', (described elsewhere as 'the cleric in mufti'[200]) and wrote of Halligan's plan to take 'the stars from the plough and the stars to fashion a new version of the miraculous medal'.[201] At the same time, individual candidates were taking a similar approach, perhaps most notoriously David Thornley, a devout Catholic whose ostentatious displays of faith soon became the stuff of legend.[202] All this represented a huge step back from the more overtly 'political' socialism expressed at the January conference, back towards the woollier type of Christian socialism preferred by Corish. But all of Labour's talk of encyclicals could do nothing to stop the party being called off the altar at masses from one end of the country to the other[203] and, as Andrew Gilchrist noted, 'the priests in Ireland may no longer tell their parishioners who to vote *for* but are quite capable of telling them who to vote *against*'.[204] It certainly could not hope to compete with Jack Lynch's infamous convent tour which he undertook the week before the poll. As Conor Cruise O'Brien later recalled:

> The press and media were not present for that series of convent chats, but the word came through all the same. A Labour colleague from Munster told me ruefully of a mothers' meeting convened in his constituency by a Reverend Mother on the day before polling day. It was not, said the Reverend Mother to the other mothers, for her to advise them on a political matter. Certainly not! She only wished to remind them of their duty, as Catholic mothers, both to vote and to be very prudent about how to vote . . . Whatever party they voted for, however, they should be sure . . . was free from any tendency to communism. If there was doubt as to whether there might be communists in a certain party, it would be better not to vote for that party.[205]

Not all nuns were as circumspect as their Munster sisters, however. One Roscommon woman remembered how

> A nun in our local convent told fifth class primary to tell their parents not to vote Labour as they were all communists in the Labour Party. Now this spread like wild fire to every home, and even though I don't know what effect it had, I know enough to know it had its effect. I heard one mother saying, 'The two parties are much of a muchness, but I won't vote Labour because O'Brien and Thornley are communists and should be shot.'[206]

For all the public statements made by Fianna Fáil about how Labour would nationalise land, and even Guinness's (as Charles Haughey told his party's final rally outside the GPO in Dublin), it was 'particularly the covert rumours' that inflicted the most damage. As John Healy concluded, 'the Labour lads might have a couple of Popes up on the masthead but when the Mercy crowd and the Sisters of Charity start to storm Heaven to spare Ireland to Jack you'll find it hard to buck him at the ballot box'.[207] It was not clear until afterwards just how hard Labour had been hit in the campaign, and in Dublin incidents of hostility towards the party were few and far between. Although Labour was coming in for a very hard time from the government party, it was seen as something of a perverse compliment, for if Fianna Fáil was devoting so much attention to them, then they must be a real threat. Even the Irish Workers' Party candidate expressed surprise afterwards that his team had failed to encounter a single 'incident of unfriendliness or opposition this time. Quite the opposite in fact.'[208] There was a feeling among Labour men and women that it had proved their best campaign to date, Corish speaking for many when he told Labour's final rally in Dublin that he had never been so confident before an election as he was on this occasion.[209] It was an optimism shared by Noël Browne, who predicted on the eve of the poll on 18 June that Labour could well find itself going into government whenever it returned to the Dáil.[210]

THE SEVENTIES WON'T BE SOCIALIST

Brendan Halligan well remembers sitting in the television studio in RTÉ as the results came trickling in. Brendan Corish sat there, his face ashen as it became increasingly apparent that far from making a major breakthrough (still less, forming a government) Labour would return to the new Dáil with a net loss of four seats. The results of the April Gallup poll proved prescient. There were significant gains in Dublin with 29.5 per cent of the vote (bringing its level of support equal there to that of Fine Gael) and the prestige candidates doing extremely well. David Thornley became the first Labour candidate to top the poll in a Dublin constituency, while Justin Keating, Conor Cruise O'Brien, John O'Donovan, Noël Browne and Barry Desmond joined sitting deputies Frank Cluskey, Michael O'Leary, Seán Dunne and John O'Connell. The success of the last two in Dublin South West represented the first occasion that Labour had ever won two seats in a Dublin constituency. The celebrations in South West were short lived, however, when Dunne became ill and died only six days after the poll. Dunne, charismatic, charming, a brilliant media performer and much loved by his constituents was a terrible loss for Labour, and rubbed salt into the wounds which had been inflicted on the party across the country. The seats lost at by-elections or through resignation (Kildare, Clare, mid-Cork) did not return to Labour, and three incumbents Tom Kyne in Waterford, and Patrick McAuliffe and Eileen Desmond in North East Cork and Mid Cork respectively, lost their seats. There was one gain outside Dublin, where Liam Kavanagh managed to regain his uncle James Everett's seat for Labour in Wicklow.

How had this happened? Tom Kyne's defeat could be explained largely by poor tactics, with the view being taken at the time that if he had been allowed to run on his own he would have held on to the seat,[211] and privately, Brendan Halligan placed a significant weight of blame on the party's two-candidate strategy. The strategy had been intended as part bravado and partly a way of picking up transfers, but if it succeeded in the former it failed in the latter. In Munster particularly, Halligan concluded, 'the internal Labour transfer was scandalous and Labour votes elected two Fine Gael deputies . . . it must be concluded that in the present state of organisation many constituencies cannot be trusted to mount a two or three candidate campaign effectively and that in

Mid Cork and Waterford two-candidate campaigns lost otherwise safe seats for Labour'.[212] Kevin Boland's revision of electoral boundaries was seen by some as having played an important role in Labour's losses in Cork, and had deprived the party of further gains in Dublin,[213] and this was the issue on which Halligan laid most of the blame in public. But while he put Labour's losses down to boundary changes, others felt ideological issues had played a more important part. Eileen Desmond believed that defeat stemmed from Labour lurching too far to the left, while others such as Conor Cruise O'Brien and David Thornley blamed the red scare. On the evidence of the April 1969 Gallup Poll, both explanations seem plausible. The poll had proved very accurate in the case of Dublin, but outside the capital its prediction of a three per cent increase on Labour's 1965 performance had been proved incorrect, with Labour's vote actually falling by one point on its previous election result. This suggests that there was a shift away from Labour in the last few weeks of the campaign which could well have been owing to the success of the Fianna Fáil campaign. Moreover, that poll had showed Labour to have the lowest party loyalty of the three main parties, and indicated that while Labour was attracting new voters it was also losing proportionately more of its older voters, increasing the likelihood that it would fare badly around the country.

Perhaps the question might be, could it have been otherwise? For as one writer noted afterwards:

> The outcome is not unduly surprising; the real wonder is that so much fevered expectation was ever aroused by the Labour bandwagon. For the extravagant left wing television and press commentators who were sure that from the tatty armoury of *New Statesman* clichés could come the perfect weapons for the political battlefield that poor Eileen Desmond and Tom Kyne were asked to storm.[214]

In other words, 'The Dublin based pundits were right, in Dublin'.[215] The devastation of the 1969 result can be understood only in the context of the inflated expectations which had proceeded it, but in a sense they were the inevitable conclusion of the developments of the previous decade. The project of transforming Labour from an umbrella for local independents to a party with a distinct left-wing identity was inconsistent with retaining the party's existing areas of representation. Those on the right of the PLP were only too aware of this and had run on their personal records (as they had always done in the past) eschewing all efforts by head office to identify them with the party. Some were successful; others, like Eileen Desmond and Tom Kyne, were not. The result was that while depleted, the rural right remained a strong force in the PLP while the urban left enjoyed significant representation for the first time in the party's history. The rural right, having seen what happened to their colleagues, were unlikely to allow the party's lurch to the left to continue unabated. Furthermore, after 16 years of Fianna Fáil government, Labour was going to have to sit on the backbenches for another five years. Labour would have to wait once again. The question was, would it tear itself apart in the meantime?

TEN

SMOKY MISDIRECTION
1969–73

—

The British Labour leader Harold Wilson once remarked of his own party: 'The Labour Party is like a vehicle. If you drive at great speed, all the people in it are either so exhilarated or so sick that you have no problems. But when you stop, they all get out, and start to argue about which way to go.'[1] It was a scenario with which Brendan Corish would become all too familiar over the next few years. Naturally there was disappointment about the result and anger following the poll about the character of Fianna Fáil's campaign, but as Labour began to settle down to business again during the new Dáil it found itself split, not only on issues which it had papered over prior to the election, most significantly on the question of coalition, but also on questions which had not been raised heretofore, most notably the violence in Northern Ireland. Quite apart from policy issues, many and varied clashes of personality were bound to arise when the volatile compound of egos that was Labour's 1969 cohort came together in a confined space. Many of the new deputies had not even met before with most of the new deputies having been strangers to the party before the election. Battling egos were by no means exclusive to Labour, however, and its only consolation for much of this period was that however bad things may have been in its own ranks, relations within Fianna Fáil and Fine Gael were, arguably, even worse.

Labour did not get off to the best of starts. The party sat at the opening of the new session on 2 July with fewer deputies than it had at the end of the last Dáil. There was a host of new faces: David Thornley, Justin Keating, Conor Cruise O'Brien, John O'Donovan and Barry Desmond in Dublin and its environs, and Liam Kavanagh in Wicklow, but these did not offset the names of the fallen. Labour's presence was reduced still further by Seán Dunne death shortly after polling. When the nominations for taoiseach opened Frank Cluskey was first in nominating Brendan Corish, complaining as he did so about the scurrilous campaign which had just passed against his party. Though there were some effective contributions from the Labour benches, the overwhelming impression was one of pique. Corish made a stab at attacking the last Fianna Fáil government's record, but in the end all he could do was gripe about the election.[2] Critiquing the day's speeches for his cousin, Conor Cruise O'Brien, Owen Sheehy Skeffington concluded, 'Brendan is well-meaning but weak. There was no need to complain so much.'[3] Though Corish's speech was interrupted throughout from the Fianna Fáil frontbench, the most savage response eventually came from the Fine Gael deputy leader T. F. O'Higgins. O'Higgins had 'listened with some exasperation' to Corish's protestations about the effect of the smear campaign on Labour's result, believing that party's claim to be seeking government as 'wholly pretentious'.[4] As far as O'Higgins was concerned, if Labour had not insisted on its go-it-alone policy during the election, both it and Fine Gael would now be looking at a fresh term of office. Instead he had sat listening to 'the Leader of the Labour Party whinging about misrepresentation and whinging about smears. We have witnessed him being interrupted by the Fianna Fáil Party but the plain fact is that he is the greatest friend Fianna Fáil have in this Dáil, and so are the horny-handed sons of toil who sit behind him.'[5]

For most of the Labour deputies, such heavy-handed sarcasm was unnecessary. There were few among them who did not believe that a change of heart over the coalition question was necessary. Most had already made up their minds; some, like Corish, were conscious of the need for change but wary of making the final step. As Labour's Brendan Halligan recalled subsequently, 'I certainly changed my mind about coalition. I changed it in the television studios looking at seats tumbling down all around me.' Though he broached the subject with Corish a few days later, no decisions were made.[6] Perhaps Labour's strategy on this issue, such as it was, could be best described as one of 'when you're in a hole, stop digging'. After the election, Labour put down their spades, but it was felt wiser to wait a while before they endeavoured to climb their way out.

The new Dáil opened with an expectation that it would be the forum for a particularly exciting time in politics, not least because its predecessor 'must surely have been one of the dullest and least well manned parliaments this country has seen since Independence'.[7] But the emphasis was on personalities rather than policies. Fianna Fáil sought a mandate for continuity, and when Lynch announced his ministers, he seemed happy to deliver more of the same. If the Lynch government had appeared bereft of ideas before the election, there was no evidence of any developments subsequently. The major issue facing the country was the question of Ireland's entry to the EEC. Now that Charles de Gaulle, whose veto of British entry to the Common Market had effectively stalled Ireland's entry since 1963, was no longer in situ (he had resigned as President in April 1969), the way now seemed clear for another application. In the meantime, there was little legislation of note under consideration but the Labour deputies, particularly the new arrivals, made their presence felt nonetheless, with Conor Cruise O'Brien and Barry Desmond particularly effective performers. From mid-August 1969, tension in the North began to ratchet up once again after the Battle of the Bogside, although it was not until the introduction of internment in August 1971 and the violence which followed that the North came to dominate the political agenda. The issue of violence in Northern Ireland was one that would cleave the Labour Party for years to come. The point to be made here, however, is that, perhaps to a greater extent than ever before, every matter of political importance was extra-parliamentary in its nature, whether it was the efforts to join Europe, or civil unrest and violence in the North. Labour's attention was often elsewhere, as the party's officers endeavoured to firefight the many and various local crises and personality clashes that threatened to sunder the party. It is these to which now we turn.

CATALOGUE OF CRISES

Years later, John O'Connell recalled his optimism returning to Leinster House after the 1969 election:

> This time, as I entered the Dáil, I did so feeling that now something was going to happen, now we had the energy and the intellect at our disposal, now we should be able to make the Labour Party into a force in the political life of Ireland. Now we had men of charisma, of intellect, of charm. Men of high profile who attracted attention: Conor Cruise O'Brien. David Thornley. Justin Keating. Frank Cluskey. Michael O'Leary. They added up to a power potential the like of which the party had never seen.
>
> Years later, when I saw television pictures of the American Challenger disaster, what it conjured up for me was what had happened to all that potential; one minute it was heading upward into the sunshine, all promise and excitement and drive, and the next minute it was breaking into smoky misdirection, worth watching mainly as an example of energy gone to waste.[8]

Only a month into its first session, a picture was being painted of a PLP riven by factionalism:

> Thornley, Keating and Desmond think Noël Browne is a 'twit' and the opinion is reciprocated . . . There is no love lost between Browne and O'Donovan. Thornley and Keating think poor Johnno [John O'Donovan] was born long after his time and Johnno thinks that David and Justin have a lot of growing up to do. Then there's Barry Desmond who has been out of favour with everybody since 1967 . . .

[not to mention] Michael Pat Murphy, Seamus Pattison, Dan Spring and Sean Tracey who as a group don't get on with anybody else and as individuals don't get on with each other.[9]

Every party had its rivalries and enmities but in a parliamentary party of only 17, this imposed a horrendous strain on Brendan Corish. He did not relish this particular type of political rough and tumble at the best of times, but now he was trying desperately to keep the party together. He was anxious to ameliorate the rural sections of the party who had lost so many of their representatives without alienating the soldiers of the New Republic. It was a tight line to walk, but Corish managed to keep his balance more often than not, frequently by addressing the New Republicans directly, while pacifying the right with more concrete actions such as the appointment of James Tully as Labour's spokesman on finance.[10]

The first conference after the election was going to be crucial in this regard. Brendan Halligan was particularly concerned that any debates on the coalition and the 1969 policy documents would not see the two issues become 'scapegoats for much organisational inefficiency and infighting that caused many of our disappointments'.[11] To avoid a public bloodletting, he proposed that the conference avoid discussing the question of coalition altogether and only discuss the policy documents in closed session. Public sessions would focus on Northern Ireland, housing, television and health. Displaying considerable bravery, however, Corish insisted that the conference should be a soul-searching one, and that it ought to 'take a long hard look at the coalition situation, and should talk about the matter honestly'.[12] His colleagues on the AC agreed and so it was that when delegates set off for Liberty Hall in February 1970, all were fully expectant of some variety of showdown on the issue. In spite of all indications, however, this did not come to pass. One observer noted how

the delegates who ill-temperedly assembled in Liberty Hall on Friday night . . . were lulled into some kind of happiness by the first of Brendan Corish's many interventions, when he declared (not for the last time) that he stood over the left wing policies adopted at the 1969 annual conference. They were further soothed in private session on Saturday by Justin Keating . . . The policies themselves were reaffirmed by an overwhelming vote, possibly made all the more solid by Corish's dropping a hint that although he stood over the existing radical policies, he was not prepared to move an inch to the left of them. The net result was that the left was appeased, the right was not offended, and it was possible to move on to the even more difficult subject of coalition.[13]

Here, Corish's and the AC's nerve was rewarded when the delegates voted unanimously to refer all motions relating to the coalition question back to the AC for further discussion, avoiding decisions and embarrassment on the subject. This was a considerable coup and amounted to 'the first chink in the anti-coalition chastity belt in which it has uncomfortably wriggled for so long'.[14] The conference minefield had been navigated with considerable skill; there was no volte-face on policy and the party's anti-coalitionism had been subtly eroded without any adverse reflection on Corish who had associated himself with the strategy in such personal terms a year earlier. Indeed, far from tarnishing his image, Corish left with his authority bolstered, proving once again that he was the only person capable of mollifying such an assortment of competing interests.

SHAMBLES IN DUBLIN AND LIMERICK

Successful as the conference had been, there were ongoing problems to disentangle. One issue now causing headaches was how to hold on to the late Seán Dunne's seat in Dublin South West, where an opportunity to restore Labour confidence[15] turned instead into a embarrassing saga. Labour had fielded four candidates there in 1969, and a constituency carve-up prior to the election had seen two Labour heavyweights, Seán Dunne and Dr John O'Connell, standing against each other as well as two other local men. Both Dunne and O'Connell were strong candidates, and popular and assiduous local deputies. The campaign saw greater rivalry between the four Labour men and their supporters than against the other candidates.[16] In the end, however, the party's first preferences amounted to 45 per cent of the poll and, in spite of the absence of any vote management, O'Connell and Dunne took two of the four seats in the constituency.

If relations were poor during the election, there was no improvement subsequently as moves began to choose a candidate to contest the by-election. Two of the four factions in the constituency supported Sean Dunne's widow, Cora, while John O'Connell endeavoured to have one of his protégés selected. By the autumn, the Administrative Council had suspended any further meetings of the Dublin South West Constituency Council after its meeting of 2 September had ended in a melee.[17] An investigation by the AC found that 'the type of election campaign run in June 1969 aggravated this with four personal campaigns and one official campaign being run.' In an effort to defuse the situation the constituency council was barred from meeting and informed that since it had proved incapable of doing so, that head office would select the candidate.[18] Finally, the AC ordered the dissolution of two of the branches in question. This was far from the end of the matter, however. Brendan Halligan, who had been earmarked as the head office candidate, declined to go forward,[19] while the dissolved branches appealed and others resigned. It was a shambolic state of affairs which was widely known in journalistic circles and only the 'goodwill which the party enjoyed with the newspaper media' had prevented 'saturation adverse publicity'.[20] This gave little solace to an increasingly beleaguered Brendan Corish, however, who complained that the protagonists in South West were displaying no evidence of concern for the good of the party.

After months of Labour procrastination, Fianna Fáil broke with convention and called the writ, forcing Labour to pick a candidate with only three weeks to go before the poll.[21] On 12 February, after a long debate, the AC chose long-time Labour activist (by then a member of the AC) and ATGWU official Matt Merrigan, and appointed John O'Connell as his director of elections.[22] Merrigan was well known locally and in better circumstances would have been well placed to win the seat, but this time he was up against some significant hurdles, not least of which being that Cora Dunne, having been deprived of the Labour nomination, was standing as 'Independent Labour' and had taken half the party machine with her. Observers felt she had little chance of winning (which would make her the first unsuccessful widow candidate in the history of the state), but that having split Labour's organisation, she could well split its vote there too. Moreover, another of the unsuccessful Labour nominees, George Butler, who was one of Labour's unsuccessful candidates at the general election, defected to the Fine Gael camp where he campaigned for the unknown Gay Mitchell.[23] In the end, there was little surprise when Seán Sherwin managed to take the seat for Fianna Fáil, beating Matt Merrigan on the fourth count by a couple of hundred votes. The result, as one commentator noted, was 'no consolation to any party. It was an unenthusiastic turnout . . . [and] no candidate reached the quota even after the fourth count',[24] but if no one had done well, Labour had fared worst. As one observer put it, 'Fianna Fáil did not take the South West Dublin seat from Labour. Labour threw it away.'[25] The campaign was an unedifying spectacle, providing a prescient display of the fractiousness that would characterise Labour for the next three years. Moreover, Labour's AC found itself trying to clean up the mess months after the result had come in, expelling individuals and branches who had aided and abetted not only Cora Dunne, but Fine Gael. Perhaps the irony of this was not lost on Matt Merrigan, who had himself been expelled from the party in 1957 for helping Noël Browne at that year's general election, rather than campaign for the Labour candidate.

The debacle of Dublin South West was nothing in comparison with that surrounding East Limerick deputy Stevie Coughlan who gained notoriety for a series of outré pronouncements which earned him the description as 'the George Wallace of Irish politics – personifying a parochialism and prejudice hitherto unknown at a national level'.[26] Coughlan had twice stood in general elections as a Clann na Poblachta candidate in Limerick before he finally took a seat under the Labour banner in 1961. He was a dogged local politician, rooted firmly in the working-class traditions and community of East Limerick, as publican, bookmaker, politician and member of the Confraternity, although from the mid-1960s he found himself in a constituency battle with Jim Kemmy and his supporters whose politics were diametrically opposed to Coughlan's. By the time of the 1969 election, Coughlan had already been fighting a ground war with the left in East Limerick for several years, but it seems that the nature of that campaign and the fate of some of his Munster colleagues made him more determined than ever to take on left wing or liberal opponents and associate himself firmly with conservative, or more accurately reactionary, thought whenever possible.

The first in Coughlan's succession of fracas occurred in December 1969. The occasion was a tour by the South African national rugby team, the Springboks, who had been invited to play in Ireland by the Irish Rugby Football Union, despite the fact that at that time South Africa was boycotted by the vast majority of sporting organisations in the world because of the government's policy of apartheid. The visit prompted national outrage and was widely opposed by many groups including the ICTU. Several Labour deputies, including Noël Browne, Conor Cruise O'Brien and Barry Desmond had been vocal opponents of the tour in the Dáil and in November the AC called upon all party members and supporters to refuse to attend any function or event at which the Springboks were present.[27] It was not a bandwagon on which Stevie Coughlan was inclined to jump. Unlike the rest of the country, rugby was a working-class sport in Limerick, and Coughlan saw no reason to object to the visit of a top international team, not only to Ireland, but to his own constituency. When Barry Desmond, who was an active member of the Irish Anti-Apartheid Movement, held a press conference in Limerick calling upon the city council not to oblige the team with a civic reception, Mayor Coughlan responded by warning 'these extremist offbeats that Limerick holds no future for them. Let them pack their bag and baggage before they are crushed without mercy', assuring Desmond personally that he would get a boot 'up the transom' if he showed his face in Limerick again.[28] Corish prevailed upon Desmond not to pour fuel on the fire and the issue died down with the departure of the South African team, although Coughlan commemorated the episode in verse on his 1969 Christmas card to constituents:

When protestors and rioters leave/ And men of goodwill sadly grieve
Who will raise up their hopes/ And show them the ropes?
No one better than Limerick's own Steve.[29]

It was only a matter of weeks before international politics and Limerick
sensibilities collided once again. Prior to the Springbok visit, Coughlan had
been waging a campaign against the presence of a handful Maoists who had
moved to the region in the Autumn of 1969 to work in Shannon. (One contemporary estimate put the numbers of Maoists in Ireland at 50, of whom six
were in Limerick.[30]) Coughlan had written to several of their employers
seeking their dismissal – with some success – and then set about accusing his
political rivals within the local Labour Party of being in cahoots with the
Maoists, claiming that they were trying to infiltrate the labour movement.
Things took an even more sinister turn during the Springbok visit to
Limerick. A Jesuit priest, who had been pushed out of the way when he tried
to stop an anti-apartheid demonstrator from running away from the gardaí,
subsequently informed pupils at the local school that he had been attacked by
Maoists who had 'pushed him on the ground, and threatened to destroy the
Arch-Fraternity', despite the fact that no Maoists had been present on that
occasion. This purported assault soon became a local cause célèbre, with the
Limerick Chronicle and local religious and laity taking up cudgels against the
Maoists and their tiny bookshop. This issue came to national prominence after
the bookshop came under fire from petrol bombs and was shot at; Coughlan's
subsequent statement in the newspapers giving the distinct impression that
he supported such treatment. Labour Chairman, Dan Browne, raised his
concerns about the damage being done to the party's image at a meeting of
the AC in March, and his sentiments were echoed by others including Justin
Keating, Frank Cluskey and Brendan Corish, with only a couple of voices
raised in Coughlan's support. Coughlan denied that he had condoned the use
of violence against the bookshop, and faced with almost blanket disapproval
he threatened the meeting that he would leave and form a breakaway
National Labour Party, which proved enough to dampen any action against
him. The meeting voted 12 to nine to issue a statement on the matter. The
statement's contents – emphasising that Labour was against violence or stepping outside the law, but was equally opposed to the doctrines of Maoism –
were passed by 18 votes to two.[31]

Worse was to follow. On the evening of 18 April, Coughlan addressed a
convention of the Credit Union League of Ireland held in Limerick, in the
course of which he followed his praise of the role played by credit unions in
making moneylenders redundant, with, as Michael Gallagher put it, 'a retro-
spective endorsement to a campaign conducted against Limerick Jews in

1904, and urged people to join a credit union instead of being exploited by "extortionist warble-fly bloodsuckers'".[32] This attracted widespread notice in the press and prompted a torrent of criticism within the party. Within a fortnight the AC had received 20 motions from branches and constituency councils around the country as well as from two individuals on the AC, Jim Kemmy and Matt Merrigan, calling for Coughlan's expulsion. By the time the AC met to discuss Coughlan's position, he had made a pre-emptive apology for his remarks which was accepted by the Chief Rabbi, but this was too little, too late for many of the deputy's opponents who were anxious that it be made clear that there was no room for anti-Semitism within the party. Corish, while clearly frustrated by Coughlan's behaviour, was wary of the consequences of disciplining him. Labour, he told the meeting, had seen itself as an expanding party until 19 June the previous year. The results that day had not been up to expectations, and he had taken responsibility for this. Rather than being allowed the opportunity to regroup, however, the party was being waylaid by diversions such as the one under consideration that day and, Corish complained, he was being forced to spend so much time on internal party problems that he was not making even an 'average contribution' in the Dáil. Corish told the AC that he had been appalled when he heard Coughlan's most recent remarks, but that he did not believe him to be an anti-Semite (a sentiment he shared with Jewish Fianna Fáil deputy Ben Briscoe[33]), nor (as had been suggested in a lengthy article in *Nusight* magazine) the potential leader of a fascist movement in Ireland. (It is worth noting perhaps, that a contemporary study on *Prejudice and Tolerance in Ireland* found that while most Dubliners were not anti-Semitic, nearly half (49.2 per cent) of those questioned believed that Jews were 'behind the money lending rackets in Dublin'.[34]) Stressing that the most important issue at stake here was the good of the party, Corish counselled the members of the AC to think of the repercussions if Coughlan was expelled. Here the split of 1944 loomed large over Corish who told the meeting that 'while no threats had been made of this nature, he had fair political experience on which to base such an expectation. The party must avoid a split such as that of 1944 from which it had not recovered until 1961, and he had to ask himself if he would endure another split as party leader.' Coughlan's expulsion would, he suggested, begin a war of contrition, with tit-for-tat expulsions between left and right, and a situation arising whereby 'every single word of every single member would be analysed and scrutinised for departures from party policy'.[35] After a long debate, a secret ballot saw the AC vote against the motion to expel Coughlan by 16 to 10. It released a statement giving Coughlan a slap on the wrist, but warning that 'the repetition of such views by any member of the party will incur immediate expulsion'.

This fell very far short of what Coughlan's opponents had sought. Jim Kemmy and two others indicated that they would withdraw from the meeting and resign from the AC, as they could not accept the Council's collective decision on this issue, while Merrigan withdrew to reconsider his position,[36] and Niall Greene, the party's financial secretary, also tendered his resignation. The press had a field day (not least because members of the AC were leaking detailed accounts of its meetings to journalists), while the left in particular, as well as the Dublin Regional Council – which had no love for Coughlan at the best of times – was up in arms over the issue. For them, Corish's fears of a split cut no ice. In fact, far from wanting to keep the party together, many on the DRC and elsewhere actually relished the idea of a split which would sunder the rural right from the rest of the party. The DRC held three anti-Coughlan meetings around this time, first after the Maoist episode and subsequently after his anti-Semitic remarks.[37] Coughlan had provided an issue on which all right-thinking people could be agreed, and if people were mobilised against Coughlan they might also be mobilised against coalition. This was now particularly pressing for the left, with Labour's leadership effectively having thrown its support behind the Fine Gael in two recent by-elections. 'Near perfect transfers' between the former inter-party colleagues had seen Fine Gael win both seats.[38] John Healy concluded it was 'all systems go for coalition' between Little Liam and Big Brendan.[39] As far as the general secretary was concerned, the meetings were an attempt to establish a 'parallel party' in Dublin which was 'sitting in judgement on the AC and the PLP and claiming to be purer than both'. Halligan told the AC:

> These meetings are in my view nothing more than a campaign for the destruction of the Dublin organisation by a group bitterly hostile to Labour who are however, receiving the unwitting co-operation of a number of key party activists. The proposition 'that the Labour Party is sick and is being taken over by the right' was sold successfully by a small minority after conference, and is now being repeated, and being believed by the majority. At the same time the democratic processes within the party are not being used fully and stand in danger of being abandoned in favour of an instant form of mass-democracy on People's Democratic lines.

Halligan noted that the DRC was going to hold a mass meeting of the Dublin rank and file in a couple of weeks' time. Tellingly, he remarked that 'although only 200 worked in [Dublin] South West for Matt Merrigan I confidently predict an attendance of 1,000, many of them members of other organisations.' He concluded that the DRC was perfectly entitled to hold its meetings, but that 'only official members of the party as notified to Head Office should be permitted to attend'. This is perhaps the first indication of anyone in the Labour leadership conceding that what Gilchrist called 'Labour's ride on a tiger' had gone too far. If there was any doubt on the matter, the platform of the Connolly Day meeting in the Mansion House organised by the Fintan Lalor branch in Dublin North East was illuminating: three from People's Democracy (Bernadette Devlin, Eamonn MacCann and Michael Farrell), one from Sinn Féin Gardiner Street (Tomás MacGiolla), and one from Labour, the TD for Dublin North East Conor Cruise O'Brien.[40]

OPERATION HOUDINI

Not even a year into the new Dáil, then, and Labour's future looked bleak. Corish sat eunuch-like amidst a party of irreconcilable factions, his main strength – his facility for conciliation – lambasted as his greatest flaw. Before the situation could degenerate further, however, other issues moved centre stage, shifting the media spotlight from events in Limerick and beyond. In the early morning of 6 May, the government information bureau issued a press release announcing that the taoiseach had sought the resignation of two members of the cabinet, Minister for Agriculture and Fisheries, Neil Blaney and the Minister for Finance, Charles Haughey, for their failure to subscribe to his government's policy on Northern Ireland. By the following day allegations were emerging that the two ministers had been involved in an attempt to import arms from the continent for northern Catholics. Several other resignations followed in protest at Lynch's treatment of Blaney and Haughey. Minister for Justice Mícheál Ó Morain had already resigned from the government some days earlier, ostensibly on health grounds. As details of the attempted arms importation slowly emerged, shockwaves went through the political establishment and beyond. In the fug of confusion surrounding the events, there was uncertainty about the extent and the nature of the alleged conspiracy. On the morning that news of the resignations broke, the AC was informed by Chief Whip Frank Cluskey that possible outcomes from the crisis ranged from a military takeover to a quick election.[41] Angry and alarmed at the turn of events, the opposition parties pressed for the government's resignation, but it was clear from an early stage that, divided as it was, the Fianna Fáil parliamentary party would stand united behind Lynch. When Lynch tabled a motion of confidence in his government, the result after long debate was 72 votes to 64.[42] Labour's speakers to a man spoke against the government, and even the Tipperary deputy, Seán Treacy, who subsequently became one of his party's hawks, accused the ministers involved of engaging in a 'mad escapade of war'.[43]

The chasm between rhetoric and reality was wider than usual that summer. Though the opposition parties expressed their grave fears for the good of the nation, their anxieties were not so great that they could not see the political capital to be made from the issue. Fine Gael's Ard Fheis a couple of weeks later was its most exuberant for years. Rather than the usual infighting between the conservative and Just Society factions, the party appeared united as Cosgrave addressed them 'flushed with triumph' over Fianna Fáil's difficulties.[44] Photographs showed the usually dour looking Fine Gael leader beaming like a Cheshire cat. Labour appeared less jubilant. Its deputies continued to express displeasure at losing the confidence motion and continued to call for a general election, but in reality it was a godsend. Reviewing the situation at a meeting of the AC almost a week later, Corish conceded that Lynch's success had been just as well.[45] The party had yet to properly consider or revise its position on coalition and, as things stood, if an election were called tomorrow Labour would still be obliged to stand on a go-it-alone policy. Breaking from the anti-coalition straightjacket would be a delicate business; it was urgent, but it could not be rushed if the members were going to acquiesce. A special delegate conference would be necessary to discuss the party's 'electoral strategy', as the coalition question was euphemistically known, and the foundations for a successful result at such a conference had to be carefully laid. Operation Houdini, as Conor Cruise O'Brien dubbed the project, would take time.[46] The government's crisis had provided Labour with the opportunity it needed to break the shackles of its go-it-alone policy, but for now it was crucial that Lynch stay put. Of course, to say so publicly was another matter, and when Noël Browne released a statement on 1 June in favour of Lynch staying on as taoiseach, his stance was immediately repudiated by Corish who reiterated his call for an election.[47]

When it came to broaching the coalition question, however, Corish was cautious as ever. Faced with branch resolutions for a special delegate conference to settle the issue, he demurred; they would have to gamble on there being no autumn election. It was too early to make a decision; there had to be more dialogue with the rank and file.[48] In public, however, Labour seemed almost to be shifting away from any détente with Fine Gael. Whereas Labour had advised its voters to give their second preferences to the Fine Gael candidates at two by-elections earlier that year, it made no such direction for two contests that took place in November. Nevertheless, by now, Corish had decided that the time was opportune to grasp the coalition nettle. For one thing, he was afraid Lynch might call a snap election if there was a dramatic change in the Fianna Fáil vote in the two by-elections. For another, the government had tabled another confidence motion in itself, following the collapse of the second Arms Trial (the jury had been dismissed after a week in the first effort to try the case in September) and Labour was still in the same situation as it had been in May. Had Lynch called an election, Labour would have found

itself in trouble. He did not, but Corish was no longer prepared to risk
holding off on the issue in the hope that Lynch would not go to the country.[49]
It was an analysis shared by the other members of the AC, and a motion to
hold a special conference the following month to settle the matter was passed
unanimously. The date was set for Sunday 13 December, the venue to be Cork.

The business of the Cork meeting was to accept, reject or amend a
resolution which would empower 'the Leader and the members of the
Parliamentary Labour Party to negotiate participation by the Labour Party in
a Government that would facilitate the implementation of Labour policies
and to participate in such a Government for such time as it is in the nation's
interest to do so'. There were 43 amendments for consideration, ranging from
efforts to copper-fasten Labour's go-it-alone policy (such as that tabled by the
ATGWU), to those advocating Labour support a minority government and
several agreeing with the motion, but requiring sanction by the AC before any
government could be formed. A number of motions laid down policies which
any future coalition would have to agree to, including the nationalisation of
the banks, the secularisation of schools and the withdrawal of the application
for EEC membership, before Labour could enter government.[50] The vast
majority came from Dublin branches and constituency councils, with others
coming from branches in Waterford and Dundalk. From the outset, there
were allegations on both sides of the debate that the conference would be
rigged by the opposing faction, with friction manifesting itself between
the general secretary, Brendan Halligan, and two members of the standing
orders committee, who were convinced anti-coalitionists, and accusations of
partiality flying back and forth before even the final agenda had even taken
shape.[51] The only faction to countenance defeat, however, were the anti-
coalitionists, who had met in UCC on the eve of the conference to discuss
what they would do after they lost. Some called for a walkout, others suggested they remain put. The dilemma was an echo of the more fundamental
decision facing anti-coalitionists of whether they ought to split from the party
or stay and fight on. Noël Browne made an impassioned plea to the left to
remain within the party and continue to fight for control,[52] but most had
already made up their minds.

The tension preceding the conference was nothing to the hostility which
characterised the event itself, which took place in an 'atmosphere of virtual
civil war',[53] and was the most antagonistic meeting Corish had ever faced as
party leader. Before they had even entered the City Hall delegates met a vigil
of several dozen placard carrying anti-coalitionists; beyond them was a three
deep cordon of stewards in front of the door to prevent anyone but card carrying
delegates from entering.[54] The meeting was held in an undecorated hall,
emphasising the occasion's solemnity. This time 'no sign proclaimed the

"Seventies will be socialist," no ghostly etching of Connolly's face gazed down from the lofty stage. No starry plough either', just a 'four man Politburo – Halligan, Browne (not Noël), Corish and Higgins – [which] dwarfed the audience in the great Cork City Hall while they ran the conference from the stage table above'.[55] Corish alighted from the platform to open proceedings, however, addressing the delegates from a rostrum at the front of the hall. He spoke of the dangers facing the 'new situation in Irish politics', the danger to democratic institutions of the state, the danger to the economy, Fianna Fáil's blind rush into the EEC and the ongoing crisis in the North as factors which demanded a change in government.[56] But Corish had not spoken long before Noël Browne rose from his seat to cry 'Shame!' 'I didn't shout shame when you joined Fianna Fáil', a furious Corish snapped back,[57] resurrecting a transgression of some 20 years earlier. Relations between Browne and his colleagues, and Corish in particular, which had never been cordial had by now reached their lowest ebb; Browne had been goading the party leader for months with a constant stream of flammable pronouncements designed to embarrass the leadership. These included his vocal adherence to Marxist based revolutionary socialism and his support for 'therapeutic legal abortion',[58] at a time when Labour was still trying to come to terms with supporting the legal provision of contraception. In an effort to bring to an end certain Labour deputies' (Browne's specifically) love affair with controversy in the print media, Corish made a speech in Oughterard, County Galway on 20 October in which he laid out the principles for parliamentary discipline. His views were endorsed by a meeting of the PLP on 3 November which an optimistic Corish told the AC had 'cleared the air in respect of policy and discipline'.[59] Events in Cork showed, however, that this was clearly not the case.

The anti-coalition amendments to the AC's resolution were voted on first. One by one they were defeated, albeit by a relatively slim majority.[60] Before the conference had even reached the substantive motion, Noël Browne rose from his seat and departed from the hall, followed by around 150 anti-coalition delegates, amidst cries of 'treachery' and 'sell out'. It was a highly emotional decision and several delegates were moved to tears.[61] Although a walkout had been mooted the previous evening,[62] it looks as if Browne's involvement in it was something of an accident. It had not been expected by his supporters, who had tried to get him to stay to the end,[63] and when Browne emerged from City Hall he appeared 'confused and disappointed'.[64] Regardless of whether or not the walkout had been planned, it undoubtedly added melodrama to the already acrimonious proceedings. With many of the anti-coalition delegates having absented themselves from the vote, the AC's motion was passed by 396 to 204.[65] In a last ditch effort to inject some harmony into proceedings, the chairman called upon one of the delegates to close the conference with a rendition of 'Watchword of Labour'. His request met with silence. The delegate who was to have led the performance had already left with Browne.[66]

Afterwards, Corish told the press that the result had been a vote of confidence in his leadership, and emphasised that there would be no pre-electoral agreements with other parties and that Labour would fight the next general election on its own policies.[67] Meanwhile, the anti-coalitionists were divided about their next move. Browne reiterated that he would stay and fight while others spoke of a split. On the evening conference closed, a meeting took place of a body calling itself the Socialist Labour Action Group. This group was dominated by members of the Young Socialists, which had effectively become a Trotskyist mouthpiece within the party, as well as Northern Trotskyists from People's Democracy such as Eamonn McCann and Bernadette Devlin, who were present at the anti-coalition meetings over the weekend. Speakers attacked Labour's coalitionism and called for a 32-county socialist alliance to be established to carry out the tasks in which Labour was failing. The meeting itself was attended by around 40 people, of whom half were elected to a committee to organise the new movement, with a conference to be held a number of weeks hence.[68] As the British Embassy's First Secretary David Blatherwick wrote in his account to the Foreign Office:

> They hope to gain the adherence if not of all the anti-coalition members of the Labour Party – which is most unlikely – then at least of the militant Young Socialists, the Trotskyist cadet branch of the Labour Party. Labour rank and file would of course by happy to see the Trotskyite leadership of the Young Socialists depart.[69]

Two members of the standing orders committee, Dermot Boucher and Des Bonass, who had made accusations of rigging during the conference (and had also participated in the walkout), went on television afterwards to repeat their claims. Others, including Una Claffey, Brendan Scott and Charlie Bird (then an executive member of the Trotskyist League for a Workers' Republic, which had close links to People's Democracy in the North[70]) subsequently appeared on *7 Days* to voice their dissent. Several members of the AC urged that disciplinary action be taken against those who appeared on the television, and particularly the two rebel members of the Standing Orders Committee, who ought to put up or shut up about their claims of rigging. Of course, while the rigging accusations were exaggerated, they were largely true, a point illustrated by Conor Cruise O'Brien's recollection of the meeting. After proceedings had concluded, Dan Spring came up to him, and draped an 'enormous arm' around his shoulders. 'That was nice speech you made there, boy', he told O'Brien, 'but that was a nice two busloads of delegates I brought up from Kerry too.'[71] A committee established to investigate the allegations of manipulation in the conference unanimously found that the allegations were 'absolutely without foundation'. It described the behaviour of the complainant, Dermot Boucher, at conference as 'reprehensible' and expressed the hope that 'he would conduct himself better in future'.[72]

Almost immediately afterwards, Labour faced into its annual conference. The temptation to postpone it and let the dust settle was resisted, although the AC decided that coalition would not appear on the agenda, the issue having been settled in Cork.[73] The annual conference in Galway, held in Salthill on 26–28 February, was far from jovial, but was nowhere near the massacre it might have been. The efforts to unite the delegates on less contentious issues, such as a demand for a new non-sectarian constitution for Ireland or opposition to joining the EEC, proved successful. (There was general agreement over Europe and the Cork South West deputy, Michael Pat Murphy, whose constituency was right in the heart of dairy country, was the only voice to speak in favour of entry.) Similarly, the avoidance of coalition prevented another row. The only time the undercurrent of tension became evident was during a private session debate on a motion to expel Stevie Coughlan from the party. Two of Coughlan's constituency colleagues spoke in his defence, attesting to the veracity of his anti-Semitic remarks and were ordered to leave the rostrum. Later, when David Thornley stood up to leave, another delegate asked him where his rosary beads were.[74] That delegate and the two Limerick men were subsequently suspended by the AC for their behaviour. Nevertheless, though the mood of this debate was unpleasant, the motion was ultimately withdrawn after a deal was struck between left and right whereby neither Coughlan nor Noël Browne would be expelled for their various misdeeds during the year.[75] Labour was still capable of compromise. Moreover, this row had taken place during private session, rather than in front of the television cameras. (Pictures from Fianna Fáil's rancorous first post-Arms Trial Ard Fheis, including delegates' scuffles and raised voices on the platform, have remained stock footage ever since.) Summing up the proceedings, one British diplomat concluded that 'the conference was orderly (in marked contrast to the Fianna Fáil shambles the week before) and presented a reasonably united front . . . the new party office holders are said to be from the right wing or middle-of-the-road section of the party . . . Meanwhile, their inconsistency is causing the party some embarrassment.'[76]

During the conference and afterwards, Corish had made the point that while Labour ought to be home to people with radical ideals, there was no place in the party's ranks for people with divided loyalties, although he stopped short at naming names or organisations.[77] However, when the new AC came to meet for the first time, it was clear that the Labour leadership had had quite

enough of the disruption being wreaked on the party by its small but vociferous
Trotskyist faction. Labour had been remarkably tolerant up to this point but
the leadership could clearly take no more. Luckily, it was helped in this regard
by the Trotskyists themselves. On the weekend of 13–14 March 1971, a socialist
unity conference was held in Dublin, in accordance with the decision made at
the meeting of the Socialist Labour Action Group after Labour's conference
in Cork the previous December. Among those present were representatives of
the Labour Party, People's Democracy, the Young Socialists, Saor Éire and the
League for a Workers' Republic.[78] The meeting adopted 13 resolutions of a
broadly militant socialist republican bent ranging from the general (point 6
condemned the position of women under capitalism) to the particular (points
11 and 12 pledged full support for Comrade Frank Keane 'in his fight against
the united forces of British imperialism and Irish capitalism'. Keane, a member of Saor Éire, had recently been extradited to Ireland on charges of shooting
dead Garda Richard Fallon in the course of a bank robbery). It was section (g)
of the basis of the alliance which pledged to 'work for the formation of an all-
Ireland revolutionary socialist *party*' (emphasis added) that landed it in trouble,
however. Labour's leaders happily decided that this clause rendered the
Alliance into a party, and in so doing had made any member of the Socialist
Labour Alliance ineligible for Labour Party membership which was open to
anyone who was '*not* a member of any other political party or of an organisation
subsidiary or ancillary thereto'.[79] The new AC Chairman Roddy Connolly
wasted no time in moving on the issue. Having reminded the new AC's first
meeting that they were answerable only to conference and not to any subsidi-
aries, Connolly called another meeting two days afterwards and announced,
on a point of order, that the recently elected Gerry Healy was ineligible for
Labour membership, since he was a member of the committee of the SLA.
Months of wrangling followed as certain branches resisted attempts to expel
members of the SLA, and ultimately while not all of those associated with the
SLA were expelled, the AC did manage to break the back of the faction. Several
SLA members and sympathisers were central to the formation of the Liaison of
the Left committee which subsequently took up the baton of anti-coalitionism.
According to the Liaison's contemporary tally, over the following 12 months 20
members were expelled and around 150 resigned or became inactive.[80]

LABOUR AND THE NORTH

The Troubles in Northern Ireland had been increasing in ferocity and
casualties since 1969. That year 19 people died as a result of the Troubles. In
1970 the figure rose to 29, and by the close of the first seven months of 1971, 31

people had lost their lives in political violence in the North.[81] During the first half of 1971, the Provisional IRA, which had broken away from the Official IRA, as it soon became known, began to go on the offensive. Included in this offensive was a bombing campaign which saw the PIRA plant an average of 47 bombs a month between April and June.[82] The Stormont government reacted by introducing internment without trial on 9 August 1971, unleashing the worst wave of violence in the north in decades. After over 300 people were picked up in early morning raids, gun battles raged across Belfast and 20 people were killed in the first two days of fighting, at least 11 of whom were civilians shot by the British Army.[83] Over the days which followed, thousands of Northern Catholics fled their homes, many seeking sanctuary in the South. The introduction of internment was opposed across the board by politicians in Dublin (even though Fianna Fáil had been threatening to bring it in in the South six months earlier), but while most voices urged caution, many others felt there was an obligation on the South to take a more active role in defending the Catholic community in the North. Labour was home to both points of view, but, significantly its leadership and its spokesman on Northern Ireland were all firm proponents of finding a peaceful approach to the Troubles. By the time the PIRA had embarked on its offensive, Conor Cruise O'Brien had taken a 'definite and distinctive' position on events in the North,[84] which he unveiled at the ITGWU conference in July 1971.[85] Until this point, Labour had not really had a policy on the North. It had supported civil rights, and still professed its support for a united Ireland, but beyond these vague goals there had been nothing concrete. Conor Cruise O'Brien's policies on the North became those of the party. O'Brien's view, which opposed violence and which believed that the end result of the IRA's campaign was sectarian civil war in the North, if not throughout the country, had the support of his party leader and kitchen cabinet (including Frank Cluskey and Michael O'Leary) and many others. Others, however, took a more traditional point of view and were outraged that Labour's spokesman on the North seemed to have been given free rein to make up policy on this issue. For instance, an irate David Thornley wrote to Corish after reading a front page of the *Irish Times* announcing Labour's view that the 'extreme position' of the 'establishment of a United Republic [would] have to be abandoned':

> The sooner some people realise the utter irrelevance to us of the *I.T.* and its readership, the better will grow our chances of preserving, say, 15 seats in 1973. When Connolly went into the GPO he sought to coerce, physically, not merely the Ulster Unionists, but about ⅓ of the population. Was he wrong? Every one of our Ard Fheisses [*sic*] takes place under huge blow-ups of his picture. Is this consistent with a reversion to the policy of Redmond?[86]

In the face of internment and escalating levels of violence, Labour sought to begin dialogue with its sister parties. The Council of Labour, which had been established in 1968, provided a framework for dealing with the NILP, and subsequently the Social Democratic and Labour Party (SDLP) which sought membership immediately after it was founded in 1970.[87] However, relations between the unionist NILP and the Irish Labour Party were poor, particularly after the former applied to the British Labour Party to become a regional branch. (The Irish party strongly lobbied her British counterpart to refuse the application.[88]) Relations between the NILP and the SDLP were even worse. Moreover, relations between comrades of the same party were often strained, and at one point in the autumn of 1971, the SDLP leader Gerry Fitt had fallen so out of sorts with his own party that he applied for membership of the Irish Labour Party, but was dissuaded by the Labour leadership. In effect, the Council of Labour was ignored more often than not in favour of bilateral talks between Labour and the SDLP. Around the same time, Labour also established fraternal relations with the British Labour Party (in opposition since June 1970) and a liaison committee of representatives from the two parties held its first meeting in April 1970. Although the liaison committee's meetings were infrequent, they did represent the first time that there had been any kind of formal relationship between the two parties.

On 24 August, Brendan Corish met with SDLP leader Gerry Fitt in Leinster House, and released a joint communiqué setting out six agreed points of principle and agreeing to future co-operation. The gist of the six points was that the sectarian Stormont regime should end and that power sharing should be introduced at all levels of administration in the North. The sixth point noted that 'whilst the objective of the Labour Movement in this island is national unity, the means to be used in its achievement must be peaceful. Since unity can only be based on consent, force must be unequivocally ruled out.'[89] Two days later, the AC announced it would initiate a series of meetings with the British Labour Party, the NILP, the SDLP, the Socialist International, European social democratic parties, the ICTU and individual affiliated unions, in an effort to work towards the goals laid out by Corish and Fitt. Within a fortnight, this flurry of meetings had been concluded. Labour had very positive meetings with the British Labour Party, with Harold Wilson alone and with the British TUC. It even managed a joint meeting of the Irish Labour Party, the British Labour Party, the NILP and the SDLP,[90] although the joint statement released after 'considerable consultation' was testament to the lack of common ground.[91] Dialogue was better than silence, but the talks achieved no tangible outcome, and the commitment of the British, in particular was questionable. Before one meeting of the four-party Irish Commission in December, Jim Callaghan privately intimated to his colleague Tony Benn that they ought 'to be careful not to be committed to the SDLP or tied with the Catholic minority when there was a Protestant majority to be thought of'. What Callaghan actually meant, Benn concluded, was that 'he would rather be talking to [Home Secretary, Reginald] Maudling informally than talking too much to the Irish representatives'.[92]

It was predictable, however, that the biggest problems were closest to home. The ICTU, as an all-Ireland body, was particularly sensitive about anything which might alienate its Northern members and precipitate a break up of the movement. The affiliated unions were, at best, lukewarm about Labour's stance. The leadership in some of the unions took a more militant line on the North than Labour. Particularly notable in this regard was the former Labour deputy and general secretary of the ITGWU, Michael Mullen. Mullen, a staunch republican whose views on the national question had changed little since he had been interned during the Emergency, found the Labour line being shaped by Conor Cruise O'Brien to be mealy-mouthed to say the least, and had publicly nailed his colours to the mast a year earlier when he had held a reception for Charles Haughey in Liberty Hall on the eve of the first arms trial.[93]

This view was by no means unique to Mullen. If Cruise O'Brien's analysis was shared by several senior members of the party, not least by Corish himself, there were many for whom it was anathema. Indeed, Labour was every bit as split on its attitude towards the North as was Fianna Fáil, prompting Corish's lamentation that every time there was a national crisis, Labour turned it into a crisis for the party.[94] While Michael Mullen was the most prominent Labour hawk outside the Dáil, David Thornley and Tipperary deputy Seán Treacy were the most vocal among the PLP, and had considerable support from several other rural deputies including Dan Spring and Michael Pat Murphy.[95] The view expressed by one such TD was that while academic philosophising was all very well for the so-called intellectuals, it was damaging the Labour image, with the party in danger of giving itself the appearance of Uncle Toms and Sleeveens or Castle Catholics.[96]

Labour's grass roots was similarly divided, and there was strong support among the Dublin membership for the IRA's stance.[97] The Dublin Regional Council was particularly vocal on the North, and publicly took the PLP to task for its 'inadequate' position on internment, and statements by Conor Cruise O'Brien against the IRA and by Noël Browne on James Connolly's role in the Easter Rising. It also put its money where its mouth was, by establishing a Northern Relief Committee. Details of an aggregate meeting of the DRC to discuss the northern crisis further were issued 'with the compliments of Dr John O'Donovan, TD'.[98] Ordinarily, Noël Browne was the darling of the DRC but he found his limit when he questioned Connolly's involvement in 1916, a sentiment shared by one of Browne's PLP colleagues who complained: 'I do not mind Noël Browne questioning the infallibility of the Pope, but I do object when he lashes into James Connolly.'[99]

There was no common ground between the two sides, and as the violence continued in the autumn of 1971 the cleavage grew wider and deeper. By 26 October, chief whip Frank Cluskey (who was himself a staunch advocate of the leadership line) was convinced that should there be 'three or four more weekends like that of 23–24 October in Northern Ireland, with several civilians shot by the military in emotive circumstances, the present party line condemning violence could not be maintained.' Brendan Halligan told the first secretary in the British embassy that, at best, his party could only contain discontent but not stifle it.[100] Moreover, the increasingly vocal militant voices in Labour had placed considerable strain on its relations with both the NILP and the SDLP, although the Labour leadership worked quickly and largely successfully to repair these links.

David Thornley, in particular, showed no signs of being stifled. At the beginning of December he resigned from the Northern Committee in protest at an article on the North by Conor Cruise O'Brien which was published in the *Independent* ('the last bloody straw' he told Frank Cluskey[101]). He continued to make speeches in direct contradiction of the party line, and efforts to rein him in had no effect. If anything, his language grew more combative, and he made his most notorious pronouncement on the Troubles in the Dáil on 16 December. John Barnhill, a Northern Ireland senator, had been shot dead in his home by two Official IRA gunmen, who then laid explosives beside the body and ordered the Senator's widow from her house before they blew her husband's body and her family home to pieces.[102] The killing, and the circumstances surrounding it, prompted widespread outrage,[103] but David Thornley's take on the matter was controversial, to say the least, when he remarked that Senator Barnhill's killing had been 'excessively deplored'. Taking issue with comments made by Michael O'Leary (deputising as Northern spokesman while O'Brien was away) that the onus was on the taoiseach and the attorney general to consider action against leaders of illegal organisations, Thornley announced 'if the implication of that statement is that Irish soldiers or Irish police are ever to be put into a position where they act as felon-setters for Mr Brian Faulkner, I want to dissociate myself totally from that statement at whatever cost it may be to myself. I think that I may speak for a great number of my party in saying that.'[104]

The Labour leadership concluded that enough was enough. The next day Halligan confided in the British first secretary that Labour now had no option but to expel the Republican element, even though this would cost them three seats in the Dáil.[105] Thornley and Seán Treacy countered this with a demand that Cruise O'Brien and O'Leary be forced to resign as the party's spokesmen on the North. (The previous day, 15 December, Treacy had sent a telegram to Corish telling him to 'Dump O'Brien and O'Leary fast only hope of saving party from national disgrace and political annihilation.'[106]) In the end, there were no expulsions. Significantly, by this stage even Barry Desmond, who was firmly on the side of the doves, was warning that the party should lay off on the Northern question for a while since 'the weight of condemnation has now become unbalanced'.[107] In the end, a joint meeting of the AC and the PLP was held early in the new year to consider a series of policy statements on the North, the Economy, the EEC and natural resources.[108] Among the policies enunciated in the document was the party's support for a socialist, non-sectarian and united Ireland, but it repudiated 'any attempt to achieve a united Ireland . . . by force of arms'. The policy was adopted by 27 votes to three, with one abstention, with Thornley among those voting for it.[109] Afterwards, Corish affirmed that the document was binding on all those who remained members of the party, whether they had voted for it or not, thus, as one British observer put it, 'cracking over his rebels Mr Lynch's favourite whip'.[110]

The document in question was to be voted on by Labour's annual conference in Wexford at the end of February, but in the intervening weeks, the situation in the North deteriorated immeasurably. On 30 January 1972 – Bloody Sunday – British paratroopers killed 13 civilians at an anti-internment march in Derry. Several reprisals followed. On 2 February the British Embassy on Merrion Square was burned during a massive protest in the city centre and on 22 February seven people, including five cleaners, were killed by an Official IRA bomb in Aldershot. Anger over Bloody Sunday remained, but for many the prospect of an escalation of violence with attack and counter-attack was enough to stop a swing towards militarism. Before Bloody Sunday the divisions within Labour on the North were such that the 1972 conference was likely to prove fractious (indeed, the reasoning behind holding it in Wexford in the first place was belief that people would be less likely to attack Corish on home territory[111]) but the tit-for-tat violence after the Derry killings had dampened the atmosphere by the time delegates met over 25–27 February. Chairman Roddy Connolly spoke of little else in his opening address. He attacked the Northern Irish and British authorities in the strongest terms ('Let us make no mistake that it is our country: the British army has no more right to shoot down Irish citizens at the behest of Governor Faulkner than the Nazi thugs had a right to murder Norwegian citizens at the behest of Governor Quisling') but further condemned the killings in Aldershot, and called for an end to the policy of reprisal and counter reprisal.[112] The Northern Ireland debate was scheduled for the following day. Corish conceded that the Northern policy was not perfect, but that it stood clearly against the use of violence. The

document was passed, and any amendments suggesting support for the
IRA were defeated. A composite motion, moved by Seán Treacy, followed,
expressing no confidence in the Conor Cruise O'Brien as spokesman on
Northern Ireland and calling for his removal from the position. Treacy
accused Cruise O'Brien of making a mockery of all those who had fought for
Irish freedom and said he could not himself conform to 'a brand of spineless,
supine, unprincipled shoneenism'.[113] But if Treacy's contribution was well
received outside the hall (no doubt that was his intention), it was Cruise
O'Brien who had the best reception inside, and was 'wildly applauded'
through his speech.[114] In fact, the mood of the hall during the debate was
described by one correspondent as 'euphoric'.[115] In the end, at the intervention of Paddy Devlin of the SDLP, O'Brien and Treacy shook hands and the
motion was withdrawn to much cheering and a standing ovation from delegates
for their 'hug-in'. Though some more cynical commentators drew parallels
with a similar scenario at Fianna Fáil's Ard Fheis the previous year, *Hibernia*'s
correspondent thought differently, remarking 'there was nothing of the limp
enthusiasm of a Jim Gibbons–Charlie Haughey handshake. This was for
real.'[116] Later that evening, there were further motions for expulsion, this time
against Coughlan, Spring and Murphy who had voted against the private
members bill to liberalise the law on the availability of contraceptives and
birth control information introduced by Noël Browne and John O'Connell in
February, but again the motion was dropped before it came to a vote. Once
more, the middle way prevailed.

Ultimately, the conference was a triumph for the Labour leadership.
Overall the standard of debate was high. That it was a more sedate conference
generally than in recent times would seem to be largely down to the party's
successful expulsions of some of the Trotskyist elements the previous year,
with one writer noting that 'the young Left was missing and the party seemed
the happier for it.'[117] In the eyes of one diplomat, the gathering had been
remarkable in several ways:

> First Conor Cruise O'Brien's moderate policy document on the North has been
> adopted as presented, and all 'rebel' deputies have agreed to stand by it. Secondly,
> what few wild speeches there were, were booed: like Fianna Fáil the week before,
> the Labour Party appears to be intent on moderation and reconciliation. Thirdly,
> the vast chasm between the rural deputies and the 'Dublin doctors' was papered
> over, at least for the present. Finally, it is apparent that whatever their internal
> differences and their numerical inferiority, the Labour Party are in a confident
> mood and are determined to stick together.[118]

Labour drew a line under the North at Wexford. From then on, the bickering subsided, and though there were lapses of discipline, the civil war in the party remained for the most part in a state of perpetual ceasefire. The first, and early, break in this uneasy truce was to come, however, from an unexpected source.

Unbeknown to his colleagues, on the morning of 27 January the Dublin South West deputy John O'Connell had travelled to London where he met with Graham Angel, private secretary to the home secretary, seeking a meeting with the home secretary in order to put to him his plans for an end to violence.[119] He explained that he had had discussions with leaders of the IRA who were proposing to call off their campaign of violence 'on the undertaking that after thirty days of peace, internment would be ended and a week thereafter talks would begin', at which the IRA would be represented. O'Connell had also established 'very close contact' with Ian Paisley, and had offered to win him a seat in the Dáil (in Dublin South West), which, apparently, Paisley was very keen on, although he was worried about 'carrying his followers if he moved in this direction'. Concluding that O'Connell was 'genuinely well-intentioned . . . [although] not . . . particularly clear-headed',[120] Angel telephoned him the following day to thank him for his visit, but explained that his terms were not acceptable.[121] Expressing 'great disappointment and some pique' that he was not being granted an interview with the home secretary, O'Connell then put forward another plan. This time, O'Connell would get the internees to petition the SDLP – which was refusing to enter talks until internment had been scrapped – to take part in talks on the North's future. Told that the Home Office would consider his proposal, O'Connell requested that he be telephoned directly rather than through the Embassy, and urged the Home Office official to travel to Dublin in order to talk with him and 'other people'. Angel made 'sympathetic noises' but was non-committal,[122] and O'Connell left London dejected. Bloody Sunday took place two days later, and the following day O'Connell telephoned Angel again to inform him that he had spoken with his IRA contacts about the meeting. The IRA wished him to make public the offer which had been made and turned down, and while he had declined to do so, he suggested that the IRA would make their own version of the discussions known regardless. On 4 February, Angel received further communication from O'Connell to the effect that he could not 'remain silent any longer in the face of continued British intransigence',[123] but in the event O'Connell failed to carry out his threat, and contact between the deputy and the Home Office ended there.

The following month, O'Connell was contacted by the Provisionals to approach the British government with its conditions for a proposed 72-hour truce. On 8 March he held a supper party where guests included three members of the American Embassy staff and one representative from the British Embassy, at which O'Connell reiterated his previous proposals to the British representative, Peter Evans. Evans expressed the view that this plan was highly dubious and told O'Connell he was making a fool of himself. Concluding that it was unlikely that either faction had been behind his contacts with Whitehall, Evans wrote he was

> more than ever convinced that Dr O'Connell's activities are inspired primarily by a desire for cheap publicity in Dublin. He is a political lightweight with a great opinion of himself . . . I think he has cooked this up himself with some assistance from Michael Mullen . . . who I know to be a patient of O'Connell's.[124]

Recognising that he was getting nowhere through official channels in London, O'Connell changed tack, and telephoned Harold Wilson to arrange a meeting.[125] Wilson, a man not adverse to cheap publicity himself, was happy to get involved. On the afternoon of 9 March, Wilson met with Ted Heath and informed him of the Provisionals' proposals for a 72 hour truce. When the prime minister related Wilson's information to the Home Office, he was told that they had already had dealings with O'Connell that the home secretary's decision not to meet him stood and that Wilson would be informed of this. O'Connell's colleagues at home remained unaware of his activities, although by now rumours of the Provisionals' 72-hour truce had reached Brendan Halligan. On 10 March Halligan informed the British Ambassador that he thought 'something funny' was going on, and expressed his fears that a deal might be struck 'which would enrage the Protestants and dismay moderate Catholics'.[126] Halligan was told that this story seemed unlikely but it would be looked into nonetheless. Later that day the Provisionals announced they would hold a cease-fire for 72 hours beginning at midnight. Whitehall still refused to negotiate.

On 13 March, the final day of the ceasefire, Harold Wilson travelled to Dublin, ostensibly for an interview on RTÉ, and while there he met with representatives from the three main parties in the South. Conor Cruise O'Brien, who met Wilson along with Brendan Halligan and Brendan Corish, recalled how he and his colleagues had impressed upon the British Labour leader of how unwise it would be to enter negotiations with the Provisionals in present circumstances. Wilson did not dissent, but gave no indication of engaging with what they had to say.[127] Later that evening, Wilson travelled to John O'Connell's house in Inchicore where he met with all bar one of the most senior Provisional leadership at that time. As far as the Provisionals were concerned, nothing ever came out of the meeting,[128] but the very fact that it had taken place was sufficient to infuriate swathes of the political establishment, not least within O'Connell's own party.

News of the meeting spread through political and diplomatic networks across North and South over the next few days,[129] before Wilson finally made a statement about his contacts.[130] When the Labour leadership discovered what had happened they were beyond fury. O'Connell was summoned for an interview on 22 March where he was told that his actions had been a betrayal of party policy and that he would have the party whip removed from him the following day. O'Connell recalled that he returned to Corish on three occasions that day to plead to keep the whip but to no avail,[131] although his case would not have been helped by the fact that he was completely unrepentant and told Corish that he would 'probably take what action on the North he thought fit in future but "in fairness" would consult with Corish in confidence.'[132] (Insult was added to injury when O'Connell reiterated this stance to the press.) More persuasive, however, was the delegation from the ITGWU executive who arrived at the Dáil and informed Corish that if O'Connell was expelled from the party the union would disaffiliate.[133] It was not the first time this threat had come to light, and it was taken very seriously.[134] O'Connell was expendable. The union was not. O'Connell retained the whip and was subjected to no sanctions or censure for his actions. Corish subsequently announced a new code of conduct, by which no member of the PLP would be allowed take any initiative or any action in the future without consulting him first. All this meant was that the next time O'Connell went on a solo run, Corish might not be the last to know.

Apart from O'Connell's breach of trust by negotiating with the Provisionals, Labour felt betrayed and humiliated that Wilson had gone behind their backs for this meeting, especially after they had just met and warned him of the dire consequences of such a move. Afterwards, significant contact between the Irish and British Labour Parties lapsed until 17 July when a deputation of Labour backbenchers travelled to Dublin for a few days. The visit was not a success. The British delegation began their itinerary with a courtesy visit to Dermot Ryan, the new Catholic Archbishop of Dublin, with whom they had a 'strictly off the record talk', during which they gathered (erroneously) that the Archbishop was eager for the introduction of reforms on contraception, divorce and the 'special position' of the Catholic Church. Later that evening, they gave a report of the meeting at a soirée attended by Donal Foley of the *Irish Times*, and awoke the next morning to discover their account had been reproduced verbatim in that day's paper. This did 'little to encourage confidence in others in the committee's discretion'.[135] If they were embarrassed by this indiscretion, worse was to follow, when later that evening the backbenchers discovered that Wilson had, in their absence, spent the day in London in a second round of negotiations with the Provisionals. None had been aware of this, although each suspected their colleagues had been in the know and all were 'volubly angry'. Quite apart from their anger at Wilson's duplicity, the Labour men did not regard their leader's efforts on the Irish question to be disinterested (one had complained to the group's chairman, Stan Orme some weeks earlier that '"That little xxxxx" Wilson was trying to get back on the Irish scene'). Paul Rose, the founder and Chairman of Campaign for Democracy in Ulster, was especially vexed, exclaiming 'xxxx Harold Wilson, double xxxx Harold Wilson, double xxxx Harold Wilson from the back'. After venting their spleen in their Ambassador's presence, however, they resolved unanimously to fight only in private thereafter.[136]

This might account for their united front the next day when the scheduled meeting with their Irish counterparts took place in an atmosphere that was less than cordial. The British contingent spoke of the need for negotiations, the defensive nature of the Provisional's violence, the need for the South to stop being so complacent and institute constitutional change and the accusation that the Irish contingent were 'over-reacting' to Wilson's talks. For their part, the Irish delegation also sang from the same hymn sheet, their tune being one about how Wilson had sold them out.[137] Relations between the two parties had reached a low ebb, and to top it all, it emerged the next day that John O'Connell had once again been the intermediary.

Afterwards, Conor Cruise O'Brien counselled against another meeting of the Joint Commission on Ireland. The British Labour Party 'have treated us with complete contempt', he complained, cataloguing the slights of the last year. 'In these circumstances I think that for us to sit down with the British Labour Party and purport to discuss the North would be to engage in an unsuccessful attempt at false pretences – false in that the discussions themselves would not be for real, unsuccessful in that the public now knows that this is the case and that our "special relation" with the British Labour Party has no more reality than Harold Macmillan's claim to a special relationship with Washington.'[138] He was not suggesting that the Irish Labour Party should break off contact, merely that they should confine themselves to 'personal contacts with individual members in whom we can have confidence'. Grimly, he concluded:

> The bitter fact is that if both the British Labour Party and the SDLP have treated us with contempt, we have given them justification for doing so by our own conduct. We have allowed the Wexford decisions to remain a dead letter and we have as a Party no position on the North. Officially the Party is supposed to be against the IRA but one of our members is the well-publicised mediator for the Provisionals, while another volubly expresses his sympathy for the Officials, and nothing is done about either. The institution of the Disciplinary Committee has done nothing to rectify this.

In short, in my opinion our Party needs to put its own house in order before it tries to engage in discussions with other Labour Parties. In our present condition, for us to engage in such discussions is only to expose ourselves to further trouble.

Relations between the Irish Labour Party and the SDLP which were poor, deteriorated further within weeks of O'Brien's letter. To begin with, Barry Desmond had upset the SDLP with a throwaway remark about the party in an interview, and as a result was censured by the AC for 'adversely affecting the Party's fraternal relationship with the SDLP'. (This was part of a censuring composite put forward by Labour's disciplinary committee which also saw – among others – Desmond censured for attacking Thornley, Thornley censured for attacking Desmond and Noël Browne censured for attacking Corish, who as usual, had failed to attack anyone).[139] More serious, however, was Labour's inimical reaction to the SDLP policy document *Toward a New Ireland*.[140] Published at the end of September, this document posited that the solution to the north's problems lay in a united Ireland, although it was prepared to accept joint authority as an interim measure. It was not an argument designed to appeal to Cruise O'Brien (he denied he took a two nations point of view, although effectively this was his stance), but if Labour's frosty reception was predictable, the SDLP took umbrage nonetheless, to the point where Paddy Devlin claimed relations between the two parties had been permanently damaged.[141] To make matters worse still, Conor Cruise O'Brien's book, *States of Ireland*, was published at the beginning of October. When John Hume described the book as giving 'the best statement of the Ulster unionist case ever written',[142] it was not meant as a compliment. Between his public spats with John Hume and the nature of his recent publication, Cruise O'Brien seemed to be courting controversy, and sensing that he finally had Cruise O'Brien on an issue he might have a chance with, David Thornley tabled a motion for his expulsion from the party. On this occasion, however, Thornley overshot the mark. His colleagues might have voted for censure or possibly even demotion, but expulsion was a bridge too far, especially in view of the embarrassment it would have caused Corish who had stood by Cruise O'Brien for so long. In the end, the motion was defeated and Cruise O'Brien remained in place.[143] Corish held out an olive branch to the SDLP, and after a meeting in Dublin on 17 October, the two parties managed to return to speaking terms, if nothing more.

IRELAND AND EUROPE

During this period, Northern issues overshadowed all others and one of the
most important issues facing the country – the question of Ireland's possible
membership of the Common Market – was put on the political long finger.
At government level, the negotiations took place in private and for most
people, including those who were politically active otherwise, the EEC and
its implications remained something of a mystery. Within the mainstream
political parties, both Fianna Fáil and Fine Gael were strong supporters of
EEC entry while Labour had spent most of the 1960s avoiding making a pronouncement on the subject (the issue conspicuous by its absence in the party's
150-page policy document in 1969). After the election, however, Labour began
to develop a more definite stance on the question of entry, beginning with the
decision to appoint Justin Keating, a firm opponent of membership, as party
spokesman on the EEC. Keating pushed Labour in a more anti-EEC direction, but in doing so he enjoyed significant support among the AC and the
party membership, including James Tully,[144] as well as among senior officials
within the trade union movement, including, most notably, Michael Mullen
of the ITGWU and Ruaidhrí Roberts of the ICTU. Inevitably there was
a split on the question. Several senior figures, including Brendan Halligan,
Conor Cruise O'Brien and Barry Desmond, were strongly in favour of membership, but for once, Labour managed to keep its divisions on the subject
behind closed doors. No doubt electoral considerations had a part to play
here, with the Gallup poll commissioned by Halligan before the 1969 election
showing the highest levels of opposition to EEC entry among Labour supporters and the urban working class generally.[145] Apart from appealing to
Labour's supporters, the policy also had the potential to dislodge traditional
Fianna Fáil support.[146] Moreover, it is likely that those in favour of membership kept quiet because they felt Labour did not have a hope of stopping it
anyway. (In August 1970, Labour was said to be hoping one third of the electorate would reject membership, making the referendum a matter of prestige
only for the party.[147]) Thus anti-EEC resolutions, as the only issue on which
there was a semblance of unanimity, were used to rally delegates during difficult
annual conferences in 1971 and 1972. Under Keating's guidance Labour's line
was that full membership would be ruinous for Irish industry, cause widespread
unemployment and redundancies, open Irish seas to foreign fishing fleets, lead
to wholesale takeover of Irish land by foreigners and jeopardise neutrality.
Finally, 'as a socialist party Labour must oppose any grouping of states based
on the capitalist philosophy of free trade and unrestricted competition'.[148]

   Labour did little to educate either its members or voters on the subject.
Keating was left to his own (most capable) devices and with little or no support

endeavoured to travel the country delivering local seminars on Europe which received a mixed response.[149] Two national conferences were planned to discuss the issue, but neither took place and it was only in November 1971 after the first reading of the Referendum Bill that the Labour leadership seriously broached the question of what type of campaign it would run. Even then, it was not until 20 March, with less than two months before polling, that Labour's EEC campaign committee held its first meeting.[150] By mid-April with only four weeks to go, *Hibernia* (the only national publication at the time to support a no vote) was reassuring its readers that Labour's campaign would be launched shortly. Less consoling was its headline, which read: LABOUR: HALF STEAM AHEAD.[151]

One important issue facing Labour in the campaign was the question of co-operating with others on the 'No' side, which by now included both Sinn Féins, the Communist Party of Ireland, Aontacht Éireann (a Fianna Fáil splinter group) and the Common Market Defence Campaign (CMDC), an umbrella group of artists, intellectuals and leftists, among whom Mícheál Ó Loinsigh, Anthony Coughlan and Raymond Crotty were the most active. There was one issue on which Corish was adamant: no matter what difficulties Labour might face during the campaign, the party should not associate with Sinn Féin.[152] This was adhered to at a national level, if not always in local campaigns. Nor was there co-operation with the CDMC, despite early soundings,[153] although at least four of its patrons were prominent Labour activists.[154] In the end, Labour's only liaison was with its affiliated unions, and even then, 'cooperation' was almost entirely financial.

Polling took place on 10 May. The result was a landslide in favour of entry, an 82 per cent 'yes' vote nationwide. Corish complained afterwards that Sinn Féin had damaged Labour's cause and had driven away votes,[155] but if there was truth in the accusation, the bulk of the blame lay closer to home. Labour had done too little too late and the lack of conviction among several senior figures meant that not everyone had worked as hard as they might have to bring out the no vote, which made Justin Keating's performance during the campaign all the more exceptional. Keating had acquitted himself brilliantly, showing himself to be a man of energy and charisma,[156] to the point where he was being mentioned in the press as a future party leader, no doubt raising the hackles of some of the more established people. There was little recrimination over the campaign, however, not least because it had put Labour's closet Europhiles out of their misery.[157] Furthermore, it had resolved an issue which had represented the most significant policy cleavage between Labour and Fine Gael in recent years. An important stumbling block on the way to coalition had been removed.

TOWARDS AN ALTERNATIVE GOVERNMENT

Labour had ditched its go-it-alone strategy in Cork in December 1970 but had done nothing since then to pave the way for a new coalition. Fine Gael had not wooed Labour, nor had Labour wooed Fine Gael. Through everything that had taken place over the 18 months since Cork, the two parties had looked like two giant pandas, snoozing in their respective bamboo patches, oblivious to each other's charms, while the political analysts waited impatiently for them to mate. Finally, on 13 June 1972, Corish signalled that the courtship could finally begin. He chose to do so at a meeting of Labour members in Inchicore, reminding them that he was addressing them on the third anniversary of the 1969 general election and that it might not be very long before the next one, so time was of the essence. Labour had to find out if it was 'possible to negotiate participation in a coalition government on terms which would ensure the implementation of basic elements of Labour policy'.[158] But Corish was still a little coy, and he stopped short of initiating discussions, merely letting it be known that he would take any advances seriously. Liam Cosgrave's response was immediate and favourable. In fact it was somewhat previous. Having received advance notification of Corish's speech, Cosgrave released a statement which noted that it had changed 'the political climate dramatically and must be so recognised by all responsible elements in the community . . . the possible seems more probable now.'[159] Nevertheless, things moved slowly. In early October the Fine Gael parliamentary party held a ten-hour meeting, at which each deputy and senator articulated their attitude towards a coalition with Labour. Their views on the question were overwhelmingly positive, and the meeting gave its support for a coalition, further giving the party's negotiators a free hand to negotiate a pre-election pact, if they wished, subject to reporting back on the subject to the parliamentary party.[160] Now with his party's support, Cosgrave issued Corish with an invitation to enter exploratory talks about forming an alternative government. On 11 October the PLP endorsed Corish's decision to accept the invitation. Corish explained that the two party leaders would be conducting the talks with their deputies, James Tully and T. F. O'Higgins. Announcing this news to the AC the following day, Corish was keen to stress that the talks were exploratory and without an agenda.[161] Some two weeks later, on 31 October, the four men met for talks.[162] It would be a full three months before they met again.[163]

Events got in the way. Cosgrave's long-standing difficulties with his front bench showed no signs of resolution, with his deputy leader T. F. O'Higgins and the Dáil newcomer Garret FitzGerald engaged in a constant campaign to undermine his leadership. In his speech to the Fine Gael Ard Fheis earlier that year, Cosgrave, a keen huntsman, had spoken of how he intended to unearth the 'mongrel foxes' and let the rank and file of the party tear them apart, but this shot across the boughs had done nothing to quell their ambition, and by the autumn, it seemed as though relations in the Fine Gael parliamentary party were deteriorating by the day. An already tense situation became more fraught towards the end of November when the government introduced its Offences Against the State (Amendment) Bill, which provided for conviction of a suspect on the sole testimony of a senior police officer that the accused was a member of an illegal organisation. The bill was itself highly contentious, and whether it would be passed was a tight run thing. It had the support of Fianna Fáil deputies but not the dissidents who had left the party after the arms trial. Many within Fine Gael, particularly on its liberal wing, were fundamentally against the legislation which they regarded as draconian and unnecessary. Cosgrave did not agree, and the issue became a battleground between the leader and his querulous lieutenants. Furthermore, Labour's implacable opposition to the bill served to cool relations between it and Cosgrave to the point where they were glacial, and his remarks about 'Communists and their fellow-travellers and soft-headed liberals [who] are always talking about repression', as well as the 'rabble' involved in the anti-apartheid marches the previous year, were unlikely to mend fences between the two sides (although he was more probably thinking about the soft-headed liberals much closer to home[164]). Labour was attacked for its stance by Fianna Fáil in the Dáil and in the *Irish Press*, and was accused of consorting with the Provisionals,[165] an accusation which was lent credibility by David Thornley's presence in a PIRA deputation to see Provisional leader Sean MacStiofain in the Mater Hospital where he was being held while on hunger strike.[166] On the evening of 1 December 1972, the Dáil was in the middle of an ill-tempered debate on the bill when news filtered in that two bombs had gone off in Dublin's city centre.[167] The scale of injury inflicted by the bombings was not yet apparent – two people were killed and 127 injured[168] – but the shock of the blasts was sufficient for Fine Gael to withdraw its amendment to the bill immediately. Fine Gael abstained in the vote, which was passed by 70 votes to 23.[169]

Cosgrave was his father's son and viewed Labour's continued opposition to this security legislation as unforgivably lax. Though pushed by T. F. O'Higgins to resume contact with Labour, Cosgrave was disinclined to do so.[170] There was also a marked reluctance on Labour's side to endorse the candidature of T. F. O'Higgins when was named by Fine Gael as its candidate for the forthcoming Presidential election.[171] Nevertheless, despite the strained relations, coalition, or at the very least co-operation, was an accepted fact. Sensing that spring would bring an election, Labour began to put together a plan of action for its campaign and its theme – 'There *is* an alternative' – belied any disagreement with Fine Gael, as did Halligan's instruction that 'a straight forward direction . . . be given to party workers to co-operate with Fine Gael by asking voters to give their lower preferences and by co-operating with their workers where appropriate'.[172]

Although the need for the two parties to reach some sort of agreement was quite urgent it was not until the end of January that things began moving once more, with a meeting of Corish, Tully, O'Higgins and Cosgrave on 31 January.[173] A memorandum written by Brendan Halligan two days earlier gives an indication of Labour's thinking at the time. He advised that the 'top four' should engage in talks in order to:

- a. Determine the agreed Policy Priorities for Government;
- b. Initiate, receive, debate and decide upon the recommendations of Front Bench Spokesmen on the detailed working out of the policy priorities;
- c. Determination of the electoral strategy of the coalition;
- d. Agree on principles for allocating Ministries, composition of cabinet, structure of government etc.[174]

It was clear that Labour had developed an interest in power without being sure about what it would do with it; as Halligan had told Corish the previous summer, 'the problem with our party is that we're strong on principle but weak on policy'.[175] The logic of this was that Labour should promise as little as possible.

> Nothing should be agreed upon as a policy priority which cannot be delivered because failure to do so will only create disillusion amongst party supporters and the electorate . . . Furthermore there should be a deliberate decision to do things which have to be done for the sake of winning votes and things which have to be done because they are the right things to do in themselves. Above all else, the task of the first coalition must be to elect the second one.[176]

Halligan identified what he felt were the possible areas of dissension between the two parties – (*a*) prices, pay and profits, (*b*) building land, (*c*) North, IRA and RTÉ and (*d*) control of credit – of which he felt the North was most likely to be problematic, with the events of the previous month highlighting the differences in means, rather than objectives, to be profound. 'Obviously, the events of December indicate serious disagreements as to how [bringing an end to violence is] to be accomplished. The question is this: what is Cosgrave's approach? Is it so right wing as to be unacceptable?'

There were other more logistical issues to be tackled, not least the make up of the new government, with Halligan adamant that Labour hold Finance. Finally there was the question of a joint electoral strategy, of which there were two elements. The first, Halligan explained, was the immediate necessity of establishing the idea among the public that a credible alternative existed. This meant the two parties would have to start co-ordinating their action, stressing their common attitudes on major policy issues, and, he emphasised, 'the two parties must *not* be caught again on opposite sides in any vote'. The second element of Halligan's proposed strategy was to 'go for Lynch and destroy as far as possible his image as Honest Jack . . . He must be drawn out into the political battle and pulled down from his olympian height . . . the attack must be concentrated on Lynch, and almost on him alone.'

Little or no progress was made at the meeting of 31 January, with both sides still 'cautious',[177] but the context of the talks changed dramatically when, on 5 February, Jack Lynch announced the general election. Coalition talks began the next day at 3 p.m. and continued for much of the day.[178] The following day, the party leaders signed a 'statement of intent', announcing that their respective parties had agreed to offer the electorate an alternative government in the forthcoming election.[179] The statement spoke of the national crisis and the need for change after 16 years of Fianna Fáil govern-ment, before listing the policy aims of the would-be new government. Its first responsibility was to 'protect the liberty and safety of the individual citizen and to uphold the democratic institutions of our state', before enunciating the many vague economic and social goals such as eliminating poverty and maximising Ireland's influence in the EEC. It may have been imprecise but its intent was clear from an early draft, which spoke of the priorities of the '*first* Coalition government'. The word *first* was excised from subsequent drafts. The statement was approved by the parliamentary party on 7 February and was put before a meeting of the AC two days later, where it was endorsed by 22 votes to one.[180]

Naturally, there was a certain amount of controversy about this move, not least because the Cork conference had empowered the party officers to nego-tiate a coalition *after* an election and not before, and on the understanding that Labour would fight on its own manifesto. This was clearly not to be the case. On 8 February, the ATGWU District Secretary, Matt Merrigan, wrote querying the strategy, and suggesting that his union might have to think twice about campaigning or funding the party in current circumstances.[181] Merrigan's signature later appeared along with 23 others under a statement put out by the Liaison Committee of the Left (which appeared in the press on 19 and 20 February) condemning the coalition policy document. Among their criti-cisms was the fact that the document had promised to stabilise prices without saying how this would be achieved, a fact later reprinted with some relish by Fianna Fáil's Dublin North East newsletter.[182] There was also significant dis-sension within the Parliamentary Labour Party. All candidates were required to sign a party pledge which was by far the strictest pledge ever imposed on the party, including a promise that the candidate would resign their seat if requested to do so by the AC.[183] Noël Browne and David Thornley refused, although the latter changed his mind and signed a day late. Browne was having none of it. He said he would never forgive Brendan Corish for what he had done, and lambasted the 14-point statement as 'the humane platitudes of public life everywhere'.[184]

The 1973 campaign could not have been more different from the election of 1969. Although there was more of a likelihood of entering government, there was none of the same excitement as the last time around. This helped. Far from inflated expectations, Labour was trying to hold on to the seats it had and see if it could pick up some of its losses from the previous election. The two-candidate strategy was scrapped, as was the policy of contesting every seat. Nor did head office repeat the mistake of imposing its posters and literature on the local parties, not least because it had still to pay off the printing bill from four years earlier. The whole thing was done on the cheap with little or no newspaper advertising, and candidates were left to their own devices. After 16 years in office, Fianna Fáil had nothing new up its sleeve. A tired, unimaginative administration, it ran on its record, which was little more than Lynch's performance on the North, such as that was. In the end, the Coalition chose not to fight Lynch but to emphasise its plans for the economy, such as they were, including a promise to abolish VAT on food, which were attacked by Fianna Fáil for being uncosted and unfeasible. Nevertheless, the Coalition's emphasis on economic issues did seem to strike a chord with the electorate, as opinion polls during the campaign showed them to be sick and tired of Northern Ireland and the security problem.[185] Apparently alarmed that his party's strategy had been misguided, Lynch changed tack as the campaign reached its end. Having insisted that the Coalition's policy of abolishing rates was impossible, he then turned around and promised to do just that.[186]

Labour's vote fell by three percentage points to its lowest share of the poll since 1961. Meanwhile Fine Gael's vote rose by over two per cent, as did Fianna Fáil's. In spite of the fall-off in Labour's vote, however, the pact had worked. Strong transfers between Fine Gael and Labour ensured that the larger party took four extra seats and Labour actually increased its tally by one. This added up to a majority of two in the Dáil for the National Coalition. After 16 years in the wilderness, the inter-party partners were back with 'government of all talents'. Every ounce of talent would be necessary over the next four years as the crisis in Northern Ireland escalated and the economy was ravaged by the oil crisis, which saw prices rocket and unemployment soar. The problems which had beset both parties in the previous years, not least the personality clashes, had not been resolved and would continue to affect the coalition partners. Like previous coalitions, the divisions in the government were often within parties rather than between them, but the government was bolstered by the closeness of the two party leaders. When Labour voted to abandon its anti-coalitionism in 1970, it was a case of throwing the baby out with the bathwater. Understandable as its decision was, it was little more than a reversion to the policy of 'put them out' at any cost. The coalition came together on little more than some jottings on the back of an envelope.

An assessment of this government is for another time and place, but its beginnings were not auspicious and bring to mind one of Karl Marx's more famous observations: 'Hegel says somewhere that all great events and personalities in world history reappear in one fashion or another. He forgot to add: the first time as tragedy, the second as farce.'[187]

LABOUR'S PROUD HISTORY?

—

It is commonplace for analyses of the Labour Party to concentrate on establishing where it all went wrong. That was not the intention of this study but it is a difficult question to avoid. Politics is the art of the possible and Labour's performance must be judged according to whether it made the most of the hand it was dealt. Perhaps the first question then is, could Labour have moved beyond its third-fiddle status in Irish politics? The factors standing in the way of Labour's success were numerous and substantial, but were they insurmountable? The short answer would appear to be yes. Labour was a sectional party. At the beginning it appealed to urban unionised workers and to rural labourers, which was a limited constituency within the Irish electorate. Even if it had successfully maximised its vote within this constituency it would have remained a minority party. The decision in 1930 to break with Congress and establish Labour as an independent party was an effort to move beyond this sectional straightjacket and expand the party's appeal, but it did not work. To all but the keenest of eyes, the Labour Party unveiled in 1930 looked little different from the version which had preceded it, and while it was now possible to become an individual member, it turned out that not many people wanted to join.

Why was this? There was undoubtedly an element of snobbishness which stopped many associating themselves with 'the Labourers' Party',[1] not to mention a certain suspicion among working-class members that middle-class members were slumming it when they joined. Few of the latter stayed long. Perhaps more important, however, was Fianna Fáil's success in attracting to its ranks those who might otherwise have found a home in Labour. What did that party have that Labour did not? The list is not insignificant – it was better resourced in people and finance, and it had better organisation from the outset. Its cumann membership was built on the foundations of the old IRA at a time when Labour did not even have individual members. Fianna Fáil sent fleets of cars to organise every corner of the country, while Labour struggled with one man and a bicycle. During the 1920s and for some time afterwards, Labour complained that Fianna Fáil had stolen its policies (and by extension, its voters), but clearly the newer party had to offer people something extra or they would not have been persuaded. Obviously, they differed on the national question, or at least, they did until William Norton decided that republicanism offered Labour its greatest chance of success, but degrees of nationalism are only part of it.

More importantly, Fianna Fail had charisma and a singleness of purpose that Labour lacked. It styled itself not as a party but as a national movement. De Valera inspired a devotion among his followers that was incomparable with any other living politician. Labour's leaders from Johnson to Norton may have been respected but they never inspired people to follow them and their party the way the Chief did his. The closest thing the labour movement had to the kind of allegiance enjoyed by de Valera was Big Jim Larkin, whom many workers loved, in Dublin especially, but the problem, as we have seen, was that Larkin did not always love Labour. Had he swung his weight behind the party during the 1920s instead of working against it, things might have worked out very differently. Difficult as it is to imagine Larkin being able to function for any length of time in Labour's relatively disciplined ranks, the fact remains that he had an innate capacity to rouse that was lacking among the Labour cadre. This is not to suggest that Labour fell down because it did not use the cult of personality to its advantage, but the fact remains that, at a time when politics was so much about identity and belonging, membership of the Labour club had little to recommend itself.

The exceptions to this are important, for when Labour *did* manage to establish organisations on the ground, they centred on successful deputies who built personal machines around themselves. Asked about the local Labour Party organisation in his constituency of Waterford, for instance, deputy Tom Kyne explained that he had 'no such thing as an organisation; he relied on hatchet-men'.[2] He found them very effective, although he noted that a hatchet man did have three disadvantages: 'one was that he might die; the second was that he might embezzle money and the third was that he might cause serious embarrassment by making the daughter of somebody important in the party pregnant'. Quite apart from the potential of unplanned preg-nancies, though, the use of machines and hatchet men had another problem, in that they bolstered the sense of individualism among the deputies who saw themselves as local representatives before they were Labour men, something which did nothing to foster the much-needed sense of party identity either in the Dáil or on the ground.

If there was an unwillingness among most Labour deputies to build the party beyond their own constituency, others were more eager. Labour leftists wanted to build up the party on socialist lines, believing that the party would blossom if it espoused the right ideology. Others who were also on the left, but outside the party, be they republicans or socialists of different hues, tried to capitalise on Labour's weakness to build a party in their own image. All were agreed that the party had to pitch its banners a little nearer to the skies, but was it really the case that Labour was too timid? There have always been suggestions that it was the party's lack of radicalism which sowed the seeds of its size and undoubtedly Labour's flatness did little to commend it to the public, but could it have done otherwise? The role of the Catholic Church here is important. The Church rarely mobilised against Labour, but only because Labour was assiduous in ensuring that it was never given cause to do so. The degree of self-censorship was enormous in both policy and language: Labour's amendment of the Workers' Republic constitution; its silence over the Spanish civil war; and its failure to support social reforms such as non-means-tested social welfare benefits or health reforms which would have, in the eyes of the Church in Ireland, been contrary to Catholic social teaching.

Had Labour heeded O'Casey's call of 'More courage!' would this have led to more votes? The answer is almost certainly no. Whenever Dublin delegates tried to push left-wing motions at conference, their right-wing comrades taunted them by pointing out their lack of representatives and it was a problem that Young Jim Larkin, for one, was only too well aware. As he opined to one colleague critical of Labour's right wing leadership: 'what to do? Those whom you castigate . . . secure and maintain the widest popular support as representatives of Labour – others barely managing to hang on by the skin of our teeth.'[3] The words of Jack McQuillan regarding his comrade Noël Browne are worth remembering here: much as he liked to think otherwise, people voted for him in spite of his socialism, not because of it. The proof of this came as late as the 1969 general election when Labour's radicalism, with its socialist rhetoric and new agendas designed to appeal to politically conscious children of the sixties, appeared to the majority who existed outside this milieu as jargon spouted by bearded dilettantes. Irish people were prepared to accept elements of the social democratic agenda, but the use of 'isms' remained problematic in a country notoriously suspicious of ideologies.

Young Jim Larkin understood this all too well. Having joined the Labour Party, he soon came to appreciate that Labour's doctrine ought to be practical, for as he told the young member of the Irish Workers' League, they could make all the resolutions they liked, but resolutions were what they would remain. Labour's role had to be to effect change. This might seem like a difficult task for a party which never even reached two dozen deputies, but proportional representation gave it influence beyond its size. In providing external support to Fianna Fáil governments in the 1930s and as a partner in the first and second inter-party governments of 1948–57 it had a shot at power, but did it make the most of the opportunities offered to it? Certainly, Labour was responsible for the introduction of important reforming legislation in housing and social welfare through its support for Fianna Fáil in the 1930s and its own periods in government in the 1940s and 1950s, but beyond this the limits of its influence were all too real. In government with Fine Gael it found itself unable to break through that party's conservatism. During the first inter-party government, Fine Gael successfully filibustered Norton's Social Welfare Bill, and while Labour concurred with the decision to abandon the Mother and Child scheme it is difficult to imagine that Labour would not have given its full support had Fine Gael done so.

The record of the second inter-party government is more damning, however. Labour's participation in what is a contender for the worst administration in the history of the state remained on its conscience for decades afterwards, and rightly so. At a time when Ireland's economy required a careful guidance, Labour was part of a government which went from paralysis to panic with disastrous results. As Norton conceded afterwards, 'we have tended to treat the symptoms rather than the disease'. Jim Larkin had been saying this throughout the government's time in office but no one seemed to pay any heed. Subsidised butter was no substitute for jobs. Labour's problem was that it realised this at the same time as everyone else and spent the rest of the decade, as Basil Chubb put it, 'complaining feebly ... that the clothes they could never quite bring themselves to put on had been stolen from the wardrobe'.[4] In an effort to overtake its rivals in the game of leftward leapfrog which had been ongoing during the sixties, Labour swung rather sharply leftward, attracting into its ranks a horde of Young Coveys who sat uneasily with the party's Uncle Paythers, as Young Coveys are wont to do. By 1973, Labour was a shambles, saved only by the vagaries of the proportional representation system which saw them return to government once again, despite losing votes across the board.

How is the success or failure of a political party to be evaluated then? In votes, transfers and seats? Or in the prosperity, health and security of a country's citizens? Judged on the former, Labour does not fare well. Judged on the latter, its results are possibly worse. Offering little and delivering less, Labour received the support that it deserved.

Notes

—

INTRODUCTION

1 Brendan Halligan (ed.), *The Brendan Corish Seminar Proceedings* (Dublin, 2006), p. vii.

2 DD vol. 34, col. 318, 2 Apr. 1930.

3 Patrick Lindsay, *Memories* (Dublin, 1992), p. 181.

4 Michael Gallagher, *The Irish Labour Party in Transition, 1957–82* (Manchester, 1982), pp. 15, 68.

5 Diarmaid Ferriter, *The Transformation of Ireland: 1900–2000* (London, 2004), p. 16.

6 Arthur Mitchell, *Labour in Irish Politics 1890–1930: The Irish Labour Movement in an Age of Revolution* (Dublin, 1974).

7 J. A. Gaughan, *Thomas Johnson, 1872–1963: First Leader of the Labour Party in Dáil Éireann* (Dublin, 1980).

8 John Horgan, *Labour: The Price of Power* (Dublin, 1986).

ONE: A VERY CONSTITUTIONAL PARTY

1 Jim Larkin junior, quoted in Noël Browne, *Against the Tide* (Dublin, 1986), p. 180.

2 David Thornley, 'The development of the Irish Labour Movement', *Christus Rex* 196, pp. 7–21 (The article is based on a paper to the Tuairim group in 1963).

3 *Labour*, 1955.

4 See Arthur Mitchell, *Labour in Irish Politics 1890–1930* (Dublin, 1974), pp. 37–8; Erhard Rumpf and A. C. Hepburn, *Socialism and Nationalism in Twentieth Century Ireland* (Liverpool, 1977), p. 12.

5 Mitchell, *Labour in Irish Politics*, p. 35.

6 Quoted in J. J. Judge, 'The Labour movement in the Republic of Ireland' (PhD thesis, UCD, 1955), p. 231.

7 See Mitchell, *Labour in Irish Politics*, p. 38.

8 A. Jay (ed.), *The Oxford Dictionary of Political Quotations*, 3rd edn (Oxford, 2006)

9 Judge, 'The Labour movement', pp. 119–20. Judge noted that Connolly in particular experienced the extent of popular and clerical antipathy towards socialism from his founding of the Irish Socialist Party. See Emmet Larkin. 'Socialism and Catholicism in Ireland', *Church History* 33: 4 (1964), pp. 462–83; Richard English, *Radicals and the Republic: Socialist Republicanism in the Irish Free State 1925–1937* (Oxford, 1994), p. 19.

10 Judge, 'The Labour movement', p. 34.

11 The Labour candidate Thomas Farren polled 1,816 to the Nationalists' 2,445. Mitchell, *Labour in Irish Politics*, p. 66.

12 M. Laffan, '"Labour must wait": Ireland's conservative revolution' in P. Corish (ed.), *Radicals, Rebels and Establishments* (Belfast, 1985), p. 206.

13 Quoted in Helga Woggon, 'Interpreting James Connolly, 1916–1923' in F. Lane and D. Ó Drisceoil (eds), *Politics and the Irish Working Class, 1830–1945* (Basingstoke, 2005), p. 175.

14 Ibid.

15 See, for example, J. A. Gaughan, *Thomas Johnson: 1872–1963: First Leader of the Labour Party in Dáil Éireann* (Dublin, 1980), pp. 116–22; Mitchell, *Labour in Irish Politics*, pp. 91–100; Laffan, 'Labour must wait', pp. 214–15; M. Laffan, *The Resurrection of Ireland: The Sinn Féin Party 1916–1923* (Cambridge, 1999), pp. 157–60.

16 B. Farrell, 'The First Dáil and its constitutional documents' in B. Farrell (ed.), *The Creation of the Dáil* (Dublin, 1994), p. 66. See Mitchell, *Labour in Irish Politics*, p. 109 for Cathal O'Shannon's (one of the Democratic Programme's authors) perception of Sinn Féin's motivation behind the writing of the programme.

17 An attempt by one delegate to insert definite socialist terminology met the resistance of Tom Johnson who argued that Congress should subscribe to 'James Connolly and George Russell rather than to Sydney Webb and Arthur Henderson'. Mitchell, *Labour in Irish Politics*, p. 100.

18 Laffan, 'Labour must wait', p. 210.

19 Mitchell, *Labour in Irish Politics*, p. 142.

20 Ibid., p. 142.

21 Ibid., p. 153.

22 ILP&TUC Annual Report, 1922, p. 81.

23 *Voice of Labour*, 21 Jan. 1922.

24 *Voice of Labour*, 4 Feb. 1922.

25 ILP&TUC Annual Report, 1922, p. 53.

26 See DD vol. 2, col. 167, 1 Mar. 1922 for Count Plunkett's motion to abolish the electoral deposit. Countess Markievicz supported the motion citing Labour's difficulties in this area.

27 ILP&TUC Annual Report, 1922, p. 53.

28 Gaughan, *Thomas Johnson*, p. 200; C. D. Greaves, *The Irish Transport and General Workers' Union: The Formative Years* (Dublin, 1982), p. 312; F. Robbins, *Under the Starry Plough: Recollections of the Irish Citizen Army* (Dublin, 1977), p. 232.

29 C. McCarthy, *Trade Unions in Ireland, 1894–1960* (Dublin, 1977), p. 63; Mitchell, *Labour in Irish Politics*, p. 156.

30 Laffan, *Resurrection of Ireland*, p. 394.

31 Mitchell, *Labour in Irish Politics*, p. 159.

32 Laffan, *Resurrection of Ireland*, pp. 392–3; Michael Gallagher, 'The pact general election of 1922', *Irish Historical Studies* XXI: 84 (September 1979), p. 409.

33 DD vol. 1, col. 101, 1 Sept. 1922.

34 *Voice of Labour*, 17 June 1922.

35 Laffan, *Resurrection of Ireland*, p. 394; Gallagher, 'Pact general election', p. 416.

36 Gallagher, 'Pact general election', p. 411.

37 *Voice of Labour*, 24 June 1922.

38 Gaughan, *Johnson*, p. 205; *Voice of Labour*, 24 June 1922.

39 ILP&TUC Annual Report, 1922, p. 160; William Davin claimed in the Dáil that members of the Gardaí wearing civilian clothes had engaged in impersonation, DD vol. 1, col. 101, 11 Sept. 1922; ILP&TUC Report 1922, p. 251; See also Mitchell, *Labour in Irish Politics*, p. 161.

40 B. Kissane, *Explaining Irish Democracy* (Dublin, 2002), p. 151.

41 Quoted in J. J. Lee, *Ireland 1912–1985* (Cambridge, 1988), p. 98.

42 *Sligo Champion*, 27 May 1922; Laffan, *Resurrection of Ireland*, p. 388.

43 Laffan, 'Labour must wait', p. 217. T. J. O'Connell later suggested that many of the votes had come from former parliamentary party voters who would later change their allegiance to Cumann na nGaedheal, Mitchell, *Labour in Irish Politics*, p. 162.

44 Mitchell, *Labour in Irish Politics*, p. 165; Michael Hopkinson, 'Civil war and aftermath' in J. R. Hill (ed.), *A New History of Ireland VII: Ireland 1921–1984* (Oxford, 2004), p. 32.

45 During these debates the minister for home affairs, Kevin O'Higgins, dismissed a Labour amendment dealing with the ownership of national resources stating that the new constitution could not possibly contain proposals which looked 'very much like a communist doctrine', DD vol. 1, col. 707, 25 Sept. 1922; ILP&TUC Annual Report, 1923, p. 30.

46 Gaughan, *Johnson* pp. 214–15; M. Hopkinson, *Green against Green: The Irish Civil War* (Dublin, 1988), p. 181.

47 See for example DD vol. 1, cols 177, 183, 12 Sept. 1922.

48 Quoted in Gaughan, *Johnson*, p. 215; see also Mitchell, *Labour in Irish Politics*, p. 174.

49 William O'Brien, *Forth the Banners Go: Reminiscences of William O'Brien as told to Edward MacLysaght* (Dublin, 1969), p. 222.

50 Ibid.; Gaughan, *Johnson*, p. 215.

51 For instance, when Peadar O'Donnell was imprisoned during the civil war, he managed to smuggle out a list of those who ought to be shot if he was executed. His future wife Lile O'Donel paid a visit to O'Donnell's fellow trade unionist, Tom Johnson, to inform him that 'he would be shot if anything happened to Peadar', See D. Ó Drisceoil, *Peadar O'Donnell* (Cork, 2001), p. 32.

52 O'Brien, *Forth the Banners Go*, p. 222.

53 See for example, William Davin's remarks nearly two decades later, see p. 12.

54 Emmet Larkin, *James Larkin* (London, 1968), p. 227.

55 Emmet O'Connor, *James Larkin* (Cork, 2002), p. 71.

56 Larkin, *Larkin*, p. 228.

57 Ibid., p. 71.

58 Ibid., p. 74.

59 Larkin surrendered Liberty Hall almost immediately and vacated Parnell Square after little more than a week.

60 See *The Times*, 7 Aug. 1923, *Voice of Labour*, 11 Aug. 1923; O'Connor, *Larkin*, p. 75.

61 It was also held on an enlarged franchise, since the age at which women could vote had been reduced from 30 to 21 years.

62 See Mitchell, *Labour in Irish Politics*, p. 186, Michael Gallagher, *Irish Elections 1922–1944: Results and Analysis* (Dublin, 1993), p. 23.

63 *The Times*, 27 Aug. 1923.

64 Gallagher, *Irish Elections*, pp. 51–2.

65 See *Manchester Guardian*, 1 Sept. 1923 quoted in Mitchell, *Labour in Irish Politics*, p. 190; *The Times*, 27 Aug. 1923; Lee, *Ireland*, p. 95. On the other hand Emmet O'Connor argued that 'the party was in fact paying the price of having distanced itself from the industrial struggle' (O'Connor, *Larkin*, p. 76).

66 *Voice of Labour*, quoted in Mitchell, *Labour in Irish Politics*, p. 189. The localised support for Larkin is evident from the numbers of ITGWU members moving to the WUI, with two thirds

of the Dublin membership joining Larkin's union, but only a small minority elsewhere (Mike Milotte, *Communism in Modern Ireland: The Pursuit of the Workers' Republic Since 1916* (Dublin, 1984), p. 77).

67 Cathal O'Shannon to C. J. Kennedy, 26 Sept. 1922, ILHM&A COS 84B.

68 See Nicholas Mansergh, *The Irish Free State: Its Government and Politics* (London, 1934).

69 DD vol. 5, cols 35–6, 20 Sept. 1923.

70 See DD vol. 5, col. 1940, 14 Dec. 1923.

71 ILP&TUC annual conference, 5 Aug. 1925.

72 Gilbert Lynch, unpublished memoir, p. 98.

73 Gaughan, *Johnson*, pp. 284–8.

74 Ibid.

75 Peter Pyne, 'The third Sinn Féin party 1923–1926: 1. Narrative account', *Economic and Social Review* 1: 1 (Oct. 1969), pp. 40–1.

76 Richard Dunphy, *The Making of Fianna Fáil Power in Ireland, 1923–1948* (Oxford, 1995), p. 70.

77 Ibid., p. 84.

78 *Voice of Labour*, 19 June 1926.

79 Brian Reynolds, 'The formation and development of Fianna Fáil, 1926–32' (PhD, TCD, 1976), p. 52.

80 Meeting of Party Officers, 28 May 1942, NLI, Owen Sheehy Skeffington papers.

81 John M. Regan, *The Irish Counter-Revolution, 1921–1936: Treatyite Politics and Settlement in Independent Ireland* (Dublin, 1999), p. 82. See also, p. 232; Michael Gallagher and Michael Marsh, *Days of Blue Loyalty: The Politics of Membership of the Fine Gael Party* (Dublin, 2002), p. 49.

82 Warner Moss, *Irish Political Parties* (New York and London, 1933), pp. 142–5.

83 The Licensed Vintners, who had come under attack through Kevin O'Higgins's Intoxicating Liquor Act, Town Tenants, British ex-service men and erstwhile Home Rulers were the key sections of the electorate being appealed to by the League.

84 Mitchell, *Labour in Irish Politics*, p. 241.

85 Campaign leaflet, ILHM&A POWU M S10/PTWU Elections.

86 *The Irishman*, 21 May 1927.

87 Mitchell, *Labour in Irish Politics*, p. 244.

88 See for example *The Times*, 30 May 1927.

89 *Irishman*, 18 June 1927.

90 Mitchell, *Labour in Irish Politics*, p. 247. Labour also won seats in Cork Borough, Longford–Westmeath and Mayo South bringing it to nine gains, while it lost one seat in Waterford and the seat won by Norton in the Dublin County by-election in Feb. 1926. See Gallagher, *Irish Elections*, p. 87.

91 Earl of Longford and T. P. O'Neill, *Eamon de Valera* (London, 1970), p. 252.

92 Gaughan, *Johnson*, p. 294; Mitchell, *Labour in Irish Politics*, pp. 251–2.

93 See Gaughan, *Johnson*, pp. 295–300.

94 DD vol. 20, col. 950, 27 July 1927.

95 Lynch, Memoir, p. 101.

96 Greaves, *Irish Transport and General Workers' Union*, p. 314.

97 Lynch, Memoir, p. 101.

98 Ibid., p. 102.

99 Ibid., p. 103. When the Fianna Fáil deputy for County Galway, Dr Seán Tubridy, met Lynch afterwards, he asked him what he had done on the 'Big Fellow', because at a meeting of the Fianna Fáil executive some days earlier 'all he said about you, a dog wouldn't lick your blood!'.

100 ILHM&A COS 93/12/74. He seemed to suggest that the support of the British government would be forthcoming, as following the next election there would more than likely be a Labour government in office.

101 After being approved by William O'Brien, Luke Duffy and R. J. P. Mortished as an accurate representation of Labour policy.

102 There were 153 seats in the Dáil, but at this time two seats were vacant following the deaths of Kevin O'Higgins and Countess Markievicz, and five seats were held by abstentionist Sinn Féin deputies, so that a majority at that point was 74 seats.

103 Certainly Cosgrave felt he was on the way out and spent the eve of the vote hosting a farewell party for his staff (see Mitchell, *Labour in Irish Politics*, p. 261).

104 Ibid., p. 265.

105 Ibid., *Labour in Irish Politics*, p. 267.

106 Lynch, Memoir, p. 105.

107 Ibid.

108 Milotte, *Communism*, pp. 90–1; O'Connor, *Larkin*, p. 88; Gaughan, *Johnson*, pp. 323–5.

109 Mitchell, *Labour in Irish Politics*, p. 272.

110 See for example *Irishman*, 1 Oct. 1927; Moss, *Irish Political Parties*, p. 170.

111 Gaughan, *Johnson*, p. 324.

112 Milotte, *Communism*, p. 92; O'Connor, *Larkin*, p. 88.

113 *Irishman*, 10 Sept. 1927.

114 Joe Deasy, *The Fiery Cross: The Story of Jim Larkin* (2nd edn, Dublin, 2004), p. 40; O'Connor, *Larkin*, p. 88.

115 Johnson to Duffy quoted in Gaughan, *Johnson*, p. 309.

116 Enda McKay, 'The Irish Labour Party, 1927–33' (MA, UCD, 1983), p. 9.

117 Johnson to Duffy quoted in Gaughan, *Johnson*, p. 309.

118 See Gallagher, *Irish Elections*, pp. 153–4, 145.

119 Labour Party Annual Report, 1930, pp. 63–4. For more complaints of absenteeism, see *The Irishman*, 14 July 1928; 20 Oct. 1928.

120 See Labour Party Annual Report, 1930, p. 16; *The Irishman*, 9 June 1928; 21 Sept. 1929; 5 Oct. 1929; 12 Oct. 1929.

121 Lemass to Gallagher, 16 Aug. 1929 quoted in Dunphy, *Fianna Fáil*, p. 133.

122 See *An Díon*, Nov. 1929.

123 See DD vol. 34, col. 179–240, 27 Mar. 1930; McKay, 'Irish Labour Party', p. 20.

124 McKay, 'Irish Labour Party', p. 20; *The Irishman*, 15 Mar. 1930; *The Times*, 3 Apr. 1930.

125 DD vol. 34, col. 292, 2 Apr. 1930.

126 *The Times*, 24 May 1927.

127 DD vol. 22, col. 1615, 21 Mar. 1928.

128 DD vol. 34, col. 318, 2 Apr. 1930.

129 DD vol. 34, cols 356–6, 2 Apr. 1930.

130 *The Times*, 3 Apr. 1930. It received comparable praise in the similarly conservative imperialist *Round Table*. See McKay, 'Irish Labour Party', p. 22.

131 Mitchell, *Labour in Irish Politics*, p. 280.

132 *An Dîon*, Oct. 1927.

133 Quoted in McKay, 'Irish Labour Party', p. 58.

134 The committee was to be comprised of three members of the National Executive (O'Brien, Norton and O'Farrell), three members of the Parliamentary Labour Party (Davin, Murphy and Tom Johnson, who was now a senator) and three members of affiliated trade Unions (Gillespie (ATGWU), Linehan (INTO) and Somerville (Amalgamated Society of Woodworkers). T. J. O'Connell was appointed Chairman. ILHM&A POWU, *Report of the Special Committee on Re-organisation*, 1930, p. 1.

135 ILHM&A POWU, *Report.*

136 Ibid.

137 See ILHM&A POWU, Provisional Draft of the National Labour Party (Confidential), 4 Dec. 1929.

138 Quoted in Donal Nevin, 'Labour and the political revolution' in Francis MacManus (ed.), *The Years of the Great Test 1926–39* (Dublin, 1967), p. 64.

139 *Irishman*, 8 Mar. 1930.

140 *Irishman*, 12 Apr. 1930.

141 'Action arising out of special congress decisions' [n.d.], ILHM&A POWU. Coburn had stood unsuccessfully as an independent Labour candidate in the 1923 general election 'urging co-operation and goodwill between employers and workers and opposing class war'. He was elected as an independent in the 1932 and 1933 elections. He was subsequently elected under the Fine Gael banner from 1937 to 1954. Vincent Browne (ed.), *Magill Book of Irish Politics* (Dublin, 1981), p. 270.

142 William Davin, Honorary Secretary to the Branch secretaries of the Labour Party, 5 Mar. 1931, ILHM&A POWU.

143 *Irishman*, 5, 19 July 1930.

144 *Irishman*, 9, 30 Aug. 1930.

145 Enda McKay, 'Changing with the tide: The Irish Labour Party, 1927–1933', *Saothar* 11 (1986), p. 32.

146 McKay, 'Irish Labour Party', p. 61.

147 Labour Party Annual Report, 1931–2, pp. 6–7.

148 The affiliated unions were as follows: the National Union of Assurance Workers; the Bakers and Confectioners Union; the Furnishing Trades Union; the Municipal Employees' Trade Union; the Post Office Workers' Union; the National Union of Railwaymen; the Railway Clerks' Association; the Tailors' and Garment Workers' trade union; the Irish National Teachers' Organisation; the Typographical Providential Society; National Union of Vehicle Builders; the Amalgamated Transport and General Workers' Union and the Irish Transport and General Workers' Union. ILHM&A POWU.

149 Reynolds, 'Fianna Fáil', p. 352.

150 Richard English, *Radicals and the Republic: Socialist Republicanism in the Irish Free State 1925–1937* (Oxford, 1994), p. 154. Surprisingly, only one person was in all five groups, although it is less surprising that this person was Maud Gonne MacBride.

151 Dermot Keogh, *Twentieth Century Ireland* (Dublin, 1994), p. 54.

152 Mary Banta, 'The red scare in the Irish Free State, 1929–37' (MA, UCD, 1982), p. 21.

153 See Moss, *Political Parties*, p. 176.

154 Labour Party Annual Report, 1931–2, p. 11.

155 DD vol. 40 cols 38–41, 43; 49, 14 Oct. 1931.

156 DD vol. 40, col. 62, 101, 14 Oct. 1931.

157 DD vol. 40, col. 199, 15 Oct. 1931.

158 Handwritten notes of the AC's interview with Morrissey and Anthony, ILHM&A POWU n.d.

159 *Watchword*, 24 Oct. 1931.

160 Johnson to Mortished, 1 Nov. 1931 quoted in Gaughan, *Johnson*, p. 474; Labour Party Annual Report, 1931–2, p. 12.

161 This point was made by Seán Lemass during the debate. Asking why, if the conspiracy dated before July when the Dáil adjourned, the legislation was being rushed through now in October, he concluded that it was more than likely because the general election was now six months nearer, and claimed that the government's failure to tackle economic issues, especially unemployment, had prompted it to used public safety legislation as camouflage behind which it could hide at the next election. DD vol. 40, cols 83, 87, 14 Oct. 1931.

162 Keogh, *Twentieth Century*, p. 59.

163 Banta, 'Red scare', p. 242.

164 Labour's address to the electors, which featured in the *Watchword*, 6 Feb. 1932, is reprinted in full in Moss, *Political Parties*, pp. 209–16.

165 T. J. O'Connell speaking in Knock, quoted in the *Watchword*, 6 Feb. 1932.

166 *Watchword*, 20 Feb. 1932.

167 Reynolds 'Fianna Fáil', p. 395; Moss, *Political Parties*, p. 181.

168 Gallagher, *Irish Elections*, p. 125.

169 See for instance *Irish Independent*, 26 Feb. 1932.

TWO: COULD LABOUR BECOME SOCIALIST?

1   *Irish Independent*, 26 Feb. 1932 quoted in *An Díon*, Mar. 1932, p. 63.

2   *The Times*, 10 Mar. 1932.

3   See for instance Fearghal McGarry, *Eoin O'Duffy: A Self-Made Hero* (Oxford, 2005), pp. 187–8.

4   Maurice Manning, *James Dillon* (Dublin, 1999), p. 53. See also Manning, *Blueshirts* (Dublin, 1970), p. 18; T. Desmond Williams, 'De Valera in power' in F. MacManus (ed.), *The Years of the Great Test* (Cork, 1967), p. 30; Deirdre McMahon, *Republicans and Imperialists: Anglo-Irish Relations in the 1930s* (London, 1984), p. 6.

5   DD vol. 41, col. 28, 9 Mar. 1932.

6   Richard Anthony in DD vol. 49, col. 1832, 28 Sept. 1933.

7   DD vol. 41, col. 906, 29 Apr. 1932

8   DD vol. 41, cols 906–7, 29 Apr. 1932. This was quite clearly de Valera mollifying Labour on whose votes he was relying for a Dáil majority, rather than an effort to use 'his alleged friendship with James Connolly to outmanoeuvre the Labour Party', or to 'posthumously enrol the father of Irish socialism behind a behind a project that relegates organised labour to a subaltern role', as Richard Dunphy has suggested. See R. Dunphy, 'Fianna Fáil and the Irish working class' in Fintan Lane and Donal Ó Drisceoil (eds), *Politics and the Irish Working Class, 1830–1945* (Basingstoke, 2005), p. 252.

9   That is, he was no longer employed by Congress by this point.

10   Duffy to Mortished, 9 June 1932 quoted in J. A. Gaughan, *Thomas Johnson: 1872–1963: First Leader of the Labour Party in Dáil Éireann* (Dublin, 1980), p. 355.

11   Johnson to Mortished, 26 May 1932 quoted in Gaughan, *Johnson*, p. 348.

12   See Extract from minutes of Cabinet meeting, 12 Mar. 1932, NAI DT S2264 in C. Crowe et al. (eds), *Documents in Irish Foreign Policy* (Dublin, 2005) v, p. 4; DD vol. 41, col. 171, 20 Apr. 1932.

13   The despatches were published in London by the Stationery Office and in *The Times*, 12 Apr. 1932.

14   See *Oxford Dictionary of National Biography*.

15   Earl of Longford and T. P. O'Neill, *Eamon De Valera* (Dublin, 1970), p. 274.

16   McMahon, *Republicans*, p. 52; Paul Canning, *British Policy Towards Ireland, 1921–1941* (Oxford, 1985), p. 131.

17   DD vol. 41, cols 739–45, 28 Apr. 1932

18   DD vol. 41, col. 935, 29 Apr. 1932.

19   Johnson to Middleton, 9 Apr. 1932, LHASCM WG/IFS/2i.

20   *The Times*, 12 Apr. 1932.

21   For instance, when the Labour organiser George Shepherd visited Dublin for a few days on a fact-finding trip it was difficult to find anyone prepared to meet him. William Davin to Norton, 22 Mar. 1932, ILHM&A POWU

22   Johnson to Middleton 9 Apr. 1932, LHASCM WG/IFS/2i; *The Times*, 12 Apr. 1932.

23   *The Times*, 13 Apr. 1932.

24   Labour Party Annual Report, 1931–2, p. 23; Gaughan, *Johnson*, p. 344; McMahon, *Republicans*, p. 65; Canny, *British Policy*, p. 138; Enda McKay, 'The Irish Labour Party 1927–1933' (MA, UCD, 1983), p. 37; *The Times*, 4 July 1932.

25   McMahon, *Republicans*, p. 65.

26   Ibid.

27   *The Times*, 15 July 1932.

28   Canning, *British Policy*, p. 138.

29   *The Times*, 15 July 1932.

30   Longford and O'Neill, *De Valera*, p. 281.

31   McMahon, *Republicans*, p. 67.

32   *The Times*, 16 July 1932.

33   J. J. Lee, *Ireland 1912–1985: Politics and Society* (Cambridge, 1989), p. 193.

34   DD vol. 41, col. 2195, 30 May 1932.

35   Labour Party Annual Report, 1931–2, p. 7.

36   *Watchword*, 17 Sept. 1932.

37   See for example *Watchword*, 1 Oct. 1932.

38   Manning, *Blueshirts*, p. 46.

39   McKay, 'Irish Labour Party', p. 44 [*Irish Press*, 17 Sept.].

40   Labour Party Annual Report, 1931–2, pp. 23–27; *Watchword*, 24 Sept. 1932.

41   See McKay, 'Irish Labour Party', pp. 49–52.

42   Labour Party Annual Report, 1931–2, p. 30.

43   Ibid., p. 38.

44   Private source.

45 Ibid. See UCDAD P150/2274 for meetings between members of the Fianna Fáil Executive and representatives of the Labour Party.

46 *Watchword*, 26 Nov. 1932.

47 Brian Farrell, *Seán Lemass* (Dublin, 1983), p. 40.

48 McKay, 'Irish Labour Party', p. 54; *The Times*, 3 Jan. 1932 Another factor which would have influenced de Valera's decision was the effort led by Dublin Lord Mayor Alfie Byrne to unite anti-government elements into a single group. De Valera's timing effectively meant that this group was thrown into an election before it had had a chance to organise itself effectively.

49 Ronan Fanning, *Independent Ireland* (Dublin, 1983), p. 114.

50 Manning, *Blueshirts*, p. 47; John M. Regan, *The Irish Counter-Revolution, 1921–1936: Treatyite Politics and Settlement in Independent Ireland* (Dublin, 1999), p. 321.

51 Quoted in McKay, 'Irish Labour Party', p. 55.

52 This was a point made by the Centre Party principal spokesman Frank MacDermott. *Irish Times*, 19 Jan. 1933 quoted in McKay, 'Irish Labour Party', p. 64.

53 Labour Party Annual Report, 1932–3, pp. 4–5.

54 Manning, *Blueshirts*, p. 47.

55 *The Times*, 25 Jan. 1933.

56 See Lee, *Ireland*, p. 179; Michael Gallagher, *Irish Elections 1922–1944: Results and Analysis* (Dublin, 1993), p. 180.

57 *The Times*, 31 Jan. 1933.

58 *The Times*, 30 Jan. 1933.

59 *The Times*, 4 Feb. 1933.

60 DD vol. 46, cols 23–4, 8 Feb. 1933.

61 Emmet O'Connor, *Reds and the Green: Ireland, Russia and the Communist Internationals, 1919–43* (Dublin, 2004), p. 179.

62 Mike Milotte, *Communism in Modern Ireland: The Pursuit of the Workers' Republic since 1916* (Dublin, 1984), p. 116.

63 Hanley, Brian, *The IRA 1926–1936* (Dublin, 2002), p. 66. Moss Twomey estimated that nine out of ten Lenten pastorals at this time were dedicated to the issue of communism.

64 O'Connor, *Reds and the Green*, p. 186.

65 Mary M. Banta, 'The red scare in the Irish Free State, 1929–37' (MA, UCD, 1982), p. 128; Dónal Ó Drisceoil, *Peadar O'Donnell* (Cork, 2001), p. 80.

66 Milotte, *Communism*, p. 119; Manning, *Blueshirts*, p. 61; Hanley, *IRA*, p. 66.

67 He was particularly angry about the way the motion had been tabled, since, he claimed, it had been forwarded to the press before it had been seen by the AC, hence his accusations of burlesque.

68 Labour Party Annual Report, 1932–3, pp. 64–5.

69 Milotte, *Communism*, p. 117.

70 Manning, *Blueshirts*, p. 82; See *An Díon*, Oct. 1933 for an example of an Irish trade union's look at Nazi Germany.

71 Manning, *Blueshirts*, pp. 84–91; Regan, *Counter Revolution*, pp. 340–4; McGarry, *Eoin O'Duffy*, pp. 217–18.

72 For instance, its amendment on the Land Bill passed with a majority of only three votes when all the opposition parties, including Labour, combined to vote against it. See *Irish Times*, 2 Aug. 1933.

73   Norton accused it of being a Jekyll and Hyde regime which was a friend of the workers only at election time. Quoted in *Irish Times*, 3 Aug. 1933.

74   *Irish Independent*, 13 Sept. 1933; *Irish Times*, 13 Sept. 1933.

75   Ibid., 14 Sept. 1933.

76   *Irish Times*, 16 Sept. 1933.

77   *Irish Times*, 14 Sept. 1933.

78   *Irish Independent*, 18 Sept. 1933. There are only three agendas for the fortnightly meetings in de Valera's papers held in UCD's archives, and on balance it seems likely that this is a complete set. UCDAD P150/2274.

79   *Irish Independent*, 14 Sept. 1933.

80   See DD vol. 49, cols 1837–8, 28 Sept. 1933.

81   DD vol. 49, col. 1854, 28 Sept. 1933.

82   Labour Party Annual Report, 1933, p. 64.

83   Labour Party Annual Report, 1933–4, p. 9.

84   DD vol. 50, col. 2237, 28 Feb. 1934. Labour's Annual Report, 1933–4 features an unusually lengthy section devoted to 'the Menace of Fascism' in which Costello's remarks and many others like it are quoted, pp. 9–14.

85   See Labour Party Annual Report, 1933–4, pp. 33–4.

86   See NAI Jus 8/338; O'Connor, *Reds and the Green*, p. 198.

87   Emmet O'Connor, *Jim Larkin* (Cork, 2002), p. 100; Gaughan, *Johnson*, p. 360.

88   Secretariat, Communist Party of Ireland 'Down tools on May 1', NAI Jus8/338.

89   O'Connor, *Reds and the Green*, p. 196.

90   ITUC Annual Report, 1934, p. 104.

91   See Labour Party Annual Report, 1933–4, pp. 62, 119.

92   Ibid., 1933–4, p. 64.

93   Ibid., p. 120. See Ben Pimlott, *Labour and the Left in the 1930s* (Cambridge, 1977), for the British Labour Party's travails in this area.

94   Labour Party Annual Report, 1933–4, pp. 113–18. He went on that 'In 1913 it was Syndicalism; in 1923 it was Bolshevism in 1934 the bogeyman was Communism.' He did not know what it would be in 1940, but he felt sure that the people who instituted these things would conjure something new by that time (as it was they didn't). The motion, while strongly anti-communist, was not as reactionary as it might seem on first examination. It was tabled by R. M. Burke of Tuam, a Protestant landowner and committed Christian socialist, who had established a farming co-operative on his land. He remained a proponent of socialist policies within the party until he left to become a missionary in Africa. The motion must not, therefore, be viewed as being part of any sort of any 'tradition of militant Catholicism', as argued by Kieran Allen, *Fianna Fáil and Irish Labour, 1926 to Present* (London, 1997), p. 56.

95   Labour Party Annual Report, 1933–4, p. 66.

96   Ibid., p. 70.

97   Ibid.

98   See Labour Party Annual Report, 1934–5, p. 41.

99   Ibid., p. 14.

100 Resolutions submitted to the General Army Convention with Reference to Making the Workers Republic a basis of rally and struggle and defining attitude towards the Irish Labour Party and the NILP. ICA GHQ 13 June 1935. NAI JUS/8/322. See also Brian Hanley 'The Irish Citizen Army after 1916', *Saothar* 28 (2003), pp. 37–48.

101 D. R. O'Connor Lysaght 'The second rise and fall of the Irish Labour Party: from separation to split, 1930–1944', unpublished manuscript.

102 Report of the Irish Citizen Army Convention at Kilkenny, 3 Nov. 1935, JUS/8/322.

103 Labour Party Annual Report, 1934–5.

104 Ibid., pp. 101–2.

105 Nora Connolly O'Brien to Leon Trotsky, 28 Apr. 1936, *Revolutionary History* (Summer 1996), p. 54.

106 *Irish Rosary*, Mar. 1936, p. 169.

107 Banta, 'Red scare', p. 209.

108 *Irish Times*, 24 Feb. 1936; *Irish Independent*, 24 Feb. 1936; See also Banta, 'Red scare', p. 219.

109 *Irish Independent*, 11 May 1936.

110 See also the remarks on Radio Éireann by Labour Chairman William O'Brien on the recent budget a number of days later, in which he complained that the government had failed to deliver its promise of prosperity from five years earlier and the burden of its policies was falling on the poor. *Irish Independent*, 15 May 1936.

111 *Irish Independent*, 22 June 1936; 10 Aug. 1936.

112 See for example Report of Garda Síochána Metropolitan division 13 Aug. 1936, NAI Jus 8/388.

113 *Irish Independent*, 8 Aug. 1936.

114 It is likely that much of this fall-off was the result of the late entry of Labour's candidate to the contest, and the Annual Report took succour from the high number of second preferences received from the Fianna Fáil and the Republican candidates. Labour Party Annual Report, 1935–6, p. 19.

115 *Irish Independent*, 2 July 1936; Labour Party Annual Report, 1935–6, p. 20. It won one extra seat on the Corporation, but this was on a new one man one vote franchise, which should have led to a much larger swing to Labour.

116 Banta, 'Red scare', p. 224; Fearghal McGarry, *Irish Politics and the Spanish Civil War* (Cork, 1999), p. 24.

117 Fearghal McGarry, '"Catholics first and politicians afterwards": The Labour Party and the Workers' Republic, 1936–39', *Saothar* 25 (2000), p. 58.

118 *Irish Independent*, 26 June 1936.

119 McGarry, *Irish Politics and the Spanish Civil War*, p. 183.

120 For instance Seán Keane in Cork, see p. 161 below.

121 See for example McGarry, *Irish Politics and the Spanish Civil War*, p. 185; O'Connor, *Larkin*, p. 100.

122 Andrew Thorpe, *A History of the British Labour Party* (London, 2001), p. 82.

123 For instance tensions over the Spanish issue within the Camberwell Labour Party prompted the setting up of a breakaway Catholic 'Constitutional Labour Party' which won around 4,000 votes in the November 1937 local elections. See Tom Buchanan 'Great Britain' in T. Buchanan and M. Conway (eds), *Political Catholicism in Europe, 1918–1965* (Oxford, 1996), p. 265.

124 Ibid., p. 268.

125 *Irish Times*, 9 Feb. 1937; *Irish Independent* 9 Feb. 1937; Labour Party Annual Report, 1935–6, p. 112.

126 Labour Party Annual Report, 1935–6, p. 120.

127 *Irish Independent*, 10 Feb. 1937.

128 McGarry, 'Catholics first', p. 59.

129 See Labour Party Annual Report, 1935–6, pp. 129–40 for a report of the debate in full.

130 DD vol. 65, cols 698–701, 19 Feb. 1937; *Irish Independent*, 20 Feb. 1937; *Labour News*, 27 Feb. 1937.

131 *Irish Rosary*, Feb. 1937; *Labour News*, 27 Feb. 1937; McGarry, 'Catholics first', p. 60.

132 The letter was reprinted in full in *Labour News*, 6 Mar. 1937 and Labour Party Annual Report, 1937–8, pp. 14–16.

133 *Labour News*, 20 Mar. 1937; McGarry, 'Catholics first', p. 60.

134 Johnson to Luke Duffy, 6 Mar. 1937, NLI, Johnson papers, MS 17231. For instance, in 1931 he had been reluctant to take too disciplinary an approach with Morrissey and Anthony when they voted for the Special Powers Bill, warning that it was unlikely to be the only instance when members of the PLP felt compelled to vote against 'specific questions as to which a majority of the Party may have decided on a certain course. (Gently as possible I referred to possible religious issues – thinking of myself!)' Quoted in Gaughan, *Johnson*, p. 474.

135 Noel Ward 'The INTO and the Catholic Church, 1930–1955' (MA thesis, UCD, 1987), p. 174; J. H. Whyte, *Church and State in Modern Ireland 1923–1979* (Dublin, 1980), p. 83; John P. Swift, *John Swift: An Irish Dissident* (Dublin, 1991), p. 93; McGarry, 'Catholics first', p. 61.

136 Ward, 'The INTO and the Catholic Church', p. 80.

137 The formal decision to write a new constitution had been made by the Cabinet in June 1936.

138 *Irish Independent*, 3 May 1937; see also DD vol. 67, col. 259, 12 May 1937; *Irish Independent*, 17 May 1937.

139 See Labour Party Annual Report, 1937, p. 22.

140 *Irish Independent*, 3 May 1937. Similarly Luke Duffy told a Connolly Commemoration in Cork that the draft constitution had 'no trace of the principles which inspired James Connolly [it was] as if the proclamation had never been written'. *Irish Independent*, 24 May 1937.

141 Confidential monthly summary for information of members of the AC, n.d. NLI, Johnson papers, MS 17,267.

142 Ibid.

143 DD vol. 64, col. 1247, 11 Dec. 1936.

144 *Irish Independent*, 18 June 1937.

145 Ibid., 13 May 1937.

146 Ibid., 14 June 1937; *Labour News*, 22 May 1937.

147 See for example, *Irish Independent*, 17, 26 June 1937. Brian Hanley has suggested that Labour's campaign for Old IRA pensions, particularly in the pages of *Labour News*, as well as its marked nationalist tone may have been the result of the ICA influence in the party (Hanley, 'The Irish Citizen Army', p. 45). It is more likely a simple case of opportunism in an effort to out manoeuvre the government.

148 *Irish Independent*, 18 June 1937.

149 *Labour News*, 20 Mar. 1937.

150 Labour Party Annual Report, 1937, p. 18.

151 *Labour News*, 24 July 1937.

152 *Irish Independent*, 29 May 1937; *Labour News*, 5 June 1937.

153 Labour Party Annual Report, 1937, p. 19; *Labour News*, 24 July 1937.

154 *Labour News*, 19 June 1937. *Labour News* may well have been selling 65,000 issues during the election campaign, but this represents around a tenfold increase on its usual circulation.

155 *The Times*, 1 July 1937.

156 *The Times*, 8 July 1937. Under PR–STV the smaller seat constituencies tend to favour the larger parties disproportionately.

157 *Irish Independent*, 2 July 1937.

158 Manning, *Dillon*, p. 134. This was a particularly poor showing for Fine Gael which lost a number of its most high profile deputies including Desmond FitzGerald and Richard Mulcahy.

159 *Irish Independent*, 7 July 1937.

160 Lee, *Ireland*, p. 210.

161 Richard Dunphy, *The Making of Fianna Fáil Power in Ireland, 1923–1948* (Oxford, 1995), p. 201.

162 Labour Party Annual Report, 1938, p. 198.

163 O'Connor, *Larkin*, p. 102.

164 *Irish Independent*, 7, 19 July 1937.

165 *Irish Independent*, 8 July 1937.

166 *The Times*, 6, 7 July 1938.

167 Lee, *Ireland*, p. 211.

168 *Labour News*, 27 Nov. 1937.

169 Luke Duffy to the Secretary of each affiliated union, 27 Oct. 1937, POWU ILHM&A.

170 *Labour News*, 18 Sept. 1937.

171 Labour Party Annual Report, 1938, p. 17.

172 *Irish Independent*, 28 Feb. 1938.

173 As Norton put it, though the editor was a capable journalist 'he appeared not to have sufficient understanding to weigh the harm which the publication of certain news items would cause'. Norton to T. Kehoe, 11 Apr. 1938, ILHM&A POWU.

174 *Labour News*, 31 July 1937.

175 Norton to T. Kehoe, 11 Apr. 1938, ILHM&A POWU; Labour Party Annual Report, 1938, p. 120.

176 *Labour News*, 26 Mar. 1938; Norton to T Kehoe, 11 Apr. 1938, ILHM&A POWU.

177 Labour Party Annual Report, 1937, p. 214.

178 See notes of meeting (18 Jan. 1938) regarding *Labour News*, ILHM&A, POWU.

179 See Owen Sheehy Skeffington, 'What is wrong with the Labour Party?' *Workers' Action*, May 1942, UCDAD P29a/90.

180 Norton to T Kehoe, 11 Apr. 1938, ILHM&A POWU.

181 Labour Party Annual Report, 1938, pp. 195–6.

182 C. Cruise O'Brien to O. Sheehy Skeffington, n.d. NLI, O. Sheehy Skeffington papers, MS 40,489/4.

183 Ibid.

184 Labour Party Annual Report, 1938, p. 193. Emphasis added.

185 McGarry, *Irish Politics and the Spanish Civil War*, p. 188.

186 See Labour Youth Movement draft scheme, as approved by the Dublin Constituencies Council 5 Apr. 1937. NLI, Johnson papers, MS 17,267.

187 *Labour News*, 20 Feb. 1937.

188 Michael Price to Cathal O'Shannon, n.d. [*c.* Aug. 1939] Cathal O'Shannon papers, Box 1 ILHM&A. Ironically Price's ICA colleagues in the Kilkenny Labour Party complained of just this a couple of years earlier, writing to GHQ that their local deputy only went near them when he needed posters put up. See Hanley, 'Irish Citizen Army', p. 45.

189 Meenan quoted in Dunphy, *Making of Fianna Fáil*, p. 171.

190 Lee, *Ireland*, p. 214.

191 *Irish Independent*, 27 May 1938.

192 Ibid., 28 May 1938; *The Times*, 28 May 1938.

193 *Irish Independent*, 30 May 1938.

194 Cornelius O'Leary, *Irish Elections 1918–77: Parties, Voters and Proportional Representation* (Dublin, 1979), p. 33.

195 *Irish Independent*, 30 May 1938.

196 For instance Labour put up three candidates in Dublin South.

197 *Irish Independent*, 30 May, 4, 7, 8, 9, 10, 14 June 1938.

198 Ibid., 31 May, 3, 4 June 1938.

199 *The Times*, 2 June 1938; O'Leary, *Irish Elections*, p. 30–4.

200 *Irish Independent*, 7 June 1938.

201 Ibid., 8 June 1938.

202 Gallagher, *Irish Elections*, p. 217. The only other time this feat has been achieved was Fianna Fáil's vote at the 1977 general election.

203 Ibid., p. 241.

204 Ibid., p. 211.

THREE: LABOUR'S RISE AND FALL

1   Fearghal McGarry, '"Catholics first and politicians afterwards": The Labour Party and the Workers' Republic, 1936–39', *Saothar* 25 (2000), p. 61.

2   Ibid.; J. H. Whyte, *Church and State in Modern Ireland* (Dublin, 1980), pp. 83–4; Noel Ward 'The INTO and the Catholic Church, 1930–1955' (MA, UCD, 1987), p. 174.

3   Whyte, *Church and State*, p. 83.

4   McGarry, 'Catholics first', p. 63; Whyte, *Church and State*, p. 84.

5   This account is based on the debates recorded in the Labour Party Annual Report, 1939, pp. 160–71.

6   No doubt the official report of proceedings was sanitised, and Nora Connolly O'Brien's recollection of her husband's contribution to the conference does not tally with that of the Annual Report. See Uinseann MacEoin (ed.), *Survivors* (Dublin, 1986), p. 213.

7   Labour Party Annual Report, 1938, p. 173.

8   89 votes to 25.

9   MacEoin (ed.), *Survivors*, p. 213.

10   Certainly of those speaking against the motion at conference, Seamus O'Brien was the only one to withdraw from the party subsequently.

11   E. Rumpf and A. C. Hepburn, *Socialism and Nationalism in Twentieth Century Ireland* (Liverpool, 1977), p. 87.

12   See also DD vol. 77, col. 3, 2 Sept. 1939.

13   Labour Party Annual Report, 1939, p. 135.

14   See for instance the opening address by Michael Keyes at the 1939 conference. Labour Party Annual Report, p. 91. See also Michael McLoughlin, 'A labour history of the Emergency' (MA, UCD 1993).

15   *Torch*, 6 May 1939.

16   *Torch*, 10 June 1939.

17   J. Bowyer Bell, *The Secret Army: The IRA 1916–1979* (Dublin, 1990), p. 155.

18   See *Report of the Committee to Review the Offences Against the State Act 1939–1998 and Related Matters* (Dublin, 1999), paragraph 4.15.

19   DD vol. 74, col. 982, 23 Feb. 1939.

20   DD vol. 74, col. 1322, 2 Mar. 1939. Similarly Deputy James Hickey said that he never remembered Cork City to have been more peaceful than in recent years (ibid., col 1354).

21   DD vol. 74, col. 1434, 3 Mar. 1939.

22   DD vol. 74, col. 1556, 7 Mar. 1939. See also James Everett, DD vol. 74, col. 1449, 3 Mar. 1939.

23   Eunan O'Halpin, *Defending Ireland: The Irish State and its Enemies since 1922* (Oxford, 1999), pp. 145, 201–2.

24   DD vol. 77, col. 95, 98, 2 Sept. 1939.

25   *Torch*, 16 Sept. 1939.

26   *Torch*, 21 Oct., 30 Sept., 14 Oct. 1939.

27   Donal Ó Drisceoil, *Censorship in Ireland, 1939–1945* (Cork, 1996), p. 20.

28   Ibid., pp. 21–2.

29   *Torch*, 7 Oct. 1939.

30   Bowyer Bell, *Secret Army*, p. 169.

31   DD vol. 77, col. 831, 19 Oct. 1939.

32   *Torch*, 28 Oct. 1939.

33   *Torch*, 18 Nov. 1939; see DD vol. 77, cols 1209–11, 9 Nov. 1939 for de Valera's response to the PLP's letter requesting McGrath's release.

34   DD vol. 79, col. 1639, 18 Apr. 1940.

35   J. J. Lee, *Ireland 1912–1985: Politics and Society* (Cambridge, 1989), p. 223.

36   D. Nevin, 'Decades of dissensions and divisions 1923–59', in Nevin (ed.), *Trade Union Century* (Cork, 1994), p. 90.

37   Emmet O'Connor, *A Labour History of Ireland* (Dublin, 1992), p. 132.

38   Ibid., pp. 132–3.

39   John Horgan, *Seán Lemass. The Enigmatic Patriot* (Dublin, 1997), p. 120.

40   O'Connor, *Labour History*, p. 133.

41   Charles McCarthy, *Trade Unions in Ireland, 1894–1960* (Dublin, 1977), p. 142.

42   Ibid., pp. 144, 153.

43   Ibid., p. 154; O'Connor, *Labour History*, p. 135.

44   O'Connor, *Labour History*, p. 135.

45   Seán T. O'Kelly, budget speech 8 Nov. 1939, quoted in Kieran Allen, *Fianna Fáil and Irish Labour, 1926 to Present* (London, 1997), p. 65.

46   Ibid., p. 66.

47   Much of the following is based on Finbarr O'Shea, 'A tale of two acts: government and trade unions during the Emergency', in Dermot Keogh and Mervyn O'Driscoll (eds), *Ireland in World War Two: Diplomacy and Survival* (Cork, 2004), pp. 213–20; Allen, *Fianna Fáil*, p. 69; S. Redmond *The Irish Municipal Employees Trade Union 1885–1985* (Dublin, n.d.), pp. 104–7.

48   O'Shea 'A tale of two acts', p. 220; Allen, *Fianna Fáil*, p. 70.

49   O'Connor, *Labour History of Ireland*, p. 142.

50   Ibid., p. 143.

51 John P. Swift, *John Swift: An Irish Dissident* (Dublin, 1991), p. 113.

52 For the Council of Action see J. Swift 'The last years', in Donal Nevin (ed.), *James Larkin: Lion of the Fold* (Dublin, 1998), p. 87; O'Shea, 'A tale of two acts', p. 221; McCarthy, *Trade Unions*, pp. 206–9; Swift, *Swift*, p. 113; Séamus Cody, John O'Dowd and Peter Rigney, *The Parliament of Labour: 100 Years of the Dublin Council of Trade Unions* (Dublin, 1986), p. 173.

53 Barney Conway to Seán O'Casey, 26 June 1941, NLI, O'Casey papers, MS 37,990.

54 M. McLoughlin, 'One step forward, two steps back: A labour history of the Emergency' (MA, UCD, 1993) [unpaginated thesis].

55 Swift, *Swift*, p. 113.

56 O'Connor, *Labour History of Ireland*, p. 144.

57 Emmet O'Connor, *Jim Larkin* (Cork, 2002), pp. 105–6; Swift, *Swift*, p. 112.

58 Andrée Sheehy Skeffington, *Skeff: A Life of Owen Sheehy Skeffington* (Dublin, 1991), p. 108.

59 O'Connor, *Larkin*, pp. 105–6.

60 Mike Milotte, *Communism in Modern Ireland: The Pursuit of the Workers' Republic since 1916* (Dublin, 1984), p. 192.

61 McCarthy, *Trade Unions*, p. 209.

62 Report of party officers' meeting 30 July 1941. NLI, O. Sheehy Skeffington papers, unlisted, Printed matter 2.

63 McLoughlin, '"One step forward, two steps back"'.

64 Quoted in O'Shea, 'A tale of two acts', p. 222.

65 State Censor to Desmond Ryan, 23 June 1941 UCDAD LA10/I/30; Ó Drisceoil, *Censorship*, 253.

66 Conference between the officers of the Labour Party and the Officers of the TUC. Precis of the report prepared by Messrs Luke J. Duffy and S. P. Campbell [n.d., July? 1941] NLI, O. Sheehy Skeffington papers, [unlisted, LP Admin Council – 2] Emphasis added.

67 Implementation of the amended legislation was delayed by the National Union of Railway Workers action against the constitutionality of the bill.

68 Labour Party Annual Report, 1941, p. 6 His only relations with Labour previously had been in the courts after he had sued *Labour News* for libel in 1937.

69 Although he was a deputy, he was not really active in public politics at the time.

70 *Watchword*, 24 Apr. 1926.

71 Sheehy Skeffington, *Skeff*, p. 107.

72 Notes on Communism in Saorstát Éireann, NAI D/J 93/4/7.

73 P. O'Connor, *A Soldier of Liberty: Recollections of a Socialist Anti-Fascist Fighter* (Dublin, 1996).

74 C. Crossey and J. Monaghan, 'The origins of Trotskyism in Ireland', *Revolutionary History* (Summer 1996), p. 5.

75 The Fourth International activists were considered subversives because they believed the war was an imperialist conflict and that workers' interests could only be achieved through a class war in Britain. Crossey and Monaghan, 'Origins', p. 7; Milotte, *Communism*, p. 188.

76 Crossey and Monaghan, 'Origins', p. 24.

77 J. Bowyer Bell, *The Gun in Irish Politics: An Analysis of Irish Political Conflict, 1916–1986* (New Brunswick, 1987), p. 102.

78 Ibid., p. 8. Armstrong returned to Britain in 1948. See Matt Merrigan, *Memoir* (forthcoming), p. 39.

79 Bowyer Bell, *Gun in Irish Politics*, p. 33.

80 Crossey and Monaghan, 'Origins', p. 9.

81 Minute book of the Pearse Street branch, Dec 1942–Oct. 1943, NLI, O'Brien papers, MS 15,661.

82 Luke J Duffy and Eamonn Lynch to members of the AC, NE, and PLP 21 Dec. 1939 ILHM&A POWU papers, unlisted.

83 See R. Fanning, *The Irish Department of Finance* (Dublin, 1978), p. 359.

84 The second minority report was written by Professor John Busteed, an economist from UCC, while the third was a treatise on distributism and the need to use Catholic social principles in economic planning, which was signed by Peadar O'Louglin (although written by Bulmer Hobson, who was not a member of the committee).

85 This was coined by Myles na Gopaleen in his *Irish Times* column. See John A. Murphy, *The College: A History of Queen's/University College Cork, 1845–1995* (Cork, 1995), p. 274.

86 When the 1939 conference dropped the Workers Republic clauses, O'Rahilly wrote to the press to express his pleasure at the party's decision. J. A. Gaughan, *Alfred O'Rahilly II: Public Figure* (Dublin, 1989), pp. 305–6.

87 Extracts from a report recently submitted by an S.I. agent in Éire on the Irish Labour Party (n.d. 1942/3), NAM.

88 Gaughan, *O'Rahilly II*, p. 339.

89 Duffy to Norton, 15 Jan. 1940, ILHM&A POWU.

90 Draft document by 'P. T' [Patrick Trench] n.d. ILHM&A, Cathal O'Shannon papers.

91 Labour Party Annual Report, 1939, p. 95.

92 Ibid., p. 146.

93 Ibid., p. 156.

94 *Torch*, 27 Apr. 1940.

95 Emmet Larkin, *James Larkin: Irish Labour Leader 1876–1947* (London, 1965), p. 270.

96 J. A. Gaughan, *Thomas Johnson, 1872–1963: First Leader of the Labour Party in Dáil Éireann* (Dublin, 1980), p. 377; Larkin, *James Larkin*, p. 270.

97 O'Connor, *Larkin*, p. 100.

98 See Memorandum on Communist Party of Ireland 28 Jan. 1944, NAI DFA A 55.1.

99 Emmet O'Connor, *Reds and the Green: Ireland, Russia and the Communist Internationals, 1919–43* (Dublin, 2004), p. 231.

100 Private source; Milotte, *Communism*, p. 191.

101 O'Connor, *Reds and the Green*, p. 231.

102 According to a contemporary account by Tom Burns (the pseudonym of leading London-based Trotskyist Gerry Healy, who, like other senior British Trotskyists, had spent the very early part of the war in Dublin as a member of the Labour Party) there was a vote of eleven to nine in favour of the dissolution, a vote which was 'carried on the votes of British communists who had come over when the war began and who acted on instructions from the central committee of the CPGB'. Milotte, *Communism*, p. 191.

103 Private source.

104 O'Connor, *Reds and the Green*, p. 232. Note however the arrest of Fred Cowan on 20 Jan. 1942, and interrogation on the subject of the DCC [P34/E/152] 'In view of the apparent desire on the part of the police to obtain detailed knowledge of party routine and party members' names and addresses, occupations etc . . .'.

105 Labour Party Annual Report, 1941, p. 102.

106 Tunney joined in December. See report of the resident officers' committee 22 Dec. 1942. NLI, O. Sheehy Skeffington papers, unlisted.

107 DCC minutes, 3, 4, 8 Aug., 15 Sept. 1942. UCDAD P34/E/104.

108 DCC minutes, 4 Aug. 1942. UCDAD P34/E/10.

109 Certainly Larkin's vehement opposition to the motion would seem to bare this out. DCC minutes 15 Sept. 1942. UCDAD P34/E/10.

110 It seems that relations between the two parties were very good on ground. Following the 1942 local elections, the Labour councillor R. M Burke recorded that he 'found the Clann na Talmhan men most friendly to Labour'. Afterwards Burke was nominated for several council positions by the Clann leader Michael Donnellan and his colleagues but he was defeated by Fianna Fáil votes. R. M. Burke to Luke Duffy, 5 Sept. 1942 in NLI, O. Sheehy Skeffington papers. For Clann na Talmhan see Tony Varley, 'Farmers against nationalists: the rise and fall of Clann na Talmhan' in G. Moran and R. Gillespie (eds), *Galway: History and Society* (1996), pp. 589–622.

111 See for example, Bowyer Bell, *Secret Army*, pp. 175–6; Eithne MacDermott, *Clann na Poblachta* (Cork, 1998), pp. 10–11.

112 General situation in Éire, July–Aug. 1942. TNA DO 121/85.

113 It managed to field 18 candidates in Dublin for the 1942 municipal elections, but without success. The following year it contested five seats in the general election and lost all its deposits.

114 Confidential list of prospective candidates for the local elections in 1942. NLI, O. Sheehy Skeffington papers, unlisted.

115 General situation in Éire, Nov.–Dec. 1942. TNA, DO 121/8.

116 Irish Affairs, the General Situation in Éire, 1 May 1943. TNA, DO 121/85.

117 Draft minutes of AC meeting 23 Mar. 1943. Private papers.

118 DD vol. 91, cols 545–6, 9 July 1943.

119 Roddy Connolly and Peadar Cowan at 1942 annual conference. Labour Party Annual Report, 1941, pp. 90, 91 'It was up to the LP to take advantage of that trend – if they did not do it, the young people of the country, dissatisfied with FF and FG would form some other party.'

120 Daniel C. O'Boyle to Peadar Cowan, 28 Apr. 1942. NLI, O. Sheehy Skeffington papers, unlisted.

121 Swift, 'The last years', p. 88.

122 Swift, *Swift*, p. 115.

123 See letter to each Labour Party member from DCC 10 June 1942, UCDAD P34/E/154.

124 Swift, *Swift*, p. 99.

125 UCDAD P29a/90.

126 Sheehy Skeffington, *Skeff*, p. 107; Owen Sheehy Skeffington to Joe [McGlinchey] 7 Sept. 1942. NLI, O. Sheehy Skeffington papers, unlisted [LP Corr 1].

127 Sheehy Skeffington, *Skeff*, p. 107; DCC minute book 29 June 1942, UCDAD P34/E/104.

128 See, p. 88 above.

129 *Torch*, 15 Aug. 1942; DCC minute book 20 July 1942 UCDAD P34/E/104.

130 John de Courcy Ireland in D. Nevin (ed.), *Lion of the Fold* (Dublin, 1978), p. 452.

131 Seán O'Casey to Jack Carney, 29 June 1942. D. Krause (ed.), *The Letters of Seán O'Casey, 1942–54*, 4 vols (New York, 1980), II, p. 65.

132 See DCC minutes 1 Dec. 1941 UCDAD P34/E/10.

133 The Labour Party, 'Official Statement relating to the disaffiliation from the Labour Party of the ITGWU', p. 2; Desmond Ryan, draft article UCDAD LA10/D/192. Indeed there were

allegations at the time that it actually engaged in a campaign of disruption against Labour. See A. Sheehy Skeffington to F. Cowan 18 Feb. 1974, UCDAD P34/E/27.

134 AC minutes 18 June 1942. Private papers.

135 In the event Roddy Connolly was unable to make the meeting and was replaced by James Everett. Draft minutes of AC meeting, 2 July 1942. NLI, O. Sheehy Skeffington papers, unlisted.

136 Ibid.

137 Ibid.

138 Minutes of officers meeting, 10 Sept. 1942 NLI, O. Sheehy Skeffington papers, unlisted.

139 McLoughlin, 'A Labour history of the Emergency'.

140 Desmond Ryan, draft article UCDAD LA10/D/192.

141 AC minutes, 18 Sept. 1942, NLI, O. Sheehy Skeffington papers, unlisted.

142 See notes on expulsion by Owen Sheehy Skeffington, Apr. 1943.

143 Draft minutes AC meeting 20 Nov. 1942. NLI, O. Sheehy Skeffington papers, unlisted.

144 Skeffington, *Skeff*, p. 110; O. Sheehy Skeffington to Seamas [McGowan], 19 Apr. 1944. UCDAD P34/D/61(1).

145 Price died just over a year later, on 17 January 1944.

146 AC minutes, 11 Dec. 1942. Private papers; Minutes Drumcondra Branch Labour Party 10 Dec. 1942. UCDAD P34/E/101; Price to Chairman Labour Party 4 Dec. 1942. UCDAD P34/E/132;.

147 O. Sheehy Skeffington to L. J. Duffy, 4 Dec. 1942. UCDAD P34/D/61 (2); AC minutes, 11 Dec. 1942. Private papers.

148 Minutes Pearse Street Branch, 9 Dec. 1942. NLI, William O'Brien papers.

149 Pollock – also known as George McLay – was originally from Scotland, and had moved to Ireland in 1917 to avoid conscription. He was active in the CPI until 1927, when intelligence reports noted he had 'dropped out of active political work, though there is no reason to doubt that he is still a communist'. See Notes on Communism in Saorstat Éireann, NAI, D/J 93/4/7, p. 10.

150 George Pollock to Owen Sheehy Skeffington, 10 Dec. 1942. NLI, O. Sheehy Skeffington papers, unlisted.

151 AC minutes, 11 Dec. 1942. Private papers. The two votes in favour were those of Skeffington and Hanley, with Roddy Connolly, Peadar Cowan and R. M. Burke abstaining.

152 See Owen Sheehy Skeffington to Luke Duffy, 24 Dec. 1942. UCDAD P34/D/61 (6).

153 DCC minutes, 3 Jan. 1942, UCDAD P34/E/104; Owen Sheehy Skeffington to Luke Duffy, 24 Dec. 1942, UCDAD P34/D/61 (6).

154 AC minutes, 20 Nov. 1942. NLI, O. Sheehy Skeffington papers, unlisted. DCC minutes, 1 Feb. 1943, UCDAD P34/E/104.

155 Report of the Resident Committee, 22 Dec. 1942. NLI, O. Sheehy Skeffington papers, unlisted. Those present at this meeting were Norton (Chair), Roddy Connolly, Luke Duffy and Peadar Cowan; copy of letter from Luke Duffy to Owen Sheehy Skeffington, 23 Dec. 1942, UCDAD P34/D/61 (6).

156 Skeffington to Duffy, 24 Dec. 1942, UCDAD P34/D/61 (6).

157 Skeffington, *Skeff*, p. 111; Minutes Pearse Street Branch, 13 Jan. 1943, NLI, William O'Brien papers.

158 Skeffington, *Skeff*, p. 112.

159 Ibid., p. 113. Skeffington's readmission to the Labour Party had been broached at the beginning of 1950, but met with stiff resistance in the AC. Skeffington had been engaged in a war of words in the letters page of the *Irish Times* in what became known as the Liberal Ethic

controversy and it was felt that his membership 'would be most inopportune' (AC minutes, 30 Mar. 1950, NLI, Corish papers, unlisted). It was not until 7 December 1950 that the AC finally came to a decision on the matter and voted that Dr Skeffington be not admitted to membership of the party (AC minutes, 7 Dec. 1950, NLI, Corish papers, unlisted). Ironically, the resurrection of the Skeffington issue resulted in the resignation of Dan Desmond from the AC for leaking information on the application to the press (Minutes of the Resident Committee, 27 June 1950, NLI, Corish papers, unlisted). Skeffington was asked to join once again some twenty years later (see chapter 9).

160 For instance, one recent popular history book claims that 'a measure of the conservativeness of the [Labour] party was that it expelled Owen Sheehy Skeffington in 1943 for publicly engaging in controversy with a priest over the nature of socialism', managing not only to telescope two separate controversies but also avoid the issue of why Skeffington was expelled at all. Diarmaid Ferriter, *The Transformation of Ireland 1900–2000* (London, 2004), p. 413.

161 It was a cultural deficit that would afflict another plaster saint, Noel Browne.

162 Skeffington, *Skeff*, p. 104; Swift, *Swift*, p. 114; Roy Johnston to Skeffington, 9 July 1946, NLI, O. Sheehy Skeffington papers.

163 See for example minutes, Pearse Street Branch 27 Jan. 1943, NLI, O'Brien papers.

164 Fred Cowan to Owen Sheehy Skeffington, 17 Feb. 1943, NLI, O. Sheehy Skeffington papers, unlisted.

165 Notes on Communism in Saorstát Éireann, NAI D/J 93/4/7.

166 Fred Cowan to Owen Sheehy Skeffington, 17 Feb. 1943, NLI, O. Sheehy Skeffington papers, unlisted. A report on 'Communism in Ireland' written by the Department of Justice in December 1947 described the setting up of the Dublin Executive [founded by Jim Larkin junior and John de Courcy Ireland and assisted by Peadar Cowan] as the second 'major success' (after establishing the Central Branch) by the communist element in Labour. (UCDAD P67/522(4)).

167 AC minutes, 13 Apr. 1943. Private papers.

168 AC minutes, 18 May 1943, UCDAD P56/299 (7).

169 *Irish Press*, 16 Apr. 1943.

170 Ibid.

171 Larkin to Norton, 14 May 1943 in minutes of the AC 23 May 1943, UCDAD P56/299 (7) Emphasis in the original.

172 Labour Party, 'Official statement', p. 5.

173 AC minutes, 18 May 1943, UCDAD P56/299 (7).

174 Larkin to Norton 22 May 1943 quoted in Labour Party, 'Official statement', p. 5.

175 AC minutes, 25 May 1943, UCDAD P56/299 (7).

176 Two AC members were absent from the meeting, neither of whom were ITGWU members, and both claimed they would have voted for Larkin had they been there. Labour Party, 'Official statement', p. 3.

177 Statement by Thomas Farren, P56/299 (15); P56/299 (15); Copy of letter [unsigned] to Luke Duffy, 8 June 1943, NLI, O'Brien papers, MSS 15680.

178 Louie Bennett to Tom Johnson 5 Feb. 1943, NLI, Johnson papers. Bennett was also on the platform at the meeting, as was Roddy Connolly and Larkin junior.

179 See Farren to Duffy, 8 June 1943, UCDAD P56/299 (22); ITGWU, 'The Union's reply to the Labour Party statement', p. 5.

180 Prognosis of election results, marked confidential. Luke Duffy, 2 June 1942. NLI, O. Sheehy Skeffington papers, unlisted.

181 Price to Labour Party chairman, 4 Dec. 1942.

182 *The Times*, 21 June 1943.

183 The inflationary potential for Labour's policies were emphasised, while, for instance, de Valera argued about the impossibility of reducing tax while increasing social services. See *Irish Press*, 5 June 1943.

184 *Irish Press*, 18 May 1943.

185 Ibid., 4 June 1943.

186 Ibid., 5 June 1943.

187 Lemass to MacEntee, 10 June 1943, UCDAD P67/363 (6).

188 MacEntee to Lemass, 10 June 1943, UCDAD P67/363 (7).

189 For instance, he devoted most of a meeting in Rathmines to critiquing Labour's policy of open inflation, although he could not resist reference to young Jim Larkin's 'beloved Russia'. *Irish Press*, 18 June 1943.

190 *The Times*, 21 June 1943.

191 Figures from Richard Sinnott, *Irish Voters Decide: Voting Behaviour in Elections and Referendums since 1918* (Manchester, 1995). Labour's vote increased across the country, but made the most significant increases in Dublin and the rest of Leinster.

192 A Labour advertisement in the *Kerryman* had listed the Fianna Fáil record as follows: 'Proclaimed George VI King of Ireland; Interned without trial 500 Republicans; Banished 150,000 Irish youths to work and fight for the Empire; Won't permit Irishmen threatened with Conscription to return Home; have kept 100,000 people in Idleness and Poverty.' Stephen Collins, *Spring and the Labour Story* (Dublin, 1993), p. 13.

193 Luke Duffy later told the TUC Congress the following month that it was 'not up to expectations', *Irish Press*, 24 July 1943.

194 MacEntee to de Valera, 28 June 1943, UCDAD P67/366 (1).

195 Each and every one of his colleagues would have recognised that in writing this letter MacEntee was throwing a tantrum, and nothing more. The suggestion that it constituted a 'near crisis' in Fianna Fáil which prompted it to 'find a new strategy for maintaining its hegemony over the working class' (see Allen, *Fianna Fáil*, p. 78) is ludicrous.

196 *Irish Press*, 16 July 1943.

197 DD vol. 91, col. 521, July 1943.

198 One woman from Galway wrote to express how impressed she had been with his speech 'with its note – so unusual in the Dáil – of intelligence and political acumen'. Angela Barry to Jim Larkin junior, 9 July 1943. ILHM&A WUI unlisted.

199 Record of communist activities, Jan. 1942–Dec. 1943, UCDAD P67/522 (4).

200 Jim Larkin to Olive Sheehy Skeffington [*sic*], 6 July 1943, NLI, O. Sheehy Skeffington papers, unlisted. Emphasis added.

201 DD vol. 91, col. 2018, 11 Nov. 1943.

202 See Carney to O'Casey, London, 17 Feb. 1945. NLI, MS 37,989.

203 AC minutes, 3 Dec. 1943, UCDAD P56/299 (7).

204 Each ITGWU member of the PLP voted for the expulsion of Larkin, with the exception of Richard Corish. See William O'Brien diary, NLI, quoted in D. R. O'Connor Lysaght 'The second rise and fall of the Irish Labour Party: from separation to split, 1930–1944', unpublished manuscript.

205 AC minutes, 3 Dec. 1943. UCDAD P56/299 (7); Labour Party 'Statement', p. 3.

206 *The Times*, 14 Jan. 1944. Hickey resigned as chairman on the orders of his union bosses, rather than of his own volition.

207 O'Connor, *Larkin*, p. 110.

208 Louie Bennett to Tom Johnson, 5 Feb. 1944, NLI, Johnson papers, MS 17,267.

209 Pollitt to Bob Stewart, intercepted letter 5 Oct. 1943, TNA KV2/1180. My thanks to Eunan O'Halpin for bringing this letter to my attention.

210 Memorandum on Communist Party of Ireland 28 Jan. 1944, NAI DFA A 55.1.

211 Report of Lecture delivered 7 Nov. 1943, UCDAD P67/522 (5). MacEntee forwarded this report to de Valera as 'confirming everything I said during the election campaign in June last regarding the plan of the Communist element in this country to capture the Labour Party organisation'. MacEntee to de Valera, 10 Nov. 1943, UCDAD P67/537 (1). The contents of this report later appeared in the *Standard* on 10 Mar. 1944.

212 See Report of the committee of inquiry 20 Apr. 1944. TCDM, Marsh papers, 8311/36 and UCDAD P56/299. Colgan never took part in its proceedings, although the report acknowledged his help. He attended the party's conference in April but by the time of the general election that summer, he had defected to National Labour, for which he stood as a candidate. He was a Knight of Columbanus (see Evelyn Bolster, *Knights of St Columbanus* (Dublin, 1979), p. 168), and a long time anti-communist. 'I daresay Colgan sleeps in a Friar's habit, "We want no Reds here," spouting out of him at a Pioneer Temperance meeting; crushed between a crowd of clergymen', Seán O'Casey once remarked of him (O'Casey to Carney, 31 Dec. 1942 in Krause (ed.), *Letters of O'Casey*, II, p. 111.) He was, in O'Casey's opinion, 'a shit' (ibid., p. 175).

213 To be fair, muckraking suggests an element of journalistic investigation, whereas all O'Rahilly did was add his by-line to leaked security documents.

214 O'Rahilly to P. J. O'Brien, 14 Feb. 1944. NLI, O'Brien papers, MS 13,960.

215 See, P. Carroll to the Secretary, Department of Justice, 20 Apr. 1944. NAI Jus/8/322.

216 Report of the committee of inquiry, 20 Apr. 1944, TCDM, Marsh papers, 8311/36 and UCDAD P56/299.

217 Ibid.

218 MacEntee took great umbrage at the accusation that the information was derived from the work of agents provocateurs, and sought legal advice on the matter, but he was told in no uncertain terms to drop the idea. P67/537 (8).

219 Swift, *Swift*, p. 122.

220 See for example Uinseann MacEoin (ed.), *The IRA in the Twilight Years, 1923–1948* (Dublin, 1997), pp. 762, 822; D. Kelleher *Buried Alive in Ireland: A Story of a Twentieth Century Inquisition* (Wicklow, 2001), p. 97.

221 Confidential Special Branch report to the Deputy Commissioner, 19 Apr. 1944, NAI Jus/8/917.

222 Milotte, *Communism*, p. 198.

223 Ibid., p. 199; B. McKevitt, 'The split in the Irish Labour Party and the general election of 1944' (MA, UCD, 1984), p. 36.

224 Milotte, *Communism*, p. 199.

225 Minute book of the Inchicore branch of the Labour Party, 4 Oct. 1944, ILHM&A Deasy papers.

226 UCDAD P67/321, *Torch*, 29 Apr. 1942.

227 Ibid.

228 The last copy in John de Courcy Ireland's papers is that of March 1944 (UCDAD P29a/28).

229 *The Spark* was regarded as a communist publication in intelligence circles (see, for example, Communism in Ireland, 31 Dec. 1947, UCDAD P67.548 (i)). Named after Lenin's old paper *Iskra*, the first issue of the Gestetnered monthly, which appeared in December 1943 was filled with references to socialism and Russia, although subsequent issues were dominated by local agitprop. The last edition was published in November 1944.

230 His successor Richard Mulcahy, did not even have a seat in the Dáil, having been one of the 11 outgoing Fine Gael deputies to lose their seat at the previous election.

231 He told the Dáil the election was 'an outrage'. *Irish Press*, 10 May 1944.

232 McKevitt, 'The split in the Irish Labour Party', p. 50.

233 The London *Times* correspondent in Dublin was quite taken aback by just how prepared the government party was for this contest.

234 Fine Gael were the second largest party, 55 seats, 32 fewer than in 1943, and its lowest ever since the pact election of 1922. Figures from Sinnott, *Irish Voters Decide*, p. 300.

235 *Irish Press*, 18 May 1944.

236 Ibid. 17 May 1944.

237 *Irish People*, 3 June 1944.

238 McKevitt, 'Split in the Irish Labour Party', p. 61.

239 This was once again solo run by MacEntee, and contrary to the wishes of many within his party. The issue of Fianna Fáil's attitude towards Labour was dealt with by the party's publicity sub-committee in early 1944. Arising out of a discussion over whether Alderman Martin O'Sullivan was getting too much publicity in the *Irish Press*, one member of the sub-committee expressed the view that the party should 'try and win over that section of Labour which is slightly favourable to Fianna Fáil rather than antagonise them, as we were inclined to do at the general election'. Discussion was deferred until the next meeting, but there is no record of the issue being resumed. Minutes of Publicity sub-committee 24 Jan. 1944. UCDAD P176/384. This thinking is evident in Seán Lemass's campaign speeches, however, in which, rather than berate Labour, he tended to stress that 'FIANNA FÁIL IS *THE* WORKERS' PARTY' (*Irish Press*, 26 May 1944) or in Crumlin the next day, 'FIANNA FÁIL FOR THE WORKERS' (*Irish Press*, 27 May 1944).

240 McKevitt, 'Split in the Irish Labour Party', p. 48. When Young Jim Larkin referred to MacEntee's use of the red scare in his maiden speech the year before, he noted that it was a tactic which had been pioneered by Cumann na nGaedheal sometime earlier. DD vol. 91, icol. 169, 2 July 1943.

241 McKevitt, 'Split in the Irish Labour Party', p. 47.

242 Ibid.

243 Corish to Norton, 16 May 1944, ILHM&A POWU deposit. To rub salt into the wound, the second candidate had, according to Corish, previously been a member of another union, and had been fast tracked into the Transport Union to make him eligible for funding in the election.

244 *The Times*, 2 June 1944.

245 Clann na Talmhan held its share of the vote, but lost two seats nonetheless.

246 Michael Gallagher, *Irish Elections 1922–1944: Results and Analysis* (Dublin, 1993), p. 305.

FOUR: PICKING UP THE PIECES

1   It is unclear when her association with Labour began, but certainly when Labour's Committee on Financial Policy was formed at the end of 1943 she was one of the original members. Minutes Committee on Financial policy, 8 Oct. 1943. NLI, Johnson papers, MSS 17,267.

2   *Irish People*, 20 May 1944.

3   Minutes of the Drumcondra branch of the Labour Party, 22 June 1944, UCDAD P34/E/101.

4   Minutes of the Inchicore Branch of the Labour Party, 25 Mar. 1945, ILHM&A Deasy deposit 90/2/1.

5   Communist Group since 1945, 23 June 1947, NAI DFA A 55/1.

6   Communism in Ireland. Department of Justice typescript 31 Dec. 1947, UCDAD P67/548 (1); Communist Group since 1945, 13 June 1947, NAI DFA A55/1.

7   *Leader*, 26 May 1951.

8   Brian Inglis, *West Briton* (London, 1962), p. 108.

9   Ibid.

10   Minutes of the Inchicore Branch of the Labour Party, 23 Feb. 1947, ILHM&A Deasy deposit 90/2/1.

11   See for example NLI, *Irish People*, 31 Mar.; 14 Apr.; 28 Apr.; 5 May 1945.

12   Sheila Greene to Fred Cowan, 28 Nov. 1946, UCDAD P34/E/57. The *Irish People* clippings present in Seán MacEntee's papers is testament to this.

13   Sheila Greene to Seán O'Casey, 7 Oct. 1946, NLI, O'Casey papers, MS 38,005.

14   Seán O'Casey to Sheila Greene, 12 Oct. 1946, O'Casey papers. O'Casey had not lived in Ireland for decades, but he was very critical at what he saw as the ostentatious piety being practised there, allied to the prevalence of vehement anti-communism. 'I can quite see that Ireland is panicking with the dint of each trying to say more prayers than the other fellow; for it has to do now with getting on in the world of Gaels. I shouldn't be surprised if there were competitions soon of endurance and speed in the recital of rosary and litany. Catholic Stakhanovites. The Campaign of Emulation. 150 per cent over quota in prayer and penance.' O'Casey to Carney, 22 Feb. 1945. David Krause (ed.), *Letters of Seán O'Casey*, 4 vols (New York, 1980), II, p. 217.

15   F. Devine and J. Horne, 'A labour consciousness in Carlow: the young Paddy Bergin, 1916–1950', *Saothar* 6 (1980), p. 116.

16   Patrick Trench was terminally ill with TB. Matt Merrigan and Johnny Byrne along with about 20 others had launched a Revolutionary Socialist Party and had withdrawn from Labour (see Matt Merrigan, unpublished memoir, p. 35), while key Labour men who had been sympathetic towards the Trotskyists were no longer around, Michael Price having died and Owen Sheehy Skeffington having been expelled.

17   Draft letter to John [de Courcy Ireland] n.d., NLI, O. Sheehy Skeffington papers, Box 2.

18   Owen Sheehy Skeffington to John Ireland, 17 May 1947, NLI, O. Sheehy Skeffington papers. This is the sent version of the draft above.

19   See for example Michael McInerney, 'Jim Larkin: a tribute', *Irish Times*, 20 Feb. 1969.

20   See for example *Sunday Independent*, 19 Dec. 1943 quoted in *The Spark*, Jan. 1944; McInerney, 'Jim Larkin', *Irish Times*, 20 Feb. 1969; T. D. Williams, 'Jim Larkin TD', *Leader*, 27 Mar. 1954 quoted in D. Nevin (ed.), *Trade Union Century* (Cork, 1994), p. 380.

21   See for instance Jack Carney to Seán O'Casey, 15 Oct. 1946. NLI, O'Casey papers, MS 37,989.

22   *Review*, July 1945.

23 Jim Larkin junior to John de Courcy Ireland, n.d. [1946], UCDAD, P29a/365.

24 Manus O'Riordan, *The voice of a Thinking Intelligent Movement: James Larkin Jnr and the Ideological Modernisation of Irish Trade unionism*, Studies in Irish Labour History, 2 (Dublin, 2001), p. 10.

25 Information from Joe Deasy.

26 Jim Larkin junior to John de Courcy Ireland, n.d. [1946], UCDAD, P29a/365.

27 See, p. 198 below.

28 B. Desmond, *Finally and in Conclusion: A Political Memoir* (Dublin, 2000), p. 32.

29 'Communism in Ireland', emphasis added.

30 Noël Browne, *Against the Tide* (Dublin, 1986), p. 110.

31 http://www.bbc.co.uk/dna/ww2/A1143578.

32 See for instance Paul Bew and Henry Patterson, *Seán Lemass and the Making of Modern Ireland 1945–66* (Dublin, 1982), p. 31.

33 A. Marsh, 'Memoirs' [unpublished manuscript], TCDM MS 8340. The book was published under Marsh's name, but its preface described the contents as the 'work of a committee' which had been examining the question for the last two years. (See Arnold Marsh, *Full Employment in Ireland* (Dublin, 1945), p. vii.) It is likely that the study originated under the auspices of the Mount Street Club.

34 See D. O'Leary, *Vocationalism and Social Catholicism in Twentieth Century Ireland* (Dublin, 2000), p. 98, Duffy replaced Senator Thomas Foran on 17 April 1939.

35 John Swift described Larkin as having held the Commission in 'silent contempt' (John P. Swift, *John Swift: An Irish Dissident* (Dublin, 1991), p. 92), but it does seem as though he got some enjoyment from his membership, deciding at one point to gift its Chairman, the Most Reverend Michael Browne, Bishop of Galway, with whom he was 'very, very friendly', a complete set of Seán O'Casey plays, signed by the playwright. See Jack Carney to Seán O'Casey, 21 Feb. 1940, NLI, O'Casey papers, MS 37,989.

36 See J. H. Whyte, *Church and State in Modern Ireland* (Dublin, 1980), p. 101. For accounts of the Dignan scheme see also S. Riordan, '"A political blackthorn": Seán MacEntee, the Dignan plan and the principle of ministerial responsibility', *Irish Economic and Social History* (2000), pp. 44–62; O'Leary, *Vocationalism and Social Catholicism*; Tom Feeney, 'The road to serfdom: Seán MacEntee, "Beveridgism" and the development of Irish social policy', *History Review* XII (2001), pp. 63–72.

37 Whyte, *Church and State*, pp. 102–3.

38 DD vol. 95, col. 1489, 24 Jan. 1945.

39 Ibid.; Riordan, 'Political blackthorn', p. 53.

40 DD vol. 95, col. 1489, 24 Jan. 1945.

41 Riordan, 'Political blackthorn', p. 51.

42 Ibid., p. 56.

43 *Irish Times*, 26–28 Oct. 1944, quoted in Riordan, 'Political blackthorn', p. 49.

44 Quoted in R. McNamara, 'Blueprints from Britain: Irish responses to post-war plans' in D. Keogh and M. O'Driscoll (eds), *Ireland in World War Two: Diplomacy and Survival* (Cork, 2004), p. 247; Bew and Patterson, *Seán Lemass*, p. 30.

45 Feeney, 'Road to serfdom', p. 64.

46 This point was made by Dr Jim Ryan in 1950 when he claimed the reason the opposition parties 'went to the country advocating Dr Dignan's scheme' was because 'it was published by a Catholic bishop.' Quoted in Riordan, 'Political blackthorn', p. 61.

47 MacEntee quoted in Riordan, 'Political blackthorn', p. 61. As Riordan points out, the opportunistic nature of Labour's support for the issue is borne out by the fact that when Norton became minister for Social Welfare in the first inter-party government he dissolved the NHIS and absorbed its functions and assets into his Department, see below, p. 174. Ironically, it was Luke Duffy who had had refused to sign the Report on Vocational Organisation who moved a motion in support of the Dignan plan in the Senate. See SD vol. 30, col. 300, 18 July 1945.

48 J. J. Lee, *Ireland 1912–1985: Politics and Society* (Cambridge, 1989), p. 241.

49 Maurice Manning quoted in Michael Gallagher and Michael Marsh, *Days of Blue Loyalty: The Politics of Membership of the Fine Gael Party* (Dublin, 2002), p. 26.

50 The exception was the 1937 contest, when it held its 1933 figure. See Richard Sinnott, *Irish Voters Decide: Voting Behaviour in Elections and Referendums Since 1918* (Manchester, 1995), p. 300.

51 Gallagher and Marsh, *Days of Blue Loyalty*, p. 26; Whyte, *Church and State*, p. 113.

52 Maurice Manning, *Irish Political Parties: An Introduction* (Dublin, 1972), p. 101.

53 See Brian M. Walker (ed.), *Parliamentary Election results in Ireland, 1918–92* (Dublin, 1992), p. 167. Clann na Talmhan fared less well in the Wexford by-election held at this time but, considering the sympathy vote for Labour and the fact that the party had not contested elections in that constituency previously, it fared reasonably well.

54 Jack Carney to Seán O'Casey, 15 Oct. 1946, NLI, O'Casey papers, MS 37,989.

55 Carney to O'Casey, 15 Oct. 1946, NLI, O'Casey papers, MS 37,989.

56 Ibid.

57 This might explain why Lemass did not see fit to mention it to his visitor during their chat. The last such party, Córas na Poblachta had been founded during the Emergency (see above, p. 88). Its immediate precursors were Cumann Poblachta na hÉireann, founded in Mar. 1936, and Saor Éire in 1931. For more on the Clann's antecedents see Eithne MacDermott, *Clann na Poblachta* (Cork, 1998).

58 See MacDermott, *Clann na Poblachta*, p. 16; David McCullagh, *A Makeshift Majority: The First Inter-Party Government, 1948–51* (Dublin, 1998), p. 10.

59 Cowan was a political maverick whose authoritarianism made him unpopular with his colleagues. He was suspected by some of being a stooge for the communist element within Labour. After the 1944 general election he resigned from the party and in Sept. 1944 he formed a socialist republican organisation called Vanguard which was organised along democratic centralist lines. (See Manifesto of the Vanguard, signed on behalf of the committee by Peadar Cowan, 19 Aug. 1944 in UCDAD P29a/106.) Among those involved in this organisation were John de Courcy Ireland and R. N. Tweedy both of whom had been expelled from Labour earlier that year. Vanguard appears to have done little or nothing apart from publish a manifesto and hold a single public meeting in the Engineers' Hall on Dawson Street on 22 September 1944. Cowan subsequently returned to Labour, joining the Fairview branch in Oct. 1945 but resigned in July 1946 when he joined the Provisional Committee of Clann na Poblachta. (See 'Communism in Ireland').

60 Bennett to John de Courcy Ireland, 7 July 1946, UCDAD P29a/140 (i).

61 Greaves to John de Courcy Ireland, 17 July 1946, UCDAD P29/I/149.

62 *Review*, Aug. 1947.

63 Patrick Staunton in *Signpost*, 4 July 1943, UCDAD P29a/20–28.

64 Martin McGovern, 'The emergence and development of Clann na Poblachta, July 1946–Feb. 1948' (MA, UCD, 1979), p. 90. See also Winifred Trench in *Review*, July 1947.

65 Anthony Jordan, *Seán MacBride* (Dublin, 1993), p. 84.

66 *Irish People*, 28 Feb. 1948.

67 Carney to Seán O'Casey, 5 Feb. 1947. NLI, O'Casey papers, MS 37,989.

68 'Dev was really sorry to learn of Jim's death. So were Lemass, Boland and McIntee [*sic*]' Carney recalled. Carney to Seán O'Casey, 5 Feb. 1947, NLI, O'Casey papers, MS 37,989.

69 James Plunkett quoted in O'Riordan, 'Voice of a thinking intelligent movement', p. 9.

70 Charles McCarthy, *Trade Unions in Ireland, 1894–1960* (Dublin, 1977), p. 378.

71 See Ross M. Connolly, *The Labour Movement in Co. Wicklow* (Bray, 1992), p. 27.

72 *Irish Times*, 14 July 1947.

73 Ibid.

74 *Irish Independent*, 21 Oct. 1947.

75 Connolly, *Labour Movement in Co. Wicklow*, p. 29; Labour Party Speakers' Notes No. 3 'The so-called National Labour Party' n.d. [Jan. 1948], NLI, Johnson papers, MSS 17197.

76 *Review*, Aug. 1947.

77 *Irish People*, 1 Feb. 1947.

78 Or to quote Erskine Childers precisely, the supplementary budget's effect was 'too small in positive effect and too great in negative effect', Childers to MacEntee, n.d. [Feb. 1948], UCDAD P67/299 (1).

79 McCullagh, *A Makeshift Majority*, p. 8.

80 Ibid., p. 10; Breandán Ó hEithir, *The Begrudger's Guide to Irish Politics* (Dublin, 1986), p. 110.

81 Putting it mildly, one writer in *Review* noted 'it is certain there is a great deal more dissatisfaction with Fianna Fáil at the present time than was the case at the time of the last election'. *Review*, Aug. 1947.

82 Maurice Manning, *James Dillon: A Biography* (Dublin, 1999), p. 209.

83 *Irish Times*, 4–5 Apr. 1947.

84 Ibid.

85 *Irish Times*, 12 May 1947.

86 *Irish Times*, 31 May 1947.

87 See for instance *Review*, Aug. 1947.

88 *Irish People*, 8 Nov. 1947.

89 *Irish People*, 15 Nov. 1947. Bennett was a long-standing opponent of co-operation, having been the 'sole dissenter' on Labour's executive in 1927 when the question of coalescing with Fianna Fáil had been raised, see p. 24.

90 Matt Merrigan, unpublished memoir, p. 39.

91 *Irish People*, 13 Dec. 1947.

92 *Irish People*, 15 Nov. 1947.

93 McCullagh, *Makeshift Majority*, p. 17.

94 *Irish Times*, 15 Dec. 1947.

95 This was nine more seats than at the previous election.

96 *The Times*, 2 Feb. 1948.

97 See for instance the Fianna Fáil advertisement in the *Leader*, 31 Jan. 1948, which responded to complaints that the price of a bottle of stout had gone up by tuppence halfpenny by arguing that at least voters could 'eat and sleep in security for tomorrow – and the next day'.

98 Again, it ought to be stressed that MacEntee was on his own, or at least in a minority in this tactic. Lemass complained at the time that Fianna Fáil would be in with a chance of winning if only 'MacEntee would just shut up and the Chief would come out fighting'. Information from

Kevin O'Doherty. Arnold Marsh, who contested Dun Laoghaire–Rathdown for Labour recalled 'a pleasant feature of the contest was the respect shown to Labour by the other candidates. A Fianna Fáil deputy on the announcement of the result [Labour receiving less than five per cent of first preferences] declared that it was a disgrace to the constituency that I had received so little support'. A. Marsh, 'Memoirs', unpublished manuscript, TCDM, Arnold Marsh papers, 8340.

99 *Irish Times*, 20 Jan. 1948.

100 See Caitriona Lawlor (ed.), *Seán MacBride: That Day's Struggle. A Memoir 1904–1951* (Dublin 2005), p. 140; MacDermott, *Clann na Poblachta* pp. 62–3.

101 See for instance *Irish Times*, 23 Jan. 1948.

102 Lawlor (ed.), *Seán MacBride*, p. 142.

103 See MacDermott, *Clann na Poblachta*, p. 63. Figures taken from Sinnott, *Irish Voters Decide*, p. 299.

104 Duffy to Marsh, 10 Feb. 1948, TCDM, Marsh papers, 8310/2.

105 Manning, *Dillon*, p. 225.

106 Seán MacEoin, memorandum on the formation of the first inter-party government. UCDAD P151/919.

107 McCullagh, *Makeshift Majority*, p. 30. Seán MacEoin reported that while those with whom he spoke had a great deal of respect for Mulcahy, they could not leave themselves open to the inevitable propagandist use Fianna Fáil would make of this. (Memorandum, UCDAD P151/919). It seems unlikely, however, that those involved (not least Seán MacBride) would be so magnanimous.

108 See McCullagh, *Makeshift Majority*, p. 30.

109 Manning, *Dillon*, p. 226. He had, for instance acted as counsel for the NUR in its successful case against the constitutionality of the 1941 Trade Union act. McBride, *That Day's Struggle*, p. 203.

110 Brian Farrell, *Chairman or Chief? The Role of Taoiseach in Irish Government* (Dublin, 1971), p. 44.

111 Mulcahy to Costello, 29 Apr. 1969, UCDAD P190/973.

112 MacEoin, memorandum, UCDAD P151/919.

113 Manning, *Dillon*, p. 225.

114 *Irish Times*, 16 Feb. 1948.

115 *Irish People*, 14 Feb. 1948.

116 The CIU's affiliated unions had pledged to give their 'full support, moral and financial', to the National Labour Party nominees at a special conference held on 28 Nov. 1947. See McCarthy, *Trade Unions in Ireland*, p. 386.

117 Ibid.

118 MacEoin, memorandum, UCDAD P151/919.

119 Ibid.

120 Note from John A. Costello to Michael McInerney, 1967, UCDAD P190/973; See also Farrell, *Chairman or Chief*, p. 44.

121 MacDermott, *Clann na Poblachta*, p. 70.

122 See Farrell, *Lemass*, p. 79.

123 MacDermott, *Clann na Poblachta*, p. 70; McCullagh, *Makeshift Majority*, p. 36.

124 McCullagh, *Makeshift Majority*, p. 37.

FIVE: IN OFFICE OR POWER?

1 See D. Nevin (ed.), *James Larkin: Lion of the Fold* (Dublin, 1998) for one account. pp. 527–8.

2 Certainly a preliminary version of the Cabinet listing does not feature his name. See UCDAD P35/208.

3 Noël Browne, *Against the Tide* (Dublin, 1986), p. 107.

4 David McCullagh, *A Makeshift Majority: The First Inter-party Government, 1948–51* (Dublin, 1998), p. 35.

5 Interview with Donal Nevin, 10 July 2001.

6 *Irish People*, 28 Feb. 1948.

7 *Irish People*, 21 Feb.; 6, 13, 20 Mar. 1948; Minutes of National Executive, 27 Feb. 1948, NAI ITUC.

8 Martin McGovern, 'The emergence and development of Clann na Poblachta, July 1946–February 1948' (MA, UCD, 1979), p. 102; Eithne MacDermott, *Clann na Poblachta* (Cork, 1998), p. 82.

9 *Worldover Press*, 12 Mar. 1948, TCDM, Marsh papers,.

10 Profile of McGilligan in the *Leader*, 28 Feb. 1953, quoted in Fanning, *Finance*, p. 458. National Labour had been adamant that McGilligan be Minister for Finance (MacEoin, memorandum. UCDAD P151/919), while Labour's Bill Davin and William Norton and Seán MacBride had also proposed his appointment. McCullagh, *Makeshift Majority*, p. 35.

11 *Worldover Press*, 12 Mar. 1948, TCDM, Marsh papers.

12 Labour Party Annual Report, 1950–52, p. 12.

13 DD vol. 110, col. 67, 18 Feb. 1948.

14 *Irish People*, 6 Mar. 1948. See also Inchicore minute book, 14 Apr. 1948, ILHM&A Deasy deposit.

15 Untitled document, 13 Apr. 1948, NLI, Corish papers.

16 Brian Inglis, *Downstart* (London, 1990), p. 166.

17 This was the subject of resolutions at Labour's annual conference in Sept. 1948. One, from the Baldoyle and Sutton Branch complained that the party's 'propaganda is totally inadequate to present the Labour point of view and to combat anti-Labour propaganda'. Agenda Annual Conference 1948, ILHM&A IWWU deposit, box 25.

18 For the inter-party government and its lack of collective responsibility see McCullagh, *Makeshift Majority*, p. 51; Basil Chubb, *The Government and Politics of Ireland* (Oxford, 1970), pp. 181–3; Brian Farrell, *Chairman or Chief? The Role of Taoiseach in Irish Government* (Dublin, 1971), pp. 45–6.

19 Chubb, *Government and Politics* pp. 184–5.

20 Maurice Manning, *James Dillon: A Biography* (Dublin, 1999), p. 228.

21 *Leader*, 24 Apr. 1954.

22 McCullagh, *Makeshift Majority*, p. 47.

23 Browne, *Against the Tide*, p. 190.

24 See McCullagh, *Makeshift Majority*, pp. 43–50.

25 Caitriona Lawlor (ed.), *Seán MacBride: That Day's Struggle: A Memoir 1904–1951*, (Dublin 2005), p. 156.

26 Ibid., p. 174.

27 See F. Devine, 'Letting Labour lead: Jack Macgougan and the pursuit of unity, 1913–1958', *Saothar* 14 (1989), p. 115.

28 Michael Gallagher, *The Labour Party in Transition* (Dublin, 1982), p. 132.

29 Devine, 'Letting Labour lead', p. 116.

30 State of the Labour Movement in Northern Ireland, June 1949, LHASC,M GS/NI/48ii.

31 Duffy to secretary NILP, 18 Dec. 1948, LHASC,M GS/NI/Gii.

32 State of the Labour Movement in Northern Ireland.

33 Philips to Duffy, 27 Feb. 1949, LHASC,M GS/NI/11.

34 C. Norton, 'The Irish Labour Party in Northern Ireland, 1949–1958', *Saothar* 21 (1995), p. 50.

35 The two parties had little to say to each other after their early efforts to end the economic war in 1932. See above chapter 2.

36 *The Times*, 8 Apr. 1947.

37 See Report of Alderman E. G. Gooch to the Irish Labour Party Conference, 12–14 Sept. 1947, LHASC,M Denis Healey papers, LP/ID Box 8.

38 *The Times*, 29 Jan. 1948.

39 See B. Purdie, 'The Friends of Ireland, British Labour and Irish Nationalism, 1945–49' in T. Gallagher and J. O'Connell (eds), *Contemporary Irish Studies* (Manchester, 1983), pp. 81–94.

40 Luke Duffy to Morgan Phillips, 30 Nov. 1948, LHASC,M GS/NI/5i.

41 Purdie, 'Friends of Ireland', p. 84. It is worth noting, nevertheless, that half of Labour's MPs tried to prevent its second reading, of whom 66 later defied the whips to vote against it.

42 Devine, 'Letting Labour lead', p. 119.

43 Ibid.; *The Times*, 11 June 1949.

44 See McCullagh, *Makeshift Majority*, p. 70; John Horgan, *Seán Lemass: The Enigmatic Patriot* (Dublin, 1997), p. 139.

45 Mel Cousins, *The Birth of Social Welfare in Ireland, 1922–52* (Dublin, 2003), p. 153.

46 See J. H. Whyte, *Church and State in Modern Ireland* (Dublin, 1980), pp. 179–83.

47 McCullagh, *Makeshift Majority*, p. 182; see also Cousins, *Social Welfare*, p. 153.

48 McCullagh, *Makeshift Majority*, p. 186; Cousins, *Social Welfare* pp. 154–5.

49 McCullagh, *Makeshift Majority*, p. 187.

50 Minute of Meeting of the Cabinet committee, 30 Aug. 1949. UCDAD P190/554 (10).

51 Confidential notes on a social security scheme, unsigned and undated, forwarded to John A. Costello by Paddy Lynch at the request of the Private Secretary to the Minister of Finance on 1 Oct. 1949, UCDAD P190/554 (12). Emphasis added by Costello.

52 See Cousins, *Social Welfare*, p. 156; McCullagh, *Makeshift Majority*, p. 188.

53 Browne, *Against the Tide*, p. 191. It is a view with which McCullagh concurs, p. 187.

54 See, for example, White Paper on social security memorandum for the government, 8 June 1949, UCDAD P190/554 (6).

55 McCullagh, *Makeshift Majority*, p. 193.

56 Quoted in *Leader*, 31 Jan. 1953.

57 M. Davidson to members of PLP, 13 Apr. 1950. NLI, Corish papers. This is by no means an isolated case. The problem of Labour deputies absenting themselves from debates and votes is one that comes up on a regular basis at party meetings over the years.

58 Minute book, Labour Party Inchicore branch, 30 Sept. 1948, ILHM&A Deasy papers.

59 Circular from J. T. O'Farrell, Secretary of Freeman Publications, 29 Oct. 1949, ILHM&A POWU deposit.

60 George Garret, 'Communist activity in Ireland'; 'Infiltration in the Press'; 'Activities of Brian O'Neill'; 'Proposed Labor Party weekly', 10 June 1949, NAM.

61 *The Citizen* 16 Dec. 1949. The communist *Irish Workers' Voice* (Feb. 1950) was scathing of its 'glowing eulogy of pro-Blueshirt Costello' and described the paper as a 'hybrid monster' of a 'Labour mouthpiece of a capitalist government'.

62 Ibid., 23 Dec. 1949; 30 Dec. 1949.

63 Ibid.

64 Brian Inglis, *Downstart* (London, 1990), p. 172.

65 Brian Inglis, *West Briton* (London, 1962), p. 134; Report to AC, 28 July 1948, NLI, Corish papers.

66 An addendum tabled at the 1948 conference by the Madame Markievitz branch argued that the party was 'already losing its identity as a progressive party by its acceptance of Fine Gael's reactionary policies'. Agenda 1948 conference, ILHM&A IWWU Box 25.

67 Liam MacAodha to J. Larkin, 18 Apr. 1950, ILHM&A JLJ/3.

68 See *Labour Newsletter*, no. 10, Mar. 1949 for Luke Duffy's appraisal of the first year in government.

69 Inglis, *West Briton*, p. 135.

70 *Hibernia*, Feb. 1952.

71 Communist Group since 1945, 23 June 1947, NAI DFA A 55/1.

72 Muldowney to Corish, 29 May 1949, NLI, Corish papers, unlisted. Emphasis in the original.

73 James O'Keefe to Luke Duffy 15 Oct. 1948, NLI, Corish papers, unlisted.

74 See Frank Coppa, 'Pope Pius XII and the Cold War' in Dianne Kirby (ed.), *Religion and the Cold War* (Basingstoke, 2003), pp. 61–2.

75 One person told me of the enormous peer pressure to contribute to this collection, recalling 'if you didn't give them money they looked at you as though you had horns'.

76 Ireland was not alone in its protests. There was also significant opposition in the USA, Britain, Canada and Latin America. See Peter C. Kent, 'The lonely Cold War of Pope Pius XII' in Kirby (ed.), *Religion and the Cold War*, p. 70.

77 Mike Milotte, *Communism in Modern Ireland: The Pursuit of the Workers' Republic since 1916.* (Dublin, 1984), p. 218. It is worth noting that there was a very strong trade union contingent in this march.

78 Four years later, the Dublin activist and one time *Irish People*, editor, Patricia [Peggy] Rushton, singled this out as one reason why she would be unwilling to sit on the Corporation: 'There are some compromises I just couldn't make . . . (I mean the sort of resolutions Dublin Corporation passes from time to time and things like Jack Breen having to speak as Lord Mayor at the Mindzenty meeting etc.)' Peggy R. to John de Courcy Ireland, 14 May 1953, UCDAD P29/I/156.

79 Private source.

80 Quoted in John Cooney, *John Charles McQuaid: Ruler of Catholic Ireland* (Dublin, 1999), p. 227.

81 See for instance Rugby to Machtig, 17 Aug. 1948, TNA DO 130/90.

82 Cooney, *McQuaid*, p. 224.

83 Evelyn Bolster, *The Knights of the Order of St Columbanus* (Dublin, 1979), p. 105.

84 Ibid.

85 Milotte, *Communism*, p. 217.

86   *Cavalcade*, 25 June 1949. NLI, O. Sheehy Skeffington papers, 82, MS 40,550/11.

87   *Sunday Independent* 15 May 1949. The *Sunday Independent* piece was published after one of that newspaper's reporters chanced upon a meeting of the newly formed Irish Workers' League at which the first edition of its paper *The Irish Workers' Voice* was on sale.

88   See Circular from the Irish Association of Civil Liberty, 23 Feb. 1948, UCDAD LA 10/Q/3(2).

89   See Hickey and O'Reilly solicitors to the publishers of *Cavalcade* 17 Aug. 1949. NLI, O. Sheehy Skeffington papers, 82, MS 40,550/11; Oswald, Hickson and Collier to Hickey and O'Reilly 16 Sept. 1949 and Christo Gore Grimes to Owen Sheehy Skeffington, 20 July 1949, NLI, O. Sheehy Skeffington papers, 82, MS 40,505/4; H. Tweedy, *A Link in the Chain: The Story of the Irish Housewives Association 1942–92* (Dublin, 1992), p. 70.

90   Interview with Joe Deasy.

91   Garret FitzGerald, *All in a Life* (Dublin, 1991), p. 48.

92   *Irish Times*, 7 June 1950.

93   Charles McCarthy, *Trade Unions in Ireland, 1894–1960* (Dublin, 1977), p. 401.

94   Fianna Fáil Parliamentary Party minutes, 7 June 1950, UCDAD P176/384.

95   UCDAD P190/161 561 (11).

96   *Irish Press*, 6 Jan. 1951.

97   *Irish Times*, 20 Dec. 1950.

98   McCullagh, *Makeshift Majority*, p. 68.

99   J. J. Lee *Ireland 1912–1985: Politics and Society* (Cambridge, 1989), p. 313.

100   Gerard Fee, 'The effects of WWII on Dublin's low income families, 1939–1945' (PhD, UCD 1996), pp. 165–70.

101   Whyte, *Church and State* pp. 130–1.

102   Ibid., p. 132.

103   Ibid., p. 135.

104   Ibid., , p. 141.

105   Ibid., p. 143.

106   Ibid., p. 200. Dillon withdrew his action soon after entering government.

107   Browne wrote a harrowing account of the loss of his parents and siblings to TB in his 1986 autobiography *Against the Tide*. A more dispassionate and accurate account of Browne's early years can be found in John Horgan's biography *Noël Browne: Passionate Outsider* (Dublin, 2000).

108   Ruth Barrington, *Health, Medicine and Politics* (Dublin, 1987), pp. 201–2.

109   Browne, *Against the Tide*, p. 153.

110   Horgan, *Browne*, p. 105.

111   Ibid., p. 108. It was not formally raised at cabinet until April the following year.

112   Cooney, *McQuaid*, p. 260.

113   Whyte, *Church and State*, p. 206.

114   Cooney, *McQuaid*, pp. 260–1; Whyte, *Church and State*, p. 208.

115   Whyte, *Church and State*, p. 208.

116   Horgan, *Browne*, p. 111.

117   See, p. 144 above.

118   Cooney, *McQuaid*, p. 259.

119   Ibid., p. 263.

120   Horgan, *Browne*, p. 130.

121 Browne, *Against the Tide*, p. 190.

122 Whyte, *Church and State*, p. 219.

123 Cooney, *McQuaid*, pp. 265–6.

124 Report to Standing Committee of Hierarchy (Handwritten note by McQuaid), 3 Apr. 1951 (emphasis in the original), DDA, McQuaid papers, Govt box 5.

125 Notes of events since the hierarchy's meeting on 4 Apr., DDA, McQuaid papers, Govt box 5 B8/B.

126 Ibid.

127 Browne, *Against the Tide*, p. 176.

128 Secretary to the Government to the Private Secretary, Minister for Health, 7 Apr. 1951, UCDAD P190/557 (9).

129 Skeffington, *Skeff*, p. 147.

130 McCullagh, *Makeshift Majority*, p. 226.

131 *Leader*, 14 Apr. 1951.

132 Browne, *Against the Tide*, p. 175.

133 McQuaid to D'Alton, 11 Apr. 1951, DDA McQuaid papers, Govt box 5.

134 Tom Garvin, 'A quiet revolution: the remaking of Irish political culture' in Ray Ryan (ed.), *Writing in the Irish Republic: Literature, Culture, Politics 1949–1999* (London, 2000), p. 193. Apart from anecdotal evidence, this is backed up by the electoral successes of candidates at the subsequent general election who took a Browneite position either during the crisis or during the contest.

135 *Leader*, 14 Apr. 1951.

136 McCullagh, *Makeshift Majority*, p. 232.

137 *Leader*, 25 Oct. 1952.

138 Manning, *Dillon*, p. 275.

139 See Mary E. Daly, *The Buffer State: The Historical Roots of the Department of the Environment* (Dublin, 1997), pp. 329, 378, 403.

140 Describing itself as 'a journal of Labour opinion' *Impact* was intended to be Irish Labour's answer to the *New Statesman*. It was published by such prominent left-wing Labour figures as Christy Ferguson, Ruaidhrí Roberts, Patricia Rushton and Donal Nevin. Memo from Advisory Committee of Freeman Publications [n.d., 1949]. Unfortunately, it met a very cold response from the few who shared its ideological viewpoint. Regarded as a rather amateur – and even boring – publication, it folded after five issues.

141 *Impact*, May 1951.

142 *Irish Press*, 18 Sept. 1948.

143 Brian Inglis, 'Why did you vote?', *The Bell*, July 1951.

144 NLI, Corish papers, Labour Party speakers' notes, 'Inter-Party government' (May 1951).

145 *Irish Times*, 30 May 1951.

146 *The Times*, 31 May 1951.

147 *Leader*, 1 June 1951.

148 Ibid.

149 Figures taken from Richard Sinnott, *Irish Voters Decide: Voting Behaviour in Elections and Referendums since 1918* (Manchester, 1995), pp. 301, 303.

150 J. J. O'Farrell to Larkin 2 June 1951 (ILHM&A WUI/3 JLJ/7/3). Connolly was a hard-working party activist but he was based in Bray and had been unpopular with his constituency

colleagues in Louth who felt he was not pulling his weight on local matters. See minute of full Administrative Council meeting, 30 Mar. 1950, NLI, Corish papers.

151 J. J. O'Farrell to Larkin 2 June 1951, ILHM&A WUI/3 JLJ/7/3.

152 *Irish Times*, 2 June 1951.

153 *Sunday Press*, 5 July 1953.

154 McCullagh, *Makeshift Majority*, p. 249; Manning, *Dillon*, p. 278.

155 *The Times*, 14 June 1951.

156 Labour Party Annual Report, 1950–2, pp. 12–13.

157 McCullagh, *Makeshift Majority*, p. 250; Manning, *Dillon*, p. 278.

158 Browne, *Against the Tide*, p. 210; Horgan, *Browne*, p. 163.

159 Horgan, *Browne*, p. 163.

160 Manning, *Dillon*, p. 279.

161 DD vol. 126, cols 21–2, 13 June 1951.

162 DD vol. 126, col. 30, 13 June 1951

163 DD vol. 126, col. 35, 13 June 1951.

164 *Cork Examiner*, 8 Jan. 1937.

165 DD vol. 126, col. 35, 13 June 1951. Keane's remarks met with adverse comment in *Impact*, June 1951.

SIX: RETURN TO THE SIDELINES

1 Labour Party Annual Report, 1950–2, p. 23.

2 *Impact*, June 1951.

3 Labour Party Annual Report, 1950–2, p. 45.

4 M. Davidson to all branch secretaries, 25 July 1951, ILHM&A JLJ/7/3.

5 J. Prendergast to J. Larkin 2 Oct. 1955, ILHM&A JLJ/3.

6 Notes of AC sub-committee on Dublin organisation, 10 Dec. 1952, ILHM&A Deasy deposit, 90/2/19(1).

7 *Leader*, 26 Jan. 1952.

8 Johnson to J. de Courcy Ireland, 10 Nov. 1951, UCDAD P29a/151(7).

9 Johnson to J. de Courcy Ireland 20 Dec. 1951 [emphasis in the original], UCDAD P29a/151(9).

10 P. Rushton to J. de Courcy Ireland, UCDAD P29/I/ 156b [n.d?].

11 John Horgan, *Noël Browne: Passionate Outsider* (Dublin, 2000), p. 152; Donal Nevin (ed.), *James Larkin: Lion of the Fold* (Dublin, 1998), p. 348. Both wrote for the short-lived journal *Impact*.

12 See *Irish Times*, 7 Mar. 1952, 15 Mar. 1952, 21 Mar. 1952.

13 *Irish Times*, 21 Apr. 1952.

14 Ibid.; *Irish Press*, 21 Apr. 1952.

15 *Irish Times*, 21 Apr. 1952.

16 *Leader*, 26 Apr. 1952.

17 *Irish Times*, 24 Apr. 1952.

18 Ibid., 21 Apr. 1952.

19 *Irish Times*, 24 Apr. 1952.

20 Rosemary Cullen Owens, *Louie Bennett* (Cork, 2001), p. 114.

21 *Leader*, 26 Apr. 1952.

22 Report of the AC Subcommittee on Party Organisation in Dublin City, 10 Dec. 1952. ILHM&A Deasy papers, 90/2/19.

23 *Irish Times*, 7 Apr. 1952.

24 See Hilda Tweedy, *A Link in the Chain: The Story of the Irish Housewives Association, 1942–1992* (Dublin, 1992), p. 70. *Roscommon Herald*, 12 Apr. 1952.

25 See for example DD vol. 130, col. 1731, 8 Apr. 1952

26 Taking the most recent available figures for branch affiliations (December 1948), Mayo is one of only three constituencies in which there is no Labour organisation. See NLI, Corish papers.

27 *Irish Times*, 9 June 1952.

28 *Leader*, 10 May 1952.

29 J. Larkin to J. Carney, 1 May 1952 in relation to the East Limerick by-election. It should be noted, however, that it was expected that an opposition candidate would beat the Fianna Fáil candidate in the poll. ILHM&A JLJ/3.

39 *Irish Times*, 29 Apr. 1953.

31 J. L. B. Deane, County Cork, to the editor, *Irish Times*, 23 May 1953.

32 Although ostensibly not affiliated or allied with any political party, most of its activists were members of the Irish Workers League, which, with a membership amounting to 79, needed all the help it could get by this time. See IWL conference 1954 – EC report. CPGB papers LHASCM. This was a net loss of 24 members (over one fifth) since the same time the previous year.

33 Patricia Rushton to J de Courcy Ireland, n.d., UCDAD P29/I/156 (6).

34 *Irish Times*, 22 June 1953.

35 Ibid., 27 June 1953.

36 For instance, Patricia Rushton's request to John de Courcy Ireland that he draw up a document which would 'summarise the objects and underlying ideas of the party, without using words which will scare the 'rightists' – to express socialist ideas without using the word socialism'. 'Peggy R.' to J. de Courcy Ireland, 14 May 1953, UCDAD P29/I/156. See also Paddy Bergin quoted on p. 113 above.

37 See Tweedy, *A Link in the Chain*; Interview with Joe Deasy 2001; Mike Milotte, *Communism in Modern Ireland: The Pursuit of the Workers' Republic since 1916* (Dublin, 1984), p. 219. See pp. 147–9 above for one contemporary attack on the IHA.

38 Séamus Cody, John O'Dowd and Peter Rigney, *The Parliament of Labour: 100 Years of the Dublin Council of Trade Unions* (Dublin, 1986), p. 201.

39 'Peggy R.' to J. de Courcy Ireland, 14 May 1953, UCDAD P29/I/156.

40 For example 'Aknefton' in the *Irish Times*, 19 Apr. 1952.

41 One wag described Browne as having the same unsettling effect on Norton as Banquo's ghost had on Macbeth and wondered whether Norton murmured to himself, 'thou canst not say I did it; never shake thy gory locks at me', when he recalled the fate of Dr Browne. This would suggest that Browne had an unsettling affect on the Labour leader's conscience, which was not the case; in contrast to Macbeth's response to Banquo's ghost, Norton's attitude towards Browne was more one of irritation than dread.

42 Michael McInerney, 'Noel Browne: Church and state', *University Review* 5 (1968), p. 205; Noël Browne, *Against the Tide* (Dublin, 1986), p. 221.

43 For an account of this see Horgan, *Browne*, p. 172.

44 The *Irish Workers' Voice* put the move down to the coalitionist tendencies within the Labour leadership and described it as a 'backward step' for progressive politics in Ireland: 'Why Dr Browne did not join the Labour Party, in our opinion, calls less for an answer from Dr Browne than it does from the Labour Party leaders. Had Labour Party spokesmen been less concerned to keep up their alliances with Fine Gael they would have helped to attract to the Party the progressive elements among the Independents. There is something wrong with a Labour Party which could so easily absorb a Dr Brennan supporter of Franco fascism and opponent of Free State medical services, and yet treat Dr Browne as if he were the greatest enemy of all time.' *IWV*, Nov.–Dec. 1953.

45 Statement adopted by Aggregate Meeting of Members of the Labour Party in Dublin, held on 17 Nov. 1953, ILHM&A WUI/3 JLJ/7/3 LP 1951–54. See also *Irish Times*, 19 Nov. 1953. This call to the hurlers on the ditch, who refused to join Labour because of its conservatism, to come in and try to change the policies they did not like was to become a frequent refrain from Donal Nevin later during the decade.

46 See also the *Irish Democrat*, Dec. 1953.

47 *Irish Times*, 13 Mar. 1954.

48 *Irish Press*, 24 Apr. 1954.

49 For example see E. A. Breen MCC in *Irish Press*, 8 Apr. 1954, J. P. Brennan, *Irish Press*, 19 Apr. 1954. A meeting of the Dun Laoghaire branch (a long-time left-wing domain) stated that 'under no circumstances could the basic principles of Labour be compromised by union with any other party'. *Irish Press*, 16 Mar. 1954.

50 *Irish Times*, 18 May 1954.

51 *Irish Press*, 14 Apr. 1954.

52 *Irish Times*, 11 May 1954.

53 Ibid. 20 Mar. 1954, *Leader* 13 Mar. 1954. Tom Johnson was also concerned by the trend of seeing Fine Gael and not Fianna Fáil as the party's natural ally. Johnson to J. de Courcy Ireland, UCDAD P29/I/151, quoted in J. Anthony Gaughan, *Thomas Johnson* (Dublin, 1980), p. 39.

54 *Irish Times*, 6 Apr. 1954.

55 *Leader*, 22 May 1954.

56 Letter from Mary Davidson, 13 May 1954, ILHM&A JLJ/3.

57 *Irish Times*, 15 May 1954.

58 Letter from Jim Larkin to Mary Davidson, 5 May 1954, ILHM&A JLJ/3.

59 *Irish Press*, 14 Apr. 1954.

60 *The Times*, 11 May 1954.

61 Ibid., 18 May 1954.

62 Ibid.

63 Larkin to P Crowley 21 May 1954; see also Larkin to Tom Kyne, 21 May 1954, ILHM&A JLJ/3.

64 *Leader*, 5 June 1954.

65 Labour Party Annual Report, 1953–4, p. 14.

66 *Irish Press*, 26 May 1954.

67 For instance, the Programme for Government drawn up by the Progressive Democrats and Fianna Fáil in 2002 zmounts to 37 pages.

68 Memorandum, n.d., on the principal objects of the government's policy, UCDAD P190/551 (1).

69 Memorandum . . . UCDAD P190/551 (2).

70 Labour Party Annual Report, 1953–4. According to the *Irish Press* the attendance figure was 750.

71 Interview with Donal Nevin, 28 Apr. 2000.

72 *Irish Press*, 31 May 1954. The suspension was claimed to have been because of the 'branch's attitude on policy matters during the general election campaign' (a reference to a disagreement over health policy) but the timing of the suspension, merely hours before the special conference led many to take a different view. The National Organiser Paddy Bergin later told one of those involved that the branch had been suspended because it was 'acting against the interests of the party, as directed by the National Executive'. *Evening Mail*, 8 Mar. 1957. Although the subject was brought up and investigated at subsequent conferences, the impromptu suspension of the Dun Laoghaire branch was never fully explained, and became the source of bitterness for years to come.

73 See Paddy Bergin to John de Courcy Ireland, 15 Sept. 1953, UCDAD P29a/5.

74 Interview with Donal Nevin, 28 Apr. 2000.

75 *Irish Press*, 1 June 1954.

SEVEN: NEVER HAD IT SO BAD

1 Basil Chubb, *The Government and Politics of Ireland* (Oxford, 1970), p. 169.

2 *Leader*, 5 June 1954.

3 Mina Carney to Seán O'Casey, 10 Apr. 1955, NLI, O'Casey papers, MS 37,989; See also Paddy Bergin, Profile of Young Jim Larkin, unpublished manuscript.

4 B. Farrell, *Chairman or Chief? The Role of Taoiseach in Irish Government* (Dublin, 1971), p. 53.

5 *Nusight*, Apr. 1970.

6 *Hibernia*, June 1969.

7 Brian Maye, *Fine Gael 1923–87.* (Dublin, 1993), p. 317. See also Maurice Manning, *James Dillon: A Biography* (Dublin, 1999), p. 293.

8 *Irish Times*, 5 June 1954; *Leader*, 5 June 1954.

9 UCDAD P190/551 (2).

10 T. F. O'Higgins, *A Double Life* (Dublin, 1996), p. 163; Ruth Barrington, *Health, Medicine and Politics* (Dublin, 1987), p. 245.

11 O'Higgins, *A Double Life*, p. 164.

12 DD vol. 146, col. 1373, 7 July 1954.

13 *Labour*, Oct. 1954.

14 *The Leader*, 3 July 1954.

15 Ibid., 28 Aug. 1954.

16 *Flagstaff*, July 1954.

17 *Leader*, 9 Oct. 1954.

18 *Fine Gael Bulletin*, 20 Oct. 1954 (UCDAD P35c/196).

19 *Labour*, Dec. 1954.

20 See for example DD vol. 148, col. 605, 17 Feb. 1955. Larkin was joined on this topic by Waterford deputy Tom Kyne see DD vol. 148, col. 717, 23 Feb. 1955.

21 *Irish Independent*, 2 May 1955; *Irish Times*, 2 May 1955.

22 Nor, Patrick Lindsay suggested, was it merely their public utterances. (See introduction.)

23 *Leader*, 14 May 1955.

24 *The Times*, 15 Jan. 1955.

25 NAI D/T CAB2/16, 11 Jan. 1955.

26 The Majority report of the Commission was dated 11 Mar. 1954, with two minority reports to follow. See NAI CAB2/16, 2 July 1954.

27 Diarmaid Ferriter, *The Transformation of Ireland 1900–2000* (London, 2004), p. 473.

28 Enda Delaney, *Demography, State and Society: Irish Migration to Britain, 1921–1971* (Liverpool, 2000), p. 201.

29 Enda Delaney, 'Emigration, political cultures and the evolution of post-war Irish society' in Brian Girvin and Gary Murphy (eds), *The Lemass Era: Politics and Society in the Ireland of Seán Lemass* (Dublin, 2005), p. 54.

30 See DD vol. 158, col. 805, 21 June 1956.

31 ITGWU annual conference; *Liberty*, Oct. 1955.

32 See for example Brian Girvin, 'Trade unions and economic development' in Donal Nevin (ed.), *Trade Union Century* (Cork, 1994), p. 125.

33 Letter from Industry and Commerce to the ITUC National Executive, reproduced in ITUC Annual Report, 1955–6, pp. 52–3.

34 *Times Pictorial*, 1 Oct. 1955.

35 He foresaw the kind of attack that his words could provoke, writing 'such a philosophy can be readily damned, and, no doubt, the attempt will be made, by tagging on to it a label or "ism" to frighten the unthinking or the prejudiced'.

36 *Pictorial*, 22 Oct. 1955. The paper described Nevin as being from the ITUC, but did not mention his role as Chairman of the Dublin Regional Council of the Labour Party.

37 *Pictorial*, 29 Oct. 1955.

38 Micheál Ó Maoláin to Jim Larkin, 25 Oct. 1955, ILHM&A JLJ/3. Emphasis in the original.

39 Jim Predergast to Jim Larkin, 2 Oct. 1955, ILHM&A JLJ/3.

40 Jim Larkin to Micheál O Maoláin, 2 Nov. 1955, ILHM&A JLJ/3.

41 See Niamh Puirséil, 'Political competition and party competition in post war Ireland' in Girvin and Murphy (eds), *The Lemass Era*, p. 21.

42 John Horgan, *Seán Lemass: The Enigmatic Patriot* (Dublin 1997), p. 165. See also John F. McCarthy, 'Ireland's turnaround: Whitaker and the 1958 plan for economic development' in McCarthy (ed.), *Planning Ireland's Future: The Legacy of T.K. Whitaker* (Dublin, 1990).

43 *Irish Times*, 14 Nov. 1955.

44 Garret FitzGerald, *Planning in Ireland* (Dublin, 1968), p. 14.

45 See for example Brendan M. Walsh, 'Economic growth and development, 1945–70' in J. J. Lee (ed.), *Ireland 1945–70* (Dublin, 1980), p. 30.

46 Statement from the PUTUO 7 Feb. 1956, reprinted in *Trade Union Information*, May 1956.

47 *Labour*, Jan. 1956. Larkin repeated these sentiments to a meeting of the Dublin Regional Council on 10 Feb. (Quoted in DD vol. 157, col. 564, 16 May 1956).

48 *Irish Times*, 18 Feb. 1956. While undoubtedly an accurate representation of Labour's situation it could equally be applied to any political party in Ireland.

49 Kieran Kennedy and Brendan Dowling, *Economic Growth in Ireland: The Experience since 1947* (Dublin, 1975), p. 220.

50 Ibid. The motion was tabled by the Crumlin and District Branch.

51 Final agenda of the annual conference held in Royal Hotel Athlone, 27–29 April 1956. The motion was withdrawn but a more anodyne motion from the Cabra branch which called on the

'Parliamentary Labour Group to take the necessary steps to ensure that the 12-point programme is put into operation forthwith' was passed.

52   This was because, following the fifth round of pay increases earlier in the year, many workers had found themselves and their families ineligible for benefits, having surpassed the minimum rate to qualify. Other more far-reaching motions relating to the health services which were on the agenda were either withdrawn or not moved, including an amendment from the Dun Laoghaire branch calling on the Party to 'prepare Health legislation on the lines of the British Health Scheme'.

53   *Irish Press*, 30 Apr. 1956.

54   *Irish Times*, 28 Apr. 1956. The taoiseach's wife, Ida Costello, died during the campaign and Fine Gael suspended its campaign as a mark of respect. However, it is unlikely that this unhappy event contributed to any great extent on the general quality of the campaign.

55   *Irish Times*, 2 May 1956 The selection of Michael Davin had not proved to be very popular with the local Labour Party, which may have contributed to the lack of a Labour campaign there.

56   In the end, Norton had to lead a one-man campaign on behalf of Labour for the Independent. The *Irish Workers' Voice* mused afterwards that 'despite Mr Norton's efforts it is doubtful if many of Labour's 5,000 voters went to the polls in Dublin North East.' *Irish Workers' Voice*, May 1956.

57   *Irish Times*, 2 May 1956.

58   Fianna Fáil described it as his third, counting his imposition of import levies in mid-March as his second.

59   *Irish Times*, 12 May 1956.

60   *Irish Times*, 1 May 1956.

61   The one encouraging sign to come from the direction of the unions was the motion put down at the ITGWU congress in June by the Thomastown branch, that the union should affiliate to the Labour Party. This positive development was negated by an amendment put down by the Cork Number 2 branch, which suggested that the question of affiliation should be dealt with at a special conference 'after the Labour Party ceases to be a unit of the inter-Party Government'. *Irish Times*, 2 June 1956.

62   *Irish Times*, 2 June 1956. The Central Statistics Office had stopped publishing annual statistics for emigration in 1951 having decided that the method they were using to derive the figure was unreliable. See Delaney, *Demography, State and Society*, p. 196.

63   NAI CAB 2/17, 6 July 1956.

64   John O'Connell, *Dr John: Crusading Doctor and Politician* (Dublin, 1989), p. 87.

65   Statement issued by the ITUC, 7 June 1956 printed in *Trade Union Information*, June 1956; Memo from PUTUO submitted to Government 21 June 1956, in *Trade Union Information* July 1956.

66   Statement by MacBride to a meeting of Clann na Poblachta constituency representatives, 30 Jan. 1957, UCDAD P35c/199. See also McCarthy (ed.), *Planning Ireland's Future*, p. 32.

67   Mary Davidson to members of the PLP, 11 May 1956, ILHM&A JLJ/3 1953–57 LP.

68   ITUC Annual Report, 1955–6, p. 193.

69   Ibid.

70   *Irish Times* 13 Aug. 1956. The vacancies were caused by the deaths of Fianna Fáil and Fine Gael deputies respectively.

71   Statement from the Standing Committee of Clann na Poblachta released 17 Aug. 1956 referred to in Statement by MacBride to Clann Dublin constituency representatives, 30 Jan. 1957 in UCDAD P35c/199. See also *Irish Times*, 20 Aug. 1956.

72 O'Higgins, *A Double Life*, p. 185.

73 UCDAD P190/708 (7).

74 McCarthy, *Planning Ireland's Future*, p. 29.

75 Pre-policy speech papers, Aug.–Oct. 1956, UCDAD P190/713.

76 Ibid.

77 Ibid.

78 *Irish Times*, 27 Sept. 1956.

79 John O'Connell to Larkin, 28 Sept. 1956, ILHM&A JLJ/3 1953–57 (LP).

80 B. Maguire to Larkin, 29 Sept. 1956, ILHM&A JLJ/3 1953–57 (LP).

81 Joe Byrne to Larkin, 30 Sept. 1956, ILHM&A JLJ/3 1953–57 (LP).

82 *Irish Times*, 28 Sept. 1956.

83 See Ronan Fanning, *The Irish Department of Finance 1922–1958* (Dublin, 1978), p. 507.

84 *Irish Times*, 6 Oct. 1956.

85 Ibid.

86 PUTUO statement in response to Costello's statement of Government policy, 8 Oct. 1956 reprinted in *Trade Union Information*, Oct. 1956.

87 *Irish Times*, 20 Oct. 1956.

88 Ibid., 13 Nov. 1956.

89 Ibid., 19 Nov. 1956.

90 T. K. Whitaker witness seminar, Centre for Contemporary Irish History, TCD, 19 Jan. 2005.

91 See for example Dominic Sandbrook, *Never Had It So Good: A History of Britain from Suez to the Beatles* (London, 2005), p. 65.

92 See p. 184.

93 Tuairim constitution.

94 P. Rushton to J. de.Courcy Ireland, 14 May 1953, UCDAD P29/I/156.

95 Memorandum on recent meeting of new political group, 16 Oct. 1956, UCDAD P7b/120.

96 Horgan, *Browne*, p. 172. See Browne, *Against the Tide*, p. 249 for Browne on May Keating.

97 Deasún Breathnach and Robert Emoe. Breathnach ultimately ended up in the republican movement.

98 Horgan, *Browne*, p. 232.

99 Rex McGall [Deasún Breathnach] to Desmond Ryan, 24 Nov. 1956, UCDAD LA 10/M/18 (1); see also Andrée Sheehy Skeffington, *Skeff: A Life of Owen Sheehy Skeffington* (Dublin, 1991), p. 262. Those putting their signatures to the proclamation included Owen Sheehy Skeffington, Máirtín Ó Cadhain and David Greene (all Trinity College lecturers), the writers James Plunkett and Brendan Behan as well as Arnold Marsh and Peadar O'Donnell.

100 Catherine Cranwell to Seán O'Casey, 16 Oct. 1957, NLI, O'Casey papers, MS 38,014.

101 Desmond Ryan to Frances, 24 Feb. 1959, UCDAD LA 10/P/90a (20).

102 Tom Johnson to John de Courcy Ireland, 10 July 1958, UCDAD P29a?151 (16).

103 Executive Committee report of the IWL, 1954, CPGB papers, Manchester.

104 Milotte, *Communism*, p. 226.

105 Ibid., p. 228.

106 See Joseph Deasy, '*Fiery Cross* and letters from James Larkin Junior', *Saothar* 21 (1996), p. 123.

107 NAI CAB2/16, 16 Nov. 1956.

108 Eilís Ward, '"A big show-off to show what we could do": Ireland and the Hungarian refugee crisis of 1956', *Irish Studies in International Affairs* 7 (1996), p. 137.

109 It was essentially a continuation of the Dublin Unemployed Action Committee of 1953–4. See E. Kilmurray, *Starve or Emigrate: A History of the Unemployed Associations in the 1950s* (Dublin 1988), p. 28.

110 After taking office again in 1954 William Norton would often respond to criticism from Fianna Fáil on any subject by saying that at least there were no unemployed people protesting on O'Connell Street Bridge. See for example DD vol. 153, col 97, 26 Oct. 1955.

111 Eunan O'Halpin, *Defending Ireland: The Irish State and its Enemies since 1922* (Oxford, 1999), p. 298; *This Week*, 19 June 1970.

112 J. Bowyer Bell, *The Secret Army: The IRA 1916–1979.* (Dublin, 1990), p. 299.

113 Review of IRA organisation, 19 Mar. 1957, UCDAD P190/708 (7).

114 *The Times*, 4 Mar. 1957.

115 Bowyer Bell, *Secret Army*, p. 300.

116 Colman Tadhg O'Sullivan, 'The IRA takes constitutional action: a history of Clann na Poblachta, 1946–1965' (MA, UCD 1995), p. 131.

117 Ibid.

118 *Irish Times*, 29 Jan. 1957.

119 See Basil Chubb, 'Ireland 1957' in D. E. Butler (ed.), *Elections Abroad* (London, 1959), pp. 188–9.

120 Michael Gallagher, *The Labour Party in Transition* (Dublin, 1982), p. 31.

121 Chubb, 'Ireland 1957', pp. 188–9.

122 See for example *Evening Mail*, 9 Feb. 1957.

123 An *Irish Times* profile had said of Larkin, 'He gives the impression that his political work as a TD comes a poor second to his trade union activities, much to the annoyance of his supporters, and more of his ex-supporters who have left the Labour Party in disgust' (18 Oct. 1952).

124 Todd Andrews recalled that when he expressed to Larkin his regret at his decision to leave politics, Larkin responded 'that the choice was not his; he had been forced out of politics by the right wing of the Labour Party and specifically by those who were associated with the first coalition government'. C. S. Andrews *Man of No Property* (Dublin, 1982), p. 259; see also ibid. pp. 192–3.

125 *Leader*, 27 Mar. 1954.

126 Interview with Vincent McDowell, 12 Apr. 2001.

127 For instance, although some difficulties had arisen over the allocation of party political broadcasts on Radio Éireann (NLI, CAB, 2/16 12 Feb. 1957), Basil Chubb noted that when the broadcasts did take place 'most of the speakers, who were party leaders, had poor scripts and were under-rehearsed. One at least was unbelievably dreadful; most were mediocre; one, Mr Lemass, was excellent.' Chubb, 'Ireland 1957', p. 201.

128 *Dublin Evening Mail*, 16 Feb. 1957.

129 *Protest*, July 1957.

130 Horgan, *Browne*, p. 185.

131 Interview with Matt Merrigan, RTÉ Dec. 1998; Francis Devine, 'Reminiscence – Socialist Trade Unionist: Matt Merrigan's political formation', *Saothar* 12 (1987), p. 96.

132 Sinn Féin had put up two candidates in the 1954 election, its first electoral outing since the June 1927 election.

133 *Irish Times*, 2 Mar. 1957.

134 The Labour candidate standing in his place won 12.8 per cent of the first preferences in the three-seat constituency in comparison with Dunne's 23.5 per cent in 1954.

135 Chubb observed that 'the most disturbing aspect of [the 1957] election for Labour was its inability to retain votes formerly given to its retiring senior members.' Chubb 'Ireland 1957', p. 216.

136 Labour had entered the Dáil after the 1954 election with 19 seats, but the party had lost William Davin's seat in Laois Offaly in 1956. Paddy Hogan, as outgoing Ceann Comhairle was returned automatically.

137 *Leader*, 25 Oct. 1952.

138 Farrell, *Chairman or Chief?* p. 53.

139 J. J. Lee, *Ireland 1912–1985: Politics and Society* (Cambridge, 1989), p. 326.

140 *Leader*, 27 Mar. 1954.

EIGHT: LABOUR'S WAY

1 Brian Fallon, *An Age of Innocence: Irish Culture 1930–1960* (Dublin, 1998), p. 257.

2 Liam Cosgrave was one who placed the blame for the government's collapse squarely on Sweetman's shoulders, and apparently told him as much. See Paddy Harte, *Young Tigers and Mongrel Foxes* (Dublin, 2005), p. 95.

3 Maurice Manning, *James Dillon: A Biography* (Dublin, 1999), p. 314.

4 Interviews with Donal Nevin, Joe Deasy, John de Courcy Ireland.

5 *Sunday Press*, 16 June 1957; *Irish Times*, 17 June 1957.

6 *Irish Times*, 17 June 1957.

7 *Irish Times*, 20 June 1957. The motion was tabled by the following: the Jim Larkin branch, Dublin; the Dun Laoghaire branch; the James Connolly branch Drogheda; Carrigaline Divisional Council; Dublin Regional Council and Meath Constituency Council. ILHM&A POWU papers.

8 Labour Party Annual Report, 1957–8, p. 17.

9 See Paddy Murphy to Larkin, 26 Oct. 1957, ILHM&A JLJ/3 1953–57 (LP), File L7; Mary Davidson to Larkin, 24 Feb. 1958, ILHM&A JLJ/7/3 1958.

10 Larkin to Paddy Murphy, 30 Oct. 1957, ILHM&A JLJ/3 1953–57 (LP), File L7.

11 B. Maguire to Jim Larkin, 28 Oct. 1957, ILHM&A JLJ/3 1953–57 (LP), File L7.

12 The speech was later published as a pamphlet entitled *Labour's Way*. See UCDAD P56/284.

13 'The re-shaping of the Labour Party – what an opportunity for youth!' *Plough*, Mar. 1958.

14 Labour Party Annual Report, 1957–8, p. 18.

15 *Plough*, Mar. 1958.

16 Interview with Jim Larkin in the *Plough*, Sept. 1960.

17 The type of candidate Larkin had in mind can be seen in two Dublin by-elections in 1958 and 1959 which were contested by Frank Cluskey and Hilda Larkin, both of the WUI. Cluskey eventually got in following the 1965 general election.

18 *Irish Independent*, 26 May 1958; *Evening Mail*, 26 May 1958.

19 MacBride to John de Courcy Ireland, 9 June 1958, UCDAD P29a/153.

20 *Evening Mail*, 12 June 1958; *Irish Times*, 12 June 1958.

21 See C. O'Leary, *Irish Elections 1918–77: Parties, Voters and Proportional Representation* (Dublin, 1979), pp. 46–58 for an account of the campaign.

22 Blythe to MacEntee, 4 Dec. 1958, UCDAD P67/420 (2).

23 *Irish Times*, 5 June 1959.

24 *Liberty*, May 1958, p. 3. Emphasis added.

25 For instance the ITGWU's journal *Liberty* began publishing articles and editorials which portrayed Labour as the natural choice for trade unionists.

26 *Liberty*, Oct. 1959.

27 *Irish Times*, 10 Oct. 1959.

28 *Liberty*, Nov. 1959.

29 *Liberty*, Nov. 1959.

30 Michael Gallagher, *The Irish Labour Party in Transition, 1957–82* (Dublin, 1982), p. 40.

31 Information from Barry Desmond.

32 *Irish Democrat*, Mar. 1960.

33 According to *Liberty*'s account, delegates faced up to the difficult problems of leadership and the apparent anomaly of a leading member holding a position as a director in a private company; they decided without a vote that this was really a matter for the individual in question (Nov. 1959).

34 Ryan to Frances, 27 Nov. 1959, UCDAD LA10/P/90a (25); John de Courcy Ireland had already expressed 'grounds for optimism' about the party during the summer. See Johnson to Ireland, 10 July 1959, UCDAD P29a/151 (16).

35 *Liberty*, Jan. 1960.

36 *Irish Times*, 11 Feb. 1960.

37 Ibid., 18, 25 Feb. 1960.

38 Ibid., 11 Feb. 1960.

39 Vincent McDowell in *Nusight*, June 1969; Noël Browne in *Nusight*, Nov. 1968; interviews with Proinsias MacAonghusa, Nov. 1999; Brendan Halligan, 8 Feb. 2002. It is worth noting, however, that none of these sources was close to the Labour or union leadership at this time, and their opinions would be reliant on hearsay.

40 Manning, *Dillon*, p. 325.

41 *Irish Times*, 26 Feb. 1960.

42 Gallagher, *Irish Labour Party*, p. 41.

43 In fact, he was foremost in the PLP on this area, as the other people who played the most significant role in this regard, James Tully and Jim Larkin, were not in the Dáil at this time.

44 Gallagher, *Irish Labour Party*, p. 41.

45 *Irish Times*, 17 May 1960.

46 *Hibernia*, 8 Apr. 1960.

47 Quoted in the introduction, p. 2.

48 Evelyn Bolster, *The Knights of the Order of St Columbanus* (Dublin, 1979), p. 96.

49 DD vol. 138, col. 839, 29 Apr. 1953.

50 *Plough*, June 1958. See for example DD vol. 167, col. 330, 17 Apr. 1958.

51 Quoted in Gallagher, *Irish Labour Party*, p. 42.

52 Information from Owen Dudley Edwards.

53 John Horgan, *Labour: The Price of Power* (Dublin, 1986), p. 37.

54 Barry Desmond, *Finally and in Conclusion: A Political Memoir* (Dublin, 2000) p. 32; John Horgan, *Noël Brown: Passionate Outsider* (Dublin, 2000), p. 208; Gallagher, *Irish Labour Party*, p. 42.

55 *Labour*, June 1960.

56 Basil Chubb, *Government and Politics of Ireland* (Oxford, 1971), p. 292.

57 *The Plough*, Nov. 1960.

58 The text was published in full in *Liberty.*

59 *Irish Times*, 6 June 1960.

60 *The Plough*, Aug. 1960.

61 Interview with Donal Nevin.

62 *Irish Times*, 10 Oct. 1960.

63 Notes of speech in ILHM&A WUI JLJ papers.

64 *Irish Times*, 10 Oct. 1960.

65 Ibid., 11 Oct. 1960.

66 *Plough*, Nov. 1960.

67 Brendan Corish pocket diary 1961, ILHM&A Corish deposit.

68 Seán MacBride to Brendan Corish, 31 Mar. 1961 quoted in O'Sullivan, 'IRA takes constitutional action', pp. 145–6.

69 Brendan Corish Pocket diary 1961, ILHM&A Corish deposit.

70 *Irish Times*, 26 Feb. 1960.

71 Emmet O'Connor, *A Labour History of Ireland* (Dublin, 1992), p. 172.

72 See ICTU Trade Union policy and political objectives. Strictly confidential circular to members of the EC n.d. [30 Dec. 1960].

73 Handwritten notes on relations with the Labour Party, NAI ICTU (Box 43).

74 Labour Party Annual Report, 1960–2, p. 10.

75 Gallagher suggests it only met on about a dozen occasions over a six-year period (*Irish Labour Party*, p. 45).

76 State department memorandum on the Irish Labour Party and the coming election, 4 Aug. 1961. NAM, courtesy of John Horgan. ICTU Annual Report, p. 253.

77 John Horgan, *Seán Lemass: The Enigmatic Patriot* (Dublin, 1997), pp. 219–22.

78 See Fintan Horihan, 'From scepticism to pragmatism: Irish trade unions and the EC' (MComm, UCD, 1996); Gary Murphy, '"Fostering a spurious progeny?": the trade union movement and Europe, 1957–64', *Saothar* 21 (1996), pp. 61–70.

79 See Michael Kennedy and Eunan O'Halpin, *Ireland and the Council of Europe: From Isolation to Integration* (Strasbourg, 2000).

80 DD vol. 191, col. 307, 5 July 1961.

81 DD vol. 191 cols 321–2, 5 July 1961.

82 State department memorandum on the Irish Labour Party and the coming election, 4 Aug. 1961.

83 Until this point, the work had been done by Donal Nevin, who was more than capable but had more pressing calls upon his time from his day job.

84 See Arnold Marsh, Memoirs [unpublished manuscript], p. 231, TCDM, Marsh papers, 8340.

85 State department memorandum, 4 Aug. 1960.

86 Although this was a step down from Michael McInerney's prediction that Labour would 'go into the election with a joint Congress–Labour manifesto'. *Irish Times*, 25 July 1961.

87 Leo Crawford and Ruaidhrí Roberts, joint secretaries of the ITUC; John Conroy (President), Edward Browne (Vice President) and Fintan Kennedy (General Secretary) of the ITGWU and Jim Larkin (General Secretary) of the WUI.

88 Labour Party Annual Report, 1960–2, p. 9.

89 O'Leary, *Irish Elections*, p. 62.

90 State department memo, 4 Aug. 1961.

91 Seamus Pattison in Carlow Kilkenny and James Tully in Meath, while the third was former Clann na Poblachta man Stevie Coughlan who had joined Labour immediately prior to the election and regained the seat vacated by Michael Keyes in 1957. Labour's report (p. 13) expressed its 'satisfaction' at winning back 'what may be described as traditional seats'.

92 Gerry Gregg, 'Dr Noël Browne: Irish political maverick 1948–1977' (MA, UCD, 1981), n. 51. This is not to say that the new arrivals did not make some favourable impact. For instance Catherine McGuinness wrote of how the 'new deputies, Mr Pattison, Mr Treacy and Mr Mullen [were] on the whole more interested in educational matters than some of the more senior deputies'. McGuinness to Ireland, 22 June 1962, UCDAD P29a/154 (3).

93 Labour Party Annual Report, 1960–1, 1961–2, p. 8; *Irish Democrat*, June 1962.

94 Notice of aggregate meeting of DRC, 14 Feb. 1962, ILHM&A JLJ/7/3 1958.

95 Ibid.

96 AC Annual Report, 1962–3, p. 8.

97 She also took over Duffy's seat in the Senate, where she sat on the Industrial panel, 1950–1 and 1954–69.

98 Interview with Betty Dowling, Jan. 2002; John O'Connell, *Doctor John: Crusading Doctor and Politician* (Dublin, 1989). p. 56.

99 Brian Inglis, *West Briton* (London, 1962), p. 109.

100 Interview with Proinsias MacAonghusa, November 1999.

101 Draft election literature by Barry Desmond and Catherine McGuinness, Apr. 1963, ILHM&A JLJ/7/3.

102 See, p. 214 above.

103 *Sunday Review*, 2 June 1963.

104 It received a somewhat mixed reception from Eustás Ó hÉideáin, OP, who reviewed it in *Doctrine and Life*, who was of the opinion that the Irish education system was not in need of a radical overhaul and that 'decapitation [was] not the cure for dandruff' (14: 7 (Aug. 1964), p. 394); the *Irish Socialist*, on the other hand, was positive but felt the document did not go far enough (Dec. 1963).

105 *Hibernia*, Mar. 1963.

106 'A Tribute to Jim Kemmy' audiocassette (tape 1, side 2).

107 *Plough*, June 1963.

108 Larkin to S. P. Irwin, 8 May 1963, ILHM&A JLJ/7/3.

109 File relating to the use of dogs, NAI Justice 2005/154/2.

110 See Richard English, *Armed Struggle: A History of the IRA* (London, 2003), p. 82.

111 Ibid., p. 85.

112 Interview with Jack Gannon, 31 Mar. 2003; Roy Johnston, *Century of Endeavour* (Dublin, 2006). Among the prime movers in the early days of Scéim na gCeardcumann were the brothers Geraghty (Sé, Des and Hugh) and Michael O'Leary, then based in Congress.

113 Johnston, *Century of Endeavour*, p. 179.

114 Private source.

115 *United Irishman*, May 1965.

116 Johnston, *Century of Endeavour*, p. 179.

117 American Embassy report, quoted in Horgan, *Browne*, p. 211.

118 File relating to the use of dogs, NAI Justice 2005/154/2.

119 Horgan, *Browne*, p. 213. The march and the photograph were mentioned in a number of interviews with activists who became active around this time.

120 Noël Browne, *Against the Tide* (Dublin, 1986), p. 255.

121 *Sunday Review*, 18 Feb. 1962.

122 Horgan, *Browne*, p. 213.

123 *Irish Times*, 7 Dec. 1963.

124 *Plough*, May 1964.

125 *Irish Times*, 9 Dec. 1963.

126 See D. R. O'Connor Lysaght, *The Irish Republic* (Cork, 1970), pp. 214–15.

127 *Irish Times*, 30 Oct. 1963.

128 Manning, *Dillon*, p. 353. Another example of Labour's aggressive policy and its willingness to break with Dáil protocol was evident when Labour moved the writ for the by-election in Cork borough following the death of Fianna Fáil deputy John Galvin.

129 *Sunday Review*, 3 Nov. 1963.

130 This was most likely John de Courcy Ireland, see clipping from *Tribune* (n.d.), UCDAD P290/C/64; see also DTUC minutes 8 Oct. 1963, ILHM&A; *Irish Socialist*, Nov. 1963; *Irish Democrat*, Dec. 1963.

131 *Tribune* (n.d.), UCDAD P290/C/64.

132 For instance, the *Plough* (May 1964) complained that while Labour had started to 'move slowly forward . . . its pace [was] much too slow'.

133 *Irish Democrat*, Apr. 1964.

134 *The Plough*, Aug. 1964. See also *Tribune*, 10 July 1964, UCDAD P29/D/1.

135 *Irish Times*, 9 June 1964.

136 *Irish Socialist*, July 1964.

137 Horgan, *Lemass*, p. 232.

138 Mike Milotte, *Communism in Modern Ireland: The Pursuit of the Workers' Republic Since 1916* (Dublin, 1984), p. 247.

139 Miriam Daly, 'Believing today', *The Furrow* 18: 10 (Oct. 1967), p. 555.

140 July 1964. The vogue for citing papal pronouncements often resulted in quite ludicrous claims. For instance, in August 1967 the *United Irishman* featured an article examining 'papal and republican parallels'. This compared quotes from Paul VI's 'On the development of peoples' with passages by Pearse, Lalor, Seamus Costello and Muintir Wolfe Tone's pamphlet 'The case against the Common Market', with the Pope found to be in full agreement with all those on this particular pantheon.

141 Milotte, *Communism*, pp. 247–8. See also *Irish Socialist*, July; Aug.; Sept. 1964; Sept.; Dec. 1965; Jan. 1966; Nov. 1967.

142 See, for example, Denis McCullough, 'Protest and the student', *UCD News Magazine*, no.1 n.d. (NLI); interview with Brendan Halligan, 8 Feb. 2002.

143 Derry Kelleher recalled a priest in the Church of the Holy Redeemer in Bray ranting 'against his parishioners for not having read Pope John's encyclical *Mater et Magistra* at Sunday mass'. Afterwards Kelleher 'went to remind him that there were no copies on the book rack for sale at the church door. He brusquely waived the matter aside stating that it was not of his concern, but one of the Archbishop.' Derry Kelleher, *Buried Alive in Ireland: A Story of a Twentieth Century Inquisition* (Wicklow, 2001), p. 223.

144 Edmund Dell, *A Strange and Eventful History: Democratic Socialism in Britain* (London, 2000), p. 309.

145 Indeed, Wilson told viewers of a party political broadcast in 1964: 'What I think we are going to need is something like what President Kennedy had when he came in after years of stagnation in the United States.' (Quoted in Anthony Jay (ed.), *The Oxford Dictionary of Political Quotations* (Oxford, 1996), p. 390.)

146 Dell, *Strange and Eventful History*, p. 312.

147 Interview with Jack Gannon; see also Ruairí Quinn *Straight Left: A Journey in Politics* (Dublin, 2005), p. 45. Some years later, the *Labour Newsletter* noted that 'Irish Labour was helped at the last election [1965] by the fact that Labour was in power in Britain and appeared to be on the up and up.' 14 Mar. 1967.

148 *United Irishman*, Nov. 1964.

149 See for example, Dónall Ó Móráin, 'Ireland and the Council, III', *The Furrow* 17: 7 (July 1966), p. 429; T. Garvin, 'Political parties in a Dublin Constituency' (PhD University of Georgia, 1974), p. 126.

150 Confidential dispatch on the 1968 referendum, 23 Oct. 1968, TNA FCO33/751.

151 Horgan, *Lemass*, p. 206.

152 *Irish Times*, 24 Mar. 1965.

153 *Hibernia*, Apr. 1965; *Irish Independent*, Mar. 1965.

154 *Irish Times*, 19 Mar. 1965.

155 Ibid., 24 Mar. 1965.

156 See O'Leary, *Irish Elections*, p. 65; Manning, *Dillon*, p. 373.

157 Browne, *Against the Tide*, p. 256; Horgan, *Browne*, p. 219.

158 *Irish Times*, 31 Mar. 1965; see, p. 243 for McQuillan and the perils of socialism.

159 Gallagher, *Irish Labour Party*, p. 56.

160 *Hibernia*, May 1965.

161 Following the result, he told party workers in Liberty Hall that Labour could 'no longer afford to refer merely to the basic principles for which [it] fought', but now needed to 'spell out in greater clarity and detail the policies for which we stand and the actions which would be taken by a Labour government'. Proinsias MacAonghusa (ed.), *Corish Speaks* (1966), p. 40.

.

NINE: 'THE SEVENTIES WILL BE SOCIALIST'

1   Máirtín Breathnach, *Republican Days: 75 Years of Fianna Fáil* (Dublin, 2002).

2   Those not given special areas were Frank Cluskey, John O'Connell, Patrick Norton, Séamus Pattison, James Everett and Patrick Tierney. See Labour Party Annual Report, 1964–5.

3   *Business and Finance*, 21 May 1965.

4   *Irish Democrat*, June 1965.

5   John O'Connell, *Doctor John: Crusading Doctor and Politician* (Dublin, 1989), p. 71. O'Connell's eagerness did not go unnoticed by political commentators. John Healy wrote of him, 'His earnestness is, at times painful. Day after day he plods away with questions to all of which he had supplementaries. So inexperienced is he that he has constantly to be reminded by his colleagues that his remarks should be in the form of a question, and not a speech.' *Irish Times*, 26 June 1965.

6   *Irish Times*, 8 Jan. 1966.

7   *Hibernia* (July 1967) complained that the Dáil was in the doldrums and missed the dissent of Browne and McQuillan.

8   *Irish Times*, 1 Jan. 1966.

9   Preliminary agenda annual conference 1965, John Goodwillie papers, ILHM&A.

10   *Munster Express*, 22 Oct. 1965.

11   *Labour News*, Nov. 1965.

12   Proinsias MacAonghusa (ed.), *Corish Speaks* (1966), p. 40.

13   *Comment* (Magazine of the Universities Branch of the Labour Party), Dec. 1965.

14   *Business and Finance*, 6 May 1966.

15   *Campus*, 3 Mar. 1966.

16   *Irish Times*, 7 Apr. 1966.

17   *New Statesman*, 1 July 1966; *Irish Times*, 26 May 1966.

18   *New Statesman*, 1 July 1966.

19   Corish to Jim Larkin, 15 Sept. 1966, ILHM&A JLJ/7/3 1958.

20   *Labour News*, Oct. 1966.

21   *Irish Times*, 1 Oct. 1966.

22   List of delegates 1967. Sixty-seven delegates represented trade unions and 14 were from the PLP and AC.

23   *Irish Times*, 17 Oct. 1966.

24   *Irish Times*, 14 Oct. 1966. The number of registered branch delegates in July 1964 was 245.

25   *Irish Times*, 17 Oct. 1966; *Irish Socialist*, Nov. 1966.

26   *Irish Socialist*, Nov. 1966.

27   *Irish Times*, 17 Oct. 1966.

28   Ibid.

29   In the *Hibernia* newspaper awards in 1968, Michael McInerney was named best political correspondent 'in spite of a certain amount of naïveté when dealing with the Labour Party and the inclination to discover progressive tendencies in politicians of whom he personally approves' (Mar. 1968). Donal Foley's father had stood for Labour in the 1932 and 1937 general elections. He would himself be the co-author of Corish's leader's speech the following year, along with another *Irish Times* journalist, Mary Maher.

30   John Horgan, *Labour: The Price of Power* (Dublin, 1986), p. 34; *Irish Socialist*, Nov. 1966.

31   *Irish Times*, 18 Oct. 1966; *Hibernia*, Nov. 1966.

32   This point was stressed by Michael O'Leary in his obituary of Corish in the *Irish Times*, 19 Feb. 1990.

33   *Hibernia*, Mar. 1967. UCD's Baby Tigers were very unhappy at their treatment at the hands of Fine Gael Head Office, complaining about the ill treatment from both Hume Street and the Fine Gael front bench in comparison with Labour's attitude to its student branches. See *Campus*, 29 Feb. 1968.

34   *Nusight*, June 1969.

35   Report of the 36th Ard Fheis, Nov. 1965; *Ógra* 1: 2 and 3 (n.d.); see Robert McNamara, 'Irish Perspectives on the Vietnam war', *Irish Studies in International Affairs* 14 (2003), pp. 75–94.

36   Michael Gallagher, *The Irish Labour Party in Transition 1957–82* (Dublin, 1982), p. 76. The only exception to this, according to Gallagher, was the Dutch Labour Party, the PvdA.

37   Brendan Corish, 'Towards equality and freedom', *Everyman*, 1969.

38 *Hibernia*, Dec. 1960.

39 This refers to the British Labour Leader Hugh Gaitskell's tooth and nail opposition to his party's wish to engage in a policy of unilateral nuclear disarmament in 1960. Gaitskell said that he would 'fight and fight and fight again to save the Party' he loved.

40 Quoted in Stephen Collins, *Spring and the Labour Story*, p. 30. Browne himself could not even keep a clinic open, and more than likely lost his seat in Dublin South East in the 1973 election as a result. See John Horgan, *Noël Browne: Passionate Outsider* (Dublin, 2000), p. 239 and Ruairí Quinn, *Straight Left: A Journey in Politics* (Dublin, 2005). p. 89.

41 *Nusight*, May 1970.

42 *Irish Times, Review and Annual 1963*, p. 55.

43 Interestingly, the cause of the Telephonists was taken up by members of Clann na hÉireann (a then recent off-shoot of the Republican Prisoners Committee in Britain). See Telex from London 28.10.65, NAI DFA 305/14/263/23.

44 Gallagher, *Irish Labour Party*, p. 72.

45 *Irish Independent*, 31 Mar. 1966.

46 Draft notes by Catherine McGuinness of meeting between Economic Committee (ICTU) and the Labour Party, 27 Oct. 1966, amended by Ruaidhrí Roberts. NAI ICTU Box 4, File 4005B.

47 Originally there had been two motions tabled on the subject. The first, from the Rathmines branch, one of the younger branches, deplored 'the fact that certain prominent members of the party are actively engaging in the fragmentation of the trade union movement, particularly in the light of the efforts of the ICTU in this regard.' The second motion, from the Capwell/Ballyphehane Branch in Cork, was very similar. Conference Programme, ILHM&A POWU MS 10/LP/1–5.

48 Larkin to Mary Davidson, 23 Nov. 1966, ILHM&A JLJ/7/3 1958.

49 See *Labour Newsletter*, Uimhir 1, 5 Nov. 1966; 19 Nov. 1966.

50 Labour Party Annual Report, 1966–7, p. 12.

51 Reports of AC meetings, 10 Nov. 1966; 14 Dec. 1966, ILHM&A JLJ/7/3 1958.

52 Report of AC meeting, 14 Dec. 1966, ILHM&A JLJ/7/3 1958. Emphasis added.

53 *Labour Newsletter*, 19 Nov. 1966.

54 Interview with Niall Greene Nov. 2001; Labour Party Annual Report, 1966–7, p. 13.

55 *Irish Times*, 21 Jan. 1967. See *New Statesman*, 3 Feb. 1967; *Labour Newsletter*, 21 Jan. 1967.

56 This was particularly the case in the *Irish Times* (See John Shields to John Goodwillie (n.d.), ILHM&A MSS 33 92/2/12); *Irish Times*, 4 Feb. 1967.

57 *New Statesman*, 3 Feb. 1967.

58 See for example *Hibernia*, May 1968.

59 See *New Statesman*, 3 Feb. 1967; *Labour Newsletter*, 21 Jan. 1967.

60 *Hibernia*, Feb. 1967.

61 *Irish Times*, 28 Jan. 1967.

62 *Irish Times*, 4 Feb. 1967; John Goodwillie to Corish, 31 Jan. 1967, ILHM&A MSS 33 92/2/12.

63 O'Connell, *Doctor John*, p. 90.

64 *Nusight*, 20 Oct. 1967; *Irish Times*, 14 Oct. 1967.

65 Some two years after his expulsion, he was to be found lauding Fine Gael's policies at a meeting of the Limerick branch of Tuairim. (John Horgan, *Broadcasting and Public Life: RTÉ News and Current Affairs, 1926–1997* (Dublin, 2004), p. 87). The Trotskyist writer D. R. O'Connor

Lysaght, a contemporary of MacAonghusa's, described his political philosophy as one of the 'bureaucratic idealism of the left wing of Fianna Fáil and Fine Gael' (Lysaght, *Republic of Ireland*, p. 215), while the *New Statesman* quoted a left-winger in Ireland as saying 'It's a bad thing that MacAonghusa was expelled – it's a good thing he's out.' *New Statesman*, 17 Feb. 1967.

66 Nevertheless, 'most of the discussion was inimical to Mac'. See Confidential report of AC meeting, 15 Dec. 1965, ILHSM&A MSS 33 92/2/9.

67 *Hibernia*, Feb. 1967.

68 *Irish Times*, 4 Feb. 1967.

69 There is more than a little irony about the source of this idea, in view of the difficulties which Coughlan would face from 'intellectuals' in the PLP after 1969. See chapter 10.

70 Description of the role of the political director, n.d., ILHM&A JLJ/7/3/1958.

71 Report of the interviewing committee for party organiser, n.d., ILHM&A JLJ/7/3/1958.

72 *Hibernia*, July 1967.

73 *Labour Newsletter*, 1 Apr. 1967. See *Irish Times*, 29 Mar. 1967; *Business and Finance*, 7 Apr. 1967; *Hibernia*, July 1967; *Labour*, Mar. 1967.

74 As the *Labour Newsletter* put it, 'Miss Davidson has made life hell for organisers who preceded Halligan. It remains to be seen if she has changed in any way over the years. The story goes that Halligan has boasted he is well able for her. We hope he is right. This unfortunate woman has done more harm to the Labour Party than any other one thousand people put together. There are many reasons for Labour's pathetic position in Irish politics. Miss Davidson may not head the list, but she's quite close to it.' 1 Apr. 1967.

75 Labour Party Annual Report, 1966–7, p. 20. According to the *Labour Newsletter*, she was 72 years old at this time. 26 Nov. 1966.

76 *Hibernia*, July 1967.

77 *Liberty*, June 1967.

78 *Impact* (Published by the QUB Labour Group), 1966.

79 Fianna Fáil took 15, Fine Gael 11. *Irish Socialist*, July–Aug. 1967.

80 *Irish Socialist*, July–Aug. 1967; Goodwillie to O'Rourke, 10 July 1967; Notes of meeting of the AC held 19 July 1967, ILHM&A JLJ/7/3; Labour Party Annual Report, 1966–7, p. 10.

81 *Hibernia*, Aug. 1967.

82 Richard English, *Armed Struggle: A History of the IRA* (London, 2003), p. 94.

83 Ibid.

84 *United Irishman*, Aug. 1967; Henry Patterson, *The Politics of Illusion: A Political History of the IRA* (2nd edn, London, 1997), p. 113.

85 See Mike Milotte, *Communism in Modern Ireland: The Pursuit of the Workers' Republic since 1916* (Dublin, 1984), p. 241.

86 See *United Irishman*, Feb. 1968.

87 As British Foreign Office intelligence put it in 1970, 'The committee has become a cause for the regular left wing protesters in Dublin and is not communist controlled, although it has probably been infiltrated.' TNA FCO 33/1204 Communism in Ireland, 1970.

88 Patterson, *Politics of Illusion*, pp. 113, 118.

89 *Grille*, Summer 1968.

90 American Embassy Dublin to State Department, 2 Nov. 1967, NAM.

91 Brendan Corish, *New Republic* (Dublin, 1967), p. 2.

92 American Embassy Dublin to State Department, 2 Nov. 1967, NAM.

93 *Irish Socialist*, Nov. 1967; see also *Irish Democrat*, Nov. 1967.

94 Circular from Corish, Desmond and Davidson to the secretaries of each branch, 19 Oct. 1967, ILHM&A JLJ/7/3.

95 Labour Information Bulletin, Jan. 1968, ILHM&A JLJ/7/3.

96 Gallagher, *Irish Labour Party*, p. 70.

97 *Irish Times*, 15 Dec. 1967.

98 *Irish Socialist*, Jan. 1968.

99 *Labour Newsletter*, 10 Dec. 1966.

100 *Irish Socialist*, Jan. 1968. Earlier during the year, Norton had been ordered in court to make repairs to rental properties. See *Irish Times*, 25 Feb. 1967. See also *United Irishman*, Apr. 1967.

101 *Irish Times*, 15 Dec. 1967.

102 Gallagher, *Irish Labour Party*, p. 73.

103 Ibid.

104 Larkin to Corish, 31 Oct. 1967, ILHM&A JLJ/7/3.

105 ICTU Executive Council minutes, 27 Oct. 1967, NAI ICTU Box 108.

106 *Irish Democrat*, June 1968.

107 ICTU EC minutes, 28 June 1968, NAI ICTU Box 108. The May Congress had referred a motion condemning the increase to the Economic Committee to be discussed with Labour representatives. ICTU Annual Report, 1967–8, p. 427.

108 Quoted in Manus O'Riordan, *Voice of a Thinking Intelligent Movement: James Larkin Junior and the Ideological Modernisation of Irish Trade Unionism*, Studies in Irish Labour History 2 (Dublin 2001), p. 35. Similar points were made by another WUI delegate at the ICTU congress during the same month. ICTU Annual Report, 1967–8, p. 278.

109 *Hibernia*, Mar. 1968.

110 Nor did he expect to. Kavanagh was playing a longer game, and expected to lose the by-election, but take back the seat at the next general election, which is exactly what he did.

111 Interview with Brendan Halligan, Feb. 2002.

112 Labour Party Annual Report, 1967–8, p. 6.

113 See for example Paddy Harte, *Young Tigers and Mongrel Foxes: A Life in Politics* (Dublin, 2005), p. 101.

114 Garret FitzGerald, *All in a Life* (Dublin, 1991), pp. 77–8. Similarly, while the idea of a new Social Democratic Party consisting of progressive elements of Fine Gael and Labour (see Harte, *Young Tigers*, p. 319) may have been floated over tea in Young Tiger circles, it was never considered within Labour.

115 Interview with Brendan Halligan.

116 *Nusight*, Nov. 1969.

117 *The Times*, 14 Oct. 1968.

118 *The Times*, 6 Mar. 1968.

119 Gallagher, *Irish Labour Party*, p. 75.

120 See memo from B. Halligan to each discussion group chairman, n.d. Courtesy of Barry Desmond.

121 *Irish Times*, 22 July 1968.

122 *Hibernia*, Sept. 1968.

123 Ibid.

124 *Irish Times*, 20 July 1968.

125 First report of the Constitutional Review Committee, 13 July 1968. Courtesy of Barry Desmond.

126 Comments on First Report by Barry Desmond; Comments on First Report by M. P. Merrigan. Courtesy of Barry Desmond.

127 See pp. 67–8 above.

128 Conor Cruise O'Brien, *Memoir: My Life and Themes* (Dublin, 1998), p. 317.

129 Keating's mother was May Keating, the prominent Browneite who had helped set up the *Plough*. His father was the painter Seán Keating RHA.

130 AC minutes, 9 Apr. 1969. Ely Place.

131 O. Sheey Skeffington to C. Cruise O'Brien, 2 Feb. 1969, NLI, O. Sheehy Skeffington papers, MS 40,489/9.

132 Information from Eunan O'Halpin.

133 Basil Chubb, *Government and Politics of Ireland* (Oxford, 1971), p. 56.

134 *Ógra*, vol. 1, no. 2, n.d.

135 *Hibernia*, 3 Jan. 1969.

136 Fergal Tobin, *The Best of Decades: Ireland in the 1960s* (Dublin, 1996), p. 180.

137 See Philip Pettit (ed.), *The Gentle Revolution: Crisis in the Universities* (Dublin, 1969); Donal McCartney, *UCD: A National Idea. The History of University College Dublin* (Dublin, 1999), pp. 345–88; Quinn, *Straight Left* pp. 60–7; FitzGerald, *All in a Life*; the SDA newspaper *Confrontation* is available in NLI.

138 *Campus*, 14 Mar. 1968.

139 A. G. Gilchrist, 'The Irish political situation', 30 Jan. 1969. Churchill College Cambridge Gilc 14 A. My thanks to Eunan O'Halpin for bringing this to my attention. The Internationalists was formed in TCD in 1966 to promote the study of international affairs, and was originally a left-wing liberal group but was soon taken over by 'a number of students of Maoist tendencies and later became completely dominated by them'. *Nusight*, May 1970.

140 *Nusight*, Apr. 1970.

141 Quinn, *Straight Left*, p. 61.

142 *Revolutionary Alternative*, n.d. Official organ of the academic freedom committee.

143 See *Campus*, 17 Nov. 1966. McCartney, *UCD*, pp. 167–8.

144 The second edition of *Grille* recorded that the first issue had garnered a 'generally positive reception' and that it had been sold on street stalls and religious shops, 'everywhere indeed except outside Haddington Road Church, where a young priest ranting about private property ejected us from church grounds calling us stupid, ignorant exhibitionists.' *Grille* 2 (Autumn 1968).

145 Tobin, *Best of Decades*, p. 191.

146 *Grille*, Winter 1968.

147 This compares with an increase of 400 per cent in Britain and of 70 per cent in France. *Irish Socialist*, June 1968.

148 For instance, three years after the event, Dr John O'Donovan complained of the presence of a Special Branch car outside the party's convention in Dublin South West in March 1967. See DD vol. 246, col. 1143, 8 May 1970.

149 *Nusight*, Nov. 1968. This is borne out by the archives of Military Intelligence.

150 Information from Tom Garvin.

151 Tobin, *Best of Decades*, p. 182. *United Irishman*, June 1967. There were frequent accusations of garda brutality, which had begun in earnest the previous year. Special Branch's

modus operandi around this time suggests more of an interest in intimidation than in intelligence gathering.

152 *Labour News*, June 1966.

153 Gilchrist, 'The Irish political situation'.

154 Ibid.

155 *Confrontation* 2: 1 (Jan. 1969).

156 Gilchrist, 'The Irish political situation'.

157 Embassy report on the Labour Party conference, NAM.

158 *Irish Times*, 27 Jan. 1969.

159 *Hibernia*, 31 Jan. 1969.

160 Horgan, *Labour: Price of Power*, p. 34.

161 Harte, *Young Tigers*, p. 104.

162 Horgan, *Labour: Price of Power*, p. 34.

163 *Irish Times*, 27 Jan. 1969. This remark drew the ire of one delegate who countered that her reference to herself as a devout Catholic mother was completely immaterial, because she had been elected by the working class and should represent them indiscriminately.

164 Final Agenda, 1969 conference.

165 Nor was it only Labour's representatives in the Oireachtas who came in for a hard time. There were also calls for Labour members on county councils, corporations and urban councils 'to be instructed in future to vote together as a party on policy issues and not be allowed divide, as in the past'. The behaviour of local representatives was also subjected to criticism by a letter written by a Cork-based member published in *Hibernia* (11 Apr. 1969). If the large numbers of Labour local authority members who did not vote the party ticket in the Seanad elections later that year is anything to go by, this slap on the wrist did precious little good. See Labour Party Annual Report, 1969–70, pp. 20–1.

166 Constitution Review Committee, Discussion document no. 1, 'Expanding the role of the party membership', p. 22.

167 *Irish Times*, 27 Jan. 1969.

168 The intention was to conduct a series of meetings in every constituency on the matter but this was upset when the general election was called. Labour Party Annual Report, 1969–70, p. 24.

169 Gilchrist, 'The Irish political situation'.

170 *Irish Times*, 27 Jan. 1969.

171 *Irish Socialist*, Feb. 1969.

172 *Hibernia*, 19 Dec. 1969.

173 The results of the poll were subsequently published in *Nusight* in November 1969.

174 Information from Brendan Halligan, 8 May 2002.

175 Gallagher, *Irish Labour Party*, p. 87.

176 *Nusight*, July 1969.

177 Halligan, 1969 Election Report, 18 Sept. 1969, Ely Place.

178 AC minutes, 14 May 1969. LPA.

179 Halligan, 1969 Election Report, 18 Sept. 1969, Ely Place.

180 Ibid.

181 *Canvassers' Notes*, courtesy of Barry Desmond.

182 Tobin, *Best of Decades*, p. 216.

183 *Irish Times*, 17 June 1969.

184 David Thornley in the *Irish Independent*, 29 June 1969.

185 Horgan, *Price of Power*, p. 70; Interview with Betty Dowling, Jan. 2002.

186 Gallagher, *Irish Labour Party*, p. 91.

187 *Irish Times*, 30 May 1969.

188 *Irish Times*, 7 June 1969.

189 Peter Berry diaries, 22 May 1969 in *Magill*, June 1980.

190 Gallagher, *Irish Labour Party*, p. 93.

191 Labour Party Annual Report, 1969–70, p. 16.

192 Cruise O'Brien, *Memoirs*, p. 319.

193 Gilchrist to Stewart, Irish Election, 25 June 1969, FCO33/1753.

194 Howard to Owen Sheehy Skeffington, n.d. NLI, Sheehy Skeffington papers, MS 40,489/10.

195 Gallagher, *Irish Labour Party*, p. 91.

196 Ibid., p. 92.

197 *Nusight*, July 1969.

198 Ibid.

199 Quoted in Stephen Collins, *Cosgrave Legacy* (Dublin, 1996), p. 99.

200 *Nusight*, July 1969.

201 *Irish Times*, 15 Mar.; 22 Mar.; 31 May 1969.

202 See, for instance, *Irish Times*, 14 June 1969 for John Healy's account of David Thornley leading a most precious blood procession through Cabra.

203 See, for example, interview with Betty Dowling, Jan. 2002.

204 Gilchrist to Stewart, Forthcoming election in Irish Republic, 29 May 1969, TNA FCO33/1753.

205 O'Brien, *Memoir*, p. 321–2.

206 *Sunday Independent*, 29 June 1969.

207 *Irish Times*, 14 June 1969.

208 Ibid., 16 June 1969.

209 Ibid.

210 Horgan, *Browne*, p. 232.

211 *Nusight*, July 1969.

212 Brendan Halligan, 1969 General Election Report, 18 Sept. 1969. Ely Place.

213 Interview with Brendan Halligan, Feb. 2002; Halligan in *Irish Times*, July 1982; Labour Party Annual Report, 1969–70, p. 14; *Nusight*, July 1969.

214 *Hibernia*, 18 July 1969.

215 *Hibernia*, 27 June 1969.

TEN: SMOKY MISDIRECTION

1 Quoted in the *New Statesman*, 1 Oct. 1965.

2 DD vol. 241, col. 32–41, 2 July 1969.

3 Sheehy Skefffington to Cruise O'Brien, 7 July 1969, NLI, O. Sheehy Skeffington papers, MS 40,489/9.

4 T. F. O'Higgins, *A Double Life* (Dublin, 1996), p. 216.

5 DD vol. 241, col. 41, 2 July 1969.

6   Stephen Collins, *The Cosgrave Legacy* (Dublin, 1996), pp. 102–3.

7   *Hibernia*, 27 June 1969.

8   John O'Connell, *Doctor John: Crusading Doctor and Politician* (Dublin, 1989), p. 99.

9   *Nusight*, Aug. 1969.

10   Ibid.

11   Memo to the AC on Annual Conference 1970, 14 Nov. 1969, LP Ely Place.

12   AC minutes, 14 Nov. 1969, LP Ely Place.

13   *Hibernia*, 6 Feb. 1970.

14   Ibid.

15   Ibid., 24 Oct. 1969.

16   Only Dublin South East, Dublin North Central and Dublin South County were found not guilty of intra-party fighting. Brendan Halligan, 1969 General Election Report, 18 Sept. 1969. Labour Party papers, Ely Place.

17   AC minutes, 18 Sept. 1969, LP Ely Place.

18   Ibid.

19   *Hibernia*, 20 Feb. 1970.

20   AC minutes, 14 Nov. 1969.

21   *Hibernia*, 20 Feb. 1970.

22   AC minutes, 12 Feb. 1970.

23   Butler campaigned for Gay Mitchell, who played up his working-class background and membership of the WUI and only ever 'pronounced the words "Fine Gael" in a whisper'. *Hibernia*, 6 Mar. 1970.

24   David Blatherwick to FCO, 10 Mar. 1970, TNA FCO 33/1203.

25   *Hibernia*, 20 Mar. 1970.

26   *Nusight*, May 1970.

27   AC minutes, 14 Nov. 1969, LP Ely Place.

28   *Nusight*, May 1970; Barry Desmond, *Finally and In Conclusion: A Political Memoir* (Dublin, 2000), p. 158.

29   The account of Coughlan and the Maoists which follows is based on an article in *Nusight*, May 1970.

30   *Nusight*, May 1970; See also *This Week*, 13 Mar. 1970.

31   AC minutes, 18 Mar. 1970, LP Ely Place.

32   Michael Gallagher, *The Irish Labour Party in Transition 1957–82* (Dublin, 1982), p. 106.

33   *Irish Times*, 27 Apr. 1970.

34   Mícheál MacGréil, *Prejudice and Tolerance in Ireland* (Dublin 1977), p. 333.

35   AC minutes, 30 Apr. 1970, LP Ely Place.

36   Ibid.

37   General Secretary's report to the AC, 30 Apr. 1970, LP Ely Place.

38   *Irish Times*, 16 Apr. 1970.

39   Ibid., 18 Apr. 1970.

40   *Irish Press*, 13 May 1970.

41   AC minutes, 6 May 1970, LP Ely Place.

42   DD vol. 246, col. 1764, 14 May 1970.

43   Ibid., col. 1566.

44   *This Week*, 29 May 1970.

45 AC minutes, 20 May 1970, LP Ely Place.

46 See Cruise O'Brien, *States of Ireland*, p. 204. The PLP met to discuss the question on 3 June.

47 See for example Blatherwick, 5 June 1970, TNA FCO 331/1202.

48 AC minutes, 25 Aug. 1970, LP Ely Place.

49 AC minutes, 4 Nov. 1970, LP Ely Place.

50 See AC minute book, LP Ely Place.

51 AC minutes, 9 Dec. 1970, LP Ely Place.

52 *Irish Times*, 14 Dec. 1970.

53 Gallagher, *Irish Labour Party*, p. 184.

54 *Irish Times*, 14 Dec. 1970.

55 *Hibernia*, 18 Dec. 1970.

56 See AC minutes, LP Ely Place.

57 *Irish Times*, 14 Dec. 1970.

58 Gallagher, *Irish Labour Party*, p. 109.

59 AC minutes, 4 Nov. 1970, Ely Place.

60 John Horgan, *Noel Browne: Passionate Outsider* (Dublin, 2000), p. 236.

61 American Embassy, Dec. 1970, NAM.

62 *Irish Times*, 14 Dec. 1970.

63 Horgan, *Browne*, p. 236.

64 *Irish Times*, 14 Dec. 1970.

65 Blatherwick to Thorpe, 17 Dec. 1970, TNA FCO 331/1202.

66 *Hibernia*, 18 Dec. 1970.

67 American Embassy, Dec. 1970, NAM.

68 *Irish Times*, 14 Dec. 1970; Blatherwick to Thorpe, 17 Dec. 1970, TNA FCO 331/1202.

69 Blatherwick to Thorpe, 17 Dec. 1970.

70 Communism in Ireland, 1970, TNA FCO 33/1204.

71 Conor Cruise O'Brien, *Memoir: My Life and Themes* (Dublin, 1998), p. 338.

72 AC minutes, 10 Feb. 1971, LP Ely Place.

73 AC minutes, 23 Dec. 1970, LP Ely Place.

74 Gallagher, *Irish Labour Party*, p. 110.

75 Blatherwick to Thorpe, 3 Mar. 1971, TNA FCO 33/1598.

76 Ibid.

77 *Irish Press*, 1 Mar. 1971.

78 Resolutions passed by the socialist republican unity conference, Ely Place.

79 AC minutes, 27 Mar. 1971, LP Ely Place.

80 Manifesto of the Liaison of the Left Committee, n.d. (1972), ILHM&A LP 170/002.

81 D. McKittrick et al. (eds), *Lost Lives* (Edinburgh, 1999), pp. 31, 47, 61.

82 J. Bowyer Bell, *The IRA 1916–1979* (Dublin, 1990), p. 380.

83 McKittrick et al. (eds), *Lost Lives*, pp. 79–88.

84 Cruise O'Brien, *Memoir*, p. 332.

85 Ibid., pp. 332–4; Conor Cruise O'Brien, *States of Ireland* (London, 1974), p. 284.

86 Thornley to Corish, 13 Aug. 1971.

87 I. McAllister, *The Northern Ireland Social Democratic and Labour Party* (London, 1977), p. 41.

88 Minutes of meeting of Liaison Committee, 24 Apr. 1970, LP Ely Place.

89 Labour Party press release, 24 Aug. 1971, LP Ely Place.

90   General Secretary's Report, 16 Sept. 1971.

91   Text of statement, n.d., ILHM&A Corish deposit, Box 2.

92   Tony Benn, *Office Without Power: Diaries 1968–72* (London, 1988), p. 389.

93   *Hibernia*, Sept. 1971.

94   AC minutes 16 Sept. 1971, LP Ely Place.

95   Blatherwick to Thorpe, 27 Oct. 1971, TNA FCO 33/1598.

96   Minutes of joint meeting PLP and AC, 23 Sept. 1971.

97   See for example minutes of joint meeting PLP and AC, 23 Sept. 1971.

98   Report of aggregate meeting of DRC, 11 Sept. 1971, ILHM&A Corish papers.

99   Minutes of joint meeting PLP and AC, 23 Sept. 1971.

100 Blatherwick to Thorpe, 27 Oct. 1971, TNA FCO 33/1598.

101 Thornley to Cluskey, 7 Dec. 1971; Thornley to Corish 7 Dec. 1971. Corish deposit, box 2 ILHM&A.

102 *The Times*, 13 Dec. 1971.

103 Ibid.

104 DD vol. 257, col. 2496, 16 Dec. 1971.

105 Blatherwick to Bone, 21 Dec. 1971, TNA FCO 33/1598.

106 Treacy to Corish, Corish deposit, box 2 ILHSM&A.

107 Barry Desmond to Conor Cruise O'Brien, 31 Dec. 1971, Corish deposit, box 2 ILHM&A.

108 AC meeting, 6 Jan. 1972, LP Ely Place.

109 Blatherwick to Bone, 13 Jan. 1972, TNA FCO 33/1598.

110 Ibid.

111 *Hibernia*, 7 Jan. 1972.

112 LP Ely Place.

113 Quoted in Blatherwick to Bone, 29 Feb. 1972, FCO 87/9.

114 Blatherwick to Bone, 29 Feb. 1972, FCO 87/9.

115 *Hibernia*, 3 Mar. 1972.

116 Ibid.

117 Ibid.

118 Blatherwick to Bone, 29 Feb. 1972, FCO 87/9.

119 For O'Connell's account of the meetings see O'Connell, *Dr John*, pp. 124–44.

120 G. L. Angel, Note of meeting with Dr O'Connell, 27 Jan. 1972, FCO 87/30.

121 Angel, note for the record, 28 Jan. 1972, FCO 87/30.

122 Ibid.

123 Telegram from O'Connell to Angel, 4 Feb. 1972, TNA FCO 87/30.

124 Evans to Bone, 9 Mar. 1972, TNA FCO87/1.

125 O'Connell, *Dr John*, p. 127.

126 Peck to FCO, 10 Mar. 1972, TNA FCO 87/1.

127 Cruise O'Brien, *States of Ireland*, p. 268.

128 Brendan Anderson, *Joe Cahill: A Life in the IRA* (Dublin 2002), p. 248.

129 The First Secretary in the Australian Embassy told Blatherwick of the British Embassy that O'Connell had told *him* about 'the whole affair', although he had 'sworn him to total secrecy' in doing so. Blatherwick to White, 20 Mar. 1972, FCO 87/32.

130 The Hansard account of his speech in the Commons on 20 Mar. 1972 was retained by FCO, headlined 'Harold Wilson's "version" of his visit'.

131 O'Connell, *Dr John*, p. 135.

132 Blatherwick to Bone, 23 Mar. 1972, FCO 87/9.

133 O'Connell, *Dr John*, p. 135.

134 *Hibernia*, 10 Sept. 1971 noted rumours of a split around the time of the first arms trial.

135 Peck to White, 19 July 1972 FCO87/32.

136 Ibid.

137 Rough notes on talks with British Labour Party delegation on 19 July 1972. ILHM&A LP 046/1.

138 O'Brien to Halligan, 17 Aug. 1972, ILHM&A LP 066/006.

139 AC minutes, 7 Sept. 1972, LP Ely Place.

140 Gallagher, *Irish Labour Party*, p. 149.

141 Ibid.; Paddy Devlin, *Straight Left: An Autobiography* (Belfast, 1993), pp. 187–8.

142 Cruise O'Brien, *Memoir*, p. 339.

143 Ibid.

144 *This Week*, 7 Aug. 1970.

145 See poll in *Nusight*, Apr. 1970, pp. 67–8.

146 *This Week*, 7 Aug. 1970.

147 Ibid.

148 Emergency report of political committee to AC meeting, 3 June 1971, LP Ely Place.

149 In the summer of 1971 Justin Keating addressed seminars on the EEC in Waterford and Cork. Fifty people turned up for the Waterford seminar which was considered 'very successful', but only 20 attended the one in Cork, a 'debacle' blamed on the poor state of the Cork organisation.

150 The committee was chaired by Keating, who was joined by Michael D. Higgins, Des Bonass, Tom O'Brien, Bill Conroy and Niall Greene. Halligan to AC, 20 Mar. 1970, LP Ely Place.

151 *Hibernia*, 14 Apr. 1972.

152 AC minutes, 25 Nov. 1971, LP Ely Place.

153 AC minutes, 15 Mar. 1972, LP Ely Place.

154 Michael D. Higgins, Niall Greene, Matt Merrigan and Liam Hamilton.

155 AC minutes, 31 May 1972, LP Ely Place.

156 See for example *Hibernia*, 3 Mar. 1972.

157 See for example Cruise O'Brien, *States of Ireland*, p. 273.

158 Press release, 13 June 1972.

159 Gallagher, *Irish Labour Party*, p. 189.

160 Ibid.

161 AC minutes, 12 Oct. 1972. LP Ely Place; Annual Report, p. 18.

162 Corish pocket diary 1972, ILHM&A Corish deposit.

163 Ibid., 1973.

164 Garret FitzGerald, *All in a Life* (Dublin, 1991), p. 107.

165 See DD vol. 264, col. 834, 1 Dec. 1972 for Labour's response.

166 *The Times*, 27 Nov. 1972.

167 DD vol. 264, col. 830, 1 Dec. 1972; O'Higgins, *A Double Life*, p. 252.

168 Dermot Keogh, *Twentieth Century Ireland* (Dublin, 1994), p. 317.

169 Those voting against the bill were the 17 members of the PLP, Neil Blaney, Paudge Brennan, Desmond Foley and Seán Sherwin (independents) and Edward Collins and Oliver J. Flannagan (FG).

170 O'Higgins, *Double Life*, p. 257.

171 AC minutes, 5 Jan. 1973, LP Ely Place.

172 General election Dec. 1972, Plan of action, 1 Dec. 1972. ILHM&A Corish deposit, box 2.

173 Corish pocket diary, 1973. ILHM&A Corish deposit, Box 1. Most accounts of this period, including O'Higgins's, fail to mention this meeting.

174 Memorandum of coalition negotiations, 29 Jan. 1973. ILHM&A Corish deposit, box 2.

175 Halligan to Corish, 28 June 1972. ILHM&A Corish deposit, Box 2.

176 Memorandum of coalition negotiations, 29 Jan. 1973. ILHM&A Corish deposit, box 2.

177 Gallagher, *Irish Labour Party*, p. 190.

178 Corish diary 1973, ILHM&A Corish deposit, Box 1.

179 Statement of intent, ILHM&A Corish deposit, Box 2.

180 AC minutes, 9 Feb. 1973, LP Ely Place.

181 Merrigan to Halligan, 8 Feb. 1973, ILHM&A Corish deposit, box 2.

182 Labour Party Annual Report, 1972–3, p. 20.

183 Ibid., pp. 30–1.

184 Horgan, *Browne*, p. 246.

185 Cornelius O'Leary, *Irish Elections 1918–77: Parties, Voters and Proportional Representation* (Dublin, 1979), p. 80.

186 Vincent Browne (ed.), *Magill Book of Irish Politics* (Dublin, 1981), p. 27.

187 Karl Marx, *The Eighteenth Brumaire of Louis Bonaparte* (1852).

CONCLUSION: LABOUR'S PROUD HISTORY?

1   See for example, p. 30 above.

2   Patrick Lindsay, *Memories* (Dublin, 1992), p. 178.

3   See p. 185 above.

4   Basil Chubb, *The Government and Politics of Ireland* (Oxford, 1971), p. 76.

Bibliography

—

PRIMARY SOURCES

MANUSCRIPTS

IRISH LABOUR HISTORY MUSEUM AND ARCHIVE (ILHM&A)
Workers' Union of Ireland/Jim Larkin Junior
John Horgan
Seán Dunne
William Norton/ Post Office Workers' Union
John Goodwillie
Joe Deasy
Irish Women's Workers Union
DTUC Council Minutes
Cathal O'Shannon
Labour Party
Brendan Corish papers

UNIVERSITY COLLEGE DUBLIN ARCHIVES (UCDA)
John de Courcy Ireland P29
Fred Cowan P34
Barry Desmond P56
Seán MacEntee P67
Desmond Ryan LA10
Richard Mulcahy P7
Seán MacEoin P151
Patrick McGilligan P35
Fianna Fáil P176
Éamon de Valera P150
Fine Gael P39
John A. Costello P190

NATIONAL LIBRARY OF IRELAND (NLI)
Brendan Corish papers 1948–51 (unlisted)
Rosamund Jacob
Seán O'Casey
William O'Brien
Owen Sheehy Skeffington
Thomas Johnson

DUBLIN DIOCESAN ARCHIVE (DDA)
John Charles McQuaid papers

TRINITY COLLEGE DUBLIN MANUSCRIPT ROOM (TCDM)
Arnold Marsh

Labour Party, Ely Place
Minutes of the Administrative Council

LABOUR HISTORY ARCHIVE AND STUDY CENTRE, MANCHESTER (LHASC,M)
William Gillies Papers
Communist Party of Great Britain papers
Denis Healey papers

NATIONAL ARCHIVES, KEW (TNA)
Foreign and Commonwealth Office

NATIONAL ARCHIVES, MARYLAND

CORK CITY & COUNTY ARCHIVES
Seamus Fitzgerald papers

PRIVATE COLLECTIONS
Donal Nevin
Barry Desmond

GOVERNMENT RECORDS

NATIONAL ARCHIVES OF IRELAND (NAI)
Irish Congress of Trade Unions
Cabinet papers
Department of Justice
Department of Finance
Military Archives 2006 release
Department of Foreign Affairs (DFA)
Department of an Taoiseach (D/T)

MILITARY ARCHIVES
Military Intelligence

LABOUR, LEFT WING AND TRADE UNION PERIODICALS AND REPORTS

Annual Reports of the Administrative Council of the Irish Labour Party (1930–73)
Annual Reports of the Irish Labour Party and Trade Union Congress (1918–29)
Annual Reports of the Irish Trade Union Congress (1930–58)
Annual Reports of the PUTUO/ Irish Congress of Trade Unions (1959–73)
The Boro' Bulletin (1967) Dun Laoghaire–Rathdown branch of the Labour Party
Bulletin (Monthly journal of the WUI)
Canvassers' Notes (Labour Party, 1969 General Election)
The Citizen (Freeman publications, 1949)
Corish, Brendan, *The New Republic* (1967).
An Díon (Post Office Workers' Union, 1926–35)
Flagstaff (Monthly newsletter, Irish Labour Party, 1952–4)
Fox, R. M., *Labour in the National Struggle* (Labour Party propaganda department, Dublin, c.1945).
Hawkins, John, *The Irish Question Today* (Fabian Society, Research series no. 54, Feb. 1941).
Impact (Freeman publications, 1951)
Irish Democrat (Connolly Association, London)
The Irishman (Labour Party, 1927–30)
Irish People (Labour Party, 1944–8)
Irish Socialist (Monthly newspaper of the Irish Workers' League, 1961–5)
Irish Workers Voice (Monthly newspaper of the Irish Workers' League, 1949–56)
Johnson, Thomas, *Planning for a New Order in Ireland: Economic Aims* (Dublin, 1943).
Labour (Dublin Regional Council of the Labour Party)
Labour (Labour Party, 1967)
Labour and Ireland – Notes for Trade Unionists (Dec 1965), Churchtown Branch of the Labour Party, Dec. 1965).
Labour News (Labour Party – Dublin South West, 1965–6)
Labour News (Labour Party, 1936–8)
Labour's Way (William Norton's speech to Labour Party special conference, March 1958)
Liberty [1957–69] (ITGWU)
MacAonghusa, Proinsias (ed.), *Corish Speaks* (1966)
New Leader (Independent Labour Party)
The Pioneer (ILP&TUC monthly newsletter, c.1924–7)
The Plough (Independent socialist monthly 1957–64)
Review (incorporating the *Irish Workers' Weekly*, 1945–8)
An Solas/ Workers' Republic (Journal of the Irish Workers' League, 1965–71)
The Spark/An Splanc (Waterford Labour Party)
Torch (Dublin Constituencies Council, Labour Party, 1939–44)
Torch (Dublin Unemployed Association, 1953–4)
Trade Union Information (ITUC 1949–)
Tribune (London, c.1963–72)
Voice of Labour (ITGWU)
Watchword of Labour

NEWSPAPERS AND JOURNALS

The Bell
Business and Finance
Campus/UCD News
Clann Bulletin
Confrontation (Students for Democratic
    Action)
Cork Examiner
Doctrine and Life
Dublin Evening Mail
Dublin Opinion
Grille
Hibernia
Irish Review and Annual (*Irish Times*)
Irish Independent
Irish Press
Irish Rosary

Irish Times
The Kerryman
The Leader
Magill
Munster Express
National Observer (Fine Gael, 1959–60)
The New Statesman
Nusight
Profile
Sunday Independent
Sunday Review
Sunday Press
The Furrow
This Week
The Times (London)
United Irishman

OFFICIAL DOCUMENTS

Dáil Debates
Report of the Commission on Vocational Organisation

INTERVIEWS

Owen Dudley Edwards, 21 October 1999
Donal Nevin, 12 November 1999, 28 April 2000
Proinsias MacAonghusa, November 1999
John de Courcy Ireland, 9 December 1999
Joe Deasy, 9 March 2000
Deasún Breathnach, 31 March 2001
Vincent McDowell, 12 April 2001
Garret FitzGerald, November 2002
Niall Greene, November 2002
Betty Dowling, January 2002
Brendan Halligan, 8 February 2002
Jack Gannon, March 2003
Ruairí Quinn, March 2003
Declan Costello, 22 August 2006

ORAL HISTORIES

Bergin, Paddy, 'A Labour consciousness in Carlow: The young Paddy Bergin: 1916–1950', *Saothar* 6 (1980), pp. 109–17.

Devine, Francis, 'Reminiscence – socialist trade unionist: Matt Merrigan's political formation', *Saothar* 12 (1987), pp. 94–106.

Kilmurray, Evanne 'Reminiscence – Joe Deasy: the evolution of an Irish Marxist, 1941–1950', *Saothar* 13 (1988), pp. 112–19.

Interview with Matt Merrigan broadcast on *A Week in Politics*, RTÉ 12 Dec. 1998.

Cathal Óg O'Shannon, 'Journeys around my father', RTÉ Radio 1, 13 Aug. 2003.

UNPUBLISHED MEMOIRS

Arnold Marsh
Gilbert Lynch
Matt Merrigan

SECONDARY SOURCES

BOOKS

Allen, Kieran, *Fianna Fáil and Irish Labour, 1926 to Present* (London, 1997).

Anderson, Brendan, *Joe Cahill: A Life in the IRA* (Dublin, 2002).

Andrews, C. S., *Man of No Property* (Dublin, 1982).

Augusteijn, Joost (ed.), *Ireland in the 1930s: New Perspectives* (Dublin, 1999).

Barrington, Ruth, *Health, Medicine and Politics* (Dublin, 1987).

Benn, Tony, *Office Without Power: Diaries 1968–72* (London, 1988).

Berresford Ellis, Peter, *A History of the Irish Working Class* (London, 1996).

Bew, Paul, Ellen Hazelkorn and Henry Patterson, *Dynamics of Irish Politics* (London, 1989).

Bew, Paul and Henry Patterson, *Séan Lemass and the Making of Modern Ireland 1945–66* (Dublin, 1982).

Bowyer Bell, J., *The Secret Army: The IRA 1916–1979* (Dublin, 1990).

Bowyer Bell, J., *The Gun in Irish Politics: An Analysis of Irish Political Conflict, 1916–1986* (New Brunswick, 1987).

Breathnach, Máirtín, *Republican Days: 75 Years of Fianna Fáil* (Dublin, 2002).

Browne, Noel, *Against the Tide* (Dublin, 1986).

Browne, Vincent (ed.), *Magill Book of Irish Politics* (Dublin, 1981).

Bolster, Evelyn, *The Knights of the Order of St Columbanus* (Dublin, 1979).

Busteed, M. A., *Voting Behaviour in the Republic of Ireland: A Geographical Perspective* (Oxford, 1990).

Callaghan, James, *A House Divided: The Dilemma of Northern Ireland* (London, 1973).

Canning, Paul, *British Policy towards Ireland: 1921–1941* (Oxford, 1985).

Chubb, Basil, *Government and Politics of Ireland* (Oxford, 1971).

Coakley, John and Michael Gallagher (eds), *Politics in the Republic of Ireland* (Dublin, 1993).

Cody, Séamus, John O'Dowd and Peter Rigney, *The Parliament of Labour: 100 Years of the Dublin Council of Trade Unions* (Dublin, 1986).

Collins, Stephen, *Spring and the Labour Story* (Dublin, 1993).

Collins, Stephen, *The Cosgrave Legacy* (Dublin, 1996).

Cooney, John, *John Charles McQuaid: Ruler of Catholic Ireland* (Dublin, 1999).

Cousins, Mel, *The Birth of Social Welfare in Ireland, 1922–52* (Dublin, 2003).

Cronin, Mike, *The Blueshirts and Irish Politics* (Dublin, 1997).

Crowe, C. et al. (eds), *Documents on Irish Foreign Policy* IV: *1932–1936* (Dublin, 2004).

Cruise O'Brien, Conor, *States of Ireland* (London, 1974).

Cruise O'Brien, Conor, *Memoir: My Life and Themes* (Dublin, 1998).

Cullen, Mary and Maria Luddy (eds), *Female Activists: Irish Women and Change 1900–1960* (Dublin, 2001).

Cullen Owens, Rosemary, *Louie Bennett* (Cork, 2001).

Daly, Mary E., *Social and Economic History of Ireland since 1800* (Dublin, 1981).

Daly, Mary E., *The Buffer State: The Historical Roots of the Department of the Environment.* (Dublin, 1997).

Deeny, James, *To Cure or to Care: Memoirs of a Chief Medical Officer* (Dun Laoghaire, 1991).

Delaney, Enda, *Demography, State and Society: Irish Migration to Britain, 1921–1971* (Liverpool, 2000).

Dell, Edmund, *A Strange and Eventful History: Democratic Socialism in Britain* (London, 2000).

Desmond, Barry, *Finally and In Conclusion: A Political Memoir* (Dublin, 2000).

Devlin, Paddy, *Straight Left: An Autobiography* (Belfast, 1993).

Dunphy, Richard, *The Making of Fianna Fáil Power in Ireland, 1923–1948* (Oxford, 1995).

English, Richard, *Radicals in the Republic: Socialist Republicanism in the Irish Free State, 1925–1937* (Oxford, 1994).

English, Richard, *Armed Struggle: A History of the IRA* (London, 2003).

Fallon, Gabriel, *An Age of Innocence: Irish Culture 1930–1960* (Dublin, 1998).

Fanning, Ronan, *Independent Ireland* (Dublin, 1983).

Fanning, Ronan, *The Irish Department of Finance 1922–1958* (Dublin, 1978).

Farrell, Brian, *Chairman or Chief? The Role of Taoiseach in Irish Government* (Dublin, 1971).

Farrell, Brian, *Seán Lemass* (Dublin, 1983).

Farrell, Brian (ed.), *The Creation of the Dáil* (Dublin, 1994).

Faulkner, Pádraig, *As I Saw It* (Dublin, 2005).

Ferriter, Diarmaid, *The Transformation of Ireland 1900–2000* (London, 2004).

Fielding, Steven, *Class and Ethnicity: Irish Catholics in England 1880–1939* (Buckingham, 1993).

Fielding, Steven, *The Labour Party: 'Socialism' and Society since 1951* (Manchester, 1997).

FitzGerald, Garret, *All in a Life* (Dublin, 1991).

Foley, Donal, *Three Villages: An Autobiography* (Dublin, 1997).

Fox, R. M., *History of the Irish Citizen Army* (Dublin, 1943).

Fox, R. M., *James Connolly: The Forerunner* (Dublin, 1946).

Fox, R. M., *Jim Larkin: The Rise of the Underman* (London, 1957).

Gaughan, J. Anthony, *Thomas Johnson* (Dublin, 1980).

Gallagher, Michael, *The Irish Labour Party in Transition 1957–82* (Dublin, 1982).

Gallagher, Michael, *Irish Elections 1922–1944: Results and Analysis* (Dublin, 1993).

Gallagher, Michael and Michael Marsh, *Days of Blue Loyalty: The Politics of Membership of the Fine Gael Party* (Dublin, 2002),

Garvin, Tom, *1922: The Birth of Irish Democracy.*

Garvin, Tom, *Preventing the Future: Why Was Ireland Poor For So Long?* (Dublin, 2004).

Gaughan, J. Anthony, *Alfred O'Rahilly*, 3 vols (Dublin, 1986–93).

Gaughan, J. Anthony, *Thomas Johnson: 1872–1963: First Leader of the Labour Party in Dáil Éireann* (Dublin, 1980).

Girvin, Brian and Gary Murphy (eds), *The Lemass Era: Politics and Society in the Ireland of Seán Lemass* (Dublin, 2005).

Greaves, C. Desmond, *The Irish Transport and General Workers' Union: The Formative Years* (Dublin, 1982).

Hanley, Brian, *The IRA 1926–1936* (Dublin, 2002).

Harte, Paddy, *Young Tigers and Mongrel Foxes: A Life in Politics* (Dublin, 2005).

Heron, Marianne, *Sheila Conroy: Fighting Spirit* (Dublin, 1993).

Hill, J. R (ed.), *A New History of Ireland*, VII: *Ireland 1921–1984* (Oxford, 2004).

Hopkinson, Michael, *Green against Green: The Irish Civil War* (Dublin, 1988).

Hogan, James, *Could Ireland Become Communist?* (Cork, 1935).

Horgan, John, *Broadcasting and Public Life: RTÉ News and Current Affairs, 1926–1997* (Dublin, 2004).

Horgan, John, *Irish Media: A Critical History since 1922* (London, 2001).

Horgan, John, *Labour: The Price of Power* (Dublin, 1986).

Horgan, John, *Seán Lemass: The Enigmatic Patriot* (Dublin, 1997).

Horgan, John, *Noel Browne: Passionate Outsider* (Dublin, 2000).

Inglis, Brian, *West Briton* (London, 1962).

Inglis, Brian, *Downstart* (London, 1990).

Jay, A (ed.), *The Oxford Dictionary of Political Quotations* (3rd edn, Oxford, 2006).

Jefferys, Kevin, *The Labour Party Since 1945* (London, 1993).

Johnston, Roy, *A Century of Endeavour* (Dublin, 2006).

Jordan, Anthony, *Seán MacBride* (Dublin, 1993).

Kelleher, Derry, *Buried Alive in Ireland: A Story of a Twentieth Century Inquisition* (Greystones, 2001).

Kennedy, Michael and Eunan O'Halpin, *Ireland and the Council of Europe: From Isolation to Integration* (Strasbourg, 2000).

Keogh, Dermot and Mervyn O'Driscoll (eds), *Ireland in World War Two: Diplomacy and Survival* (Cork, 2004).

Keogh, Dermot, *Twentieth Century Ireland* (Dublin, 1994).

Kirby, Dianne (ed.), *Religion and the Cold War* (Basingstoke and New York, 2003).

Kissane, Bill, *Explaining Irish Democracy* (Dublin, 2002).

Klaus, H. Gustav (ed.), *Strong Words: Brave Deeds: The Poetry, Life and Times of Thomas O'Brien. Volunteer in the Spanish Civil War* (Dublin, 1994).

Krause, David (ed.), *Letters of Seán O'Casey*, 4 vols (New York, 1980), II: 1942–54.

Laffan, Michael, *The Resurrection of Ireland: The Sinn Féin Party 1916–1923* (Cambridge, 1999).

Lane, Fintan and Donal Ó Drisceoil (eds), *Politics and the Irish Working Class, 1830–1945* (Basingstoke, 2005).

Larkin, Emmet, *James Larkin: Irish Labour leader 1876–1947* (London, 1965).

Larkin, Jim, *In the Footsteps of Big Jim: A family biography* (Dublin, 1996).

Layburn, Keith, *The Rise of Labour: The British Labour Party 1890–1979* (London, 1988).

Lee, J. J. (ed.), *Ireland 1945–70* (Dublin, 1980).

Lee, J. J., *Ireland 1912–1985: Politics and Society* (Cambridge, 1989).

Lindsay, Patrick, *Memories* (Dublin, 1992).

Longford, Earl of and T. P. O'Neill, *Eamon de Valera* (London, 1970).

Lyons, F. S. L., *Ireland Since the Famine* (London, 1971).

Lysaght, D. R. O'Connor, *The Irish Republic* (Cork, 1970).

MacBride, Seán, *That Day's Struggle: A Memoir 1904–1951*, ed. Caitriona Lawlor (Dublin 2005).

McAllister, Ian, *The Northern Ireland Social Democratic and Labour Party* (London, 1977).

McCarthy, Charles, *Trade Unions in Ireland, 1894–1960* (Dublin, 1977).

McCarthy, Charles, *Decade of Upheaval: Irish Trade Unions in the 1960s* (Dublin, 1973).

McCarthy, John F (ed.), *Planning Ireland's Future: The Legacy of T. K. Whitaker* (Dublin, 1990).

McCartney, Donal, *UCD: A National Idea. The History of University College Dublin* (Dublin, 1999).

McCullagh, David, *A Makeshift Majority: The First Inter-party Government, 1948–51* (Dublin, 1998).

MacDermott, Eithne, *Clann na Poblachta* (Cork, 1998).

Macdona, Anne (ed.), *From Newman to New Woman: UCD Women Remember* (Dublin, 2001).

MacEoin, Seán P., *Communism and Ireland* (Cork, 1948).

MacEoin, Uinsenn (ed.), *Survivors* (Dublin, 1980).

MacEoin, Uinseann (ed.), *The IRA in the Twilight Years, 1923–1948* (Dublin, 1997).

McGarry, Fearghal, *Irish Politics and the Spanish Civil War* (Cork, 1999).

McGarry, Fearghal, *Frank Ryan* (Dublin, 2002).

McGarry, Fearghal, *Eoin O'Duffy* (Oxford, 2005).

MacGréil, Mícheál, *Prejudice and Tolerance in Ireland* (Dublin, 1977).

McKittrick, David, S. Kelters, B. Feeney and C. Thornton, *Lost Lives* (Edinburgh, 1999).

McMahon, Deirdre, *Republicans and Imperialists: Anglo-Irish Relations in the 1930s* (London, 1984).

Maguire, Martin, *Servants to the Public: A History of the Local Government and Public Service Union 1901–1990* (Dublin, 1998).

Manning, Maurice, *Irish Political Parties: An Introduction* (Dublin, 1972).

Manning, Maurice, *James Dillon: A Biography* (Dublin, 1999).

Manning, Maurice, *The Blueshirts* (Dublin, 1970).

Mansergh, Nicholas, *The Irish Free State: Its Government and Politics* (London, 1934).

Meenan, James, *The Irish Economy since 1922* (Liverpool, 1970).

Merrigan, Matt, *Eagle or Cuckoo? The Story of the ATGWU in Ireland* (Dublin, 1989).

Milotte, Mike, *Communism in Modern Ireland: The Pursuit of the Workers' Republic since 1916* (Dublin, 1984).

Mitchell, Arthur, *Labour in Irish Politics 1890–1930* (Dublin, 1974).

Moss, Warner, *Irish Political Parties* (New York and London, 1933).

Moynihan, Maurice, *Currency and Central Banking in Ireland, 1922–1960* (Dublin, 1975).

Mulcahy, Risteard, *Richard Mulcahy: A Family Memoir* (Dublin, 1999).

Murphy, John A., *Ireland in the Twentieth Century* (Dublin, 1989).

Murray, Christopher, *Seán O'Casey* (Dublin, 2004).

Murray, Patrick, *Oracles of God: The Roman Catholic Church and Irish Politics, 1922–37* (Dublin, 2000).

Nevin, Donal (ed.), *Trade Union Century* (Cork, 1994).

Nevin, Donal (ed.), *James Larkin: Lion of the Fold* (Dublin, 1998).

O'Brien, William, *Forth the Banners Go: Reminiscences of William O'Brien as told to Edward MacLysaght* (Dublin, 1969).

O'Connell, John, *Doctor John: Crusading Doctor and Politician* (Dublin, 1989).

O'Connell, T. J., *100 Years of Progress: The Story of the Irish National Teachers' Organisation 1868–1968* (Dublin, 1968).

O'Connor, Emmet, *A Labour History of Ireland* (Dublin, 1992).

O'Connor, Emmet, *A Labour History of Waterford* (Waterford, 1989).

O'Connor, Emmet, *Jim Larkin* (Cork, 2002).

O'Connor, Emmet, *Reds and the Green: Ireland, Russia and the Communist Internationals 1919–1943* (Dublin, 2004).

O'Connor, Kevin, *The Irish in Britain* (London, 1972).

Ó Corráin, Donnchadh, *James Hogan: Radical, Historian and Political Scientist* (Dublin, 2001).

Ó Drisceoil, Dónal, *Censorship in Ireland, 1939–1945: Neutrality, Politics and Society* (Cork, 1996).

Ó Drisceoil, Dónal, *Peadar O'Donnell* (Cork, 2001).

Ó Gráda, Cormac, *Ireland: A New Economic History* (Oxford, 1994).

O'Halpin, Eunan, *Defending Ireland: The Irish State and its Enemies since 1922* (Oxford, 1999).

O'hEithir, Breandán, *The Begrudger's Guide to Irish Politics* (Dublin, 1986).

O'Higgins, T. F., *A Double Life* (Dublin, 1996).

O'Leary, Cornelius, *Irish Elections 1918–77: Parties, Voters and Proportional Representation* (Dublin, 1979).

O'Leary, Don, *Vocationalism and Social Catholicism in Twentieth Century Ireland* (Dublin, 2000).

O'Riordan, Michael, *The Connolly Column* (Dublin, 1979).

Patterson, Henry, *The Politics of Illusion: A Political History of the IRA* (2nd edn, London, 1997).

Pettit, Philip (ed.), *The Gentle Revolution: Crisis in the Universities* (Dublin, 1969).

Pimlott, Ben, *Labour and the Left in the 1930s* (London, 1977).

Pimlott, Ben, *Harold Wilson* (London, 1992).

Quinn, Ruairí, *Straight Left: A Journey in Politics* (Dublin, 2005).

Rafter, Kevin, *The Clann* (Dublin, 1996).

Redmond, Seán, *The Irish Municipal Employees Trade Union 1883–1983* (Dublin, n.d.).

Regan, John M., *The Irish Counter-Revolution, 1921–1936: Treatyite Politics and Settlement in Independent Ireland* (Dublin, 1999).

Roberts, Ruaidhrí, *The People's College* (Dublin, 1986).

Robbins, Frank, *Under the Starry Plough: Recollections of the Irish Citizen Army* (Dublin, 1977).

Rumpf, Erhard and A. C. Hepburn, *Socialism and Nationalism in Twentieth Century Ireland* (Liverpool, 1977).

Ryan, W. P. *The Irish Labour Movement* (Dublin, 1919).

Sacks, Paul Martin, *Donegal Mafia: An Irish Political Machine* (London and New Haven, 1976).

Seyd, Patrick and Paul Whiteley, *Labour's Grass Roots: The Politics of Party Membership* (Oxford, 1992).

Sinnott, Richard, *Irish Voters Decide: Voting Behaviour in Elections and Referendums since 1918* (Manchester, 1995).

Skeffington, Andrée Sheehy, *Skeff: A Life of Owen Sheehy Skeffington* (Dublin, 1991).
Swift, John P., *John Swift: An Irish Dissident* (Dublin, 1991).
Tobin, Fergal, *The Best of Decades: Ireland in the 1960s* (Dublin, 1996).
Tormey, Bill, *Ten Years Hard Labour* (Dublin, 1994).
Thorpe, Andrew, *A History of the British Labour Party* (London, 1997).
Tweedy, Hilda, *A Link in the Chain: The Story of the Irish Housewives Association, 1942–1992* (Dublin, 1992).
Waters, John, *Jiving at the Crossroads* (Dublin, 1991).
Whelan, Bernadette, *Ireland and the Marshall Plan, 1947–57* (Dublin, 2000).
Whyte, J. H., *Church and State in Modern Ireland* (Dublin, 1980).
Whyte, J. H., *Catholics in Western Democracies: A study in Political Behaviour* (Dublin, 1981).
Yeats, Michael B., *Cast a Cold Eye: Memoirs of a poet's Son and Politician* (Dublin, 1998).

ARTICLES AND PAMPHLETS

Anon, *Communism in Ireland* (British and Irish Communist Association, Belfast n.d., *c.*1977).
Brown, Tony, 'Internationalism and international politics: The external links of the Labour Party', *Irish Studies in International Affairs* 1: 2 (1980), pp. 74–94
Buchanan, Tom, 'Great Britain', in T. Buchanan and M. Conway (eds), *Political Catholicism in Europe, 1918–1965* (Oxford, 1996), pp. 248–74.
Busteed, M. A. and Hugh Mason, 'Irish Labour in the 1969 election', *Political Studies* 18 (1970), pp. 373–9.
Byrne, Patrick, 'The Irish Republican Congress revisited' (Connolly Association, London, 1994).
Chubb, Basil, 'Ireland 1957' in D. E. Butler (ed.), *Elections Abroad* (London, 1959), pp. 183–228.
Coakley, John, 'Minor parties in Irish political life', *Economic and Social Review* 21: 3 (1990), pp. 269–97.
Connolly, Ross M., *The Labour Movement in County Wicklow* (Bray, 1992).
Corish, Brendan, 'Liberty and equality', *Everyman*, 1969.
Crossey, Ciaran and James Monaghan, 'The origins of Trotskyism in Ireland', *Revolutionary History* 6: 2/3 (Summer 1996), pp. 4–57.
Deasy, Joe, 'Thomas Johnson 1872–1963: Labour leader', *Labour History News* 8 (Autumn 1992).
Deasy, Joe, 'The fiery cross and letters from James Larkin Junior' document study, *Saothar* 21 (1996), pp. 121–8.
Deasy, Joe, *Fiery Cross: The Story of Jim Larkin* (2nd edn, Dublin, 2004).
Farrell, Brian, 'Labour and the Irish political party system: a suggested approach to analysis', *Economic and Social Review* 1: 4 (1969–70), pp. 477–502.
Farrell, Brian, 'Dáil deputies: "The 1969 generation"', *Economic and Social Review* 2: 3 (1970), pp. 309–27.
Farrell, Brian, 'The first Dáil and its constitutional documents' in B. Farrell (ed.), *The Creation of the Dáil* (Dublin 1994), pp. 61–74.
Feeney, Tom, 'The road to serfdom: Seán MacEntee, 'Beveridgism' and the development of Irish social policy', *History Review* XII (2001), pp. 63–72.

Gallagher, Michael, 'Party solidarity, exclusivity and inter-party relationships in Ireland, 1922–1977: The evidence of transfers', *Economic and Social Review* 10: 1 (1978), pp. 1–22.

Gallagher, Michael, 'The pact general election of 1922', *Irish Historical Studies* XXI: 84 (Sept. 1979), pp. 404–21.

Garvin, Tom. 'A quiet revolution: the remaking of Irish political culture' in R. Ryan (ed.), *Writing in the Irish Republic: Literature, Culture, Politics 1949–99* (London, 2000), pp. 187–203.

Geoghan, Vincent. 'Cemeteries of liberty: William Norton on communism and fascism', *Saothar* 18 (1993), pp. 106–9.

Gray, M., 'Memories of Michael McInerney', *Old Limerick Journal* (Spring 1983), pp. 19–21.

Hanley, Brian, 'Irish Citizen Army', *Saothar* 28 (2003), pp. 37–48.

Hanley, Brian, 'Moss Twomey, radicalism, and the IRA, 1931–33: a reassessment', *Saothar* 26 (2001), pp. 53–60.

Hannigan, Ken, 'British based unions in Ireland: Building workers and the split in Congress', *Saothar* 7 (1981), pp. 40–9.

Hawkins, John, *The Irish Question Today*, Fabian Society, Research series no. 54, Feb. 1941.

Higgins, Michael D., 'Making sense of change', *Saothar* 10 (1985) (review article), pp. 68–75.

Honohan, Patrick and Cormac Ó Gráda, 'The Irish macroeconomic crisis of 1955–56: how much was due to monetary policy?' *Irish Economic and Social History* 25 (1998), pp. 52–80.

Horgan, John, 'Anti-Communism and media surveillance in Ireland 1948–50', *Irish Communications Review* (Online, 1997).

Hutton, Seán, 'Labour in post-independent Ireland', in Seán Hutton and Paul Stewart (eds), *Ireland's Histories Aspects of State, Society, and Ideology* (London, 1991).

Keogh, Dermot, 'De Valera, the Catholic Church and the "Red Scare", 1931–32', in J. P. O'Carroll and J. A. Murphy (eds), *De Valera and his Times* (Cork, 1986), pp. 134–59.

Kilmurray, Evanne, *Fight, Starve or Emigrate: A History of the Unemployed Associations in the 1950s* (Larkin Unemployed Centre, Dublin, 1988).

Laffan, Michael, '"Labour must wait": Ireland's conservative revolution' in P. Corish (ed.), *Radicals, Rebels and Establishments* (Belfast, 1985), pp. 202–12.

Larkin, Emmet, 'Socialism and Catholicism in Ireland', *Church History* 33: 4 (1964), pp. 462–83.

Lee, Joseph, 'Irish nationalism and socialism: Rumpf reconsidered', *Saothar* 6 (1980), pp. 59–64.

Lynch, Patrick, 'Economic planning in Ireland', *Administration* 8: 3 (Autumn 1960), pp. 181–90.

McCarthy, Charles, 'Labour and the 1922 General Election', *Saothar* 7 (1981), pp. 115–21.

McGarry, Fearghal, '"Catholics first and politicians afterwards": The Labour Party and the Workers' Republic, 1936–39', *Saothar* 25 (2000), pp. 57–66.

McInerney, Michael, 'Noel Browne: Church and state', *University Review* v: 2 (Summer 1968).

McKay, Enda, 'Changing with the tide: The Irish Labour Party, 1927–1933', *Saothar* 11 (1986), pp. 27–38.

McKee, Eamonn, 'Church-state relations and the development of Irish health policy: the Mother and Child Scheme 1944–1953', *Irish Historical Studies* 25 (1986), pp. 159–94.

McLoughlin, Barry, 'Proletarian Academics or party functionaries? Irish Communists at the International Lenin School, Moscow, 1927–1937' *Saothar* 22 (1997), pp. 63–80.

McNamara, Robert, 'Irish perspectives on the Vietnam War', *Irish Studies in International Affairs* 14 (2003), pp. 75–94.

Mair, Peter, 'Labour and the Irish party system revisited: party competition in the 1920s', *Economic and Social Review* 9: 1 (1977), pp. 59–69.

Mair, Peter, 'Explaining the absence of class politics in Ireland' in J. E. Goldthorpe and C. T. Whelan (eds), *The Development of Industrial Society in Ireland* (Oxford, 1992), pp. 383–410.

Murphy, Christina, 'The organisational structure of the Labour Party', *Leargas* 11 (Nov. 1967).

Murphy, Gary, 'Fostering a spurious progeny?' The trade union movement and Europe, 1957–64', *Saothar* 21 (1996), pp. 61–70.

Murphy, Gary, 'Towards a corporate state? Seán Lemass and the realignment of interest groups in the policy process 1948–1964', *Administration* 47 (Spring 1999), pp. 86–102.

Murphy, John A., 'The Irish party system, 1938–51', in K. B. Nowlan and T. D. Williams (eds) *Ireland in the War Years and After* (1969), pp. 147–66.

Murphy, John A., '"Put them out!" Parties and elections 1948–69' in J. J. Lee (ed.), *Ireland 1945–69* (Dublin, 1979), pp. 1–15.

Nevin, Donal, 'Industry and labour', in K. B. Nowlan and T. D. Williams (eds), *Ireland in the War Years and After, 1938–51* (Dublin, 1969), pp. 94–108.

Norton, Christopher, 'The Irish Labour Party in Northern Ireland, 1949–1958', *Saothar* 21 (1996), pp. 47–60.

O'Connor, Emmet 'A historiography of Irish labour', *Labour History Review* 60: 1 (1995), pp. 21–34.

O'Connor, Emmet 'Jim Larkin and the Communist Internationals, 1923–29', *Irish Historical Studies* XXXI: 123 (May 1999), pp. 357–72.

O'Connor Lysaght, D. R., 'William O'Brien', *Saothar* (1983), pp. 48–62.

O'Connor, Peter, *A Soldier of Liberty: Recollections of a Socialist and Anti-Fascist Fighter* (Dublin, 1995).

O'Connor, Philip, 'Socialism and religion', *Democratic Socialist* 7 (Spring 1985), pp. 3–15.

O'Riordan, Manus, *The Voice of a Thinking Intelligent Movement: James Larkin Junior and the Ideological Modernisation Of Irish Trade Unionism*, Studies in Irish Labour History 2 (Dublin, 2001).

O'Riordan, Manus, 'Who is Comrade J. Ireland?' *Democratic Socialist* 2: 2 (June 1984), pp. 3–6.

O'Riordan, Manus, 'Irish labour politics in the 1940s', *Democratic Socialist* 2: 8 (Spring 1986), pp. 9–15.

Orridge, Andrew, 'The Irish Labour Party', *Journal of Common Market Studies* 13: 4 (1975), pp. 484–91.

Orridge, Andrew, 'The Irish Labour Party', in W. Patterson and A. Thomas (eds), *Social Democratic Parties in Western Europe* (London, 1977), pp. 153–75.

Puirséil, Niamh, 'Reading between the lines: Labour Party newspapers until 1949', *Irish Archives* (Winter 2003–4), pp. 51–5.

Purdie, Bob, 'The friends of Ireland: British labour and Irish nationalism, 1945–1949' in T. Gallagher and J. O'Connell (eds), *Contemporary Irish Studies* (Manchester, 1983), pp. 81–94.

Purdie, Bob, *Ireland Unfree* (London, n.d., *c.*1973).

Pyne, Peter. 'The third Sinn Fein Party 1923–1926: 1. Narrative account', *Economic and Social Review* 1: 1 (Oct. 1969), pp. 29–50.

Thornley, David 'The development of the Irish labour movement', *Christus Rex* (1964), pp. 7–21.

Thornley, David 'Irish politics and the left' *Hibernia*, June 1963.

Thornley, David, 'Ireland: The end of an era?' *Studies* (Spring 1964), pp. 1–17.

Varley, Tony, 'Farmers against nationalists: The rise and fall of Clann na Talmhan', in G. Moran and R. Gillespie (eds), *Galway: History and Society* (Dublin, 1996), pp. 589–622.

Ward, Eilís, 'A big show-off to show what we could do! Ireland and the Hungarian refugee crisis 1956', *Irish Studies in International Affairs* 7 (1996), pp. 131–42.

Whyte, John, 'Ireland: Politics without social bases' in Richard Rose (ed.), *Electoral Behaviour: A Comparative Handbook* (New York, 1974), pp. 619–51.

UNPUBLISHED THESES

Banta, Mary M., 'The red scare in the Irish Free State, 1929–37' (MA, UCD, 1982).

Finlay, Ian, 'A history of the Labour Court, 1946–62' (MA, UCD, 1991).

Garvin, Tom, 'Political parties in a Dublin constituency' (PhD, Georgia, 1974).

Gregg, Gerry, 'Dr Noel Browne: Irish political maverick 1948–1977' (MA, UCD 1981).

Hourihan, Fintan, 'From scepticism to pragmatism: Irish trade unions and the European Community 1961–1995' (M.Comm, UCD, 1996).

Judge, J. J., 'The Labour movement in the Republic of Ireland' (PhD, UCD, 1955).

McGovern, Martin, 'The emergence and development of Clann na Poblachta, July 1946–February 1948' (MA, UCD, 1979).

McKay, Enda, 'The Irish Labour Party 1927–1933' (MA, UCD, 1983).

McKevitt, James B, 'The split in the Labour Party and the general election of 1944' (MA, UCD, 1984).

McLoughlin, Michael, '"One step forward, two steps back": a labour history of the Emergency' (MA, UCD, 1993).

Murphy, Angela, 'Dissension and disunity: the story of the industrial and political split in the Irish labour movement' (MLitt, UCD, 2000).

O'Sullivan, Colman Tadhg, 'The IRA takes constitutional action: a history of Clann na Poblachta, 1946–1965' (MA, UCD 1995).

Reynolds, Brian. 'The formation and development of Fianna Fáil, 1926–32' (PhD, TCD, 1976).

Ward, Noel, 'The INTO and the Catholic Church, 1930–1955' (MA, UCD, 1987).

OTHER SOURCES

'A tribute to Jim Kemmy', Audio tape (Earth productions 1999).

'John Charles McQuaid: what the papers say', John Bowman, RTÉ television, 1998.

Index

—

Norton, Patrick 234; resigns from Labour
    Party 250–1
Norton, William
    on Labour re-organisation 30, 31
    supports expulsion of Morrissey and
        Anthony 35
    Labour leader 37–8, 39, 115, 254
    and Fianna Fáil government (1932)
        40–2, 45; (1933) 47, 50–1;
        (1938) 74–5
    and dismantling Anglo-Irish treaty
        41–4, 62–3
    changes in direction 44, 57, 71–3, 80–1,
        82, 204–5
    on Gralton deportation 49
    protests to Cardinal Pacelli 61
    closes *Labour News* 67
    and republicans 76–7
    and Trade Union Bill 80
    on British unions 124–5
    and the Larkin crisis 92–9 passim
    and general elections (1933) 45–6;
        (1937) (1943) 99–101; (1944) 107;
        (1951) 159; (1954) 171–3
    and ITGWU disaffiliation 103
    and coalition negotiations 129–30, 161,
        175–6
    as tánaiste and minister for social
        welfare 133–7, 139–42, 144, 151, 152,
        159, 182
    and the Mother and Child scheme 153–8
    as tánaiste and minister for industry and
        commerce in second inter-party
        government 179, 183, 185–6, 200
    resigns as leader 210–11
    and EEC membership 219
    impact of his death on Labour 228, 242
    see also 21, 51–2, 60, 85, 113, 117–18, 123, 138,
        149, 165, 170, 181–2, 203–4, 208,
        214, 216, 227

O'Brien, Conor Cruise 67–8, 139
    re-joins Labour Party 256, 263, 266,
        269–70, 272–4, 278, 282–3, 286–7,
        300

spokesman on Northern Ireland 289,
    291–4, 296, 298–9
O'Brien, Louie 122
O'Brien, Nora Connolly 56, 72–3, 83
O'Brien, P. J. 102
O'Brien, Séamus 59, 72
O'Brien, William 10, 11, 12, 14, 17, 51, 59, 60,
    84, 85, 113, 114
    relationship with Jim Larkin senior 15,
        97–8
    and trade union organisation 77–82
        passim
Ó Buachalla, Domhnall 63
    retires from ITGWU 123
O'Carroll, Maureen 145, 174, 199
O'Casey, Seán 112
O'Connell, John 220, 223, 234, 237, 243, 245,
    261, 269, 276–7, 358 n. 5
    private members bill on contraceptives
        294
    as conduit between the PIRA and
        British government 295–8
O'Connell, T. J. 14, 18, 22, 40
    absent from vote on Labour-National
        League coalition 24
    Labour leader 27, 28
    nomination for President of Executive
        Council 29
    and military tribunal legislation 34–5
    supports expulsion of Morrissey and
        Anthony 35
    loses seat at 1932 election 37
O'Connor, Peter 82
O'Connor, Rev. Fergal 231, 238
O'Connor, Rory 11
O'Donnell, Pa 179
O'Donnell, Peadar 49, 53, 58, 88
    attacks on and criticism of Labour Party
        23, 31–2, 314 n. 51
O'Donovan, John 269, 272, 274, 291
O'Duffy, General Eoin 49–50
O'Faoláin, Sean 148
O'Farrell, J. T. 12, 45, 67
O'Hanlon, Fearghal 197
O'Higgins, Kevin, assassination of, 22, 23, 25